Models of Thought

Models of Thought

HERBERT A. SIMON

NEW HAVEN AND LONDON
YALE UNIVERSITY PRESS
1979

DESIGNED BY THOS. WHITRIDGE
AND SET IN MONOPHOTO BASKERVILLE TYPE
BY ASCO TRADE TYPESETTING LTD., HONG KONG.
PRINTED IN THE UNITED STATES OF AMERICA
BY VAIL-BALLOU PRESS, INC., BINGHAMTON, N.Y.

PUBLISHED IN GREAT BRITAIN, EUROPE, AFRICA, AND
ASIA (EXCEPT JAPAN) BY YALE UNIVERSITY PRESS,
LTD., LONDON. DISTRIBUTED IN AUSTRALIA AND NEW
ZEALAND BY BOOK & FILM SERVICES, ARTARMON,
N.S.W., AUSTRALIA; AND IN JAPAN BY HARPER &
ROW, PUBLISHERS, TOKYO OFFICE.

LIBRARY OF CONGRESS CATALOGING IN PUBLICATION DATA

SIMON, HERBERT ALEXANDER, 1916–
    MODELS OF THOUGHT.

    INCLUDES BIBLIOGRAPHICAL REFERENCES AND INDEX.
    I. HUMAN INFORMATION PROCESSING.   2. THOUGHT AND
THINKING.   I. TITLE. [DNLM: I. INFORMATION THEORY—
COLLECTED WORKS.   2. MODELS, PSYCHOLOGICAL—COLLECTED
WORKS.   3. PROBLEM SOLVING—COLLECTED WORKS.
4. THINKING—COLLECTED WORKS.   5. COGNITION—COLLECTED
WORKS.   BF441 S594M]
BF455.S525   153.4   78-31744
ISBN 0-300-02347-2

To
My Collaborators

It is a true saying, that a man
must eat a peck of salt with his
friend, before he knows him.

— Scottish proverb

Contents

Preface

In the Carl I. Hovland Memorial Lectures, which I delivered at Yale in the autumn of 1977, I underlook to review some of my theoretical and empirical work of the past twenty-five years in cognitive psychology. In lieu of expanding that review for publication, it has seemed more useful to assemble and annotate this collection of my research papers, published during that quarter century in collaboration with the colleagues whose names appear in the table of contents.

Carl Hovland very early appreciated the import of the new information processing ideas that began to impinge on psychology during and after World War II. He was one of the pioneers in incorporating these ideas in experimental and theoretical work during the early postwar years (Hovland, 1952). Along with George A. Miller, Allen Newell, and myself, he was one of the organizers of the influential 1958 RAND Summer Workshop, which gave a number of leading young psychologists their first introduction to the new paradigm. At the time of his death, he was deeply engaged, with his graduate student Earl Hunt, in computer modeling of the processes of concept attainment (Hunt, 1962).

THE INFORMATION PROCESSING REVOLUTION

The information processing revolution that has occurred during these years has completely changed the face of cognitive psychology. It has introduced computer programming languages as formal ("mathematical") languages for expressing theories of human mental processes; and it has introduced the computers themselves to simulate these processes and thereby make behavioral predictions for testing the theories. These new methodologies have enabled us to describe human cognitive processes with precision in terms of a small number of basic mechanisms organized into programs (strategies) and to use these descriptions to explain a wide range of phenomena that have been observed in the psychological laboratory.

It has been my privilege and pleasure to participate in the information processing revolution from its beginnings, pursuing research aimed at understanding the workings of the human mind in information processing terms. Twice during this period, I have paused for some summing up. The first occasion, in 1969, produced *The Sciences of the Artificial*, which, especially in its second chapter, offers a brief general account of the information processing approach to cognitive psychology, but does not review the research evidence in detail.

In 1972, in *Human Problem Solving*, Allen Newell and I assembled most of the evidence we had gathered, during twenty years of collaboration, about problem solving, and organized that evidence within an explicit framework of an information processing theory. In particular, the first three chapters of that treatise and the final (fourteenth) chapter contain a general theory of human cognition, not limited to problem solving, as well as an extensive discussion of the methodology for expressing theories of cognition as programs and for using computers to simulate human thinking.

SCOPE OF THIS BOOK

The present book is a companion volume to *Human Problem Solving*, covering most of my psychological research outside the domain of problem solving, as well as some problem solving research not fully reported in the other book. The assumptions, both methodological and substantive, on which this research rests are identical with those of the earlier volume—the Problem Solving Man of *Human Problem Solving* has simply been generalized to the whole (or nearly whole) Thinking Man who will be found in these pages.[1] The present volume does not, however, assume the reader's familiarity with *Human Problem Solving* (though familiarity will do no harm).

Indeed, since the chapters of this book were originally published as independent journal articles, the reader need not be bound by the sequence I have now imposed on them, but yet should be aware that the sequence is not arbitrary. All the research has been carried on within a guiding scheme which, though modified and expanded over the years, still expresses the goals that were sketched out in the early 1950s (see especially chapters 1.1 and 1.2). That scheme has governed the assembly of the articles into this book, and brief introductions have been provided to the major sections to make goals and scheme explicit.

The product of a research program is a mosaic of particular results, for the requirements of journal publication force the scientist to exhibit each separate tile, leaving the whole pattern to the imaginations or whims of readers. I hope that the organization of my papers here will show that the tiles form a coherent mosaic. The arrangement follows from two strategic principles:

1. Thinking Man is capable of expressing his cognitive skills in a wide range of task domains: learning and remembering, problem solving, inducing rules and attaining concepts, perceiving and recognizing stimuli, understanding natural language, and others. An information processing model of Thinking Man must contain components capable of humanly intelligent behavior in each of these domains; and, as these models are created, they must gradually be merged into a coherent whole.

2. There exists a basic repertory of mechanisms and processes that Thinking Man uses in all the domains in which he exhibits intelligent behavior. The models we build initially for the several domains must all be assembled from this same basic repertory, and common principles of architecture must be followed throughout.

---

1. I will always use the word "man" and pronouns of male gender generically to denote both sexes. I dislike offending those who disapprove of this conventional usage, but have occasionally, as in this instance, found no appropriate alternative. Thinking Man is a sibling of Economic Man; both are androgynous.

Thus, the strategy is incremental, following the usual principle of dividing the difficulties at the outset and attacking them piecemeal. At the same time, it is a disciplined cumulative strategy, parsimonious in its use of mechanisms and inhospitable to ad hoc solutions. It hopes to avoid, thereby, a predicament, too often encountered in psychology, where behavior in each special experimental paradigm is explained by its own special and private microtheory. The aim here is general theory—a unified explanation of human cognition in all its manifestations.

This is a book about human information processing, not about brain physiology. The revolution in cognitive psychology has greatly extended our knowledge of the basic processes that enable human beings to perform complex intellectual tasks, but it has revealed little about the connection of these information processes to the next level of theory—the neural mechanisms that store information in the brain and that execute the information processes. Information processing psychology and neurophysiology constitute independent bodies of theory, as nineteenth century chemistry and physics constituted independent bodies of theory (see chapter 2.3). At present, we have almost no knowledge of how to build a bridge from the one to the other, although most of us have no doubt that such a bridge will be constructed by future generations. Meanwhile, the lack of a bridge need not deter us, and has not deterred us, from vastly broadening and deepening our understanding of human cognition in information processing terms.

It is really more accurate to speak of three levels of theory rather than of only two. For research in information processing psychology has itself been pursued at two levels: one concerned with relatively complex human performances, the other with what is called the "immediate processor." The immediate processor comprises the basic components of the information processing system, described in information processing terms, not in neurophysiological terms. Problem solving and concept attainment are traditional areas of research at the former level. Simple cognitive tasks—e.g., the Sternberg (1969) memory-scanning tasks, or the word-picture comparison tasks of Chase and Clark (1972)—are typical of research at the latter level.

The two information processing levels of theory are separated by no such wide gap as separates both of them from neurophysiology. On the contrary, information processing theories of complex behavior rest heavily on a specification of the immediate processor. The simplest way to characterize the difference between the two levels is to note that the one employs primitive processes that are characteristically several seconds in duration, while the other seeks to identify primitive processes that are tens or hundreds of milliseconds in duration. The latter aspires to a very detailed model of short-term memory and perceptual processes, while the former builds theories of complex behavior based on the more aggregative properties of that model. The interaction between the two levels, however, is intimate. The models of complex behavior must not incorporate structural or processing assumptions that are inconsistent with our understanding of the immediate processor.

This book is concerned mainly with the more aggregated processes. The immediate processor will be discussed in section 2 to the extent necessary to support the models of complex behavior. The EPAM system described in section 3 constitutes an important link between the two levels, for it is of an intermediate character, being concerned both with rather slow learning processes and with rapid recognition processes. Hence EPAM could be viewed as belonging to either level or to both.

STRUCTURE OF THIS BOOK

The thirty-two articles included here are grouped under seven topic headings:
    1. System Principles
    2. Memory Structures
    3. Learning Processes
    4. Problem Solving
    5. Rule Induction and Concept Formation
    6. Perception
    7. Understanding

Sections 1 and 2 are mainly concerned with providing a general description of Thinking Man. The three chapters in section 1 establish abstract specifications for the more particularized models of later sections. These chapters characterize thinking as a process of serial selective search through large spaces of alternatives, guided by motivational mechanisms that operate through dynamically adapting aspiration levels. Section 2 reviews our empirical knowledge of the organization of human memory and derives specifications for the system of memories used by the thought processes. This review establishes the critical importance of short-term memory structure for the seriality of thought, the role of chunks and chunking, and the dual index-text structure of the associative long-term memory.

The organizational principles and mechanisms described in these initial chapters provide the basic modules from which all the theories described in later chapters of the book are assembled. Each of the sections, 3 through 7, takes up a particular domain of thinking tasks and, within each domain, proposes a theory of the thought processes, usually in the form of a computer program, which is then tested against several kinds of empirical data. Thus learning processes are explained in terms of the EPAM (Elementary Perceiver and Memorizer) model, problem solving in terms of GPS (General Problem Solver) and related systems for means-ends analysis, rule induction in terms of SE (Sequence Extrapolator) and GRI (General Rule Inducer), perception in terms of MAPP (Memory-Aided Pattern Perceiver), and language understanding in terms of UNDERSTAND.

These several theories are not independent structures. In particular, MAPP is essentially an elaboration of EPAM incorporating attention-directing mechanisms; GRI represents a synthesis of the Sequence Extrapolator with the General Problem Solver; while UNDERSTAND operates as a "front end" or preprocessor, for the General Problem Solver. Taking account of these interrelations, we find that Thinking Man is described in terms of three main mechanisms: a recognition system that "indexes" and gives access to the information stored in long-term memory; a system for selective means-ends search, which is capable of solving problems and inducing rules; and a system for constructing representations of novel problem domains from natural-language descriptions of those domains.

I would not like to imply that these mechanisms provide a complete portrait of Thinking Man. There remains much unfinished business on my agenda and those of other researchers in cognitive science. The work reported here says little about associative processes in long-term memory, an area now being explored vigorously by a number of research groups. It says relatively little about visual imagery (as distinguished from visual perception). While several kinds of learning are considered, EPAM and UNDERSTAND do not exhaust the varieties of learning that occur in the human system. Over the next few years, I am sure that these and other aspects of cognition will find their place in the picture. Meanwhile, I present this partial portrait of human thinking as a report of twenty-five years of progress toward the more ambitious goal.

References

Chase, W. G., and H. H. Clark, Mental operations in the comparison of sentences and pictures. In L. W. Gregg (ed.), *Cognition in Learning and Memory*, New York: Wiley, 1972, pp. 205–32.

Hovland, C. I., A "communicational analysis" of concept learning, *Psychological Review*, 59:461–72 (1952).

Hunt, E. B., *Concept Formation*, New York: Wiley, 1962.

Newell, A., and H. A. Simon, *Human Problem Solving*, Englewood Cliffs, N. J.: Prentice-Hall, 1972.

Simon, H. A., *The Sciences of the Artificial*, Cambridge, Mass.: M.I.T. Press, 1969.

Sternberg, S., The discovery of processing stages: Extensions of Donder's method, *Acta Psychologica*, 30:276–315 (1969).

Acknowledgments

As I have indicated in the preface, this book, if not written by a committee, is surely the product of an institution—the Psychology Department of Carnegie-Mellon University. Of the thirty-two chapters, twenty-one were written with coauthors, almost all associated with that department. Four chapters first appeared in volumes of the annual Carnegie Symposium on Cognition. To my colleagues I am deeply indebted for having provided me during a quarter century with constant intellectual nourishment and warm comradeship.

In his *Origin of Species* Charles Darwin discusses the advantages and disadvantages of island environments for engendering new species. There is little doubt in my mind that the support and enthusiasm of the Carnegie campus community for the tender green shoots of the new information processing psychology played a major role in their survival and growth until they were sturdy and vigorous enough to compete with the other species of psychological theory that flourished on this continent and in Europe.

Financial support for the research has come from a variety of sources, among which I should mention at least the RAND Corporation, Carnegie-Mellon University, the Ford Foundation, the Carnegie Corporation, the National Institute of Mental Health, the Advanced Research Projects Agency of the Department of Defense, the R. K. Mellon Foundation, the National Science Foundation, and the Alfred P. Sloan Foundation. Computer simulation, while it does not compete in cost with atom smashing or moon shooting, is not inexpensive. Because of the superb facilities that have been available to us, first at RAND and then on the Carnegie campus, the limits on our rate of progress have been fixed not by hardware but by our own capacities to generate fruitful ideas.

In addition to the collaborators named elsewhere, many friends and colleagues reviewed and commented upon individual chapters. Their contributions are acknowledged in the notes to those chapters, as are the specific sources of financial support.

Finally, I want to thank the following journals and publishers for permission to reprint the papers from their original sources.

Academic Press, Inc.

"Effects of Similarity, Familiarization, and Meaningfulness in Verbal Learning" (with Edward A. Feigenbaum), *Journal of Verbal Learning and Verbal Behavior*,

3:385–96. Copyright © 1964 by Academic Press, Inc. and used by permission.
"An Information-Processing Explanation of One-Trial and Incremental Learning" (with Lee W. Gregg), *Journal of Verbal Learning and Verbal Behavior*, 6:780–87. Copyright © 1967 by Academic Press, Inc. and used by permission.
"Process Models and Stochastic Theories of Simple Concept Formation" (with Lee W. Gregg), *Journal of Mathematical Psychology*, 4:246–76. Copyright © 1967 by Academic Press, Inc. and used by permission.
"The Mind's Eye in Chess" (with William G. Chase). In William G. Chase (ed.), *Visual Information Processing*, pp. 215–81. Copyright © 1973 by Academic Press, Inc. and used by permission.
"Perception in Chess" (with William G. Chase), *Cognitive Psychology*, 4:55–81. Copyright © 1973 by Academic Press, Inc. and used by permission.
"Empirical Tests of a Theory of Human Acquisition of Concepts for Sequential Patterns" (with Kenneth Kotovsky), *Cognitive Psychology*, 4:399–424. Copyright © 1973 by Academic Press, Inc. and used by permission.
"A Simulation of Memory for Chess Positions" (with Kevin J. Gilmartin), *Cognitive Psychology*, 5:29–46. Copyright © 1973 by Academic Press, Inc. and used by permission.
"The Functional Equivalence of Problem Solving Skills," *Cognitive Psychology*, 7:268–88. Copyright © 1975 by Academic Press, Inc. and used by permission.
"Modeling Strategy Shifts in a Problem-Solving Task" (with Stephen K. Reed), *Cognitive Psychology*, 8:86–97. Copyright © 1976 by Academic Press, Inc. and used by permission.
"The Understanding Process: Problem Isomorphs" (with John R. Hayes), *Cognitive Psychology*, 8:165–90. Copyright © 1976 by Academic Press, Inc. and used by permission.

American Association for the Advancement of Science

"How Big Is A Chunk?" *Science*, 183:482–88. Copyright © 1974 by the American Association for the Advancement of Science.

American Educational Research Association

"Alternative Uses of Phonemic Information in Spelling" (with Dorothea P. Simon). *Review of Educational Research*, 43:115–37. Copyright © 1973, American Educational Research Association, Washington, D.C.

American Federation of Information Processing Societies

"A Chess Mating Combinations Program" (with George W. Baylor), *Proceedings of the 1966 Spring Joint Computer Conference, Boston*, 28:431–47. Copyright © 1966 by the American Federation of Information Processing Societies and used by permission.

American Psychological Association, Inc.

"Rational Choice and the Structure of the Environment," *Psychological Review*, 63:129–38. Copyright © 1956 by the American Psychological Association, Inc. Reprinted by permission.

"Human Acquisition of Concepts for Sequential Patterns" (with Kenneth Kotovsky), *Psychological Review*, 70:534–46. Copyright © 1963 by the American Psychological Association, Inc. Reprinted by permission.

"Motivational and Emotional Controls of Cognition," *Psychological Review*, 74:29–39. Copyright © 1967 by the American Psychological Association, Inc. Reprinted by permission.

"Information-Processing Analysis of Perceptual Processes in Problem Solving" (with Michael Barenfeld), *Psychological Review*, 76:473–83. Copyright © 1969 by the American Psychological Association, Inc. Reprinted by permission.

"Complexity and the Representation of Patterned Sequences of Symbols," *Psychological Review*, 79:369–82. Copyright © 1972 by the American Psychological Association, Inc. Reprinted by permission.

The Syndics of the Cambridge University Press

"A Theory of the Serial Position Effect" (with Edward A. Feigenbaum), *British Journal of Psychology*, 53:307–20. Published 1962 by The Syndics of the Cambridge University Press. Reprinted by permission of the British Journal of Psychology.

"An Information-Processing Explanation of Some Perceptual Phenomena," *British Journal of Psychology*, 58:1–12. Published 1967 by The Syndics of the Cambridge University Press. Reprinted by Permission of the British Journal of Psychology.

Lawrence Erlbaum Associates

"Problem Solving and Rule Induction: A Unified View" (with Glenn Lea). In Lee W. Gregg (ed.), *Knowledge and Cognition*, pp. 105–28. Copyright © 1974 by Lawrence Erlbaum Associates and used by permission.

"Understanding Written Problem Instructions" (with John R. Hayes). In Lee W. Gregg (ed.), *Knowledge and Cognition*, pp. 167–200. Copyright © 1974 by Lawrence Erlbaum Associates and used by permission.

"Psychological Differences among Problem Isomorphs" (with John R. Hayes). In N. J. Castellan, D. B. Pisoni, and G. R. Potts (eds.), *Cognitive Theory*, vol. 2, pp. 21–41. Copyright © 1977 by Lawrence Erlbaum Associates and used by permission.

W. H. Freeman and Company

"A Program Modeling Short-term Memory Under Strategy Control" (with Kevin J. Gilmartin and Allen Newell). In Charles M. Cofer (ed.), *The Structure of Human Memory*, pp. 15–30. Copyright © 1976 by W. H. Freeman and Company and used by permission.

Harvard University

"A Behavioral Model of Rational Choice," *Quarterly Journal of Economics*, 69:99–118.
  Copyright © 1955 by Harvard University, Cambridge, Mass. Reprinted by
  permission of John Wiley & Sons, Inc.

Lieber-Atherton, Inc.

"The Processes of Creative Thinking" (with Allen Newell and J. C. Shaw). In
  H. E. Gruber, G. Terrell, and M. Wertheimer (eds.), *Contemporary Approaches
  to Creative Thinking*, pp. 63–119. Copyright © 1962 by Lieber-Atherton, Inc.
  and used by permission.

The M.I.T. Press

"The Information-Storage System Called 'Human Memory'." In Mark R.
  Rosenzweig and Edward L. Bennett (eds.), *Neural Mechanisms of Learning and
  Memory*, pp. 79–96. Copyright © 1976 by The M.I.T. Press and used by per-
  mission.

The Mental Health Research Institute, The University of Michigan

"Trial and Error Search in Solving Difficult Problems: Evidence from the Game
  of Chess" (with Peter A. Simon), *Behavioral Science*, 7:425–29. Copyright ©
  1962 by The Mental Health Research Institute, The University of Michigan.
  Reprinted by permission of Behavioral Science.

The Psychometric Society

"Amounts of Fixation and Discovery in Maze Learning Behavior," *Psychometrika*,
  22:261–68. Published 1957 by The Psychometric Society. Reprinted by permission
  of Psychometrika.
"A Note on Mathematical Models for Learning," *Psychometrika*, 27:417–18.
  Published 1962 by The Psychometric Society. Reprinted by permission of
  Psychometrika.
"A Note on Jost's Law and Exponential Forgetting," *Psychometrika*, 31:505–06.
  Published 1966 by The Psychometric Society. Reprinted by permission of
  Psychometrika.

John Wiley & Sons, Inc., Publishers

"Cognitive Processes in Solving Algebra Word Problems" (with Jeffery M. Paige).
  In B. Kleinmuntz (ed.), *Problem Solving*, pp. 51–119. Copyright © 1966 by
  John Wiley & Sons, Inc. Reprinted by permission of John Wiley & Sons, Inc.

I

System Principles

The three chapters of this section set forth some of the conceptual foundations for this undertaking. They seek to provide an abstract characterization of Thinking Man and thus to set specifications that any model of thinking processes must satisfy.

The point of departure is the observation that human thinking powers are very modest when compared with the complexities of the environments in which human beings live. If computational powers were unlimited, a person would simply consult his or her preferences (utility functions) and choose the course of action that would yield maximum utility under the given circumstances. That is, of course, just what the "rational man" of classical economic theory does. But real human beings, of bounded rationality, cannot follow this procedure. Faced with complexity and uncertainty, lacking the wits to optimize, they must be content to satisfice—to find "good enough" solutions to their problems and "good enough" courses of action.

The first specification, then for a model of thinking processes is that it be a model of bounded rationality, that it incorporate mechanisms for coping with complexity even when it is unable to digest it completely. Chapter 1.1 sketches some of the mechanisms a system of limited computional power can employ toward this end. Satisficing, aiming at the good when the best is incalculable, is the key device. The good, in turn, is defined by mechanisms that set aspirations and adjust these aspirations upward or downward in the face of benign or harsh circumstances, respectively.

Satisficing provides an escape from the difficulty that, in a complex world, the alternatives of action are not given but must be sought out. Since the search generally takes place in a space that is essentially infinite, some stop rule must be imposed to terminate problem solving activity. The satisficing criterion provides that stop rule: search ends when a good-enough alternative is found.

Satisficing also provides a solution to another problem of complexity (chapter 1.2). When the criterion of problem solution or action has more than one dimension, there is the matter of calculating the relative merits of several alternatives, one of which may be preferred along one dimension, another along another. The economist, unconcerned with the boundedness of rationality, solves the problem with the help of marginalism, postulating some ratio at which the decision maker would trade off an increment of value on the one dimension against an increment of value on the other. The satisficing rule, which requires no such calculation or comparison of marginal values along incommensurate dimensions, stipulates that search stops when a solution has been found that is good enough along *all* dimensions. Dynamically adjustable aspiration levels guarantee the termination of search without prior knowledge of how rich an environment is being explored.

The discussions of satisficing search in the first two chapters show that Thinking Man is a motivated creature, and that the principles of motivation provide basic specifications for the model of thought. Satisficing mechanisms will be implicit or explicit in all the descriptions of thought processes in subsequent chapters.

Chapter 1.3 carries further the analysis of the relations among cognition, motivation, and emotion and the way in which human motivational-emotional mechanisms influence thinking. This article was written initially as a direct reply to Ulric Neisser's (1963) claims that information processing theories of cognition in general, and computer simulations in particular, ignored such interactions. I will leave the reply to speak for itself. Of course this volume makes no attempt to build a full information processing theory of affective processes, but the way in which it treats the basic interactions of those processes with cognition should not be overlooked, for it is important to understanding how the specifications of our models of thinking were derived.

The first two chapters describe thinking processes as search processes, another fundamental characteristic of thought. Moreover, though the point is not much emphasized, the search is assumed to be a serial, one-thing-at-a-time, exploration. The reasons for assuming seriality instead of parallelism will be discussed in a moment.

So there emerges from the broad and rather abstract considerations of the three chapters of section 1 a picture of Thinking Man, a creature of bounded rationality who copes with the complexity that confronts him by highly selective serial search of the environment, guided and interrupted by the demands of his motivational system, and regulated, in particular, by dynamically adjusting, multidimensional levels of aspiration. This specification of Thinking Man is the essential core of all the specific cognitive models that are examined in succeeding chapters.

SERIAL OR PARALLEL?

The specification that the human information processing system is serial is a highly controversial claim. In chapter 1.3 there is some discussion of just what the claim means and what reasons there are for making it. Empirical evidence is considered further in chapters 2.2 and 2.3. However, a few additional caveats are in order here.

The claim is *not* that there are no elements of parallel activity in the human system. There is much evidence to the contrary. First, all kinds of mental activity can go on in parallel with a beating heart and breathing lungs. Second, in the sensory organs, especially the eye, there is patently a great deal of parallel activity. What *is* claimed is that the kind of mental activity that requires at least a modicum of attention is essentially serial, for it must have access to the very limited capacity of short-term memory for its inputs and outputs.

Some phenomena that seem to contradict this claim (e.g., carrying on a conversation while driving a car) are only apparent exceptions. It is easy to show, in the car-driving case for example, that what is actually going on is not parallelism but time sharing—a relatively rapid alternation in control over the short-term memory by the two competing activities. A simple but sometimes dangerous experiment to show this is to engage a driver in a conversation of varying complexity in traffic of varying density and to observe and record the rate of his or her speech as compared with the rate of speech when there is no competing activity. Fortunately, the program of most drivers gives priority to road information over conversation; but I recently had a rather exciting ride on icy roads from an airport with a driver who was trying to perform a visual imaging task while staying on the road. By good luck, as he became less attentive to his driving, he also neglected to press his foot on the accelerator, so that he came to a halt just short of a snowbank.

Apart from the casual empiricism of this anecdote, such laboratory evidence as I am acquainted with argues heavily for time sharing rather than parallelism when subjects are instructed to perform two attention-demanding tasks simultaneously. It is less certain whether there are productive "ruminating" processes that the central nervous system can carry on without conscious direction or access to short-term memory, either during sleep or in parallel with attention-demanding activities when awake. The evidence does not seem to me to be conclusive on either side, and I would at present render a Scottish verdict of "not proven." Most often this kind of claim of parallelism is raised in connection with theories of creative activity, especially the phenomenon (or supposed phenomenon) of "incubation." The introduction to section 4 and chapter 4.1 propose a theory of creative thinking that dispenses with special parallel incubation processes.

Two other cases of apparent parallelism require consideration. One is the tip-of-the-tongue phenomenon—not the fact that recall of a familiar name or word may be delayed, but the fact that the recall often occurs after attention has been turned to other matters. I see no way of explaining this phenomenon without postulating some measure of continuing search activity in memory (though it could conceivably be time-shared) and some kind of motivational activity that is capable of interrupting attention when the answer has been found.

Finally, there seems to be ample evidence for "warm-up" phenomena in long-term memory and for the gradual diffusion of activation along associative paths. The long-term memory models of Reitman (1965), Quillian (1968), and Anderson (1976) have all incorporated spreading activation processes of one sort or another. Anderson is now exploring the attractive suggestion that short-term memory is not physiologically distinct from long-term memory, but may simply be equated with the activated portion of the latter. The evidence is not yet in, but if this conjecture proves correct, it will not call for any significant abandonment of the principle of seriality in the way that principle is incorporated in the models of this book.

My present view could be summed up thus: The evidence seems overwhelming for essential seriality of attention-demanding activities. Seriality is attractive as a working hypothesis, and it is very much worth while, as a research strategy, to see how far it can be pushed before it has to be modified in important respects. The spreading activation hypothesis is a redefinition of short-term memory rather than an abandonment of seriality; evidence for extensive parallel "ruminating" activities in the mind is quite scanty and unconvincing.

HISTORICAL NOTE

Chapter 1.1 was written in 1952 and chapter 1.2 in the winter of 1953–54, before computer simulation had become a reality and just as it was beginning to be conceived as a possibility. Indeed, Allen Newell and I had our first extended discussions of the prospects of simulating thinking in the summer of 1954. It is not surprising, therefore, that neither chapter speaks of computer modeling as a possible approach to testing the theory.[1] The work on these chapters came out of my longstanding

---

1. An earlier draft of chapter 1.1, however, included an appendix that discussed the design of a chess playing program employing selective search as its central thought process.

discontent with the economist's model of global rationality, which seemed to me to falsify the facts of human behavior and to provide a wholly wrong foundation for a theory of human decision making—the central concern of my research at that time.

The notions of serial, selective, satisficing search that are recorded in these chapters provided much of the framework for our first attempts, begun in earnest in 1955, to use the computer to simulate thinking. The continuities can be seen fairly clearly from an examination of chapter 3.1, which, although not published until 1962, was drafted in the spring of 1958.

Chapter 1.3 was written in 1963, shortly after Neisser's (1963) skeptical paper on computer simulation appeared in *Science*. I delayed submitting it for publication for several years, until I had assured myself that the theory of emotion and motivation it espoused, and especially its account of the attention interruption mechanisms, were compatible with the then current theories and evidence in neurophysiology.

References

Anderson, J. R., *Language, Memory, and Thought*, Hillsdale, N. J.: Erlbaum, 1976.
Neisser, U., The imitation of man by machine, *Science*, 139:193–97 (1963).
Quillian, M. R., Semantic memory. In M. Minsky (ed.), *Semantic Information Processing*, Cambridge, Mass.: M.I.T. Press, 1968, pp. 227–70.
Reitman, W. R., *Cognition and Thought*, New York: Wiley, 1965.

A Behavioral Model of Rational Choice
(1955)

Traditional economic theory postulates an "Economic Man," who, in the course of being "economic" is also "rational." This man is assumed to have knowledge of the relevant aspects of his environment which, if not absolutely complete, is at least impressively clear and voluminous. He is assumed also to have a well-organized and stable system of preferences and a skill in computation that enables him to calculate, for the alternative courses of action that are available to him, which of these will permit him to reach the highest attainable point on his preference scale.

Recent developments in economics, and particularly in the theory of the business

firm, have raised great doubts as to whether this schematized model of Economic Man provides a suitable foundation on which to erect a theory—whether it be a theory of how firms *do* behave, or of how they "should" rationally behave. It is not the purpose of this chapter to discuss these doubts, or to determine whether they are justified. Rather, I will assume that the concept of Economic Man (and, I might add, of his brother Administrative Man) is in need of fairly drastic revision, and I will put forth some suggestions as to the direction the revision might take.

Broadly stated, the task is to replace the global rationality of Economic Man with a kind of rational behavior that is compatible with the access to information and the computational capacities that are actually possessed by organisms, including man, in the kinds of environments in which such organisms exist. One is tempted to turn to the literature of psychology for the answer. Psychologists have certainly been concerned with rational behavior, particularly in their interest in learning phenomena. But the distance is so great between our present psychological knowledge of the learning and choice processes and the kinds of knowledge needed for economic and administrative theory, that a marking stone placed halfway between might help travel-

The ideas embodied in this paper were initially developed in a series of discussions with Herbert Bohnert, Norman Dalkey, Gerald Thompson, and Robert Wolfson during the summer of 1952. These collaborators deserve a large share of the credit for whatever merit this approach to rational choice may possess. A first draft of this paper was prepared in my capacity as a consultant to the RAND Corporation. It has been developed further (including the appendix) in work with the Cowles Commission for Research in Economics on "Decision Making Under Uncertainty," under contract with the Office of Naval Research, and has been completed with the aid of a grant from the Ford Foundation.

ers from both directions to keep to their courses.

Lacking the kinds of empirical knowledge of the decisional processes that will be required for a definitive theory, the hard facts of the actual world can, at the present stage, enter the theory only in a relatively unsystematic and unrigorous way. But none of us is completely innocent of acquaintance with the gross characteristics of human choice, or of the broad features of the environment in which this choice takes place. I will feel free to call on this common experience as a source of the hypotheses needed for the theory about the nature of man and his world.

The problem can be approached initially either by inquiring into the properties of the choosing organism or by inquiring into the environment of choice. In this chapter, I will take the former approach. In chapter 1.2, I deal with the characteristics of the environment and the interrelations of environment and organism.

This chapter, then, attempts to include explicitly some of the properties of the choosing organism as elements in defining what is meant by rational behavior in specific situations and in selecting a rational behavior in terms of such a definition. In part, this involves making more explicit what is already implicit in some of the recent work on the problem—that the state of information may as well be regarded as a characteristic of the decision maker as a characteristic of his environment. In part, it involves some new considerations—in particular taking into account the simplifications the choosing organism may deliberately introduce into its model of the situation in order to bring the model within the range of its computing capacity.

SOME GENERAL FEATURES OF RATIONAL CHOICE

The "flavor" of various models of rational choice stems primarily from the specific kinds of assumptions that are introduced as to the "givens" or constraints within which rational adaptation must take place. Among the common constraints—which are not themselves the objects of rational calculation—are (1) the set of alternatives open to choice, (2) the relationships that determine the payoffs ("satisfactions," "goal attainment") as a function of the alternative that is chosen, and (3) the preference orderings among payoffs. The selection of particular constraints, and the rejection of others, for incorporation in the model of rational behavior involves implicit assumptions as to what variables the rational organism "controls"—and hence can "optimize" as a means to rational adaptation—and what variables it must take as fixed. It also involves assumptions as to the character of the variables that are fixed. For example, by making different assumptions about the amount of information the organism has with respect to the relations between alternatives and payoffs, optimization might involve selection of a certain maximum, an expected value, or a minimax.

Another way of characterizing the givens and the behavior variables is to say that the latter refer to the organism itself, the former to its environment. But if we adopt this viewpoint, we must be prepared to accept the possibility that what we call "the environment" may lie, in part, within the skin of the biological organism. That is, some of the constraints that must be taken as givens in an optimization problem may be physiological and psychological limitations of the organism (biologically defined) itself. For example, the maximum speed at which an organism can move establishes a boundary on the set of its available behavior alternatives. Similarly, limits on computational capacity may be important constraints entering into the definition of rational choice under particular circumstances. We will explore possible ways of formulating the process of rational choice in situations where we wish to take explicit account of the "internal" as well as the "external" constraints that define the problem of rationality for the organism.

Whether our interests lie in the normative or in the descriptive aspects of rational choice, the construction of models of this kind should prove instructive. Because of the psychological limits of the organism (particularly with respect to computational and predictive ability), actual human rationality-striving can at best be an extremely crude and simplified approximation to the kind of global rationality that is implied, for example, by game theoretical models. While the approximations that organisms employ may not be the best—even at the levels of computational complexity they are able to handle—it is probable that a great deal can be learned about possible mechanisms from an examination of the schemes of approximation that are actually employed by human and other organisms.

In describing the proposed model, we will begin with elements it has in common with the more global models, and then proceed to introduce simplifying assumptions and (what is the same thing) approximating procedures.

Primitive Terms and Definitions

Models of rational behavior—both the global kinds usually constructed and the more limited kinds to be discussed here—generally require some or all of the following elements:

1. A set of *behavior alternatives* (alternatives of choice or decision). In a mathematical model, these can be represented by a point set, A.

2. The subset of *behavior alternatives that the organism "considers" or "perceives."* That is, the organism may make its choice within a set of alternatives more limited than the whole range objectively available to it. The "considered" subset can be represented by a point set $\mathring{A}$, with $\mathring{A}$ included in A ($\mathring{A} \subset A$).

3. *The possible future states of affairs,* or outcomes of choice, represented by a point set S. (For the moment it is not necessary to distinguish between actual and perceived outcomes.)

4. A *"payoff"* function, representing the "value" or "utility" placed by the organism upon each of the possible outcomes of choice. The payoff may be represented by a real function $V(s)$, defined for all elements s of S. For many purposes there is needed only an ordering relation on pairs of elements of S—i.e., a relation that states that s_1 is preferred to s_2 or vice versa—but to avoid unnecessary complications in the present discussion, we will assume that a cardinal utility $V(s)$ has been defined.

5. *Information as to which outcomes in S will actually occur* if a particular alternative a in A (or in $\mathring{A}$) is chosen. This information may be incomplete—that is, there may be more than one possible outcome s for each behavior alternative a. We represent the information, then, by a mapping of each element a in A upon a subset S_a—the set of outcomes that may ensue if a is the chosen behavior alternative.

6. *Information as to the probability that a particular outcome will ensue* if a particular behavior alternative is chosen. This is a more precise kind of information than that postulated in (5), for it associates with each element s in the set S_a a probability $P_a(s)$—the probability that s will occur if a is chosen. The probability $P_a(s)$ is a real, nonnegative function with $\sum_{S_a} P_a(s) = 1$.

Attention is directed to the threefold distinction drawn by the definitions among the set of behavior alternatives A, the set of outcomes or future states of affairs S, and the payoff V. In the ordinary representation of a game, in reduced form, by its payoff matrix, the set S corresponds to the cells of the matrix, the set A to the strategies of the first player, and the function V to the values in the cells. The set S_a is then the set of cells in the ath row. By keeping in mind this interpretation, the reader may compare the present formulation with "classical" game theory.

"Classical" Concepts of Rationality

With these elements, we can define procedures of rational choice corresponding to

the ordinary game theoretical and probabilistic models.[1]

A. Max-min Rule. Assume that whatever
alternative is chosen, the worst possible
outcome will ensue—the smallest $V(s)$ for
s in S_a will be realized. Then select that
alternative a for which this worst payoff is as
large as possible.

$$\hat{V}(\hat{a}) = \underset{s \varepsilon S\hat{a}}{\text{Min}} \; V(s) = \underset{a \varepsilon A}{\text{Max}} \; \underset{s \varepsilon Sa}{\text{Min}} \; V(s)$$

Instead of the maximum with respect to
the set A of actual alternatives, we can
substitute the maximum with respect to
the set $\mathring{A}$ of "considered" alternatives. The
probability distribution of outcomes, element (6) above, does not play any role in
the max-min rule.

B. Probabilistic Rule. Maximize the expected
value of $V(s)$ for the (assumed known)
probability distribution, $P_a(s)$

$$\hat{V}(\hat{a}) = \underset{s \varepsilon S\hat{a}}{\sum} V(s) P_a(s) = \underset{a \varepsilon A}{\text{Max}} \underset{s \varepsilon Sa}{\sum} V(s) P_a(s)$$

C. Certainty Rule. Given the information that
each a in A (or in $\mathring{A}$) maps upon a specified
s_a in S, select the behavior alternative whose
outcome has the largest payoff.

$$\hat{V}(\hat{a}) = V(S_{\hat{a}}) = \underset{s \varepsilon A}{\text{Max}} \; V(S_a)$$

THE ESSENTIAL SIMPLIFICATIONS

If we closely examine the "classical" concepts of rationality outlined above, we see
immediately what severe demands they
make upon the choosing organism. The
organism must be able to attach definite
payoffs (or at least a definite range of payoffs) to each possible outcome. This, of
course, involves also the ability to specify
the exact nature of the outcomes—there is
no room in the scheme for "unanticipated
consequences." The payoffs must be completely ordered—it must always be possible

to specify, in a consistent way, that one
outcome is better than, as good as, or worse
than any other. And, if the certainty or
probabilistic rules are employed, either the
outcomes of particular alternatives must
be known with certainty or at least it must
be possible to attach definite probabilities
to outcomes.

My first empirical proposition is that
there is a complete lack of evidence that,
in actual human choice situations of any
complexity, these computations can be, or
are in fact, performed. The introspective
evidence is certainly clear enough, but we
cannot, of course, rule out the possibility
that the unconscious is a better decision
maker than the conscious. Nevertheless, in
the absence of evidence that the classical
concepts do describe the decision-making
process, it seems reasonable to examine the
possibility that the actual process is quite
different from the ones the rules describe.

Our procedure will be to introduce some
modifications that appear (on the basis of
casual empiricism) to correspond to observed behavior processes in humans and
that lead to substantial computational
simplifications in the making of a choice.
There is no implication that human beings
use all these modifications and simplifications all the time. Nor is this the place to
attempt the formidable empirical task of
determining the extent to which, and
the circumstances under which, humans
actually employ these simplifications. The
point is rather that these are procedures
that appear often to be employed by human
beings in complex choice situations to
find an approximate model of manageable
proportions.

"Simple" Payoff Functions

One route to simplification is to assume that
$V(s)$ necessarily assumes one of two values,
$(1, 0)$, or of three values, $(1, 0, -1)$, for all
s in S. Depending on the circumstances,
we might want to interpret these values
as (1) (satisfactory or unsatisfactory) or (2)
(win, draw, or lose).

As an example of (2), let S represent the
possible positions in a chess game at White's

---

1. See Kenneth J. Arrow, Alternative approaches to the theory of choice in risk-taking
situations, *Econometrica*, 19:404–37 (October
1951).

twentieth move. Then a ($+1$) position is one in which White possesses a strategy leading to a win whatever Black does. A (0) position is one in which White can enforce a draw, but not a win. A (-1) position is one in which Black can force a win.

As an example of (1), let S represent possible prices for a house an individual is selling. He may regard $15,000 as an "acceptable" price, anything over this amount as "satisfactory," anything less as "unsatisfactory." In psychological theory we would fix the boundary at the "aspiration level"; in economic theory we would fix the boundary at the price that evokes indifference between selling and not selling (an opportunity cost concept).

The objection may be raised that, although $16,000 and $25,000 are both "very satisfactory" prices for the house, a rational individual would prefer to sell at the higher price, and hence, that the simple payoff function is an inadequate representation of the choice situation. The objection may be answered in several different ways, each answer corresponding to a class of situations in which the simple function might be appropriate.

First, the individual may not be confronted simultaneously with a number of buyers offering to purchase the house at different prices, but he may receive a sequence of offers and may have to decide to accept or reject each one before he receives the next. (Or, more generally, he may receive a sequence of pairs or triplets or n-tuples of offers and may have to decide whether to accept the highest of an n-tuple before the next n-tuple is received.) Then, if the elements S correspond to n-tuples of offers, $V(s)$ would be 1 whenever the highest offer in the n-tuple exceeded the "acceptance price" the seller had determined upon at that time. We can then raise the further question of what would be a rational process for determining the acceptance price.[2]

Second, even if there were a more general payoff function, $W(s)$, capable of assuming more than two different values, the simplified $V(s)$ might be a satisfactory approximation to $W(s)$. Suppose, for example, that there were some way of introducing a cardinal utility function, defined over S, say $U(s)$. Suppose further that $U(W)$ is a monotonic increasing function with a strongly negative second derivative (decreasing marginal utility). Then $V(s) = V\{W(s)\}$ might be the approximation as shown in figure 1.

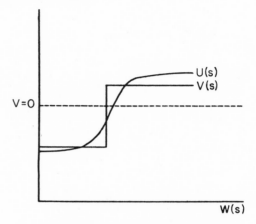

Figure 1. Approximating utility with a simple payoff function.

When a simple $V(s)$, assuming only the values ($+1$, 0) is admissible, under the circumstances just discussed or under other circumstances, then a (fourth) rational decision process could be defined as follows:

D. Satisficing Rule.

1. Search for a set of possible outcomes (a subset S' in S) such that the payoff is satisfactory [$V(s) = 1$] for all these possible outcomes (for all s in S').

2. Search for a behavior alternative (an a in $\hat{A}$) whose possible outcomes all are in S' (such that a maps upon a set S_a that is contained in S').

If a behavior alternative can be found by this procedure, then a satisfactory

2. See the appendix. It might be remarked here that the simple risk function, introduced by Wald to bring problems in statistical decision theory within the bounds of computability, is an example of a simple payoff function as that term is defined here.

outcome is assured. The procedure does not, of course, guarantee the existence or uniqueness of an *a* with the desired properties.

Information Gathering

One element of realism we may wish to introduce is that while $V(s)$ may be known in advance, the mapping of A on subsets of S may not. In the extreme case, at the outset each element, a, may be mapped on the whole set S. We may then introduce into the decision-making process information-gathering steps that produce a more precise mapping of the various elements of A on nonidentical subsets of S. If the information-gathering process is not cost-less, then one element in the decision will be the determination of how far the mapping is to be refined.

Now in the case of the simple payoff functions $(+1, 0)$, the information-gathering process can be streamlined in an important respect. First, we suppose that the individual has initially a very coarse mapping of A on S. Second, he looks for an S' in S such that $V(s) = 1$ for s in S'. Third, he gathers information to refine that part of the mapping of A on S in which elements of S' are involved. Fourth, having refined the mapping, he looks for an a that maps on to a subset of S'.

Under favorable circumstances, this procedure may require the individual to gather only a small amount of information—an insignificant part of the whole mapping of elements of A on individual elements of S. If the search for an a having the desirable properties is successful, he is certain that he cannot better his choice by securing additional information.[3]

It appears that the decision process just described is one of the important means employed by chess players to select a move in the middle and end game. Let A be the set of moves available to White on his twentieth move. Let S be a set of positions that might be reached, say, by the thirtieth move. Let S' be some subset of S that consists of clearly "won" positions. From a very rough knowledge of the mapping of A on S, White tentatively selects a move, a, that (if Black plays in a certain way) maps on S'. By then considering alternative replies for Black, White "explores" the whole mapping of a. His exploration may lead to points, s, that are not in S', but which are now recognized also as winning positions. These can be adjoined to S'. On the other hand, a sequence may be discovered that permits Black to bring about a position that is clearly not "won" for White. Then White may reject the original point a and try another.

Whether this procedure leads to any essential simplification of the computation depends on certain empirical facts about the game. Clearly all positions can be categorized as "won," "lost," or "drawn" in an objective sense. But from the standpoint of the player, positions may be categorized as "clearly won," "clearly lost," "clearly drawn," "won or drawn," "drawn or lost," and so forth—depending on the adequacy of this mapping. If the "clearly won" positions represent a significant subset of the objectively "won" positions, then the combinatorics involved in seeing whether a position can be transformed into a clearly won position, for all possible replies by Black, may not be unmanageable.[4] The advantage of this procedure over the more common notion (which may, however, be applicable in the opening) of a general valuation function

---

3. This procedure also dispenses with the necessity of estimating explicitly the cost of obtaining additional information. For further discussion of this point see the comments on dynamics in the last section of this chapter.

4. I have estimated roughly the actual degree of simplification that might be realized in the middle game in chess by experimentation with two middle-game positions. A sequence of sixteen moves, eight by each player, might be expected to yield a total of about 10^{24} (one septillion) legally permissible variations. By following the general kind of program just described, it was possible to reduce the number of lines of play examined in each of these positions to fewer than 100 variations—a rather spectacular simplification of the choice problem.

for positions, taking on values from −1 to 1, is that it implies much less complex and subtle evaluation criteria. All that is required is that the evaluation function be reasonably sensitive in detecting when a position in one of the three states—won, lost, or drawn—has been transformed into a position in another state. The player, instead of seeking for a "best" move, need only look for a "good" move.

We see that, by the introduction of a simple payoff function and of a process for gradually improving the mapping of behavior alternatives upon possible outcomes, the process of reaching a rational decision may be drastically simplified from a computational standpoint. In the theory and practice of linear programming, the distinction is commonly drawn between computations to determine the *feasibility* of a program and computations to discover the *optimal* program. Feasibility testing consists in determining whether a program satisfies certain linear inequalities that are given at the outset. For example, a mobilization plan may take as given the maximum work force and the steel-making capacity of the economy. Then a feasible program is one that does not require a work force or steel-making facilities exceeding the given limits.

An optimal program is that one of the feasible programs which maximizes a given payoff function. If, instead of requiring that the payoff be maximized, we require only that the payoff exceed some given amount, then we can find a program that satisfies this requirement by the usual methods of feasibility testing. The payoff requirement is represented simply by an additional linear inequality that must be satisfied. Once this requirement is met, it is not necessary to determine whether there exists an alternative plan with a still higher payoff.

For all practical purposes, this procedure may represent a sufficient approach to optimization, provided the minimum required payoff can be set "reasonably." In later sections of this chapter, I will discuss how this might be done, and I will show also how the scheme can be extended to vector payoff functions with multiple components. (Optimization requires, of course, a complete ordering of payoffs).

Partial Ordering of Payoffs

The classical theory does not tolerate the incomparability of oranges and apples. It requires a scalar payoff function, that is, a complete ordering of payoffs. Instead of a scalar payoff function $V(s)$, we might have a vector function $V(s)$; where V has the components V_1, V_2, ... A vector payoff function may be introduced to handle a number of situations:

1. In the case of a decision to be made by a *group of persons*, components may represent the payoff functions of the individual members of the group. What is preferred by one may not be preferred by the others.

2. In the case of an individual, he may be trying to implement a number of *values that do not have a common denominator*—e.g., he compares two jobs in terms of salary, climate, pleasantness of work, prestige, etc.

3. Where each behavior alternative a maps on a set of n possible consequences, S_a, we may replace the model by one in which each alternative maps on a single consequence, but each consequence has as its payoff the n-dimensional vector whose components are the payoffs of the elements of S_a.

This representation exhibits a striking similarity among these three important cases where the traditional maximizing model breaks down for lack of a complete ordering of the payoffs. The first case has never been satisfactorily treated—the theory of the n-person game is the most ambitious attempt to deal with it, and the so-called "weak welfare principles" of economic theory are attempts to avoid it. The second case is usually handled by superimposing a complete ordering on the points in the vector space ("indifference curves"). The third case has been handled by introducing probabilities as weights for summing the vector components, or by using principles such as minimaxing satisfaction or regret.

An extension of the notion of a simplified

payoff function permits us to treat all three cases in much the same fashion. Suppose we regard a payoff as *satisfactory* provided that $V_i \geqslant k_i$ for all i. Then a reasonable decision rule is the following:

E. Partial Ordering Rule. Search for a subset S' in S such that $V(s)$ is satisfactory for all s in S' (i.e., $\underset{s \varepsilon S'}{V(s) \geqslant k}$).

Then search for an a in A such that S_a lies in S'.

Again existence and uniqueness of solutions are not guaranteed. Rule E is illustrated in figure 2 for the case of a two-component payoff vector.

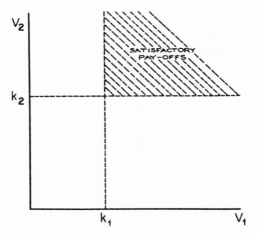

Figure 2. Partial ordering of payoffs.

In the first of the three cases mentioned above, the satisfactory payoff corresponds to what I have called a *viable* solution.[5] In the second case, the components of V define the *aspiration levels* with respect to several components of payoff. In the third case (in this case it is most plausible to assume that all the components of k are equal), k_i may be interpreted as the *minimum guaranteed payoff*—also an aspiration level concept.

5. Herbert A. Simon, A formal theory of the employment relation, *Econometrica*, 19:293–305 (July 1951) and A comparison of organization theories, *Review of Economic Studies*, 20:40–48 (no. 1, 1952–53).

Existence and Uniqueness of Solutions

Throughout this discussion, I have admitted decision procedures that do not guarantee the existence or uniqueness of solutions. This was done in order to construct a model that parallels as nearly as possible the decision procedures that appear to be used by humans in complex decision-making settings. I now proceed to add supplementary rules to fill this gap.

Obtaining a Unique Solution

In most global models of rational choice, all alternatives are evaluated before a choice is made. In actual human decision making, alternatives are often examined sequentially. We may, or may not, know the mechanism that determines the order of procedure. When alternatives are examined sequentially, we may regard the first satisfactory alternative that is evaluated as such as the one actually selected.

If a chess player finds an alternative that leads to a forced mate for his opponent, he generally adopts this alternative without worrying about whether another alternative also leads to a forced mate. In this case, we would find it very hard to predict which alternative would be chosen, for we have no theory that predicts the order in which alternatives will be examined. But in another case discussed above—the sale of a house—the environment presents the seller with alternatives in a definite sequence, and the selection of the *first* satisfactory alternative has precise meaning.

However, there are certain dynamic considerations, having a good psychological foundation, that we should introduce at this point. Let us consider, instead of a single static choice situation, a sequence of such situations. The *aspiration level*, which defines a satisfactory alternative, may change from point to point in this sequence of trials. A vague principle would be that as the individual, in his exploration of alternatives, finds it *easy* to discover satisfactory alternatives, his aspiration level rises; as he finds it *difficult* to discover satisfactory alternatives, his aspiration level falls. Perhaps it would be possible to express the ease or difficulty of exploration in terms of the cost of obtaining better information about the mapping of A on S, or the combinatorial magnitude of the task of refining this mapping. There are a number of ways in which this process could be defined formally.

Such changes in aspiration level would tend to bring about a "near-uniqueness" of the satisfactory solutions and would also tend to guarantee the existence of satisfactory solutions. For the failure to discover a solution would depress the aspiration level and bring satisfactory solutions into existence.

Existence of Solutions: Further Possibilities

I have already discussed one mechanism by which the existence of solutions, in the long run, is assured. There is another way of representing the processes already described. Up to this point little use has been made of the distinction between A, the set of behavior alternatives, and $\mathring{A}$, the set of behavior alternatives that the organism considers. Suppose now that the latter is a proper subset of the former. Then, the failure to find a satisfactory alternative in $\mathring{A}$ may lead to a search for additional alternatives in A that can be adjoined to $\mathring{A}$.[6] This procedure is simply an elaboration of the information-gathering process previously described. (We can regard the elements of A that are not in $\mathring{A}$ as elements that are initially mapped on the whole set S.)

In one organism, dynamic adjustment over a sequence of choices may depend primarily upon adjustments of the aspiration level. In another organism, the adjustments may be primarily in the set $\mathring{A}$: if satisfactory alternatives are discovered easily, $\mathring{A}$ narrows; if it becomes difficult to find satisfactory alternatives, $\mathring{A}$ broadens. The more *persistent* the organism, the greater the role played by the adjustment of $\mathring{A}$, relative to the role played by the adjustment of the aspiration level. (It is possible, of course, and even probable, that there is an asymmetry between adjustments upward and downward.)

If the payoff were measurable in money or utility terms, and *if* the cost of discovering alternatives were similarly measurable, we could replace the partial ordering of alternatives exhibited in figure 2 by a complete ordering (an ordering in terms of a weighted sum of the payoff and the cost of discovering alternatives). Then we could speak of the optimal degree of persistence in behavior—we could say that the more persistent organism was more rational than the other, or vice versa. But the central argument of this chapter is that the behaving organism does *not* in general know these costs, nor does it have a set of weights for comparing the components of a multiple payoff. It is precisely because of these limitations on its knowledge and capabilities that the less global models of rationality described here are significant and useful. The question of how it is to behave "rationally," given these limitations, is distinct from the question of how its capabilities could be increased to permit action that would be more "rational" judged from the mountaintop of a more complete model.[7]

The two viewpoints are not, of course, completely different, much less antithetical.

---

6. I might mention that, in the spirit of crude empiricism, I have presented a number of students and friends with a problem involving a multiple payoff—in which the payoff depends violently upon a very contingent and uncertain event—and have found them extremely reluctant to restrict themselves to a set of behavior alternatives allowed by the problem. They were averse to an alternative that promised very large profit or ruin, where the relevant probability could not be computed, and tried to invent new alternatives whose payoffs were less sensitive to the contingent event. The problem in question is Modigliani's "hotdog stand" problem described in *American Economic Review, Proceedings*, 39:201–08 (1949).

---

7. One might add: "or judged in terms of the survival value of its choice mechanism."

I have already pointed out that the organism may possess a whole hierarchy of rational mechanisms—that, for example, the aspiration level itself may be subject to an adjustment process that is rational in some dynamic sense. Moreover, in many situations we may be interested in the precise question of whether one decision-making procedure is more rational than another, and to answer this question we will usually have to construct a broader criterion of rationality that encompasses both procedures as approximations. Our whole point is that it is important to make explicit what level we are considering in such a hierarchy of models, and that for many purposes we are interested in models of "limited" rationality rather than models of relatively "global" rationality.

FURTHER COMMENTS ON DYNAMICS

The models thus far discussed are dynamic only in a very special sense: the aspiration level at time t depends upon the previous history of the system (previous aspiration levels and previous levels of attainment). Another kind of dynamic linkage might be very important. The payoffs in a particular trial might depend not only on the alternative chosen in that trial but also on the alternatives chosen in previous trials.

The most direct representation of this situation is to include, as components of a vector payoff function, the payoffs for the whole sequence of trials. But then optimization would require the selection, at the beginning of the sequence, of a strategy for the whole sequence (see the appendix). Such a procedure would again rapidly complicate the problem beyond the computational capacity of the organism. A possible middle ground is to define for each trial a payoff function with two components. One would be the "immediate" payoff (consumption), the other, the "position" in which the organism is left for future trials (saving, liquidity).

Let us consider a chess game in which the players are paid off at the end of each ten moves in proportion to arbitrarily assigned values of their pieces left on the board (say,

queen, 1; rook, 10; etc.). Then a player could adopt some kind of planning horizon and include in his estimated payoff the "goodness" of his position at the planning horizon. A comparable notion in economics is that of the depreciated value of an asset at the planning horizon. To compute such a value precisely would require the player actually to carry his strategy beyond the horizon. If there is time-discounting of payoffs, this has the advantage of reducing the importance of errors in estimating these depreciated values. (Time-discounting may sometimes be essential in order to assure convergence of the summed payoffs.)

It is easy to conjure up other dynamic complications, which may be of considerable practical importance. Two more may be mentioned—without attempting to incorporate them formally. The consequences that the organism experiences may change the payoff function—it doesn't know how well it likes cheese until it has eaten cheese. Likewise, one method for refining the mapping of A on S may be to select a particular alternative and experience its consequences. In these cases, one of the elements of the payoff associated with a particular alternative is the information that is gathered about the mapping or about the payoff function.

CONCLUSION

The aim of this chapter has been to construct definitions of "rational choice" that are modeled more closely upon the actual decision processes in the behavior of organisms than definitions heretofore proposed. I have outlined a fairly complete model for the static case and have described one extension of this model into dynamics. As has been indicated in the last section, a great deal remains to be done before we can handle realistically a more completely dynamic system.

In the introduction, it was suggested that definitions of this kind might have normative as well as descriptive value. In particular, they may suggest approaches to rational choice in areas that appear to be far beyond the capacities of existing or prospective computing equipment. The comparison of the IQ of a computer with that of a human being is very difficult. If one were to factor the scores made by each on a comprehensive intelligence test, one would undoubtedly find that in those factors on which the one scored as a genius the other would appear a moron—and conversely. A survey of possible definitions of rationality might suggest directions for the design and use of computing equipment with reasonably good scores on some of the factors of intelligence in which present computers are moronic.

The broader aim, however, in constructing these definitions of "approximate" rationality is to provide some materials for the construction of a theory of the behavior of a human individual or of groups of individuals who are making decisions in an organizational context. The apparent paradox to be faced is that the economic theory of the firm and the theory of administration attempt to deal with human behavior in situations in which that behavior is at least "intendedly" rational; while, at the same time, it can be shown that if we assume the global kinds of rationality of the classical theory, the problems of internal structure of the firm or other organization largely disappear.[8] The paradox vanishes, and the outlines of theory begin to emerge when we substitute for Economic Man or Administrative Man a choosing organism of limited knowledge and ability. This organism's simplifications of the real world for purposes of choice introduce discrepancies between the simplified model and the reality; and these discrepancies, in turn, serve to explain many of the phenomena of organizational behavior.

APPENDIX: EXAMPLE OF RATIONAL DETERMINATION OF AN ACCEPTABLE PAYOFF

In the body of this chapter, the notion is introduced that rational adjustment may

operate at various "levels." That is, the organism may choose rationally within a given set of limits postulated by the model, but it may also undertake to set these limits rationally. The house-selling illustration provides an example of this.

Suppose that an individual is selling a house. Each day (or other unit of time) he sets an acceptance price: $d(k)$, say, for the kth day. If he receives one or more offers above this price on the day in question, he accepts the highest offer; if he does not receive an offer above $d(k)$, he retains the house until the next day, and sets a new acceptance price, $d(k + 1)$.

Now, if he has certain information about the probability distribution of offers on each day, he can set the acceptance price so that it will be optimal in the sense that it will maximize the expected value $V[d(k)]$, of the sales price.

To show this, we proceed as follows. Let $p_k(y)$ be the probability that y will be the highest price offered on the kth day. Then:

$$P_k(d) = \int_{d(k)}^{\infty} p_k(y)dy \qquad (1)$$

is the probability that the house will be sold on the kth day if it has not been sold earlier.

$$\varepsilon_k(d) = \int_{d(k)}^{\infty} y\, p(y, k)dy \qquad (2)$$

will be the expected value received by the seller on the kth day if the house has not been sold earlier. Taking into account the probability that the house will be sold before the kth day,

$$E_k(d) = \varepsilon_k(d) \prod_{j=1}^{k-1} (1 - P_j(d)) \qquad (3)$$

will be the unconditional expected value of the seller's receipts on the kth day; and

$$V\{d(k)\} = \sum_{k=1}^{\infty} E_k(d) \qquad (4)$$

will be the expected value of the sales price.

Now we wish to set $d(k)$, for each k, at the level that will maximize (4). The k components of the function $d(k)$ are in-

---

8. See Herbert A. Simon, *Administrative Behavior*, New York: Macmillan, 1947, pp. 39–41, 80–84, 96–102, 240–44.

dependent. Differentiating V partially with respect to each component, we get:

$$\frac{\partial V}{\partial d(i)} = \sum_{k=1}^{\infty} \frac{\partial E_k(d)}{\partial d(i)} \quad (i = 1, \ldots, n)_k \quad (5)$$

But:

$$\frac{\partial E_i(d)}{\partial d(i)} = \frac{\partial \varepsilon_i(d)}{\partial d(i)} \prod_{j=1}^{i-1} (1 - P_j(d)) \quad (6)$$

and

$$\frac{\partial E_k(d)}{\partial d(i)} = \varepsilon_k(d) \prod_{\substack{j \neq i \\ j=1}}^{k-1} (1 - P_j(d)) \left(- \frac{\partial P_i(d)}{\partial d(i)}\right)$$

for $i < k$ \qquad\qquad\qquad\qquad (7)

and

$$\frac{\partial E_k(d)}{\partial d(i)} = 0 \qquad\qquad \text{for } i > k \quad (8)$$

Hence for a maximum:

$$\frac{\partial V}{\partial d(i)} = - d(i) p_i(d) \prod_{j=1}^{i-1} (1 - P_j(d))$$
$$+ \sum_{k=i+1}^{\infty} \varepsilon_k(d) \prod_{j \neq i}^{k-1} (1 - P_j(d)) p_i(d)$$
$$= 0 \qquad\qquad\qquad\qquad\qquad (9)$$

Factoring out $p_i(d)$, we obtain, finally:

$$d(i) = \frac{\sum_{k=i+1}^{\infty} \varepsilon_k(d) \prod_{j \neq i}^{k-1} [1 - P_j(d)]}{\prod_{j=1}^{i-1} [1 - P_j(d)]}$$
$$= \sum_{k=i+1}^{\infty} \varepsilon_k(d) \prod_{j=i+1}^{k-1} [1 - P_j(d)]. \quad (10)$$

For the answer to be meaningful, the infinite sum in (10) must converge. If we look at the definition (2) for $\varepsilon_k(d)$, we see this would come about if the probability distribution of offers shifts downward through time with sufficient rapidity. Such a shift might correspond to (1) expectations of falling prices, or (2) interpretation of y as the *present value* of the future price, discounted at a sufficiently high interest rate.

Alternatively, we can avoid the question of convergence by assuming a reservation price $a(n)$, for the nth day, which is low

enough so that $P_n(d)$ is unity. We will take this last alternative, but before proceeding, I wish to interpret equation (10). Equation (10) says that the rational acceptance price on the ith day, $d(i)$, is equal to the expected value of the sales price if the house is not sold on the ith day and acceptance prices are set optimally for subsequent days. This can be seen by observing that the right-hand side of (10) is the same as the right-hand side of (4) but with the summation extending from $k = (i + 1)$ instead of from $(k = 1)$.[9]

Hence, in the case where the summation is terminated at period n—that is, the house will be sold with certainty in period n if it has not been sold previously—we can compute the optimal $d(i)$ by working backward from the terminal period, and without the necessity of solving simultaneously the equations (10).

It is interesting to observe what additional information the seller needs in order to determine the rational acceptance price, over and above the information he needs once the acceptance price is set. He needs, in fact, virtually complete information as to the probability distribution of offers for all relevant subsequent time periods.

Now the seller who does not have this information, and who will be satisfied with a more bumbling kind of rationality, will make approximations to avoid using the information he doesn't have. First, he will probably limit the planning horizon by assuming a price at which he can certainly sell and will be willing to sell in the nth time period. Second, he will set his initial acceptance price quite high, watch the distribution of offers he receives, and gradually and approximately adjust his acceptance price downward or upward until he receives an offer he accepts—without ever making probability calculations. This, I submit, is the kind of rational adjustment that humans find "good

---

9. Equation (10) appears to have been arrived at independently by D. A. Darling and W. M. Kincaid. See their abstract, "An Inventory Problem," in the *Journal of Operations Research Society of America*, 1:80 (February 1953).

enough" and are capable of exercising in a wide range of practical circumstances.

References

Arrow, K. J., Alternative approaches to the theory of choice in risk-taking situations, *Econometrica*, 1951, 19:404–37.

Darling, D. A., and Kincaid, W. M., An inventory problem, *Journal of Operations Research Society of America*, 1953, 1:80.

Modigliani, F., Liquidity and uncertainty—Discussion, *American Economic Review, Proceedings*, 1949, 39:201–08.

Simon, H. A., *Administrative Behavior*, New York: Macmillan, 1947.

Simon, H. A., A comparison of organization theories, *Review of Economic Studies*, no. 1, 1952–53, 20:40–48.

Simon, H. A. A formal theory of the employment relation, *Econometrica*, 1951, 19:293–305.

Rational Choice and the Structure of the Environment (1956)

A growing interest in decision making in psychology is evidenced by the recent publication of Edwards' review article in the *Psychological Bulletin* (Edwards, 1954) and the Santa Monica Conference volume, *Decision Processes* (Thrall et al., 1954). In this work, much attention has been focused on the characterization of *rational* choice, and because this topic has been a central concern in economics, the theory of decision making has become a natural meeting ground for psychological and economic theory.

A comparative examination of the models of adaptive behavior employed in psychology (e.g., learning theories) and of the models of rational behavior employed in economics shows that in almost all respects the latter postulate a much greater complexity in the choice mechanisms, and a much larger capacity in the organism for obtaining information and performing computations, than do the former. Moreover, in the limited range of situations where the predictions of the two theories have been compared (see Thrall et al., chaps. 9, 10, 18), the learning theories

appear to account for the observed behavior rather better than do the theories of rational behavior.

Both from these scanty data and from an examination of the postulates of the economic models, it appears probable that, however adaptive the behavior of organisms in learning and choice situations, this adaptiveness falls far short of the ideal of "maximizing" postulated in economic theory. Evidently, organisms adapt well enough to "satisfice"; they do not, in general, "optimize."

If this is the case, a great deal can be learned about rational decision making by taking into account, at the outset, the limitations upon the capacities and complexity of the organism, and by taking account of the fact that the environments to which it must adapt possess properties that permit further simplification of its choice mechanisms. It may be useful, therefore, to ask: How simple a set of choice mechanisms can we postulate and still obtain the gross features of observed adaptive choice behavior?

In a previous paper (Simon, 1955) I have put forth some suggestions as to the kinds of "approximate" rationality that might be employed by an organism possessing limited information and limited computational facilities. The suggestions were

I am indebted to Allen Newell for numerous enlightening conversations on the subject of this paper and to the Ford Foundation for a grant that permitted me leisure to complete it.

"hypothetical" in that, lacking definitive knowledge of the human decisional processes, we can only conjecture on the basis of our everyday experiences, our introspection, and a very limited body of psychological literature what these processes are. The suggestions were intended, however, as empirical statements, however tentative, about some of the actual mechanisms involved in human and other organismic choice.[1]

Now if an organism is confronted with the problem of behaving approximately rationally, or adaptively, in a particular environment, the kinds of simplifications that are suitable may depend not only on the characteristics—sensory, neural, and other—of the organism, but equally upon the structure of the environment. Hence, we might hope to discover, by a careful examination of some of the fundamental structural characteristics of the environment, some further clues as to the nature of the approximating mechanisms used in decision making. This is the line of attack that will be adopted in this chapter.

The environment I will discuss initially is perhaps a more appropriate one for a rat than for a human. For the term *environment* is ambiguous. I am not interested in describing some physically objective world in its totality, but only those aspects of the totality that have relevance as the "life space" of the organism considered. Hence, what I call the "environment" will depend upon the "needs," "drives," or "goals" of the organism and upon its perceptual apparatus.

THE ENVIRONMENT OF THE ORGANISM

We consider first a simplified (perhaps "simple-minded") organism that has a single need—food—and is capable of three kinds of activity: resting, exploration, and food getting. The precise nature of these activities will be explained later. The organism's life space may be described as a surface over which it can locomote. Most of the surface is perfectly bare, but at isolated, widely scattered points there are little heaps of food, each adequate for a meal.

The organism's vision permits it to see, at any moment, a circular portion of the surface about the point in which it is standing. It is able to move at some fixed maximum rate over the surface. It metabolizes at a given average rate and is able to store a certain amount of food energy, so that it needs to eat a meal at certain average intervals. It has the capacity, once it sees a food heap, to proceed toward it at the maximum rate of locomotion. The problem of rational choice is to choose its path in such a way that it will not starve.

Now I submit that a rational way for the organism to behave is the following: (1) it explores the surface at random, watching for a food heap; (2) when it sees one, it proceeds to it and eats (food getting); (3) if the total consumption of energy during the average time required, per meal, for exploration and food getting is less than the energy of the food consumed in the meal, it can spend the remainder of its time in resting.[2]

There is nothing particularly remarkable about this description of rational choice, except that it differs so sharply from the more sophisticated models of human rationality that have been proposed by economists and others. Let us see what it is about the organism and its environment that makes its choice so simple.

---

1. Since writing the paper referred to, I have found confirmation for a number of its hypotheses in the interesting and significant study, by A. de Groot (1946), of the thought processes of chess players. I discuss the implications of these empirical findings for my model in Chapters 4.2 and 4.3.

2. A reader who is familiar with W. Grey Walter's mechanical turtle, *Machina speculatrix*, will see as we proceed that the description of our organism could well be used as a set of design specifications to assure the survival of his turtle in an environment sparsely provided with battery chargers. Since I was not familiar with the structure of the turtle when I developed this model, there are some differences in their behavior—but the resemblance is striking. See Walter, 1953.

1. It has only a single goal: food. It does not need to weigh the respective advantages of different goals. It requires no "utility function" or set of "indifference curves" to permit it to choose between alternatives.

2. It has no problem of maximization. It needs only to maintain a certain average rate of food intake, and additional food is of no use to it. In the psychologist's language, it has a definite, fixed aspiration level, and its successes or failures do not change its apirations.

3. The nature of its perceptions and its environment limit sharply its planning horizon. Since the food heaps are distributed randomly, there is no need for pattern in its searching activities. Once it sees a food heap, it can follow a definite "best" path until it reaches it.

4. The nature of its needs and environment create a very natural separation between "means" and "ends." Except for the food heaps, one point on the surface is as agreeable to it as another. Locomotion has significance only as it is a means to reaching food.[3]

We will see that the first point is not essential. As long as aspirations are fixed, the planning horizon is limited, and there is a sharp distinction between means and ends, the existence of multiple goals does not create any real difficulties in choice. The real complications ensue only when we relax the last three conditions; but to see clearly what is involved, we must formulate the model a little more precisely.

PERCEPTUAL POWERS, STORAGE
CAPACITY, AND SURVIVAL

It is convenient to describe the organism's life space not as a continuous surface, but as a branching system of paths, like a maze, each branch point representing a choice point. We call the selection of a branch and locomotion to the next branch point a

---

3. It is characteristic of economic models of rationality that the distinction between "means" and "ends" plays no essential role in them. This distinction *cannot* be identified with the distinction between behavior alternatives and utilities, for reasons that are set forth at some length in Simon, 1947, Chaps. 4, 5.

"move." At a small fraction of the branch points are heaps of food.

Let p, $0 < p < 1$, be the percentage of branch points, randomly distributed, at which food is found. Let d be the average number of paths diverging from each branch point. Let v be the number of moves ahead the organism can see. That is, if there is food at any of the branch points within v moves of the organism's present position, it can select the proper paths and reach it. Finally let H be the maximum number of moves the organism can make between meals without starving.

At any given moment, the organism can see d branch points at a distance of one move from his present position, d^2 points two moves away, and in general, d^k points k moves away. In all, it can see $d + d^2 + \ldots + d^v = \dfrac{d}{d-1}(d^v - 1)$ points. When it chooses a branch and makes a move, d^v new points become visible on its horizon. Hence, in the course of m moves, md^v new points appear. Since it can make a maximum of H moves, and since v of these will be required to reach food that it has discovered on its horizon, the probability, $Q = 1 - P$, that it will *not* survive will be equal to the probability that no food points will be visible in $(H - v)$ moves. (If p is small, we can disregard the possibility that food will be visible inside its planning horizon on the first move.) Let ρ be the probability that none of the d^v new points visible at the end of a particular move is a food point.

$$\rho = (1 - p)^{d^v} \qquad (1)$$

Then:

$$1 - P = Q = \rho^{(H-v)} = (1 - p)^{(H-v)d^v} \qquad (2)$$

We see that the survival chances, from meal to meal, of this simple organism depend on four parameters, two that describe the organism and two the environment: p, the richness of the environment in food; d, the richness of the environment in paths; H, the storage capacity of the organism; and v, the range of vision of the organism.

To give some impression of the magnitudes involved, let us assume that p is $1/10,000$, $(H - v)$ is 100, d is 10, and v is 3. Then the probability of seeing a new food point after a move is $1 - \rho = 1 - (1 - p)^{1000} \sim 880/10,000$, and the probability of survival is $P = 1 - \rho^{100} \sim 9999/10,000$. Hence there is in this case only one chance in 10,000 that the organism will fail to reach a food point before the end of the survival interval. Suppose now that the survival time $(H - v)$ is increased one-third, that is, from 100 to 133. Then a similar computation shows that the chance of starvation is reduced to less than one chance in 100,000. A one-third increase in v will, of course, have an even greater effect, reducing the chance of starvation from one in 10^4 to one in 10^{40}.

Using the same values, $p = 0.0001$, and $(H - v) = 100$, we can compute the probability of survival if the organism behaves completely randomly. In this case $P' = [1 - (1 - p)^{100}] = 0.009$. From these computations, we see that the organism's modest capacity to perform purposive acts over a short planning horizon permits it to survive easily in an environment where random behavior would lead to rapid extinction. A simple computation shows that its perceptual powers multiply by a factor of 880 the average speed with which it discovers food.

If p, d, and v are given, and in addition we specify that the survival probability must be greater than some number close to unity $(P \geq 1 - \varepsilon)$, we can compute from equation (2) the corresponding minimum value of H:

$$\log (1 - P) = (H - v) \log \rho \qquad (3)$$

$$H \geq v + \frac{\log \varepsilon}{\log \rho} \qquad (4)$$

For example, if $\rho = 0.95$ and $\varepsilon = 10^{-10}$, then $\log \rho = -0.022$, $\log \varepsilon = -10$ and $(H - v) \geq 455$. The parameter H can be interpreted as the "storage capacity" of the organism. That is, if the organism metabolizes at the rate of α units per move, then a storage of αH food units, where H is given by equation (4) would be required to provide survival at the specified risk level ε.

Further insight into the meaning of H can be gained by considering the average number of moves, M, required to discover food. From equation (1), the probability of making $(k - 1)$ moves without discovering food, and then discovering it on the k th is:

$$P_k = (1 - \rho) \rho^{(k-1)} \qquad (5)$$

Hence, the average number of moves, M, required to discover food is:

$$M = \sum_{k=1}^{\infty} k(1 - \rho) \rho^{k-1}$$

$$= \frac{(1 - \rho)}{(1 - \rho)^2} = \frac{1}{(1 - \rho)} \qquad (6)$$

Since $(1 - \rho)$ is the probability of discovering food in any one move, M is the reciprocal of this probability. Combining (3) and (6), we obtain:

$$\frac{M}{H - v} = \frac{\log \rho}{(1 - \rho)} \frac{1}{\log (1 - P)} \qquad (7)$$

Since ρ is close to one, $\log_e \rho \simeq (1 - \rho)$, and (7) reduces approximately to:

$$\frac{M}{H - v} \simeq \frac{1}{\log_e (1 - P)} \qquad (8)$$

For example, if we require $(1 - P) = \varepsilon \leq 10^{-4}$ (one chance in 10,000 of starvation), then $M/(H - v) \leq 0.11$. For this survival level we require food storage approximately equal to $\alpha(v + 9M)$—food enough to sustain the organism for nine times the period required, on the average, to discover food, plus the period required to reach the food.[4]

---

4. I have not discovered any very satisfactory data on the food storage capacities of animals, but the order of magnitude suggested above for the ratio of average search time to storage capacity is certainly correct. It may be noted that, in some cases at least, where the "food" substance is ubiquitous, and hence the search time negligible, the storage capacity is also small. Thus, in terrestrial animals there is little oxygen storage and life can be maintained in the absence of air for only a few minutes. I am not arguing as to which way the causal arrow runs, but only that the organisms, in this respect, are adapted to their environments and do not provide storage that is superfluous.

Choice Mechanisms for Multiple Goals

We consider now a more complex organism capable of searching for and responding to two or more kinds of goal objects. In doing this, we could introduce any desired degree of complexity into the choice process; but the interesting problem is how to introduce multiple goals with a minimum complication of the process—that is, to construct an organism capable of handling its decision problems with relatively primitive choice mechanisms.

At the very least, the presence of two goals will introduce a consistency requirement—the time consumed in attaining one goal will limit the time available for pursuit of the other. But in an environment like the one we have been considering, there need be no further relationship between the two goals. In our original formulation, the only essential stipulation was that H, the storage capacity, be adequate to maintain the risk of starvation below a stipulated level $(1 - P)$. Now we introduce the additional stipulation that the organism should only devote a fraction, λ, of its time to food-seeking activities, leaving the remaining fraction, $1 - \lambda$, to other activities. This new stipulation leads to a requirement of additional storage capacity.

In order to control the risk of starving, the organism must begin its exploration for food whenever it has reached a level of H periods of food storage. If it has a total storage of $(\mu + H)$ periods of food, and if the food heaps are at least $\alpha(\mu + H)$ in size, then it need begin the search for food only μ periods after its last feeding. But the food search will require, on the average, M periods. Hence, if a hunger threshold is established that leads the organism to begin to explore μ periods after feeding, we will have:

$$\lambda = \frac{M}{M + \mu} \qquad (9)$$

Hence, by making μ sufficiently large, we can make λ as small as we please. Parenthetically, it may be noted that we have here a close analogue to the very common two-bin system of controlling industrial inventories. The primary storage H is a buffer stock to meet demands pending the receipt of new orders (with risk, $1 - P$, of running out); the secondary storage μ defines the "order point"; and $\mu + M$ is the average order quantity. The storage μ is fixed to balance storage "costs" against the cost (in this case, time pressure) of too frequent reordering.

If food and the second goal object (water, let us say) are randomly and independently distributed, then there are no important complications resulting from interference between the two activities. Designate by the subscript 1 the variables and parameters referring to food getting (e.g., μ_1 is the food threshold in periods) and by the subscript 2 the quantities referring to water seeking. The organism will have adequate time for both activities if $\lambda_1 + \lambda_2 < 1$.

Now when the organism reaches either its hunger or thirst threshold, it will begin exploration. We assume that if *either* of the goal objects becomes visible, it will proceed to that object and satisfy its hunger or thirst (this will not increase the number of moves required, on the average, to reach the other object); but if *both* objects become visible at the same time, and if S_1 and S_2 are the respective quantities remaining in storage at this time, then it will proceed to food or water as M_1/S_1 is greater or less than M_2/S_2. This choice will maximize its survival probability. What is required, then, is a mechanism that produces a drive proportional to M_i/S_i.

A priority mechanism of the kind just described is by no means the only or simplest one that can be postulated. An even simpler rule is for the organism to persist in searching for points that will satisfy the particular need that first reached its threshold and initiated exploratory behavior. This is not usually an efficient procedure, from the standpoint of conserving goal-reaching time, but it may be entirely adequate for an organism generously endowed with storage capacity.

We see that an organism can satisfy a number of distinct needs without requiring a very elaborate mechanism for choosing among them. In particular, we do not have to postulate a utility function or a "marginal rate of substitution."

We can go even further, and assert that a primitive choice mechanism is adequate to take advantage of important economies, if they exist, which are derivable from the interdependence of the activities involved in satisfying the different needs. For suppose the organism has n needs, and that points at which he can satisfy each are distributed randomly and independently through the environment, each with the same probability, p. Then the probability that no points satisfying *any* of the needs will be visible on a particular move is ρ^n, and the mean number of moves for discovery of the *first* need-satisfying point is:

$$m_n = \frac{1}{(1 - \rho^n)} \qquad (10)$$

Suppose that the organism begins to explore, moves to the first need-satisfying point it discovers, resumes its exploration, moves to the next point it discovers that satisfies a need other than the one already satisfied, and so on. Then the mean time required to search for all n goals will be:

$$M_n = m_n + m_{n-1} + \cdots$$
$$= \sum_{i=1}^{n} \frac{1}{(1 - \rho^i)} \ll \frac{n}{(1 - \rho)} \qquad (11)$$

In particular, if ρ is close to one, that is, if need-satisfying points are rare, we will have:

$$M_n - M_{n-1} = \frac{1}{(1 - \rho^n)}$$
$$= \frac{1}{(1 - \rho)} \cdot \frac{1}{\sum_{i=1}^{n} \rho^i} \simeq \frac{M_1}{n} \quad (12)$$

and

$$M_n \simeq M_1 \sum_{i=1}^{n} \frac{1}{i} \qquad (13)$$

Now substituting particular values for n in (13), we get: $M_2 = \frac{3}{2} M_1$; $M_3 = \frac{11}{6} M_1$; $M_4 = \frac{25}{12} M_1$, etc. We see that if the organism has two separate needs, its exploration time will be only 50 percent greater than—and not twice as great as—if it has only one need; for four needs the exploration time will be only slightly more

than twice as great as for a single need, and so on. A little consideration of the program just described will show that the joint exploratory process does not reduce the primary storage capacity required by the organism but does reduce the secondary storage capacity required. As a matter of fact, there would be no necessity at all for secondary storage.

This conclusion holds only if the need-satsifying points are *independently* distributed. If there is a negative correlation in the joint distribution of points satisfying different needs, then it may be economical for the organism to pursue its needs separately, and hence to have a simple signaling mechanism, involving secondary storage, to trigger its several exploration drives. This point will be developed further in the next section.

A word may be said here about "avoidance needs." Suppose that certain points in the organism's behavior space are designated as "dangerous." Then it will need to avoid those paths that lead to these particular points. If r percent of all points, randomly distributed, are dangerous, then the number of available paths, among those visible at a given move, will be reduced to $(1 - r)d^v$. Hence, $\rho' = (1 - p)^{(1-r)d^v}$ will be smaller than ρ [equation (1)], and M [equation (6)] will be correspondingly larger. Hence, the presence of danger points simply increases the average exploration time and, consequently, the required storage capacity of the organism.

FURTHER SPECIFICATION OF THE ENVIRONMENT: CLUES

In our discussion up to the present point, the range of the organism's anticipations of the future has been limited by the number of behavior alternatives available to it at each move (d), and the length of the "vision" (v). It is a simple matter to introduce into the model the consequences of several types of learning. An increase in the repertoire of behavior alternatives or in the length of vision can simply be represented by changes in d and v, respectively.

A more interesting possibility arises if

the food points are not distributed completely at random, and if there are clues that indicate whether a particular intermediate point is rich or poor in paths leading to food points. First, let us suppose that on the path leading up to each food point the k preceding choice points are marked with a food clue. Once the association between the clue and the subsequent appearance of the food point is learned by the organism, its exploration can terminate with the discovery of the clue, and it can follow a determinate path from that point on. This amounts to substituting $v' = (v + k)$ for v.

A different kind of clue might operate in the following fashion. Each choice point has a distinguishable characteristic that is associated with the probability of encountering a food point if a path is selected random leading out of this at point. The organism can then select at each move the choice point with the highest probability. If only certain choice points are provided with such clues, then a combination of random and systematic exploration can be employed. Thus the organism may be led into "regions" where the probability of goal attainment is relatively high, but it may have to explore randomly for food within a given region.

A concrete example of such behavior in humans is the "position play" characteristic of the first phase of a chess game. The player chooses moves on the basis of certain characteristics of resulting positions (e.g., the extent to which his pieces are developed). Certain positions are adjudged richer in attacking and defensive possibilities than others, but the original choice may involve no definite plan for the subsequent action after the "good" position has been reached.

Next, we turn to the problem of choice that arises when those regions of the behavior space that are rich in points satisfying one need (p_1 is high in these regions) are poor in points satisfying another need (p_2 is low in these same regions.) In the earlier case of goal conflict (two or more points simultaneously visible mediating different needs), we postulated a priority mechanism that amounted to a mechanism for computing relative need intensity and for responding to the more intense need. In the environment with clues, the learning process would need to include a conditioning mechanism that would attach the priority mechanism to the response to competing clues, as well as to competing visible needs.

Finally, we have thus far specified the environment in such a way that there is only one path leading to each point. Formally, this condition can always be satisfied by representing as two or more points any point that can be reached by multiple paths. For some purposes, it might be preferable to specify an environment in which paths converge as well as diverge. This can be done without disturbing the really essential conditions of the foregoing analysis. For behavior of the sort we have been describing, we require of the environment only:

1. That if a path is selected *completely* at random the probability of survival is negligible.

2. That there exist clues in the environment (either the actual visibility of need-satisfying points or anticipatory clues) which permit the organism, sufficiently frequently for survival, to select specific paths that lead with certainty, or with very high probability, to a need-satisfying point.

Concluding Comments on Multiple Goals

The central problem of this chapter has been to construct a simple mechanism of choice that would suffice for the behavior of an organism confronted with multiple goals. Since the organism, like those of the real world, has neither the senses nor the wits to discover an "optimal" path—even assuming the concept of optimal to be clearly defined—we are concerned only with finding a choice mechanism that will lead it to pursue a "satisficing" path, a path that will permit satisfaction at some specified level of all its needs.

Certain of the assumptions we have introduced to make this possible represent characteristics of the organism: (1) It is able to plan short purposive behavior sequences (of length not exceeding v), but not long sequences. (2) Its needs are not insatiable, and hence it does not need to balance marginal increments of satisfaction. If all its needs are satisfied, it simply becomes inactive. (3) It possesses sufficient storage capacity so that the exact moment of satisfaction of any particular need is not critical.

We have introduced other assumptions that represent characteristics of the environment, the most important being that need satisfaction can take place only at "rare" points which (with some qualifications we have indicated) are distributed randomly.

The most important conclusion we have reached is that blocks of the organism's time can be allocated to activities related to individual needs (separate means-end chains) without creating any problem of overall allocation or coordination or the need for any general "utility function." The only scarce resource in the situation is time, and its scarcity, measured by the proportion of the total time that the organism will need to be engaged in *some* activity, can be reduced by the provision of generous storage capacity.

This does not mean that a more efficient procedure cannot be constructed from the standpoint of the total time required to meet the organism's needs. We have already explored some simple possibilities for increasing efficiency by recognizing complementarities among activities (particularly the exploration activity). But the point is that these complications are not essential to the survival of an organism. Moreover, if the environment is so constructed (as it often is in fact) that regions rich in possibilities for one kind of need satisfaction are poor in possibilities for other satisfactions, such efficiencies may not be available.

It may be objected that even relatively simple organisms appear to conform to efficiency criteria in their behavior, and hence that their choice mechanisms are much more elaborate than those we have

described. A rat, for example, learns to take shorter rather than longer paths to food. But this observation does not effect the central argument. We can introduce a mechanism that leads the organism to choose time-conserving paths, where multiple paths are available for satisfying a given need, without any assumption of a mechanism that allocates time among *different* needs. The former mechanism simply increases the "slack" in the whole system and makes it even more feasible to ignore the complementarities among activities in programming the overall behavior of the organism.

This is not the place to discuss at length the application of the model to human behavior, but a few general statements may be in order. First, the analysis has been a static one, in the sense that we have taken the organism's needs and its sensing and planning capacities as given. Except for a few comments, we have not considered how the organism develops needs or learns to meet them. One would conjecture, from general observation and from experimentation with aspiration levels, that in humans the balance between the time required to meet needs and the total time available is maintained by the raising and lowering of aspiration levels. I have commented on this point at greater length in my previous paper.[5]

Second, there is nothing about the model that implies that the needs are physiological and innate rather than sociological and acquired. Provided that the needs of the organism can be specified at any given time in terms of the aspiration levels for the various kinds of consummatory behavior, the model can be applied.

The principal positive implication of the model is that we should be skeptical in postulating for humans, or other organisms, elaborate mechanisms for choosing among diverse needs. Common denominators among needs may simply not exist, or may

---

5. See Simon 1955, pp. 111, 117–18. For an experiment demonstrating the adjustment of the rat's aspiration levels to considerations of realizability, see Festinger, 1953.

exist only in very rudimentary form; and the nature of the organism's needs in relation to the environment may make their nonexistence entirely tolerable.

There is some positive evidence bearing on this point in the work that has been done on conflict and frustration. A common method of producing conflict in the laboratory is to place the organism in a situation where: (1) it is stimulated to address itself simultaneously to alternative goal-oriented behaviors, or (2) it is stimulated to a goal-oriented behavior, but restricted from carrying out the behaviors it usually evinces in similar natural situations. This suggests that conflict may arise (at least in a large class of situations) from presenting the animal with situations with which it is not "programmed" to deal. Conflict of choice may often be equivalent to an absence of a choice mechanism in the given situation. And while it may be easy to create such situations in the laboratory, the absence of a mechanism to deal with them may simply reflect the fact that the organism seldom encounters equivalent situations in its natural environment.[6]

CONCLUSION

In this chapter I have attempted to identify some of the structural characteristics that are typical of the "psychological" environments of organisms. We have seen that an organism in an environment with these characteristics requires only very simple perceptual and choice mechanisms to satisfy its several needs and to assure a high probability of its survival over extended periods of time. In particular, no "utility function" needs to be postulated for the organism, nor does it require any elaborate procedure for calculating marginal rates of substitution among different wants.

The analysis set forth here casts serious doubt on the usefulness of current economic and statistical theories of rational behavior as bases for explaining the characteristics of human and other organismic rationality. It suggests an alternative approach to the description of rational behavior that is more closely related to psychological theories of perception and cognition, and that is in closer agreement with the facts of behavior as observed in laboratory and field.

References

Edwards, W. The theory of decision making. *Psychol. Bull.*, 1954, 51, 380–417.
Festinger, L. Development of differential appetite in the rat. *J. exp. Psychol.*, 1953, 32, 226–34.
De Groot, A. *Het Denken van den Sckaker*. Amsterdam: Noord-Hollandsche Uitgevers Maatschapij, 1946. Translated as *Thought and choice in chess*. The Hague: Mouton, 1965; 2nd ed., 1978.
Hunt, J. McV. *Personality and the behavior disorders*. New York: Ronald, 1944.
Simon, H. A. *Administrative behavior*. New York: Macmillan, 1947.
Simon, H. A. A behavioral model of rational choice. *Quart. J. Econ.*, 1955, 59, 99–118. Reprinted as chapter 1.1 in this book.
Thrall, R. M., Coombs, C. H., & Davis, R. L. (Eds.). *Decision processes*. New York: Wiley, 1954.
Walter, W. G. *The living brain*. New York: Norton, 1953.

---

6. See, for example, Neal E. Miller, "Experimental Studies of Conflict" in Hunt, 1944, Chap. 14.

1.3

Motivational and Emotional Controls of Cognition (1967)

Considerable progress has been made in the last decade in accounting for human cognitive performances in terms of organizations of simple information processes (Reitman, 1965; Simon and Newell, 1964). Information-processing theories, however, have generally been silent on the interaction of cognition with affect. Since in actual human behavior motive and emotion are major influences on the course of cognitive behavior, a general theory of thinking and problem solving must incorporate such influences.

Critics of information-processing theories and of computer simulation of human thinking point, quite correctly, to this lacuna as a major deficiency of the theories. Neisser (1963), whose views on simulation are perceptive and informed, argues that

Discussions with my colleague Walter R. Reitman about the relations of serial and parallel processing provided much of the motivation for the approach of this chapter. I alone accept responsibility for the particular form of the theory of emotional behavior proposed here. Reitman (1963) has described part of his own theory. An earlier version of this chapter provided the basis for one of my William James Lectures at Harvard University, March 1963. Its completion has been aided by research grants from the Carnegie Corporation and the National Institutes of Health (MH-07722).

"the view that machines will think as man does reveals misunderstanding of human thought." He observes that:

Three fundamental and interrelated characteristics of human thought . . . are conspicuously absent from existing or contemplated computer programs:

1. human thinking always takes place in, and contributes to, a cumulative process of growth and development;

2. human thinking begins in an intimate association with emotions and feelings which is never entirely lost;

3. almost all human activity, including thinking, serves not one but a multiplicity of motives at the same time [p. 195].

Our purpose here is to discuss the behavior of humans, not the capabilities of computers. Nonetheless, Neisser has characterized correctly some of the visibly gross differences between human behavior and the behavior of existing simulation programs. Even if it were to be argued that the differences are quantitative rather than qualitative, they would prove conspicuous nonetheless. Developmental processes play a small role in existing simulation programs, emotions play almost no role, and most such programs appear to be driven by a single top-level goal, or motive. Progress in theory construction will require us to remove these differences.

This chapter attempts to show how motivational and emotional controls over cognition can be incorporated into an information-processing system, so that thinking will take place in "intimate association with emotions and feelings," and will serve a "multiplicity of motives at the same time." The expanded system will therefore meet Neisser's second and third objections.

In its assumptions about the mechanisms of motivation and emotion, the theory will follow lines already laid down by Hebb, Lindsley, and others, for which there is considerable empirical support. The proposed theory contains elements of novelty mainly by showing how relatively familiar mechanisms of motivation and emotion can be integrated in a simple and natural way with the mechanisms that have been postulated in information-processing theories of cognition.

"MOTIVATION" OF BEHAVIOR IN A SERIAL PROCESSOR

Two assumptions are central to most of the existing information-processing theories of thinking:[1] (1) The central nervous system (CNS) is basically organized to operate in serial fashion; and (2) the course of behavior is regulated, or motivated, by a tightly organized hierarchy of goals.

Serial Organization

It is not easy to state rigorously what is meant by a "serial" as contrasted with a "parallel" processor. A serial processor, of course, is one in which only a few things go on at a time, while a parallel processor is one in which many things go on at a time. This distinction is meaningless, however, until we specify how to count "things"— how to recognize a unitary process or object.

The ambiguity extends not only to defining the symbolic units, but to defining the

----

1. Reitman (1965, chap. 8) outlines a model, ARGUS, that is highly parallel in operation. Development of this model has not yet reached a point where its adequacy to simulate cognitive behavior can be evaluated.

time units as well. Any serial system, given enough time, can do many things. If we only look at its behavior periodically, we cannot tell whether the processes have been carried out in serial or parallel fashion.

When we say that the human CNS is organized as a serial processor, we must have in mind, therefore, some notion of an "elementary" symbol and an "indivisible" time unit. Since the simplest reflex actions require about 100 milliseconds, we may take this as the approximate relevant time interval. Since in some memory experiments, the "chunk" (i.e., a single familiar symbol, like a familiar nonsense syllable, a digit, or a familiar short word) appears to be the significant processing unit, we may consider it the elementary symbol.

Then the postulate that the human CNS is serial can be rendered roughly as follows: The processes that operate during $\frac{1}{10}$ second affect only a few chunks (about seven, according to Miller, 1956) among all those in short- and long-term memory. More macroscopic processes are synthesized from sequences of elementary processes, organized to operate over longer time intervals. For anything "interesting" to happen in the CNS may require quite long times— for example, about 30 seconds to memorize a nonsense-syllable pair of low association value. During a relatively short interval of time during which one such process is going on, not much else can or does happen.

The plausibility of this postulate rests on several kinds of evidence. First, there is a large mass of behavioral evidence, both from everyday observation and from laboratory experiments, for a phenomenon called "attention"; and there is evidence that the span of attention—the number of things that can be attended to simultaneously—is only a few chunks. To be sure, not everything that happens in the CNS goes on at the level of consciousness. Nevertheless, certain cognitive processes, at least, require attention; the number that can be within the scope of attention at one time is very limited.

A second kind of argument for serial processing is of a more a priori character:

It is difficult to specify how to organize a highly parallel information-processing system that would behave coherently. The basic problem is this. Suppose a system, C, has two components, C_1 and C_2, operating in parallel, which interact. From time to time the behavior of C_1 depends on the current state of C_2, and vice versa. In a simple case, we might have two memories, M_1 and M_2, for communication between the two components. At certain times, C_1 would store information in M_1, and C_2 in M_2; likewise, from time to time, C_1 would take information from M_2, and C_2 from M_1.

To obtain coherent behavior from such a system, there would have to be a certain measure of temporal coordination between its components. If C_1 takes inputs from M_2, which have been placed there by C_2, then C_1 must, in some sense, "know" how recently the contents of M_2 have been updated. The higher the frequency of interaction, the more precise is the requirement of temporal coordination.

In general, if the components of a parallel system are to operate with a high degree of interdependence, there must be a correspondingly adequate system of coordination or synchronization among them. And then the coordinating or synchronizing system will itself be a serially organized system. In the case of an organism like a human being, the requirements for coordination are fairly obvious. Most behaviors call upon a considerable part of the whole sensory and motor system for their successful performance. Hence, patting one's head while rubbing one's stomach becomes feasible only under the guidance of a supervisory synchronizing program. Even extreme cases of schizophrenia take the form of alternation, rather than parallelism, of personalities.

Control Hierarchy

The obvious way to govern the behavior of a serial processor is by a hierarchy of subroutines, with an interpreter capable of executing the instructions in the proper order (Newell and Simon, 1963, pp. 380–84). For example, the program, "Walk the length of a block," could consist of a list of instructions to be executed in the following sequence:

Walk the length of a block.
1. Step with left foot, then 2.
2. Step with right foot, then 3.
3. If end of block, do 4; if not, do 1.
4. Terminate.

A similar sequence of instructions could correspond to the program, "Cross an intersection." Now by combining these two programs in a larger one we could construct, "Walk to the 1400 block," thus:

Walk to the 1400 block.
1. Walk the length of a block, then 2.
2. Cross an intersection, then 3.
3. If 1400 reached, do 4; if not, do 1.
4. Terminate.

The interpreter in such a system starts to execute the executive program—the program at the highest level in the hierarchy. Each instruction in this program will be, in general, a subprogram to be executed in the same way. Thus the interpreter must proceed downward through the hierarchy of subprograms, or subroutines, until it reaches an "elementary" process that can be executed immediately. While it is doing this, it must keep its place in the routine it is executing at each level of the hirearchy.

Now a system organized in this simple, straightforward way is likely to reveal, in its behavior, considerable single-mindedness and unity of purpose. Whatever elementary task it is performing at a given instant was assigned to it by a subroutine which was itself, in turn, called for by a higher level subroutine. Thus, everything that is done is done in the service of the highest level executive program through successive levels of delegation.

This apparently single-minded, single-purpose behavior of most existing simulations of information-processing systems provides a striking contrast with human behavior. Under many circumstances, human behavior can be interrupted by imperative demands entirely unrelated to the goal hierarchy in current control—by hunger, fear, noticing sudden motion, etc.

Moreover, even when not actually interrupted, human behavior appears to be responsive not to just one, but to a multiplicity of goals. A speaker not only attends to the content of what he is saying, but also responds in many gross and subtle ways to the feedback he gets from the facial expressions and postures of his listeners. While he is seeking to inform, he may also be seeking to please, to impress, or to earn love.

Goal Completion

Even in a purely serial system, there must be some way in which a particular subroutine can be terminated and control returned, at the next higher level, to the routine that called for its execution. What are the criteria of completion of a subgoal that might initiate this termination? There are a number of possible alternatives:

Aspiration achievement. A subroutine may terminate when its subgoal has been achieved. The subgoal may be, for example, to discover a proof for a certain theorem or to discover a move in a chess game that leads to checkmate.

Satisficing. A subroutine may terminate when its subgoal has been achieved "well enough." A subroutine may search for a course of action that will yield at least k dollars profit or for a chess move that will win at least a pawn.

Impatience. A subroutine may terminate when a certain amount of time has been used up in trying to achieve it, perhaps then selecting the alternative that is "best so far."

Discouragement. A subroutine may terminate after a certain set of processes for attaining the subgoal has been tried and has failed.

Thus, aspiration levels, satisficing criteria, impatience, and discouragement constitute mechanisms for terminating subroutines which can be combined in a variety of ways. Existing information-processing systems, for example, theories

of problem solving in chess, already incorporate these kinds of goal completion mechanisms.[2]

MULTIPLE GOALS

Even if a system is organized in the serial hierarchic fashion described, it may be able to respond to several goals simultaneously. There are at least two ways in which multiple goals can be introduced into such a system without altering basically its serial character. The first is by queuing—attending to several goals in sequence. The second involves generalizing the notion of goal to encompass multifaceted criteria against which possible problem solutions are tested. We will consider these in order.

Queuing of Goals

At a minimum, a living organism like a human being has to satisfy, periodically, its biological needs. A goal (e.g., seeking food or water) is then evoked by a drive. If the organism is quiescent at the time a new goal is evoked, a program appropriate to a goal of this kind is put into execution. If the organism is already occupied with achieving another goal, the new goal may be postponed and activated when the program associated with the earlier goal has been terminated.[3]

This scheme will accommodate any number of needs provided the total time required to realize the goals that are evoked by drives is, on the average, a small fraction of the total time available to the organism. It is necessary, also, that goals be evoked a sufficient time before their achievement becomes essential for survival. That is, the hunger mechanism must be adapted to the organism's storage capacity for food

---

2. Schemes of this general kind are described in Simon, 1957, chaps. 14, 15, reprinted as chapters 1.1 and 1.2 in this book. Some of these mechanisms are realized in the programs described in Newell, Shaw, and Simon, 1963, and in Simon and Simon, 1962.

3. For further discussion, see chapter 1.2 in this book.

and the expected length of search to find food once the goal has been evoked.

If goals are evoked more or less periodically (e.g., the need for sleep), then the queuing system can be supplemented or replaced by a time-allocation system: a fixed cycle of processing, with each phase of the cycle assigned to a particular goal.

These two mechanisms, queuing and allocation, are used continually by human beings to reconcile the competing claims upon their serial processing capacities of the multiple needs they must satisfy—not only biological needs, but the whole range of goals that characterize adult human existence.

Multifaceted Criteria

A goal need not be a unitary thing, and in actual fact it seldom is. For example, the only behaviors a human being normally regards as suitable for satisfying hunger are behaviors that lead to ingesting foods of culturally acceptable kinds in a culturally acceptable manner. A gentleman dresses for dinner and eats with knife and fork roast beef that has been obtained in a legal way (e.g., by purchase) and treated at high temperatures.

Achievement of a goal, then, characteristically calls for behavior that meets a whole set of criteria. In fact, there is no need to treat these criteria asymmetrically, to single out one of them and call it "the goal." We could as well say that the gentleman's goal is to dine in his dinner jacket as to say that his goal is to satisfy his hunger.[4] The hierarchy of programs that is associated with the goal will be responsive to the whole set of criteria.

---

4. This is not to say that the set of criteria that specifies goal achievement may not change from one situation to another or that there is not some sense in which "satisfying hunger" is a more fundamental goal than "dining in one's dinner jacket." We are considering here only short-run considerations: the set of criteria that is applied by the goal-achievement program to determine when processing should terminate. For further discussion of multifaceted goals, see Simon, 1964.

Therefore, a hierarchically organized serial system need not single-mindedly pursue a simple goal. The chess-playing simulations constructed by Newell et al., 1963, p. 402 and by Simon and Simon, 1962, though serial programs, take into account such goals as protection of pieces, development of pieces, control of the center, and restriction of the opponent's mobility in selecting a move. They limit themselves, of course, to considering only legal moves, and there is no reason why they could not take into account additional criteria, even aesthetic ones.

In conclusion, our review of the basic principles of organization of existing information-processing theories reveals that, in spite of their serial hierarchic character, they permit behavior to respond to a multiplicity of motives at the same time, in agreement, at least qualitatively, with the observed facts of human behavior. Activity toward specific goals is terminated by aspiration, satisficing, impatience, and discouragement mechanisms; distinct tasks may be queued or handled within individual time allocations; choices among alternatives may respond to multiple criteria. If the behavior of existing models frequently appears "single-minded", as compared with human behavior, this is due in considerable part to the fact that the substantive content of the choice criteria has been excessively simplified or abstracted, and not to the absence from the models of fundamental mechanisms that permit multifaceted activity in the human being.

INTERRUPTION AND EMOTION

A serial processor can respond to multiple needs and goals without requiring any special mechanisms to represent affect or emotion. We can use the term *motivation*, in systems like those described, simply to designate that which controls attention at any given time.[5] The motivation may be

---

5. This point of view toward motivation is developed at length in Taylor, 1960.

directed toward a single goal, or, more commonly, toward multiple goals.

But this is not the whole story. The mechanisms we have considered are inadequate to deal with the fact that, if the organism is to survive, certain goals must be achieved by certain specified times. The environment places important, and sometimes severe, real-time demands upon the system. In a queuing system, for example, if a new goal is evoked, it is placed on a waiting list until current goal programs have been terminated. In a mild, benign environment, a leisurely response of this kind is adequate. In the real world, it sometimes is not.

If real-time needs are to be met, then provision must be made for an *interrupt system*. Such a system sets two requirements:

1. A certain amount of processing must go on continuously, or almost continuously, to enable the system to *notice* when conditions have arisen that require ongoing programs to be interrupted. The noticing processes will be substantially in parallel with the ongoing goal-attaining program of the total system, although this parallelism may be realized, in fact, by the high-frequency time sharing of a single serial processor.

2. The noticing program must be capable of *interrupting* and setting aside ongoing programs when real-time needs of high priority are encountered. The programs thus set aside may simply be abandoned, or they may be resumed after the real-time need has been met.

Simple noticing and interruption programs of this general kind are already incorporated in some information-processing theories. EPAM, a theory of rote learning, for example, notices the turning of the memory drum and is capable of interrupting its learning processes to attend to the new syllable that has appeared on the drum (Feigenbaum, 1963).

A somewhat different kind of interrupt system fits the hunger-thirst example mentioned earlier. For each drive, the *drive level* is an increasing function of the number of hours of deprivation. The need having the smaller storage capacity will generally

have the higher time gradient. Further, a *threshold* for each drive determines at what drive level the goal becomes "urgent" and interrupts the onging program.[6]

Real-time Needs

What are the principal kinds of real-time needs that the interruption system serves in human beings. We can distinguish three classes:

1. Needs arising from uncertain environmental events—"loud" stimuli, auditory, visual, or other, that warn of danger.

2. Physiological needs—internal stimuli, usually warning of the impending exhaustion of a physiological inventory.

3. Cognitive associations—loud stimuli evoked not by sensory events, but by associations in memory, for example, anxiety arousal.

The capacity of stimuli from these sources to interrupt attention is a commonplace of daily experience. With respect to the first class of stimuli, it is especially clear that they will be more likely noticed to the extent that they are both intense and unexpected.

Sudden intense stimuli have easily observable effects on behavior. They also have well-validated effects on the CNS. These are described at length, for example, by Lindsley, 1951. These effects produce substantial disruption of the electroencephalogram pattern (Lindsley, 1951, pp. 496–500). A plausible, and not novel, interpretation of these CNS effects is that they amount to an interruption of the interpreter that manages the goal hierarchy; that is, they supplant the present goals with a new hierarchy. This interpretation has become increasingly popular as more has been learned of the role of the lower brain centers in motivation.

Second, sudden intense stimuli often produce large effects on the autonomic nervous system, commonly of an "arousal"

---

6. A system of this kind is described in chapter 1.2 in this book. More recently, Tomkins, 1963, has described a system with some similar characteristics.

and "energy marshaling" nature. It is to these effects that the label "emotion" is generally attached.[7] The weight of evidence today is that the effects result from, rather than cause, the changes in the CNS described in the previous paragraph. Thus, substantial destruction of the connections of CNS with the autonomic nervous system does not prevent normal displays of emotional behavior in animals (Lindsley, 1951, pp. 484–85).

Third, in human beings sudden intense stimuli are commonly associated with reports of the subjective feelings that typically accompany emotional behavior. We will not be particularly concerned here with these reports, but will assume, perhaps not implausibly, that the feelings reported are produced, in turn, by internal stimuli resulting from the arousal of the autonomic system.

Emotional Behavior

We see that all the evidence points to a close connection between the operation of the interrupt system and much of what is usually called emotional behavior. Further, the interrupting stimulus has a whole range of effects, including (1) interruption of ongoing goals in the CNS and substitution of new goals, producing, inter alia, emotional behavior, (2) arousal of the autonomic nervous system, (3) production of feelings of emotion. We will be concerned with the first of these effects and will largely ignore the others.

The system comprises both performance and learning processes. In the performance system, emotion is aroused (the interrupt mechanism is activated) by sensory stimuli, memory images, and drives. What response program will replace the interrupted pro-

gram will also depend on the nature of the interrupting stimulus. The response program may, and often will, activate the autonomic nervous system, producing a feeling of emotion.

As Hebb (1949, pp. 238–40, 250–58) and others have emphasized, the emotional stimulus is to be regarded as more often *interrupting* than *disrupting* behavior. The responses to interruption are largely adaptive, either because they are genetically determined or because the adaptation has been learned. Interruption is not limited to simple responses like "startle," but may evoke an elaborate goal-oriented chain of activity (e.g., the reactions of a trained soldier to the sound of approaching aircraft).

When the emotion-producing stimuli are persistent as well as intense, they sometimes become disruptive and produce nonadaptive behavior. This occurs if the stimuli continue to interrupt, repeatedly, the evoked response program and hence to prevent an organized behavioral response to the original interrupting stimulus.

Learning of Emotional Behavior

Several kinds of learning can occur in relation to an interrupt system:

1. The efficacy of particular stimuli in activating the interrupt system can change. New associations are acquired allowing stimuli not previously effective to interrupt ongoing behavior. Stimuli, on the other hand, that previously had the capacity to interrupt often lose their efficacy.

2. The organism can acquire new or modified response programs associated with the various interrupting stimuli.

In general, the tendency of a particular stimulus to evoke emotional behavior through interruption of ongoing behavior decreases with repetition. For example, an unskilled bicyclist who tries to carry on a conversation frequently interrupts his conversation to attend to the road. With greater skill, he time-shares between the conversation and the cycling without often interrupting the former. In effect the earlier single-purpose program, with frequent in-

---

7. "Emotion" like "learning" and other traditional categories, refers to a mixed bag of phenomena, which may involve diverse mechanisms. Thus, the present theory probably does not account for intense aesthetic emotion (e.g., emotion which may occur while listening to music) where arousal of the autonomic system does not stem from interruption.

terruption, has been replaced with a program having the goal: "Carry on the conversation while keeping your balance." As learning proceeds, not only does the amount of interruption decrease, but evidences of emotional behavior become less and less frequent and intense as well.

Similarly, the response after interruption usually becomes more and more adaptive with repetition. In the early stages of practice, the interrupting response often overcorrects, causing a new interruption. As practice proceeds, the response is more adequately controlled and usually does not cause a new interruption.

In two ways, then, we may expect learning to reduce the emotionality of response as a situation becomes more familiar: (1) The need for interruption is reduced by incorporation of more elaborate side conditions in the programs associated with ongoing goals; (2) the response to interruption becomes more successfully adaptive, thus forestalling new interruptions. Hence, emotionality is associated with meeting real-time needs, particularly those that arise unexpectedly and in unfamiliar circumstances.

Of course learning is not always successful. If interruption occurs and real-time needs are not met, the painful consequences may lead to more precipitous, less adaptive responses when the situation recurs. Indeed, the classical paradigms for producing neurosis experimentally place excessive real-time demands on the organism.

EMOTION AND SOCIAL INTERACTION

In human behavior, situations involving interaction with other human beings are characteristically more heavily laden with emotion than are other situations. A theory of emotional behavior, to be satisfactory, must explain this connection of emotion with social interaction.

In general, real-time needs to respond to the environment arise when the environment can change rapidly and unpredictably. What are the most active and upredictable parts of the human environment?

Suddenly appearing, rapidly moving objects, for example, flying sticks and stones, are one important class of events calling for interruption. Changes of environment through one's own relative motion, slipping or falling, are another.

But the most active part of the environment of man, and the part most consequential to him, consists of living organisms, particularly other men. Hence, a large part of the complexity of goals arises from the need, while accomplishing tasks, to attend to the responses of other human beings and to do this in real time. Thus, the behavior of problem-solving groups is commonly observed as taking place at two "levels": "task-oriented" behavior and behavior directed toward the group's social-emotional needs.

The degree to which a person exhibits emotional behavior in social interaction will vary with the progress of the two kinds of learning that may modify the interrupt system. A human being, in the course of development and socialization, acquires an increasingly sophisticated set of cues to indicate which responses of another person call for interruption of his own ongoing program. As the set of interrupting social stimuli grows, ceteris paribus, the emotionality of social situations should increase. On the other hand, the maturing individual also learns programs for anticipating (hence forestalling) interrupting stimuli and for responding to them adaptively when they occur. As the behavior of other actors becomes more predictable, the ego's behavior can more readily be planned, and the emotionality of the situation decreases. Thus, the experienced salesman finds his interaction with the customer less stressful as his ability to predict responses to his own behavior improves.

Since the one type of learning tends to increase the emotionality of social situations and the other tends to decrease it, and since both types of learning can be expected to go on simultaneously, the theory leads to no definite prediction of whether, netting these two effects, emotionality of social interaction will tend to grow or decline for the individual. Common observation suggests that it typically grows throughout adolescence, then gradually declines throughout adult life.

MOTIVATION AND LEARNING

Learning theories differ widely in the role they assign to motivation in the learning process. These differences were central to the controversy, in the 1930s and 1940s, about latent learning. The issue in its simplest form is whether the organism learns anything about aspects of its environment that are not directly relevant to its currently evoked goal system. For labeling purposes only, let us call the affirmative and negative views on this question Tolmanian and Hullian, respectively.

The theory proposed here gives a qualified Tolmanian answer to the question and predicts some circumstances under which latent learning will occur. When we try to make order out of the chaos of latent learning experiments, as Kimble, Hilgard, and Marquis have done (Kimble, 1961, pp. 226–34), we discover that they are reasonably consistent with the two following generalizations:

1. Learning only occurs when there is knowledge of results, but may proceed in the absence of any obvious reward or punishment. Punishment is often as effective in giving knowledge of results as is reward.

2. Learning without obvious punishment or reward occurs principally under conditions of *low* irrelevant drive.

The simplest explanation of these facts is that motivation is effective primarily in determining *what* goal hierarchy will be activated at any given time; hence it is effective in determining what aspects of the environment will be relevant to the organism for performance of learning. Stated otherwise, motivation controls attention and hence influences learning only through its influence on program control. *Given* the focus of attention and the established goal hierarchy, learning still requires knowledge of results, but does not call for reward or punishment mechanisms. Reward and punishment, and motivation

generally, install and replace goal systems.

This explanation leads to three predictions of circumstances under which "latent" learning will occur. First, if while achieving a particular evoked goal the organism encounters an interrupting stimulus, it may learn things that are irrelevant to the original goal but relevant to the response program activated by the interruption. Thus, a hungry rat can learn where it will receive an electric shock in the maze. But by increasing the intensity of the original drive, we should be able to reduce sensitivity to interruption and hence reduce the amount of learning producible by potentially interrupting stimuli. The fact that the interrupting stimulus does or does not have punishment associated with it is irrelevant.

Second, as goals are elaborated by the incorporation of side constraints, the organism will learn about aspects of the environment that are relevant to meeting the side constraints, as well as aspects relevant to the original goal. Thus, as a novice chess player begins to learn that he must protect his own men while attacking his opponent's, he learns to attend to his opponent's as well as to his own threats.

Third, really a generalization of the first two points, the organism may learn about any aspect of the environment that "happens" to attract its attention. Aspects of the environment with which negligible, or no, rewards and punishments are associated will generally attract attention only when other, more pressing needs are absent. Hence, consistent with the evidence, latent learning should occur principally under conditions of low irrelevant drive.

CONCLUSION

This chapter has proposed a theory of the relation of motivation and emotional behavior to man's information-processing behavior. The theory explains how a basically serial information processor endowed with multiple needs behaves adaptively and survives in an environment that presents unpredictable threats and opportunities. The explanation is built on two central mechanisms:

1. A goal-terminating mechanism permits the processor to satisfice, dealing generally with one goal (albeit perhaps a complex one) at a time, and terminating action when a satisfactory situation has been achieved.

2. An interruption mechanism, that is, emotion, allows the processor to respond to urgent needs in real time.

Rudimentary mechanisms of these kinds have already been incorporated in some of the current information-processing theories of human cognition. Elaboration of the mechanisms and assignment to them of a larger and more crucial role in the simulated behavior will permit these theories to be extended to the explanation of wider ranges of human behavior. Thus, information-processing theories must be endowed, as can readily be done, with the properties that Neisser lists as characterizing human thinking: intimate association of cognitive processes with emotions and feelings, and determination of behavior by the operation of a multiplicity of motivations operating simultaneously.

References

Feigenbaum, E. A. The simulation of verbal learning behavior. In E. A. Feigenbaum & J. Feldman (Eds.), *Computers and thought.* New York: McGraw-Hill, 1963. Pp. 297–309. (Originally published in *Proceedings of the 1961 Western Joint Computer Conference*, pp. 121–32.)

Hebb, D. O. *The organisation of behavior.* New York: Wiley, 1949.

Kimble, G. A. *Hilgard and Marquis' conditioning and learning* (2nd ed.). New York: Appleton-Century-Crofts, 1961.

Lindsley, D. B. Emotion. In S. S. Stevens (Ed.), *Handbook of experimental psychology.* New York:

Wiley, 1951. Pp. 473–516.

Miller, G. A. The magical number seven, plus or minus two: Some limits on our capacity for processing information. *Psychological Review*, 1956, 63, 81–97.

Neisser, U. The imitation of man by machine. *Science*, 1963, 139, 193–97.

Newell, A., Shaw, J. C., & Simon, H. A. Chess-playing programs and the problem of complexity. In E. A. Feigenbaum & J. Feldman (Eds.), *Computers and thought.* New York: McGraw-Hill, 1963. Pp. 39–70. (Originally published under this title in *Journal of Research and Development* [IBM], 2:320–35, 1958).

Newell, A., & Simon, H. A. Computers in psychology. In R. D. Luce, R. R. Bush, & E. Galanter (Eds.), *Handbook of mathematical psychology.* Vol. 1. New York: Wiley, 1963, chap. 7. Pp. 361–428.

Reitman, W. R. Personality as a problem-solving coalition. In S. S. Tomkins & S. Messick (Eds.), *Computer simulation of personality.* New York: Wiley, 1963. Pp. 69–99.

Reitman, W. R. *Cognition and thought.* New York: Wiley, 1965.

Simon, H. A. *Models of man.* New York: Wiley, 1957.

Simon, H. A. On the concept of organizational goal. *Administrative Science Quarterly*, 1964, 9, 1–22.

Simon, H. A., & Newell, A. Information processing in computer and man. *American Scientist*, 1964, 52, 281–300.

Simon, H. A., & Simon, P. A. Trial and error search in solving difficult problems: Evidence from the game of chess. *Behavioral Science*, 1962, 7, 425–29. Reprinted as chapter 4.2 in this book.

Taylor, D. W. Toward an information processing theory of motivation. In M. R. Jones (Ed.), *Nebraska symposium on motivation: 1960.* Lincoln: University of Nebraska Press, 1960. Pp. 51–79.

Tomkins, S. S. Simulation of personality. In S. S. Tomkins & S. Messick (Eds.), *Computer simulation of personality.* New York: Wiley, 1963. Pp. 3–58.

2

Memory Structures

The four chapters of this section complete the general specification of Thinking Man, providing the foundation for the specific subsystems considered in the subsequent sections. As serial search provides the central motif of section 1, so the *chunk*, the basic unit of memory content, provides the motif for this section.

The picture of memory that is drawn in these chapters is a familiar one. Leaving aside small, temporary sensory and motor buffers, most evidence points to the existence of a pair of principal memory structures: a short-term memory (STM),[1] and a long-term memory (LTM). The STM is characterized by rapid access times (in the 200 msec range), but very small capacity. The LTM is characterized by much slower access and store times (of the order of seconds), but essentially unlimited capacity. This specification of memory is accepted by almost all contemporary cognitive psychologists, although some would admit only a functional, and not an anatomical, distinction between STM and LTM (recall the discussion in section 1 of the hypothesis that STM may merely be the activated portion of LTM). In any event, it is only the functional difference between the two memories that is important for our purposes, and that difference has strong empirical support. These memory structures, and the evidence that points to their existence, are discussed at some length in chapter 2.3.

Before we can speak of the capacity of memory structures, however, we must define the unit for measuring capacity. Such a unit for STM, the chunk, was proposed by George A. Miller in 1956 in his celebrated "Magical Number Seven" paper, and the relevance of the same unit for measuring fixation in LTM was shown a year later in my *Psychometrika* paper reprinted here as chapter 2.1. Evidence that the STM chunk and the LTM chunk are equivalent units is presented in chapter 2.2. I will have more to say about the significance of this equivalence below.

A final task in these chapters is to distinguish between those aspects of memory that are, so to speak, "wired in" physiologically and those aspects that are modifiable by learning or change in strategy. That strategy is a crucial intervening variable interposed between physiology and behavior will be an important recurrent theme throughout this volume. That theme is first introduced, in application to the operation of STM, in chapter 2.4.

CHUNKS

The LTM described in these chapters is itself a structure having two components. In analogy with an encyclopedia, we may say that the memory has both a *text* and an *index*. The information in the encyclopedia, contained in the text, is accessed rapidly by way of the pointers comprising the index.

---

1. In some chapters, short-term memory is referred to as "immediate memory." The terms will be regarded as synonymous.

The text of LTM is an associative structure—a system of nodes interconnected by numerous links. Information can be retrieved from it not only via the index but also by following paths of links from one node to another through intermediate nodes. Retrieval using the index we call *recognition*, retrieval using sequences of links we call *association*. The latter process is considerably slower than the former.

Learning, as we will see in section 3, involves both (1) storing new nodes and links in the text of LTM and (2) elaborating the index to increase its powers of discrimination and recognition. The EPAM model, alluded to briefly in this section and examined in detail in section 3, provides a theory of the interaction of index with text in LTM and of the learning process that creates and elaborates them.

The crucial assumption with respect to chunks is that the contents of STM are symbols that give access to, or "point" to, corresponding nodes in LTM. Thus an act of recognition consists of using the index to retrieve such a symbol and to store it in STM; while an act of recall from LTM consists of placing in STM the symbol designating a particular node in LTM.

Each node in LTM, then, together with the links connected directly with it, constitutes a chunk of information, while the symbol that designates such a node constitutes the corresponding chunk in STM. If STM can hold some fixed number of such symbols, then it will have a fixed capacity measured in chunks. Moreover, if adding each new node to LTM, with its associated links and indexing entries, requires some average fixed amount of attention, the chunk will also provide a measure of learning. As will be shown in chapter 2.2, a chunk corresponds to anything that has become a familiar unit of experience (i.e., has been stored and indexed), and the measurement of chunks can be made entirely operational.

STRATEGY

Describing an adaptive system is difficult because, Proteus-like, it takes on the shape of its environment. Confronted with a particular kind of task, it gradually fits its processing capabilities, as far as it can, to the requirements of that task (see my *Sciences of the Artificial*).

The control structure governing the behavior of Thinking Man in a given task environment is a strategy or program that marshals cognitive resources for performance of the task. New and improved strategies are acquired by learning, while familiar tasks may be performed with available strategies retrieved from memory on recognition of the task environment. However the strategy is generated or retrieved, it becomes a central determinant of task behavior, so that any account of task performance requires a description of the strategy.

Of course, strategies are only feasible if they can be executed by the central nervous system. In particular, they will be infeasible if they demand more STM capacity than is available or more rapid operation of the memory processes than these are capable of. This is the reason why memory capacities and speeds are such crucial parameters in models of complex cognitive performance.

In chapter 2.4, Kevin Gilmartin, Allen Newell, and I show how a range of memory phenomena can be accounted for by postulating strategies adapted to the individual memory tasks within the limits imposed on adaptation by the structure and capacity of STM. This is the first of many occasions in this book where strategies serve as essential intervening variables. Other examples will be found in chapters 3.3, 4.2, 4.4, 4.5, 4.6, 5.4, 6.6, 7.2, and 7.3, to mention only the most prominent instances.

MISCELLANEOUS COMMENTS

1. The chapters of this section, particularly chapters 2.2 and 2.3, provide some preview of, and references forward to, later chapters—especially those that relate to the EPAM model. Forward reference could have been avoided by arranging the chapters in strict chronological order, but the arrangement I have adopted appeared to give a far more coherent picture of the entire research program than would an ordering by date of publication.

2. To avoid making a long book longer, I have omitted some of my papers that deal with the important topic of visual imagery. Some comments on that topic will be found, however, in a section so titled in chapter 2.3, and others later on in chapters 4.1, 6.1, and 6.5. The lack of a more extensive discussion can perhaps be excused by the unsatisfactory present state of psychology's under-standing of imagery phenomena and of their relation to internal representations of problem situations. I will make a few more comments on this point in the introductions to sections 6 and 7.

3. The "magical number" that measures STM capacity is assigned different values in different chapters. The number seven, proposed originally by George A. Miller, is almost certainly too large, and I would currently prefer the number four. Part of the difficulty in assigning a precise number is that STM probably holds control symbols as well as symbols designating chunks in LTM, and the relative proportions of the two kinds of symbols may vary from time to time and from task to task (see chapter 2.4). The usual methods for measuring STM capacity empirically do not count the control symbols.

References

Miller, G. A., The magical number seven, plus or minus two: Some limits on our capacity for processing information, *Psychological Review*, 63:81–97 (1956).
Simon, H. A., *The Sciences of the Artificial*, Cambridge, Mass.: M.I.T. Press, 1969.

Amounts of Fixation and Discovery in Maze Learning Behavior (1957)

To learn the correct path through a maze, a subject must first discover the path and then fixate it in memory. The distinction between the processes of discovery and fixation is well known in the psychological literature (see Melton, 1950) but has not been much used for analyzing learning experiments quantitatively. In this chapter, it is shown how amounts of discovery and fixation can be estimated from the structure of a maze learning task, how these amounts can be used to predict number of trials and number of errors to criterion, and how an analysis of maze learning in these terms brings these experiments into relationship with classical experiments on the learning of lists of nonsense syllables.

THE THEORETICAL MODEL

To run a maze successfully, the subject must make a correct sequence of responses, e.g., "left, left, up, right, left, up." At each choice point, the response must be selected from a specified list of alternatives. There is a specified number of choice points. Hence, a particular maze may be characterized by two parameters: n, the number of alternative paths, or possible responses, at each choice point; and L, the number of choice points, or length of the maze. As measures of learning only total errors

to criterion E and trials to criterion T will be considered.

It is postulated that the learning behavior involves two simple processes: one of discovery and one of fixation. It is convenient to discuss them in reverse order.

Fixation

The learning may occur under either the correction or the noncorrection method. Under the correction method, the subject makes a sequence of responses at each choice point until he makes the correct response; he is then informed that it was correct and proceeds to the next choice point. Under the noncorrection method, if the subject's first response is incorrect, he is told the correct response and then proceeds to the next choice point. Under both methods, one *correct* response is reinforced on each trial at each choice point. When animals are used as subjects, and when the learning involves a physical maze, the correction method is ordinarily used. In experiments on human learning in verbal mazes, either the correction or the noncorrection method may be used.

I am grateful to W. J. Brogden, G. A. Miller, R. F. Thompson, and J. Voss for their helpful comments on an earlier draft of this paper.

Ignoring, for the moment, the activities of the subject in searching for the correct response (i.e., the discovery activities) and the range of alternative responses open to him, it is seen that the task of *fixating* the correct response in a verbal maze learning experiment is the same as the task of fixating the correct response in learning a series of syllables or digits. Assuming that these two processes are, indeed, the same, one is justified in using the experimental findings on serial learning to predict the course of the fixation process in maze learning. This assumption will be validated by testing the predictions to which it leads and by relating it to other recent findings on memory processes.

Available data on serial learning (see Hovland, 1951, p. 620, figure 8) show, for sequences of the lengths employed in maze learning experiments (L no greater than 24), that the total number of trials to criterion increases monotonically with the length of the sequence:

$$T = f(L), \text{ with } dT/dL > 0 \qquad (1)$$

T appears to increase proportionately with L; within the range considered, the departure from proportionality is not large. Accepting the evidence for proportional increase, equation (1) may be specialized to the linear relation

$$T = bL, b > 0 \qquad (1')$$

Both the general and special forms of the function will be used in what follows.

An initial hypothesis is that these functions, obtained from the empirical data on fixation in serial learning, are applicable to the fixation process in maze learning. It may be remarked that b depends both on the ability of the subjects and the difficulty of the material to be learned. For nonsense syllables with low association value, values of b in the neighborhood of 1 are often reported; it is remarkable that values from studies carried out at widely different times are quite similar (Hovland, 1951, p. 620, figure 8). Whether or not this relative constancy carries over to learning in verbal mazes will be discusses in a later section.

Implicit in the hypothesis that the function (1) applies to the fixation process in maze learning is the very strong assumption that T is independent of n. It is not at all obvious that the difficulty in fixating the correct response at a choice point in a maze should be independent of the number of alternative responses at that point. It would be plausible to assume that the difficulty of fixation would increase with the amount of information contained in a correct response. But, by definition, the amount of information in a response is proportional to the logarithm of the number of alternative responses—one bit for a choice between two alternatives, two bits for a choice between four alternatives, three for a choice between eight alternatives, and so on. If difficulty of fixation depended on amount of information, T would depend on n.

Regardless of the plausibility of the assumption that T is independent of n, it is made tacitly in the whole body of experimentation that has been carried out on serial learning. The grounds for this assertion are these: a subject, learning a series of nonsense syllables or digits, is at each step trying to select the correct response from some range of possible responses. But (with the exception of a recent experiment mentioned below) it has not been usual for the experimenter to specify for the subject the range of possible or admissible responses. The particular nonsense syllables used are selected from a much larger class upon which the subject could presumably draw in trying to choose the correct response. The size of this class is a possible source of variance in the fixation process that has not generally been controlled in the classical experiments. In the learning of verbal mazes, the number of alternatives at each branch point is made explicit, and hence the independence of T from n can be subjected to direct test. The experimental findings are consistent with the hypothesis of independence.

The finding that the number of trials required to learn a sequence of syllables depends primarily on the number of syllables to be learned and not upon the number of bits of information per syllable is parallel with the data of Miller (1956a) on the span of immediate memory, recently corroborated directly by Miller and Smith (Miller, 1956b) for rote memory. These results suggest the need of caution and sophistication in applying measurements from statistical information theory to learning experiments. As Miller (1956b) has pointed out, information measurements appear to be directly applicable to certain experiments in perception and discrimination but not to memory span experiments. These findings provide additional justification for the absence of n from equation (1).

Discovery

For purposes of simplifying the development, assume (1) when the subject is at a particular choice point on a particular trial, he either knows or does not know the correct response; (2) if the former, he gives the correct response at once; (3) if the latter, he tries responses at random until he hits on the correct one. It is well known, empirically, that assumption (3) is not literally correct, since subjects ordinarily try alternatives in a patterned way. However, as long as the pattern is (for the average over all subjects) uncorrelated with the location of the correct response, results will be unchanged, and there may be no need for a more accurate but more complicated substitute for assumption (3).

Under the above assumptions, the expected number of errors E_t on a given trial will be proportional to the product of the average number of errors per random search, $\frac{1}{2}(n - 1)$, and the number of unlearned responses at the beginning of the trial, U_{t-1}:

$$E_t = \tfrac{1}{2}(n - 1)\,U_{t-1} \qquad (2)$$

Drawing again upon the empirical data that describe the fixation process in serial learning, some of the regularities in these data allow the derivation from (2) of an equation for E, the total number of errors to criterion. In particular, it is assumed that the Kjersted-Robinson law (see Hovland, 1951, p. 619) applies to the fix-

ation process in maze learning. This law asserts that the percentage of responses learned through the tth trial, $(L - U_t)/L$, is a function only of t/T, say:

$$(L - U_t)/L = g(t/T) \qquad (3)$$

By the definition of E as the sum of the E_t, and by using (3) to eliminate U_{t-1} from the right side of (2),

$$E = \sum_1^T E_t = \sum_1^T \tfrac{1}{2}(n - 1)\,L\,[\,1 - g(t/T)\,]$$
$$= \tfrac{1}{2}(n - 1)\,L\sum_1^T [\,1 - g(t/T)\,] \qquad (4)$$

But, by a well-known theorem on homogeneous functions,

$$\int_0^T g(t/T)\,dt = T\int_0^1 g(\lambda)\,d\lambda = KT,$$

where K is a constant $\qquad (5)$

Since the integral of (5) is an approximation to the last term of the sum on the right of (4), then (4) may be rewritten approximately:

$$E = \tfrac{1}{2}(1 - K)(n - 1)\,LT \qquad (6)$$

Finally, substituting (1) or (1′) in (6):

$$E = a(n - 1)\,Lf(L) \quad (a = \text{a constant}) \qquad (7)$$
or
$$E = a'(n - 1)\,L^2, \qquad (7')$$
respectively.

From (6) it is apparent that the number of errors to criterion will vary proportionately with the number of alternatives at each choice point, more precisely, with $(n - 1)$, and with the product of the length of the maze by the number of trials. If the number of trials is, by (1′), proportional to the length, the number of errors, by (7′), will be proportional to the square of the length. All the quantities appearing in (1′), (6), and (7′) are observables, and hence the equations can be fitted to data on learning performance in mazes. In fitting (1′) and (7′), one degree of freedom corresponding to the constant of proportionality, b or a, is lost.

From the data of Robinson and Darrow reported by Hovland (1951, p. 619, table 1), one can make a numerical estimate of

$(1 - K)$ in (6), obtaining the value 0.41. Since this constant has only an empirical basis, it cannot be expected to be exact; in what follows, the approximate value 0.4 will be used. If $(1 - K)$ is estimated at 0.4, no degrees of freedom are lost in fitting (6).

THE EXPERIMENTAL DATA

The two principal bodies of evidence for testing the model are: (1) a series of experiments by Brogden and his associates on human learning in verbal mazes of various lengths and numbers of branch points (see Brogden and Schmidt, 1954, and Thompson); (2) a series of experiments with animals by Scott and Henninger (1933) using two-alternative mazes of various lengths.

Number of Trials to Criterion

All these data support equation (1'). Brogden and Schmidt (1954) obtain an average value for b of 0.75 for 16-unit mazes, and 0.83 for 24-unit mazes. Thompson obtains an average b of 0.75 for 12-unit mazes. Since the fixation tasks in all three sets of experiments were of about the same difficulty, and since the subjects were drawn from the same population (volunteers from the introductory psychology

course at the University of Wisconsin), the relative constancy of the values of b cannot be regarded as a mere artifact. For this reason, it is justified to pool the data from all three sets of experiments, using a single averaged value of b. (On the other hand, Scott and Henninger, 1933, in experiments using a variety of maze designs and animal subjects, obtained values for b ranging from 0.7 to 2.) Finally, it is noted that Thompson compared the correction and noncorrection methods and found no significant difference between them in the relation of length of maze to trials to criterion.

That the number of trials is independent of number of alternatives at each choice point, as postulated in equation (1), is shown by the data of Brogden and Schmidt and of Thompson. In all three sets of experiments, the average number of trials to criterion was not significantly related to number of alternatives, except that the average number of trials was usually significantly low for mazes having only two alternatives at each choice point. Hence, the assumption of independence holds strictly only for n greater than 2. Thompson reports data for a 12-alternative maze with n ranging from 2 to 6; Brogden and Schmidt report data for a 16-alternative maze with n ranging from 2 to 8, and for a 24-alternative maze with n ranging from 2 to 12.

That the number of trials varies propor-

Table 1. Predicted and Actual Trials to Criterion and Errors to Criterion for Four Types of Mazes of Varying Length.

			Maze Types											
	I					II			III		IV			
	Maze Lengths					Maze Lengths			Maze Lengths		Maze Lengths			
Values of T and E	4	5	6	8	10	6	10	12	5	10	6	10	12	13
1. *T* actual	5.7	10.4	11.2	16.5	23.8	10.5	18.0	21.3	3.6	7.3	3.5	9.1	13.4	11.7
2. *T* estimate*	8.0	10.0	12.0	16.0	20.0	10.8	18.0	21.6	3.5	7.0	6.0	10.0	12.0	13.0
3. *E* actual	5.8	12.0	17.9	38.9	62.2	14.5	38.0	57.1	4.4	16.9	5.0	20.2	28.7	37.7
4. *E* estimate[†]	5.7	13.0	16.8	32.9	58.5	15.7	45.0	63.7	4.5	18.2	5.3	22.8	40.2	37.8

*Obtained from equation (1), with $b = 2$, 1.8, 0.7, and 1, estimated from the data for the four types of maze, respectively.
[†]Obtained from equation (2), with $c = 0.5$ (because of the relatively short lengths of the mazes).

Source: Data from Scott and Henninger, 1933.

tionately with maze length is shown by the near-equality in values of b obtained with mazes of similar design of lengths 12, 16, and 24. Table 1 provides additional evidence in the form of a comparison of the actual with estimated values of T for mazes of various lengths in four of the designs studied by Scott and Henninger, 1933.

Number of Errors to Criterion

Having tested that part of the theory which relates to number of trials, the data on errors is now to be considered. Brogden has made available to the writer the data on numbers of errors and trials to criterion for the 210 individual subjects in the experiments reported in the Journal of Experimental Psychology, 1954, 47, 48. Using the estimated value of 0.4 for $(1 - K)$, the experimentally determined values for n and L, and the observed values of T, call them T_i, E is estimated for each subject by equation (6). Let E_i be the observed values of E, and E_i^* be the values estimated from (6). It has been pointed out above that no degrees of freedom are lost in this process, since all the parameters in (6) are estimated independently of the observed E_i.

The mean E_i for all 210 subjects is 376.7, and the standard deviation is 347.8. Designating the error of estimate, $d_i = E_i - E_i^*$, the arithmetic mean error (the mean of d_i) is only -12.48. This implies that the least squares estimate of $(1 - K)$ is about 0.39, instead of the 0.4 estimated from the serial learning data; for the mean of the E_i, 376.7, is about 39/40 of the mean of the E_i^*, 389.2.

More remarkable, the estimates from (6) account for 93.7 percent of the variance in the E_i. The variance of the E_i is 5,334 $\times$ 10^6; the variance of the d_i is 335 $\times$ 10^6. The latter is only 6.3 percent of the former. The coefficient of variation, the ratio of the standard deviation of the d_i to the mean of the E_i, is 0.23.

The entire theory can be subjected to a severe test by estimating E in the experiments of Brogden and Schmidt and of

Thompson from equation $(7')$, employing a single average value of a' obtained from the whole set of experiments. Estimating $b = 0.75$ from the experimental data, $a' = \frac{1}{2}(0.4)(0.75) = 0.15$. Substituting in $(7')$ the values 12, 16, and 24 for L gives the corresponding equations for E: $E(12) = 21.6(n - 1)$; $E(16) = 38.4(n - 1)$; $E(24) = 86.6(n - 1)$. The least squares regressions reported by Thompson and by Brogden and Schmidt are: $E(12) = 31.1(n - 1) - 24.7$; $E(16) = 34.1(n - 1) + 21.3$; $E(24) = 93.4(n - 1) + 28.0$. Considering that the only degree of freedom lost was that used to estimate b, these equations must be regarded as a remarkably close fit. Moreover, if the regression line is constrained to pass through the origin, as required by the theory, the actual data would give $E(12) = 23(n - 1)$; $E(16) = 37(n - 1)$; and $E(24) = 96(n - 1)$. This provides, on the whole, an even closer fit.

The test of $(7')$ may also be made with the data for 210 individual subjects that were used to test (6). Let E_i' be the estimate of E_i from $(7')$, taking $b = 0.8$. Then the mean $E' = 350.1$, which is about 5 percent below the observed mean. (Stated otherwise, a least squares estimate of b would give a value of about 0.84.) The variance of the $(E_i' - E_i)$ is 1,039 $\times$ 10^6, or 19.5 percent of the variance of the E_i. Hence, the estimate from $(7')$ accounts for just over 80 percent of the variance, as compared with the nearly 95 percent accounted for by estimating the E_i from (6). The additional source of estimation error lies, of course, in the deviations of the actual values of the T_i from the values, T_i', estimated by $(1')$.

In their first experiment, Brogden and Schmidt (1954, 47, p. 239) adduce one piece of direct evidence for (2), which is required for the derivation of (6). Since U_0, the number of unlearned responses at the beginning of the first trial, is equal to L, from (2)

$$E_1 = \tfrac{1}{2}(n - 1) U_0 = \tfrac{1}{2}(n - 1) L \qquad (8)$$

Brogden and Schmidt find that the data fit (8) within sampling error.

References

Brogden, W. J. and Schmidt, R. E. The effect of number of choices per unit of a verbal maze on learning and serial position errors. *J. exp. Psychol.*, 1954, 47, 235–40.

Brogden, W. J. and Schmidt, R. E. Acquisition of a 24-unit verbal maze as a function of number of alternative choices per unit. *J. exp. Psychol.*, 1954, 48, 335–38.

Hovland, C. I. Human learning and retention. In S. S. Stevens (Ed.), Handbook of experimental psychology. New York: Wiley, 1951. Pp. 613–89.

Melton, A. W. Learning. In W. S. Monroe (Ed.), Encyclopedia of educational research. (Rev. Ed.) New York: Macmillan, 1950. Pp. 668–90.

Miller, G. A. The magical number seven, plus or minus two: Some limits on our capacity for processing information. *Psychol. Rev.*, 1956a, 63, 81–97.

Miller, G. A. Human memory and the storage of information. *IRE Trans. on Information Theory*, 1956b, IT-2, 129–37.

Scott, T. C., and Henninger, L. C. The relation between length and difficulty in motor learning; a comparison with verbal learning. *J. exp. Psychol.*, 1933, 16, 657–78.

Thompson, R. F. A comparison of correction and non-correction procedures on the acquisition of a 12-unit verbal maze (unpublished report).

2.2

How Big Is a Chunk? (1974)

During the past fifteen years, substantial progress has been made toward understanding man's problem-solving and other complex cognitive processes—toward measuring the immense search spaces in problem-solving tasks and identifying some of the heuristic principles that people use to reduce these spaces to manageable proportions. The understanding of problem solving now being acquired suggests a new significance, and a new application, for the simpler cognitive tasks of the classical psychological laboratory.

A crucial role in problem solving is played by man's short-term memory and the processes that transfer information from short-term to long-term memory (fixation processes). To continue the progress toward understanding complex cognitive behaviors, it is necessary to have good estimates of the basic parameters of short-term memory and of the memory fixation process. The classical laboratory tasks of experimental psychology provide efficient laboratory settings for estimating some of these parameters. Old experiments can be

analyzed in new ways, and their findings can take on new significance, when the analyses are guided by knowledge of the complex processes in which these same parameters reappear.

In this chapter I examine some very simple experiments of a familiar kind, but I examine them in a rather unfamiliar way. I seek to extract from earlier studies estimates of parameters that appear to be crucial to human performance in complex tasks and to illustrate how these parameter values predict behavior in a range of laboratory situations.

WHAT IS AN EXPERIMENT?

In psychology, the term "experiment" came to have a very specific meaning. An experiment required a dependent variable and one or more independent variables, the latter to be manipulated over a set of "experimental conditions." A null hypothesis was erected: that the mean values of the dependent variables were not significantly different for sets of subjects run under different experimental conditions. If the data led to rejection of the null hypothesis, one bit of information had been obtained—that the dependent variables was, apparently, affected by the independent variable.

Experiments conceived, executed, and published within this framework produced such facts as that the ease of learning

This work was supported by PHS research grant MH-07722 from the National Institutes of Health. The thesis set forth here has benefited from many discussions with my colleagues William G. Chase, Lee W. Gregg, and Allen Newell. An earlier version of this article was given as an invited address at the meeting of the Eastern Psychological Association, April 4, 1970.

nonsense syllables is related to their meaningfulness, or to their similarity. They paid little attention to the strength of the relation—whether running up the scale of meaningfulness from 0 to 100 reduced learning time by 5 percent, or 50 percent, or 500 percent.

Only in psychophysics (and, in a different way, in operant conditioning) was this orthodoxy ignored. When a subject is asked to compare the differences in pitch between two pairs of tones, the point of the experiment is to estimate the shape and parameters of a function in which physical pitch is the independent variable and "subjective" pitch the dependent variable. What is published is not the one-bit message that there is a relation between physical and subjective pitch, but the actual form of the function and the numerical values of its parameters.

What is done in the psychophysical laboratory does not fit the narrow definition of "experiment." No "control" condition is contrasted with the "experimental" condition. Instead of significance tests, there are reports of the standard or probable errors of measures—quite another matter. Probable errors are not intended to test whether a parameter may be different from zero, but to indicate the precision with which the measurements were carried out.

THE SPAN OF IMMEDIATE RECALL

The methods of experimental psychology are now shifting from the narrow view of experiment bound up with hypothesis-testing to a view of experiment that puts its principal emphasis upon estimating parameters and the shapes of functions. It is now becoming possible to obtain replicable estimates of basic parameters that characterize human memory and to draw implications from these estimates for complex performance.

Some years ago, George A. Miller, 1956, introduced a "magic number"—the number of chunks that can be held in short-term memory for immediate recall. Of the studies he cites, at least thirteen employ the parameter-estimation paradigm, and

no more than two employ the standard hypothesis-testing paradigm.

In introducing the "chunk," Miller was artfully vague (1956, p. 93):

The contrast of the terms *bit* and *chunk* also serves to highlight the fact that we are not very definite about what constitutes a chunk of information. For example, the memory span of five words that Hayes obtained ... might just as appropriately have been called a memory span of 15 phonemes, since each word had about three phonemes in it. Intuitively, it is clear that the subjects were recalling five words, not 15 phonemes, but the logical distinction is not immediately apparent. We are dealing here with a process of organizing or grouping the input into familiar units or chunks, and a great deal of learning has gone into the formation of these familiar units.

Miller makes a fundamental distinction between a conventionally defined amount (numbers of words or phonemes) of material and a chunk of that material, which is a particular amount that has specific psychological significance. Thus, when measuring quantity of material conventionally, one may define either the word or the phoneme as the unit. The words in Miller's example are either one or three units in length, depending on whether the word or the phoneme, respectively, is the standard of measurement.

There is no such freedom with respect to chunks—else there would be no magic in the magic number. The significance of the magic number lies in the assertion that the capacity of short-term memory, measured in chunks, is independent of the material of which those chunks are manufactured—five chunks worth of words, five chunks of digits, five chunks of colors, five chunks of shapes, five chunks of poetry or prose.[1] But unless there is a way of determining the chunk size of any given material

1. The magic number proposed here is five, rather than Millier's seven, because the estimates that I derive from data in the literature are closer to the former number than to the latter. But most of my analysis will depend only on the hypothesis that the capacity of short-term memory is a *constant* number of chunks, the same for all kinds of stimuli; the exact numerical value of the constant will not be crucial.

independently of the measurement of memory span, the assertion that there is a fixed chunk span loses all empirical content.

Miller saves his proposition from tautology by using two methods for estimating chunk size, one depending on knowledge of the previous experiences of his subjects, the other depending on training procedures—on experience provided in the laboratory. With respect to the former, he again determines that words, not phonemes, are to be regarded as the chunks (Miller, 1956, p. 93):

> Intuitively, it is clear that the subjects were recalling five words, not 15 phonemes, but the logical distinction is not immediately apparent. We are dealing here with a process of organizing or grouping the input into familiar units or chunks, and a great deal of learning has gone into the formation of these familiar units.

With respect to the latter, altering the chunking of material by laboratory training, he says (Miller, 1956, p. 93):

> In order to speak more precisely, therefore, we must recognize the importance of grouping or organizing the input sequence into units or chunks. Since the memory span is a fixed number of chunks, we can increase the number of bits of information that it contains simply by building larger and larger chunks, each chunk containing more information than before.

He continues (pp. 93–95) by describing the now-famous experiment of Sidney Smith, who increased the number of binary (0 or 1) digits he could recall from about 12 to 40 by recoding each sequence of three binary digits into a single, octal (0 through 7) digit. Assuming that the digit could be equated with the chunk, the length of the sequence of digits that could be recalled should be independent of the size of the alphabet of digits, whether two or eight. And so it was.

The reality of the chunk can be pursued further by using words instead of digits and past experience instead of training in experiments analogous to Smith's. The span of immediate recall for words is roughly equal to the span for unrelated letters or for digits. This is the principal reason for concluding, as Miller did, that a word is a chunk. But the implications of

the chunk hypothesis can be tested; if it is correct, the recall span for words should not depend on the number of syllables the words contain.

This prediction is easily checked. I made up lists of one-syllable, two syllable, and three-syllable English nouns and tested my own span by later reading them aloud at about two items per second, then recalling them. My span was nearly seven words for the one-syllable and two-syllable nouns, and about six words for three-syllable nouns. Thus, if words are chunks, the span was not quite constant; there was a variation of some 15 percent between the extreme conditions. But what of the alternative—of treating syllables as chunks? The span for one-syllable nouns was 7 syllables; for three-syllable nouns, 18—a ratio of 2.5 to 1. One must conclude, therefore, that the syllable is not the invariant unit that measures short-term memory capacity, but that the word *may* be.

The chunking hypothesis does not assert that the word will always be the unit. Units much larger than words may be highly familiar, hence may serve as chunks. I tried to recall after one reading the following list of words: Lincoln, milky, criminal, differential, address, way, lawyer, calculus, Gettysburg. I had no success whatsoever. I should not have expected success, for the list exceeded my span of six or seven words. Then I rearranged the list a bit, as follows:

Lincoln's Gettysburg Address
Milky Way
Criminal lawyer
Differential calculus

I had no difficulty at all. Obvious? It is only obvious if one accepts the chunk hypothesis and if one knows that, in the culture in which I was raised, the four items in the list are, in fact, familiar chunks. If these premises are accepted, I have simply performed a variant of the Smith experiment.

The prediction that I should be able to recall lists of six familiar phrases of this sort is not substantiated. Four or five seems to be about the limit, indicating that something about the additional length of the material reduces the total number of imputed chunks that can be retained—just as in the comparison of three-syllable with one-syllable words. To substantiate further this gentle decline in capacity with imputed chunk length, I extrapolated from familiar two-word and three-word phrases to longer ones. Consider the list:

Four score and seven years ago
To be or not to be, that is the question
In the beginning was the word
All's fair in love and war

Lists of three such phrases were all I could recall with reliability, although I could sometimes retain four.

To summarize the results up to this point: as one moves from one-syllable to three-syllable words, then to familiar two-word and three-word phrases, then to familiar phrases of six to ten words, the memory span, measured in syllables, words, and imputed chunks, varies as shown in table 1.

Table 1. Span of Immediate Recall for Words and Phrases (With the Author as Subject).

Words and Phrases	Span			
	Syllables	Words	Imputed Chunks	Syllables /Chunk
1-syllable	7	7	7	1.0
2-syllable	14	7	7	2.0
3-syllable	18	6	6	3.0
2-word	22	9	4	5.5
8-word	26	22	3	8.7

None of the measures remains constant, but the number of chunks retained declines only by a factor of two, while the number of words retained increases by a factor of three, and the number of syllables almost by a factor of four. I conclude that the "constant capacity in chunks" hypothesis is a rough first approximation of the true state of affairs but that it must be refined— perhaps by taking into account the additional time required to rehearse the longer passages—in order to achieve a fully satisfactory fit to the data.

TIME TO LEARN

The experiments and data reported thus far still leave the chunk in an unsatisfactory

status. Limiting the data to memory span experiments provides no evidence for the reality of the imputed chunks other than some agreement between the measured span and a priori notions of what the "familiar unit" actually is.

The difficulty arises because the number of chunks is not directly observable. Viewed in isolation, the hypothesis is not really an empirical statement at all, but a definition of "chunk": a chunk of any kind of stimulus material is the quantity that short-term memory will hold five of.

Simple examples from the physical sciences show, however, that difficulties of this sort can often be removed by compounding them. It is often observed that Newton's Second Law of Motion (force equals mass times acceleration) is not really a law, but a definition of force. By the same token, Hooke's Law, which states that the extensions of a spring are proportional to the forces applied to it, is also merely a definition of those forces. Taken together, however, the two laws can be tested empirically (for example, by whirling a weighted spring); one can determine whether the magnitudes of the forces determined by the one law (viewed as definition) agree with the magnitudes of the same forces determined by the other law.

A law of the form $y = am$, where m is an observable but y is not, can be used to estimate y, but observations can never refute the law. Suppose there is a second law, of the form $y = bp$, where p is also an observable. Taken together, the two laws imply $am = bp$, which is a testable proposition since the single free parameter, a/b, can be estimated from observations. Thus, one can use the first equation to estimate values of y and then see whether these satisfy the second equation.

In the case at hand, there is a quantity that is directly observable (number of syllables immediately recallable, say) and another, unobservable quantity that is postulated by the theory (number of syllables per chunk). Call these S and s, respectively. The hypothesis that short-term memory has a constant capacity of five chunks can be rendered as simply $S = 5s$. Given the measurement of S, the observable, this equation can be used to estimate chunk size: $s = S/5$. The theory is essentially untestable, however, because for any observed S there always exists an s that satisfies the equation.

Suppose, however, that there is another observable—the number of syllables that can be fixated per minute in a rote memory experiment. Consider the hypothesis that this number (F) is proportional to the number of syllables per chunk (s): $F = ks$. As before, the theory provides an equation for estimating an unobservable, but the theory is untestable.

If, however, one puts the two hypotheses together, one can combine the two estimating equations for s, eliminating the unobserved s between them: $F = aS$, where a is a new constant parameter. This equation makes it possible to estimate the time required per syllable to learn any particular kind of stimulus material from the memory span for that same kind of material. The constant, a, can be estimated for any single kind of material, say common English words, thus reducing by 1 the degrees of freedom. Hence, the conjunction of the two hypotheses (the span of immediate recall is five chunks; the time required to memorize a chunk of material is k seconds) is testable, even though neither hypothesis taken separately is. Moreover, if the hypotheses satisfy the empirical test, either of the original equations can be used to measure chunk size (up to a constant of proportionality) for all kinds of stimulus material.

The second of the two hypotheses above —that learning time is proportional to the number of chunks to be fixated—was introduced without any particular motivation. Before marshaling the data to test the two hypotheses, let me mention some of the evidence for the notion that quantity of material learned is proportional to time. The hypothesis rests on three legs—two empirical, the other theoretical.

Since most learning theories connected the learning of nonsense syllables with reinforcement, it was natural to measure ease or difficulty of learning by number of trials (that is, number of reinforcements)

required to reach criterion. The following statement is typical:

> When the presentation time of each syllable in a 12-syllable list is increased from 2 seconds to 4 seconds, the mean trials required to attain a criterion of 7 syllables correct out of 12 decreases from 6.05 to 3.28.[2]

Of course, if one does not start with the theoretical presumption that the trial's the thing, there is a much more parsimonious way of reporting this experiment. One can say, simply:

> When the presentation time of each syllable in a 12-syllable list is increased from 2 seconds to 4 seconds, the mean length of time required to attain a criterion of 7 syllables correct out of 12 remains almost constant, increasing only from 12.1 seconds to 13.1 seconds.

A number of other experiments done before World War II support the hypothesis that the total learning time per unit of material of any particular kind is constant. This observation was an important clue that led Feigenbaum, in 1958, to use learning *time* rather than *trials* as the key variable in his EPAM (Elementary Perceiver and Memorizer) learning theory [3].

Apparently no experiments were run before 1960 with the deliberate aim of determining whether time, rather than trials, was the decisive variable in learning, although Wilcoxon, Wilson, and Wise mentioned time constancy in 1961. The first experiment specifically designed to test the time-constancy hypothesis was conducted by Bugelski and published in 1962. He found that the time required to learn a list was essentially independent of presentation speed over a wide range of speeds. Subsequent experiments have extended his result and have clarified the range of conditions under which the constancy may be expected to hold (see Cooper and Pantle, 1967).

2. McGeoch (1962), pp. 105–06.

3. E. A. Feigenbaum, (1959). The hypothesis is used in our joint paper, (Feigenbaum and Simon, 1962), which was first circulated as a working paper in 1958. It is reprinted as chapter 3.1 in this book.

So much for the empirical evidence of time constancy in learning. The third leg of the stool is the EPAM theory of verbal learning, formulated as a simulation program for a digital computer (see Simon and Feigenbaum, 1962). Since computers are serial devices, requiring time to carry out their processes, it was natural to hypothesize the same seriality in human beings, and hence to construct EPAM in such a way that amount of learning would be roughly proportional to time. As Feigenbaum and I stated the matter in an article on the serial position effect:

> The fixation of an item on a serial list requires the execution of a sequence of information processes that requires, for a given set of experimental conditions, a definite amount of processing time per syllable. The time per syllable varies with the difficulty of the syllables, the length of the list, the ability of the subject, and other factors.[4]

While the experiments I have cited, as well as EPAM theory, support the idea that amount of material learned is proportional to learning time, they permit only comparisons of a single kind of learning material at different presentation speeds, not comparisons among different kinds of stimulus material. It still remains to define a unit quantity that permits the latter kind of comparison.

TESTING THE CHUNKING HYPOTHESIS

I have now reviewed two basic hypotheses: that short-term memory holds a fixed number of chunks and that total learning time is proportional to the number of chunks to be assembled. The weakness of each hypothesis lies in its inability to provide an independent operational definition of the chunk. But by conjoining the two hypotheses, one removes the need for a priori assumptions about what constitutes a chunk.

In the EPAM theory, fixation is identified with assembling compound symbol structures from components—a familiar notion from association theory—and storing the compound structures in memory, appropriately "indexed." ("Indexing" simply means storing information that permits recovery of the compound structure upon recognition of its stimulus component.)

Thus, in paired-associate learning, a stimulus symbol and a response symbol can be assembled into a pair, indexed to the stimulus. But before this can happen, the stimulus and the response must each be assembled into a symbol compounded from their component letters (or phonemes, as the case may be). Under ordinary laboratory conditions of nonsense-syllable learning, the component letters can be assumed already to be unitary symbols at the outset of the experiments. For each pair in a set of paired-associate nonsense syllables of low association value, a total of about seven such compounding operations is required by EPAM for learning: three to familiarize the response, two to familiarize the stimulus (which need only be recognized, not recalled), and two to compound the pair.[5] The corresponding number for a serial list is four compounding operations per syllable—three to familiarize the syllable, one to incorporate it in the list.[6]

Analogous to Miller's encoding assumptions, which allowed him to predict the span of recall for recoded digits, are encoding assumptions for rote learning that enable us to predict the relative learning times for different materials. Thus, by making the a priori (but plausible) assumption that unfamiliar nonsense syllables are initially encoded as three chunks, while familiar syllables and one-syllable words are encoded as single chunks, one can

---

4. Feigenbaum and Simon (1962), p. 310.

5. Thus, to learn the pair CEF-DAX, the letters D, A, and X must be compounded into the response; then C and F, say, must be compounded into the recognition cue (C-F) for the stimulus; and finally, stimulus cue and response must each be incorporated in the pair structure: (C-F)-(DAX).

6. Similarly, if DAX is to be learned as an item in a list, the D, A, and X must be compounded into a familiar syllable (DAX) and this syllable incorporated in the list.

predict the relative learning times for these materials.

The predictions that have been made on this basis, and tests of these predictions, are mainly reported in two articles (Simon and Feigenbaum, 1964; Gregg and Simon, 1967—reprinted as chapters 3.2 and 3.3 in this book). The EPAM theory predicts, correctly, that lists of syllables of low familiarity will take nearly three times as long to learn as lists of highly familiar syllables. In fact, syllables of low familiarity take about 2.5 times as long to learn as syllables of high familiarity (Simon and Feigenbaum, 1964). The EPAM theory also predicts accurately the circumstances under which learning will have a one-trial character, and those under which it will be incremental (Gregg and Simon, 1967).

If data from experiments on immediate recall could be directly compared with data from experiments on rote learning, a priori assumptions about chunk size would be unnecessary. There is considerable consistency in measurements of the relative memory spans for different kinds of materials—for example, the ratio of the memory span for digits to the memory span for words. No a priori assumptions about chunk size enter into this ratio. Similarly, there is fairly good consistency in the relative learning times reported for different kinds of materials—for example, the ratio of the learning time for nonsense syllables to the learning time for simple words. Again, this ratio is independent of assumptions about chunk size. If the theory proposed here is correct, the ratios obtained by these different and independent experimental operations should be the same for the same pairs of experimental materials.[7]

With respect to memory span, there is a representative set of data in an experiment conducted by Brener (1940). Table 2, taken from Brener's study, shows memory

7. Using the equation introduced previously and denoting by the subscripts i and j two different kinds of stimulus material, we will have, from $S_i = 5s_i$ and $S_j = 5s_j$, $S_i/S_j = s_i/s_j$. Similarly, from $F_i = ks_i$ and $F_j = ks_j$, we will have $F_i/F_j = s_i/s_j$; whence $S_i/S_j = F_i/F_j$.

Table 2. Spans of Immediate Recall.

Test	*Mean Span*
Digits	7.98
Nonsense syllables	2.49
Consonants (visual)	7.30
Geometrical designs	5.31
Colors	7.06
Concrete words (visual)	5.76
Paired associates (pair)	2.50
Abstract words (visual)	5.24
Commands*	2.42
Sentences (six words)	1.75

* Each command involved a relation between two objects.

Source: Brener, 1940.

spans for ten different kinds of stimulus material, ranging from digits and colors to six-word sentences. The ten mean values fall into four groups: spans of 10 (words in six-word sentences), around 7.5 (digits, consonants, colors), 5.0 (geometric designs, concrete nouns, abstract nouns), and 2.5 (nonsense syllables, paired associates, and simple commands). The task now is to compare the ratios of these spans with ratios of learning times for the same materials.

Unfortunately, data on learning times in serial or paired-associate paradigms are available for only a few of the materials for which digit spans have been measured. Those ratios that have been measured are reasonably consistent from one experiment to another. I have already mentioned the commonly observed 2.5 to 1 advantage in learning simple words over nonsense syllables. Averaging Brener's data for abstract and concrete words (the difference is only about 10 percent), one finds a span of 5.5 for words, as compared with 2.49 for nonsense syllables—a ratio of 2.2. Thus the two operations give us estimates—2.5 and 2.2, respectively—that differ by only about 15 percent.

Lyon's 1914 experiments, with himself as subject, in memorizing lists of hundreds of nonsense syllables, digits, and passages of prose and poetry provide a second source of data (Lyon, 1914). Table 3 shows the

Table 3. Fixation Times.

Material	Unit	Time (Second/Unit)
Nonsense syllables	Syllable	27.9
Digits	Digit	25.5
Prose	Word	7.2
Poetry	Word	3.0

Source: Lyon, 1914.

time, in seconds per unit of material, it took him to memorize 200 units of material by reciting them once each day.

From the Brener data (1940), the ratio of the span for sentences (measured in words) to the span for nonsense syllables is 10.5 to 2.49, or 4.2. From the Lyon data (1914), the ratio of learning times for nonsense syllables and prose (per word) is 27.9 to 7.2, or 3.9. Again, the two ratios agree within about 10 percent.

There is no such happy agreement when memory spans and learning times for nonsense syllables and digits are compared. In the Brener data, the ratio of spans for the two kinds of stimuli is 7.98 to 2.49, or 3.2. In the Lyon data, the ratio of learning times is 27.9 to 25.5, or 1.1. No significance test is needed to show that something is wrong. The theory is certainly not entirely accurate.

Lyon himself argues that the excessive difficulty in learning the digit list arose from high intralist similarity. In a list of 200 digits, each digit will appear about 20 times, and each pair, on the average, about twice. However, in experiments involving the learning of nonsense syllables, where similarity is manipulated as the independent variable, the difference in learning times between high and low similarity conditions is about 30 percent—very far from the ratio of 3 to 1 that appears in the Simon and Feigenbaum data (1964).

Another possible explanation is provided by McLean and Gregg (1967), who showed that sequences of letters were learned about twice as rapidly when the letters were presented in groups of three or more as when they were presented one at a time. Their interpretation (an extension of the

EPAM theory) was that, in the absence of cues from the experimenter, the subject was unable to group the letters consistently from one trial to the next, hence was forced to learn unnecessary additional groups. This hypothesis would account for two-thirds of the discrepancy in the Lyon data on digits.

That the length of the series learned by Lyon has something to do with the problem is shown by the fact that shorter strings of digits were learned much more rapidly than shorter strings of syllables. For example, the ratio of learning times for 16 syllables and 16 digits was almost exactly 2 to 1—still only two-thirds of the ratio predicted by the simple version of the theory.

These explanations are hardly satisfactory. The hypothesis simply does not work well with material in which there is frequent repetition of the same chunks. The difficulty in carrying out rote learning experiments with materials like digits, simple geometric designs, or colors is that, if one uses long series, one must repeat symbols; if one uses short series, one is in danger of confounding short-term with long-term memory, and hence not obtaining an independent measure of the parameters associated with the latter.

To summarize, the estimates of relative chunk size for nonsense syllables, words, and prose obtained from immediate recall experiments agree very well with the estimates obtained from rote learning experiments. There is serious disagreement, however, between the two estimates of digit chunk size; data for estimating chunk size for colors and geometric figures are apparently not available from the rote learning paradigm.

The theory had some successes, but also a clear-cut (although perhaps temporary) failure. The failure is as instructive as the successes. It did not arise from either experiment taken in isolation from the other. Each was perfectly consistent within itself—it provided the one bit of information that it was capable of giving within the classical paradigm for each experimental condition. It does not make much sense to ask, within the context of Lyon's experiment alone, whether digits "should" have been learned faster than nonsense syllables. After an independent experiment has predicted a 3-to-1 advantage of digits over syllables, this "should" becomes something that must be taken seriously.

The main importance of invariants lies in their power to strip away the complexity and diversity of a whole range of phenomena and to reveal the simplicity and order underneath. Invariants, however, not only provide explanations for simple cognitive phenomena, they are also needed in the explanation of more complicated phenomena of thinking and problem solving. Having discovered what a chunk is—if we have—it remains to be seen how it can be used in predicting human cognitive behavior in complex settings.

SIGNIFICANCE OF THE CHUNK IN COGNITION

The examples I use refer to three very different situations. The first is a modest extrapolation from the immediate recall experiments I have already examined: Does the theory of chunking have implications for the change in memory span with age? The second is an extrapolation to a relatively structured task that one might not even want to call "problem solving"— mental multiplication of relatively large numbers. The third is an extrapolation to the initial stages of problem solving, the period during which the subject characterizes for himself the problem that has been placed before him. In all three cases, the extrapolation depends not merely on having a general hypothesis that some independent variable affects some dependent variable, but on having quantitative estimates, derived from the simpler situations, of the values of parameters.

Because digit span increases with age, tests of digit span are included in most standard instruments for measuring mental age. Span is measured, of course, in common units (that is, digits) that might or might not represent the same number of chunks at different ages. In fact, the chunking hypothesis forces one to conclude that,

with cumulative experience with numbers, children should learn to encode digits in larger and larger chunks, so that an increasing number of digit pairs and even triplets might become recognizable as a single chunk.

If the capacity of short-term memory is five chunks, and if the growth in digit span is due to learning, I should be able to make at least one quantitative prediction about absolute digit span as a function of age. Specifically, a digit should be equivalent to almost exactly one chunk at an age where the child knows the individual digits well, but has not had much arithmetic practice in combining or manipulating them—that is, at about the age the child enters school.

Table 4. Stanford-Binet Norms for Digit Span.

Age (Years)	Digits
2.5	2
3.0	3
4.5	4
7.0	5
10.0	6
College	8

Source: Woodworth and Schlosberg, 1954.

Table 4 gives the revised Stanford-Binet norms for digit span (Woodworth and Schlosberg, 1954, p. 704). It shows that, in fact, the norm for digit span is five at age seven—the age of first or second grade children—while it is only four at age four and a half—the age of prekindergarten children. The digit span for college students is slightly below the value it would have if they handled pairs of digits as chunks. Both of these facts are consistent with the hypothesis that the change in digit span with age is due to the shortening of the encoded strings by the use of learned chunks. Also consistent with this hypothesis are experiments which show that digit span can be increased substantially (for example, from 4.4 to 6.4 among kindergartners, from 10 to 14 among college students) with persistent practice.

I next turn to a task where immediate recall and rote learning are only components of a process. In an endeavor to explain the relative lengths of time required for subjects to do mental multiplications of pairs of numbers, Dansereau (1969) constructed a simulation model of the process, assigning specific time parameters to each of the subprocesses and capacity parameters to short-term memory.

Since Dansereau's model was more detailed and complete than the one I have used informally throughout this article, he needed more parameters than the two I have discussed. He needed to specify the capacity of the short-term visual memory and the short-term auditory memory; he also needed to specify the times required to transfer symbols from the external stimulus to internal memories, and from each internal memory (visual, auditory, long-term) to each of the others. An important constraint that Dansereau imposed on his model was that these parameters not be selected simply to fit his data on mental multiplication speeds, but that they be consistent with estimates of the same parameters derived from simpler component tasks. By drawing on data from others' experiments as well as experiments on component tasks that he himself carried out, Dansereau greatly reduced the degrees of freedom available for fitting his mental multiplication data to his processing model.

For example, he specified 2 seconds per digit as the time required to transfer symbols from short-term to long-term memory. He based this specification on times of 5 seconds per chunk, derived from the experiments of Bugelski and others (Bugelski, 1962; Cooper and Pantle, 1967; Wilcoxen et al., 1961), together with the assumption that chunks averaged three digits each. These specifications are perhaps biased on the low side, and I might want to quarrel with the details, but the important points are (1) that it is a definite enough theoretical structure to be quarreled about meaningfully and (2) that the outcome of the quarrel could hardly change the estimate by as much as a factor of 2.

I cannot summarize Dansereau's results here. Rather, I cite his study as another example of the strategy of using parameters estimated from experiments on simple tasks to predict performance on complex tasks. Dansereau undertook to explain performance in mental multiplication on the basis of the same component processes and the same system parameters as those already encountered in laboratory experiments with simpler component tasks.

As a final example, I should like to mention some perceptual phenomena that have been studied a great deal in the past few years. Experiments by de Groot (1978), Jongman (1968), and others on the ability of subjects to reproduce the pattern of pieces on a chessboard after an exposure of 5 to 10 seconds, have yielded the following results:

If the pieces represent a position from an actual game (unknown to the subjects), then grandmasters and masters will generally reproduce the position (about 20 to 25 pieces) almost without error, while ordinary players will generally be able to place only a half-dozen pieces correctly. If the same number of pieces is placed on the board in a random pattern, grandmasters and ordinary players alike will be able to place only a half-dozen pieces correctly.

The grandmasters' performance in the first situation could be explained by attributing to them some extraordinary perceptual capability. In the second situation, however, this capability disappears. A more parsimonious explanation would be that the same number of chunks was being retained in memory by both sets of subjects in both situations. To complete this explanation, one would then have to show how a chess position composed of 24 pieces could be recoded into a half-dozen chunks by a master.

This hypothesis has been explored in a series of studies by Barenfeld, Charness, Chase, Gilmartin, and myself, with generally positive results.[8] Direct evidence for the chunking hypothesis was obtained, for

---

8. For general summaries, see chapter 6.5 and Simon and Chase (1973).

example, by timing how rapidly pieces were replaced on a chessboard from memory. The longer pauses occurred when two unrelated pieces were placed in sequence, while the shorter pauses occurred when closely related pieces were placed in sequence. Interpreting the longer pauses as chunk boundaries, it was found that more than half the variance between the numbers of pieces remembered by strong and weak players, respectively, could be attributed to the larger average chunk size of the former. The explanation for the remaining variance is still being sought.

Using simple probability models, as well as a computer simultation of the chess perception processes, quantitative estimates were made of the "vocabulary" of familiar chunks in a master's memory. The estimates obtained by several different procedures all fall in the range of 25,000 to 100,000 chunks—that is, a vocabulary of roughly the same size as the vocabulary of an educated adult in his native language. Here, again, the combination of approximate measurements of a few basic parameters and a detailed process theory permits one to make far-reaching predictions and extrapolations.

CONCLUSION

I have explored some of the interactions between research on higher mental processes over the past decade or two and laboratory experiments on simpler cognitive processes. I have shown that, by viewing experimentation in a parameter-estimating paradigm instead of a hypothesis-testing paradigm, one can obtain much more information from experiments—information that, combined with contemporary theoretical models of the cognitive processes, has implications for human performance on tasks quite different from those of the original experiments.

The work of identifying and measuring the basic parameters of the human information processing system has just begun, but already important information has been gained. The psychological reality of the chunk has been fairly well demon-

strated, and the chunk capacity of short-term memory has been shown to be in the range of five to seven. Fixation of information in long-term memory has been shown to take about 5 or 10 seconds per chunk.

Some other "magical numbers" have been estimated—for example, visual scanning speeds and times required for simple grammatical transformations—and no doubt others remain to be discovered. But even the two basic constants discussed in this chapter—short-term memory capacity and rate of fixation in long-term memory—organize, systematize, and explain a wide range of findings, about both simple tasks and more complex cognitive performances that have been reported in the psychological literature over the past 50 years or more.

References

Brener, R., An experimental investigation of memory span, *Journal of Experimental Psychology*, 26:467–82 (1940).

Bugelski, B. R., Presentation time, total time, and mediation in paired-associate learning, *Journal of Experimental Psychology*, 63:409–89 (1962).

Cooper, E. H., and A. J. Pantle, The total-time hypothesis in verbal learning, *Psychological Bulletin*, 68:221–34 (1967).

Dansereau, D. F., An information processing model of mental multiplication, Unpublished PhD dissertation, Carnegie-Mellon University (1969).

Feigenbaum, E. A., An information processing theory of verbal learning, PhD dissertation, Carnegie Institute of Technology, 1959. Published as RAND Paper P-1817, Santa Monica, Calif.: The RAND Corporation, 1959.

Feigenbaum, E. A., and H. A. Simon, A theory of the serial position effect, *British Journal of Psychology*, 53:307–20 (1962). Reprinted as chapter 3.1 in this book.

Gregg, L. W., and H. A. Simon, An information-processing explanation of one-trial and incremental learning, *Journal of Verbal Learning and Verbal Behavior*, 6:780–87 (1967).

de Groot, A. D., *Thought and Choice in Chess* (2nd ed.), The Hague: Mouton, 1978.

Jongman, R. W., *Het Oog van de Meester*, Amsterdam: van Gorcum, 1968.

Lyon, D. O., The relation of length of material

to time taken for learning and the optimum distribution of time, *Journal of Educational Psychology*, 5:1–9, 85–91, 155–63 (1914).

McGeoch, J. A., *The Psychology of Human Learning*, New York: Longmans, Green, 1942.

McLean, R. S., and L. W. Gregg, Effect of induced chunking on temporal aspects of serial recitation, *Journal of Experimental Psychology*, 74:455–59 (1967).

Miller, G. A., The magical number seven, plus or minus two: Some limits on our capacity for processing information, *Psychological Review*, 63:81–97 (1956).

Simon, H. A., and W. G. Chase, Skill in chess, *American Scientist*, 61:394–403 (1973).

Simon, H. A., and E. A. Feigenbaum, An information-processing theory of some effects of similarity, familiarization, and meaningfulness in verbal learning, *Journal of Verbal Learning and Verbal Behavior*, 3:385–96 (1964).

Wilcoxon, H. C., W. R. Wilson, and D. A. Wise, Paired associate learning as a function of percentage of occurrence of response members and other factors, *Journal of Experimental Psychology*, 61:283–89 (1961).

Woodworth, R. S., and H. Schlosberg, *Experimental Psychology* (2nd ed.) New York: Holt, 1954.

2.3

The Information Storage System Called "Human Memory" (1976)

The first purpose of this chapter is to describe human memory as it looks today to that growing group of psychologists who approach it from an information processing point of view. A second purpose is to examine the relation between an information processing account of human memory and a physiological account and the implications of that relation for the division of labor between information processing psychologists and physiological psychologists.

In the past five years there has been a great spate of books and articles that review our present knowledge about human memory and propose more or less comprehensive theories of memory organization (e.g., Anderson and Bower, 1973; Hunt, 1971, 1973; Kintsch, 1970; and Rumelhart, Lindsay, and Norman, 1972). No important purpose would be served by going over that ground again, and I will not undertake to do so. Instead, I will look at matters primarily from a methodological stand-

point and undertake to analyze the nature of the inferences that connect theories of memory with data from experiments on memory.

INFORMATION PROCESSING AND PHYSIOLOGICAL APPROACHES

There are numerous examples in modern science of the need for multiple explanations of complex phenomena at different levels of fineness of detail. Perhaps the classical example of this kind is found in chemistry. For many purposes, chemical reactions can be described and explained in terms of regroupings of basic units called atoms connected by ionic or covalent bonds, the reactions being accompanied by absorption or release of certain quantities of energy. With each type of atom is associated a number, its valence; and the admissibility of molecular structures is governed by rules on the valences. A body of theory erected on this basis served chemistry through the nineteenth century and well into the twentieth and still provides the first approximation to the description of chemical processes.

By 1916, G. N. Lewis and a number of his predecessors had found a bridge, the modern electronic theory of valence, between the empirically postulated valence

This research has been supported in part by Research Grant MH-07722 from the National Institute of Mental Health and in part by the Advanced Research Projects Agency of the Secretary of Defense (F44620-70-C-0107), a contract monitored by the Air Force Office of Scientific Research. I am grateful to my colleague Chris Frederickson for helpful comments on a first draft of this paper.

numbers of the chemist and the emerging physical theory of the atom. That bridge was based on the idea of stable electron shells (for ionic bonds) and the sharing of electrons between atoms (for covalent bonds). Almost immediately after the invention of quantum mechanics in 1926, the reduction of the theory of the chemical bond to the underlying physical level was carried very much farther by Condon, Heitler, London, Pauling, and many others. In principle at least, there no longer existed any boundary between physics and chemistry. Any chemical reaction could be explained in terms of an underlying atomic structure and the accompanying quantum-mechanical laws.

In practice, of course, the discovery of the quantum-mechanical explanation of the chemical bond has not made the classical chemical explanations of reactions superfluous. In the first place, the actual quantum-mechanical reduction of chemical phenomena has been carried out for only the simplest cases, and then only on the basis of ingenious approximations. Many of the largest computers in the nation today are laboring to carry out approximate quantum-mechanical analyses of molecules of quite modest size. We believe, of course, that the great mass of chemical systems that have not been analyzed in this way could be—given computers of unlimited power—but that belief is an article of our scientific faith in the uniformity of nature, not an inference from tested facts. Our reductionism remains in-principle reductionism.

In the second place, even if we could actually carry out the quantum-mechanical reduction of all chemical phenomena, we still would not want to dispense with the chemical level of theory. Research in problem solving has shown that the efficiency of problem-solving efforts can often be greatly increased by carrying out the search for a solution, not in the original problem space with all of its cluttering detail, but in an abstracted space, from which much of the detail has been removed, leaving the essential skeleton of the problem more clearly visible. The so-called planning method in problem solving involves just such a process of abstraction. In the same way, a chemist seeking to solve a typical problem of chemical synthesis would be ill-advised to immerse himself in the quantum-mechanical detail of the system before using classical chemical theory to discover one or more promising reaction paths. Thus theory at the chemical level, rather than the more "basic" theory at the physical level, remains the principal conceptual apparatus for most working chemists.

There are physicists who take the doctrine of reductionism so literally that they believe there are no "fundamental" scientific questions except the questions of elementary-particle theory. Most of us, I think, have a quite different picture of the scientific enterprise. We see the natural world as an immensely complex hierarchical system, understandable only by being represented alternatively at many levels of detail, and understood by constructing bodies of theory at each of these levels, in combination with reduction theories that show how the unanalyzed elementary structures at each level can themselves be explained in terms of the constructs available at the next level below. In this world there is need for chemistry as well as physics, biology as well as chemistry, and information processing psychology as well as physiological psychology. Nor should the necessity for this plurality of levels of theory construction carry any implications for vitalism or mentalism, or bring any aid or comfort to antireductionists.

Information processing psychology has sometimes been referred to as "the new mental chemistry." The atoms of this mental chemistry are symbols, which are combinable into larger and more complex associational structures called lists and list structures. The fundamental "reactions" of the mental chemistry employ elementary information processes that operate upon symbols and symbol structures: copying symbols, storing symbols, retrieving symbols, inputting and outputting symbols, and comparing symbols. Symbol structures are stored in memories, often classified as short-term and long-term memories, whose properties will be a major topic of this chapter.

Symbol structures and elementary information processes are abstract entities in exactly the same sense that the molecules and reactions of classical chemistry are abstract entities. Symbol structures "exist" in exactly the same sense that molecules exist; their presence is postulated in order to explain parsimoniously a whole host of observable phenomena. Thus, the evidence for them is indirect in the same way that the evidence for molecules—at least prior to the invention of the electron microscope —was indirect. We know them by their actions, by the macroscopic phenomena that they produce.

At the same time, all of us, I believe, are committed to the proposition that thinking and other cognitive processes are performed by a biological organ called the brain, in conjunction with the peripheral nervous system and sensory and motor organs. The symbol structures and elementary information processes of information processing psychology must therefore have their physiological counterparts in subsystems within the central nervous system that function as memory units, and subsystems that are capable of processing these physiologically stored structures. The term "system" is used here rather than "unit" to avoid commitment to any assumption of localism —any notion that each symbol structure that is stored must have its specific storage location in the brain. Nothing in contemporary information processing theories of memory requires that memories be specifically localized; and nothing in those theories is incompatible with a distributed or even holographic theory of the physiological basis for memory.

There is no reason to suppose that the "mental chemistry" of symbols is any less complex than the chemistry of atoms and molecules. On the contrary, the best information processing explanations we possess of problem solving and other complex cognitive performances employ intricate organizations, or programs, of information processes to account for the long sequences of events that occur (Newell and Simon,

1972). Hence it is likely that, when we come to have a bridge theory that provides an explanation of information processing in physiological terms, that bridge theory will deal explicitly and in detail only with relatively simple phenomena, handling more complex phenomena only in an "in-principle" sense. Moreover, however adequate the physiological theory turns out to be, we will still need a more aggregative and abstract theory at the information process level to guide our thinking about the more complex phenomena.

For these reasons, the relation between physiological psychology and information processing psychology is a complementary relation, not a competitive one. To achieve the kind of explanation of human cognition that we want to and need to have, we will have to construct an information processing theory to handle the complex phenomena, a bridge theory to show how the primitive structures and processes of the theory are realized physiologically, and a physiological theory to show what the basic biological and biochemical mechanisms are that implement the physiological functions.

In this scheme of things, there is plenty of work for all, and a very natural, if rough, division of labor between information processing psychologists and physiological psychologists. Returning again to our physico-chemical analogue, we note that it was the job of the chemist to reduce the phenomena of the test tube and the beaker to rearrangements of molecular structures. It was the job of the physicist to provide physical mechanisms that could explicate "atom" and "chemical bond." Without denying the importance of the bridging theorist—the physical chemist or chemical physicist—it should be apparent that, for the most part, the physicist did not need to concern himself with complex chemical reactions, while the chemist could ignore many of the physical details of the atom. The two disciplines, while contributing in vital ways to each other's work, could specialize with respect both to the phenomena studied and the techniques for studying them.

In psychology today, the subdisciplines already exist for implementing an analogous specialization, but in this specialization it is important that the bridging function not be lost from sight. I welcome a meeting like this as an opportunity to make contact with physiological data and theories that can explain the elementary information structures and processes that theorists on my side of the boundary have postulated in order to explain complex behavior. I hope that this chapter may provide to some physiological psychologists a corresponding opportunity to ascertain for what kinds of structures and processes physiological explanations are needed.

Points of contact between information processing psychology and physiological psychology are becoming increasingly visible. One of these concerns the extraction of features from visual stimuli and their subsequent encoding in the central nervous system. Another, closer to the topic of the present chapter, is the relation between physiological and behavioral approaches to the phenomena of amnesia and aphasia in brain-damaged subjects. Quite similar views of the architecture of human memory are emerging from these complementary approaches.

The point of view I have taken here in my excursion into the philosophy of science is quite orthodox, and it is unlikely to evoke much disagreement or controversy. I have taken the time to present it because I think it is necessary in an interdisciplinary conversation like this one to make our frames of reference and underlying methodological assumptions fully explicit.

For the same reason, it is necessary to make some preliminary remarks about one of the main research tools of information processing psychology—the digital computer. These remarks are the subject of the next section, at the end of which we can turn to matters of substance.

The Computer in Information Processing Psychology

Over the past twenty years, the electronic digital computer has played a central role as a research tool in information processing approaches to cognitive psychology. It has, in fact, had two roles. On the one hand, computer languages have proved to be the most powerful and appropriate languages for stating psychological theories formally. Computer languages have vocabularies and syntaxes specifically designed to describe symbols and symbol structures, elementary information processes, and the organizations of those processes called programs. At the same time, whenever a theory is stated in a computer language, the computer becomes available as a powerful tool for predicting the behavior of the system described by the theory, and thereby permitting a comparison of theoretical predictions with empirical data. Most of the theories of memory I will be discussing either have been, or could rather easily be, expressed formally as computer programs.

In our book *Human Problem Solving* (1972), Allen Newell and I have discussed at some length the methods and problems of stating and testing theories expressed as computer programs. I will not repeat that discussion here, but refer the interested reader to our book. In fact, such differences as exist in the methodology for handling theories expressed in computer languages and theories not so expressed are tactical rather than fundamental. The issues are the familiar ones of stating the theories in a form that makes them operationally testable and devising experiments and other forms of observation that permit the predictions of theory to be confronted with empirical facts.

I will have little to say explicitly in this chapter about the computer programs that have been constructed to simulate human memory (e.g., Feigenbaum, 1961; Simon and Feigenbaum, 1964; Gregg and Simon, 1967; Anderson and Bower, 1973). These programs have played an important (and increasing) role in exploring the mechanisms required to account for memory phenomena and in searching out the indirect consequences of hypotheses about memory organization.

The Statics of Memory: The Storage System

It is common in psychology today to use the term "memory" in the plural—to speak of "long-term memory," "short-term memory," "iconic memory," "echoic memory," and others. What is the phenomenological basis on which one makes such distinctions? How does one tell that different sets of information are held in different memories, or in the same memory?

Phenomenologically, a memory is characterized and identified by (1) the kinds of inputs that can be stored in it, (2) the time required to store new information in it, (3) the time required to access information previously stored in it, (4) the durations over which information, once stored, is retained, (5) conditions that cause loss of information over a period during which it could otherwise be retained, (6) the qualitative nature of the deterioration of stored information, (7) the nature of the cues needed for accessing stored information, and (8) the form of organization of the stored information.

Some Standard Experimental Paradigms

A brief and simplified description of some standard paradigms for memory experiments will illustrate how the parameters of memory listed above can be used to infer the existence of distinct memories from experimental data. The term "distinct" here does not imply distinct spatial localization but functional specialization.

The stimulus for all the experiments to be described is a rectangular array of English letters, selected at random and displayed in three rows of four letters each. The stimulus is displayed for 50 msec, and it is of such size and intensity that there is no question of visual confusion. In the first experimental paradigm (Immediate recall experiment), the subject is instructed to repeat back the sequence of stimulus letters as soon as he has seen them. Typically, a subject will recall an average of about four to six letters correctly (see chapter 2.2).

In the second paradigm (Sperling paradigm), an aural cue is presented shortly after the stimulus, the subject being instructed to repeat back either the upper line of letters, the middle line, or the lower line, depending on whether the cue is a tone of high pitch, intermediate pitch, or low pitch. Performance on this task varies with the interval between exposure of the stimulus and presentation of the cue. If that interval is brief (50 msec, say), performance is nearly perfect; as the interval lengthens to one second or more, performance gradually drops to its level in the immediate recall experiment—that is, an average of 50 percent or less correct (Sperling, 1960).

The third experimental paradigm (Delayed recall experiment) is like the first, except that a delay is introduced between presentation of the stimulus and the subject's response, and during this delay the subject is instructed to perform some other task (e.g., counting backward by threes or naming colors). Typically, the delay is some 30 seconds. Performance now depends upon the nature of the intervening task, but many tasks cause the subject's performance to fall to a level of one or two letters correct per trial (Peterson and Peterson, 1959).

In the fourth experimental paradigm (Rote verbal learning experiment), the stimulus is exposed for a longer time, or for a number of successive trials—say, for a total exposure of several minutes. After the lapse of some time, during which there may or may not be an explicit intervening task, the subject is instructed to recall the letters. In this experiment, with sufficient redundancy, performance may be nearly perfect for delays up to several hours. Performance varies with a number of variables, including (1) total stimulus exposure time, (2) response delay, and (3) nature of intervening activity (Underwood, 1969). The strategy the subject adopts in attending to different parts of the stimulus, and the priority he assigns to fixation relative to other task activities, also affect the rate of learning (Gregg and Simon, 1967).

Inferences to Memory Structure

Many more variants can, of course, be built upon these four experimental paradigms, which have been the basis for innumerable studies published in the literature. Instead of looking in detail at these variants on the basic four themes, let us ask what the paradigms tell us about the structure of human memory. All the inferences are based on a fundamental principle: if a subject is able to recall a stimulus that is no longer present, information about that stimulus must be stored in some memory, and if the subject is later unable to recall the stimulus, some of the stored information must have been lost or altered.

The Sperling paradigm tells us that all twelve letters can be stored for some fraction of a second—at least until the delayed cue is received that permits the perfect response. The experiment also tells us that considerable information is lost from this memory store before a second has elapsed. The immediate recall experiment tells us that some amount of briefly presented information—but nothing like twelve letters—can be retained for an indefinite number of seconds, but that most of it is lost rapidly if certain kinds of tasks are interposed.

If we put these pieces of evidence together, we are led to one of two conclusions: either there is a single memory with a capacity of at least twelve letters, a very rapid initial forgetting rate, and then a much slower forgetting rate; or there are two memories, the first of which has the larger capacity but the faster forgetting rate. Examination of the nature of the errors of commission that subjects typically make in the immediate recall and Sperling paradigms, respectively, suggests that the second alternative is more plausible than the first. In the immediate recall experiment, erroneous responses are likely to be auditorily similar to the corresponding correct responses (Conrad, 1959). In the Sperling paradigm, visual similarity plays a larger role relative to aural similarity, while confusion errors tend to be relatively much less frequent than errors of omission

(Sperling, 1960). The error data suggest that the memory involved in the Sperling paradigm contains information about the visual features of the stimulus elements, while the memory involved in the immediate recall paradigm most often contains information about phoneme features of the corresponding aural letters. Under these circumstances, a recoding process occurs in transferring information from the former to the latter memory, and the two memories must be regarded as distinct.

If we turn now to a comparison of the immediate or delayed recall experiments with the rote verbal learning experiments, we obtain evidence for the existence of a memory with properties quite different from the other two. The memory produced by a stimulus of relatively long duration is capable of surviving over intervening times and tasks that would cause the loss of storage observed in the delayed response experiments. Moreover, while there appears to be a rather definite upper limit on the amount of information that can be retained from a brief stimulus exposure, an amount which is not sensitive to the precise duration of the exposure, the amount that can be stored on longer exposure seems to be essentially unlimited—the total varying more or less proportionately with the total exposure time for the stimulus.

Again, the most parsimonious explanation for these phenomena is to postulate two memories: one that can acquire a specified small amount of information quite rapidly but cannot increase that amount or retain it over interrupting activities; and one that can acquire an indefinite amount of information and retain it for an indefinite length of time, even over intervening tasks, but that requires a substantial length of time for the acquisition process to take place.

This brief account sketches the logic and the nonphysiological evidence on which are based current widely held beliefs about the main kinds of human memory. If one looks at the recent literature, one discerns, amidst the mass of variant detail, a fair degree of agreement that the human memory system includes distinguishable iconic (sensory), short-term, "intermediate-term," and long-term memories, and even some agreement about the characteristics those memories possess.

THE PARAMETERS OF MEMORY

Let us look a little more closely at the parameters that define the storage speeds, access speeds and capacities of the memories we have identified, particularly the short-term and long-term memories. In the case of short-term memory, storage capacity is the parameter of primary interest because storage and retrieval times are very short—a few hundred msec to fill the entire STM, and a second or so to produce its entire contents. Before we can measure its capacity, however, we must have some units of measurement. George Miller (1956) has proposed that the amount of the information that can be stored in STM depends upon the familiarity of the information and thus, specifically, upon the number of symbols into which it must be encoded. For example, in an immediate recall experiment with sequences of random letters, each letter would be encoded as a symbol, or "chunk," since it can be assumed that the subjects are highly familiar with individual letters of the alphabet, but not with random pairs of them. But if the stimuli in the immediate recall experiment are random sequences of simple words, each word, being familiar to the subject, would constitute a single chunk.

Capacity of Short-term Memory

Experimental data show that the capacity of STM is reasonably constant—at least to a first approximation—when the amount of information held is measured in chunks (but not at all if it is measured in bits). To test this proposition, of course, one must have some means for determining what the chunks are. In chapter 2.2 I showed how that can be done. Short-term memory capacity measured in chunks is probably

closer to four, however, than to the number seven originally proposed by Miller.

To find a plausible interpretation of the chunking hypothesis in terms of memory structures, one cannot view the STM in isolation, but must consider its relation to long-term memory. To say that a particular symbol string, say the word "cat," is a familiar chunk is to say that there is already information available in LTM that permits that string to be recognized as a word and its meaning to be retrieved from LTM. Because this information is already stored in LTM, the lexicographical information identifying the string of letters "cat" does not need to be retained in STM; instead, one need retain only a single symbol that serves as a pointer to the relevant information in LTM. Hence what is stored in STM, under the chunking hypothesis, is the set of these pointers, each one assumed to consume just as much STM capacity as each of the others. The chunk, or symbol, stored in STM is the internal representation, in memory, of the recognized familiar stimulus.

This interpretation of the chunking hypothesis carries with it the implication that the familiar stimuli corresponding to chunks are recognized before being stored in STM. As we have just seen, the recognition mechanism is a component of LTM, not STM. Thus STM is not a buffer between the senses and LTM, but is a temporary storage for pointers to LTM that have been produced by the recognition mechanisms of LTM. If the recognition process takes place before information is stored in STM, does it occur before or after the information (if presented visually) has passed through the iconic memory? I do not know of any experiments that cast much light on this question, so I will not speculate upon the answer.

The chunking hypothesis carries no particular implications for the sensory modality of the information to which the STM symbol points. When the visual stimulus "cat" is presented to a subject who reads English, the visual string may be recognized directly, or the letters may be "sounded out," i.e., recognized, and replaced by a phoneme string, which is then recognized as a familiar sound sequence. Either process is consistent with the memory structure hypothesis, and examples of both processes can be observed in the behavior of beginning readers.

The recognition process may also take place in several stages. For example, recognition of the visual stimulus "cat" can lead to the retrieval of a chunk that points to information in LTM about the aural word "cat." Upon retrieval of this information, its passage through the recognition mechanism again would leave in STM a pointer to the stored semantic information about "cat." The experimental fact (Conrad, 1959) that phonetic similarity of stimuli is more likely to cause confusion errors in STM than visual similarity suggests that the two-stage recognition process is the more common one for verbal material. Notice that the two-stage process does not imply that the visual stimulus is "sounded out." Rather, visual recognition of the entire word retrieves the cue that points to the phonemic information. The two-stage recognition process might be expected to be the normal one for persons to whom the aural word and its meaning are already familiar at the time they acquire familiarity with its visual counterpart.

Long-term Memory Fixation and Retrieval

Turning now to the parameters of long-term memory, our interest shifts from measures of capacity to measures of storage and retrieval time. Storage capacity is uninteresting because it appears to be unlimited. To be sure, one common symptom of senility is inability or difficulty in storing new information in LTM, but this does not necessarily mean that storage capacity has been exhausted. A simpler and more plausible explanation would attribute this memory deficit to failure of the acquisition mechanism.

In order to talk about the time required to store information in LTM, or to retrieve it, we must again settle upon an appropriate unit of measurement. One candidate is the chunk—the same unit used to measure the capacity of short-term memory. Again, I discussed the empirical basis for this choice in chapter 2.2 and will therefore only sketch the argument very briefly. First, there is now a reasonably convincing body of evidence that the time required to store a given number of nonsense syllables in LTM is proportionate to that number; while, if total exposure time is held constant, the number of exposures of the stimulus is irrelevant. If the time per trial is doubled, the number of trials needed for fixation is roughly halved; while if the time per trial is halved, the number of trials is doubled. Moreover, when the fixation time for familiar words is compared with the fixation time for nonsense syllables, the time per chunk remains nearly constant, while the time per letter or phoneme varies widely. The learning time required to link together two familiar chunks into a new chunk is of the order of five to ten seconds.

Fixation of new information in LTM is a complex process because it involves not only storing the new information in semantic memory, but also elaborating the recognition memory so that the new chunks can be recognized and accessed. Very little is known about the relative amount of time or effort required for these two parts of the fixation process, but there are some slight indications, which will be discussed in the next section, that growing the recognition net is a more time-consuming process than adding chunks to the semantic store.

Probably at least two parameters are involved in defining the time it takes to retrieve information from LTM. On the one hand, a well-learned list (e.g., the alphabet) can be recovered and produced at rates not much slower than 150 msec per item. On the other hand, Dansereau (1969), in studies of mental arithmetic, found that when a subject recovered a partial product in a mental multiplication task, he might take about two seconds to retrieve the first digit of the number and then some 300 msec for each succeeding digit. Likewise, a number of investigators (e.g., McLean and Gregg, 1967) have found that when a newly fixated list (e.g., the alphabet permuted) is recited, letters are grouped by threes and fours with substantially longer latencies between groups than within groups. All these data suggest that chunks are stored in LTM in highly structured form, and that while a relatively long time may be required to retrieve the first item in a structure, succeeding items are retrieved more rapidly.

Summary

Chronometric studies of information processing tasks that have important memory components have been flourishing in recent years. Most such studies involve much more than retrieval from memory. For example, they often involve comparison processes to determine whether two symbols are identical or different, or syntactical processes to transform language strings. In this account I have limited myself as nearly as possible to the "pure memory" components of processing time. Leaving aside the iconic memory and other sense-related stores, four parameters of memory show up prominently in experimental studies: (1) the four-chunk capacity limit of STM; (2) the fixation time of five to ten seconds per chunk for LTM; (3) the initial access time to LTM of about two seconds; and (4) the access time of several hundred msec for chunks beyond the first. These parameters provide a possible point of linkage, so far relatively little explored, with psychological studies that would seek to identify physiological constants matching in relevant ways the parameters measured behaviorally. The attempt to identify the parameters of STM and LTM leads to a number of hypotheses about the structure of the various memories, and it is to those hypotheses that we turn next.

STORAGE AND ACCESS

The first responsibility of anyone writing about human memory is to avoid the homunculus fallacy—to avoid postulating pictures within the head which must then be viewed and interpreted by a little man

who sits within. The invention of the digital computer has made the avoidance of that fallacy easier than it was in the past. Computers patently have memories, and just as patently do not have little men inside to read those memories. Moreover, computers can be described in highly abstract ways that do not depend at all upon the particular hardware they employ. Vacuum tubes, transistors, relays, and solid-state circuits can all be used to realize the same abstract memory organization. Thus, when one speaks of an "associational" memory, or a "content addressed" memory, one is describing an abstract organization of structures and processes for storing and retrieving symbols, and not a particular hardware realization of that organization.

The terms "symbol" and "pattern" used in an information processing context are similarly abstract. A pattern is some kind of arrangement of a substrate associated with processes for creating and copying such arrangements, and for discriminating among them. The substrate may be mechanical, electrical, magnetic, or biochemical. And a symbol is simply a pattern that can be discriminated by an information-processing system (Newell and Simon, 1972, pp. 23–6).

Because of their abstract character, the terms used to describe memory structures and processes in computers are available for the description of human memory. In using this terminology, one makes only a few basic commitments to the nature of the memory being described. The most important of these commitments is that the contents of memory can be characterized as symbols and relations among symbols, and that the memory processes are symbol manipulating processes. The advantage of a neutral and abstract terminology of this kind will become most apparent when we come, presently, to discuss mental imagery, for it is in such a discussion that the homunculus fallacy is most to be feared. If we allow nothing in memory but abstract patterns and their relations, and if we define visual imagery in terms of such patterns and the processes operating on them, then there will be no need for the homunculus, and no role for him if he tries to intrude himself. But I am getting ahead of my story, for I intend in this section to discuss general questions of memory organization and will turn to imagery only in the next section.

Recognition and Semantic Memories

Reasons have already been presented for supposing that there are at least two different components in long-term memory possessing quite different characteristics. In general, the memory models that have been proposed in recent years have been models of one or the other of these components, but not of both. Or if both components have been included, one has been treated much more fully than the other.

The first of these components of LTM is the recognition memory, which carries out the processes of discriminating among and recognizing familiar stimulus patterns or pattern components, and retrieving for STM the chunks that point to the information about those patterns stored in LTM. The second component of LTM is the information storage itself—often called nowadays the "semantic memory." Although both components of the LTM are, in a certain sense, semantic, I will follow the current terminology and refer to recognition memory and semantic memory, respectively.

Information processing models of recognition memory in the form of computer programs date back to the late 1950s, the earliest being the EPAM system (Feigenbaum, 1961; Simon and Feigenbaum, 1964; Gregg and Simon, 1967). A later system dealing with some of the same mechanisms and phenomena is SAL (Hintzman, 1968), while MAPP (Simon and Gilmartin, 1973) employs an EPAM-like memory to simulate some aspects of chess memory. Most other models of LTM are mainly concerned with semantic memory and have little to say about recognition memory. Among these are the systems of Lindsay (1963), Reitman, Grove, and Shoup (1964), Quillian (1968), Rumelhart, Lindsay, and Norman (1972), Schank

(1972), and Winograd (1972). The Anderson and Bower (1973) HAM model, while not completely specified or programmed, contains both recognition and semantic components and is the closest approximation that exists to a theory dealing in some detail with both aspects of the memory system.

In addition to cognitive models like those just mentioned, in which memory plays the central role, there are of course a considerable number of formal theories of problem solving, concept attainment, and pattern induction that incorporate theories of memory ranging from the rudimentary to the elaborate. A problem solving theory applied to tasks in the domains of cryptarithmetic, chess, and logic is discussed in Newell and Simon (1972).

The degree of consensus among all these theories about the basic mechanisms of human memory is striking. In fact, all the mechanisms postulated are variants of two basic species: (1) discrimination nets to perform the functions of recognition memory, and (2) node-link or property-list memories to perform the functions of semantic memory. A complete theory of memory would have to include components of both kinds, linked in an effective way. Whether the logic of the experimental data has forced all these theories into the same mold, or whether their resemblances are testimony to the limitations of human imagination, is a question that must be left to the verdict of future research.

Organization of Recognition Memory

A discrimination net consists of a set of test nodes connected by branches, the aggregate of nodes and branches forming a treelike structure. At each node is stored one or more perceptual tests that can be applied to a stimulus or to a chunk in STM. The outcome of the test selects a particular one of the branches emanating from the test node and transfers the stimulus to the node at the end of that branch. After a succession of tests has been performed, and the corresponding path of branches followed, a terminal node is reached, which can be

identified with the chunk that has just been
recognized. Different stimuli will produce
different test results at some nodes and will
hence be channeled down different paths
in the discrimination net to different terminal nodes. (See Newell and Simon, 1972,
pp. 34–6.)

Organization of Semantic Memory

A node-link or property-list memory also
consists of a set of nodes connected by
relations. The whole structure takes on the
form of a net, however, rather than a tree,
for it may contain cycles and multiple paths
that reach the same node. A particular
node may, for example, correspond to a
particular class of stimuli—e.g., "cat."
Then the relations radiating from that
node and connecting it with other nodes
can be interpreted as referring to properties
or descriptors of that class of stimuli. Thus
the relation "class" might lead from "cat"
to "mammal," or "animal," the relation
"food" to "carnivore," and so on. No fixed
set of descriptors is postulated, but an
arbitrary number of arbitrary relations is
posited for each node. A general description
of such a memory can be found in Anderson
and Bower, 1973, chapter 4; and in Newell
and Simon, 1972, pp. 26–8.

Relation of the Memories

The relation of the discrimination net to
the semantic memory is analogous to the
relation of an index to a textbook. Items
of information in the semantic memory
may be retrieved in two ways. First, recognition of a stimulus by sorting it through
the recognition net gives access to its terminal node, which is a node in semantic
memory. Thus, for example, recognition
of the portrait on a penny gives access to
the node referencing Abraham Lincoln
(i.e., his physical appearance). Second,
once a node in semantic memory has been
accessed, other nodes may be reached by
processing the relational links that connect
them. That is, once Lincoln's portrait is
recognized, other information about him
may be retrieved, just as it could be if his

name, rather than his picture, were recognized. The first process may be called
retrieval by recognition, the second, retrieval by (directed) association. (The term
"directed" is included here to remind the
reader that a property-list memory is
organized much more like the directed
associations of the Würzburg School than
the simple associations of stimulus-response
behaviorism.)

Experimental evidence for the existence
of these two components in LTM, and for
their relation, comes from a variety of
sources. (I will limit my comments to experiments with normal subjects. There is
also evidence from amnesic subject of failure of access to information retained in
memory.) One source of evidence is the
set of paradigms in which the subjects'
ability to recognize information is compared with their ability to recall information. It is easy to show that much information is stored in LTM that permits successful
performance of recognition tasks, but not
of recall tasks. The EPAM theory explains
this phenomenon. Total learning time for
an item is the sum of the time for elaborating the discrimination net, so that the item
can be recognized and distinguished from
others, and the time for storing a description
of the item in semantic memory, so that
the item, once accessed, can be reproduced.
In the recall task, the information about
the item stored in semantic memory must
be complete, else the item cannot be reconstructed. Successful recognition can
take place, however, with little or no information in semantic memory as long as
the item can be discriminated from others.

A second source of data on the relations
between recognition and semantic memory
comes from rote-memory experiments that
make use of certain mnemonic devices.
(For a survey of the evidence see Norman,
1969, chapter 6.) The subject first practices
a list of words—usually concrete nouns—
until they are highly overlearned. He is
then given a second list of words to learn,
with the instruction to associate each word
on the second list with the corresponding
word on the first list. Finally, he is tested
on his ability to recite the second list.

Whereas, as we have seen, learning a list of items in the standard rote-learning paradigms requires five to ten seconds of exposure per item, in the paradigm just described most subjects can learn the second list in a single trial at a presentation rate of about two seconds per item, a savings of more than half. The EPAM theory (Feigenbaum, 1961) would explain this phenomenon provided that, in the standard rote-learning paradigm, more than half the total learning time is required for elaborating the discrimination net—building the recognition memory—and less than half for storing in semantic memory the information needed to reconstruct the item. When the mnemonic aid is employed, access to the second list is gained by the associational links with the first, hence learning the second list requires no augmentation of recognition memory, with a consequent time savings.

A theory of forgetting adequate to handle the empirical evidence at even the grossest level would also appear to require a distinction between recognition memory and semantic memory. We know that much forgetting consists in an inability to retrieve information that can be shown to be in LTM. If a subject is unable to retrieve information using the cues provided when he stored it, but can retrieve the same information on other cues, then what has been lost is not the text but the index. To explain this within the framework of an EPAM-like theory, we postulate that when a new stimulus is encountered that resembles closely one encountered some time previously, the discrimination net may not be altered except by a change in the "pointer" at the terminal node, so that reaching this terminal now accesses the semantic information about the new stimulus, instead of the old. Thus, if one meets and becomes acquainted with a new John Smith, access to information about another John Smith one had known previously may be lost, or at least become more difficult to recover. The oral or written stimulus "John Smith" now retrieves information about the new John Smith instead of the old one. Of course, recognition may also fail simply

because the cues presented by the stimulus are different from those incorporated in the discrimination net when the discrimination was originally learned—e.g., the stimulus is now presented from another viewpoint, or in a different context.

There are strong phenomenological reasons, therefore, for postulating these two components of LTM. Experiments in the literature say very little as yet, beyond what has been suggested in the preceding paragraphs, about the relative contributions of the separate components to the aggregate LTM parameters.

VISUAL IMAGERY

Visual imagery is currently a very popular topic. Whether it means the same thing in all contexts or different things in different contexts is a debatable matter (Simon, 1972). Here are some examples of recent experiments that deal, or purport to deal, with imagery:

Cooper and Shepard (1973) title a recent paper "Chronometric Studies of the Rotation of Mental Images." Subjects are presented with two successive stimuli. The first is, say, the letter "R" in its normal orientation; the second is either a normal or a backward "R," presented either in its normal orientation or rotated some number of degrees from the horizontal. The subject's task is to decide if the second stimulus can or cannot be matched to the first.

In another study, based on geographical knowledge, Shepard and Chipman (1970) show that subjects can judge which pair in a triad of states are most similar in shape, and that these judgments can be scaled. Moreover, judgments of similarity of shape when a map is in view resemble closely the judgments made when the shapes must be imagined.

Baylor (1971) instructs a subject to imagine a three-inch cube, to paint certain sides of the cube with specified colors, to slice the cube into one-inch cubes, and then to count the number of these one-inch cubes that have specified numbers of sides of specified colors.

Bower (1972) and Paivio (1971) give

subjects paired-associate verbal learning tasks. Some subjects receive standard verbal learning instructions; others are instructed to form an image associating response with stimulus. In general, subjects in the imaging condition learn faster to criterion than subjects in the standard (nonimaging) condition.

Brooks (1968) has varied simultaneously the sensory modality of stimulus and response and has shown that reaction times are longer when stimulus and response are in the same modality than when they are in a different modality. Thus an oral response to a question about a visual stimulus is faster than a pointing response, while a pointing response to a question about an aural stimulus is faster than an oral response.

Internal Representation

In order to discuss these experiments, we need some vocabulary and concepts for talking about how information is represented internally, in LTM, and possibly also in STM. If semantic memory is, as we have argued, a node-link structure whose components denote objects and relations among them, then it has no special affinity, so far as this basic, abstract structure is concerned, for any particular one of the sensory modalities. LTM, in this view, is no more "visual" than it is "auditory" or "tactual." What can we mean, then, by associating any of those modalities to a memory and speaking of "visual memory" or "auditory memory?" There is a twofold answer to this question.

In the first place, when the raw information from a particular sensory source is encoded, the encoding describes features of the stimulus. But the features that discriminate among visual stimuli are completely different from those that discriminate among auditory stimuli. Hence, by the time the encoding for storage in LTM has been carried out, information coming from different sensory sources will be represented by different nodes and different relational links. We will refer to this by saying that information from different senses has different content.

In the second place, informational structures derived from different sources may have different topologies. Stimuli such as auditorily received language strings might, after syntactical parsing, have a treelike topology, while visually received geometrical figures might retain the topology of the original stimulus in the encoding. A square, for example, might be encoded into a set of nodes denoting its corners, edges, and surface, together with links denoting incidence and directional relations that connect various of the nodes. We will refer to this by saying that information from different senses may have different topologies.

Unfortunately, matters are more complicated than this account would suggest. Suppose we try to use the content and topology of the stored information to distinguish among the modalities of memory. Then we must take account of the fact that the modality in which information is stored in LTM may not be the same as the sensory modality through which the information was initially received. In the Baylor task, for instance, the subject is given an oral or written description in natural language of a visualizable shape. There is every reason to suppose, however, that the information is held in LTM not as a parsed language string but as an "image"—i.e., in the visual modality. At least that is what the subject reports. Conversely, a subject can produce a verbal description of a geometric figure that he is viewing, thus translating information from the visual to the verbal modality. The metaphors of the "mind's eye" and the "mind's ear" are locutions for referring to these complications. Notice that the metaphors do not imply that there are actual physiological structures corresponding to this "eye" and "ear." All that is actually asserted is that information is encoded in LTM in a variety of forms, some of which have affinities, with respect to content or topology, with particular sensory modalities.

Interpretation of the Experiments

Let us return now to the list of imagery experiments. The success of the paradigms used by Bower and by Paivio depends on the internal representation of the stimulus material being affected by the "imaging" instructions given to the subjects. In general, subjects receiving imaging instructions learn sets of paired associates about twice as fast as subjects not receiving such instructions. This tells us nothing very specific about either the content or the topology of the representations the subjects use (Simon, 1972).

The experiments of Shepard, on the other hand, argue rather strongly for at least a partial isomorphism between the topology (and perhaps part of the metric description) of the stimulus on the one hand, and the internal representation on the other. In the rotation tasks, the time required for performance is roughly proportional to the angle through which the figures must be rotated. In the task involving the shapes of states, there is a large correlation between judgments of similarity made when the subject has a map before him and judgments made in the mind's eye.

Baylor found that he could simulate a subject's behavior in the cube-manipulating task by postulating as the internal representation a link-node structure topologically isomorphic with a cube and by postulating processes for operating on that structure—i.e., dividing it into smaller cubes, similarly represented. The information stored and the processes for operating upon it were substantially weaker, however, than the information-extracting processes that would have been available to the subject if he had held an actual cube before his eyes. The internal representation was in no way confusable with a "photograph" of the external scene.

Stimulus Modality and Internal Modality

Mention has been made of the possibility that information received through one sensory modality may be translated, for purposes of internal storage and processing, into another. The nature of this translation depends on the subject's strategy, determined, in turn, by previous learning and by the task demands. An experiment by by Chase and Clark (1972) illustrates why

such translation must be postulated. Subjects see a simple picture (e.g., a star above a cross) and then hear a sentence (e.g., "The star is below the cross"). Their task is to pronounce the sentence true or false. The aim of the experiment is to discover what processing takes place in this task by measuring the latencies of the answers. But the mere possibility of conducting this experiment implies that subjects can match or compare sentences with pictures in some way. Either the information extracted from the pictures must be translated into a language modality or the information extracted from the sentences must be translated into a pictorial modality or both must be translated into some common, neutral modality. Since the pictures and sentences used in experiments like these are usually very simple, once abstracted, they do not represent highly dissimilar topologies; hence the evidence does not foreclose any of the three possibilities. But the evidence does show that there is at least one common internal representation that permits the comparison of meanings. (The experiment of Baylor suggests that when the situation described—whether by word or picture—has a more complex structure, processing requirements may force the internal representation into a pictorial modality.)

Another line of research that has been very active in recent years casts some light on the mode of internal representation of information received in the form of natural language (oral or written). Bransford and Franks (1971) read a list of sentences, each with one to four clauses, to subjects. Then a new list of sentences was read, each made up of clauses from the original sentences. The subjects, when asked to judge whether they had heard the sentences before, were unable to discriminate accurately between sentences actually heard before and sentences that had not been heard but were made up of components that had been heard.

Bransford and Franks inferred from their results that subjects, while encoding the meanings of sentences, discard much of the syntactical information, including information about sentence boundaries.

Rosenberg (1973) carried the story several steps farther. After replicating the Bransford-Franks result, he showed that much the same results could be obtained even when some of the sentences were in French and others in English. Subjects were frequently unable to distinguish between a sentence that had been presented in one language and a translation of that sentence. That is, they frequently could not remember which they had seen. Rosenberg then ran an analogous experiment in which some of the sentences were presented in English, as before, while others were translated into simple pictures. Subjects were frequently unable to remember whether or not they had previously seen a picture when they had in fact seen the sentence describing that picture.

Rosenberg constructed a computer simulation of semantic memory that predicted in considerable detail the findings of his experiments as well as those of the earlier experiments of Bransford and Franks. The key postulate in the simulation was that individual sentences are not stored separately in semantic memory, but that the information from the sentences is stored in a relational form attached to the nodes corresponding to the sentence themes. Thus, if several sentences have the same theme, all the information from those sentences will be stored as a single relational structure linked to the node representing that theme. Since, under these circumstances, the sentence boundaries are nowhere represented in the semantic store, the subject cannot, of course, remember whether several clauses have originated in a single sentence or in several.

Rosenberg and Parkman (1972) had earlier demonstrated a similar point with information, verbally presented, about the members of a family—their family relationships and physical characteristics. On the basis of tests of how well the information was learned in a given time, together with response latencies for various kinds of questions about the relationships, they were able to demonstrate convincingly that the stored semantic information had a close topological similarity with the genealogical chart of the family.

Summary

From our discussion, and the experiments that have been cited, it can be seen how the topic of visual imagery in particular, and of internal representation in semantic memory in general, can be discussed in information processing terms. Different storage modalities can be distinguished in terms of their information content (the sorts of stimulus features they record) and topology (the sorts of relational structures they employ). We tend to associate a storage modality with a sensory modality when they resemble each other in content and topology. Processes are available to the memory system for translating information from one storage modality to another. In particular, information need not be stored in the same modality in which it is received through the senses: for example, verbal information can be stored in the same modality, whether received visually or aurally, while verbal information describing a visual scene can also be stored, after translation, in a pictorial modality. This does not mean that all information will be preserved by the translation: translation between memory modalities may be at least as difficult as translation between natural languages.

ARE THREE MEMORIES ENOUGH?

In an earlier section of this paper, the structure of the evidence and the inferences for postulating distinct memory systems was examined. The distinction that is made between STM and LTM, and the distinction between these two memories and the iconic memory, derives principally from the data obtained from four experimental paradigms. We now return to the question of the architecture of the memory system, and in particular to some recent experiments using the delayed recall paradigm which suggest that the three memories listed above may not be enough to account for the phenomena.

It should be mentioned, before proceeding, that we have been ignoring all the iconic or sensory memories other than the visual. For example, there is another sensory memory whose existence is quite firmly established: the "echo box," or echoic memory, which permits us to retain, for a second or two, an incoming sound stream to which we have not been attending, and to bring it into STM if our attention is called to it before it disappears. The echoic memory may be thought of as the aural analogue to the visual iconic memory, although information survives substantially longer in the former than in the latter—several seconds as against a few hundred milliseconds. In this section we will group together all the sensory memories—visual, auditory, tactile, and so on—as though they formed a single memory, and we will ask whether there is evidence for the existence of memories in the central nervous system in addition to the three kinds we have been considering.

The Delayed Recall Paradigm Revisited

Early experiments using the delayed recall paradigm showed that when a 30-second task was interposed between presentation of stimulus and response, the number of chunks that could be retained in STM was reduced from four or more to one or two. This finding has usually been explained by the hypothesis that the intervening tasks require the use of some short-term memory, and that because of the limited capacity of STM, this additional information can be stored only by displacing a portion of the information already in STM.

Subsequent experiments have shown this interpretation to be untenable. First, the subject is able to recall almost perfectly on the first trial of the experiment: it is only after three or four trials that a sizeable decrement in recall appears (Kincaid and Wickens, 1970). Second, if a time interval of ten seconds or more is inserted between trials, recall improves, and with an interval of a minute or more, it is nearly perfect again (Kincaid and Wickens, 1970). Third, when successive stimuli are highly dissimilar, recall is nearly perfect, even after three or four trials (Wickens, 1970). This "recovery" phenomenon has been called "release from proactive inhibition." This is a label for the phenomenon, not an explanation. It smacks a little of a phlogis-

ton theory: we invent an entity—interference—to explain why something is missing, then postulate the suppression of that entity when the something reappears. Perhaps we could arrive at a simpler explanation if we simply dispensed with the hypothesized inhibition from the beginning.

Let us examine the logic of the situation. If information can be retrieved after an intervening task under some conditions, then only the access to the information, rather than the information itself, must have been lost from memory. In terms of the metaphor used earlier, what appears to have been lost is not the text but the index. But where was the information stored during the intervening period? If it was held in the limited-capacity STM, then why could not the same information be held there when there was no interval between successive trials? And how can the similarity of successive stimuli make a difference?

Recall of Chess Positions

Recent experiments by Charness (1974) provide some clues for the explanation of these phenomena. Charness employed the delayed recall paradigm with visual stimuli —in particular, positions from chess games with twenty-two pieces standing on the board. The subjects were chess players of moderate playing strength. There were six different recall conditions. In the first two recall conditions, the delay interval imposed no new burden on STM; in the third and fourth conditions, there were easy and hard oral tasks, respectively; and in the fifth and sixth conditions, there were easy and hard visual tasks.

Charness found that the intervening tasks, whether easy or hard, oral or visual, caused only a slight decrement in memory (10 or 15 percent), in contrast with earlier experiments using the delayed recall paradigm.

Charness did find one significant effect of the intervening tasks, however. In most of the previous experiments using this paradigm, the subjects had been required to respond within five seconds; responses after that time were counted as wrong.

Charness did not place an upper limit on the response time. In the immediate recall condition and recall after rehearsal, average latencies were under five seconds. When recall took place after an intervening task had been performed, the latency measured to the time when the first piece was replaced on the board was increased by an average of nearly four seconds over the average latency in the no-task conditions. Thus, when subjects performed no tasks during the delay interval, they were able to begin to reconstruct the chess position almost immediately upon being given the signal to do so; when they performed a task during this interval, they needed considerable additional time to begin to recall the position. This increase in latency can be interpreted as meaning either that the subjects were not recovering the information from the same memory in the two cases, or that some initial process was required after interruption to "get back into context." The latter phrase, of course, is no more an explanation than is "proactive inhibition"; it is merely a label for the phenomenon.

Charness next used the delayed recall paradigm with consonant trigrams, presented aurally at a rate of 0.6 sec per trigram, as the stimulus material, with the same interference tasks as in the previous experiment but allowing an unlimited time for response. Only one of the intervening tasks—computing the running sum of random digits—produced a recall deficit of more than 10 or 15 percent. In all the other five conditions, recall averaged 80 percent correct or better. Thus a relatively difficult aural task interferes with recall, a simple aural task or a visual task, simple or complex, does not. The only clear difference between the conditions of this experiment and those of earlier experiments that showed large decrements in recall for a variety of intervening tasks was the unlimited time allowed subjects for responding.

A Possible Explanation

Many more experiments are in prospect before a definitive explanation can be pro-

vided for this whole range of phenomena. Let us see whether there are any hints as to the direction that explanation might take, starting from the earlier remark that what seems to be lost in these experiments is not the stimulus information—which reappears intact under a variety of conditions—but access to it. This notion is supported by Charness's findings of long access times for recovery after another task has intervened. The lengthening of the average response latency by four seconds is suggestive of retrieval from long-term memory rather than short-term memory.

In the section on Storage and Access, reasons were given for supposing that LTM has two components: recognition memory and semantic memory. The speeding up of fixation when mnemonic devices are used suggests that ability to store new information in LTM is limited more by the time required to modify and elaborate the recognition memory than by the time required to add the information to the semantic memory. We now hypothesize the following sequence of events:

1. A stimulus is presented, and its familiar components are discriminated by the recognition memory.

2. The internal symbols representing these components are stored in STM.

3. A new node-link structure relating these symbols is stored in semantic memory.

4. The recognition memory is modified to incorporate a new terminal node denoting or "pointing to" the new node-link structure in semantic memory.

The first three steps in the sequence are assumed to proceed very rapidly and to be completed in a second or less. The fourth step, elaboration of the recognition memory, is assumed to require the familiar ten seconds per chunk—or about thirty seconds for a consonant trigram. The information required to carry out this fourth step is already available, however, in semantic memory as a result of step 3. Interference occurs, with consequent loss of information, if a new stimulus, similar to the previous one, is presented and processed before the processing of the previous one has been completed. In this case, the alteration of the recognition memory is interfered with since both stimuli require modification of the same portion of the net. When the successive stimuli are dissimilar, alteration of each of the two distinct portions of the recognition memory can proceed independently.

This explantion is highly speculative, but perhaps not implausible. It has the virtue that it does not invoke any memory structures or processes whose existence has not already been postulated for other reasons and on the basis of evidence from other kinds of experiments. Even the hypothesized latencies are consistent with our other knowledge. It does not call for an inhibitory process or substance, nor for the superposition of still another process to secure release from that hypothesized inhibition. In short, it can lay claim to some measure of parsimony.

Perhaps the safest conclusion for us to carry away from the experiments with the delayed recall paradigm is that the data do not yet provide us with a convincing reason for abandoning the main outlines of the three-memory model. They do give us additional reasons, however, to look more closely at the structure and properties of long-term memory, and particularly at the special properties of the recognition and semantic components of that memory. They add further plausibility to the notion that storage of new information in semantic memory may be quite rapid, the relatively lengthy fixation time of five or ten seconds per chunk being due mainly to the requirements for modifying the recognition memory.

THE STRUCTURE OF SHORT-TERM MEMORY

As we have seen, short-term memory is defined phenomenologically by the immediate recall experiment. That experiment shows that STM has a small fixed capacity, measured in chunks—that is, familiar recognizable units. The study of confusion errors in STM tasks shows that, at least for verbal stimuli, the symbols designated by the contents of STM are usually encoded in terms of auditory fea-

tures. These two facts neatly sum up the description of the generally-agreed-upon characteristics of STM. On most other points there is either lack of information or controversy.

Our ignorance of the structure of STM is a serious impediment to reaching a better general understanding of cognitive processes. The STM stands at the crossroads of almost everything that happens in the central nervous system. It is generally believed that any active cognitive process—certainly any conscious process—must find its inputs in STM, and must place its outputs in the same memory. When 2 is added to 2 to make 4, the 2's must reside, at the outset of the process, in STM, and the 4 must reside there when the process is complete. Thus the capacity limit of STM places a strict upper limit on the complexity (in terms of numbers of inputs and outputs) of the elementary information processes that can be executed by the system and on the ability of the system to execute processes in parallel instead of serially. The narrowness of the span of attention and the general seriality of the processing (except possibly for recognition processes) stems, therefore, from the structure of STM.

An information processing system needs a memory with very fast storage and retrieval times—what is usually called "working memory"—for two important purposes. One of these, described in the last paragraph, is to hold the inputs and outputs of elementary processes. The speed at which the inputs can be loaded into working memory determines how rapidly the elementary processes can be executed, and the capacity of working memory limits the complexity of those processes. But the system has a second essential reason for needing a working memory: if its behavior is to have any organization, any shape, it must have some orderly basis for determining what to do next. The information that controls the sequence of processing is called control information, and the structure that exercises this control, the control structure.

The component of an information processing system that stores the inputs and outputs of the elementary processes may be identical to or separate from the component that stores the control information. The specific question for psychology is whether STM harbors both kinds of information, or whether there is a working memory, separate from STM, that holds the control information.

Hierarchic Control Systems

In the computer field, the traditional answer to the problem of control is to organize programs hierarchically. Each routine may contain within it one or more subroutines. When the routine is executed and reaches the subroutine, it executes the subroutine in turn. When the subroutine has completed its processing (which may involve calling its own subroutines, and so on, to arbitrary numbers of recursions of the process), it returns control to the routine that called it.

In order for such a hierarchic structure to operate properly, information must be kept in working memory of which routine called the subroutine now active, and which superroutine called that routine, and so on, all the way back up to the top of the hierarchy. This information is needed in order for control to be returned to the right place in the program when each subroutine completes its work. The usual way of mechanizing this information requirement is to provide a so-called pushdown stack, which contains the list of ascending program locations in their proper order. Thus the current program location is at the top of the list, the location in its calling routine is immediately below it, and so on. When a subroutine is finished, the stack is "popped," leaving the proper return location at the top of the stack. When a new subroutine is entered, the stack is "pushed," and the subroutine location is placed at its top. Each time a process is executed, therefore, the pushdown stack is changed in at least one respect, and these changes must be as rapid as changes in STM if the stack is not to be the limiting factor in the speed of operation of the system.

In the usual design of hierarchic programming systems, the total working memory consists of three components: a small memory equally accessible to all routines, which has much the same central position as human STM and which is used to pass information between routines; the pushdown stack for program control; and an indefinite amount of working memory to hold intermediate inputs and outputs of the separate routines. The presence of the latter storage gives such a system an essentially unlimited total amount of working memory of kinds that are almost certainly not available to the human information processor. Hence, unless additional restrictions are placed on it, such a system does not provide a good model of the limits on human STM. Let us assume, therefore, that individual routines do not have "private" working storage available to them, but must use the common and limited STM for all outputs and inputs.

Even with the latter limitation, the existence of the unlimited pushdown stack for program control would give the system an ability to keep track of its goals and subgoals which seems greatly to exceed the ability of the human information processing system. One is led to the conclusion that the human control system must have a different architecture from that usually found in hierarchically organized programming systems. It has been proposed (Newell and Simon, 1972) that production systems offer an appropriate model for the control system.

Control by Production Systems

In two recent papers (Newell, 1972, 1973), Allen Newell has carried forward a considerable distance the proposal just mentioned, to model the human control system upon a production system. I will describe the idea briefly here and indicate its main implications for the structure of STM. The reader who is interested in a fuller account will find it in the references that have been cited.

A production system consists of a set of productions. Each production, in turn, has two parts: a condition and an action. The basic principle on which the system operates is that whenever the condition of a production is satisfied, the action of that production is executed. In implementations of such a system, the productions are generally listed in some order, and if the conditions of more than one production are satisfied at the same time, the action of the production that occurs first in the list is executed.

The principle of control in a production system is, therefore, to have no control—at least no centralized or hierarchical control. Each production "does its thing" whenever the situation is appropriate, that is, whenever its condition is satisfied. It remains to be shown, of course, that such a system can ever behave in an organized, goal-directed fashion, as it surely must if it is to simulate certain kinds of human behavior.

Nothing has yet been said about the nature of the conditions that determine when a production will become active. The crucial assumption here is that the conditions are tests on the contents of STM. That is, if one or more of the symbols in STM match the conditions of a production, the action of that production will be executed. Let us see how such an arrangement can lead to coherent action.

The actions of productions may be of several kinds. One kind of production may take encoded sensory information and place it in STM (perception). Another kind of production may produce a symbol that designates a goal or subgoal and place it in STM (goal creation). Another kind of production may retrieve symbols from LTM and place them in STM (recall). Another kind of production may rearrange the symbols in STM, bringing one of them up to the front (rehearsal). Still another may initiate motor actions, which may themselves be controlled by one or more such systems. There will be many kinds of productions besides these five, but the ones that have been listed are the most important for the operation of the control system.

Because the symbols in STM determine which productions will be activated, the source of these symbols has much to do with the character of the system's operation. If most of these symbols are placed in STM by acts of perception, the system will be-

have as though it were stimulus-bound. If most of the symbols originate in goal-creating actions, the system will behave in a goal-oriented and inner-directed way. If many symbols are placed in STM by recall, the course of the system's behavior will be strongly influenced by the contents of LTM—that is, by its previous learning. If the rehearsal production is activated infrequently, information may be lost from STM: (The scheme is rather more compatible with an interference theory of forgetting from STM than with a decay theory.)

Space does not permit me to elaborate further on the nature of production systems, or the precise way in which they are applied to model psychological processes. Persons accustomed to thinking in *S-R* terms may find it helpful to view the $C \rightarrow A$ connection between a condition and its action as analogous to the $S \rightarrow R$ connection with which they are familiar. There are important differences between the two relations, but the comparison is a tolerable first approximation. With the production system organization of control, the single STM serves both of the working memory functions mentioned earlier. It holds the inputs and outputs of the information processes, and it holds the control information that determines which process will be executed next. This parsimony is one of the attractive features of the production system hypothesis, and it also has strong implications for short-term memory that should be testable in laboratory experiments.

Subject Strategies

It appears that a very few complex human responses are "wired in." Most are modifiable both by learning and by change in strategy—the latter being at least partially under the voluntary control of the subject. The modification of behavior by change of strategy (often induced by task instructions) is well attested in the literature (e.g., Gregg and Simon, 1967; Dansereau, 1969).

The dependence of behavior on strategy creates problems of great subtlety for experimentation. If we wish to get at the underlying invariants of memory, particularly those invariants most directly related to physiology, we must be able to control, or at least detect, the strategy the subject is using. This argues for the direct inducement of specific strategies by problem instructions or other means; it argues against the pooling of data from several subjects, who may arrive in the laboratory with quite different strategies as the result of differences in their previous experiences and training.

Training subjects in specific task strategies can push them against the limits of their information-processing capabilities. It appears to be a powerful technique for laying bare the underlying physiological constraints on memories and processes.

Conclusion

In view of the enormous amount of research that has been done on human memory during the past twenty years, the prospect of attempting an overview of that field from an information processing point of view was intimidating. I am not sure that the retrospect is any more comforting. My account is at best a very limited sample of all of the topics that deserve to be considered. It is very far from a random sample. By necessity it is limited to the research and theories with which I am familiar, and no one, I expect, can claim today to be familiar with the whole of the literature in this field.

In selecting topics for inclusion, I have been guided by several criteria, in addition to familiarity. I have tried to select topics that would illustrate the method of inferring memory processes and structures from observable phenomena; that would deal with the most solidly based, or at least widely accepted, conclusions about the organization of human memory; that would illustrate the nature of some of the questions that are open today; and that would show how our growing understanding of those information processing systems called computers is helping us to understand the information processing system called man.

In my introduction, I spoke of the division of labor between information processing psychologists and physiological psychologists, and of the need for cooperation between them. My list of conclusions about human memory can also be interpreted as a list of queries directed to physiological psychology. I have tried to describe a number of properties of the engram, and of the storage system that holds it, as they are inferred from the phenomena they produce. I would hope that this characterization of the engram in information processing terms may provide some clues to the physiologist in his continuing search for the biochemical basis on which it operates and the place or places where it resides in the human brain.

References

Anderson, J. R., and Bower, G. H. 1973. *Human Associative Memory*. Washington D. C.: V. H. Winston & Sons.

Baylor, G. W. Jr., 1971. A treatise on the mind's eye: An empirical investigation of visual mental imagery. Unpublished Ph.D. dissertation, Carnegie-Mellon University.

Bower, G. H. 1972. Mental imagery and associative learning. In L. W. Gregg, ed., *Cognition in Learning and Memory*. New York: John Wiley & Sons, pp. 51–88.

Bransford, J. D., and Franks, J. J. 1971. The abstraction of linguistic ideas. *Cognitive Psychology* 2:331–50.

Brooks, L. R. 1968. Spatial and verbal components of the act of recall. *Canadian Journal of Psychology* 22:349–68.

Charness, N. 1974. Memory for chess positions: The effects of interference and input modality. Unpublished Ph.D. dissertation, Carnegie-Mellon University.

Chase, W. G., and Clark, H. H. 1972. Mental operations in the comparison of sentences and pictures. In L. W. Gregg, ed., *Cognition in Learning and Memory*. New York: John Wiley & Sons, pp. 205–320.

Conrad, R. 1959. Errors of immediate memory. *British Journal of Psychology* 50: 349–59.

Cooper, L. A., and Shepard, R. N. 1973. Chronometric studies of the rotation of mental images. In W. G. Chase, ed., *Visual Information Processing*. New York: Academic Press, pp. 75–176.

Dansereau, D. 1969. An information processing model of mental multiplication. Unpublished Ph.D. dissertation, Carnegie-Mellon University.

Feigenbaum, E. A. 1961. The simulation of verbal learning behavior. In *Proceedings of the 1961 Western Joint Computer Conference*, pp. 121–32. Reprinted in E. A. Feigenbaum and J. Feldman, eds., *Computers and Thought*. New York: McGraw-Hill, 1963, pp. 297–309.

Gregg, L. W., and Simon, H. A. 1967. An information-processing explanation of one-trial and incremental learning. *Journal of Verbal Learning and Verbal Behavior* 6:780–87. Reprinted as chapter 3.3 in this book.

Hintzman, D. L. 1968. Explorations with a discrimination net model for paired-associate learning. *Journal of Mathematical Psychology* 5:123–62.

Hunt, E. 1971. What kind of computer is man? *Cognitive Psychology* 2:57–98.

Hunt, E. 1973. The memory we must have. In R. C. Schank and K. M. Colby, eds., *Computer Models of Thought and Language*. San Francisco: W. H. Freeman, pp. 343–71.

Kincaid, J. P., and Wickens, D. D. 1970. Temporal gradient of release from proactive inhibition. *Journal of Experimental Psychology* 86:313–16.

Kintsch, W. 1970. *Learning, Memory, and Conceptual Processes*. New York: John Wiley & Sons.

Lindsay, R. K. 1963. Inferential memory as the basis of machines which understand natural language. In E. A. Feigenbaum and J. Feldman, eds., *Computers and Thought*. New York: McGraw-Hill, pp. 217–36.

McLean, R. S., and Gregg, L. W. 1967. Effects of induced chunking on temporal aspects of serial recitation. *Journal of Experimental Psychology* 74:455–59.

Miller, G. A. 1956. The magical number seven, plus or minus two: Some limits on our capacity for processing information, *Psychological Review* 63:81–97.

Newell, A. 1972. A theoretical explanation of mechanisms for coding the stimulus. In A. W. Melton and E. Martin, eds., *Coding Processes in Human Memory*. New York: John Wiley & Sons, pp. 373–434.

Newell, A. 1973. Production systems: Models of control structures. In W. G. Chase, ed., *Visual Information Processing*. New York: Academic Press, pp. 463–562.

Newell, A., and Simon, H. A. 1972. *Human Problem Solving*. Englewood Cliffs, N. J.: Prentice-Hall.

Norman, D. A. 1969. *Memory and Attention*. New York: John Wiley & Sons.

Paivio, A. 1971. *Imagery and Verbal Processes*. New York: Holt, Rinehart and Winston.

Peterson, L. R., and Peterson, M. J. 1959. Short-term retention of individual verbal items. *Journal of Experimental Psychology* 58:193–98.

Quillian, M. R. 1968. Semantic memory. In M. Minsky, ed., *Semantic Information Processing*. Cambridge, Mass.: M.I.T. Press, pp. 227–70.

Reitman, W., Grove, R. B., and Shoup, R. G. 1964. Argus: An information processing model of thinking. *Behavioral Science* 9:270–81.

Rosenberg, S. 1973. A theory of semantic memory. Unpublished Ph.D. dissertation, Carnegie-Mellon University.

Rosenberg, S., and Parkman, J. 1972. Semantic memory: Aspects of storage and retrieval. CIP Working Paper, no. 170, Carnegie-Mellon University.

Rumelhart, D. E., Lindsay, P. H. and Norman, D. A. 1972. A process model for long-term memory. In E. Tulving and W. Donaldson, eds., *Organization and Memory*. New York: Academic Press, pp. 198–246.

Schank, R. C. 1972. Conceptual dependency: A theory of natural-language understanding. *Cognitive Psychology* 3:552–631.

Shepard, R. N., and Chipman, S. 1970. Second-order isomorphism of internal representations: Shapes of states. *Cognitive Psychology* 1:1–17.

Simon, H. A. 1972. What is visual imagery? An information processing interpretation. In L. W. Gregg, ed., *Cognition in Learning and Memory*. New York: John Wiley & Sons, pp. 183–204.

Simon, H. A. 1974. How big is a chunk? *Science* 183:482–88. Reprinted as chapter 2.2 in this book.

Simon, H. A., and Feigenbaum, E. A. 1964. An information processing theory of some effects of similarity, familiarity, and meaningfulness in verbal learning. *Journal of Verbal Learning and Verbal Behavior* 3:385–96. Reprinted as chapter 3.2 in this book.

Simon, H. A., and Gilmartin, K. 1973. A simulation of memory for chess positions. *Cognitive Psychology* 5:29–46. Reprinted as chapter 6.3 in this book.

Sperling, G. A. 1960. The information available in brief visual presentations. *Psychological Monographs* 74 (11, whole no. 498).

Underwood, B. J. 1969. Attributes of memory. *Psychological Review* 76:559–73.

Wickens, D. D. 1970. Encoding categories of words: An empirical approach to meaning. *Psychological Review* 77:1–15.

Winograd, T. 1972. *Understanding Natural Language*. New York: Academic Press.

2.4

A Program Modeling Short-term Memory under Strategy Control (1976)

with Kevin J. Gilmartin and Allen Newell

The model described in this chapter is an information processing model of human memory that derives its flexibility of performance from strategies controlling the use of its memory stores and processing time. More generally, this discussion is concerned with the strategy of using strategies as intervening variables between task environments and performance.

Role of Strategies

We hold as a basic assumption that the behaviors humans will show in a task environment depend on the strategies they use. The qualitative and quantitative differences in performance between subjects are due in part to differences in their strategies for processing the information available to them; the changes in a particular sub-

ject's performance as he becomes experienced at a task are largely due to progressive changes in his strategies. In fact, what psychologists refer to as an "experienced subject" is someone who has explored the effects of using various strategies in a particular task environment and who has discovered and acquired strategies that lead to effective performance.

If a model of memory derives flexibility from using strategies for accomplishing its basic processes of encoding, storage, and retrieval, then we can try to apply that model to explain the effects on behavior of changes in task instructions as well as to explain how a subject is able to act upon a suggestion for performing the task better. By viewing changes in performance as reflecting changes in strategy, we can ask how and why the strategy changes as the task environment changes. In this way we can explore the correspondence between the processing demands of a task and the strategies for its optimal performance.

A body of knowledge about this correspondence between tasks and optimal strategies for humans could, in turn, serve as the groundwork for two related projects:

Research reported in this chapter was supported in part by Research Grant MH-07722 from the National Institute of Mental Health and in part by the Advanced Research Projects Agency of the Office of the Secretary of Defense (F-44620-73-C-0074) which is monitored by the Air Force Office of Scientific Research.

first, it could provide the basis for classifying tasks in terms of the types of information processing used by experienced subjects while performing them (as opposed to a classification in terms of the types of stimuli presented and the types of responses required); and second, it could enable researchers to develop the ability to decompose a task into a number of basic information-processing requirements and, from that analysis, to predict the strategies that would allow best task performance. This latter ability, if sufficiently developed, would make it possible to suggest how new equipment should be designed to best fit the information processing limitations of humans and how operators should be trained to perform new tasks (i.e., in what strategies they should be trained to increase efficiency and decrease errors).

To summarize, we believe that there are certain advantages to making the source of flexibility in models of human performance more like what we assume to be the source of flexibility in humans. In particular, we postulate flexibility in strategies, within relatively fixed constraints of a memory model, as opposed to postulating variation from task to task in the size of short-term memory, the basic write-time of long-term memory, and other structural parameters.

BACKGROUND

The approach we describe here is not a new one, but it is a relatively neglected one in investigations of short-term memory. Much of the research on memory using standard paradigms is done without even postulating what processes subjects use to perform the tasks assigned. To find the antecedents of our approach one must generally look at the studies of more active cognitive tasks.

Bruner, Goodnow, and Austin (1956) developed in some depth the concept of strategies for performing a task. In their classic book on concept attainment, they explored the effects that various strategies would have on the utilization of informa-

tion, the memory load, and the probability of failing to identify a concept. Bruner et al., defined a strategy as being a regularity in decision making: "The phrase 'strategies of decision making' is not meant in a metaphorical sense. A strategy refers to a pattern of decisions in the acquisition, retention, and utilization of information that serves to meet certain objectives, i.e., to insure certain forms of outcome and to insure against certain others" (p. 54).

Atkinson and Shiffrin (1968) discussed various types of strategies used by subjects while performing a memory task, including control processes in the sensory registers, in short-term memory, and in long-term memory. They defined a control process as a process that is not a permanent feature of memory but is instead a transient phenomenon under the control of the subject. Atkinson and Shiffrin suggested that it might be fruitful to classify experiments in terms of the control processes the subjects would be led to use. However, in their work, the concept of control process was used simply to let the scientist formulate and fit separate models for separate situations.

Recently we (Newell and Simon, 1972) made a comprehensive examination of the methods subjects use to solve various types of problems. By analyzing thinking-aloud protocols, we were able to describe a subject's strategy for performing a task as being composed of a fixed set of elementary information processes that are evoked by both aspects of the external environment and the internal representation of the problem. The problems that we asked our subjects to perform were much more complex than the typical task in a short-term memory experiment, and consequently, the "elementary" processes that we isolated during our 1972 investigation are at a higher level than the primitive processing components in the model to be described here. Nevertheless, the methods used to solve problems in that examination are similar to the strategies in this model of short-term memory: both are major intervening variables between task environments and behavior.

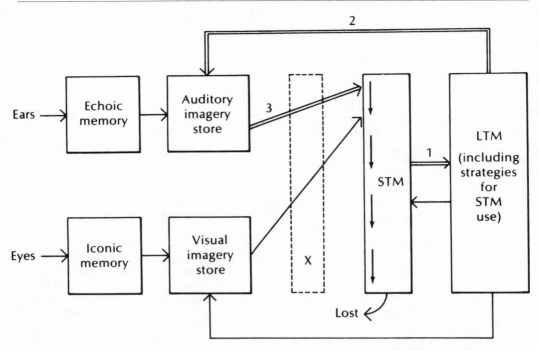

Figure 1. The memory stores and the flow of information between them in SHORT.
Arrows 1, 2, and 3 represent the flow of information during implicit auditory rehearsal;
X represents the process of recognition or perception that has access to information in LTM.

THE MODEL SHORT

Our particular model of short-term memory (STM) is a computer program written in SNOBOL, which has been named SHORT. It represents a theory of how humans use STM, and, to a lesser extent, how they use long-term memory (LTM) and the sensory-related buffers during common STM tasks. SHORT is not simply a theory of how STM tasks are performed; it is able to perform several of those tasks itself and can be tested under various experimental conditions as though it were a subject. The SHORT model is entirely deterministic, with no probability functions built into any of its processes. Only the generation of stimuli and the subsequent presentation of these stimuli to the model during a simulation can be at all random.

The structure that SHORT assumes is shown in figure 1. The memory stores are LTM, STM, and two buffers in series for each sensory modality (a sensory store and an imagery store). When an item is presented auditorily or visually to SHORT, it is automatically registered in the appropriate sensory store: echoic memory or iconic memory. The literature indicates that humans rapidly lose information from the sensory stores as a function of time: information in the visual sensory store persists for a total duration of 250 msec (Averbach and Coriell, 1961) to 500 msec or more (Sperling, 1960), while information in the auditory sensory store lasts for at least 3 or 4 seconds, even with interference (Glucksberg and Cowen, 1970; Darwin, Turvey, and Crowder, 1972). SHORT is constructed so that when a stimulus is terminated, that stimulus persists for 250 msec in the visual sensory store and for 3 seconds in the auditory sensory store. When SHORT accesses a sensory store, part of or all the information in that store is copied into the imagery store in the same modality. The contents of an imagery store are assumed to be closely

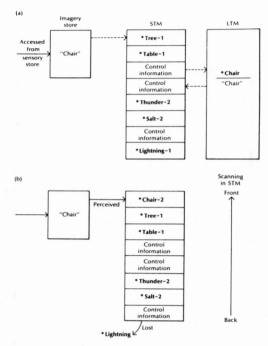

Figure 2. The structure of STM in SHORT (*a*) before and (*b*) after a new item has been perceived. Asterisks indicate names of entries in LTM; digits are rehearsal group tags.

related to the encoding of the physical characteristics of the stimulus. The process of perception (recognition) consists of a search for a match between the patterns of information in an imagery store and the patterns previously stored in LTM. If a match is found, a symbol denoting the corresponding entry in LTM is placed in STM. Figure 2 represents the contents of STM (a) immediately before and (b) immediately after a pattern is recognized; the contents of LTM are unchanged by the operation, and therefore LTM is not represented in figure 2b. In figures 2 and 3, an asterisk is the first character of the symbols in STM. This convention is used to indicate that theoretically there is no relation between the structure of a symbol in STM and the physical characteristics of the pattern it denotes. The symbols in STM are the internal names of entries in LTM.

(In our model, STM is a linear array of eight cells, each of which can hold a single symbol, or chunk. The size of STM was set at eight cells because that value produced a span of STM, in the immediate recall paradigm, of five-six chunks, the normal span for adults. The rest of the capacity of STM is occupied by various kinds of control information—place keepers or symbols that indicate the status of some part of the system. Relatively few types of such control symbols are used in SHORT.

(SHORT incorporates a first-in-first-out displacement theory of STM. That is, whenever a new symbol is placed in STM, it causes the oldest symbol in STM to be lost. Symbols entered at one end of STM move to adjacent cells down the length of STM and are finally bumped out of, and lost from, the back end of STM as newer items displace them.

(Items can be retained indefinitely in STM only by rehearsal, that is, by inserting a new copy of the item at the front of STM) Items in STM can be grouped for rehearsal; the grouping scheme is part of the system's strategy for performing a particular task. Items that are assigned to the same rehearsal group are not contiguously grouped together in adjacent cells, but rather each one has an associated label that specifies that it is a member of a particular group. In figure 2, some of the symbols in STM are tagged with the digit 1 or 2 to indicate membership in the first or second rehearsal group. An item can be assigned to one of three groups: although some subjects report dividing strings of items into more than three groups in STM (Anders, 1971), most do not, and hence SHORT has been limited to three rehearsal groups in STM. Of course, an item may not be assigned to any rehearsal group, but in that case it will not be rehearsed and will eventually be lost. (All searching, or scanning, in STM is from back to front; the basic operation, called NEXT CHUNK, moves attention to the next symbol toward the front of STM (see figure 2). There is evidence (Anders, 1971, 1973) that for short sequences of items humans search STM from the oldest items toward the newest items

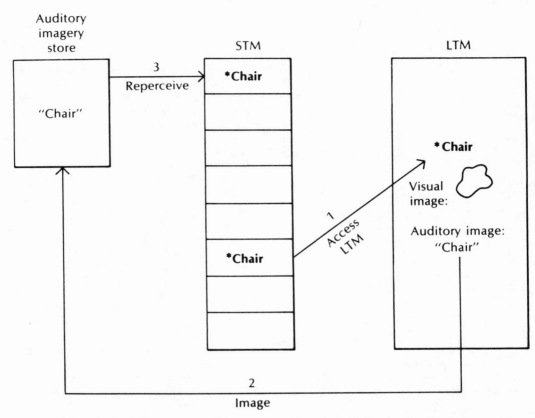

Figure 3. Three-step rehearsal in SHORT. An asterisk indicates the internal name of an entry in LTM.

in this way. As part of its strategy for performing the task, SHORT can rehearse a particular group of items, or it can start at the back of STM, search for the first occurrence of any symbol associated with a group, and then rehearse that group. Rehearsal is a three-step process. (The flow of information during implicit auditory rehearsal is indicated in figure 1 by the numbered double arrows.) First, a symbol in STM is used to access the corresponding entry in LTM (so the symbols designating entries in LTM may be thought of as addresses or pointers). Second, stored at that entry in LTM is information about the chunk, its relations to other chunks, and so on. There may also be stored at that entry small programs for saying and writing the chunk if it has an external name and for imaging the chunk visually or auditorily.

The program for imaging places into an imagery store a pattern of information identical to the information that would be in that imagery store if the item had just been entered from the external environment. That is, the act of imaging sets up symbol patterns in an imagery store that are related to the physical characteristics of the item as a stimulus. Third, this pattern in the imagery store can be reperceived, and a new symbol denoting it can be placed in the front of STM, completing the process of rehearsal. (Thus, as is indicated in figure 3, rehearsal involves (1) accessing an entry in LTM, (2) imaging the pattern designated, and (3) reperception.

All the major processes in the model (accessing the contents of a sensory store, perception or recognition, accessing LTM, imaging, outputting an item) are charged time on a simulated clock. This accounting for time limits SHORT to roughly the same amount of processing per second as a human is able to do: SHORT can rehearse 4.0 single-syllable items, or 2.9 two-syllable items, in a second.

CONSTRUCTION OF STRATEGIES

The behavior of SHORT on a particular task depends on its strategy for performing that task. A strategy comprises knowledge in LTM of the task requirements and a set of decision processes for managing the information in STM. Some of the decision processes that might be specified in a strategy are: the way that items will be grouped for rehearsal, which groups to rehearse when, whether to ignore some of the items as they are presented or to process them all, how to search STM and LTM when it is time to respond.

The following is a list of the major processes used in SHORT's strategies.

1. Access a sensory store.
2. Perceive the contents of an imagery store.
3. Assign an item to a rehearsal group.
4. Rehearse an item.
5. Rehearse a group of items.
6. Rehearse the oldest group of items.
7. Search STM for a control symbol.
8. Access an entry in LTM.
9. Search LTM.
10. Image a pattern.
11. Output an item.
12. Output a group of items.

There are also a few more specialized processes that would not be used in every task; one example is the process of recoding digits into a number and vice versa. New strategies are constructed from these basic components. The possible strategies for SHORT are limited to the various ways that the processes can be combined.

When we use SHORT to simulate performance on a particular task, we assume that the subject being simulated employs a strategy that would perform the task as well as possible. That is, the simulation assumes adaptive behavior in the subject and, hence, does not take the strategy as a free parameter to be fitted to the observed behavior. This gives us a certain advantage over many other models of STM. Most models are adjusted on each task to mimic human performance as closely as possible, thus serving mainly a descriptive role. Often the constraints built into a model are not sufficient to prevent it from outperforming humans or performing qualitatively differently from humans. On the other hand, with SHORT we have searched for those strategies that perform a task best, and then we have compared SHORT's behavior using those strategies to human behavior. This allows us to note those cases where the proper constraints have not been built into the model, where it is possible for the model to outperform humans, or where the optimal strategies lead to behavior qualitatively different from human behavior. SHORT is vulnerable to being disproved. When SHORT outperforms humans at some task, either the subjects could be taught to improve their performances by using SHORT's strategy for performing the task, or else the model is, at least partially, wrong.

LTM is represented in SHORT in a rudimentary way, consisting for the most part only of unlabeled associations. Two chunks that are being rehearsed together may be consolidated as a new entry in LTM. As soon as one act of consolidation is complete, the next two chunks to be rehearsed consecutively will be used for the next consolidation. Consolidation continues to completion even if the pair of chunks is lost from STM during the consolidation period. The process of consolidation occurs over a period of time, but it does not reduce the system's processing capacity; it is assumed that consolidation is performed concurrently with the other ongoing processes.

We have looked at a number of studies where, for various reasons, it can be assumed that recall is from LTM, not STM, and we have calculated from the subjects' performance the average time needed to consolidate a new entry in LTM. Almost all estimates are in the range of 7–10 seconds per consolidation, and most estimates are in the range of 8–9 seconds. SHORT has therefore been set to require 8 seconds to consolidate a new entry in LTM.

Experimental Tests of SHORT

SHORT, as a model, predicts a wide range of experimental findings and has been run formally in a number of simulations. The tasks that have been simulated are the STM-span paradigm, forward serial recall of supraspan lists, backward serial recall, single presentation of short lists of paired associates, and the Peterson and Peterson paradigm with a distractor task (Gilmartin, 1975). These simulations have included variations in the presentation rate, the stimulus material, the modality of presentation, the delay of the respond signal, as well as in the strategy used to perform a particular task.

SHORT does very well simulating most of these tasks. However, it may be instructive to discuss some simulations where discrepancies between model and data (as well as matches between the two) were visible. In the experiment in question, we analyzed simulations of forward serial recall of words presented visually and auditorily with variations in the strategy for performing the task. SHORT's performance was qualitatively different from the human data in some respects, raising questions about the model and about the limitations in human performance. During forward serial recall, a supraspan sequence of items is presented once, after which the subject is asked to recall the items in the order in which they were presented. In our experimental simulations, the sequences were composed of nine words from SHORT's repertoire, presented at the rate of 1/sec with a duration of 0.5 seconds for each item. In the first set of simulations, presentation was visual, the response signal following the offset of the last item by 0.5 seconds.

The strategy SHORT used to perform the forward serial recall task with visual presentation is listed below (translated from SNOBOL into English), and the same

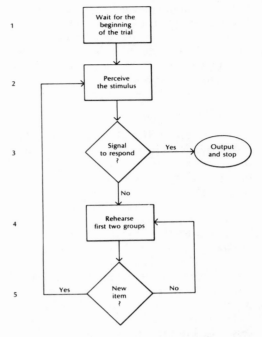

Figure 4. The strategy used by SHORT to perform forward serial recall.

strategy is represented as a flow diagram in figure 4.

1. Wait until the first item is presented, testing for the presence of a stimulus every 100 msec.

2. Access the sensory store and perceive the stimulus, entering the item in STM.

3. Is this the signal to respond? If so, output the first two rehearsal groups; output the last group, indicating that it is at the end of the list, and stop.

4. Rehearse whichever of the first two rehearsal groups has a member nearest the back of STM.

5. Has a new item been presented? If so, go to 2, if not, go to 4.

The number of items assigned to each of the rehearsal groups can affect the shape of the serial position curve. The serial position curve is the proportion of items recalled at each of the nine positions in the presented sequences. Since only the first two groups are being rehearsed in this strategy, it is the size of those groups that affects performance. The visually presented forward serial recall task was simulated three times, with the number of items in each of the first two rehearsal groups specified to be 2–2, 3–2, and 2–3, respectively. Each simulation consisted of 50 trials. The resulting serial position curves are presented in figure 5. Trials were scored as free recall even though SHORT was "told" that recall had to be in serial order. The mean number of words recalled in the three simulations was 4.56, 5.26, and 5.02, respectively. Jahnke (1965), who scored forward serial recall in the same manner, reported for human subjects means of 4.6 words recalled for lists of both 6 and 10 words.

It can be seen that the 2–2 grouping of the first two rehearsal groups leads to poorer performance than the 3–2 grouping or the 2–3 grouping. This is because a strategy to rehearse only four items underestimates the capacity of STM; when an attempt is made to rehearse five items, an average of at least 0.5 item more is recalled from the first two groups.

We have found that, on the average, SHORT's performance is just a little better than the reported human performance. The greatest discrepancy between SHORT's performance and human performance on this task occurs at the last serial position. As is evident in figure 6, humans show little or no recency effect during forward serial recall of visually presented lists (e.g., Jahnke, 1965; Conrad and Hull, 1968; Craik, 1969); SHORT can always report the last item in a list by perceiving the later items in the list without rehearsing them. An alternative strategy is to ignore the later items in the list. Although this

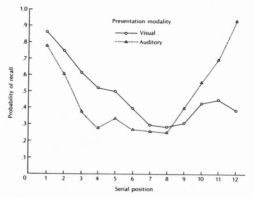

Figure 6. Forward serial recall of words presented at 1/sec, after Craik (1969), experiment I.

increases recall at the early serial positions somewhat, total recall is lower. It is curious that humans do not report one of the last items presented in each list; possibly if they were taught to do so it would improve their overall performance. In any case, this is an instance where the class of strategies that lead to the best performance of the task by SHORT causes the program to perform in a qualitatively different manner than an average human subject.

The next two simulations involve forward serial recall after auditory, instead of visual, presentation of items. The sequence length and the rate and duration of item presentation are unchanged. The strategy for recall with auditory presentation is slightly different from the strategy for recall following visual presentation, the change in strategy having the effect of accessing the auditory sensory store during recall before the information in it decays. When the response signal is perceived and the first group is output, leaving some space in STM where additional items can be stored, the contents of the auditory sensory store are accessed and perceived before the second and third groups are output from STM.

In figure 7, the results from two simulations after auditory presentation are compared to the results following visual presentation. The grouping scheme for rehearsal, 3 items in the first group and 2 in the second, was the same in all three cases.

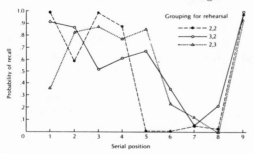

Figure 5. Simulation of forward serial recall of words presented visually at 1/sec.

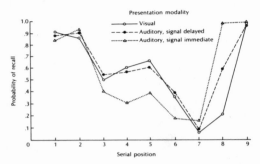

Figure 7. Simulation of forward serial recall of words presented at 1/sec.

The first "auditory" simulation was equivalent to the "visual" simulation, with the response signal being presented 0.5 seconds after the termination of the last item. The resulting serial position curve shows a modality effect, that is, better recall of the final items on the list following auditory presentation. While there is a discrepancy between SHORT's performance and human performance at the last serial position following visual presentation, their levels of performance are similar following auditory presentation (see figure 6).

One usual difference between auditory and visual presentation, other than the modality, is that the response signal follows the last item in visual presentation, but is often simultaneous with the last item in auditory presentation (the experimenter's voice drops on the last item). This earlier response signal should allow more of the contents of the auditory sensory store to be accessed before decaying, producing a larger modality effect. In the second auditory simulation, the response signal was presented simultaneously with the last item. As predicted, this produced an even larger recency effect. However, it was not foreseen that this increase would be at the expense of the middle serial positions. When the last item and the response signal are both entered into STM at the same time, there is a higher probability of an item being lost from STM than when the last item is entered into STM, followed by a period of rehearsal, and then the response signal is entered into STM. It is interesting to

note that in some studies that compare recall by humans after visual and auditory presentation, recall is slightly better over the first half of the list following visual presentation, while the recency effect is much larger following auditory presentation (Murdock, 1966; Craik, 1969).

CONCLUSION

We would like to summarize what we believe to be some of the advantages of postulating strategies as genuine variables that intervene between task environments and performance:

1. Strategies can be specified in psychologically meaningful terms, that is, in terms of processes that we believe humans use, such as perceiving, rehearsing, and searching through STM and LTM.

2. We should be able to train subjects to use several strategies for performing a task and then compare their performance using those strategies to a model's performance using the same strategies. This would allow fine tuning of a model.

3. If constraints are built into a model such that it cannot outperform humans, we can search for a strategy that performs a particular task best, rather than a strategy that mimics human performance. In that case, when we compare the model's performance to human performance, we will be testing the validity of the initial constraints. A model that has constraints built into it such that it cannot perform in a manner impossible for humans can be used to predict human performance on entirely new tasks within its domain.

This point can be restated in another way. One method of modeling the variation in human performance from task to task is to adjust parameters until the model shows the same level of performance as human subjects. The best-fitting parameter values characterize of describe the human performance of each task. But this approach provides no basis for setting the parameter values to predict human performance in a new task.

In our modeling we have tried to incorporate psychologically motivated, fixed constraints into the model so that it cannot outperform humans. The constraints impose ceilings on the model's performance so that in situations where humans perform well, the model will be able to perform well also, but in situations where humans have difficulty in performing the task, the model will be unable to perform any better than humans. With this type of model, we can predict human performance on a new task by discovering the best performance of the task that the model can exhibit. If the constraints have been specified correctly, the best performance of the model will be close to the best performance of humans in the same task.

Viewing strategies as major intervening variables between task environments and behavior also opens up some challenging research questions:

1. What is happening as a subject gets better at a task over the first few blocks of trials? What, explicitly, is he doing differently?

2. How does a subject choose between alternative methods of performing a task?

3. How does a person create new and better strategies from previous ones?

References

Anders, T. R. Retrospective reports of retrieval from short-term memory. *Journal of Experimental Psychology*, 1971, *90*, 251–57.

Anders, T. R. A high-speed, self-terminating search of short-term memory. *Journal of Experimental Psychology*, 1973, *97*, 34–40.

Atkinson, R. C., and Shiffrin, R. M. Human memory: A proposed system and its control processes. In Spence, K. W., and Spence, J. T. (Eds.), *The psychology of learning and motivation* (Vol. 2). New York: Academic Press, 1968, pp. 90–195.

Averbach, E., and Coriell, A. S. Short-term memory in vision. *Bell System Technical Journal*, 1961, *40*, 309–28.

Bruner, J. S., Goodnow, J. J., and Austin, G. A. *A study of thinking.* New York: Wiley, 1956.

Conrad, R., and Hull, A. J. Input modality and the serial position curve in short-term memory. *Psychonomic Science*, 1968, *10*, 135–36.

Craik, F. I. M. Modality effects in short-term storage. *Journal of Verbal Learning and Verbal Behavior*, 1969, *8*, 658–64.

Darwin, C. J., Turvey, M. T., and Crowder, R. G. An auditory analogue of the Sperling partial report procedure: Evidence for brief auditory storage. *Cognitive Psychology*, 1972, *3*, 255–67.

Gilmartin, K. J. An information-processing model of short-term memory. Doctoral dissertation, Carnegie-Mellon University. Ann Arbor, Michigan: University Microfilms No. 75–09–082, 1975.

Glucksberg, S., and Cowen, G. N., Jr. Memory for nonattended auditory material *Cognitive Psychology*, 1970, *1*, 149–56.

Jahnke, J. C. Primacy and recency effects in serial-position curves of immediate recall. *Journal of Experimental Psychology*, 1965, *70*, 130–32.

Murdock, B. B., Jr. Visual and auditory stores in short-term memory. *Quarterly Journal of Experimental Psychology*, 1966, *18*, 206–11.

Newell, A., and Simon H. A. *Human problem solving.* Englewood Cliffs, N. J.: Prentice-Hall, 1972.

Sperling, G. A. The information available in brief visual presentations. *Psychological Monographs*, 1960, *74*, (11, Whole No. 498).

3

Learning Processes

The first three chapters of this section describe a theory (EPAM: Elementary Perceiver and Memorizer) of human rote learning and show how this theory explains the principal phenomena that have been distilled from verbal learning experiments from the time of Ebbinghaus down to the present. Apart from its substantive interest, EPAM also illustrates the power of an information processing model, expressed as a computer program, to sum up and explain a bewildering mass of experimental results in terms of a few basic mechanisms.

The last two chapters, 3.4 and 3.5, are brief notes on learning and forgetting phenomena employing the same kinds of simple mathematical modeling techniques as were used in chapter 2.1. Chapter 3.4 warns against confusing psychological parameters with parameters that are artifactual, reflecting the experimenter's construction of the stimuli—a warning that will be taken up again in chapter 5.4. Chapter 3.5 demonstrates that the empirically derived Jost's Laws are incompatible with the hypothesis that forgetting follows an exponential curve.

Genesis of EPAM

At the time (1956) when the Logic Theorist, the first computer model of human problem solving, was constructed, the idea arose that the associative organization of memory (list structure memory) used for that model could also be employed to construct a system capable of acquiring new associations. Edward Feigenbaum took this task as his doctoral thesis project and completed the first version of EPAM in 1959.

EPAM was specifically designed to simulate human rote verbal learning by the paired associate and serial anticipation methods, paradigms that had dominated the human learning literature for nearly three-quarters of a century. EPAM accomplishes this with the help of a discrimination learning mechanism, an association learning (chunk-forming) mechanism, a performance or response mechanism, and a strategy for managing attention to the stimuli.

The Learning Strategy

The first component of EPAM to be specified, by Feigenbaum and myself in 1958, was the attention managing strategy. Independently of the other components of EPAM, this mechanism was by itself powerful enough to explain the puzzling invariance in shape of the serial position curve that had earlier been noticed by McCrary and Hunter (1953) and the independence between total learning time and memory drum speed that was later tested by Bugelski (1962). Two of the four assumptions we used in deriving the strategy are already familiar from sections 1 and 2: that processing is serial and that STM is limited in capacity. The initial version of EPAM assumed an STM capacity of six chunks; a later version, EPAM-III, required only three chunks.[1]

Strategy control of the learning behavior, which is explicit in chapter 3.1, produced two consequences that we did not anticipate when we built the model, but which explained several striking empirical findings in the literature. One, known from the old experiments of Krueger (1932), was that the shape of the serial position curve could be altered by instructions to the subject to attend to particular parts of the list. The second was the phenomenon of one-trial learning that had just been demonstrated by Rock (1957).

COMMENTS ON EPAM STRUCTURE

The most accessible description of the first EPAM can be found in Feigenbaum (1963). By 1963, Feigenbaum and I had completed an improved version used in all our later experiments. The new version, EPAM-III, is described in chapter 3.2. Since the latter chapter uses somewhat different terminology to name the components of LTM than was used in section 2, a short glossary may be helpful.

The "compound symbols" of chapter 3.2 are identical with the chunks of previous chapters. The two learning processes, discrimination learning and image building (chunking), of chapter 3.2 act upon the two distinct components of LTM proposed in section 2. Thus, "discrimination net" and "index" are simply alternate ways of referring to the component of LTM that grows through discrimination learning, while "images," "text," and "semantic memory" are synonymous names for the component that grows through the creation of new chunks.

While EPAM has distinct (but interdependent) learning mechanisms for elaborating the discrimination net and the semantic memory, respectively, the latter mechanism (chunking) serves parsimoniously both to *familiarize* EPAM with compound symbols and to *associate* responses to stimuli. Stated otherwise, stimulus-response pairs are chunks in exactly the same sense that familiar syllables or words are. Both kinds of chunks are represented by nodes in semantic memory that are accessed by the discrimination net.

EMPIRICAL TESTS OF EPAM

Chapters 3.1, 3.2 (written with Feigenbaum), and 3.3 (written with Gregg) are mainly devoted to showing how EPAM accounts for important verbal learning phenomena reported in the literature. As we have already seen, chapter 3.1 deals with the invariance of the serial position curve and of total learning time and some related phenomena. Chapter 3.2 focuses upon the effects of manipulating (1) the degree of similarity among stimulus and response symbols and (2) their levels of familiarity and meaningfulness.

Chapter 3.3 continues from chapter 3.1 the analysis of one-trial learning, showing that EPAM predicts the conditions under which learning will have a one-trial character and the conditions under which it will be incremental. The

---

1. In 1958, Feigenbaum and I submitted a paper embodying our results to the *Psychological Review*, which, finding it incomprehensible, rejected it. After several years' delay, we submitted the paper to the *British Journal of Psychology*, which published it in 1962. That paper is reprinted here as chapter 3.1.

chapter also discusses the additional evidence provided by the one-trial learning experiments for strategy control of learning.

I might call attention here to a point already discussed in the section on "Motivation and Learning" in chapter 1.3. In EPAM, learning is a function of attention and knowledge of results, independent of reward. When combined with the motivational mechanisms of chapter 1.3, EPAM therefore predicts correctly the circumstances under which latent learning will and will not occur (Kimble, 1961).

In section 6 of this book we will return to EPAM, and we will see that EPAM-like learning and recognition mechanisms are capable of explaining some important aspects of expert skill in chess playing and other domains. There are, of course, a number of learning phenomena that EPAM does not address, among them, the effects of "imaging" instructions, alluded to in chapter 2.3. In a paper not reprinted in this volume (Simon, 1972), I have speculated on how these effects might be explained within the framework of EPAM.

In spite of these and other remaining loose ends, I think it fair to claim that EPAM provides a theory of verbal learning, and more generally of recognition and chunking processes, that is both parsimonious and powerful in explaining these phenomena. While some small mysteries remain, the larger mysteries that attracted so much attention from experimental psychologists over so long a span of years have been successfully dispelled by the EPAM theory.

Adequacy of EPAM

In their *Human Associative Memory* (1973), Anderson and Bower provide (pp. 69–76) a very good description of the basic EPAM mechanisms, and then go on (pp. 76–7) to list what they regard as "its deficiencies as a general model for perceptual pattern recognition and as a general model of an associative information store." Their comments deserve our consideration.

With respect to pattern recognition, they make four points:

"First, it is clear that serial discrimination nets place far too much reliance on veridical identification of single stimulus features in a strong order of priority." This objection seems to me incorrect. There is voluminous evidence that human ability to recognize a stimulus depends on the order of processing the stimulus features—the tip-of-the-tongue phenomenon being a striking example. Moreover, there is nothing that prevents EPAM from acquiring multiple and redundant discrimination paths that point to the same node—a capability which has, indeed, been exploited in the application of EPAM to chess perception described in section 6. A parallel recognition scheme like PANDEMONIUM, which Anderson and Bower propose as an alternative to EPAM, lacks the sensitivity to order of cues that is almost certainly present in human pattern recognition. Besides, EPAM has never been proposed as a model of the visual preprocessor that extracts basic features from complex stimuli, but rather as a mechanism for discriminating among such features, once detected. Finally, the ability of a human to "recognize" blurred or degraded stimuli is often not based on perceptual recognition at all, but upon much slower and more complex problem solving processes of the sort that will be encountered in section 4.

"Second ... EPAM appears to be lacking a recognition mechanism which enables it to 'know' whether or not it has previously seen the current stimulus." Not so. EPAM need not have an image at the terminus of every path through the discrimination net. If a stimulus is sorted to a node lacking such an image, EPAM could know (or believe) it had not previously seen the stimulus.

"Third, the model is not now formulated with sufficient complexity to permit the operation of a prevailing semantic context to bias its perceptions of words in context." True, but superficial. Contextual constraints apply *after* perceptual recognition has occurred. Until the shape of the word "ball" had been discriminated (from "bull," say, or "bell"), the system cannot determine whether a spherical object is intended or a formal dance. But making the later distinction is a function of the node-link structure and its activation mechanisms, not of the perceptual discrimination process—it belongs to the text, not the index, of memory.

"Fourth, the model performs static recognition of single objects or characters, but is inadequate for dealing with realistic scenes containing multiple objects arranged in depth in a variety of relations." The objection is partly met, again, by the observation that EPAM obviously requires a preprocessor to analyze visual scenes. The Anderson and Bower HAM scheme and other semantic net proposals would need to be supplemented *both* by such a preprocessor *and* an EPAM-like discrimination net. Nor is EPAM limited to single objects. It does, in fact, discriminate among compound stimuli such as phrases consisting of words consisting of letters consisting of features, or chess positions (section 6, below) consisting of patterns of chess pieces.

Anderson and Bower next go on to criticize EPAM "as a theory of our memory store." Nolo contendere. Since EPAM has never been put forth as a complete theory of the text of memory, but simply of its index, I can only agree on this point, and agree also, that in order to model the whole LTM structure, an EPAM-like recognizer must be combined with a node-link associative structure, and both must be supplemented with visual and auditory feature-extracting preprocessors.

In sum, these deficiencies and supposed deficiencies of EPAM do not invalidate the system as a theory of perceptual recognition and of verbal learning. They simply indicate a few of the respects in which EPAM is less than a comprehensive and complete model of Thinking Man. I should like to offer a few more comments about the semantic component that is needed to complement EPAM.

SEMANTIC MEMORY

We can agree then that EPAM is not, and does not claim to be, a complete theory of memory. While it models the nodes of semantic memory (its "images"), it does not model the whole semantic network or the associative processes that operate over it. This network and its processes, while of fundamental importance to many memory storage and accessing tasks, are not much implicated in the classes of performances that EPAM was designed to explain.

Efforts to model the semantic network component of LTM began in the Carnegie group at an early data with the doctoral dissertation of Lindsay (1961) and my design of a Heuristic Compiler (1961). Reitman explored in rather different directions, involving decentralized control of network search, in his ARGUS model of 1965. Working at the same time, Quillian, in his doctoral dissertation produced a model of semantic memory that has had a seminal effect on the whole field. Its publication in 1968 produced a great rash of activity in the design of semantic networks that is still continuing in the work of Anderson, of Schank and Abelson, and of others.

The semantic network models have tended to emphasize the node-link structure of the LTM "text," and to neglect, comparatively, the discrimination net structure of its "index." In the coming years some amalgamation will be needed of these two components to give a truly comprehensive account of human long term memory. Except for the brief discussions of these issues in Section 2, they lie outside the scope of this book.

References

Anderson, J. R. *Language, Memory, and Thought*, Hillsdale, N.J.: Lawrence Erlbaum Associates, 1976.
Anderson, J. R. & G. H. Bower. *Human Associative Memory*, Washington, D.C.: V. H. Winston & Sons, 1973.
Bugelski, B. R. Presentation time, total time, and mediation in paired-associate learning, *Journal of Experimental Psychology*, 63:409–12 (1962).
Feigenbaum, E. A. The simulation of verbal learning behavior, *in* Feigenbaum & Feldman (eds.), *Computers and Thought*, New York: McGraw-Hill, 1963, pp. 297–309.
Kimble, G. A. *Hilgard and Marquis' Conditioning and Learning* (2nd ed.), New York: Appleton-Century-Crofts, 1961.
Krueger, W. C. F. Learning during directed attention, *Journal of Experimental Psychology*, 15:517–27 (1932).
Lindsay, R. K. Toward the development of machines which comprehend. Unpublished doctoral dissertation, Carnegie Institute of Technology, 1961. (A revised version under the title "Inferential memory as the basis of machines that understand natural language" appears in E. A. Feigenbaum & J. Feldman (eds.), *Computers and Thought*, New York: McGraw-Hill, 1963, pp. 217–36.)
McCrary, J. W., & W. S. Hunter. Serial position curves in verbal learning, *Science*, 117:131–34 (1953).
Newell, A., & H. A. Simon. The Logic Theory Machine: A complex information processing system. *IRE Transactions on Information Theory*, Vol. IT-2, No. 3, pp.61–79 (1956).
Quillian, M. R. *Semantic Theory*, unpublished doctoral dissertation, Carnegie Institute of Technology, 1966.
Reitman, *W. R. Cognition and Thought*, New York: Wiley, 1965.
Rock, I. The role of repetition in associative learning, *American Journal of Psychology*, 70:186–93 (1957).
Schank, R., & R. Abelson. *Scripts, Plans, Goals and Understanding*, Hillsdale, N.J.: Lawrence Erlbaum Associates, 1977.
Simon, H. A. The heuristic compiler, *in* H. A. Simon & L. Siklossy (eds.), *Representation and Meaning*, Englewood Cliffs, N.J.: Prentice-Hall, 1972a, pp. 9–43.
Simon, H. A. What is visual imagery: An information processing interpretation, *in* L. W. Gregg (ed.), *Cognition in Learning and Memory*, New York: Wiley, 1972b, pp. 183–204.

3.1

A Theory of the Serial Position Effect (1962)

with Edward A. Feigenbaum

INTRODUCTION

Intraserial phenomena have been a major focus of interest in the study of serial learning. McGeoch, 1942, for example, devoted fifty pages of his *Psychology of Human Learning* to such phenomena. And among intraserial phenomena, one of the most prominent is the serial position curve, depicting the relative number of errors made with the various syllables in a list while learning the list to some criterion.

McCrary and Hunter (1953) observed that if percentage of total errors is taken as the unit of measurement, then all the empirical serial position curves for lists of a given length are substantially identical. Earlier investigators, measuring number of errors, had concluded that relatively more errors occurred for the middle syllables when the lists were hard than when they were easy, more with slow learners than with fast learners, more with rapid presentation of syllables than with slow presentation, and so on. One can find in

the literature numerous theoretical explanations of these differences.

The findings of McCrary and Hunter leave us in the embarrassing position of having explained phenomena that do not exist, i.e., the supposed differences in amount of the position effect, and of having failed to explain a striking uniformity that does exist—the substantial identity of curves derived under a variety of experimental conditions. McCrary and Hunter themselves reach the peculiar conclusion that a single principle can hardly be expected to account for uniformity of effect under diversity of conditions, and hence that some multiple factor is needed to explain the outcome.

The thesis of this chapter is the opposite one—that if a uniformity underlies experiments performed under a wide variety of conditions, this uniformity should be traceable to a single simple mechanism that is invariant under change of conditions. We will propose such a model of the information processing activity of a subject as he organizes his learning effort in a serial learning task. The serial position effect will be shown to be a consequence of the information processing strategy postulated in the model; the model predicts both

We are indebted to our colleague Allen Newell for numerous helpful discussions about this project and to the Ford Foundation for financial assistance that made it possible.

qualitatively and quantitatively the shape of the curve and the percentages reported by McCrary and Hunter and by others.

Some Relevant Data

Before we state the theory of the serial position effect, we will review some important empirical findings on serial learning of nonsense syllables:

1. Under the usual experimental conditions and with experienced subjects there is generally a characteristic curvilinear relation between number of errors to criterion for a given syllable and the serial position of that syllable in the list. The syllable with the largest number of errors is generally beyond the middle of the list, though this effect becomes less noticeable as the length of the list increases (Ribback and Underwood, 1950); the first syllable almost always exhibits the fewest errors (Hovland, 1938).

2. McCrary and Hunter (1953) have shown that, for lists of a given number of syllables, all serial position curves obtained with the usual experimental procedures are virtually identical when errors are plotted on a percentage, rather than an absolute, basis. About the same degree of bowing is exhibited with nonsense syllables as with names, with massed as with distributed practice, with slow as with fast learners, with rapid as with slow presentation. Typical data for lists of twelve and fourteen syllables are given in tables 1 and 2.

3. In spite of this uniformity under normal conditions, it is easy to produce large deviations from the characteristic curve. Such deviations can be produced in at least the following four ways: (*a*) by varying the difficulty of particular items in the list; (*b*) by introducing an item sharply distinguishable from those that precede it or follow it (McGeoch, 1942, p. 107); (*c*) by introducing distinguishable sublists within the main list (Wishner, Shipley and Jurvich, 1957); (*d*) by explicit instructions to the subjects (Krueger, 1932; Welch and Burnett, 1924). Not surprisingly, difficult items are learned with more errors than easy items in the same serial position; distinguishable items are learned with fewer errors; items that the subject is instructed to learn first are learned with fewer errors.

4. For lists of a given length, average learning time per syllable is almost independent of: (*a*) the rate of presentation— though this result is not given explicitly by Hovland (1938), we have used his reported data to compute the average learning time per syllable; this constancy has been independently reported by Wilcoxon, Wilson, and Wise (1961); and (*b*) the order in which subjects are instructed to learn the items—though this result is not given explicitly by Krueger (1932), we have computed it from his data. Hence, number of trials to criterion is inversely proportional to seconds per syllable.

5. Distribution of practice reduces the number of trials to criterion, but not sufficiently to compensate for the additional total time. The advantages of distribution, measured in trials to criterion, almost disappears when the presentation rate is as slow as 4 seconds per syllable (Hovland, 1938).

In the next section we will propose a theory of the serial learning process that accounts quantitatively for the data mentioned in items 1, 2, and 4, and qualitatively for the observation of item 3. In the present paper, we will not discuss the effects of distribution of practice, since these effects almost certainly derive from mechanisms that go beyond the simple theory proposed here. We wish merely to observe that when time to criterion is taken as the measure of learning rate, these effects are of rather small magnitude compared with those we will consider.

An Information Processing Theory of Serial Learning

We hypothesize that serial learning is an active, complex process involving the manipulation and storage of symbols by means of an interacting set of elementary information processes; and that these processes are qualitatively similar to those used in problem solving, concept formation, and other higher mental processes (Newell, Shaw, and Simon, 1958*a*). Thus, we will argue that the stimulus-response sequences postulated by *S-R* theory are simple only in surface appearance—that beneath them lies an iceberg of complex information processing activity.

We will not defend this viewpoint in detail here although it has proved exceedingly fruitful in research in which we and our associates have been engaged (see, for example, Feigenbaum (1959); Newell and Simon (1961); Newell et al. (1958*b*)). We should like to offer three brief observations to persuade the reader that our conjecture does not entirely fly in the face of common sense or previous psychological observation. First, expectancy and mediation theories, like those of Tolman (Hilgard, 1956, pp. 185–221), or of Osgood (Hilgard, 1956, pp. 464–5), attribute as much complexity to the stimulus-response connexion as does our conjecture; what they fail to indicate is the nature of the mechanisms that might provide the complexity. Secondly, equally elaborate and more explicit mechanisms are postulated in concept-formation theories such as those of Gibson (1940) and the recent one of Bruner, Goodnow, and Austin (1956). Indeed, we will see that one of our postulates involves a conception closely related to Bruner's notion of 'cognitive strain'. Thirdly, the time an experienced subject needs, per syllable, to memorize a list of a dozen nonsense syllables is of the order of 30 seconds. In comparison with the times required by familiar electronic systems for simple processes, this is an enormous time interval. It is large—by a factor of 500 or more—even in comparison with the 50 msec or thereabouts required for the central processes in the simplest responses to stimuli. If a theory is to fill up this 30-second time interval in at all a plausible manner, it will have to attribute considerable complexity to the processes that take place. Feigenbaum (1959) reports on such a theory of verbal learning, dealing in a complete manner with discrimination learning, association learning, responding, etc. The theory predicts a variety of the phenomena of rote learning of nonsense syllables in serial and paired associate learning tasks.

Underlying Assumptions of the model

For the purposes of this paper, we will not need to examine the elementary information processes in detail, for the shape of the serial position curve will prove to be independent of their microstructure. This point is examined in detail by Feigenbaum (1959), where a distinction is drawn between macroprocesses of verbal learning and microprocesses. We require, instead, the assumption that in order for a connection between a stimulus and a response to be formed, a certain (unspecified) sequence of elementary processes needs to be carried out, and that the execution of this sequence requires a definite interval of time, the length of the interval depending on the "difficulty" of the task and other parameters of the experimental situation.

We suppose the information processing mechanism to be operating predominantly in a serial rather than a parallel manner—it is capable of doing only one, or a few things at a time. The narrowness of the span of attention is a familiar aspect of conscious activity; we assume that it is also an attribute of the subconscious.

Information Processing Postulates

The structure of the theory is embodied in four postulates about the processing mechanism.

Postulate 1. Serial Mechanism. The central processing mechanism operates serially and is capable of doing only one thing at a time. Thus, if many things demand processing activity from the central processing mechanism, they must share the total processing time available. This means that the total time required to memorize a collection of items, when there is no interaction among them, will be the sum of the times of the individual items. (In serial learning of syllables there is, in fact, interaction among individual items; and total learning time increases more than proportionately with number of items. We will not be concerned with this point in the present chapter because we are dealing not with total learning time or total errors, but with the relative number of errors made on different syllables in a list.)

Postulate 2. Average Unit Processing Time per Syllable. The fixation of an item on a serial list requires the execution of a sequence of information processes that requires, for a given set of experimental conditions, a definite amount of processing time per syllable. The time per syllable varies with the difficulty of the syllables, the length of list, the ability of the subject and other factors. In a well-known series of experiments by Hovland (1938), for example, it averaged approximately 30 seconds.

Postulate 3. Immediate Memory. There exists in the central processing mechanism an immediate memory of limited size capable of storing information temporarily; and all access to an item by the learning processes must be through the immediate memory. There is a great deal of experimental evidence to support the concept of an immediate memory. The evidence points to a span of immediate memory of about five or six symbols (Miller, 1956). We postulate that each symbol stored separately in the immediate memory must be a familiar, well-learned symbol. For unfamiliar nonsense syllable materials, the familiar symbols are the letters. Thus, for the three-letter nonsense syllables ordinarily used, we postulate that the immediate memory has the capacity to hold two syllables (six letters). This means that it will ordinarily hold at any moment one S-R pair being learned.

Postulate 4. Anchor Points. In the absence of countervailing conditions—the nature of which will be specified presently—the information processing will be carried out in a relatively systematic and orderly way which will limit the demands that are placed on the small immediate memory. This postulate is related to the generalization, which Bruner and his associates (1956)

have tested in certain concept-forming experiments, that subjects develop strategies for limiting the "cognitive strain" involved in concept formation, and that these strategies involve handling newly acquired information in a systematic and orderly way.

We assume that subjects learning the syllables of a serial list will reduce the demands on memory by treating the ends of the list as "anchor points," and by learning the syllables in an orderly sequence, starting from these anchor points and working toward the middle. This procedure reduces demands on memory because, at each stage of the learning task, the next syllable to be learned is readily identified as being adjacent to a syllable that has already been learned. Thus, no special information about position in list needs to be remembered.

The idea of learning from anchor points is not new, though it does not seem to have been previously formalized. Woodworth (1938), for example, makes use of it in describing the process by which a list of digits is learned. Wishner et al. (1957) mention it in their discussion of the serial position curves obtained in their list-sublist experiment.

The first three postulates differ from the fourth in that the former describe built-in characteristics of the processing mechanism that are probably not learned or readily modified; while the latter describes a method of proceeding that is apparently habitual with most subjects, at least in our culture, but which is modifiable by experimental instructions and by certain attention-directing stimuli.

It has been observed frequently that in serial memorization subjects not only develop associations between syllables but also use various position cues and other cues. They learn, for example, that a particular syllable occurs in the early or in the late part of the list. (From this reliance on "irrelevant" cues, one can develop an explanation for such phenomena as anticipatory errors and "remote associations" that is much simpler than the usual one; but these topics would take us beyond the scope of our present task.) The use of position cues gives a unique status to the beginning and end of a serial list, for these items have the special property that they have no neighbors "before" and "after" respectively, i.e., the first item is always preceded, and the last item succeeded, by the intertrial activity. Once the items at the anchor points are memorized, the items contiguous to them become the first un-learned items "after" or "before" syllables already memorized; and so on, as the learning proceeds. More than this, the first two items are unique in that they represent the first *S-R* pair presented to the subject in the experiment. Thus, we can make out at least a plausible case that a learner can reduce the demands on immediate memory by memorizing in a more or less systematic fashion from the ends of the list toward the middle.

This postulate is sufficient to explain the bowed form of the serial position curve— although it says only a little more than the observed fact of the bowing. Its advantage over explanations like the Lepley-Hull hypothesis (which will be discussed later) is that it is not inconsistent with the ease (item 3, above) with which changes can be induced by the experimenter in the serial position curve.

In order to make quantitative predic-tions as to the amount of bowing that will be observed, we use the notion of anchor points to strengthen postulate 4, as follows:

Postulate 4a. Processing Sequence. We postulate the following information processing strat-egy for organizing the serial learning task using anchor points: (*a*) the first two items presented in the experiment are learned first; (*b*) attention is next focused for learn-ing on an item immediately adjacent to an anchor point. (In the ordinary serial list, this will be the third item or the last.) The probability that any specific item adjacent to an anchor point will be selected for learning next is $1/p$, where p is the number of anchor points (in the ordinary serial list, $p = 2$. Thus, for example, the probability that the last item will be learned after the second item is 0.5); (*c*) attention is focused,

and learning proceeds, item by item in this orderly fashion until the criterion trial is completed.

One can picture the subject building up over time an internal representation of the serial list he is learning. It will be seen, then, that the postulate specifies only a minimal amount of organizational activity: namely, the ability to add an item immediately after or immediately before an item already learned (or a "special" stimulus like the intertrial interval). Our explorations with other processing strategies have shown that this strategy reduces greatly the informa-tion processing demands on the learner.

Predictions from the Postulates

The postulates describe a learning mech-anism that memorizes serial lists in a prescribed way. This mechanism generates a serial error curve as it learns (i.e., some particular serial error curve is deduced as a consequence of the postulates). We wish to compute this serial error curve and com-pare it with the McCrary and Hunter curve.

Computer simulation is the most general and powerful method for doing this. We and others have used this method exten-sively in building theories of problem solv-ing (Newell et al., 1958*a*), binary choice behaviour (Feldman, 1959), concept at-tainment (Hovland and Hunt, 1960), and other cognitive phenomena. It is described in detail elsewhere (Newell and Simon, 1961). Briefly the idea is this. The digital computer is a universal information pro-cessing device, capable of carrying out any precisely specified information process. Thus a computer can carry out exactly the information processing required by the postulates of the model. We program the model on a computer, use it qua subject in verbal learning experiments (simulated inside the computer), observe the learning behavior of the model, and thereby gener-ate the consequences of the postulates in particular verbal learning situations. We have used this method in constructing and exploring an information processing theory of verbal learning (Feigenbaum, 1959). In particular, for the purposes of this chapter, we have generated the serial error curve for a few simple serial learning experiments. We have done this in two different ways: first, following postulate 2, we introduced a unit processing time per syllable without specifying the microprocesses of the learning that take place during this time interval; secondly, we removed the latter artificiality and substituted the full complement of microprocesses postulated by the more complete theory.

For the particular case of the serial position curve, the postulates are simple enough so that there is no real need to employ computer simulation to generate the predictions. The postulates can be formalized in a simple mathematical model, from which the quantitative predictions can be generated. As this method is likely to be more familiar to the reader, we give the mathematical model in the appendix and present the serial error curves which it predicts (for lists of twelve and fourteen syllables) in tables 1 and 2. The results obtained by the computer simulation technique are substantially identical (though slightly more discontinuous).

What can we specifically say about the fit? First, the ordinates of the first and last syllable of the predicted curves are in almost exact agreement with those of the empirical curves. Secondly, the syllable position of the peak of the predicted curves is substantially the same as that of the observed curves. Thirdly, the ordinates of the predicted curves and the empirical curves at each syllable position are very close, especially in the critical first and last third of each list, where very good agreement is important to any claims about goodness-of-fit. Furthermore, this fit was obtained without any arbitrary parameters, other than the specification of the sequence in which incoming syllables are processed.

The goodness-of-fit of the observed frequency distribution to the predicted distribution was tested by the Kolmogorov-Smirnov test of association. The test accepted the null hypothesis at the 99 percent level of significance.

ELABORATION AND DISCUSSION

In this section, we wish to compare the predictions of our information processing theory with those derived from the Lepley-Hull hypothesis and to extend our predic-

Table 1. Percentage of Total Errors Made during Acquisition at Each Syllable Position of a 14-item Serial List of Nonsense Syllables Predicted and Observed.

	Syllable Position													
	1	2	3	4	5	6	7	8	9	10	11	12	13	14
Predicted	0.95	1.9	4.7	5.6	8.1	8.9	10.5	10.8	10.8	10.5	8.9	8.1	5.6	4.7
*Observed**	1.0	3.5	4.3	6.0	8.0	8.9	9.2	10.0	9.5	10.6	8.8	8.9	7.2	4.0

*These values are approximate.
Source: From figure 4 of McCrary and Hunter (1953, p. 133).

Table 2. Percentage of Total Errors Made during Acquisition at Each Syllable Position of a 12-item Serial List of Nonsense Syllables Predicted and Observed.

	Syllable Position											
	1	2	3	4	5	6	7	8	9	10	11	12
Predicted	1.3	2.6	6.3	7.5	10.5	11.3	12.5	12.5	11.3	10.5	7.5	6.3
*Observed**	1.5	2.3	4.5	7.0	10.3	11.6	14.0	12.4	11.0	10.0	8.5	7.0

*These values are approximate values for the median percentages at each position for the four curves presented in figure 2 of McCrary and Hunter (1953, p. 132).

tions to two important experiments, one of which was published after we had specified our model.

The Lepley-Hull Hypothesis

There have been few attempts to account for the serial position effect in quantitative terms. Hull et al. (1940) attempted to do so on the assumption of some inhibitory processes, or intralist "interference." Atkinson (1957), drawing on statistical learning theory, has exhibited a stochastic process which generates a curve of the general shape of the serial position curve. We will discuss Hull's results in some detail and comment briefly on Atkinson's.

Although Hull's equations provide a good fit to the empirical data, this fit is not a convincing test of the Lepley-Hull theory for the following reasons:

Hull's theory leads to a set of equations having three free parameters: the reaction threshold, the ratio of inhibitory potential to excitatory potential per trial, and the remoteness reduction factor. These are used to fit the serial error curve, or, more precisely, the curve of number of repetitions to reaction threshold—see Hull et al. (1940, pp. 103–7). Hull fits the theoretical curve by passing it through three points of the empirical curve. Since the empirical data form a relatively smooth, bow-shaped curve, it is not surprising that a three-parameter curve can be made to fit them closely; an equally good approximation can be obtained by fitting a parabola empirically to the data.

This means that Hull's hypothesis will fit almost any data (provided the serial position curve has the characteristic bowed pattern), and hence is almost impossible to disprove from the data. It is therefore an exceedingly weak hypothesis. By the same token—because of the three free parameters—Hull's theory does not predict the constancy on a percentage scale observed by McCrary and Hunter.

Conversely, given the constancy observed by McCrary and Hunter, we can draw certain conclusions from Hull's theory regarding the growth of excitatory and inhibitory potential and the reaction threshold. For example, it can be shown by an examination of Hull's equations that the ratio of the increment of inhibitory potential per trial to the increment of excitatory potential must be a constant (independent, for example, of intralist similarity). See Hull et al. (1940, pp. 104–5).

The McCrary and Hunter result implies that the Rs are related: they are proportional to each other. The variables q_i are homogeneous of degree two in R, and the D_i are homogeneous of degree one in R. The Js are homogeneous of degree zero in R. By equation (3) of p. 104, $\Delta e/\Delta k$ is homogeneous of degree zero in R, hence a constant.

This is surprising and contrary to the whole spirit of the Lepley-Hull hypothesis. For we would expect that with high intralist similarity the inhibitory potential would rise more rapidly than with low intralist similarity. On the contrary, if Hull's model is correct the only parameter that changes as lists become more difficult to learn is the ratio of the threshold to the increment of excitatory potential per trial—by equation (2), p. 104, of Hull et al. (1940). Finally, the Lepley-Hull hypothesis does not explain how a subject can voluntarily or through a shift in his attention greatly alter the shape of the curve.

There are four reasons, therefore, why Hull's mathematical model for the serial position effect is unsatisfactory: since it contains three adjustable parameters its predictions are very weak; it does not predict the constancy in the percentage-error curve; this constancy hardly seems compatible with the mechanism assumed as a basis for the model; and finally, the model is difficult to reconcile with well-known attention-shift and set-change phenomena.

The preceding discussion of the curve-fitting aspects of Hull's equations applies also to Atkinson's equations. Atkinson (1957) has available four free parameters. He estimates these parameters from data for an 18-syllable list and uses these estimated values to make predictions for lists of 8 and 13 syllables. However, a careful examination of Atkinson's equations shows that even after the parameters have been estimated, there are enough degrees of freedom left in the system almost to ensure a reasonably good fit to the other curves. Thus, his theory suffers the same infirmity that we have pointed out in Hull's.

Furthermore, to make workable the difficult mathematics of the stochastic process, Atkinson has had to introduce a number of very constraining assumptions. His equations hold only for serial lists of highly dissimilar words which are familiar and easily pronounced; the presentation must be at a moderate rate, with a long interval provided at the conclusion of each trial. Yet the same bowed curve is obtained empirically when these conditions are not met as when they are. Finally, as in Hull's theory, there is difficulty in predicting the constancy observed by McCrary and Hunter. Given a set of parameter values, Atkinson's theory does not predict the constancy over the experimental conditions reported by McCrary and Hunter. On the other hand, if one admits that these values may change from situation to situation, then one must reestimate them for each experimental condition, and therein the theory loses much of its power.

The Two-part List

A simple extension of ordinary nonsense syllable experiments is to differentiate the first half of the list from the second half by printing the former in one color (say black) and the latter in another color (say red), dividing the total list perceptually into two smaller sublists.

What will be the shape of the serial position curve? One can predict this from Hull's theory by the unsatisfying procedure of assuming that the total list is learned as two separate sublists, and by fitting each sublist with a three-parameter curve such as we have discussed previously. The total fit will have six free parameters.

We should like to be able to predict the shape of the curve from the theory we have already presented. There are two important issues involved in making such a prediction:

1. Consider those subjects who perceive the total list as being constructed of two sublists. One possible reasonable strategy for dealing with the learning task is to use the end points of each sublist as anchor points, in the type of learning process described earlier. Another plausible strategy is to use as anchor points the ends of the total list and one point in the center to identify the point of bifurcation, say the first red syllable.

In making a prediction of the serial position curve for the two-part list, we have assumed simply that of those subjects who perceived the list as being two sublists, one half used the first strategy and the other half used the second strategy. The assumption is, of course, a relatively crude one, but the prediction is not very sensitive to the actual percentages assumed. Alternatively, we could have estimated the percentage from the data.

2. In the experiment which we will discuss shortly, we have no way of knowing precisely how many subjects perceived the task as one of memorizing two sublists and how many perceived it as learning one long serial list. In the absence of this knowledge, we can estimate these percentages from the observed ordinate of the first red syllable and weight our prediction at each syllable position appropriately using this estimate. This procedure essentially "fits" our predicted curve to the empirical curve at one point, the "break" between black and red syllables. But it guarantees nothing about the quality of the prediction at the other points.

As part of a larger experiment, Wishner et al. (1957) performed an experiment with a two-part list. They had an experimental group memorize lists of 14 syllables, half of which were printed in black capitals, the other half in red lower case letters. The experimental group was told that the object of the experiment was to discover how people learned two lists simultaneously.

In table 3 the predicted values for the percentage of errors at each syllable position are compared with the observed values.

The predictions were generated by the

Table 3. Percentage of Total Errors, Predicted and Observed, Made at Each Syllable Position during Acquisition, for a Two-color, 14-item Serial List of Nonsense Syllables.

Syllable Position

	1	2	3	4	5	6	7	8	9	10	11	12	13	14
Predicted	1.9	3.1	4.7	6.7	9.1	10.1	8.9	5.9	6.0	8.3	8.7	9.8	9.9	5.5
*Observed**	2.2	4.3	6.5	7.3	8.2	8.5	8.1	6.0	6.0	9.0	9.5	9.9	8.5	6.0

* These values are approximate, and were derived from data taken from Wishner et al. (1957, p. 260).

methods previously described. Three anchor points were used. In the mathematical treatment, the three-anchor-point predictions were corrected by a factor which ensured an exact fit of the ordinate of syllable 9 (the middle anchor point). In the computer simulation method, whole-list and sublist strategies were both run and the predicted ordinates averaged in a weighted fashion such that the ordinate of syllable 9 fitted exactly. What this procedure comes down to is the assumption that approximately two-thirds of the subjects learned the list as two sublists and approximately one-third learned it as a single long list (note that these fractions were not assumed a priori but were obtained by working backwards from the observed ordinate of the ninth syllable).

The agreement at all syllable positions is very close. As contrasted with our other predictions, in this one we had available the one free parameter already mentioned. The goodness-of-fit of the observed frequency distribution to the predicted distribution was tested by the Kolmogorov-Smirnov test of association. The test accepted the null hypothesis at the 99 percent level of significance.

The Experiments of Krueger

We turn now to some important experiments, the results of which were alluded to previously, and which have important implications for the information processing theory.

In a well-known series of experiments, Krueger (1932) presented various kinds of lists of "easy" and "hard" paired nouns to subjects who either received instructions to learn the list in some specified order or no instructions at all. These studies demonstrated that the order in which the various items were learned was influenced markedly by the instructions given to the subjects. As McGeoch puts it (1942, p. 102), "The relation between rate of learning and position in the series is, then, a function of the direction of the subject's effort or attention." As we have indicated, this is entirely consistent with the information processing theory, which regards particular learning sequences as "strategies" for dealing with the learning problem—as adaptive response to task.

What about our more specific hypothesis that in the usual serial learning experiment the "end points" of the list will be taken as anchor points in the learning process? Krueger's experiments showed that subjects given *no* instructions produced essentially the same serial position curves as those subjects who were instructed to learn the *ends* of the list first.

Because the fixation of an item requires a fixed amount of processing time, and because the sequence of learning is considered a "strategy" and not a built-in characteristic of the learning process, our theory predicts that the total number of syllables learned will be proportional to the total learning time and independent of the order of learning. On this point Krueger reports, "When the attention given is constant, the total amounts learned are the same, irrespective of whether this effort is directed to the beginning, center, or the final sections of the unit which is to be memorized" (1932, p. 527).

Although we assume that there is a constant fixation time associated with each particular item on a list, items of different kinds (e.g., "easy" items against "difficult" items) will have different processing times. The theory we have proposed predicts that the total learning time will be the sum of these processing times per syllable, and as such will be independent of the order in which the syllables are learned. Confirming this prediction, Krueger reports, "When materials of unequal difficulty appear within the same unit to be mastered, the total number of trials required to memorize the unit is approximately the same whether attention is given at first to the more difficult or the easier sections of the unit" (1932, p. 527).

This is consistent with the McCrary and Hunter results. If one plots the McCrary and Hunter curve by ordering the abscissa values not by serial position in the list but by the apparent order in which the syllables were learned, the ordinates lie on a straight line. This, of course, is in exact agreement with our model. Recent additional information on this phenomenon was obtained by Jensen (1962) for the learning of nonsense figures.

Thus, Krueger's experiments, though they were performed with serial lists of paired nouns rather than nonsense syllables, demonstrate (1) that the serial position curve can be "shaped" by the experimenter with suitable instructions to subjects, so that the order of learning syllables is itself a learned response; (2) that the total amount of material learned within a given time is independent of the order in which various items, sometimes heterogeneous with respect to difficulty, are learned.

SOME RECENT RESULTS

Subsequent to the specification of the model proposed in this chapter, some important new experiments have been published on the effect of replacing syllables on a list during learning. Rock (1957) used the following procedure on his experimental groups: on each test trial, those syllables incorrectly responded to by the

subject were removed and new syllables were substituted in their place for the next learning trial. Rock found no impairment of the rate of learning for the experimental groups (as compared with the control groups). This important result casts further doubt on Hull's incremental build-up hypothesis. Criticism of Rock's technique led Estes, Hopkins, and Crothers (1960) to replicate and extend Rock's experiment, but their results substantiate Rock's.

Estes et al. say of these experiments, "No hitherto published theory with which we are familiar gives a reasonable account of our principal findings" (1960, p. 338). The information processing theory we have proposed here predicts the Rock result. A computer simulation of the Rock experiment using the information processing model generated behaviour substantially identical with that reported by Rock. In terms of our theory (postulate 4a) the explanation, of course, is that items on a list are learned one at a time in the processing sequence. Items presented when attention is focused on some other particular item are simply ignored by the learner and are picked up on a later trial, as determined by the processing sequence. Hence, no time is lost by the learner if the experimenter replaces an item that has not yet been processed.

CONCLUDING REMARKS

In this chapter we have surveyed the principal known facts about the shape of the serial position curve in serial learning of nonsense syllables by the anticipation method. We have examined the Lepley-Hull hypothesis as an explanation for the shape of the curve and have concluded that the hypothesis is unsatisfactory. We have proposed an alternative hypothesis formulated in terms of information processes. We have shown that the hypothesis not only predicts the constancy of the serial position curve when the ordinates are plotted in percentage terms, but also predicts the quantitative values of the ordinates. Since the hypothesis allows no free parameters, its success in fitting the observed data provides rather persuasive evidence for its validity.

The information processing hypothesis is built on the following assumptions:

1. that the brain is a serial processing mechanism with a limited span of processing attention;

2. That the fixation of an item uses up a definite amount of processing time.

3. That there is a small immediate memory which holds information to be processed.

4. That the subject employs a relatively orderly and systematic method for organizing the learning task, using items with features of uniqueness as anchor points.

In this chapter, we have offered no explanation of the fixation process itself, i.e., we have talked not at all about what occurs during the processing time assumed in item (2) above.

APPENDIX

Given the unit processing time per syllable, one can, from the postulates, compute the average time after the beginning of a learning experiment that will pass before any specified syllable is learned. This time, in turn, determines uniquely the number of errors that will be made with that syllable. While the actual number of errors will be a function of the unit processing time, the percentage that this number represents of the expected total errors is independent of the unit processing time.

The numerical estimates given in the text tables were obtained as follows: By the postulates, the syllables will be learned in an orderly sequence, each syllable requiring a certain processing time, say k. Each syllable can be identified by its serial order, i, in the list as presented by the experimenter, and also by the order, r, in which it is learned by the subject. Since learning takes place from both ends of the list, these two orders will not, in general, be identical. Thus, s_i, the ith syllable in order of presentation, may be the same syllable as s'_r, the rth syllable in order of learning. (Technically, the list of syllables in order of learning is a permutation of the original list.) Let T'_r be the time that elapses before the first successful response to syllable s'_r—that is, until the rth syllable is learned. Then $T'_r = kr$. The number of errors, W'_r, the subject will make on the rth

syllable is equal to the number of learning trials prior to the trial on which that syllable is learned and will be proportional to r:

$$W'_r = mr \qquad (1)$$

where m is a proportionality constant, equal to k divided by the time per trial.

The numerical value of m is a function, of course, of the difficulty of the items and the rate of presentation. However, we are only concerned with the fraction of total errors made on a given syllable, and this fraction is clearly independent of m. For let W be the total number of errors, summed over all syllables, and $w'_r = W'_r/W$, the fraction of total errors made on the rth syllable.

$$w'_r = mr \left/ \sum_{r=1}^{n} mr = r \right/ \sum_{r=1}^{n} r = \frac{2r}{n(n+1)} \quad (2)$$

where n is the number of syllables in the list. Suppose, for example, that we are dealing with a list of twelve syllables, then $\sum_{r=1}^{12} r = 78$. Hence, the fraction of total errors that will be made on the fourth syllable learned will be $4/78 = 0.051$.

Now, to obtain the serial position curve, we need merely to relabel the syllables from the order in which they are learned to their order of presentation. That is, if r_i is the rank, in order of learning, of the ith syllable in order of presentation, then the fraction of total errors for the ith syllable will be simply:

$$w_i = w'_{r_i} = r_i / \sum_r r_i \qquad (3)$$

To apply this result, we must calculate the rank, r_i, of the ith syllable in order of presentation, as determined by postulate 4a. We assume (postulate 3) that the immediate memory capacity is two syllables and, for simplicity in the calculation, will assume that the items are picked up pairwise in the processing sequence, and stored in the immediate memory for learning. The first two syllables in the list will be learned first (will have rank, $r = 1$ and $r = 2$, respectively), followed either by the last two syllables on the list, or by syllables three and four, each with probability one-half. The result is that in a list of 12 syllables the third syllable, for example, will have a probability of one-half of being the third syllable in order of learning, a probability of one-quarter of being the fifth syllable, a probability of one-eighth of being the seventh, and of one-sixteenth of being ninth or eleventh. Averaging these ranks, weighted by their respective probabilities, we find that the average rank of the third is

$r_3 = 4.875$. The fraction of total errors on the third syllable will then be $w_3 = 4.875/78 = 0.063$ (see table 2). All the other predicted values in the tables were computed in the same way.

The fact that the third syllable has zero probability of being learned fourth, sixth, eighth, etc., is artificially introduced by the calculation simplification introduced above of handling the syllables in pairs. It does not materially affect the serial position curve prediction, as is shown by the fact that the computer simulation (which does not use the pairwise learning simplification) generated the same serial position curve prediction.

References

Atkinson, R. C. (1957). A stochastic model for rote serial learning. *Psychometrika*. **22**, 87–95.

Bruner, J. S., Goodnow, J. J. & Austin, G. A. (1956). *A Study of Thinking*. New York: Wiley.

Estes, W. K., Hopkins, B. L. & Crothers, E. J. (1960). All-or-none and conservation effects in the learning and retention of paired associates. *J. Exp. Psychol.* **6**, 329–39.

Feigenbaum, E. A. (1959). *An Information Processing Theory of Verbal Learning*. The RAND Corporation, Paper P-1817.

Feldman, J. (1959). Analysis of predictive behavior in a two choice situation. Unpublished doctoral dissertation, Carnegie Institute of Technology.

Gibson, E. J. (1940). A systematic application of the concepts of generalization and differentiation to verbal learning. *Psychol. Rev.* **47**, 196–229.

Hilgard, E. R. (1956). *Theories of Learning* (2nd ed.). New York: Appleton-Century-Crofts.

Hovland, C. I. (1938). Experimental studies in rote learning theory. III. Distribution of practice with varying speeds of syllable presentation. *J. Exp. Psychol.* **23**, 172–90.

Hovland, C. I. (1951). Human learning and retention. In S. S. Stevens (ed.), *Handbook of Experimental Psychology*. New York: Wiley, pp. 613–89.

Hovland, C. I. & Hunt, E. B. (1960). The computer simulation of concept attainment. *Behavioral Science*, **5**, 265–67.

Hull, C. L. et al. (1940). *Mathematico-deductive Theory of Rote Learning*, New Haven: Yale University Press.

Jensen, A. R. (1962). Is the serial position curve invariant? *Brit. J. Psychol.* **53**, 159–66.

Krueger, W. C. F. (1932). Learning during directed attention. *J. Exp. Psychol.* **15**, 517–27.

McCrary, J. W. & Hunter, W. S. (1953). Serial position curves in verbal learning. *Science*, **117**, 131–34.

McGeoch, J. A. (1942). *The Psychology of Human Learning*. New York: Longmans, Green.

Miller, G. A. (1956). The magical number seven, plus or minus two: Some limits on our capacity for processing information. *Psychol. Rev.* **63**, 81–97.

Newell, A., Shaw, J. C. & Simon, H. A. (1958a). The elements of a theory of human problem solving. *Psychol. Rev.* **65**, 151–66.

Newell, A., Shaw, J. C. & Simon, H. A. (1958b). *The Processes of Creative Thinking*. The RAND Corporation Paper P-1320. Revised version published in H. E. Gruber, G. Terrell, & M. Wertheimer (eds.), *Contemporary Approaches to Creative Thinking*. New York: Atherton Press, 1962, pp. 63–119, and reprinted as chapter 4.1 in this book.

Newell, A. & Simon, H. A. (1961). Computer simulation of human thinking. *Science*, **134**, 2011–17.

Ribback, A. & Underwood, B. V. (1950). An empirical explanation of the skewness of the bowed serial position curve. *J. Exp. Psychol.* **40**, 329–35.

Rock, I. (1957). The role of repetition in associative learning. *Amer. J. Psychol.* **70**, 186–93.

Welch, G. B. & Burnett, C. T. (1924). Is primacy a factor in association-formation? *Amer. J. Psychol.* **35**, 396–401.

Wilcoxon, H. C., Wilson, W. R. & Wise, D. A. (1961). Paired-associate learning as a function of percentage of occurrence of response members and other factors. *J. Exp. Psychol.* **61**, 283–89.

Wishner, J., Shipley, T. E., Jr. & Jurvich, M. S. (1957). The serial position curve as a function of organization. *Amer. J. Psychol.* **70**, 258–62.

Woodworth, R. S. (1938). *Experimental Psychology*. New York: Holt.

3.2

Effects of Similarity, Familiarization, and Meaningfulness in Verbal Learning (1964)

with Edward A. Feigenbaum

Among the most commonly used paradigms in the study of verbal learning is the learning of nonsense syllables by the paired associate or serial anticipation methods. The variables that have been shown to have important effects on the rate of learning include the levels of familiarity and meaningfulness of the syllables, the amount of similarity among them, and the rate of presentation. In addition, in the learning of lists, there are well-known serial position effects.

In previous papers (Feigenbaum, 1959, 1961; Feigenbaum and Simon, 1962*b*), a theory has been set forth that undertakes to explain the performance and learning processes underlying the behaviour of *S*s in verbal learning experiments. The theory, in its original version, makes correct quantitative predictions of the shape of the serial position curve (Feigenbaum and Simon, 1962*a*) and the effect of rate of presentation on learning (Feigenbaum, 1959; Feigenbaum and Simon, 1962*a*) as well as predic-

tions of certain qualitative phenomena (for example, oscillation) (Feigenbaum and Simon, 1961).

In this chapter, a simplified and improved version of the theory is reported that retains these properties of the earlier theory while providing correct quantitative predictions of the effects of the other important variables: familiarization, meaningfulness, and similarity. The tests of the theory discussed here are based on comparisons of the performance of human *S*s, as reported in published experiments on paired associate learning (Bruce, 1933; Chenzoff, 1962; Underwood, 1953; Underwood and Schulz, 1960), with the performance predicted by the theory in the same experimental situations with the same, or equivalent, stimulus material.

The theory to be described is a theory of the information processes underlying verbal learning. The precise statement of such a theory is most readily made in the information processing language of a digital computer, i.e., the language of computer programs.

The formal and rigorous statement of the theory is a program called the Elementary Perceiver and Memorizer (third version),

This research has been supported by the Carnegie Corporation of New York and The RAND Corporation (Computer Science Department).

or EPAM-III. This program is a closed model and is used as an "artificial subject" in standard verbal learning experiments (the latter being also simulated within the computer by means of an Experimenter program). Imbedded in the theory are hypotheses about the several kinds of processes that are involved in the performance of verbal learning tasks. These hypotheses take the form of subroutines that are component parts of the total program. Thus, there are performance subroutines which allow the program to produce responses that have previously been associated with stimuli, subroutines for learning to discriminate among different stimuli, and subroutines for acquiring familiarity with stimuli. Top-level executive routines, which organize these subroutines into a program, represent hypotheses about the *S*'s understanding of the experimental instructions and the learning strategy he employs. The computer simulation of verbal learning behavior using the EPAM-III theory is, in essence, generation (by the computer) of the remote consequences of the information processing hypotheses of the theory in particular experimental situations.

In the first part of the chapter, a brief description of EPAM-III is provided. Since other descriptions of the program are available in the literature (Feigenbaum, 1959, 1961; Feigenbaum and Simon, 1962*b*), only so much of the detail will be presented as is essential to an understanding of the experiments and the interpretation of their results. In the second part of the chapter, the results will be reported of comparisons of the behavior of EPAM-III with the behavior of human *S*s in paired associate learning where similarity is the independent variable. In the third part of the chapter, the results will be reported of comparisons in which familiarization and meaningfulness are the independent variables.

A BRIEF DESCRIPTION OF EPAM-III

The computer language in which EPAM-III is written is known as IPL-V (Newell,

Tonge, Feigenbaum, Green, and Mealy, 1964). A companion program simulates an experimental setting, more specifically, a memory drum capable of exposing stimulus materials to EPAM, in either the serial or paired associate paradigm. The simulated drum rotation rate can be altered as desired, as can the stimulus materials. An interrupt system is provided so that the simulated experimental environment and the simulated *S* can behave simultaneously, to all effects and purposes, and can interact, the *S* having access to the stimulus material presented in the memory drum window.

The Performance System

EPAM-III incorporates one major performance system and two learning processes (Feigenbaum, 1959, 1961; Feigenbaum and Simon, 1962*b*). When a stimulus (a symbol structure) is presented, EPAM seeks to recognize it by sorting it through a *discrimination net*. At each node of the net, some characteristic of the stimulus is noticed, and the branch corresponding to that characteristic is followed to the next node. With each terminal node of the net is associated an *image* that can be compared with any stimulus sorted to that node. If the two are similar, in the characteristics used for comparisons, the stimulus has been successfully recognized. We call such a stimulus *familiar*, i.e., it has a recognizable image in the discrimination-net memory.

An image is the internal informational representation of an external stimulus configuration that the learner has stored in memory. An image, thus, is comprised of the information the learner knows about, and has associated with, a particular stimulus configuration. An image may be elementary or compound. A compound image has, as components, one or more elementary or compound images which may themselves be familiar and which may possess their own terminal nodes in the discrimination net. For simplicity, in the current representation, letters of the Roman alphabet are treated as elementary stimuli whose characteristics may be noticed but which are not decomposable into more elementary familiar stimuli. On the other hand, syllables are compound stimuli, their components being, of course, letters.

A compound stimulus image, viewed from the bottom up, may be regarded as an association among the component stimuli. Thus, the net may contain stimulus images that represent pairs of syllables, these compound images having as components other compound images, the individual syllables.

In performing the paired associate task, the program uses the stimulus, present in the window of the memory drum, to construct a compound symbol representing the pair comprised of the stimulus and its associated responses. We may designate this compound symbol by $S-$ —, for the second response member is not then visible in the drum window. The compound symbol, $S-$ —, is sorted through the net, and the image associated with the terminal is retrieved. We will designate this image by $S'-R'$, for if the previous learning has been successful, it will be comprised of two components: an image of the stimulus syllable and an image of the associated response syllable. The response image, R', which has just been retrieved as the second component of the compound image, $S'-R'$, identifies a net node where an image, say R'', is stored. R'' will have as its components symbols designating the constituent letters of the syllable, say X'', Y'', and Z''. Each of these, in turn, identifies a terminal node. Associated with the terminal for a letter is not only an image of the usual kind (an afferent image) but also the information required to produce the letter in question, i.e., to print it. This information, which we may call the efferent image, is used to produce the response. Thus, the final step in the sequence is for the program to respond, say, XYZ.

It is a fundamental characteristic of this program that elementary symbols and compound symbols of all levels are stored in the discrimination net in exactly the same way. Thus, a syllable is simply a list of letters, and an $S-R$ is simply a list of syllables. A single interpretive process suffices to sort a letter, a syllable, an $S-R$

pair, or any other symbol, elementary or compound. Moreover, the symbols discriminated by the net are not restricted to any specific sensory or effector mode. All modes can be accommodated by a single net and a single interpretive process. Afferent symbols belonging to different sensory modes will possess different attributes: phonemes will have attributes like "voicing," "tongue position," and so on; printed letters will have attributes like "possession of closed loop," "possession of diagonal line," and so on. Because they possess entirely different attributes, they will be sorted to different parts of the net. Finally, symbols may be of mixed mode. In a symbol, $S-R$, for example, S may be in the visual mode, R in the oral.

The Learning System

EPAM-III uses just two learning processes, one to construct and elaborate images at terminal nodes of the net (*image building*),[1] and another to elaborate the net by adding new branches (*discrimination learning*). The first learning process also serves to guide the second.

When a stimulus S is in view and is sorted to a terminal, the stimulus can be compared with the image S' stored at the terminal. If there is no image at the terminal, the image-building process copies a part of S and stores the copy S' as the initial image at the terminal. If there is already an image, S' at the terminal, one or more differences between S and S' are detected, and S' is corrected or augmented to agree more closely with S.

When a positive difference (not a mere lack of detail) is detected between a stimulus S and its image S', the discrimination learning process can use this difference to construct a new test that will discriminate between S and S'. The terminal node with which S' was associated is then

---

1. We use the term "image building" rather than the less clumsy and more descriptive term "familiarization" to resolve a dilemma of nomenclature that will become obvious in a later section.

changed to a branch node, the test associated with the node S', is associated with a new terminal on one of the branches, and a new image of S is associated with a new terminal on another branch. Thus the discrimination learning process adds a new pair of branches to the discrimination net and attaches initial images to the branches.

Note that a stimulus S can be sorted to a terminal T only if S satisfies all the tests that point to the branches leading to T. But the image S' stored at T must also satisfy these tests. Hence, there can be a positive difference between S' and S only if S' contains more information than is necessary to sort S to T. For instance, let S be the syllable KAW, and suppose that all the tests leading to the terminal T happen to be tests on the first letter, K. Then the image S' stored at T must have K as its first symbol, but, it may differ from KAW in other characteristics. It might be, for example, the incomplete syllable K-B. The discrimination learning process could detect the difference between the W and the B in the final letters of the respective syllables, construct a test for this difference, and append the test to a new net node. The redundancy of information in the image, in this case the letter B, permits the further elaboration of the net.

Thus, learning in EPAM-III involves cycles of the two learning processes. Through image building, the stimulus image is elaborated until it contains more information than the minimum required to sort to its terminal. Through discrimination, this information is used to distinguish between new stimuli and the stimulus that generated this terminal and grew its image. On the basis of such distinctions, the net is elaborated. The interaction of these two processes is fundamental to the whole working of EPAM. It is not easy to conjure up alternative schemes that will permit learning to proceed when the members of a pair of stimuli to be discriminated are not present simultaneously.

The stimuli that EPAM-III can make familiar and learn to discriminate are symbols of any kind, elementary or compound. Thus the letters of the alphabet can be first made familiar, and the net elaborated to discriminate among them. Then EPAM can make familiar and learn to discriminate among syllables, using the now familiar letters as unitary building blocks. But now, paired associate learning can take place without the introduction of any additional mechanisms. Instead of postulating a new associational process, we suppose that an S-R pair is associated simply by making familiar and learning to discriminate the compound object SR.

The entire EPAM-III paired associate learning scheme is completed by an executive routine that determines under what circumstances the several image-building and discrimination learning processes will be activated. The executive routine makes use of a kind of knowledge of results. When the simulated S detects that he has made an incorrect response to a stimulus syllable, he engages in a rudimentary diagnostic activity: distinguishing between no response and a wrong response and determining to what extent the response syllable, the stimulus syllable, and the S-R pair are familiar. Depending on the outcome of the diagnosis, various image-building and discrimination learning processes are initiated.

There are many details of the EPAM-III program we have not described here, but this general sketch will give us a sufficient basis for discussing the behavior of the program in standard paired associate learning situations.

EFFECTS OF INTRALIST AND INTERLIST SIMILARITY

The adequacy of EPAM-III as a theory of human rote verbal learning has been tested initially by replicating, with the program, experiments of Underwood (1953) on intralist similarity; of Bruce (1933) on interlist similarity; and a number of authors (Underwood and Schulz, 1960) on stimulus and response familiarization and meaningfulness. In this section, the experiments employing similarity as the independent variable will be discussed; in the next section, the experiments on familiarization and meaningfulness will be considered.

Table 1. Comparison of EPAM with Underwood's (1953) Data on Intralist Similarity
(Relative Number of Trials to Criterion, $LL = 100$).

	Condition of Stimulus and Response Similarity				
Data	L-L	L-M	M-L	L-H	H-L
Underwood	100	96	109	104	131
EPAM-III ("visual only")	100	88	141	91	146
EPAM-III ("aural only")	100	100	100	100	114
EPAM-III ("visual" and "aural" mixed, 1 : 1)	100	94	121	96	130
EPAM-III ("visual" and "aural" mixed, 1 : 2)	100	96	114	97	125

Underwood (1953) studied paired associate learning of nonsense syllables under various conditions of intralist similarity of stimulus syllables and response syllables. If we use L, M, and H to designate low, medium, and high intralist similarity, respectively; and let, e.g., *L-M* stand for "low intralist similarity of stimuli, medium intralist similarity of responses," then Underwood's five experimental conditions are *L-L, M-L, H-L, L-M*, and *L-H*. Underwood also studied three different conditions of distribution of practice, but since he found no significant differences in his data, we will not consider this variable further.

In summary, Underwood found (1) that intralist similarity of *responses* had virtually no effect on ease or difficulty of learning;[2] (2) that trials required for learning increased with degree of intralist similarity of *stimuli*, the difference being about 30 percent between the *LL* and *HL* conditions. The first row in table 1 summarizes Underwood's findings averaged over the three conditions of distribution of practice. The numbers are relative numbers of trials to criterion, with the number for the *LL* condition taken as 100.

The syllables employed in the EPAM simulation were the same as those used by Underwood.[3] Row 2 in table 1 summarizes the data from the EPAM tests. Response similarity facilitated learning very slightly, while stimulus similarity impeded learning by as much as 40 percent. Since relative learning times are reported in both cases, there is one free parameter available for matching the two series. (In the normal course of events, the compound images S'-R' are discriminated from each other on the basis of stimulus information, not response information. High intralist stimulus similarity makes difficulties for EPAM in discriminating and retrieving these images, and hence impedes learning. Response similarity, of course, has no such effect.)

The qualitative fit of the EPAM predictions to the Underwood data is better than the quantitative fit, although, considering the (a priori) plausible range of impact of the similarity variable on difficulty of learning, even the quantitative fit is not bad. Nevertheless, we sought a much better quantitative prediction. This search led us into the following considerations. The prediction that is seriously out of line in table 1 is the prediction for the *M-L* condition. The more carefully one scrutinizes the Underwood experiment and the Underwood materials, the more puzzling the

---

2. In the Underwood experiment, the effect of response similarity is inconsequential. In general, the evidence on the impeding or facilitating effects of response similarity is mixed. What does stand out, however, is this: The effects of response similarity, if any, are quantitatively small and insignificant when compared with the large effects of stimulus similarity.

---

3. We are indebted to Underwood for making these sets of syllables available to us.

experimental results become. Why do *S*s, as the results indicate, respond in the *M-L* condition so similarly to the way they respond in the *L-L* condition, while their responses in the *H-L* condition are so different from responses in either the *M-L* or *L-L* conditions? The answer is not to be found in the Underwood materials. We have analyzed the Underwood definition of "medium similarity" in terms of the information necessary to discriminate the items on a list of a given length (in EPAM-like fashion) and have found that Underwood's definition is quite careful and correct. By his definition, one should expect "medium similarity" lists to be midway in effect between his "low similarity" and his "high similarity" lists.

The answer, we believe, lies in the recoding, or "chunking," behavior of *S*s, which would make the "medium similarity" stimulus list formally identical with the "low similarity" stimulus list under Underwood's definition. Suppose that many *S*s were pronouncing the Underwood CVCs, i.e., recoding the items into the aural mode, instead of dealing with them directly in the visual-literal (presentation) mode. The recoded ("aural") syllables will be "chunked" into two parts: a consonant-vowel pair, and a consonant. In other words, the visual-literal stimulus objects of three parts (CVC) quite naturally recode into "aural" stimulus objects of two parts (C'C or CC''). In Underwood's "medium similarity" lists, none of the C' chunks are duplicated, nor any of the C'' chunks. The recoding, therefore, has transformed the "medium similarity" list into a "low similarity" list, by Underwood's definition.

To test this hypothesis for sufficiency from the point of view of the theory, we reran the EPAM (simulated) experiments using "aural" recodings of the original syllables. The modified predictions are given in row 3 of table 1. As the analysis above indicates, the *M-L* condition is now no different from the *L-L* condition, but the prediction of difficulty for the *H-L* condition is too low. Assuming that some *S*s are processing in the visual-literal mode and some in the "aural" mode, we have computed the average ($1:1$) of the two sets of EPAM predictions. This is given in row 4 of table 1. If we weight the average $2:1$ in favor of *S*s doing "aural" recoding, the result is as given in row 5 of table 1. Each of these averaging procedures gives a prediction which is much better than that for the Underwood lists nonrecoded.

It is clear that we still have much to learn about this low versus medium similarity problem. In this regard, we are currently attempting a direct experimental test of the "aural" recoding hypothesis.

Bruce's *S*s (1933) learned two successive lists of paired associate nonsense syllables. On the second list, response syllables, or stimulus syllables, or neither, could be the same as the corresponding syllables on the first list. Thus, using current designations, Bruce's three conditions were (A-B, C-D), (A-B, A-C), and (A-B, C-B), respectively. In summary, he found that learning of the second list was somewhat easier than learning of the first when all syllables were different (A-B, C-D), much easier when the response syllables were the same (A-B, C-B), and a little harder when the stimulus syllables were the same (A-B, A-C) (see table 2). The relative difficulties are compared using the A-B, C-D group as the norm.

Nonsense syllable lists of low Glaze value and low intralist similarity were used when the experiment was replicated with EPAM.

Table 2. Comparison of EPAM with Bruce's Data on Interlist Similarity
(Relative Number of Trials to Criterion).

	Condition of Stimulus and Response Similarity		
	A-B, A-C	*A-B, C-B*	*A-B, C-D*
A-B, C-D condition = 100	130	75	100
EPAM-III A-B, C-D condition = 100	112	75	100

The normalized results are shown in the second line of table 2. The effects in the simulated experiment were qualitatively the same as in the actual data. If we compare the conditions A-B, A-C and A-B, C-B with A-B, C-D, we find that identity of stimulus syllables impeded learning less, and identity of response syllables facilitated learning to the same degree in the simulation as for the human Ss. The ratio of difficulty for the A-B, A-C compared with the A-B, C-B conditions, where total number of different syllables discriminated and learned was the same, was 1.73 for the human Ss and 1.49 for EPAM.

From our analysis of the data of the Underwood and Bruce experiments, we conclude that EPAM provides satisfactory explanations for the main observed effects of intralist and interlist stimulus and response similarity upon the learning of paired associate nonsense syllables. The effects predicted by EPAM-III are in the right direction and are of the right order of magnitude, although there is room for improvement in the quantiative agreement.

FAMILIARITY AND MEANINGFULNESS

Among the other independent variables that have been shown to have major significance for the ease or difficulty of learning nonsense syllables are familiarity and meaningfulness. A thorough discussion of the definition of these two variables can be found in Underwood and Schulz (1960).

The degree of familiarity of a syllable is usually not measured directly; instead, it is measured by the amount of *Familiarization training* to which S has been exposed with that syllable. In the following discussion, they are not synonymous. "Familiarization" will be used when reference is made to specific experimental conditions and operations. "Familiarity," on the other hand, will refer to a condition internal to an S: the state of information about a syllable in the memory of an S who has gone through some kind of familiarization training. Thus, familiarity is an intervening variable not directly observable. The use of an intervening variable hardly needs to be defended, since it is the rule rather than the exception in theory-building in the natural sciences as well as the behavioral sciences.

Familiarization training is accomplished by causing S to attend to the syllable in question in the context of some task other than the paired-associate learning task to be given him subsequently. It should be noted that there is no way of discovering, with this definition, how familiar a syllable may be for an S due to his experience prior to coming into the laboratory. Although the syllables are not meaningful words, the consonant-vowel combinations contained in them occur with varying frequency in English. The meaningfulness of a syllable, on the other hand, is generally determined by measuring the number of associations that Ss make to it in a specified period of time. Nonsense syllables for learning experiments are generally selected from available lists that have been graded in this way for meaningfulness.

Since high familiarity and high meaningfulness both facilitate nonsense-syllable learning, there has been much speculation that the two phenomena might be the "same thing." This, in fact, is the central hypothesis examined in the Underwood and Schulz monograph. In one sense, meaningfulness and familiarity are demonstrably not the same, for a substantial amount of familiarization training can be given with low-meaningful syllables without significantly increasing their meaningfulness. However, Underwood and Schulz (1960) adduce a large body of evidence to show that there is a strong relation running the other way i.e., that meaningfulness of words is correlated with their frequency of occurrence in English, and that ease of learning nonsense syllables is correlated with the frequency, in English, of the letters that compose them (for syllables of low pronunciability), or with their pronunciability.

The data are of course greatly complicated by the fact that Ss may handle the material in either the visual or the aural mode, and that most Ss probably encode into the latter, at least part of the time. Hence, for relatively easily pronounceable syllables, frequency of phoneme pairs in the aural encoding is a more relevant measure of frequency than frequency of the printed bigrams or trigrams. Thus, the finding by Underwood and Schulz that pronunciability is a better predictor than trigram frequency of ease of learning does not damage the hypothesis that familiarity of the component units is the critical variable, and that familiarity, in turn, is a function of previous exposure.

We conclude that high meaningfulness implies high familiarity, although not the converse.

If this is so, then the correlation of meaningfulness with ease of learning may be spurious. Familiarity may be the variable that determines ease of learning, and meaningful syllables may be easy to learn only because they are highly familiar.

The idea that familiarity is the critical variable in learning rests on the idea, certainly not new with the EPAM model, that there are two stages in paired associate learning: (1) integration of responses, and (2) association of responses with stimuli. Underwood and Schulz (1960) have used this idea, and it plays an important role in their analysis. It also plays an important role in the structure of EPAM (Feigenbaum, 1959, 1960). From our earlier description, it can be seen that these two stages of learning are also present in EPAM-III, but that both stages make use of the same pair of learning processes: image building and discrimination learning.

If response integration is the mechanism accounting for the relation between meaningfulness and familiarity, on the one hand, and ease of learning, on the other, then there should be a point of saturation beyond which additional familiarization will not further facilitate learning, i.e., the point at which the syllables are so familiar that they are completely integrated. In the EPAM-III mechanism, this would be the point where the syllable images were complete and where the tests in the net were fully adequate to discriminate among them.

There is strong empirical support for the hypothesis of saturation. At the high end of the meaningfulness scale, further increases in meaningfulness of syllables have relatively little effect on ease of learning, but the effects are large over the lower range of the scale. In fact, and this is the most striking evidence relevant to the issue, the experiments on meaningfulness in the literature reveal a remarkably consistent upper bound on the effect of that variable. Underwood and Schulz (1960) survey a large number of the experiments reported in the literature, of both paired associate and serial learning of CVC syllables, and find rather consistently that the ratio of

trials to criterion for the least and most meaningful conditions, respectively, lies in the neighborhood of 2.5. That is to say, syllables of very low meaningfulness take about two and one-half times as long to learn as syllables of very high meaningfulness (and about two and one-half times as many errors are made during learning).

Before the significance of this 2.5/1 ratio is considered further, it is necessary to discuss one difficulty with the hypothesis that familiarization and meaningfulness (via familiarity) facilitate learning primarily by virtue of responses being integrated prior to the associational trials. The effects reported in the literature with meaningfulness as the independent variable are generally much larger than the effects reported for familiarization. No one has produced anything like a 2.5/1 gain in learning speed by familiarization training.

There is now some evidence, primarily in a doctoral dissertation by Chenzoff (1962), that the main reason for this discrepancy is that the familiarization training in experiments has been too weak, has stopped too soon. It appears that no one has carried out familiarization training with his Ss to the point where the syllable integration achieved is comparable to the integration of syllables of high meaningfulness.

Chenzoff's experiment can be summed up as follows. First, in his experiment he manipulated both meaningfulness and familiarization of both stimuli and responses. Thus, he had 16 conditions: all possible combinations of *H-H*, *L-H*, *H-L*, and *L-L* for stimulus and response meaningfulness[4] with *F-F*, *U-F*, *F-U*, and *U-U* for familiarity. Second, he employed a more thorough familiarization training technique for the *F* condition than had any previous investigator. The syllables were presented one at a time to *S* at about a 2.5-sec rate. The *S* was required to pronounce each syllable. After five trials, *S* was asked to recall the syllables in any order. If an incorrect syllable was given, *S* was told that it was not a member of the list. If, within 30 sec, *S* could not perform completely correctly, five more familiarization trials were adminis-

---

4. The two levels of the meaningfulness variable were constructed as follows (using CVC's):

H: 53–100 Glaze, 85–100 Krueger, 67–97 Archer, 2.89–3.66 Noble (*m'*), 3.08–3.87 Noble (*a'*).

L: 0–53 Glaze, 39–72 Krueger, 9–48 Archer, 0.92–1.83 Noble (*m'*), 1.38–1.94 Noble (*a'*).

Table 3. Effects of Familiarization and Meaningfulness.

Meaningfulness (or Familiarity)	Chenzoff's (1962) Data*				EPAM-III†	
	(1) High Meaning-fulness	(2) High Familiar-ization	(3) Low Meaning-fulness	(4) No Familiar-ization	(5) No Previous Familiar-ization	(6) Previous Familiar-ization
H-H or F-F	1.0	1.0	1.0	1.0	1.0	1.0
L-H or U-F	1.0	1.1	1.2	1.2	1.3	1.0
H-L or F-U	1.0	1.2	1.6	1.2	1.8	1.5
L-L or U-U	1.0	1.2	1.8	2.2	2.5	1.7

* Reciprocal of number of correct responses; H-H or F-F = 1.0.
† Relative number of errors to criterion; H-H or F-F = 1.0.

tered. This continued until S learned the list. The range of number of trials for the various Ss was 10–30; the median and mode were 15 trials.

With this training, the effects of familiarization were qualitatively similar to, and more than half as large in magnitude as, the effects of meaningfulness. Specifically:

1. For the H-H (high meaningfulness) conditions, amount of familiarization of stimuli, responses, or both had no effect on ease of learning; the saturation was complete [table 3, column 1].

2. For the L-L (low meaningfulness) conditions, unfamiliarized syllables (U-U) took 1.8 times as long to learn[5] as familiarized syllables (F-F). Response familiarization (U-F) had a greater effect than stimulus familiarization (F-U); the ratios were 1.2 and 1.6, respectively [table 3, column 3].

3. When familiarization training was provided, the effects of meaningfulness upon ease of learning were reduced by about two thirds. In the F-F conditions, the L-L pairs took only 1.2 times as long to learn as the H-H pairs, the L-H and H-L pairs falling between the two extremes. Saturation was not quite complete but was clearly visible [table 3, column 2].

4. In the absence of familiarization training, the usual large effects of meaningfulness were visible. In the U-U conditions, the L-L pairs took 2.2 times as long to learn as the H-H pairs [table 3, column 4].

5. Because of the form in which Chenzoff presented his data, the actual measure of speed of learning used here is the reciprocal of the number of correct responses between particular (fixed) trial boundaries, relative to the (H-H, F-F) condition taken as a norm of 1.0 (see table 3).

Thus, except for the quantitative deficiency in the effect of familiarization, Chenzoff shows meaningfulness and familiarity to be equivalent. But they are not additive because of the saturation effect.

Further and very strong evidence for the syllable integration hypothesis is obtainable from the predictions of EPAM-III. By presenting syllables with appropriate instructions, EPAM can attain familiarity with stimulus syllables, response syllables, or both. Amount of familiarity can be manipulated by varying the number of familiarization trials. In particular, familiarity can be carried to saturation— to the point where complete syllable images are stored in the discrimination net. The maximum effects predicted by EPAM-III for familiarization are of the same magnitude as the maximum effects of meaningfulness observed in the empirical studies.

Table 3 shows, for the four conditions, and taking the L-L conditions as the norm, the relative rates of learning as predicted by EPAM-III [column 5], and as reported by Chenzoff's Ss [column 4]. Except for the rather high value for the H-L condition for Chenzoff's Ss, which is in disagreement with the other experiments in the literature on this point, the quantitative agreement with the EPAM-III predictions is remarkably close. In particular, EPAM predicts the 2.5 maximum ratio that has been so often observed. Since syllable integration is the mechanism that EPAM employs to achieve this result, this implication of the theory provides support for the hypothesis that syllable integration is the mediating mechanism in producing the effect of meaningfulness (and familiarization) upon ease of learning.

DEGREE OF FAMILIARIZATION

If the present interpretation of the mechanism of familiarity is correct, then the effects of a given amount of familiarization training will depend, in a sensitive way, upon how familiar the syllables were at the beginning of training. There is no way of knowing this exactly, although it is reasonable to assume that nonsense syllables of low association value are close to the zero level of familiarity. (See, however, the findings of Underwood and Schulz on differential pronunciability of such syllables.)

To examine the effects of varying amounts of familiarization training upon the ease or difficulty of paired associate learning, EPAM was tested with various combinations of zero to five trials of stimulus- and response-syllable familiarization. The results are shown in table 4 in terms of number of errors to criterion.

Table 4. Effects of Stimulus and Response Familiarization (Number of Errors to Criterion in Paired Associate Learning).

Response Familiarization (Trials)	Stimulus Familiarization (Trials)			
	0	1	2	3
0	52	44	38	38
1	48	35	32	32
2	39	24	24	24
3	27	21	21	21

Under the conditions employed in these experiments, the maximum possible effects of familiarization were obtained with a combination of three trials of response familiarization and one trial of stimulus familiarization; additional familiarization did not facilitate learning. The asymptote, 21 errors, for this amount of familiarization was not attainable with any amount of response familiarization in the absence of

stimulus familiarization, or with any amount of stimulus familiarization without response familiarization. The asymptotes in the latter two cases were 27 errors and 38 errors, respectively, and were reached with three trials and two trials, respectively, of familiarization.

The detail of table 4 shows some exceedingly complicated relations. For example, if syllables have received no prior familiarization, one trial of stimulus familiarization reduces errors more than one trial of response familiarization (reductions of eight and four errors, respectively) from 52 in the no-familiarization case. On the other hand, for syllables that had already received one trial of stimulus and response familiarization, an additional trial of stimulus familiarization reduced errors only by three, while an additional trial of response familiarization reduced errors by 11, from a level of 35. Other similar results may be read from table 4. Many of the numerous small anomalies in the literature on familiarization training may be attributable to the lack of control over the amount of prior familiarity that *S*s had with the syllables used in the experiments.

In table 3, column 6, we show the predicted effect, estimated from the EPAM data of table 4, of familiarization training with syllables that were already somewhat familiar before the experiment began (i.e., that had previously received one simulated trial each of stimulus and response familiarization). Under the *F-F* condition, we would have 21 errors to criterion; under the *U-F* condition (one stimulus familiarization trial, three response trials), 21; under the *F-U* condition (three and one stimulus and response familiarization trials, respectively), 32; and under the *U-U* condition (one *S* and one *R* familiarization trial), 35. The resulting indexes of relative difficulty for the four conditions are 1.0, 1.0, 1.5, and 1.7, respectively, as shown in column 6. These may be compared with the values 1.0, 1.2, 1.6, 1.8, for the actual data in column 3. In other words, the fact that the effects shown in column 3, and even in column 4, are somewhat smaller than the predictions in column 5 may be due simply to the fact that the syllables were already slightly familiar to the Ss at the beginning of the experiment.

CONCLUSION

In this chapter we have compared the predictions of EPAM-III, a theory of human verbal learning, with data from the experiments of Bruce, Chenzoff, Underwood, and others, on the effects of intralist and interlist similarity, of familiarization, and of meaningfulness upon difficulty of learning. We find that there is good quantitative, as well as qualitative, agreement between the published data and the predictions of the theory. Finally, we have used our findings to discuss the relation between familiarity and meaningfulness, and have shown that most of the known facts can be explained by supposing that a symbolic structure necessarily becomes familiar in the process of becoming meaningful, but that the converse is not necessarily the case.

References

Bruce, R. W. Conditions of transfer of training. *J. exp. Psychol.*, 1933, **16**, 343–61.

Chenzoff, A. P. The interaction of meaningfulness with S and R familiarization in paired associate learning. Unpublished doctoral dissertation, Carnegie Institute of Technology, 1962.

Feigenbaum, E. A. *An information processing theory of verbal learning.* Report P-1817. Santa Monica, Calif.: The RAND Corporation, 1959.

Feigenbaum, E. A. The simulation of verbal learning behavior. *Proceedings of the 1961 Western Joint Computer Conference*, 1961, **19**, 121–32. Reprinted in E. A. Feigenbaum and J. Feldman, *Computers and thought.* New York: McGraw-Hill, 1963, pp. 297–309.

Feigenbaum, E. A., and Simon, H. A. Forgetting in an association memory. *Reprints of the 1961 National Conference of the Association for Computing Machinery*, 1961, **16**, 2C2-2C5.

Feigenbaum, E. A., and Simon, H. A. A theory of the serial position effect. *Brit. J. Psychol.*, 1962, **53**, 307–20. (a). Reprinted as chapter 3.1 in this book.

Feigenbaum, E. A., and Simon, H. A. Generalization of an elementary perceiving and memorizing machine. *Information processing 1962, Proceedings of IFIP Congress 62.* Amsterdam: North-Holland Publishing Co., 1962, 401–06. (b)

Newell, A., Tonge, F. M., Feigenbaum, E. A., Green, B. F., Jr., and Mealy, G. H. *Information processing language V manual.* (2nd ed.) Englewood Cliffs N.J.: Prentice-Hall, 1964.

Underwood, B. J. Studies of distributed practice: VIII. Learning and retention of paired nonsense syllables as a function of intralist similarity. *J. exp. Psychol.*, 1953, **45**, 133–42.

Underwood, B. J., and Schulz, R. W. *Meaningfulness and verbal learning.* Philadelphia: Lippincott, 1960.

3·3

One-trial and Incremental Learning (1967)

with Lee W. Gregg

Determining to what extent rote verbal learning is incremental, and to what extent it takes place in a single trial has been a central problem of learning theory during the past decade. In the light of the accumulated experimental evidence, the answer to "Is rote learning incremental?" can only be "Sometimes." The problem, as Atkinson, Bower, and Crothers (1965, p. 118) observe, is to define the "sometimes." "At present writing," they say, "a challenging task confronting the theorist is (1) to identify those experimental conditions where the one-element (i.e., all-or-none) model works, and those where it does not, and (2) to construct a more general model which essentially reduces to the one-element model in the former cases but accounts for the discrepancies in the latter cases."

It is the aim of this chapter to show that an information processing theory, EPAM (Elementary Perceiver and Memorizer), makes quantitative predictions about one-trial learning and departures from it that are consistent with the main body of empirical evidence. The first version of EPAM was constructed by Feigenbaum and Simon, as an explanation of the serial position effect in serial rote verbal learning, and without awareness of Rock's first experiments on one-trial learning and hence without intent to explain them.[1] EPAM was later generalized to account for a range of phenomena in serial and paired-associate learning, including some of the main effects of meaningfulness, familiarity, and similarity upon rate of learning.

POSTULATES

The mechanisms that appear relevant to the problem of one-trial learning are common to all three versions of EPAM that have been tested thus far. These mech-

This investigation was supported by public Health Service Research grant MH-07722 from the National Institute of Mental Health. The authors are greatly indebted to Edward A. Feigenbaum, with whom they have had numerous discussions of the implications of the EPAM theory for one-trial learning. They are grateful also to Andrew P. Chenzoff and Kenneth R. Laughery, who participated in conducting the experiment, and whose data are reanalyzed here.

1. The earliest public description of EPAM is in Edward A. Feigenbaum (1959). The predictions of EPAM for the serial position effect are developed more fully in chapter 3.1.

anisms are summed up in the following postulates (cf., Feigenbaum, 1959; Feigenbaum and Simon, 1962, pp. 310–11):

1. *Serial Mechanism.* The central processing mechanism operates serially; so that the total time required to memorize a set of noninteracting items is the sum of the times of the individual items.

2. *Chunks.* The basic units on which the system operates are *chunks*, i.e., the largest stimulus components that are familiar units, either by virtue of the system's previous history or familiarization procedures.

3. *Processing Time.* The fixation of an item requires a definite amount of processing time per chunk. (Empirically, the time for "normal college sophomores" appears to be about 10 seconds per chunk. cf. Bugelsky, 1962; Hovland, 1938.)

4. *Immediate Memory.* An immediate memory with a capacity of a few chunks is capable of storing information temporarily.

5. *Attention.* The central processing mechanism fixates any part of the stimulus material to which it attends (i.e., holds in immediate memory for the requisite length of time). The management of attention is modifiable by experimental instructions, attention-directing stimuli (e.g., anchor points), habit, and *S*'s strategies.

In previous publications, it has been shown that these postulates lead to correct quantitative predictions of the shape of the serial position curve (Feigenbaum and Simon, 1962) and predict correctly that CVC syllables of very low familiarity should take about three times as long to fixate as syllables of very high familiarity (Simon and Feigenbaum, 1964).

IMPLICATIONS OF THE POSTULATES

The central issues about one-trial learning have been reviewed by Underwood and Keppel (1962) and Postman (1963). They have pointed to chunk size (in our terminology), length of trial, and *S*'s strategy as variables likely to affect materially whether one-trial learning will or will not occur. Since these variables and others are incorporated in the structure of EPAM, we can consider whether EPAM will or will not predict correctly their effects on the possibility of one-trial learning. We will review these qualitative predictions briefly, then turn to a specific analysis of some experimental data where sharp quantitative predictions can be made and tested.

From the EPAM postulates, one-trial learning is more likely to occur with highly familiar responses than with unfamiliar responses, in agreement with the evidence reviewed by Postman (1963). Since in the EPAM model, the same processes account for both "response learning" and "associative learning," and the theory predicts from the nature of the stimulus material how much is required of each, the conclusion that one-trial learning is most compatible with familiar material does not require independent ad hoc assumptions.

Under the EPAM postulates, learning can take place in a single trial only if the material remains in short-term memory long enough to be fixated—about 10 seconds per chunk. The data of Peterson and Peterson (1959) suggest that counting backwards from a three-digit number may prevent even a single syllable from remaining very long in short-term memory. In general, a slow rate of presentation and the absence of distracting interpolated tasks are likely to be conducive to keeping a particular item in immediate memory long enough to fixate it completely. Hence, we would expect one-trial learning to occur more frequently under such circumstances than with a fast rate of presentation or when other tasks are interpolated. (The evidence is reviewed in Gregg et al., 1963; Postman, 1963; and Underwood and Keppel, 1962.)

Finally, even when the chunk and the time unit are specified, whether one-trial learning occurs will depend on how long the processor continues to work on any given item—how attention is directed. Brackett and Battig (1963) showed that the differences between groups learning under replacement and nonreplacement conditions disappeared when *S*s were instructed to learn one or a few pairs at a time.

In the next section, we show again, by reanalyzing the raw data to bring new evidence to bear on a previously published experiment of Gregg et al. (1963), how rates of learning under replacement and nonreplacement conditions depend on the management of attention. The new findings, based on a classification of Ss by attention strategies, not reported in the previous analysis, support the results of Brackett and Battig (1963) and resolve some puzzling anomalies in the data in the form in which they were first analyzed.

THE EXPERIMENT

Method and Results

Gregg et al. (1963) tested the generality of Rock's findings on one-trial learning, using his replacement method but more difficult tasks. Under all but one of the conditions (involving the easiest of their tasks) the experiments showed substantial differences in performance between the replacement and nonreplacement conditions, differences that are usually interpreted as antithetical to the one-trial hypothesis.

Their first experiment was carried out with 20 Ss in each of four conditions, formed from the possible combinations of Fast (F) and Slow (S) rates of presentation with replacement (R) or nonreplacement (N) of a new syllable after an erroneous response. We will designate the conditions FR, SR, FN and SN, respectively. The total times per trial in S and F conditions (including the intertrial interval) were 79 seconds and 55 seconds, respectively.

The total number of correct responses by the 20 Ss on the tenth test trial is shown in table 1, columns 1 and 2 for each of the four experimental conditions. In table 1, column 3 shows the total number of correct responses predicted for the same conditions, assuming (1) that amount of learning is simply proportional to time available for learning (postulate 3) and (2) that replacement causes no deficiency in learning. It requires no tests of significance to see from the tables that: (1) the relative amount of learning in the FN and SN conditions is consistent with postulate 3 (the second assumption is not involved in

Table 1. Actual and Predicted Performance: Simple-Learning Model.

	No. Correct Responses*		
	Actual		Simple-model prediction
Condition	R	N	
	(1)	(2)	(3)
Slow (79″ per trial)	57	146	151
Fast (55″ per trial)	59	110	105

*The entries in columns 1 and 2 are the total number of correct responses in the tenth trial of a paired-associates learning experiment (Gregg, Chenzoff, and Laughery, 1963). Presentation rate and Replacement (R) versus nonreplacement (N) of incorrect pairs were the independent variables, $N = 20$ for each cell. In column 3, numbers of correct responses are predicted on the assumption of equal learning rates per minute in the F and S conditions, the assumed rate being the average of the actual rates for the SN and FN conditions.

these conditions); (2) much less learning than predicted occurs in the R condition, when the N conditions are taken as the norm; and (3) the deficiency is much more severe in the S than in the F condition. In the SR condition, Ss learned only about 40 percent, and in the FR condition, only about 55 percent as much as would be predicted from the learning rate of the Ss in the N conditions. Can we account for the deficiency in learning under the replacement conditions, using the mechanisms postulated for EPAM?

In the R condition, any syllable pair not learned in a single trial is removed from the list. If a relatively fixed processing time is required to fixate each syllable (postulate 3), then S could fail to learn a pair in a single trial for any of several reasons, among them: (1) he may be interrupted or distracted by another task before a pair is learned; or (2) he may stop processing a pair because he thinks, erroneously, that it has been fixated. The extent of the former difficulty would depend on his attention strategy. The extent of the latter difficulty would depend on the feedback available to him about how well the pair was already learned, and his alacrity in turning to a new pair.

In the N conditions, the time required, on the average, to learn a pair is greater than the exposure time per syllable per trial. In fact, with 2-second presentation, Ss learned, on the average, about one-half syllable per *trial* (eight pair presentations), and with 4-second presentation, on the average, about two-thirds syllables per trial. This suggests that, unless an S attends to one or a few specific pairs on each trial, he is unlikely to learn any syllables at all under the R conditions.

Analysis of Learning Strategies

We now have direct evidence for this hypothesis from raw data gathered in the experiment but not presented or used in the analysis of the findings in the earlier publication. After the experiment, Ss in the R conditions were asked what strategies they used in learning. On the basis of their replies, they were classified into those who attempted to focus on one or two syllable pairs at a time (O Strategy), versus those who tried to learn many, or all, of the syllables on each trial (A Strategy). Of 15 Ss in the FR condition whose replies could be classified, 10 reported that they tried to learn one or two syllables on each trial, five that they tried to learn all or most. On the tenth trial, Ss in the O group made an average of 3.4 correct responses each; those in the A group made an average

of only 1.4 correct responses each. Of 16 Ss in the SR condition whose replies could be classified, only 4 replied that they tried to learn one or two at a time, 12 that they tried to learn all or most. On the tenth trial, Ss in the O group made an average of 5 correct responses each, those in the A group an average of only 2.4 correct responses each. (Two A Ss account for half these correct responses).

The data confirm our conjecture that Ss who adopted a One-at-a-time (O) strategy under R conditions learned much more rapidly than those who adopted an All-at-once (A) strategy. Under N conditions, as expected, there was no difference between learning rates of O and A Ss. The RA Ss, indeed, with two exceptions in the S condition, learned very little at all.

This result can be expressed quantitatively. Extrapolating from the O Ss to the entire group of 20 for each condition, we would predict 68 correct responses (3.4×20) on the tenth trial for the FR Ss, and 100 correct responses (5×20) for the SR Ss (table 2, column 2). These values are now two-thirds as large as would be predicted (105 and 151, respectively) from the responses of the corresponding N groups (table 2, column 5), and the relative learning rates of the F and S Ss are in the predicted ratio of nearly $55 : 79$.

Quantitative allowance can also be made for the second source of disadvantage of the R groups—that if they make an incorrect response on a pair previously re-

Table 2. Actual and Predicted Performance One-at-a-Time (O) Strategy.

No. Correct Responses*

Condition	Actual: R Condition (From Table 1, Col. 1)	Actual: "Efficient" Ss (O) Strategy	Same as Col. 2 with Backsliding Adjustment		Simple Model: N Condition (from Table 1, Col. 3)
			Conservative	Liberal	
	(1)	(2)	(3)	(4)	(5)
Slow	57	100	120	160	151
Fast	59	68	88	108	105

* The entries are the total number of correct responses on the tenth trial extrapolated to an N of 20 from reports of Ss of the R conditions who adopted the O strategy. There were 10 Ss in the FR and 5 Ss in the SR conditions.

sponded to correctly, the pair is replaced. For the entire experiment, in about one case in ten an incorrect response was made on a pair that had been responded to correctly on the previous trial (2189 correct responses on the first ten trials for all *S*s, with 199 instances of "backsliding"). The relative frequency of backsliding was about the same in *R* and *N* conditions (53 instances and 669 correct responses in the former, 146 instances and 1510 correct responses in the latter).

In the *N* conditions, backsliding was often followed by a "jump"—that is, more than one syllable pair learned on a subsequent trial. This seldom occurred in the *R* conditions. The numbers of jumps were 7 for the *FR*, 10 for the *SR*, 35 for the *FN*, and 49 for the *SN* conditions, respectively. The difference largely reflects the fact that if an *S* in an *N* condition missed a nearly-learned pair on one trial, he could recover that pair on a later trial with little interference with his other learning.

If we assume that the pairs for which backsliding occurs are almost completely learned, then, to measure total amounts of learning, we should add to the number of syllables learned by the *S*s in the *R* conditions the number responded to correctly at least once but lost through backsliding. We can estimate this number in several ways. Since the "efficient" *O S*s exhibited less backsliding than the others, we can take the actual rate of the former as the basis for the estimate. We will call this the "conservative" estimate. Alternatively, we can use the average backsliding rate for all subjects as a more "liberal" estimator.

Conservative Estimate: The ten *O S*s in the *FR* condition backslid 10 times—a rate of 20 additional correct responses for 20 *S*s (cf. table 2). The four *O S*s in the *SR* condition backslid 4 times—also a rate of 20 responses for 20 *S*s. Adding these numbers to the previous adjustments, we obtain total estimated correct responses for the *FR* and *SR* conditions of 88 and 120, respectively, as compared with the predicted values from the *N* conditions, of 105 and 151, respectively (table 2, columns 3 and 5). These estimates for the *R* conditions

are about 80 percent of the values for the *N* conditions in each case.

Liberal Estimate: In the *SR* condition, the four *O S*s made 119 correct responses in the first 10 trials, which would give an estimated 12 cases of backsliding, or 5 × 12 = 60 for a group of 20 *S*s. Similarly, the ten *O S*s in the *FR* condition made 201 correct responses, which would correspond to an expected 20 cases of backsliding, or 20 × 2 = 40 for a group of 20 *S*s. Adding these numbers to the earlier estimates based on the learning of the *O S*s, we obtain expected correct responses for 20 *S*s on the tenth trial of 68 + 40 = 108 and 100 + 60 = 160 for the *FR* and *SR* groups, respectively; which are very close to the predicted values for the *FN* and *SN* groups: 105 and 151 (table 2, columns 4 and 5).

In summary, the *S*s in the *R* conditions performed far less well than *S*s in the *N* conditions. However, those *S*s in the former condition who stated that they had followed a One-at-a-time strategy performed about two-thirds as well as *S*s in the non-replacement condition. When adjustment is made for the fact that a single error on an almost-learned pair loses the prior learning on that pair in the replacement condition, the adjusted learning rates of the One-at-a-time *S*s in the replacement condition are approximately as high as the rates of *S*s in the nonreplacement condition. Comparing *F* and *S* conditions, amount of learning is also proportional to learning time in both (efficient) replacement and nonreplacement conditions. The experiment can therefore be taken as a strong confirmation of quantitative predictions of the EPAM model.

Predictions by Simulation

The predictions we have just made can be checked in a more precise way by using the EPAM program to simulate the exact conditions of the Gregg et al. (1963) experiment. Except for the modifications to be listed in a moment, the same version of EPAM was used in the present simulation as in the simulations reported by Simon and Feigenbaum (1964). Eight conditions are to be simulated, deriving from the two dichotomous variables manipulated by the *E*s (rate of presentation and replacement), and the strategy determined by *S*.

Rate of Presentation: Slow (S) *or Fast* (F). This variable was manipulated directly by changing the drum speed parameter in EPAM. The total time per trial in the *S* condition was 79:55 the time per trial in the F condition.

Syllable Replacement: Replacement (R) *or Nonreplacement* (N). After each test of a syllable pair, the program checked the correctness of the response. In the *R* condition, if no response was made, or the response was wrong, the syllable pair was replaced by another pair stored in the computer memory. The syllables employed in the simulation were drawn from the same population as that used by Gregg et al. (1963).

Subject Stralegy: One-at-a-time (O) *or All-at-once* (A). A particular subroutine in the EPAM program determines when *S* will replace the syllable pair he is holding in immediate memory with a new pair read from the meory drum. In the *O* conditions, on each learning trial presentation, EPAM checked whether it could make a correct response to the stimulus already held in immediate memory; if so, the pair in im-

mediate memory was replaced by the pair in the memory drum window; if not, learning continued with the part already in immediate memory, and the pair currently in the memory drum window was ignored. In the *A* condition, each time the memory drum turned during a learning trial, EPAM replaced the syllable pair in immediate memory with the pair in the memory drum window. This was the only difference in the EPAM programs for the two strategies.

In analyzing the data from Gregg et al. (1963), we have used number of correct responses on the tenth trial as the measure of learning rate. In the simulation, learning was more rapid than for the average of the human *S*s in all conditions. (The simulated syllable exposure times proved to be longer than the corresponding times in the human experiment). Hence, EPAM learned the lists in less than 10 trials in all conditions except one, and a different measure of learning rate had to be used. Since both numbers of errors to criterion and number of trials to criterion vary inversely with learning rate, the reciprocals of these quantities were used to measure learning speed. In order to adjust for the difference in average learning speed in the simulation and the human data, all learn-

Table 3. Comparison of EPAM Learning Rates with Human Rates.

Experimental Conditions

Rates	One-at-a-time				All-at-once			
	Fast		Slow		Fast		Slow	
	N	R	N	R	N	R	N	R
EPAM* $\left(\frac{1}{\text{errors}}\right)$	43	39	116	71	49	20[†]	84	44
EPAM* $\left(\frac{1}{\text{trials}}\right)$	50	38	114	69	69	19[†]	86	50
Human *S*s*	69[‡]	45	100[‡]	67	69[‡]	19	100[‡]	32

* Entries in the EPAM rows are the reciprocals of the numbers of errors and numbers of trials, while the entries in the last row are numbers of correct responses on the tenth trial, both expressed as ratios to the average of the *SNO* and *SNA* conditions (See text).

[†] List not learned in 11 trials. See text for method of estimating learning rate.

[‡] In the *N* conditions, there was no difference in the learning rates of *O* and *A* *S*s. The rates used here are those for the entire group of 20 *S*s in each condition.

ing rates are expressed as ratios to the average of the rates for the *SNO* and *SNA* conditions. One *df* is lost in this adjustment, and 7 *df* remain. In the presentation of the data, since there was no difference in learning rates between *NO* and *NA Ss*, the average rates are used for the combined groups in the *FN* and *SN* conditions.

Table 3 compares the two measures of learning rates in the eight conditions of the simulation with the actual rates for the *Ss*. The product-moment coefficient of correlation between the EPAM (errors) and human learning rate indexes was 0.87; the coefficient between the EPAM (trials) and human indexes was 0.93. Both coefficients are significant at the 0.05 level. It will be observed that in the *FRA* conditions, EPAM did not succeed in learning the list by the time all replacement syllables had been exhausted after 11 trials. Fifty-six errors had been made, and only five pairs learned. Thus, the learning in this condition was about half as fast as in the *FRO* condition, where the entire list was learned in nine trials with 24 errors.

The EPAM simulation also gave excellent quantitative predictions of the rate of backsliding. We have noted that, while making 2,189 correct responses, the human *Ss* "backslid" 199 times, a rate of 0.087 syllables lost per correct response. For EPAM, the corresponding figures were 232 responses and 18 losses, for a backsliding rate of 0.078. As with the human *Ss*, there were in the EPAM runs no big differences in the backsliding rates for different conditions, but the samples were not large enough to detect small differences reliably.

CONCLUSION

This chapter has sought to meet the challenge of Atkinson et al. quoted earlier "(1) to identify the experimental conditions where the . . . all-or-none . . . model works . . . and (2) to construct a more general model . . . [that] accounts for the discrepancies." The EPAM model predicts, and the data support, these generalizations:

1. Whether learning will be all-or-none or incremental depends not only on the experimental conditions but also on the learning (i.e., attention) strategies that *Ss* can, or do, adopt. The *E* can establish necessary, but not sufficient, conditions for all-or-none learning when he sets the parameters of the experiment. These conditions, in turn, *may* influence the strategy *S* adopts.

2. Under nonreplacement conditions, learning will be all-or-none if *S* adopts a one-at-a-time strategy. It may be incremental otherwise.

3. Under replacement conditions, if *S* follows a one-at-a-time strategy, learning will be all-or-none provided that the total time per *trial* (for all the syllables) is about as long as, or longer than, the time required for fixating a syllable pair. For shorter exposure times, and for *Ss* who follow an all-at-once strategy, little or no learning will occur.

4. For *Ss* who follow a one-at-a-time strategy, the speed of learning under replacement conditions will fall short of the speed under nonreplacement conditions only by an amount that can be attributed to backsliding. Under both conditions, fixation will occur at a rate of about 10 seconds per chunk, where the number of chunks in a syllable pair can be derived from the familiarity (to these *Ss*) of the syllables.

5. Severe experimental conditions, e.g., replacement with short exposure times, may induce more *Ss* to follow a one-at-a-time strategy than easier conditions, hence increasing average learning rates under the former relative to the latter conditions.

References

Atkinson, R. C., Bower, G. H., and Crothers, E. J. *An introduction to mathematical learning theory.* New York: Wiley, 1965.
Brackett, H. R., and Battig, W. F. Method of pretraining and knowledge of results in paired-associate learning under conditions of repetition and non-repetition. *Amer. J. Psychol.*, 1963, 76, 66–73.
Bugelski, B. R. Presentation time, total time, and mediation in paired-associate learning. *J. exp. Psychol.*, 1962, 63, 409–12.

Feigenbaum, E. A. An information-processing theory of verbal learning. Doctoral dissertation. Pittsburgh: Carnegie Institute of Technology, 1959. Printed as The RAND Corporation Paper P-1817, 1959.

Feigenbaum, E. A., and Simon, H. A. A theory of the serial position effect. *British J. Psychol.*, 1962, **53**, 307–20. Reprinted as chapter 3.1 in this book.

Gregg, L. W., Chenzoff, A. P., and Laughery, K. R. The effect of rate of presentation, substitution, and mode of response in paired-associate learning. *Amer. J. Psychol.*, 1963, **76**, 110–15.

Hovland, C. I. Experimental studies in rote learning theory; III. Distribution of practice with varying speeds of syllable presentation.

J. exp. Psychol., 1938, **23**, 172–90.

Peterson, L. R., and Peterson, Margaret J. Short-term retention of individual verbal items. *J. exp. Psychol.*, 1959, **58**, 193–98.

Postman, L. One-trial learning. In C. N. Cofer and Barbara S. Musgrave (Eds.), *Verbal behavior and learning*. New York: McGraw-Hill, 1963. Pp. 295–321.

Simon, H. A., and Feigenbaum, E. A. An information-processing theory of some effects of similarity, familiarization, and meaningfulness in verbal learning. *J. verb. Learn. verb. Behav.*, 1964, **3**, 385–96. Reprinted as chapter 3.2 in this book.

Underwood, B. J., and Keppel, G. One-trial learning? *J. verb. Learn. verb. Behav.*, 1962, 1, 1–13.

3·4

A Note on Mathematical Models for Learning (1962)

In a recent paper Estes (1961) shows that certain data on paired associate learning can be fitted very well by the rational learning curve

$$E_t = (1 - 1/N)(1 - c)^{t-1} \qquad (1)$$

where E_t is the number of errors made on the tth trial, N is the total number of alternative responses available, and c is a parameter, so that $(1 - c)^{t-1}$ is the number of *unlearned* items at the beginning of the tth trial.

Estes' data show that the error curves for different values of N (in particular, $N = 2$ and $N = 8$) are almost precisely similar; that is, they can be factored into products of a function of N and a function of t:

$$E_t = \phi(N)\psi(t) \qquad (2)$$

where the particular form of (2) that Estes uses in fitting the data has already been shown in (1) above. That is, Estes makes the special assumptions that

$$\phi(N) = (1 - 1/N) \text{ and } \psi(t) = (1 - c)^{t-1} \qquad (3)$$

and shows that, with these special assumptions, the functions fit the data well.

The fact that the learning curves for different N are similar, as hypothesized in (2), follows from the assumption that the number of trials required to learn a set of associations is independent of the size of the class of possible responses. The derivation does not depend on the forms of the functions ϕ and ψ; all it requires is that E_t be expressible as a product of two such functions. In psychological terms, the assumption underlying the derivation means simply that discovery and fixation are independent aspects of learning; it implies nothing about the nature of the fixation process. An equation equivalent to (2) was derived by Simon (1957, p. 264) from this assumption and was shown to be consistent with data from maze learning experiments, as well as rote learning experiments.

What Estes has shown, then, are three things: (1) the discovery and fixation aspects of learning are independent in his data, as in data analyzed previously in Simon (1957); the number of errors, produced in discovery can be explained by a simple model of random search, from which the form of $\phi(N)$ follows; (3) the number of trials required for fixation can be explained by a simple stimulus conditioning model, from which Estes obtains his form of $\psi(t)$.

What implications does this analysis have for the comparison Estes (1959, pp. 136–140) makes between his learning model and the earlier models of Robertson and Thurstone? First, if we consider these

133

models to be concerned only with the fixation process, we should compare them (suitably transformed to make E_t the dependent variable) with the function ψ, rather than with the product $\phi\psi$. By premultiplying the alternative function ψ with $(1 - 1/\mathcal{N})$, we could obtain fits to the data as good as those obtained with Estes' form of ψ. Moreover, the parameters estimated for $\mathcal{N} = 8$ would still fit the data for $\mathcal{N} = 2$—for the same reason that they do under Estes's assumptions.

We may still prefer Estes' form of ψ, since his function has only a single parameter, while those of Robertson and Thurstone have three and two, respectively. However, its claim for superiority as an explanation of the fixation process must rest entirely on its parsimony in parameters, since it is neither more nor less powerful than the alternatives in fitting data for different $\mathcal{N}$ without reestimating these parameters.

Of course there are other tests, beyond those applied by Estes, to determine whether the one-element stimulus sampling

model defined by (1) fit the data better than other models. Bower, for example, (1961) tested the same model by examining certain conditional probabilities, i.e., sequential dependencies, of correct and wrong responses, and found that his model fitted the data better than did some alternative models. The point of the present note is not to argue that the form of $\psi(t)$ is untestable—which is patently false—but that it is not tested sharply in the analysis presented by Estes.

References

Bower, G. H. Application of a model to paired-associate learning. *Psychometrika*, 1961, **26**, 255–80.
Estes, W. K. Growth and function of mathematical models for learning. *Current Trends in psychological theory*, *1959*, pp. 134–51. Pittsburgh: Univ. Pittsburgh Press, 1961.
Simon, H. A. Amounts of fixation and discovery in maze learning behavior. *Psychometrika*, 1957, **22**, 261–68. Reprinted as Chapter 2.1 in this book.

3.5

A Note on Jost's Law and Exponential Forgetting (1966)

The description of forgetting as "decay" might well suggest the exponential function as a suitable form for a law of forgetting. Then, letting $x(t)$ be the measure of amount of material retained at time t, we could write

$$x(t) = x_0 e^{-k(t-t_0)} \qquad (1)$$

where t_0 is the time of original learning and $x_0 = x(t_0)$.

Taking the derivative, we obtain:

$$\frac{1}{x}\frac{dx}{dt} = -k \qquad (2)$$

It has perhaps not been observed that this forgetting law is incompatible with the well-established empirical generalizations about memory usually called Jost's Laws. Jost's second law is stated by McGeoch [1942, p. 140] as follows:

If two associations are of equal strength but of different age, the older diminishes less with time.

In equations, this would mean

$$\frac{1}{x}\frac{dx}{dt} = -f(t-t_0) \qquad (3)$$

where $f(t)$ is positive and monotone decreasing with increase in $(t-t_0)$. But, since k in (2) is a constant, the right-hand sides of

(2) and (3) are obviously mutually incompatible.

A forgetting curve compatible with Jost's Law can be obtained by assuming that learning is not homogeneous—that, for example, the rate of forgetting depends on the extent of overlearning, and that the latter is not the same for all portions of the material learned. Thus, suppose that the material, x_0, learned at t_0, is composed of two parts, x_{1_0} and x_{2_0},

$$x_0 = x_{1_0} + x_{2_0} \qquad (4)$$

where x_{1_0} has been more highly overlearned than x_{2_0}. Suppose that x_{1_0} is subject to exponential decay with time constant k_1, and x_{2_0} to decay with time constant k_2, where $k_2 > k_1$. Then

$$\frac{1}{x}\frac{dx}{dt} = -k_1\frac{x_1}{x} - k_2\frac{x_2}{x} \qquad (5)$$

But, since x_2 is decaying more rapidly than x_1, x_2/x will go to zero and x_1/x will go to unity as t increases, and the absolute magnitude of the right-hand side of (5) will consequently decrease asymptotically

This investigation was supported in part by the Public Health Service Research Grant MH-07722, from the National Institutes of Health.

to k_1. We see that (5) satisfies the conditions of (3), and hence is compatible with Jost's Law.

Thus the validity of Jost's Law may imply that the rate of loss of retained material is dependent on the age of the memory, or that the rate of loss is dependent on the completeness of the original learning, or on some combination of these.

Reference

McGeoch, J. *The psychology of human learning.* New York: Longmans, Green and Company, 1942.

4

Problem Solving

The first chapter of this section will serve as a link to the comprehensive treatment of its topic in *Human Problem Solving*, reminding the reader how the selective search mechanisms of the Logic Theorist and the means-ends analysis of the General Problem Solver account for some of the main phenomena of human problem solving behavior. However, chapter 4.1 is included here primarily because it states and develops the claim that there is no qualitative gulf between ordinary, garden-variety problem solving and that kind of problem solving which, because of its impressiveness, we judge worthy of the label "creative." The same mechanisms, it argues, are at the root of both kinds of problem solving—creativity is simply problem solving writ large.

Although not published until 1962, chapter 4.1, reporting collaborative work with Allen Newell and J. C. Shaw, was written quite early, for a conference in Boulder, Colorado, in May 1958 and for subsequent use in the RAND Workshop on Cognitive Simulation held that summer. Hence, the General Problem Solver, which had not yet been christened, is not mentioned by name in the chapter, although an explicit description of that program is given there under the rubric of "functional analysis." This article constitutes the earliest written description of GPS.

Chapters 4.2 (with Peter A. Simon) and 4.3 (with George W. Baylor) pursue the topic of creativity further, describing and analyzing the behavior of a program, MATER, that is able, using a quite simple mechanism of selective search, to discover chess mating combinations that were regarded as highly creative when discovered by human chessmasters. Of course, since these chapters were written, there has been enormous progress in designing computer programs for playing chess, one such program now (1978) performing at the skill level of a master. However, these newer and more powerful programs are exercises in artificial intelligence, not cognitive simulation, for they all make extensive and essential use of the arithmetic brute force of the computer. What the MATER program of chapters 4.2 and 4.3 demonstrates is that the same results can be achieved, at least for mating combinations. with only the modest amounts of selective search that have been observed in human play. Hence, as a psychological theory of this aspect of chess playing, MATER has not been outmoded. The perceptual aspects of chess skill will be treated extensively in section 6.

The remaining three chapters in section 4 take up again the theme of alternative strategies for performing identical tasks. Chapter 4.4 (in collaboration with Jeffery M. Paige) describes an empirical study of the processes used by students to solve algebra story problems. It was motivated by an interest in testing to what extent the STUDENT program (Bobrow, 1968) could be regarded as a theory of human cognitive processing in this task domain. The human experiments revealed important differences among the strategies used by different subjects, and only one of these strategies was simulated adequately by STUDENT. The different strategies were associated with different problem representations. Hence, the results of the study reported in this chapter provided one important motivation for the research on understanding processes described in section 7.

Chapters 4.5 and 4.6 continue the exploration of alternative problem solving strategies. The former chapter provides a taxonomy of strategies that can be used to solve the Tower of Hanoi puzzle, while chapter 4.6 (written with Stephen K. Reed) shows how some data of human performance on the Missionaries and Cannibals puzzle can be explained by a hypothesis of strategy learning and adaptation.

CREATIVITY

Chapter 4.1 has nothing to say about the phenomenon—so often referred to in discussions of creativity—of sudden "illumination" (problem solution) after "incubation" (putting the problem aside). How can it come about that a problem solver, after interrupting his work on a problem, should suddenly, and without conscious effort, find a solution?

Although the evidence for sudden illumination is largely anecdotal, I see no reason to deny that the phenomenon is genuine. The question is not whether it occurs, but whether it can be explained without postulating special mechanisms for creative thinking. In a paper not reprinted in this volume (Simon, 1966), I have shown how forgetting mechanisms of a quite ordinary sort could account for the relatively sudden appearance of problem solutions after work on a problem had been interrupted for a longer or shorter period of time. I should like to summarize that argument here.

In typical human problem solving activity, a person starts out with the goal of solving the original problem and, in trying to reach this goal, generates a subgoal that will take him part way. If the subgoal is achieved, attention may then return to the now modified original goal; if difficulties arise for achieving the subgoal, sub-subgoals may be erected to deal with them.

The subgoal hierarchy has to be held in memory. Once achieved, a goal may be forgotten, but the tree of unattained goals must be retained. Sometimes, of course, subjects forget exactly where they are in the subgoal structure, and they may have to repeat some earlier work to get back into the context of the current goal. Since the subgoal hierarchy is constantly changing as subgoals are achieved or abandoned, it is usually held only in STM. Hence, in case of interruption or temporary abandonment of problem solving activity, much of this structure is lost from memory. When work is resumed on the problem, it does not resume at the same point— aimed at the same subgoals—at which it left off, but usually returns to an earlier, higher level goal.

Meanwhile, during the course of problem solving, a second body of information is being built up in LTM. The problem solver is noticing various features of the problem environment and is storing some of these in LTM. If he is studying a chess position, for example, he may notice that a particular piece is undefended or that another piece is pinned against the queen. Although this information is generated while specific goals are being attended to, it often has general significance beyond these particular goals and is used by the control process that generates new subgoals and governs the course of the search. Hence, over the longer run, the information influences the growth of the subgoal tree. The information transferred to LTM during the course of search may be thought of as being recorded on a sort of "blackboard," readable by all subsequent processes.

What happens if the problem solver removes himself from the task temporarily? Information that has been held in STM begins to disappear, while information that has been transfered to LTM remains in memory longer. Hence, when the problem solver takes up the task again, many or most of the subgoals in the goal tree will have disappeared, while the blackboard information will still be available. The new search for a problem solution, under the influence of the richer set of blackboard information, will now follow a different path from the original search, and more often than not, a path more likely to lead to the goal. Under these circumstances (and remembering the large difference a few hints can produce in solving problems) solutions may now appear quickly that had previously eluded a protracted search.

Here, then, is an explanation for sudden illumination that invokes only mechanisms that have already been incorporated in problem solving theories. It accounts for the suddenness of solution without calling on the subconscious to perform elaborate processes, or processes different from those it and the conscious perform in the normal course of problem solving activity. While no direct empirical evidence yet exists for the correctness of this explanation, it does demonstrate that suddenness of solution is quite compatible with the basic tenets of information processing theories of thinking.

Chapters 4.2 and 4.3 attempt no general theory of creativity, but rather describe a specific program that demonstrates its ability to do things that have been judged creative when done by humans. In the past five years, a number of computer programs have appeared on the scene that are creative in task domains other than chess. Most of these have been written in the spirit of artificial intelligence and do not necessarily simulate human processes closely, but they do again provide tests of the sufficiency of the mechanisms of selective search for intelligent performance in complex task domains.

One example is Lenat's AM program (1977). AM is provided with certain information about elementary set theory: a definition of set, examples, the notions of union and intersection of sets, and so on. It is given the goal of generating "interesting" new concepts, where "interest" is defined for it in terms of the relation of the new concepts to old ones, the ease or difficulty of generating examples, and so on. AM is also given some heuristics for generating interesting new concepts: for example, generating examples; generalizing a concept if examples are hard to find and specializing it if they are too easy to find; paying particular attention to borderline examples that barely fit the concept definition.

In a few hours of central processor time on a large computer, AM discovered the concept of the natural numbers; of addition, subtraction, multiplication, and division; of odd and even numbers; of the prime numbers; of the prime number decomposition theorem (the so-called basic theorem of arithmetic), and others. In a human, this performance (without access to the mathematical literature in which these concepts are put forth) would be spectacular and would certainly be judged highly creative. The general explanation of the processes involved in creative thinking proposed in chapters 4.1, 4.2, and 4.3 has gained additional support from the evidence of recent information processing research such as Lenat's.

Use of Knowledge in Problem Solving

With the major exception of research on chess, most work on human problem solving has been carried on in task domains where the solver's skill does not depend on the possession of large amounts of task-dependent information. Almost everything one needs to know about the Tower of Hanoi problem, or the Missionaries and Cannibals puzzle, is contained in the problem instructions. Even algebra story problems call on only a little knowledge of the real world, outside the language of the problem statements. On the other hand, a physician faced with a medical problem is distinguished from a layman less by his possession of particular problem solving procedures than by his possession of a large amount of knowledge about such subjects as physiology, biochemistry, and pharmacology. Therefore, we must be cautious in extrapolating what we learn about problem solving in puzzle-like domains to problem solving in information-rich domains.

In later sections of this book, I will have something more to say about problem solving in semantically rich domains. In particular, the papers of section 6 will have a good deal to say about the chess player's use of his chess knowledge; while the introduction to section 7 will discuss the use of subject matter knowledge to guide the construction of problem representations in familiar task domains.

Strategy Learning

The realization that people may use a great variety of strategies to solve the same problems leads directly to the question of how these strategies are acquired. Research progress has been more rapid in modeling strategies than in modeling processes for changing strategies adaptively. Even chapter 4.6, which deals with the learning of strategies in the Missionaries and Cannibals puzzle, assumes that the strategies are already available to the subjects and have merely to be evoked from memory when situational cues suggest that they are appropriate.

With the recent introduction, by Waterman (1970), of the idea of *adaptive production systems*, rapid progress is now being made toward devising plausible models of strategy learning processes. A production system (see chapter 4.5) is a program, each component of which consists of two linked parts: a *condition* part and an *action* part. The condition part of a production determines whether certain conditions are satisfied by the stimulus (perceptual production) or by the contents of STM (general production). If the condition part of the production is satisfied, the action part is executed immediately. (A condition-action pair can be viewed as a kind of stimulus-response pair, although the resemblance is only approximate.) The production system structure is a quite general format for describing programs, hence strategies.

A production system can be modified simply by introducing new productions into it. Waterman showed that a system using this principle could learn to play poker at a respectable level of skill. More recently, adaptive production systems have been built that are capable of learning in other domains. Neves (personal communication) has now constructed a system that learns to solve linear algebraic equations by examining a worked-out textbook example. It uses the information embedded in the example to generate a small set of productions (about four) that constitutes a general algorithm for solving such equations. Anzai and I (1979) have constructed an adaptive production system that simulates closely the behavior of an intelligent human subject in acquiring sophisticated strategies for solving the Tower of Hanoi problem, using information gathered during solution attempts made without the help of these strategies.

Final Comments

Problem solving continues to be a very active area of research into human information processing. Two recent surveys of the field have been published by Greeno (1978) and myself (1978). Greeno's work on understanding (e.g., Greeno, 1977), and the work of Polson and his associates (Atwood and Polson, 1976; Jeffries, et al., 1977) on means-ends strategies deserve particular attention. The page limits of this volume prevent me from including two of my own most recent pieces of work on problem solving in semantically rich domains (Bhaskar and Simon, 1977; and Simon and Simon, 1978).

References

Anzai, Y., and H. A. Simon. The theory of learning by doing. *Psychological Review* 86:124–40 (1979.)

Atwood, M. E., and P. G. Polson. A process model for water jug problems, *Cognitive Psychology*, 8:191–216 (1976).

Bhaskar, R., and H. A. Simon. Problem solving in semantically rich domains: An example from enginering thermodynamics, *Cognitive Science*, 1:193–215 (1977).

Bobrow, D. G. Natural language input for a computer problem-solving system. *In* M. Minsky (ed.), *Semantic Information Processing*, Cambridge, Mass.: M.I.T. Press, 1968, pp. 135–215.

Greeno, J. G. Process of understanding in problem solving. *In* N.J. Castellan, D. B. Pisoni and G. R. Potts (eds.), *Cognitive Theory*, Vol. 2, Hillsdale, N.J.: Lawrence Erlbaum Associates, 1977, pp. 43–84.

Greeno, J. G. Natures of problem-solving abilities. *In* W. K. Estes (ed.), *Handbook of Learning and Cognitive Processes*, Vol. 5: *Human Information Processing*, Hillsdale, N.J.: Lawrence Erlbaum Associates, 1978, pp. 239–70.

Jeffries, R., P. G. Polson, L. Razran, and M. E. Atwood. Model for missionaries-cannibals and other river-crossing problems, *Cognitive Psychology*, 9:412–40 (1977).

Lenat, D. Automated theory formation in mathematics, *Proceedings of the 5th International Joint Conference on Artificial Intelligence*, 1977, Vol. 2, pp. 833–42.

Newell, A., and H. A. Simon. *Human Problem Solving*, Englewood Cliffs, N.J.: Prentice-Hall, 1972.

Simon, D. P. and H. A. Simon. Individual differences in solving physics problems. *In* R. S. Siegler (ed.), *Children's Thinking: What Develops?*, Hillsdale, N.J.: Lawrence Erlbaum Associates, 1978, chap. 13.

Simon, H. A. Scientific discovery and the psychology of problem solving. *In* R. Colodny (ed.), *Mind and Cosmos*, Pittsburgh: University of Pittsburgh Press, 1966, pp. 22–40.

Simon, H. A. Information-processing theory of human problem solving. *In* W. K. Estes (ed.), *Handbook of Learning and Cognitive Processes*, Vol. 5: *Human Information Processing*, Hillsdale, N.J.: Lawrence Erlbaum Associates, 1978, pp. 271–95.

Waterman, D. Generalization learning techniques for automating the learning of heuristics. *Artificial Intelligence* 1:121–70 (1970).

4.1

The Processes of Creative Thinking (1962)

with Allen Newell and J. C. Shaw

What is meant by an "explanation" of the creative process? In the published literature on the subject, the stages of thought in the solution of difficult problems have been described, and the processes that go on at each stage discussed. Interest has focused particularly on the more dramatic and mysterious aspects of creativity —the unconscious processes that are supposed to occur during "incubation," the imagery employed in creative thinking and its significance for the effectiveness of the thinking, and, above all, the phenomenon of "illumination," the sudden flash of insight that reveals the solution of a problem long pursued. Experimental work —to the limited extent that it has been done—has been most concerned with directional set, including the motivational and cognitive conditions that produce set and that alter set, and interpersonal differences in "inappropriate" persistence of set (stereotypy).

All the topics we have mentioned are interesting enough, and are appropriate parts of a theory of creative thinking. In our own orientation to creativity, however, we have felt the need for a clearer idea of the overall requirements and aims of such a theory. We propose that a theory of

creative thinking should consist of:

1. Completely operational specifications[1] for the behavior of mechanisms (or organisms) that, with appropriate initial conditions, would in fact think creatively.

2. A demonstration that mechanisms behaving as specified (by these programs) would exhibit the phenomena that commonly accompany creative thinking (e.g., incubation, illumination, formation and change in set.

3. A set of statements—verbal or mathematical—about the characteristics of the class of specifications (programs) that includes the particular examples specified.

Stated otherwise, we would have a satisfactory theory of creative thought if we could design and build some mechanisms that could think creatively (exhibit behavior just like that of a human carrying on creative activity), and if we could state the general principles on which the mechanisms were built and operated.

Put in this bald way, these aims sound

---

1. As we will explain later, we propose that such a set of specifications take the form of *a program*, as that term is used in the digital computer field. We will henceforth refer to them as "programs."

utopian. How utopian they are—or rather, how imminent their realization—depends on how broadly or narrowly we interpret the term "creative." If we are willing to regard all human complex problem solving as creative, then—as we will point out—successful programs for problem solving mechanisms that simulate human problem solvers already exist, and a number of their general characteristics are known. If we reserve the term "creative" for activities like discovery of the special theory of relativity or the composition of Beethoven's Seventh Symphony, then no example of a creative mechanism exists at the present time.

But the success already achieved in synthesizing mechanisms that solve difficult problems in the same manner as humans is beginning to provide a theory of problem solving that is highly specific and operational. The purpose of this chapter is to draw out some of the implications of this theory for creative thinking. To do so is to assume that creative thinking is simply a special kind of problem solving behavior. This seems to us a useful working hypothesis.

We start by discussing the relation of creative thinking to problem solving in general and by inquiring to what extent existing problem solving programs may be considered creative. Next we sketch the theory of problem solving that underlies these programs, and then use the theory to analyze the programs and to compare them with some human problem solving behavior exhibited in thinking-aloud protocols of subjects in the laboratory. Finally, we consider some topics that have been prominent in discussions of creativity to see what this analysis of problem solving has to say about them.

PROBLEM SOLVING AND CREATIVITY

In the psychological literature, "creative thinking" designates a special class of activities, with somewhat vague and indefinite boundaries (see, e.g., Johnson, 1955). Problem solving is called creative to the extent that one or more of the

following conditions are satisfied:

1. The product of the thinking has novelty and value (either for the thinker or for his culture).

2. The thinking is unconventional, in the sense that it requires modification or rejection of previously accepted ideas.

3. The thinking requires high motivation and persistence, taking place either over a considerable span of time (continuously or intermittently) or at high intensity.

4. The problem as initially posed was vague and ill-defined, so that part of the task was to formulate the problem itself.

Vagueness of the Distinction

A problem solving process can exhibit all these characteristics to a greater or lesser degree, but we are unable to find any more specific criteria separating creative from noncreative thought processes. Moreover, the data currently available about the processes involved in creative and noncreative thinking show no particular differences between the two. We may cite, as examples, the data of Patrick (1935, 1937) on the processes involved (for both professionals and amateurs) in drawing a picture or writing a poem, or the data of de Groot (1946) on the thought processes of chess players. Not only do the processes appear to be remarkably similar from one task to another—agreeing well with Wallas's (1926) account of the stages in problem solving—but it is impossible, by looking solely at the statistics describing the processes, to distinguish the highly skilled practitioner from the rank amateur.

Similarly, there is a high correlation between creativity (at least in the sciences) and proficiency in the more routine intellective tasks that are commonly used to measure intelligence. There is little doubt that virtually all the persons who have made major creative advances in science and technology in historic times have possessed very great general problem solving powers (Johnson, 1955).

Thus, creative activity appears simply to be a special class of problem solving activity characterized by novelty, unconventionality, persistence, and difficulty in problem formulation.

Simulation of Problem Solving

As we indicated earlier, the theory of problem solving we are putting forth derives from mechanisms that solve problems in the same manner as humans— mechanisms whose behavior can be observed, modified, and analyzed. The only available technique for constructing problem solvers is to write programs for digital computers; no other physical mechanisms are complex enough.

The material in the present chapter rests mostly on several programs that we have constructed.[2] These are:

1. *The Logic Theorist.* The Logic Theorist is a computer program that is capable of discovering proofs for theorems in elementary symbolic logic, using heuristic techniques similar to those used by humans. Several versions of the Logic Theorist have been coded for a computer, and a substantial amount of experience has been accumulated with one of these versions and some of its variants (Newell and Shaw, 1957; Newell, Shaw, and Simon, 1957, 1958*a*; Newell and Simon, 1956).

2. *The Chess Player.* We have written a program that plays chess. It is just now being checked out on the computer, but we have done a good deal of hand simulation with the program so that we know some of its more immediate characteristics (Newell, Shaw, and Simon, 1958*b*).

When we say that these programs are simulations of human problem solving, we do not mean merely that they solve problems that had previously been solved only by humans—although they do that also. We mean that they solve these problems by using techniques and processes that resemble more or less closely the techniques and processes used by humans. The most recent version of the Logic Theorist was designed explicitly as a

simulation of a (particular) human problem solver whose behavior had been recorded under laboratory conditions.

Although the Carnegie-RAND group is the only one to our knowledge that has been trying explicity to construct programs that simulate human higher mental processes, a number of workers have been exploring the capabilities of computer programs to solve complex and difficult problems. Many of these programs provide additional information about the nature of the problem solving process. Some of the more relevant are:

3. *Musical Composition.* A computer program has been written and run on the ILLIAC that composes music employing Palestrina's rules of counterpoint. Some of its music has been performed by a string quartet and tape-recorded, but as far as we are aware, no description of the program has been published. Other experiments in musical composition have also been made.

4. *Chess Playing.* Two programs besides ours have been written that play chess. Although both of these proceed in a way that is fundamentally different from the ways humans play chess, some of their features provide illuminating comparisons (Newell, Shaw, and Simon, 1958*b*).

5. *Design of Electric Motors.* At least two, and probably more, computer programs have been written, and are now being used by industrial concerns, that design electric motors. These programs take as their inputs the customers' design specifications and produce as their outputs the manufacturing specifications that are sent to the factory floor. The programs do not simply make calculations needed in the design process, but actually carry out the analysis itself and make the decisions that were formerly the province of the design engineers.

The main objective of these motor design programs, of course, is to provide effective problem solving routines that are economical substitutes for engineers. Thus these programs simulate human processes only to the extent that such processes are believed to enhance the problem solving capabilities and efficiency of the programs.

6. *Visual Pattern Recognition.* A program

---

2. This brief survey reflects the state of affairs at the time this chapter was first prepared, in the spring of 1958.

has been written that attempts to learn a two-dimensional pattern—such as an "A" —from examples. The program was developed by Selfridge (1955) and Dineen (1955). Although only partly successful, it was a pioneering attempt to use computer simulation as a technique for investigating an area of human mental functioning.

Is the Logic Theorist Creative?

The activities carried on by these problem solving computer programs lie in areas not far from what is usually regarded as "creative." Discovering proofs for mathematical theorems, composing music, designing engineering structures, and playing chess would ordinarily be thought creative if the product were original and of high quality. Hence, the relevance of these programs to the theory of creativity is clear —even if the present programs fall short of exact simulation of human processes and produce a fairly mundane product.

Let us consider more specifically whether we should regard the Logic Theorist as creative. When the Logic Theorist is presented with a purported theorem in elementary symbolic logic, it attempts to find a proof. In the problems we have actually posed it, which were theorems drawn from chapter 2 of Whitehead and Russell's *Principia Mathematica* (1925–27), it has found the proof about three times out of four. The Logic Theorist does not pose its own problems—it must be given these— although in the course of seeking a proof for a theorem it will derive the theorem from other expressions and then attempt to prove the latter. Hence, in proving one theorem, the Theorist is capable of conjecturing other theorems and then trying to prove these.

Now no one would deny that Whitehead and Russell were creative when they wrote *Principia Mathematica*. Their book is one of the most significant intellectual products of the twentieth century. If it was creative for Whitehead and Russell to write these volumes, it is possibly creative for the Logic Theorist to reinvent large portions of chapter 2—rediscovering in many cases

the very same proofs that Whitehead and Russell discovered originally. Of course the Logic Theorist will not receive much acclaim for its discoveries, since these have been anticipated, but, subjectively if not culturally, its product is novel and original. In at least one case, moreover, the Logic Theorist has discovered a proof for a theorem in chapter 2 that is far shorter and more elegant than the one published by Whitehead and Russell.[3]

If we wish to object seriously to calling the Logic Theorist creative, we must rest our case on the way it gets the problems it tackles and not on its activity in tackling them. Perhaps the program is a mathematical hack, since it relies on Whitehead and Russell to provide it with significant problems and then merely finds the answers to these; perhaps the real creativity lies in the problem selection. This certainly is the point of the fourth characteristic we listed for creativity. But we have already indicated that the Theorist has some powers of problem selection. In working backward from the goal of proving one theorem, it can conjecture new theorems—or supposed theorems—and set up the subgoal of proving these. Historically, albeit on a much broader scale, this is exactly the process whereby Whitehead and Russell generated the theorems that they then undertook to prove. For the task they originally set themselves was to take the basic postulates of arithmetic (as set forth by Peano and his students) and to derive these as *theorems* from the axioms of logic. The theorems of chapter 2 of *Principia* were generated, as nearly as we can determine the history of the matter, in the same way that subproblems are generated by the Logic Theorist—as subproblems whose

---

3. Perhaps even this is not creative. *The Journal of Symbolic Logic* has declined to publish an article, coauthored by the Logic Theorist, describing this proof. The principal objection offered by the editor is that the same theorem could today be proved (using certain metatheorems that were available neither to Whitehead and Russell nor the Logic Theorist) in a simpler way.

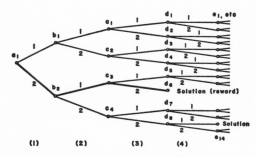

Figure 1. A problem maze. Alternatives at choice points, $m = 2$; minimum length of path to solution, $k = 3$. The shortest path to a solution is given by the choices 2-1-2; it runs from choice point a_1, through b_2 and c_3 to d_6, the solution.

solution would lead to the solution of the problem originally posed.

We do not wish to exaggerate the extent to which the Logic Theorist is capable of matching the higher flights of the human mind. We wish only to indicate that the boundary between its problem solving activities and activities that are important examples of human creativity is not simple or obvious.

AN ABSTRACT MODEL OF PROBLEM SOLVING BEHAVIOR

We turn next to the general theory of problem solving, only returning later to issues that are specific to the "creative" end of the problem solving spectrum.

Definition of "Problem"

The maze provides a suitable abstract model for most kinds of problem solving activity. A maze is a set of paths (possibly partly overlapping), some subset of which are distinguished from the others by having rewards at their termini (see figure 1). These latter are the "correct" paths; to discover one of them is to solve the problem of running the maze.

We can abstract one stage further and characterize problem solving by the following rubric: Given a set, P, of elements, to find a member of a subset, S, of P having

specified properties. Here are some examples:

1. Solving a crossword puzzle. Take as P all possible combinations of letters of the English alphabet that will fill the white squares of the puzzle. The subset S comprises those combinations in which all consecutive linear horizontal and vertical sequences are words that satisfy specified definitions.

2. Finding the combination of a safe. Take as P all possible settings of the dials of the safe; and as S those particular settings that open the safe. As safes are usually constructed, S consists of a single element.

3. Making a move in chess. Take as P the set of all possible (legal) moves; as S, the set of "good" moves, where the term "good" reflects some set of criteria.

4. Proving a theorem in logic or geometry. Take as P the set of all possible sequences of expressions in a formal language for logic (or geometry, respectively); and as S the subset of sequences that: (a) are valid proofs and (b) terminate in the specified theorem.

5. Programming a computer to invert a matrix. Take as P the set of all possible sequences of computer instructions; and as S a particular sequence that will perform the specified matrix inversion.

6. Translating a German article into English. Take as P the set of all possible sequences of English words (of length, say, less than L); take as S the subset of sequences that: (a) satisfy certain criteria of English syntax and style and (b) have the same meaning as the German original.

7. Designing a machine. Take as P the set of all possible parameter values for a machine design; take as S the subset of parameter values that: (a) satisfy the design specifications (b) meet certain criteria of cost minimization.

In examples 4, 5, and 6, the interpretation in terms of the maze model can be carried a step further by identifying the elements of the sequences mentioned there with the succssive segments of the maze that constitute a path.

A Preliminary View of Problem Solving Processes

There are any number of ways of classifying the processes that are used by humans to solve problems. One useful distinction differentiates processes for finding possible solutions (generating members of P that may belong to S), from processes for determining whether a solution proposal is in fact a solution (verifying that an element of P that has been generated does belong to S). This is a distinction that is often made in the literature, in one set of terms or another. Johnson (1955), for example, distinguishes "production" processes from "judgment" processes in a way that corresponds closely to the distinction we have just made. We prefer to call the first class of processes *solution generating* processes, and the second class *verifying processes*.

Solution generators range all the way from exceedingly "primitive" trial-and-error searches that take up the elements of P in a fairly arbitrary order to extensive calculations that select an appropriate solution at the first try or to elaborate analytic processes that construct a solution by some kind of "working backward" from the known properties of solutions. In spite of the primitive character of trial-and-error processes, they bulk very large in highly creative problem solving; in fact, at the upper end of the range of problem difficulty there is likely to be a positive correlation between creativity and the use of trial-and-error generators.

How Large is the Maze?

In a sufficiently small maze where a member of S, once discovered, can be identified easily as a solution, the task of discovering solutions is trivial (e.g., a T-maze for a rat with food in one branch). The difficulties in complex problem solving arise from some combination of two factors: the size of the set of possible solutions that must be searched and the task of identifying whether a proposed solution actually satisfies the conditions of the problem. In any particular case, either or both of these may be the sources of problem difficulty. By using our formal model of problem solving we can often obtain meaningful measures of the size and difficulty of particular problems and measures of the effectiveness of particular problem solving processes and devices. Let us consider some examples.

The Logic Theorist. We have made some estimates of the size of the space of possible solutions (proofs) for the problems handled by the Logic Theorist. By a possible proof —which we will take as the element of the set P in this case—we mean a sequence of symbolic logic expressions. If we impose no limits on the length or other characterisitics of such sequences, their number, obviously, is infinite. Hence, we must suppose at the outset that we are not concerned with the whole set of possible proofs, but with some subset comprising, say, the "simpler" elements of that set. We might restrict P, for example, to proofs consisting of sequences of not more than twenty logic expressions, with each expression not more than twenty-three symbols in length and involving only the variables p, q, r, s, and t and the connectives "or" and "implies." The number of possible proofs meeting these restrictions is about 10^{235}—one followed by 235 zeros!

The task is also not trivial of verifying that a particular element of the set P, as we have just defined it, is a proof of a particular problem in logic; for it is necessary to determine whether each expression in the sequence is an axiom or whether it follows from some of the expressions preceding it by the rules of deductive inference. In addition, of course, the expression to be proved has to be contained in the sequence.

Clearly, selecting possible proofs by sheer trial and error and testing whether each element selected is actually the desired proof is not a feasible method for proving logic theorems—for either humans or machines. The set to be searched is too large and the testing of the elements selected is too difficult. How can we bring task down to manageable proportions?

First of all, the number we have just computed, 10^{235}, is not only exceedingly large but also arbitrary, for it depends entirely on the restrictions of simplicity we impose on P. By strengthening these conditions, we reduce the size of P; by weakening them, we increase its size. We must look for a more meaningful way to describe the size of the set P. This we do by considering a simple solution generator that produces members of the set in a certain order and asking how many members the generator would have to produce, on the average, to obtain solutions to problems of a specified class. Let us generate elements of P according to the following simple scheme, which we call the British Museum algorithm in honor of the primates who are credited with employing it (Newell, Shaw, and Simon, 1957):

1. We consider only sequences of logic expressions that are valid proofs—that is, whose initial expressions are axioms—and each of whose expressions is derived from prior ones by valid rules of inference. By generating only sequences that are proofs (of something), we eliminate the major part of the task of verification.

2. We generate first those proofs that consist of a single expression (the axioms themselves), then proofs two expressions long, and so on, limiting the alphabet of symbols as before. Given all the proofs of length k, we generate those of length $(k + 1)$ by applying the rules of inference in all permissible ways to the former to generate new derived expressions that can be added to the sequences. That is, we generate a maze (see again, figure 1), each choice point $(a_1, b_1, b_2,$ etc.) representing the legitimate ways of deriving new expressions as immediate consequences of the expressions contained in the proof. Thus, in the figure, d_4 is a proof that can be derived as an immediate consequence of c_2, using path 2.

We estimate that of the sixty-odd theorems that appear in chapter 2 of *Principia Mathematica* about six (all of which are among the first ten in the chapter) would be included in the first 1,000 proofs generated by the algorithm, but that about a

hundred million more proofs would have to be generated to obtain all the theorems in the chapter. (The actual number may be much greater; it is difficult to estimate with any accuracy.) That is to say, if we used this scheme to find the proof of a theorem selected at random from the theorems of chapter 2, we would, on the average, have to generate some fifty million possible solutions before finding the one we wanted; and the chances of finding the proof among the first thousand generated would be only one in ten. One hundred million (10^8) is a large number, but a very small number compared with 10^{235}. Thus a proof has a very much higher probability of turning up in chapter 2 of *Principia* if it is relatively simple than if it is complicated. On the other hand, something more effective is needed than the British Museum algorithm in order for a man or a machine to solve problems in symbolic logic in a reasonable time.

Before leaving the Logic Theorist, we wish to mention a variant of the Whitehead and Russell problems which we have also studied, and which will be the subject of some analysis later. At Yale, Moore and Anderson (1954) have studied the problem solving behavior of subjects who were given a small set (from one to four) of logic expressions as premises and asked to derive another expression from these, using twelve specified rules of transformation. (For details see the discussion in the next section and in the appendix.) If we again suppose derivations to be generated by working forward from the premises, we can, in the case where there is a single premise, make simple estimates of the number of possible derivations of given length—and hence characterize this particular problem maze.

Assuming (and this is an oversimplification) that each rule of transformation operates on one premise, and that each such rule is applicable to any premise, this particular maze branches in twelve directions (one for each rule of transformation) at each choice point. That is, we start out with a single premise; depending on which rule of transformation we apply, we obtain one of twelve possible new expressions from each of these, and so on. Thus, the number of possible sequences of length k is 12^k. If the problem expression can be derived from the premise in a minimum of seven steps, then a trial-and-error search for the derivation would require, on the average, the construction of $\frac{1}{2} \times 12^7 = 1.8 \times 10^7 = 18{,}000{,}000$ sequences.

If only four rules of transformation, on the average, were actually applicable at each stage (a more realistic assumption, since expressions must be of particular forms for particular rules to be applicable to them), the number of sequences of length 7 would still be $4^7 = 16{,}384$.

Chess Playing. Let us turn now to a second example—choosing a move in chess. On the average, a chess player whose turn it is to move has his choice among twenty to thirty alternatives. There is no difficulty, therefore, in "finding" possible moves, but great difficulty in determining whether a particular legal move is a good move. The problem lies in the verifier and not in the generator. However, a principal technique for evaluating a move is to consider some of the opponent's possible replies to it, one's own replies to his, and so on, only attempting to evaluate the resulting positions after this maze of possible move sequences has been explored to some depth. The maze of move sequences is tremendously large. If we consider the number of continuations five moves deep for each player, assuming an average of twenty-five legal continuations at each stage, we find that P, the set of such move sequences, has about 10^{14} (one hundred million million) members.

Opening a Safe. We can make similar estimates of the sizes of the set P for the other examples of problem solving tasks we have listed. In all cases the set is so large as to foreclose a solution generating process that makes a completely random search through the set for possible solutions.

Before we leave our estimates, it will be useful to consider one additional "synthetic" example that has a simpler structure than any we have discussed so far, and that will be helpful later in understanding how

various heuristic devices cut down the amount of search required to find problem solutions. Consider a safe whose lock has ten independent dials, each with numbers running from oo to 99 on its face. The safe will have $100^{10} = 10^{20}$, or one hundred billion billion possible settings, only one of which will unlock it. A would-be safecracker, twirling the dials at random, would take on the average fifty billion billion trials to open it.

However, if the safe were defective, so that there was a faint click each time any dial was turned to its correct setting, it would take an average of only fifty trials to find the correct setting of any one dial, or five hundred trials to open the safe. The ten successive clicks that told him when he was getting "warmer" would make all the difference to the person opening the safe between an impossible task and a trivial one.

Thus, if we can obtain information that tells us which solutions to try, and in particular, if we can obtain information that allows us to factor one large problem into several small ones—*and to know when we have successfully solved each of the small ones*—the search task can be tremendously reduced. This guidance of the solution generator by information about the problem and its solution and this factorization of problems into more or less independent subproblems lie at the heart of effective problem solving processes.

HEURISTICS FOR PROBLEM SOLVING

We have seen that we can describe most problems abstractly in terms of a maze whose paths are possible solutions, with some small proportion of these being actual solutions. Then we can analyze the problem solving processes into those that determine the order in which the paths will be explored (solution generators) and those that determine whether a proposed solution is in fact a solution (solution verifiers).

Our examples show that solution generation and verification need not operate in an inflexible sequence. In the Logic Theorist, as we saw, certain of the verifying conditions are built into the generator, so that only valid proofs are generated and other sequences of logic expressions are never considered. On the other hand, in chess playing, to verify that a proposed move is satisfactory, it is necessary to consider a large maze of possible continuations and to search some part of this maze.

In the present section we will examine some actual examples of successful problem solving programs to see just what is involved in solution generation and verification, and how the programs reduce the problems to manageable size. We use the term *heuristic* to denote any principle or device that contributes to the reduction in the average search to solution. Although no general theory of heuristics exists yet,[4] we can say a good deal about some of the heuristics employed in human complex problem solving. Our data derive largely from symbolic logic and chess problems that are formal and symbolic. This characteristic of the tasks undoubtedly limits the range of of heuristics that we have observed. However, the kinds of heuristics we have found and can describe (e.g., planning and functional analysis) seem to have rather general applicability.

Efficient Generators

Even when the set P is large, as it usually is in complex problem solving, it is possible for the solution generator to consider at an early stage those parts of P that are likely to contain a solution and to avoid the parts that are most likely to be barren. For example, many problems have the following form: S, the set of solutions, consists of all elements of P with property A, property B, and property C. No generator is available that will generate elements having all three properties. However, generators may exist that generate elements satisfying any two of the properties. Thus there are three possible schemes: (1) to generate elements with properties A and B

4. See, however, the work of G. Polya (1954, 1957), who has analyzed the use of heuristics in mathematics.

until one is found that also has C; (2) to generate elements A and C until one is found with property B; (3) to generate elements with B and C until one is found with property A. Which generator should be chosen depends on which constraints are the most difficult to satisfy and on the relative costs of generation. If there are lots of elements satisfying A, then generating elements with B and C is reasonable, since an "A" can be expected to show up soon. If "As" are rare, it is better to generate elements that already have property A.

The Logic Theorist provides a clear example of this type of heuristic. Recall that the problem of the Logic Theorist is to find proofs. A proof is a list of logic expressions satisfying the following properties:

A. The beginning of the list consists of known theorems (any number of them).

B. All other expressions on the list are direct and valid consequences of expressions higher on the list.

C. The last expression on the list is the expression to be proved.

Now, although there is no generator that will turn out sequences satisfying all three of these conditions, there are generators that satisfy any two of them. It is easy to write down lists that start with theorems and end with the known expression. The difficult condition, however is B: that the list must consist of valid inference steps. Hence, it would be obviously foolish to choose a generator that automatically satisfied A and C and simply wait until it generated a list that also satisfied B.

It is also possible to construct a generator satisfying A and B—one that produces lists that are proofs of something. This generator could find a proof by producing such lists until one appeared containing the desired expression—condition C. The British Museum algorithm discussed earlier is a generator of this kind. Finally, one can build a generator that satisfies conditions B and C. Fixing the last expression to be the desired one, lists are produced that consist only of valid inference steps leading to the last expression. Then the problem is solved when a list is generated that satisfies condition A, so that the expressions on the front of the list are all theorems. With this kind of generator, the list is constructed "backward" from the desired result toward the given theorems. This is the way the Logic Theorist actually goes about discovering proofs.

How do we choose between these two generators—the one that requires a search to satisfy C or the one that requires a search to satisfy A? In the case of logic, the answer is reasonably clear. There is only one terminal expression (the theorem to be proved), but there are many known theorems.

It should be clear that there is nothing inherently superior in working backward as opposed to working forward. The choice between them resolves itself into a question of which constraints are the most binding. It may well be, of course, that the particular situation found here (many possible starting points versus a single end), which predisposes toward working backward, is relatively common.[5]

Simple Selection Heuristics

When a problem solver faces a set of alternatives, such as the branches from a choice point in the maze in figure 1, a common heuristic procedure is to screen out possible paths initially, using a relatively inexpensive test. To see the worth of this procedure, consider a maze having m alternatives at each branch point and length k. If there were a single correct path to the goal, finding that path by random search would require, on the average, $\frac{1}{2}m^k$ trials. If a heuristic test were available that could immediately weed out half the alternatives at each branch point as unprofitable, then a random search with this heuristic would require only $\frac{1}{2}(\frac{1}{2}m)^k$

trials on the average. This is a reduction in search by a ratio of 2^k, which, if the maze were only seven steps in length, would amount to a factor of 128, and if the maze were ten steps in length, a factor of just over a thousand.

The Logic Theorist uses a number of such selection heuristics, for example, working backward as described above. In this way, it generates a maze of subproblems which corresponds exactly to the abstract pictures we have been giving (Newell and Simon, 1956).

In figure 2, two mazes are shown, derived from two attempts, under slightly different conditions, to prove a particular theorem from the same set of known theorems. In each maze, the desired theorem (*2.45) is represented by the top node; and each node below corresponds to a new expression generated (as a subproblem) from the node immediately above it. In both cases, the Logic Theorist found the same proof, which is designated in each maze by a heavy line.

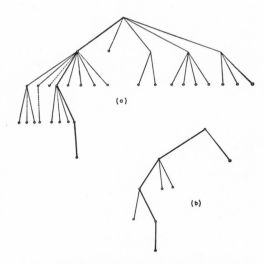

(a)

(b)

Figure 2. Mazes of two proofs of theorem 2.45 from the same initial theorems. Identical programs generated the two mazes, except that the program of maze (b) had two additional selective heuristics. The heavy line is the proof. Dotted lines show additional branches eliminated by selective heuristics already in the first program.

---

5. Duncker (1945) calls working backward an "organic" procedure and distinguishes it from the "mechanical" procedures of working forward. Our analysis shows both why the former might be generally more efficient than the latter and why there is nothing qualitatively different between them.

When it was generating the lower maze, the Logic Theorist had available two selective heuristics it did not have during the run that generated the upper maze. One of these heuristics weeded out new expressions that appeared "unprovable" on the basis of certain plausible criteria; the other heuristic weeded out expressions that seemed too complicated, in the sense of having too many negation signs. These two heuristics reduced the amount of search required to find the solution by a factor of 24/9 or 2.7. However, when the cost of the additional testing is taken into account, the net saving in total problem solving effort after allowing for this testing was 2.3. On the other hand, we have experimented with heuristics that were excellent in their performance characteristics (reducing search by factors of 10) but that required so much effort to carry out as to cancel out the gain.

A heuristic need not be foolproof—indeed, most are not. Both heuristics mentioned above eliminate paths that lead to solutions. In rare cases, they can even eliminate all paths to solutions. To take another example, a chess heuristic that would instantly remove from consideration any move that left the queen under attack would be an excellent rule of thumb for a novice player, but would occasionally lead him to miss a winning queen sacrifice. Occasionally, heuristics are found that are foolproof. These are usually called algorithms. The British Museum algorithm is an example, for it will always generate a proof, given enough time. ("Enough time" may, as we have seen, sometimes be centuries or millenia.)

Strategies in Solution Generation

Usually the information needed to select promising paths becomes available only as the search proceeds. Examination of paths produces clues of the "warmer-cooler" variety that guide the further conduct of the search. We have already given a simple, but striking, example of this in the clicking safe. As any particular dial is turned to the correct setting, the person opening the safe is informed by the click that he should stop manipulating that dial and go to the next. As a result he need attempt, on the average, only five hundred of the enormous total number of possible settings of the dials.

The sequential availability of cues derives from a deep property of problem solving tasks that we must examine closely. There are, in general, two distinct ways to describe any particular choice point in a problem solving maze. In chess, for example, a particular position can be specified by stating (verbally or with a diagram) what piece occupies each square on the board. Alternatively, the position can be specified by giving a sequence of moves that leads to it from the opening position.

Similarly, in logic an expression can be specified by writing it explicitly in the usual way or equally well by giving a sequence of operations on the axioms (a proof) that will produce it. (In figure 1, the solution may be described as d_6 or as 2−1−2.) Or, in arithmetic, if we use the symbol x' to mean the integer that follows x, we can write the number five as 5 or as $0''''$. Or, as a more familiar example, we can designate a house by an address—5936 Phillips Avenue—or by the sequence of turns (go two blocks, turn right, go nine blocks, turn right, go one block) necessary to get there from a given starting point.

In all these cases, we will call the first method of specifying an element of P *specification by state description*; the second method, *specification by process description*. Often problems are set by providing the problem solver with a partial or complete state description of the solution, the state descriptions of one or more starting points, and a list of allowable processes. The task, in these terms, is to find a sequence of processes that, operating on the initial state, will produce the final state.

We can now see how cues become available sequentially, and why, consequently, strategies of search that use the cues are possible. Each time a process is applied to an initial state, a new state with a new description is produced. If there are relations (known to or learnable by the problem solver) between characteristics of the state description and distance from the goal (i.e., the final description that represents the solution), these relations can be used to tell when the problem solver is getting "warmer " or "colder," hence, whether or not he should continue along a path defined by some sequence of processes. If, for example, in figure 1, the state description corresponding to b_2 indicates that it is closer to the solution than the description corresponding to b_1, then the problem solver at a_1 with take path 2 instead of path 1 and will be relieved of the necessity of exploring the entire upper half of the maze.

Let us examine a concrete example, for which we have data. Consider the following sequence of logic expressions that was written down by a subject solving one of O. K. Moore's problems in our laboratory. (The reader does not need to know what the symbols mean to understand the example. The task involved in these problems is described briefly in the appendix.)

Step	Expression	Justification for Step
(1)	$R \cdot (-P \supset Q)$	Given
(2)	$R \cdot (\quad P \vee Q)$	Rule 6
(3)	$R \cdot (\quad Q \vee P)$	Rule 1 (inside parenthesis)
(4)	$(Q \vee P) \cdot R$	Rule 1 (outside parenthesis)

The first line is the expression given to the subject as the starting point of the "maze." The last line is the expression he was instructed to produce by applying the allowable operations. The number at the right of each line is the number of the rule he applied to obtain that line from the previous one. In this example, the state description of the solution is the expression: "$(Q \vee P) \cdot R$." The process description is: "The expression obtained by applying rules 6, 1, 1 to expression '$R \cdot (-P \supset Q)$.'" It is, of course, not at all obvious, except by hindsight, that these two descriptions refer to the same logic expression—if it were obvious, the problem would be no problem.

How can the problem solver in this instance obtain new information as he proceeds each step down the maze? If we compare the final expression with the intermediate ones, we note that at each stage the newly derived expression resembles the final expression more closely than did the previous ones. For example, expression (1) contains two symbols that do not appear in the final expression; these have disappeared from expression (2). The next step rectifies the order of the symbols within parentheses, while the final step rectifies the order of the symbols in the expression as a whole.

A simple heuristic to follow in such cases is to apply an operator if the result of its application is to produce a new expression that resembles the final expression more nearly than did the previous one. To apply the heuristic, the problem solver needs some criteria of similarity, but it is easy to see what they might be in the present case. These criteria provide the "clicks" that reduce the amount of search required.

We can test this explanation further by comparing it with the thinking-aloud protocol that the subject produced as he performed the task. We produce here an excerpt from his protocol, slightly edited to make it more comprehensible to the reader:

E. What are you looking at?
S. I'm looking at the idea of reversing the Rs. Then I'd have a similar group at the beginning.
But I can easily leave something like that until the end. . . .
Now I'm trying to see what operation I might apply to expression (1). . . . (He goes down the list of operations.) Rule 4 looks interesting . . . but there's no switching of order. I need that P and Q changed. . . . That doesn't seem practical with any of these rules. . . . I'm looking for a way, now, to get rid of that horseshoe ($\supset$). Ah . . . here it is, rule 6. So I'd apply rule 6 to the second part of what we have up there.
E. That gives you (writing) (2) $R \cdot (P \vee Q)$.
S. Okay. And now I'd use rule 1 on P and Q and then with the entire expression.
E. We'll do them one at a time (writing) (3) $R \cdot (Q \vee P)$.

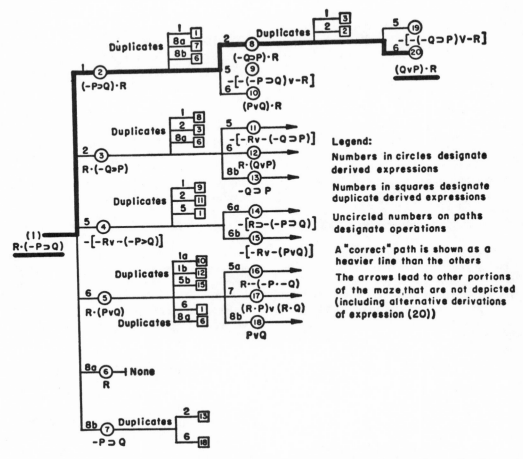

Figure 3. Partial diagram of problem maze for deriving $(Q \vee P) \cdot R$ from $R \cdot (-P \supset Q)$

Now the total expression?

S. Yeah.

E. You get (writing) (4) $(Q \vee P) \cdot R$, and . . . that's it.

S. That's it all right. Okay . . . that wasn't too hard.

It will be observed that the subject thought through the successive changes (bringing the R to the left side, interchanging P and Q, eliminating the horseshoe) in the order opposite to that in which he actually carried them out, but that his process—that of making the expression at hand more and more like the final expression—is precisely the one we have described.

To give a picture of the selectivity involved in this particular piece of problem solving, we show in figure 3 a somewhat simplified picture of a portion of the problem maze, including only those branches that would actually be explored if the problem were solved by a systematic search without selectivity. Note that the path to the goal (1–2–6) discovered through systematic search is different from the one (6–1–1) discovered by the subject's selective processes and that the systematic search generated many expressions that—from the protocol evidence—did not even enter the subject's awareness.

The same kind of alternation between state description and process description is involved in choosing a move in chess. Because of the tremendous size of the maze of continuations, only a few of all the possible lines of play can be examined. When the player considers a particular move, he can construct in his imagination a picture of the board after the move has been made. He can then examine this new state description to see what features of it are favorable, what features unfavorable, and what likely continuations it suggests. In this way, he is guided to examine a few paths through the maze (if he is a good player, his heuristic will usually lead him to examine the important ones), and he can explore these to some depth—deeply enough to be able to evaluate directly the final positions he reaches. The best evidence we possess indicates that the strongest chess players do not examine more than (at the very most) a few dozen continuations, and these to depths ranging from several moves to ten or even more (see figure 4). The ability of the chess master, so amazing to the novice, to explore in depth derives from

his ability to explore very selectively without missing important alternatives. The "clicks" he notices, inaudible to the novice, are loud and obvious to him.

Functional Analysis

Underlying the heuristic of "reducing differences" is the general concept of functional analysis. Functional or means-end analysis provides a generalized heuristic that can be applied to a wide range of problems. We will describe a program for functional analysis that we have now incorporated in a revised version of the Logic Theorist, and which, while not completely general, can almost certainly transfer without modification to problem solving in trigonometry, algebra, and probably other subjects such as geometry and chess.

The entities that the program recognizes are *expressions*, *differences* between expressions, *operators*, *goals* and *subgoals*, and *methods*. The program can be used as a problem solving heuristic for problems of the form: "given expression *a* and a set of admissible operators, to derive expression *b*." We have already observed that logic problems can be put in this form—and so can most other problems formulated in terms of the maze model.

Associated with each goal in the heuristic is a set of methods—procedures that may help attain the goal in question. A method may, in turn, involve establishing subgoals and applying the methods associated with these. At some point, if the heuristic is successful, a subgoal is attained by one of its methods; this success reactivates the goal at the next higher level in the hierarchy, and so on.

Let us be more concrete. There are three types of goals in the functional problem solver:

Type 0 Goal: Find a way to transform expression *a* into expression *b*.
Type 1 Goal: Reduce the difference *d* between expressions *a* and *b*.
Type 2 Goal: Apply operator *q* to expression *a*.

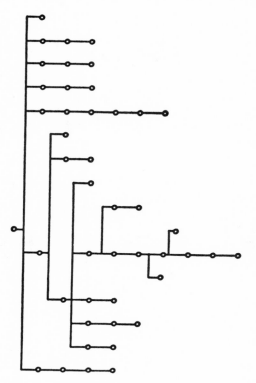

Figure 4. Portion of maze of continuations examined by chessmaster in middle-game position. (From de Groot (1946), p. 207.)

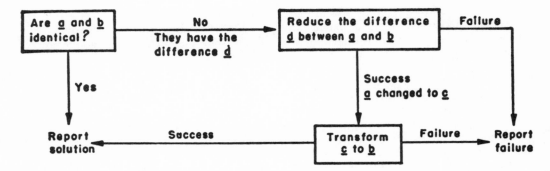

(a)— Type 0 goal: Transform $\underline{a}$ to $\underline{b}$

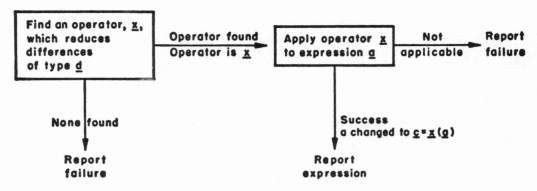

(b)— Type 1 goal: Reduce the difference $\underline{d}$ between $\underline{a}$ and $\underline{b}$

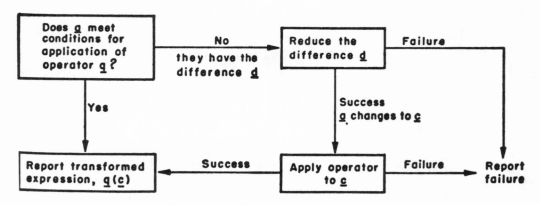

(c)— Type 2 goal: Apply operator $\underline{q}$ to expression $\underline{a}$

Figure 5. Goals in functional heuristic.

At present, one method is associated with each of these goals. Briefly, the method associated with the type 0 goal consists of (figure 5*a*): (a) matching the two expressions to find a difference, *d*, between them; (b) setting up the type 1 subgoal of reducing *d*—if this is successful, a new transformed expression, *a'* is obtained; (c) setting up the type 0 subgoal of transforming *a'* into *b*. If the last step is successfully carried out, the original problem has been solved.

The method associated with the type 1 goal consists of (figure 5*b*): (a) searching for an operator that is relevant to the reduction of the difference, *d*; and (b) setting up the type 2 goal of applying the operator.

The method associated with the type 2 goal consists in (figure 5*c*): (a) determining if the conditions are met for applying *q* to *a*; (b) if so, applying the operator; or, if not, setting up the type 1 subgoal of reducing the difference between *a* and the conditions for applying *q*.

Let us see how this functional problem solver would approach the particular logic problem we examined in the last section. The problem solver is given a type 0 goal of transforming expression (1) into expression (4). In trying to reach this goal (figure 5*a*), it first matches (1) with (4) to see what differences there are and notes that the symbols *P* and *Q* occur in reverse order in (1) from the order in (4). This generates the type 1 subgoal (figure 5*b*) of eliminating this difference. The problem solver remembers (from instruction or previous description) that operator 1 is relevant to reducing differences of this kind and sets up the type 2 subgoal (figure 5*c*) of applying rule 1 to (1). The conditions for applicability are not met, for operator 1 requires a $\vee$ between *P* and *Q* while actually there is a $\supset$. Hence a new type 1 goal is created to change the $\supset$ into a $\vee$. Operator 6, which has this function, is found, and the type 2 goal of applying it is set up and achieved. The transformed expression (2) now satisfies the conditions for applying operator 1. This is now applied, achieving the type 2 subgoal and yielding expression (3). A similar but simpler sequence of events leads to expression (4)—at which time the problem solver notes that it has eliminated all differences between the initial and terminal expressions, and hence has solved the original problem. Reference back to the protocol will show how closely this program models the behavior of the subject.[6]

It will be observed that neither the goals nor the methods of the functional problem solving program make reference to logic or any other subject matter. Simply by acquiring new definitions of the terms "expressions," "differences," and "operators," the problem solver can use the functional heuristic to solve problems relating to quite different subject matter. We hope, in the near future, to test whether this heuristic will, in fact, solve trigonometric identities.

The Heuristics of Planning

Another class of heuristics of great generality that increase the selectivity of solution generators are those that come under the rubric of "planning." Consider again a maze *k* steps in length with *m* branches at each choice point. Suppose that, instead of cues at each choice point, there was a cue at every second step to mark the correct path (see figure 6). Then the task of traversing the maze successfully could be divided into a number of subtasks—specifically, the tasks of reaching successively each of the choice points that were marked by the cues.

---

6. Our aim here is to illustrate, and not deal with the scientific problems of how well these programs explain the protocols. In the sketch of the program given in the text, we generate the expressions in the order in which the subject wrote them down. The protocol indicates clearly that he proceeded initially in the opposite order. To simplify the exposition, we have not tried to describe the program that would simulate the subject's behavior most closely, and we have taken the liberty of editing the protocols. At another time we will undertake a more systematic analysis of the protocols as evidence.

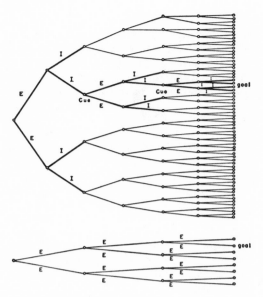

Figure 6. Problem space (top) and planning space (bottom) for a simple task. The plan is used to find the cues in the larger maze; then only the darkened paths in the maze need be explored. The steps marked *E* are essential, and those marked I are inessential —see text.

Such a set of subtasks would constitute a plan. In place of the original task of traversing a maze k steps in length, the problem solver would now have the task of traversing $(k/2)$ mazes each two steps in length. The expected number of paths that would have to be searched to solve the first problem is, as before $\frac{1}{2}m^k$. The expected number of trials to solve the second problem is $\frac{1}{2}(k/2)m^2$.

If, as in the figure, the original maze was six steps in length with two alternatives at each choice point, the average amount of search required would be reduced from thirty-two trials to six—to which would have to be added the effort required to find the plan.

We use such a planning technique whenever we take a cross-country trip. First we sketch a general route from major city to major city; then, taking these cities as subgoals, we solve the subproblem of reaching each from the previous one.

We have devised a program of this kind to describe the way some of our subjects

handle O. K. Moore's logic problems, perhaps the easiest way to show what is involved in planning is to describe that program. On a purely pragmatic basis, the twelve operators that are admitted in this system of logic can be put in two classes, which we will call, respectively, "essential" and "inessential" operators. Essential operators are those which, when applied to an expression, make "large" changes in its appearance—change "$P \lor P$" to "P," for example. Inessential operators are those which make "small" changes —e.g., change "$P \lor Q$" to "$Q \lor P$." (See appendix.) As we have said, the distinction is purely pragmatic. Of the twelve operators in this calculus, we have classified eight as essential and four as inessential. Roughly speaking, the inessential operators are those that change the order of the symbols in expressions or change the connectives ("$\lor$" to "$\cdot$", for example) but make no other changes.

Next, we can take an expression and abstract from it those characteristics that relate only to inessential changes. For example, we can abstract from "$P \lor Q$" the expression (PQ), where the order of the symbols in the latter expression is regarded as irrelevant [i.e., (PQ) is treated as identical with (QP)]. Clearly, if inessential operations are applied to the abstracted expressions, the expressions will remain unchanged, while essential operations can be expected to change them [e.g., the operator that will change "$P \lor P$" to "P" will change (PP) to (P)].

We can now set up a correspondence between our original expressions and operators, on the one hand, and the abstracted expressions and essential operators, on the other. Corresponding to the original problem of transforming a into b, we can construct a new problem of transforming a' into b', where a' and b' are the expressions obtained by abstracting a and b respectively. Suppose that we solve the new problem, obtaining a sequence of expressions, $a'c'd' \ldots b'$. We can now transform back to the original problem space and set up the new problems of transforming a into c, c into d, and so on. Thus, the solution of the problem in the planning space provides

	Proof			*Plan*	
Step	*Expression*	*Justification*		*Expression*	*Justification*
(1)	PvQ	Given		PQ	Given
(2)	−R ⊃ −Q	,,		RQ	,,
(3)	S	,,		S	,,
(4)	R ⊃ −S	,,		RS	,,
(5)	S ⊃ −R	Rule 2 on (4)			
(6)	S ⊃ −Q	Rule 12 on (2), (5)		SQ	Rule 12 on (2), (4)
(7)	−Q	Rule 11 on (3), (6)		Q	Rule 11 on (3), (6)
(8)	−P ⊃ Q	Rule 6 on (1)			
(9)	−Q ⊃ P	Rule 2 on (8)			
(10)	P	Rule 11 on (7), (9)		P	Rule 11 on (1), (7)
(11)	PvT	Rule 9 on (10)		PT	Rule 9 on (10)

Figure 7. Solution of problem A4 by subject 8.

a plan for the solution of the original problem.

Let us examine (figure 7) an actual example of the application of the planning heuristic to the O. K. Moore problems. This example follows the protocol of one of our subjects and shows quite clearly that he used the planning heuristic in precisely this way to solve the problem in question. The left-hand side of figure 7 shows the sequence of expressions the subject wrote down in solving Moore's problem A4. The subject was given the expressions in lines (1) through (4) and told to derive the expression in line (11). He carried through the derivation in seven steps, the prior expressions and rules used in each step being given to the right of the derived expression.

The subject's protocol shows, however, that prior to obtaining the rigorous derivation, he had worked out a complete plan for the proof. The plan is shown, in terms of abstracted expressions, in the right-hand half of the figure. The planning activity took place immediately after the problem was presented to the subject, and before he instructed the experimenter to write down any transformations of the expressions given him as premises. Here is the protocol segment that discloses the planning activity:

S. Well, one possibility right off the bat is when you have just a *P* ∨ *T* like that (the problem expression) the last thing you might use is

that rule 9. I can get everything down to a *P* and just add a ∨ *T*. So that's one thing to keep in mind. . . . I don't know if that's possible; but I think it is because I see that expressions (2) and (4) are somewhat similar. If I can cancel out the *R*s that would leave me with just an *S* and *Q*; and if I have just an *S* and *Q*, I can eventually get—expression (3)—get the *S*s to cancel out and end up with just a *Q*. And if I end up with just *Q*, maybe the *Q*s will cancel out; so you see all the way down the line. I don't know, it looks too good to be true, but I think I see it already.

At this point the subject has already constructed a four-step plan, which will lead him, as he executes it, to two sub-problems of filling in the gaps (the other two subproblems are trivial, since they are solved simply by the translation of the abstracted expressions back into the original space). One of these subproblems is three steps in length, the other is two. Thus, for the original seven-step maze, the subject has substituted a four-step maze, a three-step maze, and a two-step maze.

To complete our illustration, let us see how the subject goes about solving the first subproblem—eliminating the *R* between expressions (2) and (4):

S. (Immediately following previous excerpt) Expressions (2) and (4)—we'll have to do something with them. If I invert expression (4)—apply rule 2 to it—I will have (*S* ⊃ −*R*). Good. O.K. Apply rule 2 to expression (4).

E. That gives (writing): (5) $S \supset - R$.
S. Now apply rule 12 to expressions (2) and
   $(4) - (2)$ and (5), I mean.
E. That gives (writing): (6) $S \supset - Q$.
S. Right. I got rid of the Rs. Now. . . .

It will be observed that only rules 9, 11, and 12 are used in the derivation of the plan. All these are essential rules. Rules 2 and 6, both of which are inessential, are used to solve the subproblems.

We can estimate how much reduction the planning heuristic accomplishes in the size of the maze to be searched. The number of alternative operations at each step is of the order of 10. (Because we distinguish between essential and inessential operations, it may be smaller when the planning heuristic is used than when the problem is solved without it, but we will ignore this additional source of efficiency of the planning heuristics.) If m is 10, then the average number of paths to be searched without planning is $\frac{1}{2}$ $10^7 = 5,000,000$. With planning, the number of paths is $\frac{1}{2} \cdot 10^4 + \frac{1}{2} \cdot 10^3 + \frac{1}{2} \cdot 10^2 = 5,550$. The search required in the first case is larger by a ratio of 900:1.

Of course these ratios assume that no other selective heuristic—apart from the planning heuristic—is employed. If the planning heuristic were superimposed, for example, on the functional analysis heuristic, the latter would reduce m to a much smaller number; hence there would be much less search either with or without planning. Suppose, for example, that the functional analysis heuristic reduced m to 4. Then the search without planning would involve $\frac{1}{2} \cdot 4^7 = 8,192$ paths; the search with planning would require $\frac{1}{2} \cdot 4^4 + \frac{1}{2} \cdot 4^3 + \frac{1}{2} \cdot 4^2 = 168$. The savings ratio is now *only* 49:1.

The subject, understandably, was pleased with his heuristic. His comment on solving the problem was "See, I'm acquiring an insight." Since his protocol gives evidence of other bits of heuristic in addition to the ones we have been discussing, his value of m was probably 2 or less, and the total number of paths he searched was probably less than a dozen. The combination of heuristics he used, simple

though they were, secured him a saving over blind trial and error of a factor of perhaps 500,000. These rough statistics give us a good picture of the reason for the "aha!" that goes with "insight" into the problem structure (which we would translate, "acquisition of an additional piece of heuristic").

Summary: The Nature of Heuristics

In this section, we have seen that the success of a problem solver who is confronted with a complex task rests primarily on his ability to select—correctly—a very small part of the total problem solving maze for exploration. The processes that carry out this selection we call heuristics. We have seen that most heuristics depend on a strategy that modifies subsequent search as a function of information obtained in previous search; and we have discussed at some length several of the most significant and powerful classes of heuristics that we have encountered in our attempts to simulate human problem solving.

Among the heuristics we examined were: processes for working backward from the problem solution, selection heuristics, functional or means-end analysis, and planning. We provided operational meanings for these terms by sketching out what the actual processes would be in the Logic Theorist and in a chessplaying machine. We referred to our evidence from protocols of human subjects that such processes actually do occur in human problem solving behavior. We also constructed quantitative estimates of the reduction in search that results from the selectivity of these heuristics and used the estimates to account for the ability of humans—and of machines simulating them by using the same processes—to solve the particular problems in question.

Some Conditions of Creativity

In the remaining pages of this paper, we will use the theory of problem solving developed in preceding sections to cast light on three topics that are often discussed in relation to creativity:

1. The use of imagery in problem solving.
2. The relation of unconventionality to creativity.
3. The role of hindsight in the discovery of new heuristics.

These three topics were chosen because we think our theory has something to say about them. We have not tried to include all the traditional topics in the theory of creative activity—we do not, for example, discuss the phenomenon of incubation—nor will we try to treat definitively the topics we have included. We are still far from having all the mechanisms that will be required for a complete theory of creativity: these last pages are necessarily extrapolations and are more speculative than the earlier sections.

PLANNING AND IMAGERY

Among the issues that have surrounded the topic of imagery in the literature on thinking the following have been prominent:

1. What internal "language" is used by the organism in thinking? To what extent is this "language" related to the sense modalities, and is the thinking represented by elements that correspond to abstract "symbols," or to pictures or to something else?
2. To what extent do the internal representations, whatever their nature, involve generalization and abstraction from that which they represent?

Using the example of planning we have been considering, we believe some clarification can be achieved of both issues.

Some Comments on Representation

How are the objects of thought represented internally? We are asking here neither a physiological nor a "hardware" question. We wish an answer at the level of information processing, rather than at that of neurology or electronics. In a state description of an information processing system, we can talk of patterns of elementary

symbols. These symbols may be electric charges, as in some computer memories, or they may be the cell assemblies of Hebb's theories, or they may be something quite different. We are not interested in what they are made of. Given that there are some such patterns—that the system is an information processing system—our question is in what way the patterns within mirror, or fail to mirror, the patterns without that they represent.

Let us take a simple example from logic. We may write on a piece of paper the expression "$(p \lor q) \supset p$." What would it mean to say that the "same" expression was held in memory by the Logic Theorist? With the present program, it would mean that somewhere in memory there would be a branching pattern of elementary symbols (or the internal counterparts of elementary symbols) that would look like:

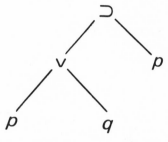

Of course, there would not literally be mounds of ink like "p," but there would be internal elementary patterns in one-one correspondence to these. Note, however, that the correspondence between the internal and external representations as a whole is far more complicated than the correspondences between elementary symbols. The external representation of the expression in the illustration is a linear array of symbols; the internal representation has branches that make it topologically distinct from a linear array. The external representation uses symbols like "("and")"; these are absent from the internal representations—the grouping relations they denote being implicit in the branching structure itself (i.e., the cluster $p \lor q$, which is enclosed in parentheses in the external representation, is a subtree of the entire expression in the internal representation).

The implicitness of certain aspects of the internal representation goes even deeper than we have just indicated. For the tree structure we represented on the paper above by connecting symbols with lines is represented within the computer memory by the fact that there are certain information processes available that will "find the left subtree" and "find the right subtree" of such a tree structure. The actual physical locations of these elements in memory can be (and usually are) completely scattered, so long as these information processes have means of finding them.

Let us take another example. If we wish to represent on paper the concept of a pair of elements, P and Q abstracted from the order of the pair, we can write something like: (PQ), and append it to the statement that (PQ) is equivalent for all purposes with (QP). In an internal representation, order independence of the terms of the pair might be secured in a quite different way. Suppose that the symbols P and Q were stored (in some order) on a list in memory, but that the only information processes available for dealing with lists were processes that produced the same output regardless of the order of the items on the list. Suppose, for example, that the "print list" process always alphabetized the list before printing. Then this process would always print out "(PQ)" regardless of whether the items were stored on the list as PQ or QP. In this case, the order independence of the information processes applicable to the lists would be an implicit internal representation of the equivalence of (PQ) with (QP).[7]

The main lesson that we learn from these examples is that the internal representation may mirror all the relevant properties of

the external representation without being a "picture" of it in any simple or straightforward sense. It is not at all clear whether a human subject would be aware that his internal representation of a logic expression "carried" the information about the expression in quite a different way from the string of symbols on paper, or that, if he were aware, he could verbalize what the differences were.

A similar point has been made in discussions of "encoding." Our examples show, however, that encoding may involve something far more complex than translating a string of symbols in one alphabet into another string of symbols in another alphabet. The encoded representation may not be a string at all, and there may be important differences in what is explicit and what is implicit in the two representations.

Representation and the Sense Modalities

Since the internal representation of information need not be a simple mapping of what is "out there," or even of what is received by the sense organs, it is not easy to know what is meant by saying that a particular internal representation is or is not "visual" or "auditory." Is the internal branching structure that represents the logic expression inside the Logic Theorist a visual image of the string of symbols on paper or is it not?

There is an obvious fallacy in saying that it is, not just because the spatial (or even the topological) relations are not the same in the two. The internal representations we carry around in our heads of even the most visual of pictures cannot possibly have the same metrical relations within (and possibly not even the same topologic relations) as without.

We believe that the explanation of why some memories are visual, some auditory, and some verbal lies in a quite different direction from a simple "mapping" theory. Since our explanation rests on considerations that have not even been touched upon in the present chapter, we cannot discuss it at length. However, a very brief statement

---

7. A simple example of this in humans is well known to teachers of matrix algebra. Since all the elementary arithmetic and algebraic systems that students have encountered previously contain the commutative law, students must be *taught* that the matrix product AB is not equivalent to the product BA.

of it may help us understand the role of imagery in creative thought.

We will assert that an internal representation is visual if it is capable of serving as an input to the same information processes as those that operate on the internal representations of immediate visual sensory experiences. These information processes that can be applied to visual sensations literally serve as a "mind's eye," for they can operate on memories that have been encoded in the same way as sensory inputs, and when they are so applied they produce the phenomena of visual imagination. Since there must be processes that can deal with sensory inputs, there is nothing mysterious in the notion these same processes can deal with inputs from memory, and hence there is nothing metaphysical or nonoperational about the concept of "mind's eye" or "mind's ear."

But the mind's eye is used not only to process inputs that "nature" coded in visual form. Often we deliberately construct visual representations of abstract relations (e.g., we draw boxes to represent states of a system and arrows connecting the boxes to represent the processes that transform one state into another). What can be the advantage of the imagery? The advantage lies in the fact that when we encode information so as to be accessible to visual processes, we have automatically built into the encoded information all the relations that are implicit in the information processes that constitute the mind's eye. For example, when we represent something as an arrow, we determine the order in which the items connected by the arrow will be called into attention.

We are led in this way to the concept of systems of imagery. A system of imagery comprises a set of conventions for encoding information and, coordinated with these, a set of information processes that apply to the encoded information. As we have seen, the information processes for interpreting the encoded information may be just as rich in implicit conventions as the processes for encoding. It is the fact that the encoding makes available the former as well as the latter that sometimes makes

it useful to represent information in a modality for which we have a rich and elaborate system of imagery.

Abstraction and Generalization

Bishop Berkeley founded his epistemology on the personal difficulty he experienced in imagining a triangle which is "neither oblique nor rectangle, equilateral, equicrural nor scalenon, but all and none of these at once." Hume, on the other hand, found this feat of imagination perfectly feasible!

The Logic Theorist would have to take Hume's side against Berkeley. For in the planning program the problem solver has the capacity to imagine a logic expression comprised of two variables joined by a connective, in which the connective is neither $\vee$ nor $\cdot$ nor $\supset$, but all and none of these at once. For this is precisely what the representation (PQ) stands for and the way in which it is used by the planning processes.

Once we admit that the relation between the object sensed and its internal representation is complex, there is no difficulty in admitting as corollary that the internal representation may abstract from all but a few of the properties of the object "out there." What we call "visual imagery," for example, may admit of colorless images even if all light that falls on the retina is colored.

The fact that the planning heuristic of the Logic Theorist possesses generalized or abstracted images of logic expressions does not prove, of course, that humans construct similar abstractions. What it does prove is that the notion of an image of a triangle "neither oblique nor rectangle, equilateral, equicrural, nor scalenon, but all and none of these at once" is not contradictory, but can be given a straightforward operational definition in an information processing system. Finally, since the information processes that can operate on the abstracted expressions in the Logic Theorist are of the same kind as those that operate on the full-bodied expressions, we would be forced, by any reasonable criterion, to regard the two images as belonging to the same modality.

The Uses of Imagery

We have already hinted at the uses of imagery, but we would like now to consider them a little more explicit. In order for us to think about something, that something must have an internal representation of some kind, and the thinking organism must have some processes that are capable of manipulating the representation. We have called such a combination of representation and processes a system of imagery.

Often, the term image is used somewhat more narrowly to refer to those representations that correspond to one or another of the sense modalities. Thus, we have visual images, auditory images, and tactile images, but we would not, in this narrower usage, speak of "abstract images"—i.e., representations and processes not used to represent any of the sensory inputs.

When a particular representation is used for something, a large number of properties are imputed implicitly to the object represented because these properties are imbedded in the information processes that operate on representations of the kind in question. Thus, if we represent something as a line, we are likely—because that is the way our visual imagery operates —to impute to it also the property of continuity.

Herein lie both the power and the danger of imagery as a tool of thought. The richer the properties of the system of imagery we employ, the more useful is the imagery in manipulating the representation, but the more danger there is that we will draw conclusions based on properties of the system of imagery that the object represented doesn't possess. When we are aware of the danger—and are conscious that we have encoded information into a system of imagery with strong properties—we are likely to call the image a "metaphor."

Often we are not aware of the danger. As has often been observed, Aristotle's logic and epistemology sometimes mistook

accidents of Greek grammar for necessary truths. From this standpoint, the significance of modern mathematics, with its emphasis on rigor and the abstract axiomatic method, is that it provides us with tests that we can apply to the products of thinking to make sure that only those assumptions that we are aware of are being used.

The imagery used in the planning heuristic drastically reduces the space searched by the solution generator by abstracting from detail. This is probably not the only function of imagery for humans, although it is the one best documented by our present programs. We think there is evidence from data on human subjects that, even in those cases where there is not a rich set of processes associated with the representation, imagery may provide a plan to the problem solver at least in the sense of a list of the elements he is dealing with and a list of which of these are related.

Summary: Imagery

We have applied our problem solving theory to the classical problem of the role of imagery in thought. Although our analysis of imagery is admittedly speculative, it provides a possible explanation of the relation of internal representations to the sense modalities, and it provides an example from one of the computer programs of generalization or abstraction and of an abstract "visual" image. Finally, the theory shows how images of various kinds can be used as the basis for planning heuristics.

UNCONVENTIONALITY AND CREATIVITY

Thus far, our view of the problem solving process has been a short-range one. We have taken as starting point a system of heuristics possessed by the problem solver and have asked how it would govern his behavior. Since his initial system of heuristics may not enable the problem solver to find a solution in a particular case, we must also understand how a system of heuristics is modified and developed over time when it is not adequate initially.

Change of Set and Learning

Although all adaptive change in heuristics might be termed "learning," it is convenient to distinguish relatively short-run and temporary changes from longer-run, more or less permanent changes. If we use "learning" to refer only to the latter, then we may designate the former as "changes in set."

There is a basis for the distinction between set change and learning in the structure of the problem solving organism. The human problem solver (and the machine simulation) is essentially a serial rather than a parallel instrument, which because of the narrow span of its attention, does only one or a few things at a time. If it has a rich and elaborate system of heuristics relevant to a particular problem, only a small part of these can be active in guiding search at any given moment. When in solving a problem one subsystem of heuristics is replaced by another, and the search, as a consequence, moves off in a new direction, we refer to this shift as a change in set. Change in set is a modification of the heuristics that are actively guiding search, by replacing them with other heuristics in the problem solver's repertoire; learning is change in the repertoire of heuristics itself.

Stereotypy

A major function of heuristics is to reduce the size of the problem space so that it can be searched in reasonable time. Effective heuristics exclude those portions of the space where solutions don't exist or are rare and retain those portions where solutions are relatively common. Heuristics that have been acquired by experience with some set of problems may be exceedingly effective for problems of that class but may prove inappropriate when used to attack new problems. Behaviorally, stereotypy is simply the subject's persistence in using a system of heuristics that the *experimenter*

knows is inappropriate under the circumstances.

It is a very common characteristic of puzzles that the first steps toward solution require the solver to do something that offends common sense, experience, or physical intuition. Solutions to chess mating problems typically begin with "surprising" moves. In the same way, a number of classical experiments with children and animals show that a simple problem of locomotion to a goal can be made more difficult if a barrier forces the subject to take his first steps away from the goal in order ultimately to reach it. When the task has this characteristic, the problem solver is obviously more likely to succeed if his repertoire of heuristics includes the injunction: "If at first you don't succeed, try something counterintuitive."

Is Unconventionality Enough?

It sometimes seems to be argued that people would become effective problem solvers if only we could teach them to be unconventional. If our analysis here is correct, unconventionality may be a necessary condition for creativity, but it is certainly not a sufficient condition. If unconventionality simply means rejecting some of the heuristics that restrict search to a limited subspace, then the effect of unconventionality will generally be a return to relatively inefficient trial-and-error search in a very much larger space. We have given enough estimates of the sizes of the spaces involved, with and without particular heuristics, to cast suspicion on a theory of creativity that places its emphasis on increase in trial and error.

Let us state the matter more formally. Associated with a problem is a space of possible solutions. Since the problem solver operates basically in a serial fashion, these solutions must be taken up and examined in some order. If the problem solver has no information about the distribution of solutions in the space of possibilities, and no way of extracting clues from his search, then he must resort to a solution generator that is, to all intents and purposes, "random"—that leads him to solutions no more rapidly than would a chance selection. At some later stage, the problem solver learns how to change the solution generator so that—at least for some range of problems —the average search required to find a solution is greatly reduced. But if the modified generator causes some elements in the solution space to be examined earlier than they would otherwise have been, it follows that the examination of others will be postponed.

The argument for unconventionality is that at some point a class of problems may be faced where the generator looks at just the wrong elements first, or even carefully filters out the right ones so that they will never be noticed (as in the chess example of queen sacrifices). A return to the original trial-and-error generator would eliminate this perverse blindness of the generator, but at the expense of reinstating a search through an enormous space. What is needed in these cases is not an elimination of the selective power of a solution generator, but the replacement of the inappropriate generator by an appropriate one.

We have neither the data nor the space to illustrate this point from classical instances of scientific creativity, but we can give a simple example from chess. A chess novice is always stunned when his opponent demolishes him with a "creative" unconventional move like a sacrifice of a major piece. The novice has carefully trained himself to reject out of hand moves that lose pieces (and kicks himself for his oversights). If he tries to imitate his more experienced opponent, he usually loses the sacrificed piece. Clearly the opponent's secret is not simply that he is willing to be unconventional—to consider paths the novice rejects. The secret is that the experienced player has various additional pieces of heuristic that guide him to promising "unconventional" moves by giving him clues of their deeper and less direct consequences. It is the possession of this additional selectivity that allows him, in appropriate positions, to give up the selectivity embodied in the novice's rule of always preserving major pieces. The

evidence we possess on the point indicates rather strongly that the amount of exploration undertaken by the chess master is no greater than that undertaken by relatively weak players (de Groot, 1946). He does not generate more solution possibilities; he does generate them in a different sequence.

Nature Abhors a Vacuum

We see that set change in particular, and unconventionality in general, are likely to facilitate the solution of a problem only if the problem solver has an appropriate new heuristic to replace the inappropriate heuristic that has been "blinding" him. Accordingly, to understand the success of effective and creative problem solvers, we must examine not only the motivational and attitudinal factors that enable them to change an initial set or to violate accepted conventions; we must pay equal attention to the richness of their systems of heuristics that makes any particular piece of heuristic dispensable and to their learning processes that generate new heuristics to fill the vacuums created by the rejection of the ones previously used.

LEARNING BY HINDSIGHT

Our experience with the simulation of learning has been much more limited than our experience with the simulation of problem solving. The chess-playing program is, to date, entirely a performance program; and only a few experiments have been carried out with learning heuristics for the Logic Theorist. Nevertheless, from these explorations and from our theoretical model, we can draw some implications about learning processes that help us understand how the creative problem solver can gradually improve his heuristics.

In the next two sections, we will describe two kinds of learning that have actually been tested with the Logic Theorist. Both kinds of learning involve "hindsight." In the third section, we will undertake a more general analysis of the role of hindsight in the acquisition of new heuristics.

Memory of Specific Results

The simplest kind of learning in a maze is to remember the path to a solution so that the same solution can be reached at once in a later trial. There is no difficulty in programming a machine for this kind of learning, provided that its memory is large enough, and little enough difficulty for a human. Thus it is probable that most high school geometry students, unless they have an enlightened teacher, focus their energies on memorizing theorems and their proofs.

The Logic Theorist stores in memory the theorems it has proved (it could also remember the proofs themselves, but at present is not programmed to do so) and hence can use these as starting points in exploring new parts of the maze.

One should not underestimate the enhancement of problem solving power that can be obtained even with this "routine" kind of learning, particularly if the teacher is careful to present tasks to the problem solver in an appropriate order. We have already seen how much the search for a long proof can be reduced if a plan is provided first; but a plan consists simply in dividing the original problem into a series of smaller problems—marking the path the problem solver is to follow. Exactly the same effect can be secured if the subproblems generated by the planning heuristic are instead provided by the teacher.

On the other hand, storage of specific information about paths in the maze is not always helpful in subsequent problem solving. We have conducted some experiments with the Logic Theorist in which a theorem is presented for proof (1) after all previous theorems have been stored in memory and, alternatively, (2) after a carefully selected small set of "powerful" theorems has been stored in memory. In a considerable number of cases, the program proves the theorem more quickly, and with far less search, in the second condition than in the first. For example, in one case (theorem *2.48 of *Principia Mathematica*) the Theorist achieved a three-step proof when it had in memory only the axioms and one prior theorem (*2.16) in one-third the time it took to find a two-step proof when it held in memory all prior theorems. We are reminded by this example of the blinding effects of excesses of pedantry on human problem solvers also. A small arsenal of good general purpose weapons may be much more effective than a storehouse of specific, narrowly useful ones.

A graphical impression of the qualitative difference that is produced in the Logic Theorist's problem solving behavior when different numbers of prior theorems are held in memory can be obtained from figure 8. The upper half of the figure shows the maze of subproblems the Theorist explored while proving theorem *2.17 with all axioms and prior theorems (twenty in all) held in memory; the lower half shows the maze explored while proving theorem *2.17 with only the axioms and five theorems (ten in all) held in memory. In the former case, twenty-three branches had to be explored to find a three-step

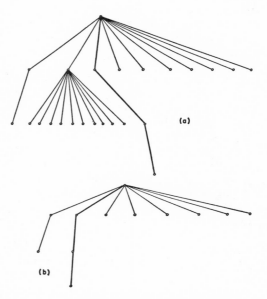

Figure 8. (*a*) Subproblem maze of *2.17 with 20 axioms and theorems in memory and (*b*) subproblem maze with 10 axioms and theorems in memory.

proof; in the latter case only eleven branches to find the same proof.

Differentiation: Specialized Methods

As the problem solver accumulates a larger and larger store of results and techniques, his problem of selection becomes more difficult unless he acquires at the same time additional clues on the basis of which to differentiate parts of the problem space in order to use special techniques under special circumstances. We have developed one example in the Logic Theorist of a process for learning specialized techniques. The Logic Theorist uses four basic methods of attack on problems. In each method it employs theorems already proved as its "raw materials." It turns out, empirically, that some theorems are used principally in connection with certain methods, other theorems with other methods. The Logic Theorist, when it has used a particular theorem in connection with a particular method to solve a problem, associates the theorem with that method. The next time it has occasion to use the same method, it tries theorems that have had a history of success with that method before it tries the other theorems.

To study the effects of introducing this learning of associations between particular methods and particular theorems, we performed the following experiment. As a *pretest*, we instructed the Logic Theorist to attempt in sequence the first fifty-two theorems in chapter 2 of *Principia Mathematica*, allowing it, when attempting a particular theorem, to use all prior theorems (whether it had succeeded in proving them or not), but not to use the special methods learning program. Then, we erased the results of this experience from memory, and as a *test* of the learning, instructed the Theorist to attempt the same fifty-two theorems, this time using the special methods learning program. The main result of the experiment can be seen by comparing the times required by the program to obtain proofs for the twenty theorems that were proved in both pretest and test and whose proofs were not trivial. (We disregard eighteen

additional theorems proved on both runs, but having trival, one-step proofs.)

The abcissa of each point in figure 9 shows the time required to prove a theorem in the pretest; the ordinate of that point, the time to prove the same theorem in the test run. The remarkable fact about this scatter diagram is that it consists of two straight lines, each containing about half the points. For the points on the upper line, almost twice as long was required to discover a proof on the test run as on the pretest; for the points on the lower line, less than half as long was required on the test as on the pretest.

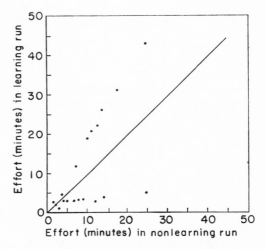

Figure 9. Effect of special methods learning on performance.

Closer examination of the machine's protocols provides a simple explanation. In the test run, the program tried its special high-priority theorems first. Only when these failed—i.e., when the problem was of a new "type" that did not yield to any methods that had worked on previous problems—did the program fall back on its full store of available theorems. The additional time required in the test run for these problems was the time spent in the futile attempt to use the special theorem lists it had learned. On the other hand, where a problem yielded to proof by a method that had worked on a previous problem, this was soon discovered in the test run with a corresponding large improvement in performance. Comparison of the mazes for pretest and test runs of the latter group of problems reveals the characteristic difference—quite similar to that in figure 2—between shallow, widely branching trees involving much search in the former case, and deep, sparsely branching trees in the latter.

The Contribution of Hindsight to Heuristics

The learning programs we have mentioned have two important characteristics in common: (1) they consist in a gradual accumulation of selective principles that modify the sequence in which possible solutions will be examined in the problem space; (2) the selective principles are obtained by hindsight—by analysis of the program's successes in its previous problem solving efforts. We believe that both these characteristics are to be found in most of the important learning processes in humans. Since we have already discussed the first at length, we will turn next to some comments on the second.

Creative problem solving is mysterious because it is hard to see how needles are found in haystacks without interminable search. We have tried to dispel the mystery of the performance by exhibiting devices that are capable of narrowing search to a very small part of the haystack. In one sense, however, this only pushes the mystery back. We can now regard the task of learning an effective problem solving heuristic as itself a problem solving task. The space of possible heuristics for problem solving is a space that must be enormous, even as problem spaces go. How do we find solutions in that space? How do we learn effective heuristics?

We must be careful not to overexplain the phenomenon by discovering learning mechanisms far more powerful than would be needed to account for the historical facts of scientific discovery. One of the key heuristics that underlie physical intuition in dynamics is the notion that forces produce changes in velocity (rather than producing velocities). Evidence from which this idea might be derived is available to anyone with eyes. Yet at least hundreds of man-years of search by highly intelligent men were required to discover this idea, and even after it was enunciated by Galileo another century of work was required before even the most intelligent scientists had cleared it of all obscurity and confusion. We have an even better documented case in chess, where the game had a large literature and numbers of professional players for two centuries or more before Steinitz discovered some of the principles of positional play. From these and other examples we might conclude that the spaces that have to be searched to find important new heuristics are indeed large and that the heuristics available for searching them are not generally very effective.

With this caution we can return to the question of how learning takes place—granted that it doesn't take place very often or very fast. Let us suppose that the Logic Theorist solves a difficult problem, and that it retains for a time in memory not only the correct path (the proof) that it finally discovered but also a record of the other paths it tried. One could then program it to reexamine some of the choice points at which it had not selected the correct branch on the first trial to look for relations between the state description at that point and characteristics of the correct branch. It could also be programmed to examine expressions just beyond the choice point along correct and incorrect paths in order to determine whether there were consistent differences between the expressions along the correct paths and those along the incorrect. Whatever differentia were discovered by such a program between correct and incorrect paths could be incorporated in the path generator. With the use of such procedures, a single successful experience of solving a problem after much trial-and-error search could become the basis for a great deal of learning.

More formally, suppose we wish to search a space of possible clues to determine which of these clues should be incorporated in a solution generator for maze paths. In terms of our general problem solving theory, we need a clue generator and a clue verifier. Hindsight contributes nothing to the construction of the clue generator, but it provides a cheap and effective verifier, since any possible clue we generate can be tested at once against a considerable number of instances.

We wish to offer a final comment on the "hindsight" aspects of learning. Suppose that, in terms of available computing power, the problem solving organism can afford to explore only a few hundred paths in searching any particular problem space. Then an effective strategy for dealing with a large class of problems would be to abandon problems that did not yield solutions after moderate effort had been applied, to do learning by hindsight on the easier problems that proved solvable, and thus gradually to add to the number of problems that could be handled successfully.

Assume that we have a class of problems with an initial value of $m = 10$. Then, if the problem solver had a limit of 500 paths per problem, he would only be able to solve problems of length $k = 2$ or less. As learning proceeded, however, the new heuristic would reduce the effective value of m. By the time that m had been reduced to 6, problems of length 3 could be solved; when m reached 2, problems of length 8 could be solved; and reductions of m below an average level of 2 would increase very rapidly the lengths of the problems that could be handled.

Concluding Remarks

In this chapter we have treated creative activity as problem solving activity characterized by the novelty and difficulty of the task. We have proposed an explanation for creative problem solving, developing this explanation along three parallel lines: (1) by constructing an abstract model of problem solving behavior that provides operational meaning to such concepts as "problem difficulty" and "power of a heuristic"; (2) by specifying programs for digital computers that simulate human problem solving behavior, and using the

abstract model to understand the effectiveness of the programs for solving problems; and (3) by reexamining some of the classical problems in the literature of problem solving and creativity to see what light the theoretical model, the computer programs, and data on human behavior cast on them.

The main results of our investigations up to the present time are embodied in a number of computer programs, some of which have actually been run on a machine, some of which are coded but have not been run, and some of which are specified at the level of flow diagrams. The computer programs that we have referred to specifically here include: (1) the original program of the Logic Theorist, adapted to proving theorems in Whitehead and Russell's *Principia Mathematica*; (2) a learning program that modifies this basic program, permitting the Logic Theorist to learn to use special methods for special classes of problems; (3) a revision of the Logic Theorist that adapts it to solving logic problems in the form used by O. K. Moore in his experiments with human subjects and that incorporates a program for functional means-end analysis; (4) a supplement to this last program that gives it the capacity to construct plans; (5) a program for a chessplaying machine. A number of other programs that are in process of construction by members of the Carnegie-RAND group and by others are not specifically mentioned here, but have provided some of the background for our theorizing.

Data obtained by comparing in detail the operation of these programs with the behavior of human subjects are limited. We have now accumulated human protocols that will permit such comparison for both the logic and chess programs, but our main tests of the theory have so far been of a grosser sort. We would chiefly rely on the fact that we have specified programs enabling mechanisms to solve complex problems so large that they would not yield to a brute force approach, using even the most powerful computers. The success of these programs in obtaining problem solutions is the primary evidence for the theory of the problem solving process that underlies their design.

We should like to stress our specific findings less than the methodology we have described for understanding the human mind. The use of computer programs to simulate information processes allows us to study the behavior of systems of great complexity—far greater complexity than can be handled reliably with either verbal or classical mathematical techniques. We have constructed a theory of human thinking in terms of its underlying information processes, and we have indicated how the theory can give precision to topics that, however important, have in the past been discussed in exceedingly vague terms. We have, for example, identified in the program of the Logic Theorist notions such as "grasp of problem structure," "visual image," "abstraction," and "set."

Some of the programs we have described perform work that is considered difficult, and even mildly creative, when it is done by humans. Although these programs fall considerably short in performance of the highest levels of creativity of which humans are capable, there is every reason to suppose that they are qualitatively of the same genus as these more complex human problem solving processes. In another place, we have predicted that within ten years a computer will discover and prove an important mathematical theorem and compose music that is regarded as aesthetically significant. On the basis of our experience with the heuristics of logic and chess, we are willing to add the further prediction that only moderate extrapolation is required from the capacities of programs already in existence to achieve the additional problem solving power needed for such simulation.

Appendix

It may be helpful to the reader, in following the specific examples in the text, to have a brief description of the problem solving task involving logic expressions that was designed by O. K. Moore and Scarvia B. Anderson.

A logic expression is a sequence of symbols of two types: (1) variables—P, Q, R, and so on— and (2) connectives—not (—), and ($\cdot$), or ($\vee$), and implies ($\supset$). An example from the text is

$R \cdot (-P \supset Q)$, which may be interpreted as "R and (not P implies Q)." The subjects are not provided with this interpretation, however, but are told that the expressions are code messages and that the connectives are named "tilde" ($-$), "dot" ($\cdot$), "wedge" ($\vee$), and "horseshoe" ($\supset$).

The following rules are provided for transforming one or two given logic expressions into a new expression (recoding expressions). We will state them here only approximately, omitting certain necessary qualifications.

One-line Rules

1. $A \vee B \Leftrightarrow B \vee A$
   $A \cdot B \Leftrightarrow B \cdot A$
2. $A \supset B \Leftrightarrow -B \supset -A$
3. $A \vee A \Leftrightarrow A$
   $A \cdot A \Leftrightarrow A$
4. $A \vee (B \vee C) \Leftrightarrow (A \vee B) \vee C$
   $A \cdot (B \cdot C) \Leftrightarrow (A \cdot B) \cdot C$
5. $A \vee B = -(-A \cdot -B)$
   $A \cdot B = -(-A \vee -B)$
6. $A \supset B \Leftrightarrow -A \vee B$
   $A \vee B \Leftrightarrow -A \supset B$
7. $A \vee (B \cdot C) \Leftrightarrow (A \vee B) \cdot (A \vee C)$
   $A \cdot (B \vee C) \Leftrightarrow (A \cdot B) \vee (A \cdot C)$
8. $A \cdot B \Rightarrow A$
   $A \cdot B \Rightarrow B$
9. $A \Rightarrow A \vee X$, where X is any expression

The rules can be applied to complete expressions, or (except rule 8) to subexpressions. Double tildes cancel—i.e., $- - A \Leftrightarrow A$, but this cancellation is not stated in a separate rule.

Two-line Rules

10. If A and B are given, they can be recoded into $A \cdot B$.
11. If A and $A \supset B$ are given, they can be recoded into B.
12. If $A \supset B$ and $B \supset C$ are given, they can be recoded into $A \supset C$.

Subjects were instructed in the use of these rules, then were given problems like those described in the text. They were asked to think aloud while working on the problems, and each time they applied a rule to recode one or two given expressions, the new expression was written on the blackboard by the experimenter, together with the numbers of the expressions and rule used to obtain it.

By inspection of the rules it can be seen that in the planning space, where connectives and the order of the symbols are disregarded, rules 1, 2, 5, and 6 would leave expressions unchanged. These are the inessential rules; the others, in altered form, become the essential rules. Rule 8, for example, becomes simply: $AB \Rightarrow A$.

References

Dineen, G. P., "Programming Pattern Recognition," *Proceedings of the Western Joint Computer Conference*, Institute of Radio Engineers (1955), pp. 94–100.

Duncker, K., "On Problem-Solving" (trans. L. S. Lees, from 1935 original), *Psychol. Monogr.*, 58, 270 (1945).

De Groot, A. D., *Het Denken van den Schaker* (Amsterdam: Noord-Hollandsche Uitgevers Maatschappij, 1946); Translated as *Thought and Choice in Chess*. (The Hague: Mouton, 1965; 2nd ed., 1978).

Johnson, D. M., *The Psychology of Thought and Judgment*. (New York: Harper, 1955).

Moore, O. K. and Scarvia Anderson, "Search Behavior and Problem Solving," *Amer. Sociol. Rev.*, 19 (1954), 702–14.

Newell, A. and J. C. Shaw, "Programming the Logic Theory Machine," *Proceedings of the Western Joint Computer Conference*, Institute of Radio Engineers (1957), pp. 230–40.

———, ———, and H. A. Simon, "Empirical Explorations of the Logic Theory Machine: A Case Study in Heuristic," *Proceedings of the Western Joint Computer Conference*, Institute of Radio Engineers (February 1957), pp. 218–30. Reprinted in E. A. Feigenbaum and J. Feldman (eds.), *Computers and Thought*. (New York: McGraw-Hill, 1963, pp. 109–33).

———, ———, and ———, "Elements of a Theory of Human Problem Solving," *Psychol. Rev.*, 65 (1958a), 151–66.

———, ———, and ———, "Chess-playing Programs and the Problem of Complexity," *J. Res. and Development* (IBM), 2 (1958b), 320–35. Reprinted in E. A. Feigenbaum and J. Feldman (eds.), *Computers and Thought*, (New York: McGraw-Hill, 1963, pp. 39–70).

——— and H. A. Simon, "The Logic Theory Machine: A complex information processing system", *IRE Transactions on Information Theory*, Vol. IT-2, No. 3 (September 1956).

Patrick, Catherine, "Creative Thought in Poets," *Archives of Psychology*, 178 (1935) whole issue.

———, "Creative Thought in Artists," *J. Psychol.*, 4 (1937), 35–73.

Polya, G., *Mathematics and Plausible Reasoning* (Princeton, N. J.: Princeton University Press, 1954).

———, *How to Solve It* (New York: Doubleday, 1957).

Selfridge, O. G., "Pattern Recognition and Modern Computers," *Proceedings of the Western Joint Computer Conference*, Institute of Radio Engineers (1955), 91–93.

Wallas, G., *The Art of Thought* (New York: Harcourt, 1926).

Whitehead, A. N. and B. Russell, *Principia Mathematica* (Cambridge, Eng.: Cambridge University Press, 1925–1927).

4.2

Trial and Error Search in Solving Difficult Problems (1962)

with Peter A. Simon

The game of chess provides often-cited examples of insightful discovery and prodigious human memory. Grandmasters frequently "see" decisive, winning moves whose force is not obvious to weaker players even after the moves have been pointed out to them. A number of chess masters can play many games simultaneously without sight of the board. Since the possible lines of play on a chessboard increase geometrically to astronomical numbers (e.g., one million possibilities, on the average, if the position is analyzed only two moves deep for each player; one billion possibilities, three moves deep), these feats of memory and discovery pose a problem for theories that would seek to explain human thinking and problem solving in terms of relatively simple processes operating in real time.[1]

Mating combinations—series of checking moves that end in a mate the opponent cannot escape—provide much of the spectacular in chess, the "brilliancies" comparable to the final smashing charge of an army that has first moved into position. In this chapter we will examine a number of mating combinations, including

two of great historical renown, in order to measure the amount of search and memory capacity required to discover the combinations in over-the-board play. In this way, we will arrive at some quantitative estimates of the processing and storage requirements for problem solving achievements that are viewed as lying at the limits of human ability—acts regarded by connoisseurs of chess as highly creative.

We have observed that looking ahead even three moves in a chess position, considering each legal possibility for the players in turn, on the average calls for the exploration of a billion branches of the game tree. Nevertheless, some of the

This investigation was carried out as part of the Carnegie Tech-RAND research on cognitive processes and complex information processing. We have had numerous helpful discussions with our colleagues G. Baylor, A. Newell, and J. C. Shaw. We are grateful also to the Carnegie Corporation for a grant in support of this work.

1. An excellent analysis of chess playing from a psychological standpoint will be found in de Groot (1946). The theoretical position of the this chapter stems from Newell, Shaw, and Simon (1958) and the literature cited there.

recorded mating combinations are as many as eight or more moves deep (that is, eight moves for each player), and it is these that give rise to much of the mythology that is current about the mnemonic and visualizing powers of grandmasters. Given the known facts about the proliferation of the analysis tree—perhaps 10^{24} branches in eight moves—how can a man see ahead so far and remember so much? We will try to show that a man cannot and need not in order to discover such combinations.

Our central hypothesis is that the behavior of a chess player in searching for a mating combination is governed by a *program* that determines which moves he will consider and which branches of the game tree he will examine. We use the term "program" exactly as it is used in the digital computer field, to denote an organized sequence of instructions, executed serially in a well-defined manner. We will describe in detail a specific program for discovering and verifying mating combinations that is powerful enough to discover a great many such combinations, including some of the most spectaclar in chess history. We will show that a player "programmed" in this way would discover these combinations with a moderate amount of search and relatively modest demands on his memory capacity. The program is, in fact, so simple in construction and execution that we have been able to test it by hand simulation, carrying out its instructions step by step without recourse to a digital computer. We do not argue that the program we will describe is exactly like that followed by any chess player, but that any one of a number of programs of equivalent power could account for the combinatorial prowess of chess grandmasters. Hence, the program provides at least rough quantitative estimates of the magnitude of these problem solving tasks.[2]

---

2. The methodological issues on which this approach to the study of human problem solving is based are discussed in Newell and Simon (1961).

THE MATING COMBINATIONS PROGRAM

The basic idea of the mating combinations program is that the tree of possible moves must be examined in a highly selective fashion, and not exhaustively. Three principles govern the selection:

1. The attacker only examines moves that are "forceful"—the specific program we will describe only examines checking moves. Since the attacker is seeking a line of play that leads to checkmate, he is under no obligation to examine all the moves legally available to him, but only those he thinks promising.

2. All legal alternatives open to the opponent, when it is the opponent's turn to move, must be explored. The essence of a mating combination is that the opponent is unable to escape checkmate no matter what he does.

3. If any move the attacker examines, no matter how forceful, allows the opponent numerous moves in reply, the attacking move is abandoned as unpromising. This principle has a double function. First, it reduces the size of the tree of alternatives that has to be explored. Second, restricting the freedom of action of the opponent is an essential aspect of entangling him in a mating net he cannot avoid. Hence, the fact that a move allows few replies increases both the likelihood that it will lead to a mate and the feasibility of tracing out its consequences.

The mating combinations program can now be described very briefly. The program generates all checking moves for the attacker, and lists them in priority order on the basis of the following criteria:

1. Give highest priority to double checks (moves that attack the opponent's King with two or more pieces simultaneously) and discovered checks (moves that take another man out of a piece's line of attack on the opponent's King).

2. Check with a more powerful in preference to a less powerful piece.

3. Give priority to checks that leave the opponent with the fewest replies (don't consider interposition of an undefended piece a reply).

4. Give priority to a check that adds a new attacker to the list of active pieces.

5. Give priority to the check that takes the opponent's King farthest from its base.

Experiments (some of which we will report) show that the exact priority order does not much affect average performance of the program. We consider the above criteria in lexicographical order. If two or more alternatives are tied as "best" on a criterion, we move down to the next criterion. The highest-priority attacker's move is to be evaluated as + (leads to mate), o (leads to material gain, but not mate), or − (does not lead to gain or mate) before the next move is considered. If the evaluation is +, analysis terminates and the move is played; if o, the move is retained as "possible" but search continues; if −, the evaluation is kept but the move rejected.

In the evaluation, all the opponent's legal replies are considered, in a priority order based on gains in material and increase in King's mobility. The highest priority defense is explored until it can be evaluated, then the next, and so on.

At any point at which the attacker has no further checks, or his opponent has four or more legal replies, analysis terminates with a value of o or −. At any point at which the attacker checkmates, the analysis terminates with a value of +.

A number of strong chess players—including one former grandmaster, a master, and an expert—who have examined this program agree that it incorporates an important part of the heuristics they use in discovering mating combinations. Certain heuristics well known to chess players are missing from the program, however. In particular, good chess players do not limit their search entirely to checking moves, but also examine certain other forcing moves—for example, attacks that threaten mate in one move and sacrificial moves that weaken the pawn protection of the opponent's King. Hence, the program undoubtedly underestimates selectivity of a chess master's analysis program and probably exaggerates the amount of search required to discover and evaluate strong moves.

Hand Simulations

The 136 positions discussed in the chapter on mating attacks in Fine (1952) provide material for studying the performance of the program by hand simulation. Taking one of these positions, we use the program rules to search for the mate, recording each of the alternatives that is examined, and thus build up a "tree" of possibilities. The positions in Fine were not used in constructing the program.

It appears that the program will discover the combinations in about 52 of the 136 situations—for the mates in these situations all come from sequences of checking moves. Ten more combinations would be discovered if the one-move mating threat were added to the list of possibilities explored by the attacker.

Table 1 provides an evaluation of the exploration required in four cases, including two that were undoubtedly among the most difficult. To interpret the data, we have to distinguish two trees of move possibilities: the *exploration* tree, and the *verification tree*.

The Exploration Tree

The attacker has to *discover* a branching sequence of moves, one subtree of which leads to a checkmate. The discovery usually involves exploring some branches that turn

Table 1. Evaluation of Exploration Required for Four Mating Attacks.

Combination	Depth (D)	Exploration (E)	Verification (V)	E/V	V/D	E/D
37	4	69	14	4.9	3.5	17.3
39	2	9	5	1.8	2.5	4.5
141	3	77	5	15.4	1.7	25.7
152	8	62	19	3.3	2.4	7.8

out to be false leads. The exploration tree is precisely analogous to the paths tried by a subject in a maze-running experiment, except that it includes branches for defender's choices as well as branches for the attacker's tries.

The Verification Tree

Analyses of mating combinations, as printed in chess books, do not include the whole exploration tree, but only that part of it which is necessary to verify that the combination is valid, or sound. That is, the analysis shows a single "correct" choice at each node for the attacker, but every legal reply at each node for the defender. We will call this tree the verification tree. It is precisely analogous to the correct path in the maze. It is a tree instead of a single path because all alternatives allowed to the defender must be tested.

Table 1 shows the maximum depth of exploration, the number of positions in the exploration tree produced by the program, the number of positions in the verification tree, and certain ratios of these quantities for the four positions mentioned above. The first of these positions is the four-move mate in Anderssen-Dufresne, one of the celebrated brilliancies of chess history; the fourth is a well-known position from Lasker-Thomas, in which Lasker announced and delivered mate in eight moves. The inclusion of these examples demonstrates that a program no more complicated than the one described here would discover brilliant mating combinations of grandmaster stature.

If we regard depth, positions in the exploration tree, and positions in the verification tree as measures of the difficulty of these combinations, then we see that these positions are not ordered in the same way with respect to the different measures of difficulty. Between depth and the size of the verification tree there is a fairly close correlation—there are, on the average, between two and three positions per move in depth. Notice that the size of the tree varies linearly, not exponentially, with depth. This characteristic, which results

from the forcing character of most of the attacker's moves, is what makes deep analysis possible in combinations.

There is little correlation between the respective sizes of the verification and exploration trees. The sizes of the exploration tree and the verification tree correspond, at least approximately, to amounts of discovery and fixation, respectively, involved in the problem solving task (Simon, 1957).

What do the numbers in table 1 tell us about human problem solving processes and memory? Let us, to use a round number, take 100 as the upper limit of the exploration tree for a combination that a chess grandmaster would actually discover in over-the-board play. Since a player may ponder fifteen minutes or more in a complex situation, he would take perhaps ten seconds per position examined in the exploration tree. Since all the positions in the tree are closely related—each differs from the adjacent ones by the move of only one piece—the information contained in them is highly redundant, and the rate at which information has to be handled under these assumptions is not great.[3]

Moreover, not all the positions in the exploration tree need to be fixated by the player. Some can be stored momentarily in immediate memory and, once they are evaluated, only the evaluation and not the position needs to be retained in memory. The number of positions in the combination that need to be in memory at any one time will depend on the shape of the verification tree, and it is likely that a measure of depth could be worked out comparable to Yngve's measure of the depth of English sentences. Lacking a detailed processing

---

3. Our knowledge of human information processing does not yet give us any good norms. In human speech, transmission rates of 10 to 20 bits per second are common (Luce, 1960, pp. 69–79). We know that a substantial amount of processing can occur in 10 seconds. We know also that a nonsense syllable of low association value can be fixated in about 30 seconds. From these considerations, a processing time of 10 seconds per position considered appears to be of a not unreasonable order of magnitude.

model of the kind he has constructed for syntax, we can reasonably assume that the skilled chess player will so organize his analysis as to keep the depth—in terms of immediate memory requirements—within tolerable limits. Since it would not be particularly difficult for a skilled writer to produce and memorize in the course of fifteen minutes or an even shorter time an entirely grammatical English sentence of 75 or 100 words, especially if the sentence contained one or more sequences of clauses and phrases of parallel construction and similar wording, the immediate memory requirements for the chess combinations do not appear to be greater than the requirements for producing complex, grammatical prose. (The preceding sentence contains just 77 words.)

VARIANTS OF THE PROGRAM

Table 2 reports some further experiments with the mating combinations program. The program described above (which we call MCP–1) is compared with a later version (MCP–4) that has different rules to determine the order in which alternatives are to be explored. The positions in table 2, which were taken from the problems page of the January and March 1957 issues of the *Chess Review*, are representative of the kinds of mate-in-two and mate-in-three problems that can be found in actual games (as distinguished from socalled "composed" problems that are deliberately created). Reasonably strong chess players

can usually discover the solutions in a few minutes, and this is reflected in the fact that the exploration trees are generally smaller than those for the Anderssen-Dufresne and Lasker-Thomas positions.

Table 2 illustrates the effects of relatively small changes in program structure using basically the same heuristics. The revised program is superior in three cases, inferior in two. In three cases, both programs generate the same exploration trees. Each of the programs would in one case have failed to discover the combination in a reasonable computing time (taking 100 positions as the limit), and the failure occurs in different positions in the two cases. This experiment suggests that we cannot create a program uniformly better than both of these simply by permuting the order in which moves are considered.

A discussion of other experiments of the same kind we have made would be of interest from the chess standpoint, but would add nothing essential to our picture of the human problem solving process. Our findings are consistent with the other knowledge that is available on human thinking in chess. De Groot (1946) has obtained thinking-aloud protocols from grandmasters and other strong chess players and has estimated the sizes of the exploration trees. In a complex middle game position (not a mating position), for example, he found that five grandmasters examined 20, 21, 22, 36, and 76 positions, respectively; five experts examined 16, 17, 29, 31, and 61. The average for the grandmasters was 35, for the experts, 31. Thus, there was no significant difference in amount of verbalized exploration between grandmasters and experts. Four out of five of the grandmasters, however, and *none* of the experts found the best move in the position. Clearly the grandmasters had a more effective selective heuristic to guide their exploration than did the experts.

Table 2. Comparison of Mating Programs 1 and 4

Problem	Verification Tree	Exploration Trees	
		MCP–1	MCP–4
Jan. 1957	1	3	10	5
	2	5	19	19
	3	3	4	4
	6	9	128	26
	9	9	24	28
March 1957	1	3	60	500+
	2	11	77	26
	4	8	12	12

CONCLUSION

The conclusion we reach from our investigations is that the discovery of "deep" mating combinations by expert chess players requires neither prodigious memory, ultra-rapid processing capacities, nor flashes of insight. Combinations as difficult as any that have been recorded in chess history will be discovered by the selective heuristics we have outlined, with amounts of search and with processing speeds that do not appear extravagant in relation to the measures we have of simpler kinds of human information-processing performance. The evidence suggests strongly that expert chess players discover combinations because their programs incorporate powerful selective heuristics and not because they think faster or memorize better than other people.

References

De Groot, A. D. *Het Denken van den Schaker.* Amsterdam: Noord Hollandsche Uitg. Mij.,
1946. Translated as *Thought and choice in chess.* The Hague: Mouton, 1965; 2nd ed. 1978.
Fine, R. *The Middle game in chess.* New York: David McKay, 1952.
Luce, R. D. (Ed.), *Developments in mathematical psychology.* Glencoe, Ill.: Free Press, 1960.
Newell, A., Shaw, J. C., & Simon, H. A. Chess-playing programs and the problem of complexity. *IBM J. Res. Devel.*, 1958, 2, 320–35. Reprinted in E. A. Feigenbaum and J. Feldman (eds.), *Computers and thought.* New York: McGraw-Hill, 1963, pp. 39–70.
Newell, A., & Simon, H. A. Computer simulation of human thinking. *Science*, 1961, 134, 2011–17.
Simon, H. A. Amounts of fixation and discovery in maze learning behavior. *Psychometrika*, 1957, 22, 261–68. Reprinted as Chapter 2.1 in this book.

4·3

A Chess Mating Combinations Program (1966)

with George W. Baylor

INTRODUCTION

The program reported here is not a complete chess player; it does not play games. Rather, it is a chess analyst limited to searching for checkmating combinations in positions containing tactical possibilities. A combination in chess is a series of forcing moves with sacrifice that ends with an objective advantage for the active side (Botvinnik, 1960). A checkmating combination, then, is a combination in which that objective advantage is checkmate.[1]

This investigation was supported in part by Research Grant MD-07722-01 from the National Institutes of Health and by the System Development Corporation.

1. Sometimes the defender is able to avert the checkmate by incurring a heavy loss in material (pieces and/or Pawns). If the attacker's gain in material is indeed an "objective advantage"— the defender being left with no compensatory attacking changes—then such combinations would generally be called mating combinations, even though not ending in mate. The current version of the program confines itself to mating combinations in the narrow sense—those from which there is no escape. Inclusion of the broader class is an obvious extension.

Thus the program described here—dubbed MATER—given a position, proceeds by generating that class of forcing moves that put the enemy King in check or threaten mate in one move and then by analyzing first those moves that appear most promising.

The organization of this chapter centers around MATER's ability to analyze chess positions. After a brief look at the program's history, the overall organization of the program is presented, an organization which is designed to allow flexible movements in an analysis tree of possibilities. Then in the section entitled The Executive and Heuristics of Search the "top level" comes under consideration; MATER's heuristics of analysis—the search rules and priorities, the search evaluators—that enable it to find a mate in the maze of possibilities. In the last section data on the performance of the program are presented. Finally, the programming language representation of the chessboard and chess pieces and the basic chess capabilities this affords are reported in the appendix (they are reported in yet finer detail in Baylor, 1965).

History of the Program

MATER has led a checkered life. The original mating combinations program, as conceived by Simon and Simon (1962) was a hand simulation setting forth a strategy of search. According to hand simulations, the program discovered mating combinations in 52 of the 129 positions collected in Fine's chapter on the mating attack (Fine, 1952). But a hand simulation is not a rigorous model and, as such, is itself sometimes prone to the imprecisions and ambiguities of many verbal theories. Indeed, Myron and May (1963) pointed out two such ambiguities in the specifications laid down by Simon and Simon (1962).

Newell and Prasad (1963) coded an IPL–V program which set up a chessboard, recorded positions, made moves, tested their legality, and performed a few other functions (see appendix). This they overlaid with the beginnings of a mating program.

The first version of a mating program described here—MATER I—is the work of Baylor (1965), Simon and Simon (1962), using the Newell-Prasad (1963) chessboard. The program was revised during 1964 by Baylor into a second version, MATER II.

Organization of the Analysis Tree

The Problem

As stated in the Introduction, the mating program analyzes chess positions. An analysis of a position—as the term is used here[2]—consists of the set of moves and evaluations made in the course of resolving the choice-of-move problem. Taken together, moves and positions make up a tree of possibilities in which moves operate on positions to produce new positions (see

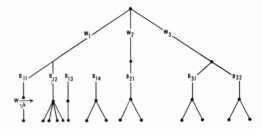

Figure 1. The analysis tree. The Ws are White moves; the Bs, replies.

figure 1) and on which evaluations of positions and of moves in achieving desired positions can be hung as desired.

The dots or nodes in figure 1 denote positions (static states), and the lines between dots denote moves (operators) that transform one position into another.[3]

How should the analysis of a position be conducted? Figure 2 presents one simple scheme. Would this scheme be workable if it were made operational? For example, let:

1. X be defined as checkmate and the program be given the capability of generating moves in its service.

2. The criteria for deciding among moves be specified by certain rules of selection.

3. The program be given the capability of making moves and updating board positions.

4. A test be provided so that the program "knew" if it had achieved X.

5–8. The corresponding provisions be made for Y, defined as escaping check, and for choosing among replies.

The answer is no, not quite. The scheme lacks a means for recovering from false starts, for retracing its steps when it runs

---

2. Chess players would probably prefer to define "analysis" as the finished product rather than the process of search, laying stress on the "right" moves and continuations rather than emphasizing how these were arrived at.

3. Simon and Newell (1956) have often drawn this difference equation analogy to the problem solving process: given an initial state description and a desired state, the problem is to find a process description that operates on the initial state to produce the desired one. In discussion of the Logic Theorist (Newell, Shaw, and Simon, 1962) for example, the logic expressions correspond to the static states and the rules of inference, to the operators.

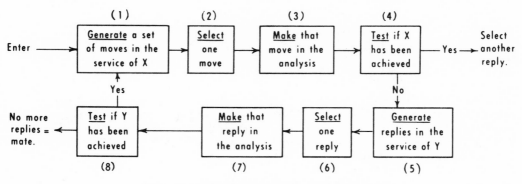

Figure 2. A simple recursive mating scheme.

into blind alleys. Indeed, what is lacking can be seen by considering the difference between actually playing a game of chess and analyzing a chess position: the course of analysis is fickle and reversible, whereas in an actual game a move once made cannot be unmade. In other words, the scheme outlined above needs provisions for unmaking moves and for abandoning seemingly unpromising positions as much as it needs the capability of making moves and pursuing promising positions. Ideally, one should like to be able to enter and reenter the move tree at any node (position) at any time and from there to proceed down any branch, old or new. Providing such capabilities for reinstating the right position at the right time is probably the central problem of organization at this level of the program, while making operational and making sense out of steps 1–8 above is probably the central problem at the next higher conceptual level. This section reports on the former problem: implementation of a flexible move tree. The next section is devoted to the latter: defining the problem and the heuristics of search.

Building the Tree

The notion of analysis as a tree search is misleading to the extent that it implies that each step consists solely of selecting a move from the many available alternatives. Actually, the process is more one of generating moves as one goes along, of building one's own tree. This is the very

distinction Maier (1960, p.218) has drawn between decision making under conditions of uncertainty[4] and problem solving: "Decision making implies a given number of alternatives, whereas in problem solving the alternatives must be created. Thus, problem solving involves both choice behavior and the finding or creating of alternatives."

In every chess position, of course, the rules of the game place an upper limit on the number of possibilities that can be created; de Groot (1965) found that, averaged across the course of a game, the mean number of legal move possibilities lies somewhere between 30 and 35. This is a full-grown tree; the one the searcher actually builds is much smaller: on the average, four or five branches at the top node and smaller thereafter.

The first question addressed in this section is the technical one: How does one build a tree? How are limbs and nodes—moves and positions, respectively—structured into a tree of possibilities? (See the appendix for the details of construction of moves and positions.) Second, and pursuing the metaphor, think of the chess player climbing the tree as he builds it. Crawling along a branch in one direction corresponds to making a move in the current position (node), while traversing

---

4. According to Luce and Raiffa (1957) decision making under uncertainty is the condition in which the outcomes of the various known alternatives are unknown.

it in the opposite direction corresponds to unmaking a move and restoring the previous position (node). This ability to back up the tree is what enables a player to abandon unpromising lines of investigation and start afresh. In starting afresh, moreover, the player may either reinvestigate branches he has previously built or build new ones.

Third, as the player builds and climbs he also accrues and retains information. The information garnered en route and the use to which it is put are in large part what *Denk*psychologists have called the development of the problem. That is, the searcher's conception of the problem at any one time consists of the information he has about the problem, how he has evaluated this information, and even how it has shaped his definition of what the problem is (cf. Duncker, 1945, and de Groot, 1965). Provisions for gathering information are considered in both this section and the next; the use to which information is put and the matter of problem development are more properly treated in the subsequent sections.

Most of the organizational problems are solved via the description lists of moves. For convenience of reference the entire list of possible attributes a move can take on is set forth in table 1.

With respect to the first question—provisions for holding the tree together—a signal cell and attributes A46 and A47 do the job. The signal cell contains the name of the most recent move made on the board—the contemporary—while attributes A46 and A47 are its ancestor and its list of

Table 1. Move Attributes.

A40	From square
A41	To square
A42	Special move (yes or no)
A43	Man removed from castle list
A44	Man captured
A45	Square of captured en passant Pawn
A46	Ancestor
A47	List of descendants
A48	Irreversibility of move (reversible; or irreversible)
A49	Value of move (mate, no mate, no value)
A50	Number of descendants
A51	Man moved
A52	Double check (yes or no)
A53	Discovered check (yes or no)
A54	Checking move (yes or no)
A55	Descendant's list of mate threats
A56	Threatened mating square
A58	Mating piece on V(A56) square
A63	Reply NOMV (no move)
A65	Number of checking moves generated to date
A66	Number of replies generated to date
A70	List of King replies
A71	List of capturing replies
A72	List of interposing replies

descendants, respectively. The log of the analysis is preserved by defining a dummy move, L31, which has on its description list the list of descendants attribute, A47. Thus the course of analysis is linked together as a chain of moves with contemporaries linked by ancestor and descendant relations, as in the example of an analysis tree in figure 3.

Second, because of the strong family ties just described, one can eventually crawl

Figure 3. Course of analysis linked as contemporaries, ancestors, and descendants.

one's way down any branch of any node and then back up. That is to say, one can make or unmake any move. Two routines, E65 and E66, make and unmake moves, respectively. Unmaking a move is exactly the reverse of making one. With the help of routine E11 the position list is restored, that is, the description lists of the pieces and squares affected are restored and the signal cells reset.

At any node a new limb may also be constructed (by routines E51 and E52; see appendix) simply by specifying the "from square" and the "to square" (and special move status, if any) whereupon the move is added to the list of descendants, $V(A47)$, and assigned an ancestor, $V(A46)$.

Third, information gathered in the search for mate is stored on the description list of the move that gathers it. (See table 1.) When a move is constructed, its ancestor is always assigned as a value of $A46$ and the man moved in always assigned as a value of $A51$. Conditionally, a move is assigned a value of $A43$ if a Rook or King is removed from the castle list, a value of $A44$ if a man is captured, a value of $A45$ if a Pawn is captured *en passant*, a value of $A52$ if it is a double check, a value of $A53$ if it is a discovered check, and a value of $A54$ if it is a checking move at all.

Evaluative information is also gathered: attribute $A49$ records the win-loss value of a move: mate, no mate, or no value. If a checking move has no descendants, that move mates; consequently, attributes $A70$, $A71$, and $A72$ record the kinds of replies to check. Attribute $A47$ lists the descendants in toto, and the value of $A50$ is a count of them.

The point here is to illustrate how information is hung on the move tree as it is gathered. How the information is retrieved and utilized is a topic for the next section.

THE EXECUTIVE AND HEURISTICS OF SEARCH

Introduction

In a given position, what moves should be considered and in what order? Human chess players are known to be highly selective in the moves they look at, a selectivity based on their heuristics of search. Computers must also incorporate such selectivity. What follows then is a discussion of the search heuristics incorporated into the early version of the mating program, some measures on its search behavior, a brief description of the routines that effect the move generation, and, finally, later developments added to a second version of the program, MATER II.

MATER I

Restricting the mobility of the opponent's pieces is a recognized principle of chess strategy. It is particularly important in checkmating combinations, since checkmate is defined as an unopposed attack on an enemy King whose mobility has been reduced to zero. Strategically this means the attacker strives to gain control over (1) the square the enemy King occupies, as well as (2) all the squares contiguous to it that do not contain an enemy piece. If just condition (1) obtains, the enemy King is simply in check; if just condition (2) holds, the enemy King is stalemated; while if both (1) and (2) hold, he is checkmated. Viewed in this light, checkmate is a process of acquiring controls, or more and more restricting the enemy King's mobility. This principle is the cornerstone of the mating program.

The restriction of mobility principle applies to the generation and selection of moves as well as to decisions about when to abandon search in certain directions. Thus in the mating program: Only checking moves (in MATER I) and moves that threaten mate in one move (in MATER II) are generated for the attacker; the move selected for investigation is the one that most restricts the opponent's mobility; and search is continued down a chosen path only so long as the opponent's mobility is on the decline. This—the rate of growth of the search tree—is an alternative formulation to an evaluation function for terminating search in a particular direction.

Before illustrating the flow of control and

the program's executive structure, it is necessary to introduce the notion of a try-list, a notion similar to the "pool of subgoals" in the Logic Theory Machine (Newell, Shaw, and Simon, 1963*b*). Since only one move can be tried out at a time in any particular position, other "eligible" checking moves must wait their turn on a list, L_{35}—the try-list. This list has two noteworthy properties: first of all, it is an ordered list, and second it is independent of a move's level.[5] Such independence proves powerful in directing search.

The list is ordered by a fewest replies heuristic: highest priority goes to moves with the fewest number of legal replies, while checking moves with more than four legal replies are discarded entirely. Ties are broken by giving priority to double checks, then to checks that have no capturing responses, then to the order in which the checks were generated. The second property—that checks from all levels are mixed—effects the evaluative principle that search is continued down a particular path only so long as the opponent's mobility is on the decline: when the number of replies at some node in the current line of investigation is equal to or greater than the number of replies at some prior node, the current line is abandoned, the prior node restored, and the alternative that had once been passed over is tried. This nips in the bud unpromising proliferations in the move tree.

In addition to the notions just described —rate of growth serving to terminate search in a particular direction, the set of considerable moves serving to restrict the set of applicable operators in the given position, the try-list ordered by the fewest replies heuristic serving to stipulate the application of offensive operators—some heuristics of chess strategy serving to stipulate the order of application of defensive

operators—can also be seen more clearly from the following illustrative position taken from Fine (1952) and MATER I's performance on it.[6]

The following layout is adapted to the simple recursive scheme of figure 2.

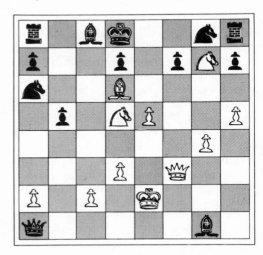

1. Generate checking moves: 1.N-K6ch; B-K7ch; B-B7ch; Q-B6ch.

2. Select one move for further analysis:

a. 1.N-K6ch   1.B-K7ch
    1 . . . K-K1   1 . . . N × B
    1 . . . QP × N   *1.*
    1 . . . BP × N
    3.

    1.B-B7ch   1.Q-B6ch
    1 . . . N × B   1 . . . N × Q
    1.   1 . . . N-K2
                          2.

b. Transfer checks to try-list; order them by their *u* values (number of replies):

L_{35}	*u*
1.B-K7ch	1
1.B-B7ch	1
1.Q-B6ch	2
1.N-K6ch	3.

c. Select and delete top move from try-list L_{35}: 1.B-K7ch.

3. Make that move (1.B-K7ch) in the analysis.

4. Test if checkmate has been achieved: No.

---

5. The level of a move refers to its depth in the move tree, i.e., how many moves out it is from the starting position.

6. They can also be seen more clearly within the picture of heuristic search in general in Newell and Ernst (1965)

5. Generate replies to relieve check: 1 . . . N × B.

6. Select "best" reply*: 1 . . . N × B.

7. Make that reply (1 . . . N × B) in the analysis.

8. Test if check has been relieved: Yes.

1. Generate checking moves: 2.N-K6ch.

2. Select one move for further analysis.

a. For each check generate and count replies:

2.N-K6ch
2 . . . K-K1
2 . . . QP × N
2 . . . BP × N
3.

b. Transfer check to try-list: order them by their *u* values:

L_{35}	*u*
1.B-B7ch	1
1.Q-B6ch	2
1.N-K6ch	3
2.N-K6ch	3.

c. Select and delete top move from try-list L_{35}: 1.B-B7ch.

3. Make that move (1.B-B7ch) in the analysis, restoring the board to the initial position.

4. Test if checkmate has been achieved: No.

5. Generate replies that relieve check: 1 . . . N × B.

6. Select best reply: 1 . . . N × B.

7. Make that reply (1 . . . N × B) in the analysis.

8. Test if check has been relieved: Yes.

1. Generate checking moves: 2.N-K6ch; Q-B6ch.

2. Select one move for further analysis.

a. For each check generate and count replies:

2.N-K6ch	2.Q-B6ch
2 . . . K-K1	2 . . . N × Q
2 . . . QP × N	2 . . . N-K2
2 . . . BP × N	*2.*
2 . . . N × N	
4.	

---

* "Best" is defined in the text immediately following this example.

b. Transfer checks to try-list; order them by their *u* values:

L_{35}	*u*
1.Q-B6ch	2
2.Q-B6ch	2
1.N-K6ch	3
2.N-K6ch	3
2.N-K6ch'	4.

c. Select and delete top move from try-list: 1.Q-B6ch.

3. Make that move (1.Q-B6ch) in the analysis, restoring the board to the initial position.

4. Test if checkmate has been achieved: No.

5. Generate replies to relieve check: 1 . . . N × Q; N-K2.

6. Select best reply: 1 . . . N × Q.

7. Make that reply (1 . . . N × Q) in the analysis.

8. Test if check has been relieved: Yes.

1. Generate checking moves: 2.N-K6ch; B-K7ch; B-B7ch.

2. Select one move for further analysis.

a. For each check generate and count replies:

2.N-K6ch	2.B-K7ch	2.B-B7ch
2 . . . K-K1	*0.*	2 . . . N × B
2 . . . QP × N		*1.*
2 . . . BP × N		
3.		

b. Transfer checks to try-list; order them by their *u* values:

L_{35}	*u*
2.B-K7ch	0
2.B-B7ch	1
2.Q-B6ch	2
2.N-K6ch	3
1.N-K6ch	3
2.N-K6ch	3
2.N-K6ch'	4.

c. Select and delete top move from try-list L_{35}: 2.B-K7ch.

3. Make that move (2.B-K7ch) in the analysis.

4. Test if checkmate has been achieved: Yes.

6'. Select next best reply: 1 . . . N-K2.

7'. Make that reply (1 . . . N-K2) in the

analysis, restoring the board to the appropriate position.

8'. Test if check has been relieved: Yes.

1. Generate checking moves: 2.N-K6ch; B × Nch; B-B7ch; Q × Nch.

2. Select one move for further analysis.

a. For each check generate and count replies:

2.N-K6ch	2.B × Nch
2 ... K-K1	*o.*
2 ... QP × N	
2 ... BP × N	
3.	
2.B-B7ch	2.Q × Nch
2 ... N × B	*o.*
1.	

b. Transfer checks to try-list; order them by their *u* values:

L35	*u*
2.B × Nch	0
2.Q × Nch	0
2.B-B7ch'	1
2.B-B7ch	1
2.Q-B6ch	2
2.N-K6ch"	3
2.N-K6ch"	'3

1.N-K6ch 3
2.N-K6ch 3
2.N-K6ch' 4.

c. Select and delete move from try-list L35: 2. B × Nch.

3. Make that move (2.B × Nch) in the analysis.

4. Test if checkmate has been achieved: Yes.

6'. Select next best reply: None.

7'. Make that reply (None) in the analysis.

8'. Test if check has been relieved: No. Make MATE and print move-tree (figure 4).

This example also illustrates the criteria by which the order of application of defensive moves is accomplished: by "best" reply is meant that reply that seems most likely to give the attacker trouble. Thus the priority of defensive moves Black tries is, first, the capture of the most valuable White pieces by the least valuable Black pieces followed by King moves, interpositions, then order of generation. Again this is an attempt to clip unnecessary proliferations in the move tree: if there is a "killing" reply to a checking move, further

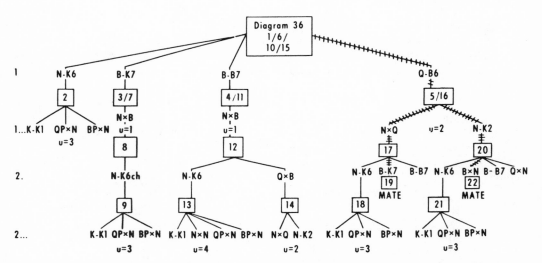

Figure 4. MATER I's analysis tree of diagram 36, Fine (1952). The u's are a tally of the number of replies by which the priority of moves on the try-list is established. The boxes represent positions and the numbers in them trace the course of the investigation—the order in which the positions were taken up. The crosshatched branches trace the mating path.

analysis of that checking move would seem futile.[7]

Measures of Search Behavior. Many measures of search behavior can be picked off an analysis tree like MATER I's of diagram 36 (figure 4). For example, the tree can be characterized by counting the number of positions or the number of moves. Simon and Simon (1962) call the total number of positions examined the "exploration tree"; in diagram 36, the position count yields an exploration tree of size 16. In general, however, more moves are seen than positions are investigated, which is to say that some moves remain unexplored, such as the replies to 1.N-K6ch in diagram 36. The count of moves seen—the uninvestigated as well as the investigated ones—will be called the discovery tree; in diagram 36, this move tally yields a discovery tree of size 36 (14 checks and 22 responses). One further refinement can be carved out of the exploration and discovery trees; namely, the "verification tree," which Simon and Simon (1962) define as the total number of positions required to prove the combination—the positions resulting from the single best move at each node for the attacker and from every legal move at each node for the defender; respectively, the positive and negative parts of the proof schema (see de Groot, 1965). The verification tree "is precisely analogous to the correct path in a maze. It is a tree instead of a single path because all alternatives allowed to the defender must be tested" (Simon and Simon, 1962, p. 427). In diagram 36 (figure 4), the branches of the verification tree are crosshatched, yielding a position count of size 6, or alternatively, a move count of size 5.

These measures do not reveal the time order in which the tree was generated.

Human chess players are fickle tree climbers, "progressive deepeners," to use de Groot's (1965) term for the phenonenon: "The investigation not only broadens itself progressively by growing new branches, countermoves, or considerable own-moves, but also literally deepens itself: the *same* variant is taken up anew and is calculated further than before" (de Groot, 1965, p. 266). In other words, the search strategy is an important structural characteristic of the thought process. In figure 4, the order in which positions are taken up is captured by numbering the nodes (positions) in the analysis. These measures will be used for comparative purposes in the next section.

Routines. How are checking moves and replies actually generated in any given position? There would seem to be two tacks, corresponding to a one-many approach and a many-one approach. In trying to find all the checks in a given position, for example, one could either radiate out from the enemy King and from each square, search for a piece that can get there and give check (the one-many approach), or converge from the squares along the move directions of each attacking piece onto the enemy King's square (the many-one approach). If there are many pieces on the board, the former is the more efficient; if few, the latter.

G1 is a master routine that procures all checks in a given position. It employs the many-one approach, calling subroutine G11 for Queen, Bishop, and Rook checking moves: G12 for Knight and regular Pawn checks; and G13 for double Pawn moves that adminster check. Similarly, R21 procures all replies to a given checking move: R11 generates all the King moves that get out of check, R12, all the captures of the checking piece, and R13, all the interpositions. In this way the mating program is able to enumerate all checks and all replies in a particular position.

MATER II

In designing search programs it is useful to distinguish the strategy of search from the information that is gathered during the search. The

---

7. This is the minimax assumption; namely, that the opponent will make his strongest reply at every opportunity. McCarthy's *killer heuristic* (see Kotok, 1962) assumes that a killing reply to one checking move may be a killing reply to other checking moves and thus should be looked at first.

search strategy tells where to go next, and what information must be kept so that the search can be carried out. It does not tell what other information to obtain while at the various positions, nor what to do with the information after it is obtained. There may be strong interaction between the search itself and the information found, as in the decision to stop searching, but we can often view this as occurring within the confines of a fixed search strategy.[8]

MATER II adds a modification to MATER I's search strategy by bypassing the fixedness in the order of application of operators inherent in the try-list. The new search rule states: in the given position pursue immediately and in depth all checking moves that keep the enemy King stalemated (or nearly so), i.e., moves that can only be answered by captures and/or interpositions or, in the absence of both, by one and only one King move (the "nearly so" condition). In addition to altering the program's search strategy by telling it "where to go next," this procedure also gathers information about the position. In this respect it resembles what de Groot (1965) has called a "sample variation," a kind of trial balloon sent up for the express purpose of gathering information to direct subsequent investigation; in this sense it is orientative. Before turning to what information is gathered and how it is used, it should be mentioned that sometimes a sample variation pays off directly—the "sample moves" may be a path to a quick mate.

Specifically, a routine G10 conducts the preliminary search and, if no "easy mate" is found, records the sequence of moves investigated on a list B4. A routine G17 makes use of this information later in drawing up a plan of attack. Just how these routines operate can best be seen by considering in three parts MATER II's analysis for a particular position, diagram 97 from Fine (1952).

The first part has to do with the preliminary search; the second with the use to which the recorded information is put in drawing up a plan; and the third with

8. Newell and Simon, 1965, pp. 24–25.

the exploration and verification of that plan.

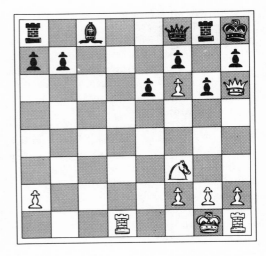

The first ten moves of the discovery tree are those in figure 5a. (Note that both the 1.Q-N7ch and 1.Q × RPch sample variations are recorded on list B4.)

Clearly, the "wishful thinking" goal of the sample variations went unfulfilled; the preliminary excursions did not yield mate. They do yield two sequences of forcing moves, however, that may be useful in constructing a plan of attack. Indeed, the routine G17 searches list B4 for the first move candidates and finds, in this example, 1.P × R and 1.N-N5. The former is rejected as illegal in the current position while the latter is deemed considerable. Note that the set of operators that may be applied in the initial position is expanded in MATER II to include moves other than just checking moves, yet the means by which these are generated continues to ensure a high degree of selectivity.

Routine G17 asks if a proposed move, in this case 1.N-N5, threatens mate in one move. It determines the answer by assuming that Black does nothing on his turn, that is, by playing a "No Move" and then seeing if White can enforce an immediate checkmate. And, indeed, 2.Q × RP is mate. In other words, White leaves the actual problem space to seek a mate in a simplified planning space (see Newell,

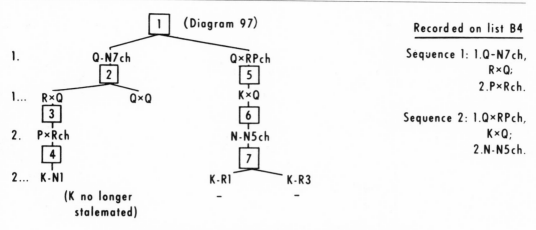

Figure 5*a*. MATER II's preliminary search in position 97.

Shaw, and Simon, 1962) and, in fact, the second part of the move tree is given over to solving the problem in the planning space (see figure 5*b*).[9]

Finally, the third stage is devoted to testing the soundness of the plan; that is, suppose Black tries to avert 1.N-N5 and 2.Q × RPmate. Can he? It happens that in this position he cannot, so that the exploration tree and the verification tree are identical in this stage of the analysis. (The rather lengthy third stage is omitted here.)

MATER II contains one other highly selective mechanism for finding moves that threaten mate in one. Controls exerted over the enemy King's square and the squares in this immediate vicinity are built into a list structure called the King's Sector. For a given square, five kinds of control have been defined:

1. No control—the enemy King can move to the given square.

2. Attacking control—the attacker can move to or capture on the given square.

3. Occupation control—one of the attacker's pieces occupies the given square.

4. Block control—one of the defender's pieces occupies the given square.

5. X-ray control—the attacker can unmask an attacker control by removing one of his own pieces (corresponding to a "discovery" in chess jargon) or he could unmask an attacking control but for an enemy interposer (corresponding to a "pin").

The King's Sector, L40, is constructed by the four routines E91-E94. The complete structure of L40 and the information contained therein can best be seen in figure 6, the King's Sector for diagram 70 from Fine (1952). Attribute Y3 has data term XO as its value, a tally of the number of uncontrolled squares in the sector (see figure 6).

---

9. A hybrid version of MATER I and II would first have reinvestigated 1.Q-N7ch and 1.Q × RPch, invoking the fewest replies heuristic, transferring these two checks to the try-list, and elaborating them, before even considering moves which threaten mate in one. Unfortunately, the statistics gathered on various versions of the program are too incomplete to say which search strategy is superior across positions, if in fact a correct strategy can be determined independent of position.

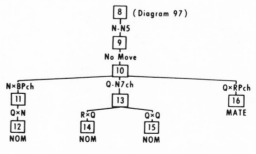

Figure 5*b*. MATER II's plan formation in position 97.

L40 9-0
9-0 0
  S64 (KR8)
  9-1   (KR8) 9-1 0
                              MO (Man on KR8?)
  S63 (KN8)
  9-2   M29 (Black King) 0
  S55 (KN7)   (KN8) 9-2 0
  9-3   Y7 (X-ray control)
                              9-10   9-10 0
  S56 (KR7)   Y6 (Attacking   M6 (White Bishop
  9-4   control)   X-rays KN8)
                              9-11 0   M22 (Black Pawn
  Y3 (No control   is X-rayed) 0
      over how
      many   (KN7) 9-3 0   9-11 0
      squares?)   Y6 (Attacking   M2 (White Knight
  XO = 1   control)   attacks KN8) 0
                              9-12   9-12 0
  ———————   Y4 (Block control)   M7 (White Knight
                                                      attacks KN7) 0
                       M23 (Black Pawn
Knight   S54 (KB7)   blocks KN7) 0
directions   9-5
not used in   S47 (KN6)   (KR7) 9-4 0
tallying XO   9-6 0   Y4 (Block control)
                       M24 (Black Pawn
                       blocks KR7) 0
            (KB7) 9-5 0
                       Y6 (Attacking
                       control)
                            9-13   9-13 0
                       Y4 (Block control)   M6 (White Bishop
                                                        attacks KB7) 0
                       M22 (Black Pawn
                       blocks KB7) 0
            (KN6) 9-6 0
                       Y6 (Attacking
                       control)
                            9-14 0   9-14 0
                                           M4 (White Queen
                                           and White
                                           M2 Knight attack
                                           KN6) 0

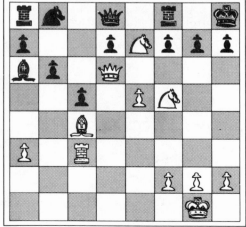

Figure 6. IPL-V list structure of king's sector controls (arranged in attribute value pairs) of Fine's (1952) diagram 70, from a game Alekhine-Supico, 1942.

How is all this information retrieved and used by the program? First, a routine G14 tries to generate mate-threatening moves by converting an X-ray control into a second attacking control. For example, in diagram 70, routine G14, seizing on the White Bishop's X-ray control of KN8, proposes 1.B × BP but then rejects the move because 2.B-N8 does not administer check, let alone mate. Second, a routine G19, given one attacking control, tries to add a second. Routine G19, seeing an attacking control over KN7 in position 70, proposes to add another with the moves 1.Q-KB6, 1.Q-N6, and 1.Q-R6. Since all three produce mate if Black does nothing, all three are accepted as considerable moves in the plan.

In summary, MATER II contains several mechanisms for generating a selective set of considerable moves. Incorporating MATER I's ability to generate all checking moves and all replies in a given position, MATER II goes on to generate mate-threatening moves based either on their earlier appearance in forced sequences of checking moves or on the function they serve in controlling key squares around the enemy King. Moreover, MATER II has a set of routines, R15, R16, R22, for generating defensive replies to a threatened mate.

MATER II also contains three principal mechanisms in its search strategy specifying the order in which moves are to be considered. Defensively, in reply to checking moves, captures are preferred to King moves, which, in turn, are preferred to interpositions; while in reply to one-move mate threats, captures are preferred to moves that defend the mating square as well as to interpositions and King runs. Offensively, search is directed by pursuing particular moves in depth as long as the enemy King remains very highly constricted, and then later by pursuing the move that leaves the opponent with the fewest replies. Each of these search evaluators rests on a single criterion: sometimes a line of search is terminated because the defender is left with King moves in reply (nodes 4 and 7 in the move tree of position

97); sometimes a move is rejected because it does not produce immediate mate (nodes 11 and 12 in position 97); sometimes a move just never gets off the waiting list (node 2 in position 36); and checking moves with more than four legal replies are always rejected out of hand. Indeed, it is the thesis here that these kinds of criteria, criteria based on features of the task area, are what regulate chess players' choice-of-move decisions and form a good alternative representation to complicated weighting functions of the sort employed by Samuel (1963) in checkers and Bernstein and Roberts (1958) in chess. Even though mating combinations are the only facet of the game in which the final evaluators, MATE and NOMATE, are well defined[10]—a degree of certainty attained nowhere else in the game—the search-directing decisions intermediate to the final choice of move must all be made on far less than certain criteria, just like the rest of the game.

Except for the sample variations recorded on the list B4, the information-gathering mechanisms rely on the description list of the move that gathered it, including the final evaluations, MATE or NOMATE, which are propagated back up the tree by the minimax inference procedure in an attempt to demonstrate the proof of a combination.

INTERPRETATION AND RESULTS
Introduction

With respect to the verification of simulation models in general, and problem solving models in particular, two criteria for assessment seem to have emerged clearly: an achievement criterion and a process criterion. That is, can the model solve the class of problems it was designed to handle and are its mechanisms for doing so equivalent to, or even comparable to, a human problem solver's? The answer to

---

10. "Well defined" is used in the sense that there exists a satisfactory test that enables the player to recognize the solution to his problem. (See McCarthy, 1956)

the first question is relatively straightforward; not so to the second, however, since the requirements for equivalence or comparability of process are themselves open to question. In the present report, we will not consider questions of human simulation but will confine ourselves to a discussion of the achievement of the programs.

MATER I solves combinations which consist of uninterrupted series of checking moves, given that the defender at no node in the verification tree has more than four legal replies; MATER II solves combinations that begin either with checks or with one-move mate threats and checking moves thereafter. This limitation on the class of moves the program can see restricts severely the class of combinations on which the model can be tested. Nevertheless, the program has been tested on material taken from Fine's (1952) chapter on the mating attack. Solutions to one class of positions in the chapter call for an uninterrupted series of checking moves ending in mate (51/129 positions). Another class of positions is solved with one-move mate threats and checking moves thereafter (5/129 positions). In the residual class, mate can either be averted through a sacrifice of material or the mate is not "forced," as the term was defined in the Introduction to this chapter (73/129 positions).

MATER I's Achievement

MATER I found solutions to 43 of the 51 mating positions. The machine missed one combination entirely by failing to move a Pawn that gave a discovered check and exhausted available space before finding the other seven.[11] Table 2 breaks these 43

11. In particular, MATER I failed to see 2.P-B6ch in position 148. The seven positions that exhausted available space did so because the fewest replies heuristic failed to discriminate among alternative checking moves: among six alternative discovered checks in positions 41 and 100; among a large number of initial checks available in positions 109 and 140; and among a large number of checks in depth involved in a King hunt on the open board in positions 111, 130, and 157.

Table 2. MATER I's Performance on 43 Positions from Fine (1952).

N (positions)	D	$\overline{VT}$	$\overline{DT}$	$\overline{VT}/D$	$\overline{DT}/D$	$\overline{VT}/\overline{DT}$
15	2	3.5	15.5	1.8	7.8	4.4
11	3	5.4	24.6	1.8	8.2	4.6
14	4	9.9	61.5	2.5	15.4	6.2
2	5	11.0	56.0	2.2	11.2	5.1
1	8	17.0	108.0	2.1	13.5	6.4

positions down according to certain structural measures of search behavior: the depth of search to mate (D), the mean size of the verification tree necessary to prove the combination ($\overline{VT}$ measured in moves), and the mean size of the discovery tree generated in searching for mate ($\overline{DT}$ measured in moves.) In a previous section of this paper, on measures of search behavior, definitions were provided for these latter two quantities.

Simon and Simon (1962, p. 428) suggest depth, number of positions in the exploration tree, and number of positions in the verification tree as measures of the difficulty of combinations. They remark that the four positions in their sample "are not ordered in the same way with respect to the different measures of difficulty." Using depth, number of moves in the discovery tree ($\overline{DT}$), and number of moves in the verification tree ($\overline{VT}$) as equivalent measures, the data of table 2 do show, with but one exception, the same ordinal relationship across measures, at least when averaged over the 43 positions.

Between depth and the size of the verification tree ($\overline{VT}/D$) there is a fairly close correlation—around two moves in the verification tree per move in depth. This confirms the Simon and Simon (1962) observation: the tree varies linearly, not exponentially, with depth, and it probably is this property that makes deep analysis possible in combinations. Neither $\overline{DT}/D$ nor $\overline{VT}/\overline{DT}$ shows any consistent relationship.

The only roughly constant ratio, $\overline{VT}/D$, has more to do with characteristics of mating positions than with characteristics of the mating program. The only measure

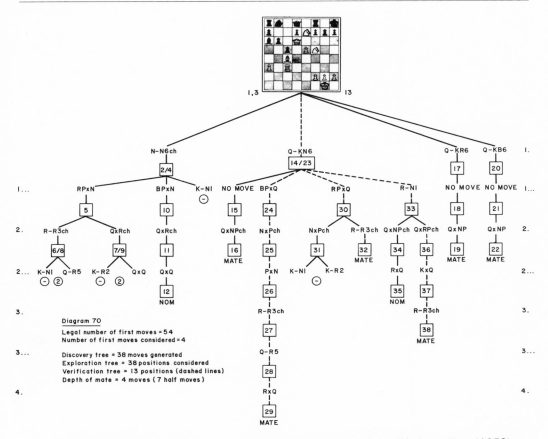

Figure 7. MATER II's analysis tree and order of search on diagram 70, from Fine (1952).

on the program's search behavior is $\overline{DT}$, and there seems to be no consistent relationship between it and the two measures on the combinations ($\overline{DT}/D$ and $\overline{VT}/\overline{DT}$).

MATER II's Achievement

MATER II has been tested on all five positions from Fine (1952) that necessitated an initial threat of mate in one and checks thereafter. It solved three directly, the other two, because of a change in computer facilities, by hand simulation. The search tree for position 97 has already been described. In position 107 the initial Queen sacrifice as well as an unexpected Bishop sacrifice were easily spotted in the service of mate. The analysis tree of position 70 is given in figure 7. Note that the correct

move and theme in position 70 derive from the celebrated game of Marshall's for which spectators showered the chessboard with gold coins![12] Of the two hand simulated runs, position 95 required but the simple addition of a second control on the KN7 square via 1.Q-R6, while position 113 required the move 1.R-R5, which had been discovered in one of the exploratory sample variants.

___

12. The program also finds the correct sequence of moves from the immortal Lewitzky-Marshall game, played in Breslau in 1912 (diagram 69 in Fine, 1952); it is excluded from the count here since Lewitzky, had he not chosen to resign, could have averted mate at the cost of a piece.

Conclusion

In conclusion, MATER's power stems from its ability to generate a small selective set of moves that merit investigation. Since most of the earlier chess programs (see the review in Newell, Shaw, and Simon, 1963*a*; and Kotok, 1962) spent their analysis time processing the wrong moves, it would seem that MATER II's two major mechanisms for generating relevant moves—its reliance on the sample variations and on the control of key squares—warrant further research. MATER II's major weakness, on the other hand, lies in its poorly organized search strategy for using its selectivity at all points in the analysis process.

On the horizon, proposals have been made for strengthening the program's perceptual capabilities as well as altering its search strategy.

APPENDIX: THE BASIC REPRESENTATION

Statement of the Problem

In this appendix we describe the basic representation implemented by Newell and Prasad (1963). Two interrelated questions guided the choice of representation:

1. What are the necessary components of a chess representation?
2. How should this information be organized?

In response to (1): The program should be able to "see" the same things a human sees when he looks at a chessboard. Thus the program requires an internal representation of the squares and pieces on a chessboard and the relations among them and a set of processes that can pick off and make use of these relations as needed. The former requirement is called "setting up the chessboard," the latter "move-making and board processing capabilities."

In response to (2): The game of chess provides an inhomogeneous collection of information out of which moves must be forged. Thus there must be enough variety in the representation to discriminate all the different kinds of moves; given that, the information should be stored in such a way that little space is allotted to moves that seldom occur (such as Pawn promotions, castling, etc.), and the dependence and division of information between routines and data should remain flexible and open to change and never solidify into a resistant collection of conventions (Newell, 1962). List processing languages are specifically designed to cope with such problems.

A chessboard is made up of squares, which lodge pieces, which make moves from one square to another. Objects in chess, like the 64 squares and 32 men, can be represented as symbols on lists, and moves can be represented as names of description lists with certain prescribed associations (such as the square *from* which a piece comes, the square *to* which it moves, and the kind of move in question). A chess position, moreover, can be fully described as a list of pieces and squares and a chess game as a list of moves that originate from a standardized initial position and terminate in a well-defined checkmate position.

Setting up the Chessboard

A chessboard is made up of eight ranks and eight files which rule off 64 squares. The sequence of symbols S1 . . . S64 is used to denote these 64 squares.

In the data section of the program there are a list of ranks, L1, containing members R1 through R8, and a list of files, L2, containing members F1 through F8. Each rank is itself the name of a list containing eight member squares; e.g., R1 contains S1, S2, . . ., S8.

In the routines section of the program a superroutine, E1, sets up a chessboard; it calls nine routines E2-E7, E9, E10, and E12, which do the work. Routine E2 builds the eight file lists, F1 through F8, out of the rank lists, R1 through R8. Then routine E12 takes each of the 64 squares and assigns it rank and file (x, y) coordinates, which are later used to compute another set of relations among squares.

Squares. For each square on a chessboard it is essential to know: (1) the name of its occupant, if there is one, and (2) the name of all its neighboring squares in the chess-legal directions. The first desideratum is effected by defining an attribute MO, "Man on Square?" on the description list of every square and assigning as its value the name of the piece occupying it— if there is one.

The extensive network of relations among squares, constituting all legal move directions in chess, is captured by defining 16 directions on the chessboard, beginning with D1 for the forward direction and continuing clockwise to D16 for forward and left (e.g., the Knight's move KN1 to KB3).

Thus the even numbers (D2, D4, ..., D16) define the eight possible Knight move directions; half the odd numbers (D1, D5, D9, D13) define rank (horizontal) and file (vertical) directions; the other half (D3, D7, D11, D15), diagonal directions.

Routines E3, E4, E5, and E8 use lists L1, L2, L5, and L6 to build the network of relations among squares by assigning to each of the 64 squares all surrounding squares as values of each of the 16 directions that obtain. In the initial position, for example, the list structure of the square S8—White's KR1 in standard American chess notation—would look like this:

Name of list	*Attribute*	*Value*
Square KR1 (S8)	Man on Square (MO)?	White King Rook (M8)
	Square to the North (D1)?	Square KR2 (S16)
	Square to the West (D13)?	Square KN1 (S7)
	Square to the WNW (D14)?	Square KB2 (S14)
	Square to the NW (D15)?	Square KN2 (S15)
	Square to the NNW (D16)?	Square KN3 (S23)

Note that in such a list structure representation only those five of the 16 legal directions that are needed are defined; space in memory is not consumed by providing the "information" that the other 11 directions have *no* values, as it would seem to be in a matrix representation of this kind of data. (cf, the argument in Newell, 1962, pp. 411–12, for a fuller statement of this view.)

Men. The 32 men take and retain their designations from their placement in the initial position; they are denoted by the sequence of symbols M1 ... M32.

For each piece, it is essential to know:
1. The square he occupies (attribute S0).
2. His type (attribute A1).
3. His color or side (attribute A2).
4. His legally permissible move directions (attribute A20).
5. His legally permissible capture directions (attribute A21).

The first of these is effected by defining an attribute SO, "Square on?" on the description list of every piece and assigning as its value the name of the square the piece currently occupies.

The other four attributes assume the complete range of values in accord with the rules of chess.

In the data structure there are 11 lists that group the chess men by types or otherwise useful categories: White Pawns; Black Pawns; Bishops; Rooks; Knights; Queens; Kings; White Rooks, Bishops and Queen; Black Rooks, Bishops, and Queen; White Knights; and Black Knights.

For each side, moreover, there is a list giving the type of each man on that side, and another list giving the move directions of each type of man.

Routines E6 and E7 assign to each man his type, color, move directions, and capture directions. In the initial position, for instance, the list structure of M8 would look like this:

Name of list	*Attribute*	*Value*
White King Rook (M8)	Man on what square (SO)?	Square KR1 (S8)
	Type of man (A1)?	A Rook
	Color of man (A2)?	White (K10)
	Move directions (A20)?	A list of directions D1, D5, D9, D13
	Capture directions (A21)?	A list of directions D1, D5, D9, D13

Positions. A chess position can be described fully in terms of squares and pieces. Since MATER is supposed to find a checkmate in any given position, obviously some representation is necessary for encoding a particular position. This representation is a describable list called the position list, L10. Its main list consists simply of the name of each man present on the board and the name of the square each man occupies, arranged in attribute-value pairs. Its description list contains a set of special attributes pertinent to the characterization of the position; in particular, S65, the "Whose move is it?" attribute that flip-flops between K10 (White on move) and K11 (Black on move); S66, the name of the castle list that contains the Kings and Rooks still "eligible" for castling; S67, the signal cell that gets set when an en passant capture is in the offing; and S69, the name of the most recent move made on the board.

Routine E10 takes as input any position list—either the initial position or the mating position, which is read in from cards by routine E90—

and converts it into a set of associations between pieces and squares such that every piece has an attribute SO ("Square on?") with the square that piece occupies as value, and very square has an attribute MO ("Man on?") with the name of the chess piece—if there is one— occupying that square as its value.

This ends our description of what might be called the "static" perceptual relations on the chessboard.

Move-making Capabilities

Moves are the operators that transform one chess position into another. What are the common properties of chess moves? Each involves a piece, or sometimes two, going from one square to another. If the "to square" is already occupied, the move is called a capture. If the "to square" is on the eighth rank and the piece a Pawn, it is called a promotion. But in all cases the common "from-to" property holds.

This permits a move to be represented as the name of a description list containing a "from square" (as the value of an attribute A_{40}) and a "to square" (as the value of an attribute A_{41}). This information is sufficient to specify most moves. There is a special class of moves, however, which, while adhering to this "from-to" pattern, introduce some idiosyncratic properties of pieces. Each of the following five members in this class is assigned a different value to the special move attribute A_{42}: King's side castling, Queen's side castling, a double Pawn move, an en passant response thereto, and a Pawn promotion.

Five steps are required to make a move: first, the move must be constructed; second, it must be tested for legality; third, for repetition of position; fourth, it must actually be made on the board; and fifth, it should be printed.

Routines E_{51} and E_{52} construct regular moves and special moves, respectively. Both create a new cell or symbol, which becomes the name of the move. Both take as input the square from which the piece is to move and the square to which it is to move and assign these as values of attributes A_{40} and A_{41}, respectively. For the special move routine, E_{52}, the type of move must also be specified as input; it is assigned as the value of attribute A_{42}. The name of the man moved is also received as the value of another attribute A_{51}, for reasons that will appear under step 3 below. The move $1.P-K_4$, for example, would be represented as follows (where a_1 and a_2 are internal cell names):

Name of list	Attribute	Value
a_1	From Square (A_{40})?	Square K2 (S13)
	To Square (A_{41})?	Square K4 (S29)
	Man moved (A_{51})?	White King Pawn (M13).

Similarly, the special move $P-K8 = Q$ would be represented in the following format:

Name of list	Attribute	Value
a_2	From Square (A_{40})?	Square K7 (S53)
	To Square (A_{41})?	Square K8 (S61)
	Special Move (A_{42})?	Promotion to Queen
	Man moved (A_{51})?	White King Pawn (M13).

Second, a routine E_{18} checks to ensure that a newly constructed move is legal. The routine tests, for example, whether a Bishop is moving through a Pawn, whether a Rook is making a Bishop move, whether a player is castling through check, and the like. The output is a simple " + " ("yes, the move is legal") or " − " ("no, the move is illegal").

Third, according to the laws of chess, a three-fold repetition of position constitutes a draw, and, according to the laws of computers, a loop. Before a move is executed, therefore, a routine E_{55} tests if the move under consideration has been played before in this same position. The position could not have occurred before if the move is irreversible, that is, if once the move is made on the board no subsequent set of legal moves can ever regain the exact same position. Captures, Pawn moves, and castling are all irreversible. Thus when a capturing move is constructed (step 1), it is given an attribute A_{44} with the man captured as its value. When a castling move is constructed, its status as a special move is recorded as the value of attribute A_{42}. And for a Pawn move, a record is kept via the man moved attribute, A_{51}. Routine E_{56}, called by E_{55}, tests for any of these three conditions to declare a move irreversible. If none of them obtains, E_{55} must make some further comparisons between the A_{40} and A_{41} values of the proposed move and earlier moves.

Fourth, a routine E_{65} makes a regular move on the board; routines $E_{71}-E_{75}$ and $E_{81}-E_{85}$ execute the special moves. A move is made by updating the position list, which is done in two steps: first, with the assistance of routine E_{11}, the description lists of the pieces and squares affected by the move are updated. Second, the signal cells—S65, S66, S67, and S69—affected by the move are reset.

Since different routines are needed to make each of the five special moves, these routines are simply associated with their respective special move values in the data section of the program.

Fifth, there is a print routine, E16, which prints out the name of the move, the "from square," the "to square," and the man captured, if any.

Additional Board Processing Capabilities

In addition to the move-making capabilities just described, there is a second group of routines intended to provide the machine with some more of the perceptual capabilities a human possesses; these are the board processing routines which provide answers to questions asked of the board. Routine E13 finds the direction, if one exists, between two given squares. Routine E14 tests to see if there is a piece between two squares in a given direction, and E24, if there is one and only one piece between two squares in a given direction. E15 tests if a piece is under attack, and routine E26 asks specifically if that piece is the enemy King. Routine E33 tests whether a given square is under attack, while E34 builds up the list of men of a particular color attacking a given square. Routine E36 tests if a given square is defended. These are some of the more important "building block" routines used in constructing the move tree.

Processing Speed

It might be supposed that since the program was written in an interpretive language, IPL-V, without any attempt to provide a special machine-language representation for primitive board manipulations, that it would be a very slow player. This has not proved to be the case—a tribute to the advantages of selectivity over machine brute force. The most difficult mates, requiring the examination of about 100 positions, were achieved in about 10 minutes on a CDC G-20—which would be equivalent to about three minutes for the IPL-V system on the IBM 7090. An excellent human player might be expected to take ten minutes or more to discover and verify the mate in a position of this difficulty.

We would like to acknowledge the assistance of G. A. Forehand, B. F. Green, A. Newell, M. R. Quillian, and R. F. Simmons.

REFERENCES

Baylor, G. W. Report on a mating combinations program. *SDC Paper*, No. SP-2150, Systems Development Corporation, Santa Monica, Calif. (1965).

Bernstein, A., and Roberts, M. DeV. Computer vs. Chess Player. *Scientific American*, 1958, 198:96–105.

Botvinnik, M. M. *One Hundred Selected Games* (translated by S. Garry), Dover Press, New York, 1960.

Duncker, K. On problem solving (translated by L. S. Lees from the 1935 original). *Psychological Monographs*, 1945, 58, whole no. 270.

Fine, R. *The Middle Game in Chess*. David McKay, New York, 1952.

de Groot, A. D. *Thought and Choice in Chess* (2nd. ed.). Mouton and Company, The Hague, 1978.

Kotok, A. A chess playing program for the IBM 7090. Unpublished bachelor's thesis. Massachusetts Institute of Technology, 1962.

Luce, D., and Raiffa, H. *Games and Decisions*. John Wiley & Sons, New York, 1957.

McCarthy, J. The inversion of functions defined by Turing Machines. In P. E. Shannon and J. McCarthy (eds.), *Automata Studies*. Princeton University Press, Princeton, N. J., 1956, pp. 177–81.

Maier, N. R. F. Screening solutions to upgrade quality: A new approach to problem solving under conditions of uncertainty. *Journal of Psychology*, 1960, 49:217–31.

Myron, S. M., and May, W. H. A note on serendipity, aesthetics, and problem solving. *Behavioral Science*, 1963, 8:242–43.

Newell, A. Some problems of basic organization in problem-solving programs. In M. Yovitts, G. T. Jacobi, and G. D. Goldstein (eds.), *Self-organizating Systems*. Spartan Books, New York, 1962, pp. 393–423.

Newell, A., and Ernst, G. The search for generality. *Proceedings of IFIPS Congress 65*, Spartan Books, Washington, D.C., 1965, vol. 1, pp. 17–24.

Newell, A., and Prasad, N. S. IPL-V chess position program. Unpublished working paper, Carnegie Institute of Technology (1963).

Newell, A., and Simon, H. A. An example of

human chess play in the light of chess playing programs. *Progress in Biocybernetics*, 1965, 2: 19–75.

Newell, A., Shaw, J. C., and Simon, H. A. Chess-playing programs and the problem of complexity. In E. A. Feigenbaum and J. Feldman (eds.), *Computers and Thought*. McGraw-Hill, New York, 1963, pp. 39–70.

Newell, A., Shaw, J. C., and Simon, H. A. Empirical explorations with the logic theory machine. In E. A. Feigenbaum and J. Feldman (eds.), *Computer and Thought*. McGraw-Hill, New York, 1963, pp. 109–33.

Newell, A., Shaw, J. C., and Simon, H. A. The processes of creative thinking. In H. E. Gruber, G. Terrell, and M. Wertheimer (eds.), *Contemporary Approaches to Creative Thinking*. Atherton Press, New York, 1962, pp. 63–119. Reprinted as chapter 4.1 in this book.

Samuel, A. L. Some studies in machine learning using the game of checkers. In E. A. Feigenbaum and J. Feldman (eds.), *Computers and Thought*. McGraw-Hill, New York, 1963, pp. 71–105.

Simon, H. A. and Newell, A. Models: Their uses and limitation. In L. D. White (ed.), *The State of the Social Sciences*. The University of Chicago Press, Chicago, 1956, pp. 66–83.

Simon, H. A., and Simon, P. A. Trial and error search in solving difficult problems: Evidence from the game of chess. *Behavioral Science*, 1962, 7:425–29. Reprinted as chapter 4.2 in this book.

4·4

Cognitive Processes in Solving Algebra Word Problems (1966)

with Jeffery M. Paige

Almost all the thinking and problem solving that people do requires that they handle natural language. Often they must perform tasks that also require simple arithmetic or even algebraic manipulations. The study of information processing systems, using computer languages as research tools, has reached the point where programs can now be constructed (indeed, have been constructed) that are capable of interpreting simple natural-language expressions and simple mathematical questions. In this chapter we will use one such computer program, which is capable of solving algebra word problems, as a point of reference and departure for investigating the processes that humans use in solving such problems.

The two following parts of this introduction describe the task environment (algebra word problems) for the human behavior we wish to explain and comment on the methods of inquiry we will use. Following the Introduction, section 1 sets out a theory, due primarily to Daniel G. Bobrow, that explains the behavior of subjects solving word problems, to at least a reasonable first approximation, in simple situations.

Section 2 presents empirical data of human behavior to illustrate some modifications in the basic theory that are required to accommodate individual differences in performance and identifies some processes, visible in the human behavior, that are treated inadequately in the theory.

Section 3 introduces a distinction between "direct" and "auxiliary" translations of natural-language expressions and presents data to show that human subjects often make use of auxiliary processes that are absent from the original form of the theory of section 1. Section 4 shows how auxiliary representations permit the problem solver to use physical assumptions that are not explicit in the problem statement, but that are essential to its solution. Section 5 summarizes the empirical findings and sketches the extensions of the theory that are required to encompass them. This

This investigation was supported in part by the Public Health Service Research Grant MH–07722 from the National Institute of Mental Health. We are indebted to David Klahr and Allen Newell for comments on an earlier draft of this paper.

201

summary section also discusses the relation of problem solving in algebra with the processes that have been identified in theoretical and empirical explorations of other task domains—proving theorems, for example, and playing chess. Our aim is not merely to account for human performance in solving algebra word problems but to do so in a way that will make apparent the relation of this performance to performance on other cognitive tasks.

Algebra Word Problems

The tasks of manipulating natural-language and mathematical symbols are both combined in answering the questions posed in simple algebra word problems:

> If the number of customers Tom gets is twice the square of 20 per cent of the number of advertisements he runs, and the number of advertisements he runs is 45, what is the number of customers Tom gets?

At a common-sense level, it seems plausible that a person solves such problems by, first, translating the problem sentences into algebraic equations and, second, solving the equations. In fact, that is exactly what textbooks instruct students to do. The following example is typical (Hawkes, Luby, and Touton, 1929):

> In the solution of problems involving the use of simple equations, the following steps are necessary:
> 1. Read the problem carefully and find the statement which will later be expressed in an equation.
> 2. Represent the unknown numbers by means of numerals and letters.
> 3. Express the conditions stated in the problem as an equation involving these symbols.
> 4. Solve the equation.
> 5. Check, by substituting in the problem the values found for the unknowns.

Assuming that these recommendations describe at least roughly what equation solvers actually do, we postulate two main subprocesses, corresponding respectively to the first three, and the last two, of the steps listed above:

TRANSFORM INPUT TEXT INTO EQUATIONS
SOLVE EQUATIONS

In this chapter we will be concerned almost exclusively with the first of these two subprocesses—with exploring how problem solvers set up an algebraic equation to correspond to a problem stated in English.

Information Processing Theories

The explanations we will propose for the behavior belong to the class of theories known as *information processing theories*. An information processing theory, usually stated as a computer program in a formal programming language, postulates in detail a precise set of mechanisms to account for the observed behavior. In a problem solving task, the behavior to be explained consists of what human subjects do, in writing or orally, under specified experimental conditions, while solving the problems.

An information processing theory is tested, as all theories are tested, by comparing its predictions with the observed behavior. The test can be extremely detailed and severe, for, using a computer programmed to behave in accordance with the information processing theory, the program can be confronted with exactly the same problems that are given to the human subjects, and either the broad outlines or the minutiae of its behavior, or both, can be compared with the corresponding aspects of the human behavior. This chapter will provide a number of examples of such comparisons.

The theory must first pass a gross test of sufficiency. That is to say, since human beings who have had some training in algebra can solve simple algebra word problems, we would consider a theory of this performance unsatisfactory if its processes were not sufficiently powerful to solve simple problems of the same kind. The theory that will be described in section 1 passes the test of sufficiency; in solving algebra word problems it is roughly comparable with a human being having better-than-average manipulative skill in algebra but possessing a rather limited knowledge of English grammar and vocabulary.

Of course the flight of airplanes does not much resemble the flight of birds, except in the fact that both can sometimes stay aloft. Having satisfied ourselves of the sufficiency of the theory in the limited sense just indicated, additional evidence is needed to determine to what extent the problem solving processes used in the theory resemble, or differ from, the processes used by humans when they handle the same tasks.

Sections 2 through 4 carry out such comparisons for the theory introduced in section 1. We will see that the main mechanisms postulated in the theory appear to be present in the behavior of most of the human subjects, but additional mechanisms have to be postulated to account for some aspects of the human behavior. Hence, the theory may be regarded as a first approximation that explains some of the broad outlines of the human behavior, and, by allowing us to abstract from these, brings into sharp focus additional phenomena that might otherwise escape our gaze. A next task (carried out only informally here) is to enlarge the theory into a second approximation so that still finer detail of the behavior can then be detected as deviations from this more accurate model.

The procedure just outlined has become a standard method for testing information processing theories. To be worthy of consideration, such a theory must pass the test of sufficiency. It must be able to handle cognitive tasks comparable to those handled by human subjects at some level of skill. If it passes the sufficiency test, it is tested in more detail by comparing its behavior with human behavior on sets of identical or similar tasks. The differences between predicted and actual behavior then provide the basis for a new round of theory modification and testing. If fortune smiles, the cycle of theory construction and testing will show forward motion—its path will be helical rather than circular, produc-ing successively more adequate explanations of behavior.[1]

1. DIRECT PROCESSES FOR SOLVING WORD PROBLEMS

Fortunately, the work of constructing a sufficient system of processes for solving algebra word problems has already largely been done for us. During 1958–60, Sylvia Garfinkel (1960) developed and hand-simulated a program for solving such problems. More recently, the work has been carried further by Daniel G. Bobrow (1964a, 1964b) who, in his M.I.T. doctoral dissertation, constructed a running computer program that solves a considerable range of algebra word problems. Garfinkel's and Bobrow's programs differ in one important respect: the former translates all problems using a single unknown, whereas the latter allows more than one unknown and simultaneous equations. Because it is more specific, and embodied in an actual running computer program, we will in general take Bobrow's program, called STUDENT, as our base of reference. In fact, however, the task given our subjects resembles more closely the one handled by Garfinkel's program, since we restricted the subjects to using a single unknown.

In proposing the STUDENT program as a theory of human problem solving, we are departing from the intent of its author. STUDENT was constructed in an investigation of artificial intelligence: "to discover how one could build a computer program which could communicate with people in a natural language within some problem domain." (1964a, p. 7.) The author did not intend to simulate human problem solving, nor does he make claims in this respect for the program. Hence, our analysis is in no sense an "evaluation" of the STUDENT program, but rather an inquiry into its relevance to a question quite different from the one it was designed to answer. Since the processes in the pro-

---

1. For a survey of information processing theories of cognition see A. Newell and H. A. Simon (1963b).

gram do, as we will see, parallel human processes in important respects, the fact that its author had other goals in mind does not make it less useful to us.

Example of a Transformation

Before trying to describe the processes used in STUDENT to translate English statements into algebraic equations, we will give an illustration, using the word problem mentioned in the introduction. "Translation" here means substantially what it does in translating from one natural language to another. We know, roughly, how to go about translating a statement from English into French: First, the French equivalent of each English word is looked up in a dictionary, and the string of French words substituted for the English string. Then certain rearrangements (and inflectional modifications) are made in the resulting string so that it will satisfy the rules of French syntax rather than English syntax. Of course this is only a rough paraphrase of how the translation would actually be done, but it indicates the essential elements. It is an example of what we will call a *direct process*.

To simplify the corresponding task of translating from English to algebra, let us preedit the text a bit. After we have analyzed the simplified form of the translation, we will return to the original problem.

> If the-number-of-customers-Tom-gets is twice the-square-of two-tenths times the-number-of-advertisements-he-runs, and the-number-of-advertisements-he-runs is 45, what is the-number-of-customers-Tom-gets?

Now we might find the following in an English-algebra dictionary:

$$
\begin{aligned}
&\text{If} &:& \text{ [not translated]}\\
&\text{the-number-of}\\
&\text{customers-Tom-}\\
&\text{gets} &:& \; x_1\\
&\text{is} &:& \; =\\
&\text{twice } [= 2 \text{ times}] &:& \; 2 * [\text{we write} *\\
& & & \text{for ``times'']}\\
&\text{the-square-of} &:& \; (\ldots)^2\\
&\text{two-tenths} &:& \; 0.2\\
&\text{times} &:& \; *
\end{aligned}
$$

$$
\begin{aligned}
&\text{the-number-of-}\\
&\text{advertisements-}\\
&\text{he-runs} &:& \; x_2\\
&\text{, and} &:& \text{ (end of sentence)}\\
&\text{, [question word]} &:& \text{ (end of sentence)}\\
&\text{what} &:& \; ?\\
&45 &:& \; 45
\end{aligned}
$$

Replacing the English by the algebraic string, we get something like

$$
\begin{aligned}
x_1 &= 2 * (0.2 * x_2)^2\\
x_2 &= 45\\
? &= x_1
\end{aligned}
$$

These equations are the algebraic equivalent of the original word problem, for solving the equations for x_1 gives the answer to that problem. Now, in order to simplify the problem and make it manageable for our crude dictionary-lookup translator, we have "cheated" in several ways. Most obvious and important: no dictionary exists that has "the-number-of-customers-Tom-gets" as an English entry and "x_1" as its algebraic translation. The use of x_1, rather than some other symbol, as the translation for the noun phrase is purely conventional. In the actual program, the translator did not find the equivalence in the dictionary; it simply assigned x_1 as an arbitrary name corresponding to the noun phrase. The only essential condition is that the translator use the *same* name to translate a particular noun phrase wherever it occurs in the problem. Thus, in the algebraic equations, x_1 and x_2 each occur twice, as did the noun phrases they stand for in the original problem statement. We have also simplified the translation by introducing the notation "$(\ldots)^2$" to handle the function "square of."

Outline of the STUDENT Program

Having shown very crudely what a translation amounts to, we may now look in more detail at the STUDENT program for accomplishing it.[2] Figure 1 is a general flowchart of the STUDENT program. The

---

2. The program is described in Bobrow (1964*a*, 1964*b*) and a listing is provided in Bobrow, 1964*a*, Appendix B.

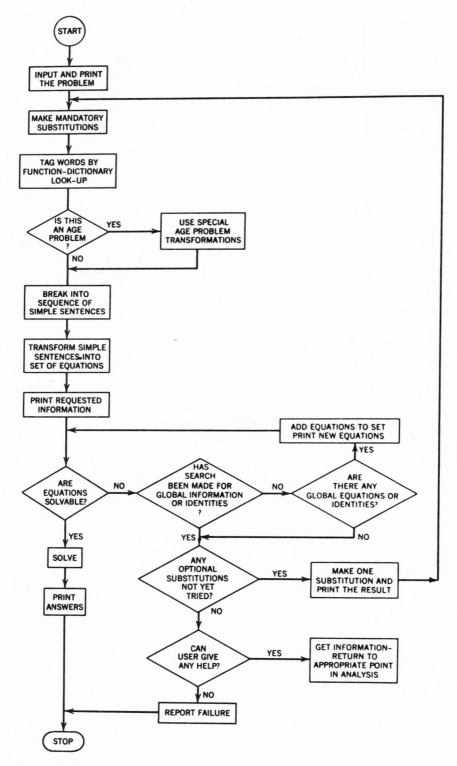

Figure 1. Flowchart of the STUDENT program. (From Bobrow, 1964*a*, p. 104.)

processes in the upper half of the flowchart transform the input text into equations; the processes in the lower half solve the equations. We will confine our attention to the upper half. Two of the processes represented in the flowchart are concerned only with a special class of word problems —age problems. These are the test labeled "Is this an age problem?" and the process labeled "Use special age problem transformations." We will omit these also from our present discussion.

What remains is the following sequence of processes (See figure 1, top half):

INPUT AND PRINT THE PROBLEM
MAKE MANDATORY SUBSTITUTIONS
TAG WORDS BY FUNCTION—DICTIONARY LOOKUP
BREAK INTO SEQUENCE OF SIMPLE SENTENCES
TRANSFORM SIMPLE SENTENCES INTO SET OF EQUATIONS

The operation of these processes on the illustrative word problem discussed above is shown in figure 2. This figure shows the successive transformations of the problem from the input text to the formal equations.

Mandatory Substitutions

The first step in transformation reduces certain words and phrases that appear in the input text to standard or canonical form, thus reducing the variety of expressions that have to be handled subsequently. As a comparison of the first and second versions of the text in figure 2 shows, the mandatory substitutions in this problem are 2 TIMES for TWICE, SQUARE for SQUARE OF, and PERCENT for PER CENT. The mandatory transformations are accomplished with the aid of a simple dictionary of synonyms.

Function Tags

The next main step in the transformation applies tags to some of the words in the

text, indicating what grammatical functions these words perform. This transformation is also accomplished by a dictionary lookup. *Functions* are what a grammarian

The problem to be solved is:

(If the number of customers Tom gets is twice the square of 20 per cent of the number of advertisements he runs, and the number of advertisements he runs is 45, what is the number of customers Tom gets Q.)

With mandatory substitutions the problem is:

(If the number of customers Tom gets is 2 times the square 20 percent of the number of advertisements he runs, and the number of advertisements he runs is 45, what is the number of customers Tom gets Q.)

With words tagged by function the problem is:

(If the number (of/op) customers Tom (gets/verb) is 2 (times/op 1) the (square/op 1) 20 (percent/op 2) (of/op) the number (of/op) advertisements (he/pro) runs, and the number (of/op) advertisements (he/pro) runs is 45, (what/Q word) is the number (of/op) customers Tom (gets/verb) (Q mark/DLM))

The simple sentences are:

(The number (of/op) customers Tom (gets/verb) is 2 (times/op 1) the (square/op 1) 20 (percent/op 2) (of/op) the number (of/op) advertisements (he/pro) runs (period/DLM))

(The number (of/op) advertisements (he/pro) runs is 45 period/DLM))

((What/Q word) is the number (of/op) customers Tom (gets/verb) (Q mark/DLM))

The equations to be solved are:

(Equal G02515 (number of customers Tom (gets/verb)))

(Equal (number of advertisements (he/pro) runs) 45)

(Equal (number of customers Tom (gets/verb)) (times 2 (expt (times 0.2000 (number of advertisements (he/pro) runs)) 2)))

(The number of customers Tom gets is 162)

Figure 2. Example of direct transformation of algebra word problem. (Bobrow, 1964*a*, p. 110.)

would call *parts of speech*, but STUDENT uses only a very simplified classification of parts of speech, containing three main categories (See Bobrow, 1964a, pp. 53–54).

The first category consists of strings of words which name objects in the model; I call such strings, variables. Variables are identified only by the string of words in them, and if two strings differ at all, they define distinct variables. . . .

The second class of words and phrases are what I call "substitutors." Each substitutor may be replaced by another string. Some substitutions are mandatory; others are optional and are only made if the problem cannot be solved without such substitutions. . . .

Members of the third class of words indicate the presence of functional linguistic forms which represent functions in the deductive model. I call members of this third class "operators." . . . One simple operator is the word "plus," which indicates that the objects named by the two variables surrounding it are to be added. An example of a more complex operator is the phrase "percent less than," as in "10 percent less than the marked price," which indicates that the number immediately preceding the "percent" is to be subtracted from 100, this result divided by 100, and then this quotient multiplied by the variable following the "than." . . .

Some words may act as operators conditionally, depending on their context. For example, "of" is equivalent to "times" if there is a fraction immediately preceding it; e.g., ".5 of the profit" is equivalent to ".5 times the profit"; however, "Queen of England" does not imply a multiplicative relationship between the Queen and her country.

Only certain words in the text are tagged —those called operators in the paragraph just quoted. Operators divide, in turn, into three subclasses: operators (proper), verbs, and delimiters. As examination of the transformed example shows, the operators there are "of," "times," "square," and "percent," the verb is "gets," and the delimiter, "?". In addition, the pronoun "he," and the question word "what" are also tagged. Note that in this case, the dictionary did not list "runs" as a verb, and the verb "is," which plays a special role, is not tagged.

Simple Sentences

Using the tags, and certain specific syntactical words as clues, the text is now divided into a sequence of simple sentences. For example, if an input sentence has an "if," followed by a string of words, followed by a comma, a question word, and a second string of words, then the first string, between the "if" and the comma, is made into a sentence, and the string following the comma into a second sentence. In the example before us, the text is divided into three sentences.

Algebraic Equations

The final step, the translation into equations, is now quite straightforward. Question words and noun phrases are interpreted as variables and are assigned names. Thus, "what" is given the arbitrary name "G02515," which is equated with "number of customers Tom gets." The other variable is "number of advertisements he runs."

In the particular notation used in STUDENT (so-called "Polish notation"), operators precede their operands. Thus we have "Equal G02515 (Number of customers Tom gets)," that is "Equals (a, b)," instead of the more familiar algebraic notation: "$a = b$." The only remaining subtlety in the transformation program is the set of rules that determines the order in which the various operations are to be performed. Partly this is handled by distinguishing "levels" of operators. Thus, in the example, "percent" is tagged "op 2," and "square" is tagged "op 1," so that the percentage will be taken before the result is squared. The program uses these tags, together with the sequence in which operators occur in the text, to assign the right phrase structure.

We have not described in detail the exact grammatical rules embodied in the syntactical routines of STUDENT because they are unimportant for our purpose. Much more complex and complete schemes for parsing English sentences than the STUDENT scheme have been programmed for computers. What is chiefly interesting about STUDENT in this respect is that a rather elementary scheme of syntactical analysis is in fact sufficient for handling an interesting range of algebra word problems.

Some STUDENT-like Human Behavior

The remainder of this chapter will largely be devoted to a comparison of the direct translation processes that enable STU-DENT to solve algebra word problems with the processes that human subjects have been observed using. The raw data for the comparisons are the thinking-aloud behavior of some twenty-eight subjects who were tape-recorded while setting up equations for algebra word problems. Ten of the subjects were college students (except one, a technical school graduate in electronics) between the ages of 19 and 21. Six of these were male (three majoring in engineering, two in physics, and one in mathematics), four were female (two majoring in mathematics, one in history, and one in psychology). Fifteen subjects were high school students, aged 15 and 16, eleven male and four female, enrolled in a special summer program of advanced, college preparatory courses for culturally deprived children. These students all had IQs in the same general range, averaging 118, and had taken at least a year of high school algebra. They had been selected for the summer program as having high intellectual potential but relatively poor motivation. The remaining three subjects were a male, aged 48, holding a PhD and with extensive mathematics training; a female, aged 27, holding an M.A. degree in psychology; and a male, aged 8, a student in the third grade.

Using this rather diverse group of subjects, and some variations on the basic task (the eight-year-old subject was given arithmetic rather than algebraic problems), we were able to get some impression of the diversity of human behaviors with a number of algebra problems of familiar types. In most parts of this chapter we will be dealing in detail with the behavior of individual subjects. For some purposes, however, we will use aggregate data from the

behavior of thirteen of the high school students, all of whom were given the same tasks.

The subjects in the main series of experiments were instructed as follows:

We are interested in how people solve problems. This experiment is not designed to test your problem-solving ability. It is simply to discover what methods you would use to attack an algebra word problem. There are no time limits on these problems. . . .

All the problems involve one algebraic equation with a single unknown. You should not attempt solutions using more than one unknown. A problem is completed when you are able to dictate to me an algebraic equation which is equivalent to the verbal statement. . . .

In order to follow your thoughts we ask that you think aloud, explaining each step as thoroughly as you can. It is a well-known psychological fact that such verbalization is not a handicap to problem solving. The problems will be presented on 5-by-9 cards, and you should begin by reading the problem aloud. Try to mention even details which you consider trivial, as they may be useful in understanding the total thought sequence.

To help you remember your place during the solution, I will write down on the blackboard parts of the equation, formulas, and so on, which you feel are useful in solving the problem. You must specify exactly what I am to write. . . . You will not be told whether or not the solution is correct. . . .

The subjects in the main series of experiments were given the three practice problems followed by the five test problems that are listed in the appendix of this chapter. Some of the early subjects were given a partially different set of problems, but all the data reported here refer to the problems in the appendix.

Much of the human behavior, especially on the simpler practice problems, resembles closely the sample given previously of STUDENT'S direct translation. A single sample will suffice at this point for illustration. Subject 8 was a woman undergraduate student of mathematics who employed (more than any of the other subjects) careful, direct translation processes. Here is her protocol on practice problem 2:

'If three more than a certain number is

divided by 5 the result is the same as twice the number diminished by 12. What is the number?'

'Three more than a certain number' is *x* plus ... *x* plus 3. Write down '*x* + 3.' 'Divided by 5,' so divide the whole thing by 5. 'The result is' ... 'is'—an equals. Write ' = ' 'The same as twice the number,' which would be 2 times *x*. 'Diminished by,' minus—minus 12. That's the completed equation.

The single quotation marks have been supplied in the transcription of the tape-recorded protocol to indicate where the subject is obviously reading from the printed problem statement, or dictating something to the experimenter at the blackboard. The wording of the text, taken together with inflectional cues in the tape recording, leave little or no ambiguity in the interpretation.

Clearly, the subject is carrying out a phrase-by-phrase translation, operating in a single pass over the problem statement from beginning to end. In this latter respect, her processing is organized in even a simpler manner than STUDENT's. Implicitly, but not explicitly, she reduces the first sentence to the simpler form, "A certain number divided by five is the same as twice the number diminished by 12." In translating phrase by phrase, she does not notice that the last part of the sentence is ambiguous—could be translated "2 (*x* − 12)" instead of "2*x* − 12". At a gross level, the general translational approach of STUDENT gives a pretty good explanation of what the student is doing in solving the problem.

2. Some Direct Translational Processes in Human Subjects

In this section, we will examine a number of interesting phenomena that emerge when we compare, in detail, the STUDENT scheme with some examples of human behavior. First, we will illustrate the range of individual differences, all within a general translational framework, in handling a simple problem. Second, we will examine some processes for naming quantities that are absent from the STUDENT program, but which are essential if the subjects are to formulate the equations using only one unknown. Third, we will investigate how ambiguities in naming quantities are handled by STUDENT and by some of the subjects.

In these explorations, we will use the protocols of three college-level subjects. Subject 8, as already mentioned, is a female undergraduate majoring in mathematics. Subject 5 is a female college graduate in psychology. Subject 6 is a male undergraduate majoring in physics.

An Example of Individual Differences

Figure 3 gives the complete protocols of these three subjects on practice problem 1. The protocols show that the subjects proceeded in quite different fashions.

The subjects were instructed to set up the equation, using a single variable, not to solve it. Subject 5 disobeyed the instructions. Instead of translating the problem into an equation, she simply finds the

PROBLEM: If a certain number is multiplied by 6 and the product increased by 44 the result is 68. Find the number.

Subject 5	Subject 6	Subject 8
So I would begin by subtracting 44 from 68 and getting 24 and therefore the number is 4.	We'll call the number *n*. It says that if we multiply it by 6 and add 44 to it, 'the result is 68.' This presents a simple equation of 6*n* plus 44 equals 68.	The unknown is a 'certain number,' which would be *x*. Multiply *x* by 6. Write down '6*x*' please. 'Increased by' means add, so you put a plus 44. 'The result is'— indicates equals—write please—'68'.

Figure 3. Three protocols on practice problem 1

answer, working backward from end to beginning, performing arithmetic operations sequentially, and holding the partial answer in memory. If we designate by A the partial answer, we could describe her process thus:

Set $A = 68$
Subtract 44 from $A [= 24]$
Divide A by 6 $[= 4]$
Report: $A = 4$

That this sequence is not simply a hindsight invention is demonstrated by the fact that the subject actually was aware of the partial result $68 - 44 = 24$. We may therefore have some confidence that she went through approximately this sequence in obtaining the answer. In order to do this, she had to replace each operation in the problem statement by its inverse: subtracting for "increased by," dividing for "multiplied by," and she had to interpret the terms "product" and "result."

Subject 8 represents the other extreme— a process corresponding very closely to a direct syntactical translator, as in her handling of practice problem 2. The subject treats "the number" as synonymous with "a certain number," and assigns it the name "x." "Is multiplied by 6" is interpreted as transforming "x" to "$6x$." "Increased by 44" is interpreted as transforming "$6x$" to "$6x + 44$." "The result is" is translated "$=$," so that the sentence is translated "$6x + 44 = 68$."

Subject 6 uses a somewhat different process to set up the equation. Like subject 8, he sets up an algebraic equation, but, like subject 5, he uses the device of successively modifying a partial result. In the case of subject 6, however, the partial result is an algebraic expression rather than a number. Again, let us call the partial answer A. The processes of subject 6 may then be described thus:

Set $A = n$
Set $A = 6A [= 6n]$
Set $A = A + 44 [= 6n + 44]$
Write equation: $A = 68 [6n + 44 = 68]$

That the subject is actually proceeding in this way is shown by the fact that he first

calls the number n, then multiplies "*it*" by 6, and adds 44 to "*it*." Only on the interpretation we have given above can the "it" refer in both cases to the same object—that is, to the partial answer, A.

To explain how the STUDENT program handles this problem, we will have to supplement our previous description of it with some new detail. There is involved a new concept here—indicated by the words "produce" and result." Instead of setting up a new equation for each clause of the sentence, the subjects identify the first clause as designating a new number (the product) that results from performing the operation described by the clause. The clause provides for this new number a *relational name*, "$6x$," that *relates* it to the name, "x," of the "certain number," Similarly, the second clause, "and the product increased by 44," provides a relational name, "$(6x) + 44$," that relates the "result" to the "product." The main clause now equates this relational name with the number 68, providing the required algebraic equation: $[(6x) + 44] = 68$, where, to emphasize the way in which the equation was developed, we put parentheses around the relational name of "the product" and square brackets around the relational name of "the result."

The STUDENT program in fact contains some processes, not described earlier, that allow it to handle this problem in much the way it is handled by subjects 6 or 8. For these processes to operate properly, the problem must be slightly reworded, although the present wording could be retained if a few sophistications were added

---

The problem to be solved is:
(A number is multiplied by 6. The product is increased by 44. The result is 68. Find the number.)

The equations to be solved are:
(Equal G02528 (number))
(Equal (plus (times (number) 6) 44) 68)

The number is 4

Figure 4. STUDENT solution of (modified) practice problem 1.

to STUDENT's dictionary and syntactical routines. Figure 4 shows how STUDENT solved the slightly reworded problem: "A number is multiplied by 6. This product is increased by 44. This result is 68. Find the number." The device STUDENT uses is described as follows:

The sentence "A number is multiplied by 6" only indicates that two objects in the model are related multiplicatively, and does not indicate explicitly any equality relation. The interpretation of this sentence in the model is the prefix notation product:

(TIMES (NUMBER) 6)

The latter phrase is stored in a temporary location for possible later reference. In this problem, it is referenced in the next sentence, with the phrase "THIS PRODUCT." The important word in this last phrase is "THIS." STUDENT ignores all other words in a variable containing the key word "THIS." The last temporarily stored phrase is substituted for the phrase containing "THIS." Thus, the first three sentences in the problem shown above yield only one equation, after two substitutions for "this" phrases.

In summary, in this problem we find subject 8 behaving in a manner closely resembling that predicted by STUDENT. Subject 6 also sets up the equation by direct translation, but uses processes a little different from those used by subject 8.

Conventional and Relational Names

The single simple example of an algebra word problem that we have been considering already discloses some interesting ingredients of the process for handling such problems. Of particular interest are the processes for *naming* variables. The names used are of two kinds: *conventional* and *relational*. Since the same distinction can be made among names used in ordinary English prose, we will first consider it as a general linguistic distinction, then apply it to algebra.

A particular automobile can be identified (that is, named) by its license number, or by naming its owner. Thus, we can speak of "the automobile F34–338," or of "John Smith's automobile." The former

method of naming is conventional, the latter is relational, for it identifies the object by a particular relation (ownership) to another object (John Smith). A variety of syntactic devices are used in English to permit relational naming. One of the most common is the noun phrase with "of": "The X of the Y of the Z." "Of" may designate a much more general relation than property ownership: "The prow of the largest ship of the fleet." The definite article, "the," implies that there is one and only one object satisfying the relation— that it defines a function, in the mathematical sense.

In algebra, we use letters of the alphabet to name numbers conventionally. In the problem we have been considering, subject 6 says, "We'll call the number n," and subject 8 says, "The unknown is 'a certain number,' which would be x." In both cases, a conventional name in English, "the number," "a certain number," is replaced by a conventional algebraic name: "n" or "x."

The two subjects also use relational naming, however. They translate the phrase, "the result," by the function $(6n + 44)$, or $(6x + 44)$ respectively. Knowing that "the result" is also equal to the number 68, they then state that these two numbers are equal: the number named "$(6n + 44)$" and the number named "68." It is because the former name relates "the result" to "a certain number" that it permits the numerical name for the latter to be found.

The point may be restated in another way. The statement of such an algebra problem asserts that certain relations hold among various numbers, some of them known, some of them unknown. In translating the problem statement into algebra, the information that a particular relation holds can be used in two ways: (1) To state an equation, whose left-hand side is one name for a number and whose right-hand side is another name for the same number (cf. "John is Fred's uncle"); or (2) to name one number by its relation to another number (cf. "Fred's uncle").

These alternatives may be illustrated if we solve the sample problem we have been examining by setting up three equations in three unknowns, instead of a single equation in one unknown. Call "a certain number" x, "the product" y, and "the result" z. Then we can state immediately the three equations:

$$y = 6x$$
$$z = y + 44$$
$$z = 68$$

We have the same alternatives in English prose. Consider: "His father's car is blue." Let X, Y, and Z be objects (or persons). We can then translate: "X is a person such that Y is the father of X, Z is the car of Y, and Z is blue." Ordinarily, we would have no occasion to make such a translation, but the fact that it is grammatical shows us that there is nothing peculiarly "algebraic" or mathematical about it. There are even certain linguistic devices that allow us to dispense with letters for names of variables: "A certain person is the father of a second person; a certain car belongs to the former; that car is blue."

Returning to the algebra problems, we see that certain trade-offs are possible between naming variables conventionally or relationally, on the one hand, and setting up more or fewer equations, on the other. In another simple problem (practice Problem 3), we see how different subjects make use of these alternatives:

The difference between two numbers is 12, and 7 times the smaller number exceeds the greater by 30. Find the numbers.

As before, the subjects were instructed to set up the equation using a single unknown, but again, Subject 5 unintentionally disobeyed the instructions. Her protocol begins:

X minus—would you write—"$x - y = 12$," and "7 times the smaller number" which is gonna by y, so would you write "$7y$," ah, . . .

Here the two numbers are named, conventionally, "x" and "y", whereas "7 times the smaller number" is named relationally, "$7y$." The other two subjects succeed in formulating the problem with a single variable. Subject 6 begins:

O.K. We'll call one number n—and you may write "n", just jot it down—and the other number $(n - 12)$. Just write it down for my reference.

Subject 8 begins in almost the same way, but chooses the smaller, rather than the larger, number to be named conventionally:

The first number we will let be represented by x. Write down "x" please. The second number is then $(x + 12)$ since "the difference is 12." Write down "$(x + 12)$."

Since the subjects were instructed to use only a single unknown, they were forced by these instructions to introduce relational names for the remaining variables. (In some cases, as with subject 5 on practice problem 3, they found themselves unable to do so, or forgot the instructions.) In this respect, STUDENT provides an inadequate description of the human behavior, for it introduces relational names only in the special case already illustrated by practice problem I, where it is cued by the occurrence of the word "this." Even had the subjects not been restricted as to the number of unknowns used, they almost certainly would have used the relational naming process more freely than STUDENT and limited themselves to smaller numbers of simultaneous equations.

We have here an example of how the technique of computer simulation can be used to identify a simple but important process that enters into the human performance. The difference between using information to create a relational name and using that same information to create an equation can be detected readily in the protocols.[3]

Ambiguity of Names

Frequently, variant phrases are used to name the same quantity in the statement

---

3. We noted earlier that Garfinkel's program (1960) translates all problems using a single unknown. Hence, it contains more elaborate processes than STUDENT for relational naming, and in this respect constitutes a more adequate theory of our subjects' behavior.

of a problem. Most often, the second time a quantity is mentioned, it is denoted by an abridgement of the phrase that named it on the first mention. Thus: "If three more than *a certain number* . . . What is *the number?*" Presumably "the number" of the question is the "certain number" of the first statement. Often, abridgement involves substitution of a pronoun for a noun: "the number of customers he has" for "the number of customers Tom has." In these cases, the rules for pronoun reference allow the identification to be made. In other cases, an identifying phrase is omitted: "the liter" for "one liter of a 90 percent alcohol-water mixture."

These examples show that a person solving an algebra word problem must be prepared sometimes to identify with a single quantity two names that are similar, but distinct. On the other hand, mere similarity of two phrases does not mean that the variables they denote are necessarily identical. Consider this example:

The number of quarters a man has is seven times the number of dimes he has. The value of the dimes exceeds the value of the quarters by two dollars and fifty cents. How many has he of each coin?

In the first two sentences, there are four noun phrases denoting quantities: "the number of quarters a man has," "the number of dimes he has," "the value of the dimes," and "the value of the quarters." In spite of the fact that the first two phrases (after replacement of the pronoun by the appropriate noun) differ in only a single word ("quarters" versus "dimes"), as do also the last two, a native speaker of English would not be likely to identify the members of either the first pair or the second pair.

But what about the first and fourth, and the second and third? Is "number of quarters" the same as, or different from "value of the quarters"? In this case we would probably decide they are different, as would any sufficiently careful reader. This decision, however, certainly does not derive from any inflexible general rule saying that identical quantities must always

have identical names. As a matter of fact, the use of "value" as a synonym for "number" is sometimes idiomatic in English: If the number of dollars a man has is 15, the value of the dollars (in dollars) is also 15.

The STUDENT program provides for matching slightly different phrases referring to the same object, and assigning the same name to them, when the second of the two phrases to appear in the problem statement is contained completely in the first, in the sense that it is a contiguous substring within the first. STUDENT initially undertakes to solve the problem without such identifications and matches variables if it has been unsuccessful (Bobrow, 1964a, p. 71).

Thus, if necessary in order to solve a problem, STUDENT will assume that "gas consumption" is the same variable as "*gas consumption* of my car," if the second phrase occurs in the problem statement earlier than the first phrase; and under the same conditions will assume that "number of gallons of gas used" is the same as "*number of gallons of gas used* on trip between New York and Boston." It would not, however, identify "number of gallons of gas used" with "number of gallons used between New York and Boston." Thus, although the program illustrates the process—commonly used in interpreting natural language—of identifying "similar" phrases, it is rather inflexible in the way it does this.

Our subjects differed a great deal in the precision with which they handled these kinds of variations in noun phrases. Consider, for example, the protocol of subject 8 on the coin problem:

Let's represent—the fir— $-x$ as the dimes. Write down x please. The number of quarters is—is seven times the dimes. Therefore, the number of quarters is represented by $7x$. Put "$7x$." "The value of the dimes exceeds the value of the quarters by two-fifty"; therefore, x equals —represented by the value of the dimes—write down "x" again.

This subject, who was generally quite careful in handling the problem sentences phrase by phrase, actually writes down the equation: $x = 250 + 7x$, but then continues:

Since it really is a money problem we will check this and discover that we really should multiply to make this—ah—to make it equal in value. Since we have 250 pennies we have to multiply the dimes by 10. So that should be 10*x* and a plus. Since it's quarters it would be 7 times 25 times *x*, on the other side. That's the correct solution.

In the initial stages of solving the problem, this subject equated *x* with "the dimes," "the number of dimes," and "the value of the dimes." Perhaps the simplest explanation is to assume that her parsing program identified all noun phrases containing "dimes," and that, operationally speaking, *x* was defined as "the variable associated with dimes."

The same subject exhibited similar behavior on another problem. Here the problem was:

Mr. Stewart decided to invest 4,000 dollars, some at 3 percent and the rest at 4 percent. How much should he invest at each rate to produce equal incomes?

Here again, four quantities are under consideration: the amount of money invested at 3 percent, the amount invested at 4 percent, the income from the money invested at 3 percent, and the income from the money invested at 4 percent. The subject refers to these quantities in quite ambiguous language: "*x* equals 3 percent invested," "Write down (4,000 − *x*). This represents the amount invested at 4 percent, so write down 4 percent invested." "We want the number invested at 4 percent to equal the amount invested at 3 percent." Although the last sentence sounds like an incorrect statement of the problem, subject 8 in fact set up the right equation.

The difficulty many subjects have in identifying the variables in the coin problem is vividly illustrated by the protocol of subject 6 (italics added):

All right. He has quarters and dimes. I'd like to represent *a dime by x and a quarter by 2.5x*, because a quarter is two and one-half times the dime, so if you'd write down my reference "*x*" for dimes and "2.5*x*" for quarters. O.K. "The value of the dimes exceeds the value of the quarters by two-fifty" and he "has 7 times as many quarters as he has dimes" so—put 7 times

the denomin—*the notation for quarters*—which is (2.5*x*)—in parentheses. Seven times that exceeds *the value*—oh, let's see, he "has seven times as many quarters as he has dimes." "The *value of the dimes*" which is *x* "exceeds the value of the quarters by two-fifty" so—"a man has seven times as many quarters"—and these are to be solved with one variable only. *X* represents the dimes; 7*x* might represent the quarters. All right. May I change that? "A man has seven times as many quarters as he has dimes," so *call x dimes but call 7x quarters please*. That's a bit of foggy thinking right there. "*The value of the dimes*," which is *x* "exceeds the value of the quarters by two-fifty." O.K. *The number of quarters is 7x, the value of the quarters is 25 cents times 7x.* Would you write that down please? Just write "25 cents times 7*x*." O.K. Now "the value of the dimes exceeds the value of the quarters by two-fifty," so that 10 cents times *x* minus the 25 cents—no, all right—just put a minus; you already have the 25 cents down, 7*x* equals two-fifty. . . . Ten cents times *x* minus 25 cents times 7*x* equals two-fifty.

3. Auxiliary Representations and Cues

We have used the phrase "direct translation" for the kinds of processes examined thus far, for they amount mostly to a step-by-step substitution of algebraic symbols and expressions for the English words and phrases of the original problem statements. These translation processes involve the meanings, hence the translation, of only those terms in the problem statement that are mathematical in character ("number of," "two times"), or that perform syntactic functions in the sentence ("if," "and"). Other words and phrases are either ignored or replaced by conventional or relational names. Consider again the example:

If the number of customers Tom gets is twice the square of 20 percent of the number of advertisements he runs, and the number of advertisements he runs is 45, what is the number of customers Tom gets?

To set up the algebraic equations for this problem requires no knowledge of the meaning of "customers" or "advertisements," or for that matter, who Tom is; as is readily seen from:

If the number of glubs *X* biks is twice the square of 20 percent of the number of quonks he dobs, and he dobs 45 quonks, how many glubs does he bik?

On the other hand, even small changes in terms like "number of," "twice," "how many" could change entirely the meaning of the problem, or make it meaningless. Certain grammatical cues are also essential: it is important to know that "customers" or "glubs" is a noun, and that "he" is a pronoun that can stand for a person, but not for an inanimate object. Nor can the problem be solved without the knowledge that "is," in this kind of context, stands for "equals numerically."

A distinction is sometimes made between words that carry a substantive meaning and those that are primarily syntactic or grammatical in function. A noun like "customers" is clearly substantive, whereas "if," "the," "and," and "of," for example, are largely syntactic. Taking into consideration words that have special arithmetic meanings ("number," "twice," "times," "square," for example) we can say, as a rough approximation, that translating the word problems into equations requires a knowledge of the meanings of words that play a grammatical role, or an arithmetic one, but not the meanings of those that play a substantive role. The substantive terms, or the phrases constructed of them ("the number of advertisements he runs") are for the most part simply translated into conventional names of variables. All that is required is to be able to decide whether two such phrases name the same variable or different variables.

Let us now return to the coin problem:

The number of quarters a man has is seven times the number of dimes he has. The value of the dimes exceeds the value of the quarters by two dollars and fifty cents. How many has he of each coin?

The subject cannot solve this problem unless he possesses certain substantive information about dimes, quarters, dollars, and coins. He must know that the value of a quantity of coins equals the number of coins times the value per coin: $V_i = N_i * v_i$. He must also know that the value per dime (v_d) is 10 cents, the value per quarter (v_q) is 25 cents, and the value per dollar (v_D) is 100 cents. The subjects who were successful in setting up the equation for this problem made use of precisely this information.

To a limited extent, the STUDENT program simulates the subjects' use of substantive information. This is accomplished by storing in memory certain definitional equations. For example, "the perimeter of a rectangle sometimes means twice the sum of the length and width of the rectangle," "distance equals speed times time," or "distance equals gas consumption times number of gallons of gas used." If a problem proves unsolvable, STUDENT searches for relevant relations of this kind in memory, and, if it finds some, adds the corresponding equations.

We will refer to information of this sort, stored in the memories of the subjects, as "auxiliary information." We see that in handling many typical algebra word problems, such information is indispensable as a supplement to the direct translation processes.

Auxiliary Information

In a number of situations, the behavior of the subjects gives evidence that they are using stored substantive information that goes beyond the definitional equations we have just considered. The reader may or may not have noticed by now that the coin problem we have been using is substantively meaningless since it describes a physical impossibility. The problem states that there are *more* quarters than dimes (seven times as many, in fact). The value of a quarter is also more than the value of the dime; hence, the total value of the quarters must exceed the total value of the dimes. [$N_q > N_d$ and $v_q > v_d$, therefore $V_q = N_q * v_q > N_d * v_d = V_d$.] But the problem states: "The value of the dimes *exceeds* the value of the quarters. . . ."

If we translate the problem as given, as our three subjects did, we obtain the equation: $10x - 7 * 25x = 250$, which has as its solution, $x = -(50/33)$. Neither subject 5 nor subject 8 gave any evidence of noticing that the solution would be negative. Subject 6, however, immediately on dictating the equation to the experimenter (see the previous quotation of his protocol), continued as follows:

> Now, I've found an incongruity in this problem. When I first saw it—it looked—it looked impossible, I think. I don't know if you want me to say this but if a man has seven times as many quarters as he has dimes and the value of the dimes exceeds the value of the quarters by two-fifty, the quarters must really not be worth too much, because if he has 7 times as many quarters as he has dimes, the number of—the value of the quarters must exceed the dimes by $7 * 2.5 - x$, or what not. The value of the dimes, if they are ordinary dimes, can't exceed the value of the quarters in this case. Therefore, if you solve out you get a negative answer, I believe, which doesn't jibe with—negative quarters—no such thing exists. So, my conclusion is this problem is impossible to solve, in two denominations—quarters, and so forth.

Subject 8 was asked to solve the problem a second time, and immediately set up the equation again—this time without hesitation:

> The number of dimes is x—the number of quarters would be $7x$, and the value of the dimes would be, then, 10 times x, which would equal $250 + 7 * 25 * x$.

The experimenter and subject then continued with the following conversation:

E: Okay. Now let me show you a diagram—you probably already have this concept in mind, but tell me if looking at that changes the problem in any way. What do you make of that diagram?
S: It just has a—a dime—just has pennies and a dime—and 25 pennies and quarters.
E: Anything else strike you about that diagram?
S: That a quarter is larger than a dime, that's all.
E: Okay. Now look at that problem again.
S: Now, wait a minute here! If you have more —oh, sure, if you have more quarters than you have dimes of course the value of the dimes can't be larger than the value of the quarters. That one's illogical too.

In both cases, noticing the physical impossibility of the problem was equivalent to noticing that, under the terms of the problem, $V_q > V_d$, and hence one could not have "the value of the dimes exceeds the value of the quarters." Noticing this inequality is in no way essential to using direct grammatical cues to translate the problem statement into an equation—and the STUDENT program would have performed exactly as subject 8 did initially.

Spatial and Physical Cues

In the protocols there are numerous instances of subjects, in handling word problems, applying processes that involve the spatial or physical relations in the problems. Such cues sometimes lead subjects to discover that a problem represents a physically impossible situation. They are also used (intentionally or unintentionally) to substitute for the original "impossible" problem a similar one that involves no physical contradiction. We have some examples of this for another "impossible" problem (problem 4):

> A board was sawed into two pieces. One piece was two-thirds as long as the whole board and was exceeded in length by the second piece by 4 feet. How long was the board before it was cut?

Subject 6, who was in general the quickest of the three to discover contradictions, notices this one immediately:

> This is another incongruous one because the first piece is two-thirds as long as the whole board means the second piece is one-third as long as the whole board. If you want to write this down to show the incongruity, put $(\frac{2}{3})L$ represents the first piece. The second piece is represented by $(\frac{1}{3})L$ . . . Now, $(\frac{1}{3})L$ exceeds the length of the first piece by 4, so that we have $(\frac{2}{3})L + 4 = (\frac{1}{3})L$. . . . If we solve this, we have $(\frac{1}{3})L + 4 = 0$, or $(\frac{1}{3})L = -4$, or $L = -12$, and this is a negative length and that doesn't exist either.

Subject 8 did not notice a contradiction, but in fact changed the problem to make it physically possible. Her equation was: $(2/3)x = +4 + [x - (2/3)x]$. There is no clear indication in the protocol of how the transposition took place. The protocol simply reads:

We want to know the length of the board, therefore, write down "x equals length of the board." "One piece is $\frac{2}{3}$ of the whole board," so $(\frac{2}{3})x$, write down please, was "exceeded in length by the second piece by 4 feet" so—we want an equals plus 4 for the "exceeded in length." Now "the second piece" would be the whole board minus the other piece, which is $\frac{2}{3}$, so it would be times the quantity—no, plus the quantity, $[x - (\frac{2}{3})x]$.

Later subject 8, now aware that some of the problems represent physically impossible situations, is asked to do the problem again. She now notices the impossibility immediately:

Of course, the—the one piece is $\frac{2}{3}$ and the other is $\frac{1}{3}$. The $\frac{1}{3}$ piece can't be longer than the $\frac{2}{3}$ piece is. So that is also illogical.

Subject 5 also substituted a physically possible problem for the given one:

You can just put x equals length for me if you want to. Ah, $\frac{2}{3}$ of x is . . . "One piece was $\frac{2}{3}$ as long as the whole board and was exceeded in length" . . . plus 4 feet—no, you won't need that—ah, equals x.

Thus, subject 5 assumes that the 4 feet represent the difference between the first piece and the whole board, not between the two pieces. Now perhaps we could merely say that subjects 5 and 8 did not know how to interpret the phrase "was exceeded . . . by," and hence translated incorrectly. This may well be so, but it is notable that in both cases the result of the incorrect translation was to substitute a physically possible problem for a physically impossible one. One possible explanation would be to suppose that the subjects were using physical cues as well as grammatical and arithmetic ones in their processing.

Suppose the problem were reworded as follows:

A board was sawed into two pieces. One piece was two-thirds as long as the whole board, and the difference in length between the two pieces was 4 feet. How long was the board before it was cut?

Using only grammatical cues, this problem is ambiguous. If we let x be the length of the board, we know that "one piece" is $(2/3)x$. But the problem does not state whether the other piece is $(2/3)x + 4$ or $(2/3)x - 4$. Hence, from grammatical information alone, we do not know whether to write $x = (2/3)x + (2/3)x - 4$ or $x = (2/3)x + (2/3)x + 4$. Of course, if we calculate that the second piece is $x - (2/3)x = (1/3)x$, and that $2/3 > 1/3$, we will be able to deduce that the "one piece" is longer than the other, hence that the first equation we have written is the one intended.

Auxiliary Representations

What processes would lead a subject to calculate that, since the one piece of the board is $2/3$ its length, the other must be $1/3$? This calculation, in the original problem, is not required in order to set up the equation. Let us hypothesize that some subjects carry out the following "semantic" processing:

1. Construct a number line. (See figure 5)
2. Represent the quantities given in the problem on the number line.
3. If certain quantities are named, but their numerical values are not given, try to compute their numerical values or relational names by use of the number line.

In the board problem, we construct the number line of length L (figure 5). We mark off the interval from the origin to $(2/3)L$ as the length of the one piece. The distance from the end of this to the end of the line is the length of the other piece, which is not given. By subtraction on the number line, we find that it is $(1/3)L$, and label it accordingly.

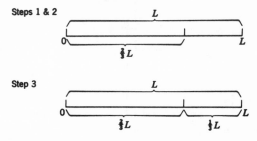

Figure 5. Auxiliary representation for problem 4.

We see clear evidence of this kind of processing in subject 8's handling of another problem—a mixture problem (problem 5):

A car radiator contains exactly one liter of a 90 percent alcohol-water mixture. What quantity of water will change the liter to an 80 percent alcohol mixture?

First, it must be noted that the problem is ambiguous. It is not clear whether the water is to be added, changing the total quantity of mixture; or whether some of the mixture is to be drawn off and replaced by water to make, again, a total of one liter of liquid. Subject 8 took the second interpretation. After reading the problem, she says:

Ah, the only way I can solve one of these is to draw a picture.

The subject then asks the experimenter to draw a picture, and later another picture that is actually used in solving the problem. The second picture is shown in figure 6. The protocol reads:

So we draw another picture. Then we draw another line across. Now, draw another line below that somewhere—it doesn't matter where. That's *x*. That's the amount we're going to take out. Let's see—that's one liter when we take out *x*, and that leaves us 1 minus *x* liters— quick—put it—write down beside it 0.9 times— parentheses 1 minus *x*, and put after that alcohol, please. ... Okay. Ah—now, I want to get a 90 percent so I want—I want that, okay, now the amount of alcohol we want to have left is 0.8 times 1 liter, so I want 0.9 times the quantity $(1 - x)$ to equal 0.8. That's the equation.

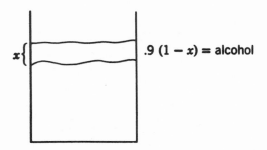

Figure 6. An auxiliary representation for problem 5.

How Representations Affect Problem-solving Performance

The three subjects whose behavior we have been examining in some detail were college students or college graduates, all of whom had studied mathematics through the calculus. Table 1 gives some data obtained from thirteen of the tenth grade students.

Most of the subjects succeeded in setting up an equation for the board-sawing problem (problem 4) and for the first two practice problems, but for few or none of the other problems. We may take this as evidence that the problems are really "hard" for high school students (even those above average in ability) or that these particular students had had poor high school algebra courses. There is probably considerable truth in both explanations.

After the subjects had undertaken to solve the three practice problems and the five test problems, they were asked by the experimenter to go to the blackboard and make diagrams for the board-sawing, riverboat, and alcohol-water mixture problems. Each diagram was to contain all the information given in the verbal statement. The diagram was to be complete enough to allow the subject to explain the problem to another student who had not read it.

Table 1 provides some information about how the subjects handled problem 4, the board-sawing problem, about the diagrams they drew for that problem, and about their performance on the other practice and test problems. The first column of the table identifies the subjects, the second column shows which of the three practice problems they solved correctly. In column (3) is the subject's self-rating of his performance in high school algebra. Column (4) shows for which of the five test problems the subject was able to construct an equation—whether correct or incorrect. Column (5) identifies the subjects who noticed contradictions in one or more problems. (problems 1, 3, and 4 were physically impossible; 5 was ambiguous.) Column (6) indicates whether the equation the subject constructed in Problem 4 followed the verbal or a physical translation

Table 1. Auxiliary Representations Used by High School Subjects.

| | | | Problems for which: | | Problem 4 | | |
Subject (1)	Practice Problems Solved (2)	Self-rating (3)	Equations Written (4)	Contradiction Noticed (5)	Type of Equation (6)	Diagram (7)	Equation (8)
Group P1 ("Physical" equation, good problem solvers)							
20	1, 2	Good	1, 4	4	(Physical)*	I, i, P	"contradictory"
28	1, 2	Fair to Good	1, 2, 4	4, 5[†]	Physical	I, i, P	$2/3x - 4 = 1/3x$
Group V1 ("Verbal" equation, good problem solvers)							
16	all	Good	2, 3, 4	None	Verbal	I, i, V	$2/3x + 2/3x + 4 = x$
21	all	Fair	1, 4	None	Verbal	U, c, P	$2/3x = 2/3x + 4$
24	all	Good	2, 3, 4	1	Verbal	I, c, V	$2(2/3x) + 4 = x$
25	1, 2	Fair	1, 4	None	Verbal	U, c, V	$2/3x + 2/3x + 4 = x$
Group P2 ("Physical" equation, poor problem solvers)							
18	1, 2	Poor	None	None	(Physical)*	U, c, P	————
22	1, 2	Fair to Poor	4	None	Physical	I, c, P	$2/3x + 4 = 0$
26	1, 2	Fair	4	None	Physical	U, c, V	$x = 2/3x + 2/3x - 4$
Group V2 ("Verbal" equation, poor problem solvers)							
17	1, 2	Fair	4	None	Verbal	U, i, P	$2/3x + (2/3x + 4) = x$
19	1, 2	Poor	4	None	Physical Verbal[‡]	I, c, V	$2/3x = 1/3x + 4$ $2/3x + (2/3x + 4) = x$
23	1, 2	Poor	4	None	Verbal	U, c, V	$2/3x + 2/3x + 4 = x$
27	all	Good	4	None	Verbal	U, c, V	$4/3x + 4 = x$

* No equation constructed, but evidence of physical interpretation.
[†] Noticed the ambiguity in problem 5.
[‡] First produced P equation; when asked to explain, produced V equation.

of the problem. Column (7) shows certain characteristics of the diagram for problem 4 each subject later drew (See figure 7): whether the diagram was integrated (I) (a single figure for the board and its parts) or unintegrated (U) (separate drawings for board and parts); whether the diagram was complete (c) (contained all the information in the problem statement) or incomplete (i); whether the diagram represented the verbal (V) problem or the physical (P) situation. Column (8) of the table shows the equation each subject actually constructed for problem 4. In interpreting these data, it should be kept in mind that the subjects constructed the diagrams some time after they derived the equations, with their work on problem 5 intervening between these two performances.

In table 1, the subjects are arranged in four groups, on the basis of whether they set up the verbal (V) or the physical (P) equation for problem 4, and whether they were successful (groups 1) or unsuccessful (groups 2) in setting up an equation for at least one test problem in addition to 4. Thus, the four groups are labeled P1, V1, P2, and V2 respectively.

Figure 7 provides an example of a diagram drawn by a member of each group. The diagrams in the top half of figure 7 are integrated. The one belonging to subject 20 (P1) is an incomplete (since "4 feet" is nowhere mentioned) diagram of the physical situation. The diagram of subject 24 (V1) is a complete diagram of the verbally described situation. The diagrams in the bottom half of figure 7 are unintegrated, consisting of three parts each. The diagram on the left, belonging to subject 18 (P2), is complete but represents the physical situation (the "4 feet" is added to the one-third piece). The dia-

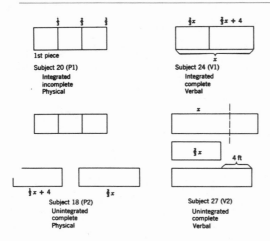

Figure 7. Types of diagrams for problem 4.

gram of subject 27 (V2) is also complete but represents the verbally described situation.

It will be noticed in the figures that the diagrams that are integrated belong to subjects in the 1 groups and the unintegrated diagrams to subjects in the 2 groups. The physical diagrams belong to subjects in the P groups and the verbal diagrams to subjects in the V groups. In the entire set of thirteen subjects these correlations are not perfect, but are visible. Four out of six integrated diagrams, but only two out of seven unintegrated diagrams, were produced by the subjects in the 1 groups.[4] Four out of six P diagrams, but only one out of seven V diagrams, were produced by the subjects in the P groups.[5] If we call the subjects in the 1 groups the "good" problem solvers, we can summarize these generalizations by saying: good problem solvers tend to construct integrated diagrams, and problem solvers who set up the physical equation tend also to represent the physical situation in their diagrams.

Next, we observe in table 1 that the subjects themselves are generally able to

predict their own performance. All the subjects who rated themselves as having been "poor" in algebra were unable to construct equations for test problems other than 4, and hence were assigned to a 2 group on the basis of performance. Three of the four subjects who were able to solve practice problem 3 were assigned to 1 groups.

Only subjects in the 1 groups noticed contradictions in any of the problems, and both subjects in P1, and only these, noticed the contradiction in problem 4 as they were attempting to set up the equation. Both of these subjects also drew integrated, incomplete, diagrams on which they represented the physical situation.

With a sample as small as the one before us, we can draw only very tentative conclusions. The data, however, are quite consistent with what our earlier discussion would lead us to expect. In trying to set up the equations for problem 4, the subjects may use either grammatical or physical clues for translation of the problem statement or some combination of these. The better problem solvers may use either, but if they use primarily the grammatical clues, they will set up the V equation and will not notice the contradiction; whereas if they use the physical clues also (particularly if they notice that $2/3 > 1/3$), they will likely notice the contradiction. If asked to represent the problem in a diagram, the subjects (five of six subjects in 1 groups) will give primacy to representing those types of clues that they responded to in setting up the equations.

About the subjects who are weaker in algebra, similar comments may be made. They may respond to either grammatical or physical clues. Those who respond to physical clues, however, will in this case not notice the contradiction—presumably because they do not also carry out the direct translation in detail. In five out of seven cases, the cues that are given primacy in the diagrams correspond with those that are given primacy in setting up the equations.

From our examination of the behavior of our subjects (at both college and high

4. The probability of this result, given no relation between integration of diagrams and problem solving ability, is 0.13.

5. The probability of this result, given no association between type of equation and type of diagram, is 0.05.

school level) we obtain considerable evidence that some of these subjects use processes that go well beyond the direct translation processes of STUDENT, even when the latter are supplemented by additional definitional equations. These auxiliary processes used by the subjects involve the construction of some kind of physical representation of the situation described by the problem statement. When the problem statement defines a physically impossible situation, subjects who employ auxiliary representations may discover the "contradiction" in the problem, or, if they rely primarily on the auxiliary representation rather than the grammatical cues in interpreting the problem, may replace the problem as stated by a similar, but physically possible one.

Since the problem statements themselves were not literally contradictory (in each case an equation could be written that accurately translated the statement), the contradictions the subjects detect must depend on additional premises imported into the problem through the auxiliary representations. In the next section, we will consider specifically how the representations serve as a source of additional assumptions about the problem situation.

4. Representations as Sources of Information

In this section we take up three related topics. First, we analyze in detail the assumptions used by subjects to set up an equation in the mixture problem (problem 5). Next, we consider the organization of their reasoning on that same problem. Finally, we look for evidences of auxiliary representations in a problem involving rates and distances (problem 3).

Introduction of Conservation Assumptions

Returning to the three college-level subjects, we examine in more detail their handling of the alcohol-water mixture problem. We noted previously that the problem is ambiguous. For definiteness, let us suppose that water is to be *added* to the mixture, changing the total quantity.

There are at least nine distinct quantities of substances that are involved in the physical situation described in this problem, and to some or all of which the subject might attend in solving it (see table below).

The statement of the problem mentioned explicitly that: (1) The total quantity of the original mixture is 1 liter; (2) 90 percent of the original mixture is alcohol; (3) water is added to the original mixture; and (4) 80 percent of the final mixture is alcohol. That is:

$$T_1 = 1 \text{ liter}$$
$$A_1 = 0.9 \, T_1$$
$$\Delta W \neq 0$$
$$A_2 = 0.8 \, T_2$$

This information is not sufficient to solve the problem (try it). In addition, the derivation of the solution must also make use of one or more of the following premises:

$$T_2 = T_1 + \Delta T; A_2 = A_1 + \Delta A;$$
$$W_2 = W_1 + \Delta W; \Delta A = 0;$$
$$T_1 = A_1 + W_1; T_2 = A_2 + W_2;$$
$$\Delta T = \Delta A + \Delta W$$

These sets of relations are postulates about the physical situation. They are not logically necessary, although they may seem "obvious" to some persons given the problem. To see that they are actually physical assumptions, consider what would happen if water were a compound containing alcohol as a component. Then when water was added to the original mixture,

Initial Situation	Changes	Final Situation
T_1—total quantity of original mixture	ΔT—quantity of liquid added	T_2—total quantity of final mixture
A_1—quantity of alcohol in original mixture	ΔA—quantity of alcohol added	A_2—quantity of alcohol in final mixture
W_1—quantity of water in original mixture	ΔW—quantity of water added	W_2—quantity of water in final mixture

some of the new water might dissociate in reaching the new equilibrium, and we could not assume that $\Delta A = 0$, even though no alcohol were added. In the same way, $T_2 = T_1 + \Delta T$ is a physical assumption, whose truth can be known only by adding one substance to another and determining whether the volume relation is in fact additive (when the one substance dissolves in the other, it isn't additive).

The physical postulates are precisely the sorts of *conservation laws* that Piaget has emphasized in his analysis of the cognitive development of children. $\Delta A = 0$ and $A_2 = A_1 + \Delta A$, for example, might be translated: "If you add no alcohol to a mixture, then the amount of alcohol in the final mixture is exactly the same as the amount in the original mixture." The subjects who succeed in solving the mixture problem supply these additional premises (usually without comment) from their own previous store of knowledge. Before turning to their protocols, let us examine a rigorous derivation of the solution, to see exactly how the physical premises enter in (see below).

At five points in this derivation, conservation assumptions, not explicitly included in the problem statement, are required. Of course, different derivations are possible, but they would not differ essentially in this respect—all would use the conservation assumptions.

New let us compare this derivation with the transcript of subject 6. In the left-hand column, we will indicate the numbers of the equations, in the above derivations, that correspond with the subject's statements.

ΔW
T_1

(2)
(13)
(3)
(6)

(1)

(7), (9)

(14)

(15)

The quantity of water which we will add we will call q. The car radiator already contains 90 percent alcohol-water mixture. O.K. Which means it contains 90 percent—ah—alcohol, which means it contains 10 percent of—of—water. O.K. What quantity will change the liter to an 80 percent alcohol mixture? The alcohol content will remain the same. Ah—90 percent of the original mix. This is another one that can't be done exactly for this reason: we can only give a percentage of water—It says 'what quantity of water will change' . . . O.K. The car contains one liter. Good. We can do it, I'm sorry. Ah—the total volume of alcohol is 0.9 of one liter—would you write that down as $0.9L$ please, for me, and I'll remember, I think, that it's alcohol. All right, the total water in this final mixture will be $0.1L$ (just write that down to the right of it) + q. O.K. Now the total mixture is comprised of $0.9L$ of alchol plus ($0.1L + q$) water, so we'll take the $0.9L$ and divide it by—just put $0.9L$ divided by $0.1L$ plus q plus the alcohol—plus $0.9L$—just add plus $0.9L$ in the denominator—those L's are irrelevant and you can erase them if you want because we know that that's a liter and the answer will be in liters. Upon solving that, 0.9 over 1 equals—I

(1)	$T_1 = 1$	(given)
(2)	$A_1 = 0.9T_1$	(given)
(3)	$A_2 = 0.8T_2$	(given)
(4)	$A_2 = A_1 + \Delta A$	(conservation assumption)
(5)	$\Delta A = 0$	(conservation assumption)
(6)	$A_2 = A_1$	[(4) + (5)]
(7)	$A_1 = 0.9$	[(1) + (2)]
(8)	$A_2/T_2 = 0.8$	[(3)]
(9)	$A_2 = 0.9$	[(7) + (6)]
(10)	$T_2 = A_2 + W_2$	(conservation assumption)
(11)	$W_2 = W_1 + \Delta W$	(conservation assumption)
(12)	$T_1 = A_1 + W_1$	(conservation assumption)
(13)	$W_1 = 0.1$	[(7) + (12)]
(14)	$W_2 = 0.1 + \Delta W$	[(11) + (13)]
(15)	$T_2 = 0.9 + 0.1 + \Delta W$	[(10) + (9) + (14)]
(16)	$0.9/(0.9 + 0.1 + \Delta W) = 0.8$	[(8) + (15) + (9)]

guess we'll have to add about 0.9 liters —0.09 liters, I'm sorry. O.K.

Experimenter: Is this your final analysis?

(16)   *Subject:* That would be my final—ah—what will—what will I equate that to? Let's see—equals 0.80.

The first thing we note about this transcript is that it follows closely the second derivation we gave above. The crucial steps are (6), "The alcohol content will remain the same," and (8), which the subject does not mention explicitly, but which guides his whole derivation from "Now the total mixture is comprised of . . ." to the end.

The second thing we note is that the subject in his derivation mentions premises, like (1) and (2), that are explicit in the problem statement, and that he mentions all steps in the derivation *except* (8) and *except* for those steps [(4), (5), (10), (11), and (12)] that are simply statements of conservation assumptions.

The third point of interest in the transcript is the way in which the subject identifies and names the various quantities that are represented in the physical situation. The problem statement itself mentions explicitly only T_1, "one liter of a 90 percent alcohol-water mixture"; ΔW, "what quantity of water will change the liter?"; and T_2, "80 percent pure alcohol." The derivation (omitting the unmentioned conservation assumptions) refers also to A_1, A_2, W_1, and W_2. These quantities (with a qualification mentioned below) are also named specifically by the subject. The subject refers to ΔW as "the quantity of water which we will add," and as "q." He refers to A_1 as: "90 percent alcohol," "the alcohol content," "90 percent of the original mix," "the total volume of alcohol," "$0.9L$ of alcohol," "the alcohol," and "$0.9L$." Since he early notes that $A_1 = A_2$, he does not adopt distinct names for these two quantities. W_1 is alluded to by "it contains 10 percent of water." The quantity W_2 is identified as "the total water in this final mixture," which he subsequently denotes as "$(0.1L + q)$."

Especially interesting are the subject's references to the total mixture. For T_1, the subject uses the phrases, "90 percent alcohol-water mixture," "the original mix," while for T_2, he uses "80 percent alcohol mixture," "this final mixture," "the total mixture." Note that in all these examples, a quantity is usually first called by a name that is close to the language of the problem statement. Names used later are often clearly relational, for example, "90 percent of the original mix." When the same object is referred to by different names, the name used in a given instance is usually determined by the particular relation in view at that moment. So, we have "the total water in this *final* mixture," when $W_2 = W_1 + \Delta W$ is in consideration; but "the *total* mixture," when the subject is using $T_2 = A_2 + W_2$. That is to say, terms like "original" and "final" are used when a relation is being considered between the mixture before and after the water is added, while "total" is used when the composition of the mixture at a given point in time is in question.

The evidence from the protocol, then, including the subject's choices of words and phrases, suggests strongly that he followed something like the second derivation. If so, where did he obtain the appropriate conservation assumptions which are not contained in the problem statement? Let us propose a hypothesis. We suppose (figure 8) that the subject constructs an internal representation of the problem situation from the problem statement. We do not insist that this representation be "visual" in any literal sense, but we do require that it contain in implicit form the same relations (for example, among T_1, A_1, and W_1) that are implicit in the diagram.

We note that the four crucial conservation assumptions can be read off the figure: (6) $A_2 = A_1$; (10) $T_2 = A_2 + W_2$; (11) $W_2 = W_1 + \Delta W$; and (12) $T_1 = A_1 + W_1$. Two of these [(10) and (12)] are obtained by adding lengths vertically; the other two [(6) and (11)], referring to the "before" and "after," are obtained by comparing lengths on the left and right sides of the diagram. Again, the details are not important; many variants on the basic

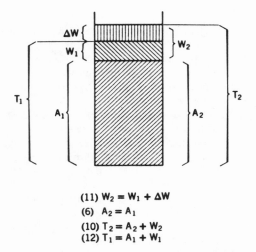

(11) $W_2 = W_1 + \Delta W$

(6) $A_2 = A_1$

(10) $T_2 = A_2 + W_2$

(12) $T_1 = A_1 + W_1$

Figure 8. A hypothetical representation for the mixture problem.

diagram would permit the same deductions, or equivalent ones, to be made.

For what it is worth, this interpretation of the derivation of the conservation assumptions is confirmed by the subject's later introspections. First, after he solved the problem, the subject was asked to explain his equation. He says,

> Now 0.9 is the percentage, if you want to call it percentage, the percentage of one—ah— liters of alcohol. This doesn't change when you add water. O.K. Now the denominator—the $0.1L$ refers to the water that's already in there. There's a tenth of a liter of water already in there. To this we add q, the—the quantity of water which is to be added. That's the total quantity of water—ah—however, since this is a percentage of alcohol in the entire mix, we have to add $0.9L$ at the bottom too, so that the numerator represents the alcohol in there to start out with and to finish with and—and the denominator represents the whole final mixture, so that what we have is 0.8 is a—is a percentage —it represents the amount of alcohol divided by the total mixture.

Later, the experimenter asked the subject what imagery he had used. The subject stated that he had had a "picture" of the container with blue alcohol and red water. The experimenter then produced a diagram, much like figure 8, but colored, asking: "Like this?" The subject exhibited

considerable amazement since, he said, that except for the fact that the colors of water and alcohol were reversed, the diagram was identical with his mental image.

The important issue here is not whether the subject employed imagery—some subjects may not. It is whether he employed some kind of, conscious or unconscious, representation, functionally equivalent to a diagram like figure 8, that enabled him to "read off" the conservation assumptions directly. The evidence seems rather overwhelming that subject 6 proceeded in this way.

Conservation Assumptions and Representation

In a previous section, we have already commented briefly on the behavior of subject 8, who explicitly had the experimenter draw a diagram for her. Let us now consider subject 5, who failed to solve the mixture problem.

Subject 5 also interprets the problem as one of changing an initial situation into a new situation. Unlike subject 6, she does not immediately identify the specific quantities involved in each situation and their relations. (She also suffers from some confusion as to whether the unit of measurement was an "unknown" or not, but we will leave this difficulty aside.) She refers to T_1 as "the liter" and T_2 as "80 percent pure alcohol," echoing literally the problem statement.

Subject 5s crude model seems to be something like this:

(initial mixture) + (water added)
= (final mixture),

We've got 90 percent of a liter that is now alcohol and you want to add some water to it. So you really want $0.90L + x$—you don't have to write this—$0.90L + x = 0.80 - 0.90 + x = 0.80$. That's just too simple. Don't write it because I don't think it's right.

This translation involves a kind of vague metaphor, a metaphor that represents the physical situation inadequately. "Initial mixture" is translated as "90 percent of a liter that is now alcohol," which becomes, in turn, "$0.90L$." Similarly, "final mixture" is identified with "80 percent pure alcohol," which is translated "0.80." By simple substitution, then,

(initial mixture) + (water added)
= (final mixture)

becomes:

$$0.90 + x = 0.80$$

With further thought, the subject begins to disentangle the several quantities involved. A little later, she says

> Ninety percent of a liter is alcohol now, and you want 80 percent of the liter plus x to be alcohol.

Here she appears to be on the point of solving the problem but fails to set up the equation. The protocol is unclear as to the nature of the remaining difficulty, but probably it is her failure to note the crucial conservation assumption—that the amount of "alcohol now" equals the amount of "to be alcohol."

Much later, after being shown a diagram, the subject solves the problem. Summarizing her solution, she says,

> One liter plus x is the new—the new quantity, x being the amount of water. Eighty percent of that has got to be the alcohol in it, so that's got to be equal to 90 percent of—because you didn't add any alcohol—90 percent of the liter.

In this final statement, the subject has unambiguous names for most of the important quantities: T_2 is "the new quantity," ΔW, "the amount of water," A_2, "the alcohol in [the new quantity]." She has also used the information in the problem statement to deduce $A_1 = 0.9 T_1$ and $A_2 = 0.8 T_2$. Finally, she expresses two crucial conservation laws, $T_2 = T_1 + x$ and $A_1 = A_2$. With these, she is able to solve the problem.

Solving the mixture problem, then, depends on identifying and naming the principal quantities involved and using the important conservation assumptions that relate them to each other. But these conservation assumptions do not derive from direct transformations of the problem statement. They are physical assumptions supplied by the problem solver, and the

principal means he has for supplying them is to construct some kind of physical or spatial representation in which they lie implicit, and from which he can extract them by processing the representation.

The protocols of the high school students on the alcohol-water mixture problem provide further evidence for some parts of our analysis and cast further light on the differences between the subjects who tend to handle problems verbally (that is, by direct translation) and those who handle them physically (that is, who use auxiliary representations of the physical situation).

None of the high school students solved the mixture problem, although eight of the thirteen set up some kind of equation. Seven of the eight equations were essentially the same as the original incorrect equation set up by subject 5 (90 percent + x = 80 percent). Four of the five subjects who, on the basis of their protocols from the board-sawing problem, we classified as "physical" set up this equation, but only three of the seven subjects we classified as "verbal" did so.[6]

As mentioned previously, each of the subjects was asked, at the end of the experimental session, to draw a diagram that would explain the problem. The diagrams can be classified in three groups (figure 9): (1) diagrams (W) that show the "water added" as a separate quantity, or as being poured into the original mixture, (2) "before-and-after" diagrams (B–A), showing the original mixture and the final mixture separately, and (3) diagrams (C) in which all the percentages are marked on a single container of liquid. Of the seven subjects who produced the incorrect "additive" equation, five drew the W diagram and two the B–A diagram. Of the six subjects

---

6. As a matter of fact, two of the three V subjects who set up the faulty equation in problem 5 also behaved anomolously (in comparison with other V subjects) in some other respects. Subject 24 was the only one among the V subjects who noted a contradiction in any problem (problem 1). Subject 19 first produced the P equation on problem 4 and then the V equation. See table 1.

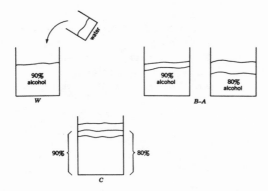

Figure 9. Examples of (*W*), (*B–A*), and (*C*) diagrams for the alcohol-water mixture problem.

who did not produce this equation, three drew the *B–A* diagram and three drew *C* diagrams; none drew the *W* diagram.[7]

Thus, our earlier interpretation of subject 5's behavior on this problem is confirmed. Underlying the translation is a representation that identifies the physical process of "adding" water with the arithmetic process of adding x to the original mixture. But, through inability to deal with percentages, or for some other reason, the subjects are unable to sort out the various quantities contained in the mixtures, hence to determine exactly to what "initial mixture" the water is to be added to obtain the "final mixture." They use the conservation assumption, $T_2 = T_1 + \Delta W$, but are unable, because of the inadequacies of their representations or of their understanding of percentage, to find the other conservation assumptions—in particular, the crucial assumption $A_1 = A_2$.

Organizing the Solution Process

We have left unexplained one important part of the procedure used by someone like subject 6 to solve an algebra problem as complicated as the mixture problem. The

───────────

7. The probability of this result, on the null hypothesis of no connection between drawing the *W* diagram and producing the erroneous equation, is less than 0.01.

derivation of the solution, in all its detail, contains a substantial number of steps. How is the problem solver able to take these steps in approximately the right order? What prevents him from wandering aimlessly, rather than moving relatively directly to the solution?

From other research on problem solving, particularly the General Problem Solver, we would hypothesize that the subject compares the "givens" of the problem with the desired result (Newell and Simon, 1963a; Simon and Newell, 1964). Finding one or more differences between them, he tries to transform one or the other to reduce, and finally eliminate, these differences. There is one important difference between the algebra problems and problems of proving theorems, which were the original task environment tests of the GPS theory. In theorem proving, the subject knows the desired result in detail—the theorem to be proved; whereas in setting up equations, he only has a general description of the desired result—an algebraic equation in which the "unknown" appears together with one or more of the known given quantities, but in which no other unknown quantities appear.

One way in which a subject can proceed to this goal, under the conditions of algebra word problems, is to set up some equation, from the problem statement, containing one or more unknown quantities, and then, by substituting relational definitions for the unknown quantities, to arrive at an equation with the necessary properties. Let us examine the sequence from equation (8), above, to equation (16) from this viewpoint. The initial equation the subject sets up (8) makes use of the fact that the percentage of alcohol in the final mixture is 80. Since "percentage of alcohol in total" is translatable "A_2/T_2", a rather direct translation process will yield $A_2/T_2 = 0.8$. Neither A_2 nor T_2 are known quantities, and the unknown, ΔW, does not appear in the equation; hence it must be transformed.

Taking A_2 under consideration, the only other known relation in which it appears is (6) $A_2 = A_1$. Taking A_1 under consideration, it is also unknown, but appears in the relation (2) $A_1 = 0.9 T_1$. Considering T_1 next, by (1) $T_1 = 1$, hence is a known quantity. Hence, the first equation, (8), can be transformed into $1/T_2 = 0.8$. This equation is still unsatisfactory, since it has the unknown T_2, and does not contain the unknown ΔW. But T_2 occurs in the conservation assumption (10) $T_2 = A_2 + W_2$. Repeating the same process, we replace the A_2 in this relation by 0.9; and using another conservation assumption, we express W_2 as $W_2 = W_1 + \Delta W$. Again, from $W_1 = T_1 - A_1 = 1 - 0.9 = 0.1$, we get, eventually, $T_2 = 0.9 + 0.1 + \Delta W$, which is exactly what the subject substitutes in the denominator of (8) to obtain (16).

Thus, it appears that the mechanisms that provide direction in GPS are also appropriate to explain the sequence of expressions that subject 6 considers in solving the mixture problem. He starts by setting up an equation—any equation, and then proceeds to try to modify any part of that equation which contains an unknown other than ΔW. This process leads him fairly directly to the solution.[8]

When the process is organized in this way, it tends to keep the cognitive strain —the load on the subject's immediate memory—within reasonable bounds. He starts out with a single relation (in this case, $A_2/T_2 = 0.8$), and by application of relations explicit in the written problem statement, or derived from conservation assumptions stored in permanent memory, modifies this relation, step-by-step, by substituting new quantities for the unknowns. At any given moment in this process, there is only a single statement (the most recent modification of the initial relation) that he has to retain in immediate memory.

---

8. Garfinkel's program (see part 2, 1960), which also requires that a single equation in one unknown be set up, uses a somewhat different process, more syntactic in spirit, to remove the superfluous unknowns. The program also makes provision for introducing certain conservation assumptions.

Further Comments on Conservation Assumptions

Problem 3, involving a launch traveling up and down stream, provides another situation where the introduction of conservation assumptions, and their physical nature, is particularly clear. The problem states the rate of flow of the stream and the speed at which a launch can go in still water. To set up the equations, the subjects had to determine the speed of the launch downstream and upstream. All three of the college subjects, and most of the high school subjects, *added* the two rates to obtain the downstream speed, and *subtracted* them to obtain the upstream speed.

Subject 8 makes the assumptions with a single comment about their physical character: "Now the distance [misspoken for "rate"] downstream is going to be 8 miles per hour plus two. Write down 8 plus 2, so that the stream helps." And later: "rate of the launch which is 8, minus the rate of the stream, which is 2."

For subject 6, the relation of the rates is also "natural":

Going downstream the launch will travel at the velocity of 8 miles an hour plus 2 miles an hour because it—the stream will carry it along, naturally, so that the rate of the launch will be 10 miles an hour downstream.

Subject 5 is explicitly aware that the physical assumption may be incorrect:

The launch can go at the rate of 8 miles per hour in still water, so it's going downstream at the rate of 10 miles per hour . . . it goes 10 miles per hour, and coming back upstream, ah, I assume—I don't know much about motors—it goes 6 miles per hour . . . so I think those two values are correct, because I assumed that all this is additive, although I'm not really certain, but I assume that if you can go 8 miles per hour and the stream is flowing 2 miles per hour, it's 10.

From these protocols, we conclude that addition of velocities is an assumption the subjects, particularly subject 5, do not make quite automatically. They are still aware of the physical origin of the assumption to an extent they are not in the case of the conservation of quantities and additivity of quantities in the mixture problem. What holds only "naturally" in the former case, holds "obviously" and without comment in the latter.

Characterizing the conservation assumptions as "physical" does not imply, of course, that direct translation processes could not be incorporated in an algebra-word-problem processor to handle them. For example, if we assume that some means (radar, for example) exists for measuring speed directly, then "distance equals rate times time" is a physical assumption. STUDENT incorporates this assumption directly in its direct translation scheme, permitting the term "distance," when it appears in a problem statement, to be replaced by "rate times time."

All three of the college-level subjects use the relation among distance, rate, and time in trying to solve the launch problem. Subject 5 uses the relation as though it were physically derived, and never mentions the formula. Subjects 6 and 8, however, behave like STUDENT, as though they had the formula stored in memory and employ it for direct translation. Subject 6 says: "There's a little equation that says that in these cases distance equals velocity times time." And subject 8 says: "Distance equals rate times time—so that you want to divide x by that. . . . Dividing the distance by the rate equals . . . "

Summary

We have examined the behavior of human subjects setting up equations for algebra word problems, using as our base of reference the direct translation schemes proposed by Garfinkel and Bobrow. Our particular interest has been in detecting the extent to which the human subjects make use of direct processes like those incorporated in the STUDENT program, and the extent to which they employ auxiliary cues and internal representations of the physical situation.

We have seen that the human subjects differ a great deal in the extent to which they rely on direct and auxiliary processes respectively. Among our college-level subjects, subject 8 (a mathematics major) is an example of a good problem solver who usually relies chiefly on direct translation —in close parallelism with the STUDENT program. Subject 6 (a physics major) is an example of a good problem solver who makes extensive use of auxiliary cues and physical representations.

A set of "contradictory" problems that represent physically impossible situations has proved to be a useful tool for detecting the relative uses of direct and auxiliary cues by the subjects. In the face of a contradictory problem, the subject can respond in three main ways: (1) He can set up an equation for the problem as it is stated literally; (2) he can set up an equation for a related, physically possible, situation; or (3) he can recognize the physical impossibility of the situation. If he is using primarily direct cues, he will make the first response; if primarily physical cues, the second; if he is attending to both, the problem description will be redundant, and he may detect the contradiction.

We were able to classify a group of high school students into those who were primarily "physical" in their responses and those who were primarily "verbal." The differences between the two groups showed up quite consistently in (1) the extent to which they detected the contradiction— the "verbal" solvers didn't, the "physical" sometimes did; (2) whether the equations set up represented a physical situation or were literal translations of the words; and (3) whether the diagrams they drew contained the physical relations that were implicit in the problems. The data from these high school students were consistent with the hypotheses derived from more detailed examination of the protocols of the college-level subjects.

In addition, we identified some of the important processes that a person must acquire in order to do algebra word problems successfully. A number of these had already been incorporated in Bobrow's STUDENT program. Several of the others, present but not emphasized in that program, have to do with identifying the quantities that have to be handled in setting up the equations and devising relational names for these quantities that incorporate part of the information in the problem statement. The processes for constructing auxiliary representations of the problem situation are not currently part of the STUDENT program and will have to be added to that program if it is to provide a satisfactory theory of the human behavior observed in handling these problems.

APPENDIX: ALGEBRA WORD PROBLEMS
USED IN EPERIMENTS

Practice Problems:

1. If a certain number is multiplied by 6 and the product increased by 44, the result is 68. Find the number.
2. If 3 more than a certain number is divided by 5, the result is the same as twice the number diminished by 12. What is the number?
3. The difference between two numbers is 12, and 7 times the smaller number exceeds the greater by 30. Find the numbers.

Test Problems:

1. A man has 7 times as many quarters as he has dimes. The value of the dimes exceeds the value of the quarters by $2.50. How many has he of each coin?
2. Mr. Stewart decided to invest $4,000, some at 3 percent and the rest at 4 percent. How much should he invest at each rate to produce equal income?
3. A stream flows at the rate of two miles per hour. A launch can go at the rate of 8 miles per hour in still water. How far down the stream does the launch go and return if the upstream trip takes half as much time as the downstream trip?
4. A board was sawed into two pieces. One piece was two-thirds as long as the whole board and was exceeded in length by the second piece by 4 feet. How long was the board before it was cut?
5. A car radiator contains exactly one liter of a 90 percent alcohol-water mixture. What quantity of water will change the liter to an 80 percent alcohol mixture?

References

Bobrow, Daniel G. Natural Language input for a computer problem-solving system, MAC-TR-1, Project MAC, Massachusetts Institute of Technology, 1964*a*. Reprinted in M. Minsky (ed.), *Semantic information processing.* Cambridge, Mass.: M.I.T. Press, 1968, pp. 135–215.

Bobrow, Daniel G. A question-answering system for high school algebra word problems, *AFIPS Conference Proceedings.* Vol. 26. Fall Joint Conference. Baltimore: Spartan Books, 1964*b*.

Garfinkel, Sylvia. Heuristic solution of first-year algebra problems, Working Paper #11, Management Science Group, Institute of Industrial Relations, University of California, (Berkeley), February, 1960.

Hawkes, H. E., Luby, W. A., and Touton, F. C. *New second course in Algebra.* (enlarged ed.) Boston: Ginn & Co., 1929.

Newell, A., and Simon, H. A. GPS, A program that simulates human thought. In E. A. Feigenbaum & J. Feldman (eds.) *Computers and thought.* New York: McGraw-Hill, 1963*a*, pp. 279–96.

Newell, A., and Simon, H. A. Computers in psychology. In R. D. Luce, R. R. Bush, and E. Galanter (eds.) *Handbook of Mathematical Psychology,* Volume 1. New York: Wiley, 1963*b*, pp. 361–428.

Simon, H. A. and Newell, A. Information processing in computer and man. *Amer. Scientist,* 1964, 52, 281–300.

4.5

The Functional Equivalence of Problem Solving Skills (1975)

For most task environments, the classical problem of "What is learned?" is still largely unsolved. We do not know what a subject has stored in long-term memory when he has learned to perform a task or in exactly what form he has stored it. Yet the precise nature of what is learned may have a considerable influence on both retention over time and ability to transfer skills to new tasks (Katona, 1940).

Discovery of what subjects learn can be approached experimentally, but important preliminary insights can be gained by analyzing the structure of the task itself to determine the possible alternative ways of performing it (Newell and Simon, 1972; Greeno and Simon, 1974). Different subjects may in fact learn different things in the same task environment, and a formal analysis of the environment can help define the range of possibilities. It can also help define the differences in the demands that

different methods of task performance place upon the subject.

The Tower of Hanoi puzzle has proved to be a suitable task environment in which to study a variety of problem solving processes (Gagné and Smith, 1962; Hormann, 1965; Klix, 1971; Egan, 1974; Hayes and Simon, 1974). Analyses of the structure of the task environment for that puzzle have revealed some interesting trade-offs between the perceptual, short-term memory, and long-term memory demands imposed by different methods of solution. In particular, by using certain "sophisticated" perceptual strategies, the solver can greatly reduce the demands of the task upon his short-term memory. It is the purpose of this chapter to carry out a formal analysis of the major alternative solution strategies that are known for this problem in order to demonstrate the relation between specific strategies and their perceptual and memory demands.

This research has been supported in part by research grant MH-07722 from the National Institute of Mental Health, and in part by the Advanced Research Projects Agency of the Secretary of Defense (F44620-70-C-0107) which is monitored by the Air Force Office of Scientific Research. I am indebted to D. E. Egan and J. G. Greeno for helpful discussions on the topic of this chapter.

THE TOWER OF HANOI PUZZLE

The Tower of Hanoi puzzle involves three vertical pegs or posts and a number of doughnut-like disks of graduated sizes that fit on the pegs. At the outset, all the disks are arranged pyramidally on one of the pegs, say A, with the largest disk on the

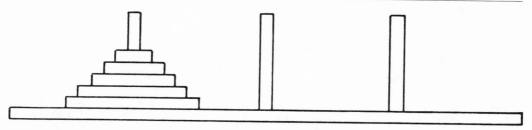

Figure 1. The Tower of Hanoi puzzle.

bottom (see figure 1). The task is to move all of the disks to another peg, C, say, under the constraints that (1) only one disk may be moved at a time, and (2) a disk may never be placed on top of another smaller than itself. Any number of disks may be used; the minimum number of moves for a solution is 2^n-1, where n is the number of disks.

STRATEGIES: INFORMAL DESCRIPTION

Before the problem representation and the various solutions are introduced formally, it will be helpful to provide an informal description of the main alternative solution methods.

1. Goal-Recursion Strategy

The pyramid of disks can be moved from A to C in the following three stages: (1) the pyramid consisting of all save the largest disk is moved from A to the third peg, B; (2) the largest disk is moved from A to C; (3) finally, the pyramid on B is moved to C.

Only the second stage, of course, corresponds to a legal move. The first stage, which clears A and C for move (2), and the third stage, which brings the remaining disks to C, are themselves Tower of Hanoi problems with one less disk than the original problem; hence they can be solved by decomposing them into the same three stages, for the location of the largest disk places no constraints on the movements of smaller disks. Since the original number of disks is finite, say n, we can continue to decompose each problem into smaller problems until, after n-1 recursions, the "pyramids" to be moved have been reduced to

single disks—that is to goals of making single legal moves. The recursion can be described succinctly, thus:

To move Pyramid(k) from A to C,
  Move Pyramid(k-1) from A to B,
  Move Disk(k) from A to C,
  Move Pyramid(k-1) from B to C.

If we apply this scheme for, say, three disks, we generate the following sequence of goals and moves:

1.   Goal: Move Pyramid(3) from A to C
2.   Goal: More Pyramid(2) from A to B
3.*   Move Disk(1) from A to C
4.*   Move Disk(2) from A to B
5.*   Move Disk(1) from C to B
6.*   Move Disk(3) from A to C
7.   Goal: Move Pyramid(2) from B to C
8.*   Move Disk(1) from B to A
9.*   Move Disk(2) from B to C
10.*   Move Disk(1) from A to C

Although the only legal moves are the moves of individual disks, marked by asterisks (*), and pyramids can only be moved disk by disk, nevertheless, the subject can have the concept and goal of moving a whole pyramid. Thus, in the sequence for the three-disk problem, there are seven moves and three additional goal-setting steps. For a subject to use this recursive strategy, he must have some way of representing goals internally and holding them in short-term memory while he carries out the subgoals. How large a STM this strategy calls for depends on how many goals have to be retained in STM simultaneously. We will examine this question later, after we have introduced the formal machinery needed for the analysis.

The information in STM about goals is not only necessary for executing the goal-recursion strategy, it is also sufficient. At any given stage in the solution, all the information needed to establish the succeeding steps is obtainable from the goal statements. At each stage, the problem solver can decide what to do next without any reference to the current distribution of the disks among the pegs. If only he can retain the unaccomplished part of the goal hierarchy in memory, he can calculate what needs to be done without sight of the puzzle and without holding a visual image of it.

Later, a variant of the goal-recursion strategy will be described that needs retain only the top goal in its goal stack but that keeps track of where it is by simple perceptual observations of the problem situation. In particular, if its current goal is to move disk k to peg A, it examines the pegs to determine if k is already on the target peg, or, if not, if it is the top disk of its own peg and smaller than the top disk of the target peg. The action it takes next is conditioned on these perceptual tests.

It is easy but tedious to show, by mathematical induction, that the path produced by the goal-recursion strategies is of minimal length.

2. A Perceptual Strategy

A second method for solving the Tower of Hanoi problem can be described as follows: To rebuild the pyramid on Peg C, the largest disk must be placed on C first, then the next largest, and so on. But a disk can only be moved when two conditions are satisfied: (1) there are no small disks on its peg (the source peg), and (2) there are no smaller disks on the target peg. Therefore, the move of a particular disk, say k, to a target peg, say X, can be accomplished by: (1)· moving any movable disk smaller than k off the source peg; (2) repeating step (1) until there are no disks smaller than k on the source peg; (3) moving any disk smaller than k off the target peg; (4) repeating (3) until all the disks smaller

than k are off the target peg; (5) moving disk k to the target peg.

This strategy is not quite straightforward, however, because there is no guarantee that clearing the target peg—steps (3) and (4)—will not again obstruct the previously cleared source peg—steps (1) and (2). Thus, the strategy in this simple form could produce nonterminating cycles of moves. In fact, this occurs when the strategy is used to attempt moving a pyramid of four or more disks. In the four-disk problem, the following situation is reached after the fifth move:

PEG A: 4   PEG B: 1 3   PEG C: 2

In this situation, Disk 2 must be moved to Peg B to permit Disk 4 to be moved to Peg C. But the former move is blocked by Disk 1; hence the subgoal is generated of moving Disk 1 to A, leading to the following situation after the sixth move:

PEG A: 1 4   PEG B: 3   PEG C: 2

The strategy now calls for Disk 1 to be moved again to B, in order to unblock the source peg of Disk 4. But this move restores the previous situation and leads to a nonterminating cycle. To avoid the cycle, using this basic strategy, it would be necessary to retain a stack of subgoals in STM. That is, in the present case, Disk 1 was first moved from B to A in order to unblock the move of 2 from C to B, in order to unblock the move of 4 from A to C. If this chain of subgoals were retained, the move of Disk 2 could be carried out after it had been enabled by the move of 1; and the move of 4 after it had been enabled by the move of 2. Hence, the strategy can be rescued, but at the cost of retaining a stack of goals in STM.

3. A Sophisticated Perceptual Strategy

A third solution strategy resembles the second one, but with one important alteration. The essential steps are: (1) identifying, as previously, the largest disk—call it k— that is not yet on the target peg; (2) by examining both the source peg and the target peg of k, identifying the largest disk that is obstructing its move to the target peg; (3) if there is no obstructor, making the indicated move: (4) if there is such a largest obstructor, establishing the goal of moving the obstructor to the other peg (neither source nor target of k), then recursing, for the obstructor, through steps (2) and (3).

While the first strategy we described determined its next action by referring only to a goal stack, the second and third strategies determine what to do next by perceiving features of the actual current problem situation. Of course, as we saw in discussing strategy 2, it may be necessary to consult both the problem situation and a goal stack in order to avoid cycling.

4. A Move-Pattern Strategy

All the strategies described so far have been "reasoned"—that is, they involve decomposing the goal of the whole task into a number of subsidiary goals, accomplishment of which will complete the task. Another procedure would be simply to store the solution steps in memory and execute them one after the other. There are at least two difficulties with this procedure. First, it requires a great deal to be committed to memory (e.g., fifteen steps even for the four-disk problem). Second and more important, a different sequence would have to be memorized for each specific number of disks.

There exist strategies that do not suffer from this second difficulty, but which nevertheless are, in a certain sense, "rote" procedures. They can be regarded as rote because the reasons for the successive moves are not easily discerned from the definition of the problem, as was the case for the three strategies described previously. Hence, what is to be done next cannot be reasoned out, by means-ends analysis, but must be calculated from the formula of the strategy. After a preliminary comment about legal moves, we will describe a well-known rote strategy for the Tower of Hanoi puzzle.

In any given Tower of Hanoi situation, there are at most three legal moves: (1) and (2), the smallest exposed disk can move to

either of two pegs; and (3) the next-smallest exposed disk, if there is one, can be placed atop the largest exposed disk or on an empty peg. The largest exposed disk, if no pegs are empty, cannot be moved, because the top disks on the other pegs are smaller than it is.

Consider now the following strategy:

1. On odd-numbered moves, move the smallest disk; 2. On even-numbered moves, move the next-smallest disk that is exposed; 3. Let peg S be the initial source peg, T the target peg, and O the other peg. Then if the total number of pegs is odd, the smallest disk is always moved from S to T to O to S, and so on; while if the total number of pegs is even, the smallest disk is always moved in the opposite cycle: from S to O to T to S, and so on.

To execute this strategy, one must keep track of (1) the parity of the move, and (2) the cycling direction for the smallest disk. Since the latter piece of information remains unchanged while the problem is being solved, it can be stored in long-term memory. Only the parity information needs to be retained in STM. Perception of the external situation is required for identifying the location of the peg to be moved (smallest or next-smallest), and, if the next-smallest is to be moved, for identifying its legal target peg. Hence the strategy, once learned, makes very small demands upon either perceptual pattern recognition or STM. The strategy is relatively easy to execute and retain, and it is applicable to any number of disks.

Summary

Four strategies, and a variant of one of them, have been described for solving the Tower of Hanoi problem for an arbitrary number of disks. One of the four strategies uses goal and subgoal structures to determine what to do next: it is primarily goal driven. The Goal-Recursion Strategy, but not the others, requires the concept of moving a pyramid of disks, as well as a single disk. The perceptual strategies are primarily stimulus driven. The simpler of the two perceptual strategies sometimes finds itself in an infinite loop if a stack of subgoals is not retained. The more sophisticated perceptual strategy requires the ability to perceive "the largest disk blocking the movement of a given disk." The Move-Pattern Strategy requires the concept of odd and even move and the concept of "cycling" a disk through the pegs in a particular order.

Thus, the strategies make different demands upon short-term memory, require different sets of concepts, and require different perceptual tests to be made for their execution. In the remainder of this chapter, these properties of the strategies will be developed more formally and their psychological significance will be discussed in more detail.

STRUCTURE OF THE PRODUCTION SYSTEM

In order to make explicit the psychological assumptions underlying the analysis, and to facilitate precise comparisons between the different strategies, the programs for the strategies will be expressed in a formal programming language. This programming language belongs to the species known as production systems. This section of the paper explains what a production system is, and what psychological assumptions—in particular, assumptions about perception and about short-term memory—are incorporated in the structure and vocabulary of the programming language.

A production system (Newell and Simon, 1972) is simply an ordered set of processes called productions. Each production has two parts: a condition (C) and an action (A), which are usually written with an arrow connecting them:

$$C \rightarrow A.$$

The reader will not mislead himself badly if he equates the arrow in a production with the link in a special kind of S-R structure. The productions fall into two classes: a general class and a special class called perceptual tests. The condition of a production belonging to the general class is some kind of test—usually for the presence or absence of a particular kind of symbol—on the contents of short-term memory. The test is either satisfied or not. Whenever the test in the condition part of a general production is satisfied, and only then, the action part is executed. The action may be a motor act, the performing of a perceptual test (see the next paragraphs), an act of retrieving information from long-term memory, or an act of changing the contents of short-term memory. The condition part of a production may involve a conjunction of several elementary tests, and the action part may involve a sequence of elementary actions. A simple example of a general production is:

$$\text{"Problem-solved"} \rightarrow \text{Halt.}$$

The condition side of this production calls for a test whether the symbol, "Problem solved," has been stored in STM. The action taken in this case is to halt the entire process. If the symbol is not found in STM, no action is taken.

The production subsystem representing perceptual tests is activated by executing a Test action in one of the general productions. The condition of a perceptual test is a perceivable feature of the task environment, or a conjunction of such features. If the feature or conjunction of features is present, and only then, the action part of the perceptual test is executed. The only action of a perceptual test is to change the contents of STM. Execution of a perceptual test makes the system "aware" of some perceivable feature of its environment by storing information about that feature in STM.

Thus, perceptual tests carry information from the sensory system to STM, while general productions carry on all internal communications among memories and cause the execution of motor actions and perceptual tests. It is not certain whether any special psychological significance is to be attached to this particular feature of the system architecture. It would be easy enough to embed the perceptual tests in the action parts of the general productions, but at the expense of making the operation of the system more complex and less transparent.

An S-R interpretation of the two-class

production system would equate a perceptual production with a connection between an external stimulus and a mediating response—S-r_m; and would equate a general production with a connection between a mediating stimulus and a response—s_m-R. In this interpretation, the symbol stored in STM by the action of the perceptual production plays the dual role of r_m and s_m, which thus become identical.

The production system and the perceptual subsystem are each assumed to operate serially—only one production may be activated at a time. If the conditions for more than one production are satisfied simultaneously, only the first of these on the list of productions is activated. Hence, the order of productions on the list is an integral part of the definition of the program; changing the order could (and usually will) cause significant changes in the system's behavior.

The advantages of production systems as programming formalisms and the reasons for thinking that strategies stored in the human central nervous system may be organized as production systems are discussed in Newell and Simon (1972, pp. 803–06), and in Newell (1973). The particular kind of production system we are using here has two advantages worth mentioning. First, it makes explicit exactly what information is held in short-term memory, so that processing assumptions that would place unrealistic demands on STM are immediately detectable. Second, the system makes equally explicit what assumptions are being made about perceptual capabilities. Features of the environment can only be taken into account by means of specific perceptual tests, and these tests can lead directly only to knowledge, not to action.

The specific production systems described here assume that the perceptual processes use STM only as the depository of the symbols they produce and do not place demands upon STM for the execution of their own processes. This is an empirical assumption that needs to be tested, and which is important, because our conclusions about the relative STM loads imposed by different strategies depend on it.

As a simple example of a program for solving the Tower of Hanoi problem, we exhibit here the production system for making the moves by rote from information stored in LTM. The production system for the rote strategy requires only three productions (figure 2). Long-term memory holds the sequence of moves in the form of a simple list, whose successive members are linked by the relation "next," and which is terminated with the symbol "end." Short-term memory holds the most recent move that has been made, which is called "Last-move."

Translating into English, the first production says that if short-term memory contains the symbol "end," the problem is solved, and the program should halt. The second production says that if short-term memory contains any symbol, X, labeled as "last-move," then the move that is next to X in the list of moves in LTM should be retrieved and called Y. The move Y should then be executed, and its name stored in STM as *last-move*. (The move process is so defined that *Move(end)* is the null process.) The third production says that, unconditionally, the first move on the list "Hanoi" should be retrieved from LTM, executed, and stored as *last-move* in STM. Of course, this third production will only be executed when the conditions of the first two productions are not satisfied: that is, when there is no symbol for *last-move* in STM.

Let us see how this production system solves the Tower of Hanoi problem. Initially, *last-move* has not been assigned a value, so only the (empty) condition of the third production is satisfied. Hence, the

Last-move = end → Halt [problem solved]
Last-move = X → Y = Retrieve(next(X)), Move(Y),last-move ← Y
      else   → Y = Retrieve(first(Hanoi)), Move(Y),last-move ← Y

Figure 2. Production system for rote strategy.

first move is executed and assigned the value *last-move*. Now the second production will be evoked repeatedly, and the corresponding succession of remembered moves will be made. Finally, *last-move* will be assigned "end" as value, the first production will be evoked, and the process will halt. As suggested earlier, the order in which the productions are listed is important. If the first and second were transposed, the process would never halt; if the third were placed first, the first move would be attempted repeatedly. Except for this one subtlety, nothing could be simpler than the production system for executing the rote strategy. Moreover, to execute the strategy, only a single place-keeping symbol need be retained in short-term memory, and no perceptual tests need be made.

Strategies: Formal Description

Using the production system language, we can now provide formal descriptions for the several Tower of Hanoi strategies in the same form as the description of the rote strategy that has just been presented. Each of these strategies will be analyzed to reveal what it assumes the person who uses it knows (i.e., has stored in LTM) and what demands it makes upon STM and perception.

The Goal-Recursion Strategy

Two variants of the goal-recursion strategy were introduced earlier. One required no perceptual tests at all, operating entirely off the goal stack to keep its place; the other kept only the current goal in the goal stack and used some simple perceptual tests for place-keeping purposes. This latter

strategy can be implemented by a system of six general productions (figure 3) and four perceptual tests (figure 4).

In this system, short-term memory is assumed to have the form of a stack, a list of symbol structures on which items can only be added or dropped from the front end. The symbols in STM describe goals (of moving pyramids) and the state of the current goal ("problem solved," "done," "can," or "can't"). Thus, the system can keep track of two items of information at a time—the goal it is working on and the state of "executability" of that goal. Looking at the right-hand side of Productions 2–4, we see that the contents of STM are deleted at each step, so that never more than the two items of information will be present at any one time.

The system employs five different kinds of actions: it can halt, it can delete the STM stack, it can add a goal to STM, it can execute a move, and finally, it can test the status of a move. The expression "Move(Pyramid(k),A)" should be read "Move the pyramid consisting of the k smallest disks to Peg A," and "Move(k,P-(k),A)" as "Move Disk k from its peg to peg A." O(P(k),A) is the "other" peg, that is, the peg which is neither P(k) nor A. Notice that the system has the concept of moving an entire pyramid and can express its goals in terms of this concept. Note also that if it has the goal of moving Pyramid k, and discerns that it can move that pyramid, the action it actually takes (P3) is to move disk k to the target peg. The "can" really means that it can move the largest disk of the pyramid in question.

The second component of this strategy is the test (P5) and its associated system of perceptual tests. As was explained earlier,

P1.   State = Problem-solved → Halt
P2.   State = Done, Goal = Move(Pyramid(k),A) → Delete(STM), Goal ← Move(Pyramid(k − 1), A)
P3.   State = Can, Goal = Move(Pyramid(k),A) → Delete(STM), Move(k,P(k),A)
P4.   State = Can't, Goal = Move(Pyramid(k),A) → Delete(STM), Goal ← Move(Pyramid (k − 1),O(P(k),A))
P5.   Goal = Move(Pyramid(k),A) → Test(Move(k,P(k),A))
P6.   else → Goal ← Move(Pyramid(n),Goal-peg)

Figure 3. Production system for goal recursion strategy.

Test(Move(X),P(X),A)

T1.   (Y)On(Y,Goal-peg) → State ← Problem-solved, Exit.

T2.   On(X,A) → State ← Done, Exit.

T3.   (X = Top(P(X))) & Free(X,A) → State ← Can, Exit.

T4.   else → State ← Can't, Exit.

Figure 4. Production system for perceptual tests.

by testing is meant noticing something about the current problem situation and recording information about it (the "state" of the goal) in STM. The tests can themselves be defined as a system of four productions. Recall that while the conditions of the six original productions all referred to symbols in STM, the conditions in the perceptual tests refer to the problem situation—the actual current arrangement of disks on pegs (see figure 4).

Each time the test is executed, one and only one of its productions is executed. Production T1 is to be read, "If for all disks, Y, Y is on the goal peg, declare the problem solved." Note that the action of this, as of all the perceptual tests, is to change the symbol, "state," in STM. T2 is to be read, "If disk X is on Peg A, declare the current goal to be done." T3: "If disk X is the top disk on its peg, and is free to move to peg A, declare that the desired move can be made." T4: "Else, declare that the desired move cannot be made."

Comparing the actions of the test productions with the conditions of the six general productions, we see that T1 sets the condition for P1, T2 for P2, T3 for P3, and T4 for P4. P5 will be executed when "state" is undefined and there is a goal in STM, while P6 will be executed when "state" is undefined and there is no goal in STM. Productions P4, P3, and P2, taken together, define the recursive solution of the k-peg Tower of Hanoi problem.

Examining the condition sides of the perceptual tests, we see that the strategy calls on the system to perceive when particular disks, or all disks, are on specified pegs; to see whether a specified disk is the top disk on its peg; and to see whether a specified disk can legally move to a specified target peg. It is implicit in the perceptual processes that each disk has some charac-

teristic (e.g., its size or color) that permits it to be identified. Notice that a perceptual predicate like "free" is derived from the conditions for legal moves in this task environment. To determine that a disk is free to move to a particular peg, the perceptual system must compare the size of the disk to be moved with the size of the top disk of the target peg.

If we compare the goal recursion strategy with the rote strategy previously described, we observe that the latter pays no attention to the actual problem situation but simply executes moves in a specified order. The rote program halts when it runs out of moves and does not even have a production like T1 to notice that it has actually solved the problem. The goal recursion strategy, on the other hand, determines what to do next on the basis both of its current goal and the current state of the problem situation.

It would be possible, however, to construct a different version of the goal-recursion strategy that would be more completely "inner-directed"—whose next step would be determined solely by the state of short-term memory. This alternative system is described in figure 5. This variant requires only four general productions and no perceptual tests. Initially (P4), it places in STM the goal: "Move(Pyramid(n), Goal-peg)." If the goal is of the form "Move(Pyramid(1),A)", then it makes "Move(1,P(1),A)." If the goal is of the form "Move(Pyramid(k),A)", with k not equal to 1, it replaces the goal by a list of three goals: "Move(Pyramid(k-1),O(P(k),A)), Move(k,P(k),A), Move(Pyramid(k-1),A)." If the top goal is of the form "Move(k,P(k),A)" it executes the move and removes the goal from the STM stack. This is called "popping" the stack. New goals are added to the stack, without re-

P1.   Goal = Move(k,P(k),A) → Move(k,P(k),A), Pop(Goal)
P2.   Goal = Move(Pyramid(1),A) → Move(1,P(1),A), Pop(Goal)
P3.   Goal = Move(Pyramid(k),A) → Pop(Goal),
         Push[Goal = Move(Pyramid(k − 1),A)]
         Push[Goal = Move(k,P(k),A)],
         Push[Goal = Move(Pyramid(k − 1),O(P(k),A))]],
P4.   else → Push[Goal = Move(Pyramid(n),Goal-peg)]

Figure 5. Variant of the goal-recursion strategy.

moving those already there ("pushing" the stack); only the top goal is "seen" by the tests on the condition side of the productions. This program halts when its goal stack is empty. The system never has to look at the external situation in order to know what to do next. With this "inner-directed" version of the goal recursive strategy, however, the goal stack must be retained in STM, and this stack will grow to depth n in solving an n-disk problem.

While the rote strategy rested on the ability of the system to execute a fixed sequence of moves, the goal-recursion strategies rest on the ability of the system to make its behavior conditional on the actual state of the problem, on a hierarchy of goals and subgoals, or on some combination of these.

The Perceptual Strategies

To employ the Goal Recursion strategy, the subject must invent the pseudomove of "move a pyramid." He can avoid this concept, still without retaining a deep goal stack, at the expense of using somewhat more sophisticated perceptual predicates than are required by the Goal Recursion strategy. We will describe the sophisticated perceptual strategy in a manner as nearly parallel as possible to the previous ones,

numbering the productions in such a way as to emphasize the correspondences (figure 6).

In P4′, "Can't (J)" may be read: 'Can't achieve goal because of Disk J.' The new productions P6′ and P7′, corresponding to the old P6, are best explained in the context of the perceptual tests. Two changes are needed in the perceptual tests: Test T4 is altered to T4′, and a new production, T5′, is introduced to perceive the biggest disk that has not yet been placed on the target peg. These two changes can be formalized as follows:

T4′.   else → State ← Can't(J),
         J ← Bigger-of[Next-smaller(k,P-(k)),Next-smaller(k,A)]

Test(Biggest-remaining)

T5′.   → J ← Biggest(Not-on-goal-peg),
         State ← Biggest(J)

The meaning of the new T4′ and P4′ is that whenever a disk cannot be moved, the goal is established of moving the largest disk blocking the movement, regardless of whether the latter is on the source peg or the target peg of the former. T4′ is the perceptual test that identifies this blocking disk. A somewhat similar concept is used in P6′ and P7′ with T5′, for the biggest disk not on the goal peg is the bigger of the

P1′.   State = Problem-solved → Halt
P2′.   State = Done, Goal = Move(k,P(k),A) → Delete(State), Delete(Goal)
P3′.   State = Can, Goal = Move(k,P(k),A) → Delete(State), Move(k,P(k),A)
P4′.   State = Can't(J), Goal = Move(k,P(k),A) → Delete(STM), Goal ← Move(J,P(J),O(P(k),A))
P5′.   Goal = Move(k,P(k),A) → Test(Move(k,P(k),A))
P6′.   State = Biggest(J) → Goal ← Move(J,P(J),Goal-peg)
P7′.   else → Test(Biggest-remaining)

Figure 6. Production system for perceptual strategy.

biggest disks on each of the other two pegs. Hence, when the state is undefined, P_7' is activated and executes T_5' to identify this largest disk. P_6' then becomes active in turn, establishing the goal of moving this disk. Thus for this perceptual strategy to be operative, the system must be capable of perceiving these disks, which are called "J" in the formal description of the program.

The perceptual strategy of figure 6 needs to retain only its current goal and state symbol, hence STM requirements do not increase with number of disks. Moreover, the perceptual strategy will solve the Tower of Hanoi problem for any number of disks starting from any situation, whether on the optimal solution path or not. The rote strategy, as well as the move-pattern strategy to be described next, will only work from the initial starting position.

In a previous section, we mentioned a variant of the perceptual strategy in which P_4' is divided into two productions. If the goal is to move a disk, and another is above it on its peg, then the goal is established of moving the other. If the goal is to move a disk that is the top one on its peg, but a disk blocks it on the target peg, the goal is established of moving the largest blocking disk from the target peg. With this scheme, clearing the source peg of a disk to be moved is given priority over clearing the target peg, independently of the sizes of the blocking disks on these pages. This variant is weaker than the strategy described previously, in the following sense. Provided that a goal stack is kept, it will work satisfactorily, but it will not always find the optimal path from an arbitrary starting position. Moreover, as we have seen, if only the top goal is kept in STM, this strategy will get into a per-

petual loop in trying to solve a problem of four or more disks. The two variants of the perceptual program differ with respect to the power of the perceptual predicates they have available—the weaker variant not having the concept that defines J in T_4' and T_5'.

If the more sophisticated perceptual strategy is used, and a goal stack is not retained, then some extra processing must be done to regenerate the goal hierarchy after each move has been made. That is, the largest unmoved disk must be identified, then the largest disk blocking its move, then the largest disk blocking the latter's move, and so on, until a realizable goal is reached. However, only the most recently generated goal in this hierarchy need be retained at any given moment.

The Move-Pattern Strategy

The strategy described previously that is based on a pattern in the moves themselves is formalized in figure 7.

As explained earlier, "next" is applied to a list of the pegs in cyclic order, the order depending on whether an even or an odd number of disks are to be moved. Hence, the program must be initiated by determining the proper cycle and setting "Parity" to "Odd." The principal perceptual discrimination the program must make (T_1) is to find the smallest disk on odd moves and the next smallest exposed disk on even moves.

Means-Ends Analysis: The General Problem Solver

A distinction was made earlier between "reasoned" and "rote" strategies, the goal-

P1.   State = Problem-solved → Halt
P2.   Parity = Odd → Move($1,P(1),$Next$(P(1))$), Parity ← Even
P3.   Next-smallest = J → Move($J,P(J),O(P(1),P(J))$), Parity ← Odd, Delete(Next-smallest)
P4.   else → Test(Next-smallest)
Test(Next-smallest)
T1.   J ← Smallest-not-on-P(1)
           J = Null → State ← Problem-solved
           Else → Next-smallest ← J

Figure 7. Production system for move-pattern strategy.

recursion and perceptual strategies being placed in the former class and the move-pattern strategy in the latter. The meaning of this distinction becomes clearer when we compare the organization of the "reasoned" strategies with the organization of the General Problem Solver (Newell and Simon, 1972), a program whose principal problem-solving tool is means-ends analysis.

The General Problem Solver is a program that appears to describe well the organization of human problem solving in certain kinds of task environments: in particular, environments in which a given situation can be compared with a goal situation to discover one or more differences between them, and in which there exist operators associated with each difference that are sometimes capable of eliminating a difference of that kind. If the operator can be applied, it is; if it cannot be, the current situation is compared with the conditions for applying the operator, and a difference is discovered between them. The entire GPS apparatus is then applied recursively to eliminate this difference.

Consider the simple case where there is just one operator relevant to eliminating each difference, so that we can number operators and differences correspondingly, from 1 to N. Then a GPS applicable to such a case can be described by the production system of figure 8. Now a comparison of figure 8 with either figures 3, 5, or 6 shows that GPS is essentially

isomorphic with either the goal-recursion or the perceptual-pattern strategy for solving the Tower of Hanoi problem. Stating the matter this way really puts the cart before the horse. A better statement would be that these Tower of Hanoi strategies are simply instantiations of the General Problem Solver.

Let us examine the isomorphism between figures 6 and 8 a little more closely. The function of the test in the Tower of Hanoi program is to determine if a move can be made legally; the function of the test in GPS is to determine if an operator can be applied. In the Tower of Hanoi program, if the test shows the move to be illegal, it also determines the most important block to its legality (the disk J). In the GPS program, if the test shows the operator to be inapplicable, it also determines a difference (j) that must be removed to make it applicable. Goals in the Tower of Hanoi production system become operators in the GPS system.

We conclude that except for the "rote" programs, the programs described here for solving the Tower of Hanoi problem owe their power to the use of means-ends analysis organized in the general way defined by the General Problem Solver.

Concepts Required by the Strategies

In the preceding discussion, alternative strategies for the Tower of Hanoi problem were compared and contrasted in terms of whether or not they required a goal stack,

G1.   Difference = Problem-solved → Halt
G2.   Difference = Applied, Operator = i → Delete(Difference), Delete(Operator)
G3.   Difference = Null, Operator = i → Apply(i), Delete(Difference)
G4.   Difference = j, Operator = i → Delete(STM), Push[Operator = j]
G5.   Operator = i → Test(i)
G6.   Difference = j → Push[Operator = j]
G7.   else → Test(Remaining-difference)
Test(i)
GT1.   Present-situation = Goal → Difference ← Problem-solved, Exit
GT2.   Applied(i) → Difference ← Applied, Exit
GT3.   Applicable(i) → Difference ← Null, Exit
GT4.   else → j ← Difference(Present-situation, Operator-input), Difference ← j, Exit
Test(Remaining-difference)
GT5.   → j ← Difference(Present-situation, Goal), Difference ← j, Exit

Figure 8. Production system for the general problem solver.

whether or not they employed the concept of a "pyramid," and what perceptual tests they made use of. This section looks more closely at the concepts and perceptual tests with a particular view to determining which of these are explicit in the problem instructions and which must somehow be inferred by the subject before he can invent and use a particular strategy.

The problem instructions mention one disk being on top of another (ABOVE), and one disk being larger than another (GR). They speak also of a disk being moved from one peg to another. They do not mention the concepts of a pyramid of disks, a disk being the top disk on a peg (TOP), a peg being free for a particular disk (FREE), a disk being the largest of those not on the goal peg, and so on. They do not mention the parity of a disk, nor the next-to-smallest disk that is top disk of some peg.

Suppose that a subject confronted with the Tower of Hanoi problem has available perceptual tests for determining that one disk is larger than another and that a particular disk is on a particular peg—both relations that are mentioned in the task instructions. It can now be shown that all of the tests that are required for the goal-recursion and perceptual strategies can be defined in terms of these, using only the Booleian connectives, not (NOT), and (&) and or ($\vee$). The definitions follow:

$$X = BG(X,Y) \quad .=. \quad GR(X,Y)$$
$$A = P(X) \quad .=. \quad ON(X,A)$$
$$ABOVE(X,Y) \quad .=. \quad ON(X,P(Y))$$
$$\& \; GR(Y,X)$$
$$FREE(A,X) \quad .=. \quad (Y)[ON(Y,A)$$
$$\rightarrow GR(Y,X)]$$
$$X = TOP(A) \quad .=. \quad ON(X,A)$$
$$\& \; FREE(A,X)$$
$$X = NSM(Y,A) \quad .=. \quad GR(Y,X)$$
$$\& \; ON(X,A)$$
$$\& \; [(ON(Z,A)$$
$$\& \; GR(Y,Z))$$
$$\rightarrow GR(X,Z)]$$
$$X = BOT(A) \quad .=. \quad ON(X,A)$$
$$\& \; [ON(Y,A)$$
$$\rightarrow GR(X,Y)]$$
$$C = O(A,B) \quad .=. \quad NOT(C = A)$$
$$\& \; NOT(C = B)$$

The predicates and relations in these definitions can be read as follows: "X is the bigger of X and Y," "A is the peg of X," "X is above Y," "X is free to move to A," or "A is free for X," "X is the top disk of Peg A," "X is the disk next smaller to Y on peg A," "X is the bottom disk on Peg A," and "C is the peg other than A and B.

None of these concepts—or percepts—is particularly complex. It is reasonable to assume that any normal subject comes to the laboratory equipped to apply any of them. Of course whether he does in fact apply it may well depend on whether it is evoked from his long-term memory—whether it occurs to him that it is relevant. Examination of the strategies shows that all he needs in addition to these is the concept of the largest disk not on the goal peg, which is defined by: $NOT(ON(X, GOAL) \& [GR(X,Y) \vee ON(Y,GOAL)]$; and the largest disk that blocks disk X from peg A: $BG(NSM(X,P(X),NSM(X,A)$.

The move-pattern strategy calls for concepts of a different kind from those used by the other strategies; for it involves patterns on the sequence of moves instead of perceptual predicates describing features of the situation. In particular, the move-pattern strategy requires keeping track of the parity of the move, something that is not directly perceivable but must be held in memory; and it requires establishing an order of cycling of the pegs. Although the basic ideas of "odd-even" and "cycle" are undoubtedly known to almost all subjects, nothing in the task instructions or task situation evokes them directly.

Keeping in mind these comments about the concepts employed by the several strategies, we can now discuss what is involved in learning to solve the Tower of Hanoi problem.

LEARNING THE STRATEGIES

Each of the strategies that has been described is a definite program which, if executed, will undertake to solve the Tower of Hanoi problem. Unless he has solved the problem before, the subject who comes to the laboratory does not have such a program stored in his memory, but must acquire it from information that he gleans from the problem instructions and from the physical arrangement of pegs and disks. Let us consider, for the various things he needs to learn, how he might acquire them.

Program Organization

While a subject cannot be expected to arrive in the laboratory with a Tower of Hanoi strategy, he may well arrive with something like the GPS production system of figure 8 stored in memory. This production system can be viewed as a very general template, an abstract framework on which specific problem solving systems for particular task environments can be built. We have already seen that there is almost a one-to-one mapping between the GPS production system and the production systems described in figure 3, 4, 5, and 6 for the various Tower of Hanoi strategies. The latter might have been derived from the GPS system used as template.

Production G1, for example, simply indicates that the system is to halt when it has been noticed that the problem is solved; while Perceptual Test GT1 compares present situation with solution situation to determine whether the latter has been reached. Thus Productions P1 of the various strategies are virtually identical with G1, while the test T1 defines a specific perceptual test for determining whether the Tower of Hanoi problem has been solved. T1 can be derived from GT1 by applying the specific information as to what constitutes a solution of that problem.

In the same way, T2 is an instantiation for the Tower of Hanoi of GT2, and T3 of GT3. Perceptual tests T4 (or T4′) and T5 correspond to GT4 and GT5, respectively. Thus, the general organization of each of these problem solving strategies can be regarded as arising out of the organization of GPS.

The "Pyramid" Concept

The idea of moving a subpyramid of the disks, required for the goal recursion strategies, must be invented by the subject. One way in which it could be invented is

by noticing that, at one point in solving the problem of moving k disks from A to C, the following situation is reached:

PEG A: k   PEG B: Pyramid (k-1)
PEG C:

Recognizing the possibility of a recursion here would depend on remembering the starting situation and perceiving Pyramid (k-1) as similar to the initial Pyramid (k).

Noticing the similarities between the pyramids is not the whole story, of course. In addition, the subject must have, in some form, the concept of a "recursion." This is a concept he could have acquired in high school or college mathematics courses that made use of the method of mathematical induction. Whether subjects without such mathematical training in their backgrounds are likely to invent the goal recursion strategy is a question on which there does not appear to be any empirical evidence.

Perceptual Predicates

We have seen that the basic perceptual primitives for the Tower of Hanoi problem are GR ("X is larger than Y") and ON ("Disk X is on Peg A"). A system that could generate new tests by forming Boolean combinations of the previous ones could arrive at all the perceptual tests that are used by the strategies. This is guaranteed by the definitions we provided for the perceptual predicates.

To generate the appropriate tests, the system would have to have an induction process that could extract from the problem situation the information needed to indicate which tests would be relevant. The space of possible tests is too large to be left to a blind trial-and-error generator. The problem instructions and observation of problem situations encountered on the way to a solution could be the major sources of information for guiding the generation process.

Move Patterns

The task of inducing the move pattern predicates appears to bear a close resemblance to the task of solving letter sequence or number sequence problems. To find these patterns, it is necessary that the subject be able to remember subsequences of moves that lie on the solution path.

Consider, for example, the sequence:

1 2 1 3 1 2 1 4 1 2 1 3 1 2 1.

There are several readily detected elements of pattern in the sequence. Most obvious is the fact that the odd members are all 1s. The sequence that remains when these are deleted is: 2 3 2 4 2 3 2, the odd members of which are all 2s. If we delete the 2s, in turn, we are left with: 3 4 3, the odd member's of which are 3s, and so on. Most of production P2 of the move-pattern strategy can be induced from this observation. The cyclical character of the moves of disk 1 could also be derived from memory of a sequence of such moves by a similar induction procedure.

CONCLUSION

At first blush, the Tower of Hanoi problem would appear to provide a rather austere task environment for demonstrating that there may be multiple answers to the question of "What is learned?" The problem elements—disks and pegs—and the instructions are all very simple. In spite of this simplicity, we have shown that there are at least four quite distinct classes of strategies that might represent the knowledge a subject holds after he has learned to solve the problem: a rote strategy, goal recursion strategies, perceptual strategies, and move-pattern strategies. Each of these classes of strategies, in turn, admits of one or more variants; and there are hybrid strategies that cut across classes.

The psychological significance of this multiplicity of available strategies is severalfold. First, different strategies may have different degrees of transferability. The rote strategy, memorized for the four-disk problem does not transfer to the five-disk problem. The simple perceptual strategy will not even work for the four-disk problem unless a goal stack is maintained.

The different strategies place different amounts of burden on short-term memory. In particular, those strategies that depend on a goal stack will require up to n chunks of information to be held in short-term memory—n goals—in the course of solving the n-disk problem.

Finally, different learning processes may be required for acquiring the different strategies. The production systems for all the "reasoning" strategies follow the general outlines of GPS in their overall organization. However, a concept like "pyramid" may be acquired by observing configurations of disks along the route to a problem solution, while perceptual tests (e.g., "X is free to move to B") may be derived from interpretation of the rules of the problem, and move patterns by review of a memorized list of moves already made.

This task analysis can serve as a prolegomena to research of several kinds. First, one can undertake "ecological" research to determine, in samples of subjects drawn from different populations, which of the different Tower of Hanoi strategies will be acquired, and by whom. Second, one can undertake, by training and instructions, to influence subjects in their choice of strategies. This technique should provide a powerful means of investigating the learning processes that underlie the acquisition of the different strategies. If subjects can be reliably induced to adopt particular strategies, the technique will also provide a means for investigating differences in retention and transfer of the different strategies.

Finally, this analysis of the Tower of Hanoi problem may serve as a warning, illustrating the diversity of behavior that may be hidden under a blanket label like "problem-solution process" even in a very simple task environment. If we are to understand human problem solving behavior, we must get a solid grip on the strategies that underlie that behavior, and we must avoid blending together in a statistical stew quite diverse problem solving behaviors whose real significance is lost in the averaging process.

References

Egan, D. E. The structure of experience acquired while learning to solve a class of problems. Unpublished doctoral dissertation, University of Michigan, 1973.

Gagné, R. M. & Smith, E. C., Jr. A study of the effects of verbalization on problem solving. *Journal of Experimental Psychology*, 1962, 63, 12–18.

Greeno, J. G. & Simon, H. A. Processes for sequence production. *Psychological Review*, 1974, 81, 187–98.

Hayes, J. R. & Simon, H. A. Understanding complex task instructions. In D. Klahr (Ed.), *Cognition and instruction*. Hillsdale, NJ: Lawrence Erlbaum, 1976, pp. 269–86.

Hormann, A. M. Gaku: An artificial student. *Behavioral Science*, 1965, 10, 88–107.

Katona, G. *Organizing and memorizing*. New York: Columbia University Press, 1940.

Klix, F. *Information und Verhalten*. Berlin: VEB Deutscher Verlag der Wissenschaften, 1971.

Newell, A. Production systems: Models of control structures. In W. G. Chase (Ed.), *Visual information processing*. New York: Academic Press, 1973. pp. 463–562.

Newell, A. & Simon, H. A. *Human problem solving*. Englewood Cliffs, NJ: Prentice-Hall, 1972.

4.6

Modeling Strategy Shifts in a Problem Solving Task (1976)

with Stephen K. Reed

This chapter reports an investigation in which a computer simulation model was fitted to human laboratory data for the Missionaries and Cannibals task in an endeavor to explain (1) the effects upon problem performance of giving a hint and (2) the effects of solving the problem a second time after one successful solution had been achieved. The first section of the chapter describes the task and model, while the second compares the output of the model with the data from the human experiments and discusses the import of the findings for our understanding of cognitive processes in complex tasks.

A person attempting to solve a problem often has to make numerous choices of path before he finds a solution. When the problem constraints are well defined, as they are in the Missionary–Cannibal task, the task environment specifies clearly what legal moves are available in each problem state (Newell and Simon, 1972). The task environment therefore tends to reduce to this space of legal moves the alternatives the problem solver has to evaluate. His choices can be reduced further if he adopts a strategy of selective search that he be-

lieves will lead to a correct solution. The strategy, by specifying that some legal moves are to be preferred to others, biases the subject's preferences among moves.

The degree of sophistication of the strategies on which subjects are likely to hit also depends on the structure of the task environment. For example, the structure of the Tower of Hanoi problem admits several kinds of subgoals which, if discovered, enable the problem solver to plan a number of moves ahead (see chapter 4.5). The Missionary–Cannibal environment has a less elegant formal structure, and subjects must rely on simple local strategies

This research was supported by Public Health Service Grant MH-07722 from the National Institute of Mental Health to the first author and by Public Health Service Grant MH-23297 from the National Institute of Mental Health to the second author. Computer time for the simulation was supported by the Advanced Research Projects Agency of the Office of the Secretary of Defense (F44620-73-C-0074) which is monitored by the Air Force Office of Scientific Research. The work was carried out while the second author held a postdoctoral fellow position at Carnegie-Mellon University.

—selecting moves that balance the numbers of missionaries and cannibals, or those that take the greatest number across the river—which permit only a short look ahead.[1]

Some strategies may be suggested directly by the constraints on legal moves. The strategy of keeping an equal number of missionaries and cannibals on each side of the river is of this kind. We will seek to explain some data on performance in this task by assuming that most subjects use this strategy initially but have to abandon it because it does not lead to a problem solution. We propose further that the facilitating effects of experience with the task and of being provided by the experimenter with a subgoal can be accounted for by the greater speed with which subjects then switch to a more efficient strategy.

THE TASK AND THE MODEL

The task is a variant of the familiar Missionaries and Cannibals problem. In this variant (5MC Problem), five missionaries and five cannibals are initially on the left bank of a river, with a rowboat having a maximum capacity of three persons. The task is to find a sequence of crossings that will leave all 10 persons on the right bank. No missionaries may ever be left with a larger number of cannibals (on either bank or in the boat), for the cannibals would overpower and eat the missionaries. (The more familiar task involves three each of cannibals and missionaries, and a boat with a capacity of two. In all other respects it is identical with the problem described here. The variant used here, having a larger space of legal moves, is more difficult than the other.)

Figure 1 shows the space of legal moves for the 5MC problem, each state that can

1. Anders Ericsson (personal communication) has proposed that a sequence of rapidly executed moves indicates that the subject is carrying out a previously constructed plan. He suggests that the lack of such sequences in the experiment discussed here indicates that subjects did not construct plans involving more than two moves.

be reached by some sequence of legal crossings being represented by a box containing four numbers. The first number is the number of missionaries on the left (initial) bank; the second, the number of cannibals on the left bank; the third, the number of missionaries on the right bank; and the fourth, the number of cannibals on the right bank. The position of the asterisk (left or right) corresponds to the location of the boat. Each line connecting two boxes represents a possible move (in either direction). The pair of numbers associated with each move shows how many missionaries (first number) and how many cannibals (second number) are transfered by that move. State A is the initial state, with all persons and the boat on the left bank; and State Z is the goal state, with all persons and the boat on the right bank. It can be seen from the figure that the problem space is not large (27 nodes), and that there are only a few legal moves in each problem state. Nevertheless, the problem is a difficult one for most human subjects (who, of course, are not shown the problem maze in explicit form).

METHOD

We will be concerned with data from two experiments, and two conditions in each experiment, a total of four experimental conditions. In the *Control* condition of experiment 1, subjects solved the Missionaries and Cannibals problem after it was described to them essentially as it has been presented above. In the *Subgoal* condition of this experiment, subjects were told, in addition, that along the path to solution, a state would be reached with three cannibals across the river by themselves, without the boat (state L in figure 1).

In experiment 2, subjects were told they were in a learning experiment and would have to solve the Missionary-Cannibal problem twice (with a one-minute unfilled interval between the two solution attempts). Performance on the first solution attempt was compared with performance on the second. We call these the *Trial 1* and *Trial 2* conditions, respectively.

In the computer simulation model, the

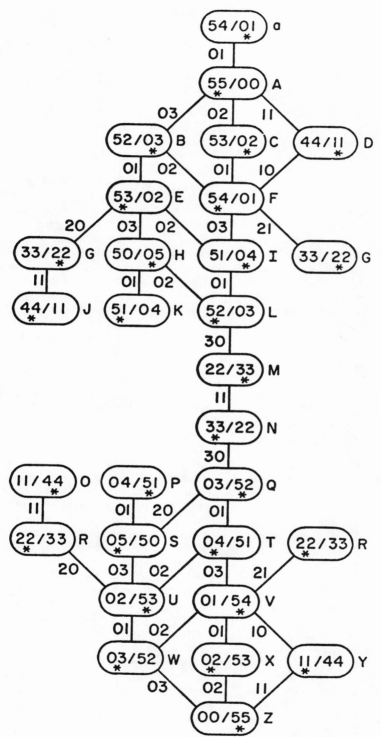

Figure 1. Space of legal moves for the 5MC problem.

fundamental assumption is made that all behavior takes place within the maze of legal moves depicted in figure 1. This assumption does not necessarily hold for human subjects, who may generate and try illegal moves before they are aware of their violation of the rules. However, since the illegal move rate of human subjects is typically low (about 20 percent), we have chosen to ignore these errors in this first approximation to a model for their behavior.

The model postulates that the subject uses a *strategy* to choose his move at each step from among the legal moves available. The strategy may incorporate both systematic and random elements. That is, the subject, according to the strategy, may choose among the alternatives on the basis of a preference ordering or may select one of the alternatives at random (with equal probability for all). From move to move in the course of a trial, a subject's strategy may change suddenly (strategy shift) or gradually (learning).

As applied to the data from the two experiments, the model incorporates two systematic strategies: (1) a *balance* strategy, and (2) a *means-ends* strategy. In addition, subjects are assumed to avoid, to a specified extent, reversing the move they have just made—an *antiloop* test. The random components in the strategies can be interpreted as genuine randomness in the subjects' behavior or (this seems more plausible to us) as behavior based on a mixture of other strategies not incorporated in the model.

The *balance* strategy selects that legal move which balances the number of missionaries with the number of cannibals on each side of the river. For example, move AD is preferred by this strategy over AB or AC. We postulate that this strategy will be evoked by subjects when they first encounter the Missionaries-Cannibals problem because of the rules, which forbid more cannibals than missionaries on either side of the river (hence, also forbid more missionaries than cannibals on either side unless the other side has no missionaries at all).

The *means-ends* strategy prefers that move

which takes the maximum number of persons across the river (on odd-numbered moves) or the fewest number back to the left bank (on even-numbered moves). For example, this strategy prefers move AB over moves AC and AD. We postulate that subjects will, in time, shift to this strategy from the balance strategy.

The balance strategy prefers the same moves as the means-ends strategy whenever it is impossible to balance missionaries and cannibals. It differs from the means-ends strategy by preferring move AD over AB, EG over EH, FG over FI, and GJ over GE.

It can be seen from figure 1 that a subject who used a pure means-ends strategy, combined with an antiloop test, would follow the path A-B-E-H-K-H-L-M-N-Q-T-V-X-Z, solving the problem in thirteen moves, only two more than the minimum. On the other hand, a subject who persisted in using the pure balance strategy with an antiloop test would follow the path A-D-F-G-J-G-F-D-A-C-F-G-etc., and would get into a large loop that would never permit him to solve the problem.

Our basic hypothesis, applicable to all subjects in all experimental conditions, is that a subject begins his search using the balance strategy combined with a random element. At each move he may switch, with a certain probability, to the means-ends strategy. Also, at each move the probability increases that he will invoke the antiloop test and that he will select his move according to the strategy's preference ordering rather than at random. Differences in behavior from one experimental condition to another are produced by manipulating the strategy-switching probability (p_s), the initial probabilities of moving according to strategy rather than randomly (p_d), and of testing for a loop (p_l), and the rates (determined by parameters a and b, respectively) at which the latter two probabilities change—five parameters in all. In addition, we tested the effects of changing the preference orderings among the moves at certain of the nodes in the problem space.

The exact sequence of steps at each move is this:

1. With probability p_s, switch to the

means-ends strategy (unless this strategy is already being followed).

2. Increment p_d, the probability of selecting the move preferred by the current strategy rather than a random move.

3. Increment p_l, the probability of checking for a loop.

4. With probability p_d, select the move preferred by the current strategy; with probability $(1 - p_d)$, select a move at random.

5. Check if the move selected in step 4 reverses the previous move. If it does not, make the move; if it does, then, with probability p_l, return to step 1 and repeat (unless this is the only legal move, in which case make it); with probability $(1 - p_l)$, make the move.

The increment in p_d at each move (step 2) is $[a(1 - p_d)^2]/[a(1 - p_d) + 1]$, where a was set equal to 0.05 in most runs of the model. The particular algebraic form of the increment has no psychological significance, but was selected for its computational convenience in the program. Similarly, the increment in p_l at each move (step 3) is $[b(1 - p_l)^2]/[b(1 - p_l) + 1]$, where b was set equal to 0.1.

In the next section, the computer simulation models will be compared with human data. The basis for comparison is the frequency with which each of the seventy legal moves of figure 1 occurs in the course of solving the problem (frequencies are averaged over subjects). Thus, we will have a total of seventy data points for each comparison and only five parameters to adjust the model to the human data. Hence, sixty-five degrees of freedom will remain for judging the quality of the approximation.

There are no known systematic procedures for finding best estimates of the model's parameters in order to fit it to a set of data. Lacking such procedures, the model was "tuned" with the aid of the data from the control condition of the first experiment, by adjusting parameters until the mean number of moves per trial was essentially identical for model and human data for this condition, and until the number of moves in the first half of the problem space of figure 1 and in the second half

each matched the human data separately. The first part of the tuning was accomplished mainly by adjusting p_d and p_l, the second part by adjusting a and b. For the larger are p_d and p_l, the more goal-oriented will be the behavior and the smaller will be the expected number of moves to solve the problem. Similarly, with faster learning (larger a and b), performance in the last half of the search will be correspondingly improved over performance in the first half. For the control condition, p_s was retained at a low value (about 0.07).

Having tuned the model for the Control condition, the other experimental conditions were simulated by making appropriate changes in the parameters. It was postulated that the hint given to the Subgoal group in the first experiment would have the effect of increasing the probability of their switching from the balance to the means-ends strategy; accordingly the value of p_s was increased for that group from 0.07 to 0.25. Again, this value was estimated by matching the average number of trials to solution for the simulation with the human data. The remaining parameters retained their previous values. The new value for p_s of 0.25 implies that it will take subjects in the Subgoal condition only about four moves on the average to discover and apply the means-ends strategy, instead of an average of about fifteen moves in the Control condition. The rationale for interpreting the effect of the hint as producing a change in p_s is that the hint established for the subjects as an intermediate goal that they must pass through a state in which the sides were thoroughly *unbalanced*: with five missionaries and two cannibals on the left bank and three cannibals by themselves on the right bank. To achieve this state, the goal of balancing missionaries and cannibals on each bank must be abandoned. The test, of course, of whether this interpretation is justified must lie in the accuracy with which the simulation approximates the human data on moves.

A similar procedure was used to simulate the difference between the performance on the first and second trials in the second experiment. The model was tuned to match the human performance on the first trial,

Table 1. Simulation of Subjects' Legal Moves in Subgoal and Learning Experiments.

Experiment	Condition	Mean	SD	Correlation	Percentage of Variance Explained
Subgoal	Control group	30.6	17.1	0.95	90%
	Simulation	30.7	13.7		
	Subgoal group	20.3	6.7	0.94	88%
	Simulation	20.2	7.7		
Learning	Trial 1	21.2	5.7	0.86	74%
	Simulation	20.6	8.3		
	Trial 2	16.0	3.5	0.89	79%
	Simulation	15.6	3.4		

resulting in a value of about 0.08 for p_s. It was assumed that the result of the first trial's experience would again be to cause a more rapid shift to the means-ends strategy in the second trial. Thus, p_s was set at 0.25 for the second trial.

For all four experimental conditions, the initial values of p_d and p_l were kept constant at 0.5, and the learning parameters, a and b, at 0.05 and 0.1, respectively.

The two pure strategies operate, as has been explained, by designating a preferred move at each of the twenty-seven nodes of the search space. By altering this preference ordering at single nodes it is easy to test the sensitivity of the behavior of the system to local changes in strategy. In particular, we noticed two nodes at which the subjects in the first experiment appeared to reverse the preference predicted by the means-ends strategy: They tended to prefer move EI to move EH and NM to move NQ. The same preference for EI over EH showed up in the second experiment, but not the preference for NM over NQ. We tested the effect of these alterations upon the goodness of approximation of the model to the human data, with results that are described in the next section. We also tested the effect of eliminating the learning processes by setting parameters a and b equal to zero.

Fianlly, it is easy to modify the model (by setting p_d and p_l equal to zero) into a completely random search through the problem space and to compare the relative frequencies from more directed searches or in the subjects' data.

RESULTS

Data from the two experiments already mentioned were used to test the model. The first experiment was conducted by Reed and Abramson (1976) as part of their study on the effect of the task environment on subgoal facilitation. Subjects who were given a hint (that the solution path passed through State L) averaged 20.3 legal moves in solving the problem; subjects who did not receive the hint averaged 30.6 legal moves in solving the problem.[2] The strategy shift model proposes that subjects solved the problem in fewer moves when given a subgoal because they shifted more rapidly to the means-ends strategy. Since only the parameter p_s differed between the models for the two conditions, the model accounts for performance differences between the two groups solely by the different rates of switching strategies.

Table 1 shows the mean and standard deviation of the number of legal moves required by the subjects and the simulation model to solve the problem. All simulation results are based on twenty-five runs except for the simulation of the Control condition which is based on the average of two sets of twenty-five runs. The results for human subjects are based on twenty-five subjects in a group. Table 1 also shows the correlation between the average number of moves in each problem state for the subjects and

---

2. The mean of 27.6 reported by Reed and Abramson did not include one subject who took 103 moves to solve the problem. All subjects are included in the analysis reported here.

the model. The correlation of 0.95 for the Control group and 0.94 for the subgoal group indicates that the model predicts the subjects' moves with considerable accuracy. As shown in the last column of the table, 90 percent of the variance in the data is explained for the Control group and 88 percent for the subgoal group. There is also reasonably good agreement in the standard deviations of numbers of moves to solution between models and subjects. Significance tests are not used to examine the differences between simulations and human data, since they are inappropriate when the hypothesis under consideration is an extreme hypothesis (i.e., a set of point predictions) as it is in this case.

The average numbers of moves between each pair of problem states for subjects and

Table 2. Simulation of Moves between Legal States for the Subgoal Experiment.*

	Forward Moves				Backward Moves			
	Subgoal		Control		Subgoal		Control	
States	Subjects	Model	Subjects	Model	Subjects	Model	Subjects	Model
AB	0.5	0.3	0.4	0.2	0.1	0	0.3	0.1
AC	0.2	0.2	0.1	0.2	0	0	0.1	0.1
AD	0.5	0.6	1.1	1.2	0.1	0.1	0.3	0.3
BE	0.7	0.5	0.8	0.4	0.2	0.1	0.7	0.3
BF	0.1	0	0.2	0.2	0.1	0.2	0.2	0.2
CF	0.2	0.2	0.2	0.2	0	0	0.1	0.2
DF	0.5	0.6	1.2	1.0	0	0	0.3	0.2
EG	0.5	0.2	1.0	0.5	0.8	0.8	1.7	1.4
EH	0.2	0.1	0.5	0.2	0	0.1	0.4	0.3
EI	0.7	1.1	0.9	1.3	0	0.1	0.2	0.2
FG	0.8	0.8	1.7	1.6	0.5	0.2	1.0	0.7
FI	0.2	0.2	0.2	0.2	0	0.2	0.2	0.3
GJ	0.8	0.3	2.0	2.0	0.8	0.3	2.0	2.0
HK	0.2	0.2	0.7	0.9	0.2	0.2	0.7	0.9
HL	0.3	0.1	0.5	0.3	0.2	0.1	0.2	0.4
IL	0.9	1.4	1.0	1.5	0	0.3	0.3	0.4
LM	1.6	1.6	1.4	1.7	0.6	0.6	0.4	0.7
MN	1.8	1.9	1.7	2.0	0.8	0.9	0.7	1.0
NQ	1.0	1.0	1.0	1.1	0	0.1	0	0.1
OR	0	0	0	0	0	0	0	0
PS	0	0	0	0	0	0	0	0
QS	0.1	0.1	0.1	0.1	0	0	0	0
QT	0.9	0.9	0.9	1.0	0	0	0	0
RU	0	0	0	0	0	0	0	0
RV	0	0	0	0	0	0	0	0
SU	0.1	0.2	0.1	0.1	0	0	0	0
TU	0.2	0.1	0.1	0	0	0	0	0
TV	0.8	0.8	0.8	1.0	0	0	0	0
UW	0.2	0.2	0.2	0.1	0	0	0	0
VW	0	0	0	0.1	0.1	0.1	0.1	0
VX	0.9	0.9	0.8	0.9	0	0	0	0
VY	0	0	0	0	0	0	0	0
WZ	0.1	0.2	0.1	0.1	—	—	—	—
XZ	0.9	0.8	0.8	0.8	—	—	—	—
YZ	0	0	0	0	—	—	—	—

*Average frequency of move per subject.

Table 3. Alternative Versions of the Simulation Model.

Condition	Version	Mean	SD	Correlation	Percentage of Variance Explained
Control group	Strategy shift	30.7	13.7	0.95	90%
	Move EH/EI	26.2	10.3	0.91	83%
	Move NQ/NM	27.0	14.1	0.86	74%
	No learning	31.9	15.0	0.87	76%
	Undirected search	133.0	126.0	0.64	41%
Subgoal group	Strategy shift	20.2	7.7	0.94	88%
	Move EH/EI	19.4	8.1	0.83	69%
	Move NQ/NM	15.6	3.4	0.66	44%
	No learning	26.6	15.3	0.89	79%
	Undirected search	133.0	126.0	0.40	16%

model in each experimental condition are shown in table 2. "Forward moves" are moves in the direction toward the goal (e.g., from A to B) and "backward moves" are moves in the opposite direction (e.g., from B to A).

The results shown in tables 1 and 2 represent the closest approximations we achieved of models to subjects' behavior. In these particular simulations, the preference ordering appropriate to the means-ends strategy was violated in two respects mentioned in the previous section: The simulation preferred move EI to move EH and move NM to move NQ. Although both of the preferred moves are inconsistent with a means-ends strategy, move NM is consistent with the balance strategy. Table 3 shows the effect upon the approximations of removing these violations. If move EH is preferred to move EI, the correlation of model with subjects is reduced to 0.91 for the Control group and 0.83 for the Subgoal group (with 83 and 69 percent of the variance explained, respectively). If move NQ is preferred to move NM, the correlations are reduced to 0.86 for the Control group and 0.66 for the Subgoal group (with 74 and 44 percent of the variance explained, respectively).

Although we have no insight into why the violations of the preference ordering associated with the strict strategies occurred, that they did occur is evident from the data on move choices (see table 2). Whatever caused them, these isolated deviations from the means-ends strategy produced a major part of the unexplained

variance of the models. We have therefore shown the correlations both with these ad hoc modifications included and with them eliminated.

We also investigated the degree to which learning influenced the predictions of the model by setting the learning parameters equal to zero. As table 3 shows, this change reduced the correlations slightly, to 0.87 and 0.89 for the Control and Subgoal groups, respectively (variance accounted for 76 and 79 percent, respectively).

These correlations between the predictions of the model and its variants and the human behavior, ranging from 0.86 to 0.95 for the Control group, and 0.66 to 0.94 for the Subgoal group, may be compared with the correlation that is obtained from a model using undirected, wholly random, search. Here, the correlation is only 0.64 (41 percent of variance accounted for) in the Control group, and 0.40 (16 percent of variance accounted for) in the Subgoal group. The behavior of the random model gives some indication of the degree to which the built-in characteristics of the problem maze, as contrasted with the strategy of the subjects, is contributing to the predictions of the directed search models.

The high mean (133 moves) and standard deviation (126 moves) of the undirected search model indicate how poorly it predicts overall subjects' performance. Subjects, even in the Control condition, were able to solve the problem with little more than one-fifth the number of moves required by the random process. However, when we compare the *relative* frequencies with which different moves were made (which is closely related to the *relative* frequencies with which the different nodes in the problem space were visited), we obtain a high correlation ($r = 0.64$) between the undirected search model and the performance of the Control group. One important determinant, then, of the relative times spent in different portions of the problem space is the structure of the space itself, apart from subjects' efforts to move through that space in a consistent direction toward the goal state. We must note, however, that the undirected model accounts for only 41 percent of the variance in the Control group's move frequencies, compared to 90 percent of that variance accounted for by the strategy shift model. The undirected search model is even less able to account for the performance of the subgoal group, accounting for only 16 percent of the variance, compared to 88 percent for the strategy shift model.

According to Newell and Simon (1972, p. 788), "The task environment (plus the intelligence of the problem solver) determines to a large extent the behavior of the problem solver, independently of the detailed internal structure of his information processing system." The present data support that proposition, in that the shape of the problem space itself accounts for a significant part of the variance in behavior (41 percent for the Control group) and the assumption that the subject chooses his moves on the basis of simple local strategies for most of the remaining variance. From this, little or nothing can be inferred about the "detailed internal structure" of the subject's information processing system, except possibly that it operates with rather limited short-term memory.

In order to gain some impression of the generality of the strategy shift model, we applied the model to data from a second experiment (Reed and Johnsen, unpublished data), previously described, in which the subjects solved the 5MC problem twice. Subjects reduced the average number of legal moves from 21.2 to 16.0 between their first and second solutions. According to the strategy shift model, subjects

achieved this improvement by switching more rapidly to the means-ends strategy during their second attempt—from a probability of 0.08 per move of switching during the first solution attempt to a probability of 0.25 during the second.

Table 1 shows the mean and standard deviation of the number of moves to solution for the subjects and the model. The results are based on twenty-five subjects and twenty-five simulation runs. The correlation between the model and subjects' performances is 0.86 for the first problem solution and 0.89 for the second solution. These correlations are not quite as high as those found for the first experiment, but they are higher than those achieved with an alternative model for the second experiment. This alternative model proposes that all subjects started with the means-ends strategy when solving the problem for the second time and that the two learning parameters began at the values that obtained at the end of the first solution, rather than being reset to 0.05 and 0.1, respectively. The correlation between the alternative model and subjects' performance was 0.78, compared with 0.89 for the strategy shift model.

Table 4 shows the average number of moves between individual problem states for the subjects and the simulation model. The simulation results incorporate one ad hoc assumption, instead of the two introduced in the simulation of experiment 1. The simulation of the means-ends strategy assumed a preference for move EI over move EH (but also assumes a preference for NQ over NM). Subjects in the learning experiment showed less of a tendency to make a backward move at state N, particularly on trial 2, than did subjects in the first experiment, with a resulting improvement in overall performance. The reasons for this difference are unknown.

CONCLUSION

The frequencies with which individual moves were selected provide a rather detailed picture of the behavior of human

Table 4. Simulation of Moves between Legal States for the Learning Experiment.*

	Forward Moves				Backward Moves			
	Trial 1		Trial 2		Trial 1		Trial 2	
States	Subjects	Model	Subjects	Model	Subjects	Model	Subjects	Model
AB	0.2	0.3	0.4	0.4	0	0.1	0	0.1
AC	0.1	0.1	0	0.1	0	0	0	0.1
AD	0.9	0.8	0.6	0.8	0.2	0.2	0	0.2
BE	0.7	0.3	0.4	0.5	0.3	0.3	0.1	0.1
BF	0.2	0	0.1	0	0.2	0.1	0.2	0.1
CF	0.1	0.2	0	0.2	0	0	0	0.1
DF	1.0	0.8	0.7	0.6	0.2	0.1	0	0
EG	0.7	0.3	0.4	0.2	1.1	1.0	0.8	0.6
EH	0.4	0.2	0.4	0	0.1	0.2	0.1	0
EI	0.6	1.0	0.5	0.9	0.1	0	0	0
FG	1.1	1.1	0.6	0.6	0.7	0.4	0.2	0.2
FI	0.2	0.1	0.3	0.2	0	0.1	0	0
GJ	0.9	1.6	0.5	0.2	0.9	1.6	0.5	0.2
HK	0.2	0	0.2	0	0.2	0	0.2	0
HL	0.3	0.2	0.3	0.2	0	0.2	0	0.1
IL	0.8	1.1	0.8	1.0	0.1	0.1	0	0.1
LM	1.1	1.1	1.0	1.0	0.1	0.1	0	0
MN	1.4	1.1	1.2	1.2	0.4	0.1	0.2	0.2
NQ	1.0	1.0	1.0	1.0	0	0	0	0
OR	0	0	0	0	0	0	0	0
PS	0	0	0	0	0	0	0	0
QS	0	0.1	0	0.2	0	0.1	0	0
QT	1.0	1.0	1.0	0.8	0	0	0	0
RU	0	0	0	0	0	0	0	0
RV	0	0	0	0	0	0	0	0
SU	0	0.1	0	0.3	0	0.1	0	0
TU	0.1	0.2	0	0.1	0	0	0	0
TV	0.8	0.8	1.0	0.7	0	0	0	0
UW	0.2	0.2	0	0.3	0	0	0	0
VW	0	0	0	0	0	0	0	0
VX	0.8	0.9	0.9	0.8	0	0	0	0
VY	0.1	0	0	0	0	0	0	0
WZ	0.1	0.2	0	0.3	—	—	—	—
XZ	0.8	0.8	0.9	0.7	—	—	—	—
YZ	0.1	0	0	0	—	—	—	—

*Average frequency of move per subject.

subjects in the Missionaries and Cannibals task environment. In this chapter we have sought to show that these frequencies can largely be explained by postulating that the subjects employ rather simple local strategies for choosing among alternative moves at each problem node. These strategies can be modified by simple hints or by previous experience with the problem.

The demonstration was accomplished by constructing a computer program with which alternative strategies could be simulated by changes in a few parameters. Because the simulation makes detailed predictions of the frequencies of seventy individual legal moves, discrepancies between model performance and the human data can be pinpointed as a first step toward seeking their explanation.

Viewed in the general context of the theory of problem solving, our analysis has shown again the great importance of the structure of the problem space in determining the course of search for a problem solution and the way in which means-ends analysis, which is the central heuristic of programs like the General Problem Solver, gives direction to problem solving search.

References

Newell, A., & Simon, H. A. *Human problem solving*. Englewood Cliffs, N.J.: Prentice-Hall, 1972.

Reed, S. K., & Abramson, A. Effect of the problem space on subgoal facilitation. *Journal of Educational Psychology*, 1976, 68, 243–46.

Simon, H. A. The functional equivalence of problem solving skills. *Cognitive Psychology*, 1975, 7, 268–88. Reprinted as chapter 4.5 in this book.

5

Rule Induction and Concept Formation

As important as problem solving ability, and often a component of it, is the human ability to discover pattern and order in the world. The chapters in this section are concerned with modeling the rule induction and concept attainment processes that incorporate this ability. The first three chapters propose a theory of serial pattern induction and advance empirical evidence in support of it. Chapter 5.4 describes information processing models of concept attainment. Chapter 5.5 describes a general rule induction model that embraces a wide range of rule induction tasks and provides a unified theory of the psychological processes that are involved in both problem-solving and inductive activities.

INDUCTION OF SEQUENTIAL PATTERNS

The first three chapters of this section need little introduction. Detecting the regularities in nature, extracting information about the world from these regularities, is a human capability of the highest significance for intelligent behavior. In a wholly unstructured world, random search is as efficient or inefficient as any other kind. Only in a world with structure can search be selective and systematic; and only by extracting from the world information about its structure can that selectivity be implemented. Chapters 5.1, 5.2, and 5.3 (the first two written in collaboration with Kenneth Kotovsky) propose and test a theory of how people induce patterns in sequences of events.

The key to simulating pattern induction lies in the observation that most complex patterns are generated from a few very simple components, of which two are predominant: repetition of elements and orderly progression down a sequence of elements. Hence, the basic capabilities needed in a flexible pattern discovery system are the abilities to recognize the relations of "same" and "next" among symbols and to manipulate simple relations like these combinatorially into arbitrarily complex hierarchical patterns.

Although the pattern induction system described in chapters 5.1 and 5.2 was designed to model behavior on a specific task, the Thurstone Letter Series Completion Test, its motivation was considerably more general. In the artificial intelligence literature, several earlier, and largely unsuccessful, attempts at constructing rule induction systems had been reported. Because they did not take account of the crucial role of "same" and "next" relations, these systems did not extract enough information from the stimulus whose pattern they were endeavoring to detect, and as a result, they commonly bogged down in excessive and largely unsystematic search through large spaces of possible patterns.

Once the new system had shown its competence to handle the Thurstone Test, its applicability to other tasks in the psychological literature could be explored. As the reference lists for chapters 5.1, 5.2, and 5.3 show, the psychological study of pattern extrapolation dates back at least to the 1930s; it has been pursued under such diverse titles as "binary choice," "partial reinforcement," and "per-ceptual processing of sequential stimuli." It is ironic that, while much of this research employed random sequences of stimuli, we can now see by hindsight that human subjects (and even rats) did not accept the experimental situation in the spirit in which the researcher designed it. Instead, subjects quite generally persisted in searching for pattern (and often believed they had found it) in the random sequences that were presented to them. The urge to find order in the environment appears to be a rather deep-seated human drive.

As with the other tasks discussed in this volume, small variations in the task or in the task instructions can induce changes in the fine structures of the strategies that human subjects employ. Such modifications of strategy, all within the general framework of the system described here, have been explored by Mari Riess Jones (e.g., Jones and Zamostny, 1975) and Frank Restle (1976). Additional references will be found in their papers.

A doctoral dissertation by Donald Williams (1972) showed how the pattern generating scheme could be generalized, but still using primarily the relations of "same" and "next," to a number of intelligence test items in addition to the Thurstone Test: specifically, letter and number sequences, symbolic analogies, and other items involving rule detection. In fact, Williams built a system that, given either the instructions for an intelligence test item or a worked-out example, could program itself to take a test composed of items of that kind. Generalization in another direction is shown in a paper, not reprinted in this volume, which I wrote with Richard Sumner (1968), and which demonstrated how the same pattern-detecting capabilities could be used to carry out rhythmic, melodic, and harmonic analysis of classical and twelve-tone music. In the case of music, the scales (diatonic, chromatic, circle of fifths, tone row, etc.) constitute the basic "alphabets" on which the relation on "next" is defined.

In doctoral work now being completed at Carnegie-Mellon University, Pat Langley has extended these pattern discovery ideas further to build a scheme that is capable of inducing scientific laws from data. For example, with only a modest amount of search in the space of hypotheses, his system discovers Kepler's Third Law, which relates the periods of orbit of the planets to their distances from the sun. These successful extensions of the theory to quite complex domains, such as music analysis and scientific discovery, demonstrate its generality and the fundamental significance in human cognition of the skills it simulates.

Concept Attainment

Concept attainment has been the task most used by psychologists to study human processes for discovering order in stimuli. Hull's doctoral dissertation addressed itself to this domain, and Carl Hovland devoted a large part of his effort to it in the period after World War II. In 1956, the influential book by J. S. Bruner, J. J. Goodnow, and G. A. Austin, *A Study of Thinking*, introduced the idea that strategies are essential intervening variables in explaining human concept attaining behavior.

Chapter 5.4, written with Lee W. Gregg, shows how concept attainment can be modeled and explained in information processing terms. The theory amounts to a formalization of the ideas put forth by Bruner and his coauthors. In addition to showing the dependence of behavior on strategies, it demonstrates how the range of strategies that subjects can adopt depends, in turn, on limits of STM capacity and the availability of external aids to memory. The study of concept attainment, at least within the usual laboratory paradigms, turns out to be largely a study of STM capacity.

A large part of chapter 5.4 is devoted to two methodological issues: (1) the relation between the information processing theory of concept attainment and stochastic models for the same tasks, and (2) the problems of testing models empirically, including the special problems of applying statistical tests of significance to them. I will not anticipate either discussion here, except to remark that I have experienced more frustration from the statistical issue than from almost any other problem I have encountered in my scientific career.[1] To be accurate, the frustration lies not in the statistical issue itself, but in the stubbornness with which psychologists hold to a misapplication of statistical methodology that is periodically and consistently denounced by mathematical statisticians.'

The misapplication is the use of standard statistical tests, whether parametric or nonparametric, to test so-called extreme hypotheses. An extreme hypothesis is a hypothesis that makes point predictions of parameter values of models, instead of the usual "null" prediction that a hypothesis is false. All the information processing models of this and other chapters incorporate extreme hypotheses, as do the stochastic models of this chapter. The practice of applying significance tests to them is wholly wrong, for reasons discussed in chapter 5.4 and in Grant's paper referenced there; yet denunciation of the practice seems not to diminish it in the least. But I cannot refrain from protesting once more.

GENERAL THEORY OF RULE INDUCTION

In the interests of parsimony, it is important that we not treat the abilities that human beings exhibit for discovering pattern in sequences and for identifying concepts as separate and independent. Parsimony would be even better served if we could show a basic relation between these abilities and the processes used in solving problems. Chapter 5.5, written with Glenn Lea, undertakes such a synthesis between theories of how rule induction is accomplished in different task environments and between these theories and the theory of problem solving discussed in section 4 and in *Human Problem Solving*.

The basic idea of the chapter is that rule induction is itself a form of problem solving search, but search carried on simultaneously in two spaces: a space of instances and a space of rules. It is the existence of this dual space, and the use of information drawn from one space to increase the selectivity of search in the other, that distinguishes rule induction from other forms of problem solving.

Thus, Chapter 5.5 unifies much of the theory that has preceded it in sections 4 and 5. We can then leave the topics of problem solving and rule induction, and turn to several quite different (or at least apparently different) task domains.

---

1. There is a possible competitor—the reaction of economists to suggestions that human beings may be not global optimizers. But this is not the place to enlarge on the follies of economists.

References

Bruner, J. S., J. J. Goodnow, and G. A. Austin. *A Study of Thinking*, New York: Wiley, 1956.

Grant, D. A. Testing the null hypothesis and the strategy and tactics of investigating theoretical models. *Psychological Review*, 69:54–61 (1962).

Hovland, C. I. A "communicational analysis" of concept learning, *Psychological Review*, 59:461–72 (1952).

Hull, C. L. Quantitative aspects of the evolution of concepts, *Psychological Monographs*, 28 (1920), Whole No. 123.

Jones, M. R. and K. P. Zamostny. Memory and rule structure in the prediction of serial patterns, *Journal of Experimental Psychology: Human Learning and Memory*, 104:295–306 (1975).

Newell, A. and H. A. Simon. *Human Problem Solving*, Englewood Cliffs, N.J.: Prentice-Hall, 1972.

Restle, F. Structural ambiguity in serial pattern learning, *Cognitive Psychology*, 8:357–81 (1976).

Simon, H. A. and R. K. Sumner. Pattern in music, *in* B. K. Kleinmuntz (ed.), *Formal Representation of Human Judgment*, New York: Wiley, 1968, pp. 219–50.

Williams, D. S. Computer program organization induced from problem examples, unpublished doctoral dissertation, Carnegie-Mellon University, 1969. Revised version published in H. A. Simon and L. Siklóssy (eds.), *Representation and Meaning*, Englewood Cliffs, N.J.: Prentice-Hall, 1972, pp. 143–205.

5.1

Human Acquisition of Concepts for
Sequential Patterns (1963)

with Kenneth Kotovsky

In most research on the acquisition of concepts, a *concept* is taken to mean a subclass of some class of objects, or, alternatively, a procedure for identifying a particular object as belonging to, or not belonging to, such a subclass. The usual behavioral evidence that a subject has attained a concept is that he is able to sort objects that embody the concept from objects that do not. For example, we would say that a subject had attained the concept "red" if, on instructions to sort a pile of variously colored objects, he placed all the red objects in one pile and all the others in another.

There is no necessary relation between the ability to identify objects exemplifying a concept and the ability to produce examples of the concept. A familiar example of the lack of relation between these two abilities is the discrepancy between an

individual's reading vocabulary and his speaking vocabulary (his ability to understand and his ability to produce words in a language). In experiments on memorization, the same discrepancy is familiar as the difference between ability to recognize and ability to recall.

There are some kinds of concepts, however, where we commonly measure attainment by ability to *produce* an object satisfying the concept rather than mere ability to *identify* an object as belonging to the concept. Prominent among these are concepts in the form of *serial patterns*. For example, the sequence abababa embodies the concept of "simple alternation of the characters a and b." We might test the subject's attainment of the concept by presenting him with a sequence of characters and asking him to decide whether it embodies the concept or not. More often, however (e.g., in the Thurstone Letter Series Completion Test), we ask him to demonstrate his attainment of the concept by presenting him with a sequence that embodies it and requiring him to extrapolate the sequence. Thus, we would say that he had attained the concept, or rec-

We are grateful to the Carnegie Corporation for a research grant that assisted us in this work and to several of our colleagues, including L. W. Gregg and K. R. Laughery, who turned our attention to the problems of serial pattern acquisition.

ognized the pattern, embodied in the sequence given above if he were able to write down ba as the next two characters in the sequence.[1]

In this chapter we propose to explain in what form a human subject remembers or "stores" a serial pattern; how he produces the serial pattern from the remembered concept or rule; and how he acquires the concept or rule by induction from an example. The theory takes the form of a computer program that simulates the processes of sequence production and rule acquisition, and that creates in the computer memory symbolic structures to represent the stored concept.[2]

Three kinds of evidence will be offered in support of the theory. First, an "existence" proof is provided—it is shown that the kinds of symbolic representations and information processes postulated in the theory are sufficient to permit a mechanism endowed with them to induct, produce, and extrapolate patterns. Second, the theory is shown to be parsimonious in a certain sense—the processes and forms of representation postulated in it are basically the same as those that have previously been used to explain certain forms of problem solving and rote learning behavior. A mechanism possessing the basic capabilities for performing these other tasks has also the capabilities for performing tasks of the kind we are considering here. Third, the predictions of the theory show good qualitative agreement with the gross behavior of human subjects in the same tasks, in

particular, predicting the relative difficulty of different tasks.

The theory casts considerable light on the psychological processes involved in series completion tasks. It indicates that task difficulty is closely related to immediate memory requirements. It suggests what kinds of errors may be expected from human subjects in series completion tasks. It provides a clear-cut and operational referent for the notion of "meaningful" as distinct from rote organization of material in memory.

CHARACTERIZATION OF SEQUENTIAL PATTERNS

Table 1 shows twenty-five Thurstone letter series completion problems. The first ten problems, designated by the letters A through J, were used as training problems with our human subjects, the last fifteen, designated by the numbers 1 through 15, as test problems. The test problems vary widely in difficulty, the number of subjects in a group of 67 who solved each problem ranging from 27 to 65.

In explaining human behavior in this problem solving task we seek, first, to form a plausible hypothesis about "what is learned": about the way in which a subject stores such patterns in memory in order to remember them, reproduce them, and extrapolate them. The first part of our theory, based on a simple "language" for characterizing serial patterns, postulates that such patterns are represented in memory by symbolic structures built from the vocabulary of such a language.

It is obvious that if a subject is able to extrapolate a sequence, he holds in memory something different from the bare sequence with which he was presented. The sequence, taken by itself, provides no basis for its own extrapolation. Indeed, from a strict mathematical standpoint, there is no uniquely defined correct answer to a serial pattern extrapolation task. Consider, for example, the sequence 1, 2, 3, 4, ... What is its continuation? One answer might be 5 but another, equally valid, would be 1

---

1. Notice that neither in concept identification nor in concept production is it essential that the concept be referred to by a name, or even have a name. We will not consider in this chapter the relation between concept naming, on the one hand, and concept identification or production, on the other.

2. On the methodological issues involved in the use of computer programs to express and test psychological theories see Newell and Simon (1961). Laughery and Gregg (1962) and Feldman, Tonge, and Kanter (1963) have incorporated similar mechanisms for detecting and generating serial patterns in tasks somewhat different from the one considered in this chapter.

Table 1. Letter Series Completion Problems.

Training Problems

Your task is to write the correct letter in the blank.

Read the row of letters below.

A.　abababab___

The next letter in this series would be a.
Write the letter a in the blank.
Now read the next row of letters and decide what the next letter should be. Write that letter in the blank.

B.　cadaeafa___

You should have written the letter g.
Now read the series of letters below and fill in each blank with a letter.

C.　aabbccdd___

D.　abxcdxefxghx___

E.　axbyaxbyaxb___

You will now be told what your answers should have been.
Now work the following problems for practice. Write the correct letter in each blank.

F.　rsrtrurvr___

G.　abcdabceabcfabc___

H.　mnlnknjn___

I.　mnomoompom___

J.　cegedeheeeiefe___

You will now be told the correct answers.

Test Problems

1.　cdcdcd___
2.　aaabbbcccdd___
3.　atbataatbat___
4.　abmcdmefmghm___
5.　defgefghfghi___
6.　qxapxbqxa___
7.　aduacuaeuabuafua___
8.　mabmbcmcdm___
9.　urtustuttu___
10.　abyabxabwab___
11.　rscdstdetuef___
12.　npaoqapraqsa___
13.　wxaxybyzczadab___
14.　jkqrklrslmst___
15.　pononmnmlmlk___

(i.e., 1, 2, 3, 4, 1, 2, 3, 4, 1 . . . . Still another would be 2 (i.e., 1, 2, 3, 4, 2, 4, 6, 8, 3, 6, 9, 12, . . .).

What is common to all these alternative solutions is that each is produced by a rule that is capable of continuing the sequence indefinitely. It is pragmatically true, although not logically necessary, that for the items commonly used on serial pattern tests it is easy to get consensus about the correct continuation. Presumably, the reason for this is that one sequence is sufficiently "simpler" or "more obvious" than others, that almost all persons who find an answer find that one first. But it must be emphasized that this is a psychological, not a logical, matter.

It is also not logically necessary that a given continuation be associated uniquely with a particular rule. There may be several different ways of obtaining the same continuation, or of representing a particular rule. Indeed, we will encounter some examples of such multiple possibilities as we go along.

We must begin, then, by saying something about what the subjects bring to the task—for what they bring will certainly affect their criteria of simplicity, the kinds of patterns they will discover, and how difficult it will be for them to discover them. We assume the subjects have in memory the English alphabet and the alphabet backward. (There are some alternatives to the latter assumption, but we make it, at present, for simplicity.) We assume the subjects have the concept of "same" or "equal"—e.g., c is the same as c. We assume they have the concept of "next" on a list—e.g., d is next to c on the alphabet, and f to g on the backward alphabet. We assume they are able to produce a cyclical pattern—e.g., to cycle on the list a, b in order to produce abababababa. . . . Finally, we assume that they are able to keep track of a small number of symbols in immediate memory—for present purposes, we need to assume only the capacity to keep track of two symbols simultaneously. We may call these the first and second symbols in immediate memory, respectively.

Now, using a simple language capable of handling only the concepts that have just been described, representations can be constructed for all of the serial patterns in table 1, and many others. It will be easiest to show how this is done by considering four examples of gradually increasing complexity.

Pattern 3: atbataatbat___. This sequence can be described most simply if we mark it off in periods of three-letter lengths: atb ata atb at___. Having done this, we observe that the first position in each period is occupied by an a, the second position, by a t. We refer to these patterns as *simple cycles* of a's and t's, respectively. The third position in the period is occupied by the cycle ba ba... We refer to a pattern of this kind as a "cycle on the list b, a." Hence, we can describe the entire pattern 3 by the notation:

$$3. \quad [a, t, (b,a)]$$

Pattern 2: aaabbbcccdd___. Again, this sequence can be marked off in periods of three letters; but in this case, there are simple relations among the letters *within* each period (they are, in fact, identical). One way in which we can describe pattern 2 is by the notation:

$$[M_1 = Alph; a]$$
$$2. \quad [M_1, M_1, M_1, N(M_1)]$$

The notation is interpreted as follows: we set a variable, M_1, equal to the first letter, a, of the alphabet. Each period is executed by producing M_1 three times, and then replacing M_1 by the *next* (N) letter of the alphabet. An alternative representation of this pattern is shown as example 2b in table 2. We will refer to it later.

Pattern 13: wxaxybyzczadab___. This sequence is more complicated than the previous two, but can again be analyzed in terms of a period of three symbols; with internal relations among the first two symbols of each period. One description of this pattern is:

$$[M_1 = Alph; w: M_2 = Alph; a]$$
$$13. \quad [M_1, N(M_1), M_1, M_2, N(M_2)]$$

Here are two variables, M_1 and M_2, corresponding to alphabetic sequences; but the M_1 sequence begins with w, while the M_2 sequence begins with a. Notice that when we come to the end of the list for such a sequence, we begin again at the beginning—z is followed by a. Thus, these alphabetic sequences are identical with what we have called cycles on a list; in this case, the list is the alphabet, (a . . . z).

Pattern 15: pononmnmlmlk___. Our final example, also based on a period of three, can be represented in the same notation as the others, with the addition of one new operator:

$$[M_2 = M_1 = Balph; p]$$
$$15. \quad [M_2, N(M_2), M_2, N(M_2), M_2, N(M_1), E(M_2, M_1)]$$

There are two variables, M_1 and M_2, which follow the sequence of the alphabet backward (Balph), starting with the letter p. The variable M_2 is produced, then the next letter of the sequence, then the next; then the next in sequence to M_1 is found, and M_2 is set equal (E) to the new M_1.

Table 2 gives pattern descriptions for the entire set of fifteen test problems in the notation we have just introduced. We remark again that the descriptions are not necessarily unique—in many, if not all, cases, it is fairly easy to find alternative descriptions of the patterns. Those provided appear intuitively to be the simplest among the alternatives we have found. In the case of patterns 1, 2, and 6, we give two alternatives.

The pattern descriptions contain all the information contained in the sequences from which they were derived. They can be used to reconstruct the sequences. More than that, they can be used to extrapolate the sequences indefinitely—hence they can be used to perform the task with which the subjects were confronted in the Letter Series Completion Test. Thus, we may assert that anyone who has learned the pattern description has learned the concept embodied in the corresponding sequence. Our central hypothesis about human concept attainment in situations involving

Table 2. Pattern Descriptions of the Test Problems.

Example	Initialization	Sequence Iteration
1a.	$M_1 = (c, d)$; c	$M_1, N(M_1)$
1b.	—	c, d
2a.	$M_1 = $ Alph; a	$M_1, M_1, M_1, N(M_1)$
2b.	$M_1 = $ Alph; a	$M_1(3), N(M_1)$
3.	$M_1 = (b, a)$; b	a, t, $M_1, N(M_1)$
4.	$M_1 = $ Alph; a	$M_1, N(M_1), M_1, N(M_1)$, m
5.	$M_1 = M_2 = $ Alph; d	$M_1, N(M_1), M_1, N(M_1), M_1, N(M_1), M_1, N(M_2),$ $E(M_1, M_2)$
6a.	$M_1 = (q, p)$; q: $M_2 = (a, b)$; a	$M_1, N(M_1), x, M_2, N(M_2)$
6b.	—	q, x, a, p, x, b
7.	$M_1 = $ Alph; d: $M_2 = $ Balph; c	a, $M_1, N(M_1)$, u, a, $M_2, N(M_2)$, u
8.	$M_1 = $ Alph; a	m, $M_1, N(M_1), M_1$
9.	$M_1 = $ Alph; r	u, $M_1, N(M_1)$, t
10.	$M_1 = $ Balph; y	a, b, $M_1, N(M_1)$
11.	$M_1 = $ Alph; r: $M_2 = $ Alph; c	$M_1, N(M_1), M_1, M_2, N(M_2), M_2$
12.	$M_1 = $ Alph; n: $M_2 = $ Alph; p	$M_1, N(M_1), M_2, N(M_2)$, a
13.	$M_1 = $ Alph; w: $M_2 = $ Alph; a	$M_1, N(M_1), M_1, M_2, N(M_2)$
14.	$M_1 = $ Alph; j: $M_2 = $ Alph; q	$M_1, N(M_1), M_1, M_2, N(M_2), M_2$
15.	$M_1 = M_2 = $ Balph; p	$M_1, N(M_1), M_1, N(M_1), M_1, N(M_2), E(M_1, M_2)$

Note: Alph = alphabet; Balph = alphabet backward.

serial patterns is the converse of this assertion, namely: *subjects attain a serial pattern concept by generating and fixating a pattern description of that concept.*

GENERATING SEQUENCES

We have now achieved our first objective: to formulate a simple, parsimonious language of pattern description, based on plausible hypotheses about what subjects bring to the serial pattern task. Our next tasks are (1) to propose a mechanism that would enable a subject, holding such a pattern description in memory, to produce and extrapolate a sequence; and (2) to propose a mechanism that would enable a subject to induce such pattern descriptions from segments of letter sequences. We consider first the possible structure of a sequence generator.

Information processing theories already exist that seek to explain how humans perform certain other tasks, including problem solving—the General Problem Solver (GPS)—and rote memory—the Elementary Perceiver and Memorizer (EPAM). In constructing our present theory, we wish to avoid creating elaborate mechanisms ad hoc and seek, instead, to build the hypothesized system from the same elementary mechanisms that have been used in GPS and EPAM. Our language of pattern description makes this easy to do, since the processes required to produce sequences fitting the list descriptions can be formulated naturally and simply in the list processing language that has been used in constructing these earlier theories.

A list processing language, as its name implies, is a system of processes for acting upon symbolic information represented in the form of lists and list structures (lists of lists). Among the fundamental processes in such a language are the process of writing or producing a symbol, the process of copying a symbol (i.e., writing a symbol that is the same as the given symbol), and the process of finding the symbol that is next to a given symbol on a list. In addition, there are processes for inserting symbols in lists, deleting symbols from lists, and otherwise modifying lists and list structures.

We can see rather immediately that processes of these kinds will enable the subject, having stored the pattern description, to produce and extrapolate the sequence.[3] By way of example, let us consider in detail pattern 9 in table 2. To produce the sequence described by the pattern, we simply interpret the pattern description, symbol by symbol, as follows:

1. *Hold* the letter "*r*" on the list named "Alphabet" *in immediate memory.*
2. *Produce* the letter "*u*."
3. *Produce* the letter that is in immediate memory (initially, this will be "*r*").
4. *Put the next* letter on the list in immediate memory (on the first round, this will move the pointer to "*s*").
5. *Produce* the letter "*t*."
6. Return to step 2, and *repeat* the sequence as often as desired.

Any mechanism that follows the program outlined in steps 1 through 6 will produce the sequence: urtustuttuut.... Thus, all that is required to construct such a mechanism is to give it the capacity to interpret the symbols in the pattern description and to execute the actions they signify—actions like "hold in immediate memory," "produce," "find next on a list," "repeat."

The second part of our theory, then, is a program, written in IPL-V—that is capable of generating sequences from pattern descriptions by executing the elementary list processes called for by the descriptions. As we have seen, the program is

extremely simple. We postulate: *normal adult beings have stored in memory a program capable of interpreting and executing descriptions of serial patterns. In its essential structure, the program is like the one we have just described.*

Our main evidence for these assertions is that the program we have written, containing the mechanisms and processes we have described, is in fact capable of generating and extrapolating letter series from stored descriptions. We are not aware that any alternative mechanism has been hypothesized capable of doing this. Further, the basic processes incorporated in the program are processes that have already been shown to be efficacious in simulating human problem solving and memorizing behavior.

PATTERN GENERATOR

We come, finally, to the question of how subjects induce a pattern description from the pattern segment that is presented to them. Our answer to this question again takes the form of a program that is capable of doing just this, in cases where the pattern is not too complex. We will describe the program and then consider the reasons for supposing it bears a close family resemblance to the programs used by human subjects.

The inputs to the pattern generator are the letter sequences presented to the subject. The outputs of the generator are the corresponding pattern descriptions. By considering what is involved in translating a sequence (table 1) into its pattern description (table 2), we can achieve some understanding of what is involved in the generator. Basically a description characterizes a sequence in terms of some initial conditions—for example, the symbol to be stored at the outset in immediate memory—and some relations among symbols—for example, that one symbol follows another in the alphabet. The main task, then, of the pattern generator is to detect these initial conditions and relations in the given sequence, and to arrange them in the corresponding pattern.

---

3. We cannot enter here into a full discussion of the reasons for supposing that human thinking processes are fundamentally list processes. For a general nontechnical introduction to this point of view see Miller, Galanter, and Pribram (1960). The particular list processing language that has been used to define GPS, EPAM, and the theory set forth in this paper is IPL-V (Information Processing Language V). The language is described in Newell et al. (1964). Investigators who wish more detail about the program of the Sequence and Pattern Generators can obtain a program listing from the authors. The program can be run on most of the large computers that are available on university campuses, for example the Bendix G-20; IBM 704, 709, and 7090; the CDC 1604; or the Univac-Scientific 1507.

There is gross behavioral evidence that the subjects accomplish these tasks by first discovering a periodicity in the sequence. Sequence 1, for example, has a period of two, for every other symbol is a c. Similarly, sequence 2 has a period of three, for it consists of segments of three equal symbols each. The pattern generator seeks periodicity in the sequence by looking for a relation that repeats at regular intervals. Thus, it discovers that the *same* symbol occurs in every second position in sequence 1, and that the *next* symbol occurs at every fourth position starting with the first in sequence 5. If this kind of periodicity is not found, the pattern generator looks for a relation that is *interrupted* at regular intervals—sequence 2 provides an example, where the relation of "same" is interrupted at every third position. Thus, to discover periodicity in the sequence, the pattern generator needs merely the capacity to detect relations like "same" and "next" with familiar alphabets.

Once a basic periodicity has been discovered, the details of the pattern are supplied in almost the same way—by detecting and recording the relations—of equal and next—that hold between successive symbols within a period or between symbols in corresponding positions of successive periods. The pattern of sequence 9, for example, records that a period of three was discovered; that the first position in the period is always occupied by the same symbol—u, and the third position always by t. In the second position, however, each successive period has the symbol next in the alphabet to the second symbol in the previous period.

A number of different variants of the pattern generator have been written, all of them, however, based on these same simple relation recognizing processes. The several variants show different degrees of success in describing the fifteen test sequences. A particular pattern generator may fail to describe a given pattern for either one of several reasons. It may be unfamiliar with an alphabet used in constructing the pattern. It may not have a sufficiently wide repertoire of relations it

can test. It may have inadequate means for organizing and recording as a coherent pattern description the relations it discovers. All these reasons for failure can be identified in our experiments.

We would expect that among our human subjects, also, different levels of performance on the Letter Series Tests might be associated with the same kinds of limitations. We will raise this point again when we look at some of the data on human performance and its comparison with the computer simulation.

Some information on the performance of four variants of the program—A, B, C, and D—is provided in table 3. The program became progressively more powerful, Variant A solving 3 of the 15 problems; Variant B, 6; Variant C, 7; and Variant D, 13. Except for problem 3, all problems solved by a less powerful variant were solved by the more powerful variants. There is no *logical* necessity for this ordering relation to hold, but as an empirical matter it would be rather difficult to construct a variant that would succeed on the "hard" problems and fail on the "easy" ones. Thus, the programs reveal a "natural" metric of difficulty—a point we will discuss further in the next section.

The pattern generator—we will not attempt to distinguish among the several variants—constitutes the third part of our theory of human serial pattern learning. We postulate: *normal adult human beings have stored in memory a program, essentially like the pattern generator just described, capable of detecting relations and recording a pattern description for a simple sequence.*

EXAMINATION OF SOME EMPIRICAL DATA

Thus far we have been concerned primarily with describing a set of programs capable of doing what human subjects demonstrably can to: discover, remember, and produce simple serial patterns. We have been able to find some quite simple mechanisms, incorporating elementary symbol manipulating and list manipulating processes, that have this capacity. The next stage in inquiry is to see what light these

Table 3. Problems Failed by Group of Twelve Subjects and by Variants of the Computer Program.

Problem Number	Subjects (In Order of Appearance)												Program Variants			
	1	2	3	4	5	6	7	8	9	10	11	12	A	B	C	D
1																
2													X			
3			X		X								X	X	X	
4													X			
5		X	X	X	X		X	X	X	X	X	X	X	X	X	X
6			X				X			X	X					
7				X	X	X	X	X	X	X	X	X	X	X	X	X
8								X	X	X	X					
9			X		X			X	X	X	X	X	X			
10								X	X		X	X	X	X		
11				X	X	X	X	X	X	X	X	X	X	X	X	
12				X	X	X	X	X		X	X	X	X	X	X	
13			X	X	X	X			X				X	X	X	
14		X						X	X	X	X	X	X	X	X	
15			X			X	X	X	X		X	X	X	X	X	
Total correct	15	14	12	10	10	9	8	8	7	6	6	6	3	6	7	13

Note: X = problem missed.

mechanisms—hypothesized as an explanation of human performance in these tasks—can cast on the behavior of subjects in the laboratory; and conversely, to seek more positive tests of the validity of the explanation.

The data we will discuss here were obtained by giving the Letter Series Completion Test to two sets of subjects. Since our main interest was in analyzing differences in difficulty among problems rather than differences in ability among subjects, no special care was taken to obtain samples representative of any particular population. The first group, twelve subjects, ranged from college graduates to housewives. The second group, sixty-seven subjects, comprised an entire class of high school seniors. Problems 1–15 of table 1 were administered to the twelve subjects individually and to the sixty-seven subjects as a group.

The three columns of table 4 show for each problem: (1) the number of subjects in the first group who solved it (2) the number of subjects in the second group who solved it, and (3) whether it was solved (S), or left unsolved (U) by variant C of the computer program.[4] The problems of less than median difficulty, as defined by the numbers of subjects solving them, are shown in boldface type in columns 1 and 2.

The three columns of table 5 show: (1) the average time per problem for those subjects in the group of twelve who obtained the problem solution, (2) the average time spent by all subjects in the first group on each problem, and (3) the time spent per problem by Variant D of the program (which solved thirteen of the fifteen problems). The times that were below median in columns 1 and 2 are shown in boldface type.

Considering both tables together, we have four measures of problem difficulty for the human subjects—two measures of numbers of subjects who solved the problems and two measures of problem solving time. Not surprisingly, there is a high level of agreement among the four measures as

---

4. Variant C was used for this comparison because it solved about half (7 out of 15) of the problems, thus permitting them to be divided evenly into "easy" and "hard."

Table 4. Problem Difficulty: Comparison of Human Subjects with Variant C of Program.

Problem Number	Number of Subjects Obtaining Correct Solution		
	Group of 12	*Group of 67*	*Program**
1	**12**	**65**	**S**
2	**12**	**61**	**S**
3	**10**	**60**	U
4	**12**	57	**S**
5	2	45	U
6	**8**	**48**	**S**
7	5	27	U
8	**9**	**49**	**S**
9	5	43	**S**
10	**9**	**51**	**S**
11	4	39	U
12	5	42	U
13	7	43	U
14	6	**43**	U
15	5	34	U

Note: Problems shown in boldface were below median in difficulty for subjects in question.

*S = solved, U = failed.

to which problems were easy and which hard. On all four measures, problems 1, 2, 3, 4, 8, and 10 ranked below the medians in difficulty, as did problem 6 on two measures (number solving) and problem 9 on two measures (problem solving time). Problems 14 and 11 were each below median on one measure, while problems 5, 7, 12, 13, and 15 were above the median in difficulty on all four measures. For purposes of gross comparison, we will call the eight problems in the first two groups the easy ones and the seven problems in the last two groups the hard ones.

To see whether there is anything in our theory that would account for these differences in difficulty, we examine the pattern descriptions in table 2. By common-sense inspection of the pattern descriptions, it is clear that the easier problems have simpler descriptions—we could have made an almost perfect prediction of which problems would be above median in difficulty simply by counting the number of symbols in their pattern descriptions. (There is some ambiguity for problem 6, which is neither

as difficult as description 6a would suggest nor as simple as description 6b would imply.)

But the lengths of the descriptions do not tell the whole story. If we now examine the patterns more closely we see that *all* the patterns for the hard problems, and *none* of the patterns for the easy one (except 6a) call for two positions in immediate memory. To extrapolate these more difficult sequences, the subject has to keep his place in two separate lists, but only in one at most, for the easier sequences. Moreover, to build up the patterns for the former sequences, the subject had to detect and keep track of relations on two distinct lists, as against one for the latter sequences.

An alternative hypothesis would be that the length of period was the source of difficulty. It is true that all the patterns with a period of four or more symbols (patterns 5, 7, 11, and 14) are among the hard ones; but patterns 12, 13, and 15, which have periods of three, are hard; while patterns 3, 4, 8, and 10, which also have periods of three, are easy. Although the evidence is far from conclusive,

Table 5. Comparison of Twelve Subjects with Variant D of Program: Time per Problem.

Problem Number	Seconds per Subject		Seconds
	Subjects Who Solved	*All Subjects*	*Program D*
1	**6.0**	**6.0**	**9**
2	**3.8**	**3.8**	28
3	**24.7**	**23.0**	18*
4	**16.8**	**16.8**	**23**
5	27.5	40.6	35
6	37.0	31.4	**19**
7	37.8	49.2	19*
8	**24.9**	**24.9**	**23**
9	**18.8**	**28.7**	**17**
10	**20.9**	**20.7**	**18**
11	**21.5**	37.3	35
12	49.8	49.0	**24**
13	61.7	65.5	29
14	41.2	47.8	36
15	48.0	56.8	30

Note: Times below median shown in boldface.

*Program D failed to solve problem.

number of positions in immediate memory appears to be more closely related to difficulty than length of period.

We cannot undertake here a detailed analysis of the errors made by our subjects, but we can make one observation that helps explain why problem 9 appeared rather more difficult (in terms of failure to solve, not solution time) than its pattern description would have predicted. The main process, we have hypothesized, for solving these problems is to detect relaions between adjoining symbols, or symbols in corresponding positions of successive periods. But toward the end of the sequence in problem 9—the symbols tuttu—there are a number of spurious relations of "equals" and "next" that are not part of the pattern. Discovery of these relations, and failure to check them through the earlier part of the sequence, would lead to wrong answers. For example, the partial sequence given above could reasonably be extrapolated by annexing the symbol t:

COMPARISONS WITH PROGRAM
PERFORMANCE

We have seen that one part of our theory —the pattern descriptions—allows us to make predictions about the relative difficulty of serial pattern problems for human subjects. It may be objected that the test is subjective, since we cannot know that the patterns used by the subjects are the same as those we have written down. The objection would be more convincing if it could be shown that the patterns could be described in a manner quite different from the one we have proposed. But there is additional evidence we can bring to bear on the question, derived from the programs used to generate the patterns—the third part of our theory.

Of the several variants of the pattern generating program we have studied, variant C will be considered here, because it solved seven of the fifteen problems, hence found about half of them "easy" and half "hard." From table 4 it can be seen that the program solved none of the problems we have previously labeled hard and all

but one (problem 3) of the problems previously labeled easy. Hence the pattern generator also provides excellent predictions of the relative difficulty of the problems for human subjects.

A closer investigation of the program's failure with the hard problems showed that the difficulties arose specifically in keeping track of the lists associated with distinct positions in immediate memory. The program was incapable of organizing the parts of the pattern into an overall structure when two immediate memory positions were involved. We take this as additional evidence for the plausibility of our hypothesis that this was the locus, also, of the difficulties the less successful human subjects encountered. A more powerful version of the program, Variant D, overcame most of these difficulties and failed only on problems 3 and 7. A still more powerful version has solved all but problem 7.

A few more words are in order about problems 3 and 6. Problem 6 was solved by Variant C relatively rapidly, but the pattern discovered was 6b rather than 6a. With respect to problem 3, we must simply say that the program of Variant C was different from that of most of the human subjects. (It might be mentioned, however, that the fourth and sixth ranking in the group of twelve adult subjects also missed this problem.) The occurrence of a following b in sequence 3 led the program to attempt to use the relation of "next on the backward alphabet" instead of describing the pattern in terms of the circular list (a, b). It did not do enough checking to discover and correct its error. The majority of the human subjects either did not make that error or were able to correct it.

In the third column of table 4 we have recorded the times spent by Variant D on each of the fifteen problems. There is a modest positive correlation between the times taken by the program and the subjects (column 1), but the agreement cannot be claimed to be close. Analysis suggests that the time required by the program depended much more on *length of period* than did the time required by the human subjects. If we consider only the nine patterns of period 3, the correlation of times is very much improved. Since the theory does not postulate that the relative times required for the several elementary processes will be the same for the computer as for human subjects, there is no real justification for comparing human with computer times between tasks that have quite different "mixes" of the elementary processes.

Among the patterns of period 3, pattern 2 took the human subjects a very short time, but the program a rather long time. We would conjecture that in this case, the program was slow because it lacked a concept that most of the subjects had— the concept of repeating a symbol a fixed number of times (see tables 1 and 2). Thus, while the program discovered pattern 2a, we believe that most subjects represented the pattern in a manner more nearly resembling 2b.

We have mentioned these details because they illustrate how a theory of the sort we have proposed permits one to examine the microstructure of the data and to develop quite specific hypotheses about the processes that human subjects use in performing these tasks. Of course, to test these hypotheses we will require additional observations, particularly observations like those we have reported on problem solving tasks, which record not simply the success or failure of the subject, but as much detail as can be detected of behavior during the problem solving process. The possibility of confronting the theory with such detail greatly facilitates its testing and improvement.

CONCLUSION

In this chapter we have set forth a theory, comprising a language for pattern description and a program, to explain the processes used by human subjects in performing the Thurstone Letter Series Completion

task. We have devised measures of problem difficulty based on the pattern descriptions and upon the ability of variants of the program to solve particular problems. These measures of problem difficulty correlate well with measures derived from the behavior of the human subjects. By analysis of the pattern descriptions and programs, we have been able to form, and partially test, some hypotheses as to the main sources of problem difficulty. By detailed comparison with the human behavior, we have formed some conjectures about the detail of processes that can be subjected to additional tests in the further development of the theory.

We conclude on the basis of the evidence presented here that the theory provides a tenable explanation for the main pattern forming and pattern extrapolating processes involved in the performance of the letter series completion task. Different variants of the theory can be used to account for individual differences among human subjects in performing this task.

References

Feldman, J., Tonge, F. M., Jr., & Kanter, H. Empirical explorations of a hypothesis-testing model of binary choice behavior. In A. C. Hoggatt & F. E. Balderston (eds.), *Symposium on simulation Models*. Cincinnati: South-western Pub. Co., 1963, pp. 55–151.

Laughery, K. R., & Gregg, L. W. Simulation of human problem-solving behavior. *Psychometrika*, 1962, 27, 265–82.

Miller, G. A. Galanter, E., & Pribram, K. H. *Plans and the structure of behavior*. New York: Holt, 1960.

Newell, A., & Simon, H. A. Computer simulation of human thinking. *Science*, 1961, 134, 2011–17.

Newell, A. Tonge, F. M., Feigenbaum, E. A., Green, B. F., Jr., & Mealy, G. H. (eds.), *Information processing language-V manual*. (2nd. ed.) Englewood Cliffs, New Jersey: Prentice-Hall, 1964.

Empirical Tests of a Theory of Human Acquisition of Concepts for Sequential Patterns (1973)

with Kenneth Kotovsky

In chapter 5.1, we proposed an information processing theory of human acquisition of concepts for sequential patterns—specifically, patterns of the sorts used in the Thurstone Letter Series Completion Test. The theory was embodied in a computer program for performing the task, consisting of two parts: a *pattern generator* and a *sequence generator*. The pattern generator takes a patterned sequence of letters as input and abstracts from it a pattern description, "concept," or "rule" of the sequence; the sequence generator takes the pattern description as input and uses it to extrapolate the letter sequence.

Some empirical evidence was presented for accepting the computer program as a valid description of the processes used by human Ss in performing the same task. The evidence, however, was only aggregative, showing mainly that there was a substantial correlation between the diffi-

culty of the several problems for the human Ss (as measured by the number who failed to solve them) and the difficulty of the same problems for the programs (as defined by the number of variants of the program that failed to solve them). Additional evidence is needed before we can be satisfied that the theory gives even an approximate explication of the human processes.

The purpose of the present chapter is to present and examine a larger body of empirical evidence, from the behavior of fourteen Ss during the problem solving process; the order in which they looked at letters in a sequence, the hypotheses they formed about probable solutions, their methods for recognizing periodicity in the sequence, the manner in which they extrapolated it once they had discovered the concept, the types of errors they made, and so on. On the basis of this evidence, we can test the detailed hypotheses that are implicit in the organization and behavior of the computer program.[1]

This study was supported by Public Health Service Research Grant MH-07722 from the National Institute of Mental Health, Department of Health, Education and Welfare.

1. Additional data and analysis from this experiment can be found in Kotovsky (1970).

Since the publication of our previous paper, our theory has been examined and extended by several other investigators, including Pivar and Finkelstein (1964), Williams (1969), and Klahr and Wallace (1970). In the following discussion, we will draw upon their investigations as well as our own data. (See also Restle, 1970; Simon and Sumner, 1968; Gregg, 1967.)

HYPOTHESES

The basic components of the theory can be summarized in a set of hypotheses about the characteristics of the human behavior in this task. Each hypothesis describes some important characteristic of the computer program and its variants.

Processes

These hypotheses predict the manner in which *S*s proceed through the problem situation.

A1. *S* first discovers the periodicity in the sequence, then induces the pattern description (the *rule*) using this periodicity. (Example: abmcdm . . . has the period 3—abm, cdm, ...)

A2. When extrapolating a sequence, *S* first initializes the rule (marks his place on certain lists), then uses the relations of *same* (I, for "identical") *next* (N) and *backward next* (BN), or *predecessor*, to extrapolate.[2]

A3. *S* experiences difficulty when he must keep his place on more than one list in extrapolating. (Information for place-keeping is assumed to be held in short-term memory along with other dynamic information during extrapolation.)

---

2. We will later discuss a difference between the program and *S*s behavior on this point. The program executes its extrapolation by initializing at the *beginning* of the letter sequence as presented; *S*s usually initialize at some point near the end of the letter sequence, and extrapolate from there. Thus, the program, given abmcdm . . . , would initialize the alphabet at "a," and produce the extrapolation, abmcd-mefmg. . . . The human *S* would more often initialize at "c," say, and produce only cdme-fmg. . . .

Mechanisms

These hypotheses are assertions about the mechanisms or abilities that *S*s have available (stored in long-term memory) for solving these kinds of problems.

B1. *S* can recognize the relations of "same," "next," and "backward next" (or "predecessor") on the slphabet and breaks in sequences of such relations.

B2. *S* can induce a new list ("alphabet") from a given sequence and apply the N relation to extrapolate with it. (Example: from atbataatb . . . induce the list or alphabet b-a, and extrapolate—b . .a . .b . . , etc.) Such alphabetic lists are treated circularly, as in the example just given.

B3. *S* solves problems by generating and fixating a pattern description based on the relations (I, N, BN) named above.

B4. *S* can extrapolate a sequence by interpreting the pattern description.

B5. The language proposed by Simon and Kotovsky (see chapter 5.1), based on the above relations and processes, gives an empirically valid explication of *S*'s internal representations of patterns (pattern descriptions) and the behavior attendant on their acquisition and use.

Individual Differences

While our main concern will be with the communalities among *S*s, we will also comment on individual differences, in order to indicate the relative independence among the various submechanisms.

C1. The computer program can be varied by rearranging or subtracting small sets of instructions to simulate these individual differences.

Sources of Human Error

D1. *S* may be unfamiliar with an alphabet used in the sequence; may have an inadequate repertoire of relations; may detect, and be confused by, spurious relations in the sequence (example: the italicized I relation in urtustu*tt*); or may be unable to organize and record the relations he detects in a coherent pattern description.

METHOD

Fourteen *S*s were given fifteen Thurstone-type letter series completion problems. The *S*s' thinking-aloud verbalizations were recorded, and the order in which they observed the letters in the sequence was automatically recorded. The *S*s only observed one letter of the sequence at a time.

Subjects

The *S*s were fourteen Carnegie Institute of Technology (now Carnegie-Mellon University) male and female freshmen and sophomore students who were fulfilling an Introductory Psychology course requirement by participating in psychology experiments.

Materials and Apparatus

The test problems were presented on a display device consisting of a board containing fourteen vertical sliding wooden slats, each displaying a single letter of each of the fifteen test sequences. The next slat after the last letter displayed a large dot that signaled the end of the sequence for that problem. A set of horizontal black

pieces of heavy cardboard could be arranged to cover the entire surface of the display device with the exception of a narrow horizontal zone located just below the information for the current problem.

S viewed a letter of the sequence by pressing down on a slat, thus pushing the letter on that slat into the visible zone. Pressing the slat activated a switch connected to a keypunch, recording which slat was moved. Releasing the slat returned it to its original position, thus removing the letter from view.

The problems were of the type used by Thurstone (1941) except that *S* was required to extrapolate four letters instead of one. (The problems are shown in table 1.)

Procedure

S was seated at a table containing the display device and pencils. A microphone was placed about his neck and he then read a page of standard thinking-aloud instructions. Next, he was given a series of practice problems and, if he did not talk much while solving them, was encouraged to verbalize more. During the performance of the practice problems, his questions

Table 1. Difficulty Measures.*

	Mean Time		Number Correct			Variant C of Program; Solved (s) or unsolved (u)
Problem	Group of 14 Ss	Group of 12 Ss	Group of 14 Ss	Group of 12 Ss	Group of 67 Ss	
P1 cdcdcd	19.6/1	6.0/2	14/1	12/2	65/1	s
P2 aaabbbcccdd	33.7/2	3.8/1	11/6.5	12/2	61/2	s
P3 atbataatbat	114.5/10	23.0/5	10/10	10/4	60/3	u
P4 abmcdmefmghm	39.1/3	16.8/3	13/3	12/2	57/4	s
P5 defgefghfghi	111.1/9	40.6/10	11/6.5	2/15	45/9	u
P6 qxapxbqxa	162.4/12	31.4/8	8/12.5	8/7	48/7.5	s
P7 aduacuaeuabuaf	177.0/14	49.2/13	7/14	5/11.5	27/15	u
P8 mabmbcmcdm	73.9/5	24.9/6	10/10	9/5.5	49/6	s
P9 urtustuttu	87.1/7	28.7/7	6/15	5/11.5	43/10.5	s
P10 abyabxabwab	52.2/4	20.7/4	13/3	9/5.5	51/5	s
P11 rscdstdetuef	86.4/6	37.3/9	11/6.5	4/14	39/13	u
P12 npaoqapraqsa	149.6/11	49.0/12	13/3	5/11.5	42/12	u
P13 wxaxybyzczadab	175.8/13	65.5/15	8/12.5	7/8	43/10.5	u
P14 jkqrklrslmst	100.1/8	47.8/11	11/6.5	6/9	48/7.5	u
P15 pononmnmlmlk	199.6/15	56.8/14	10/10	5/11.5	34/14	u

*Rank order after slash /.

about the procedures or the problems were answered. At the end he was told the correct answers to the practice problems and asked if he had any questions. *S* then read the instructions for use of the display device, after which the operation of the device was demonstrated to him. The answer and information sheet was then given to *S*.

He was told that while he should work through the problems as rapidly as he conveniently could, he was to "work for accuracy and not speed in performing the problems, since speed is not an important factor in this experiment." He was then told to begin the first problem. At the conclusion of each problem, *E* announced "OK," to provide a clear indication on the tape of when the problem ended. The time for solution is the time between the first punch (first letter looked at) and the "OK" by *E*.

RESULTS

A brief sample of the data obtained from the card punch records is presented below. The tape-recorded verbalizations were transcribed, but analysis had to involve the original tapes as well as the type-written versions in order to correlate *S*'s verbalizations with the particular letter he was observing. The tape was also used to identify voice pitch changes, rhythmic punching, and voice cadences in naming letters—an important source of information about the processes used by *S*—and to obtain solution times.

In summary, the data we obtained were: what *S* said, his correct or incorrect extrapolations, the order in which he looked at the letters, the temporal patterns in his naming of letters, and the time it took him to solve each problem.

The data were organized into six categories: measures of problem difficulty, the feature or features of each sequence first noticed by *S*, descriptions of the concepts attained by *S*, the initialization of the concepts prior to extrapolation, the method of extrapolation, and *S*'s errors and sources of problem difficulty.

Difficulty

Numerous alternative measures of problem difficulty were computed from the data:

Subject 1—Problem 13

Punching Sequence	*Verbal Protocol*
W X A X Y B Y Z C Z A D A B	

W X A X Y B	. . . . Ah . . . my anticipation got fouled up.
W X A X Y B Y Z C Z A D A B	WXAX . . YB . . YZ . . AD . . AB. I'll go back over
W X A X Y B	these again . . . . . the same sequence . . . . .
W X A X Y B Y Z C Z A D A B	WXY . . BYZ . . CZA . . DAB
W X A X Y B Y Z C Z A D A Z	WX . . AXY . . BYZ . . CZA . . DAB. This works its way down through the alphabet. The first
Y B Y Z C Z A D A B	part confused me because I didn't know
C Z A D A B	where it came from . . BYZ . . CZA . . CZA . . DAB
A	

Subject 8—Problem 12

Punching Sequence	*Verbal Protocol*
N P A O Q A P R A Q S A	

N P A O Q A P R A Q S A	NPAOQAPRAQSA There seem to be a number of
N P A O Q A P R A Q S A	As. Let's go back and see if we can find
N P O Q P R Q S	the A over there. NPA . . OQA . . PRA . . QSA. So
N O P Q A	then the third letter of this thing would be
P O	an A. NP . . OQ . . PR . . QS . . NP . . OQ . . PR . . QS. So
P Q R S	NOPQ . . . . R . . P . . O . . . wait a minute—let's get
	this straight. P . . Q . . R . . S . . T and then RS.

median and mean times and numbers of runs through the sequence for all *S*s, for *S*s solving the problem, and for *S*s not solving it, and median and mean numbers of punches. The intercorrelations among these were so high (the lowest rank-order correlation was 0.81, and most of the correlations were over 0.9) that they can all be represented adequately by mean time for all *S*s (table 1). Table 1 also shows the number of *S*s, from among our 14, solving each problem; the numbers from the earlier groups of 12 and 67 *S*s, respectively, reported in chapter 5.1; the mean times for the earlier group of 12 *S*s and the list of problems solved and left unsolved by variant C of the computer program.

Table 2 gives the correlation coefficients (rank-order correlations, and in one case the point biserial) among the difficulty measures of table 1. There are high correlations between the times required by the *S*s in the two previous studies, run under different experimental conditions. The rather lower correlations between the items correct in the present and previous studies is probably due mainly to the fact that the range of the data was very small. A difference of four in the number of *S*s missing a problem in the present study meant a difference between first and tenth rank in difficulty. Similarly, in the group of twelve *S*s a difference of four in the number of subjects obtaining a correct solution could

determine whether a problem ranked seventh or fourteenth in difficulty.

We will see later that the specific conditions under which the *S*s worked affected the difficulty of solving particular problems. The fourteen college *S*s of the present study viewed the letters of each sequence singly, as we have seen. The sixty-seven high school *S*s of the one earlier study were tested as a group, with all the letters and problems visible at once; the twelve *S*s of the other previous study were tested individually, with all letters visible, and with the importance of speed emphasized in their instructions.

Table 2 also shows high correlations among the difficulty measures of all three studies (except the number-correct measure of the present study), on the one hand, and the difficulties experienced with the different problems by variant C of the computer program, on the other. Among the fourteen *S*s in the present study, the mean number of problems missed (out of fifteen) was 3.9, and the range was 0 to 8.

First Feature Noticed

Table 3 summarizes which features of each sequence were noted first by *S*s. Features may be noticed after a smaller or larger part of the sequence has been examined. For example, on P1, S14 noticed the periodic repetition of the letter C (an ⟨I⟩

Table 2. Intercorrelations of Difficulty Measures.

		(1)	*(2)*	*(3)*	*(4)*	*(5)*	*(6)*
Mean time (group of 14 *S*s)	*(1)*	—					
Number correct (group of 14 *S*s)	*(2)*	0.62					
Number correct (group of 12 *S*s)	*(3)*	0.59	0.34*				
Number correct (group of 67 *S*s)	*(4)*	0.78	0.48	0.87			
Mean time (group of 12 *S*s)	*(5)*	0.88	0.45	0.75	0.87		
Program C (point biserial correlation)	*(6)*	0.68	0.16*	0.58	0.62	0.78	

Note: * = not significant at 0.05 level; underline = not significant at 0.01 level.

Table 3. Priorities in Noticing Features.

Problem	Features Present	Number of Ss Noticing First
1	⟨I⟩	2
	N/	—
2	I/	3
	⟨N⟩	—
3	⟨I⟩	4
	⟨N⟩	1
4	⟨I⟩	4
	N/	1
	⟨N⟩	—
5	⟨I⟩	2
	N/	7
	⟨N⟩	—
6	⟨I⟩	8
	⟨N⟩	1
7	⟨I⟩	7
	⟨N⟩	—
	⟨BN⟩	—
8	⟨I⟩	3
	N/	1
9	⟨I⟩	7
	⟨N⟩	—
10	⟨I⟩	4
	N/	—
	⟨BN⟩	2
11	⟨I⟩	—
	N/	3
12	⟨I⟩	11
	N²/	1
	⟨N⟩	—
13	⟨I⟩	3
	N/	3
	⟨N⟩	2
14	⟨I⟩	—
	N/	3
15	⟨I⟩	1
	BN/	5
	⟨BN⟩	—

(Problems, reading down the first column: cdcdcd; aaabbbcccdd; atbataatbat; abmcdmefmghm; defgefghfghi; qxapxbqxa; aduacuaeuabuaf; mabmbcmcdm; urtustuttu; abyabxabwab; rscdstdetuef; npaoqapraqsa; wxaxybyzczadab; jkqrklrslmst; pononmnmlmlk)

Note: / = broken sequence; ⟨ ⟩ = periodic recurrence of relation.

feature) after he had looked only at the letters CDC. By contrast, on P5, S2 noticed the broken sequence (defg/), an N/ feature, on his second run through the entire sequence.

The evidence that S has noticed a feature may be his explicit verbalization of it, or it may be the beginning of rhythmic punching after a pause. Each noticing act attributed to an S was assigned a confidence rating (from 1—low—to—5—

high), based on the quality of the evidence available. Explicit mention of the feature was assigned a rating of 5; close rhythmic punching based on the feature, a rating of 4. In the following analysis, only inferences with confidence ratings of 3 ("Moderate"), 4, and 5 ("high") are included. In 89 of the total of 210 possible instances (14 Ss × 15 problems) we were able to determine with confidence rating 3 or greater what features S had noticed first (see table 3).

Let us see how consistent the data of table 3 are with the hypotheses we stated earlier.

"Same" Relation ⟨I⟩. Each of the fourteen *S*s noticed in one or more problems the relation ⟨I⟩, supporting the hypothesis that *S*s can recognize the periodic recurrence of the same letter through a sequence.

Periodic "Next" Relations ⟨N⟩ and ⟨BN⟩. Only 7 *S*s gave evidence of noticing the relation N when it occurred periodically through a sequence (hypothesis B2), and only two, the periodic occurrence of BN (hypothesis B3). This does not mean, of course, that the remaining *S*s were not able to detect these relations, but only that on no occasion was there evidence that these were the first relations detected.

These observations lead us to consider whether there was a consistent priority in noticing order.

Noticing Order. The priorities can be pretty well summarized by two "ceteris paribus" generalizations: (1) the I relation is noticed before the N relations and (2) relations involving broken sequences—I/, N/, and BN/—are noticed before periodic relations ⟨N⟩, ⟨BN⟩.

Let us consider features in the order: I/, ⟨I⟩, N/, BN/, ⟨N⟩, $N^2/$ (double next), ⟨BN⟩. In the one problem where I/ occurs, it is the sole feature that is noticed first (three instances). In the 14 problems where ⟨I⟩ occurs, it is noticed first 56 times out of 86. Of the remaining 30 instances where another feature is noticed first, N/ is involved 18 times, BN/ 5 times, ⟨N⟩ 4 times, $N^2/$ once, and ⟨BN⟩ twice. In the 8 problems where N/ occurs, it is the feature noticed first in 18 instances, yielding to ⟨I⟩ in 18. BN/ is noticed first 5 times, in one problem, and gives precedence to ⟨I⟩ once. ⟨N⟩ is noticed first only 4 times in 7 problems, and yields to other features 59 times. $N^2/$ precedes ⟨I⟩ (in 1 problem) only once in 12 instances; and ⟨BN⟩, in 3 problems, is noticed first only twice out of 18 instances. Thus, only when the two rules given above are in conflict (when both ⟨I⟩ and N/ or BN/ are present) is

there much ambiguity as to which feature will be noticed first.

Four problems, of two special types, account for 18 of the 23 instances where N/ or BN/ take precedence over ⟨I⟩. Two of these, P5 and P15, begin with a broken sequence (defg/ and pon/, respectively). The method of presenting the problems undoubtedly contributes to this result. All *S*s (even though they were not required to do so) began almost all problems by punching the slats in order from left to right.

This interpretation is supported when we compare the ranks of these problems in their difficulty for the present *S*s with their difficulty for the two previous groups of *S*s. It will be recalled that in the previous experiments, all the letters of the sequence were visible to *S*s at all times. Hence, attention was not directed to the initial sequence in P5 and P15 as strongly as it is by the arrangement of the present study, and these problems should have been relatively more difficult for the *S*s in the earlier studies. P5 tied for rank 6 in number of solvers in the present study; in the two previous studies, it ranked fifteenth and ninth. P15 ranked tenth in the present study; in one of the previous studies, it tied for eleventh rank, in the other it ranked fourteenth (see table 1). Thus, the altered arrangements of the present study made these problems easier.

P11 and P14, two of the other problems in which N/ took precedence over ⟨I⟩, also share a common characteristic: they consist of two "intertwined" sequences, each of period 2. These also proved easier, on the average, for the present *S*s than for the previous groups (see table 1).

In none of these four problems, P5, P15, P11, or P14, does a single letter recur periodically ⟨I⟩ through the entire sequence. However, there is such a persistent recurrence in the five problems, P1, P4, P8, P10, and P12, where ⟨I⟩ has precedence over N/. Hence, most of the inconsistency in ordering disappears if we make a distinction between an ⟨I⟩ relation that holds only for symbols in two successive periods and an ⟨I⟩ relation that persists through the sequence. The distinction would be more persuasive, of course, if it were not introduced *a posteriori*.

Nevertheless, the same distinction arises in the processes of the computer programs. A process that first detected the periodicity of the sequence, then looked for ⟨I⟩ relations in corresponding positions in successive periods and checked for consistency throughout the sequence, would notice the ⟨I⟩ relation in problems P1, P4, P8, P10, and P12, but not in P5, P11, P14, or P15. It will be noted that program variant C (see appendix 1), which behaved precisely in this way, succeeded in solving P1, P4, P8, and P10, but not P5, P11, P14, or P15. (It failed, however, on P12). We may conclude, that our theory gives us a good understanding of the order in which the *S*s noticed features of these sequences. In addition, the above data support hypothesis B1.

Additional Features

Several features of the sequences were noticed and mentioned by the *S*s that were not incorporated in our theory or programs. For example, at least eight different *S*s noticed in one or more problems that some items of the sequence were drawn from one end or another of the alphabet. If we represent by B, M, and E letters belonging to the beginning, middle, and end of the alphabet, respectively, then the sequence of problem 4 might be abstracted as: BBMBBMBBMBBM, and the sequence of P6 as MEBMEBMEB.

Another type of relation not hypothesized in the original model is based on counting. Thus, P12 involves a "double next" relation (labeled above N²), which can be derived simply by applying N twice. Similarly, the pattern in P2 is perhaps most easily characterized as "groups of 3," an iteration of the I relation. Counting abilities have been included in other models of sequential concept attainment (Pivar and Finkelstein, 1964; Gregg, 1967; Restle, 1970), and the theory would clearly be improved by incorporating them. This involves no fundamental change in the structure of the program.

Some *S*s went so far as to change parts of the sequences to counting sequences (substituting numbers for the letters and then employing the N relation on the alphabet of integers).

Periodicity

After noticing some significant feature or features, most *S*s find a periodicity in the sequence that they then use in constructing a pattern description. Where they do not find such a period or where they find the wrong one, they almost invariably fail to solve the problem. Explicit verbalizations indicating the discovery of a periodicity before going on to form a concept are frequent, occurring in 125 of the 210 problem protocols (60 percent). This evidence supports hypothesis A1. The hypothesis is also supported by the eye movement studies that were carried out by Williams (1969).

The *S*s' behavior departs in one respect from the model. Periodicity is determined by noticing I and N relations. In the computer program, information about relations that are noticed at this stage is not retained, but is regenerated during the second stage, when the pattern description is being built up. *S*s clearly retain much or all of this information and use it while building the pattern description. Thus, the current program separates the two phases of problem solving activity—detection of periodicity and pattern description—more sharply than do the *S*s.

Concepts (Pattern Descriptions)

The principal concepts attained by *S*s are described in table 4 in a language similar to that used in chapter 5.1, but with the proviso that additional elements necessary or useful for the adequate description of the concepts are introduced as needed. The chunks held in short-term memory are designated by M_1, M_2, M_3, M_4, etc. The N relation (finding the item next to the current contents of chunk M_1) is designated $N(M_1)$; repetition of the same letter, I, is designated by the name of the letter; and

Table 4. Concepts.

Problem	No. of Ss Exact Concept	Variants	Concept No.	Concept	Program Concept*	Initialization†
1	9		1	[C, D]	+	
2	7	1	1	$[3M_1, N(M_1)]$	+	$M_1 = A, D$
	4	1	2	$[M_1, M_1, M_1, N(M_1)]$	+	$M_1 = C, D$
3	2		1	$[A, T, M_1, N(M_1)]$	+	$M_1 = B$ on A, B
	2	2	2	[A, T, B, A, T, A]		
	1		3	[A, A, T, B, A, T]		
4	13		1	$[M_1, N(M_1), M_1, N(M_1), M]$	+	$M_1 = G, H, E, A$
5	8		1	$[N(M_2), M_1 = M_2, M_1, N(M_1),$ $M_1, N(M_1), M_1, N(M_1), M_1]$	+	$M_2 = F, D, E$
	4			Other		
6	7	2	1	[Q, X, A, P, X, B]	+	
	2	1	2	$[M_1, N(M_1), X, M_2, N(M_2)]$	+	$M_1 = Q$ on P, Q; $M_2 = A$ on B, A
7	5	1	1	$[A, M_k, N(M_k), U]$ $M_k =$ $(M_1, N(M_1))(M_2, BN(M_2))$		$M_1 = D, F$
		1	2	$[A, M_t + 1 \rightarrow M_t, M_k, N(M_k),$ $N(M_k), U]$ $M_k = (M_t, N(M_1), M_1)$ $(M_t, BN(M_1), M_1)$		$M_1 = D, C$
	1			Other		
8	11	2	1	$[M_1, N(M_1), M_1, M]$	+	$M_1 = A, C$
9	11	1	1	$[U, M_1, N(M_1), T]$	+	$M_1 = R, S, T$
10	13	1	1	$[A, B, M_1, BN(M_1)]$		$M_1 = W, Y$
11	8	2	1	$[M_1, N(M_1), M_1, M_2,$ $N(M_2), M_2]$	+	$M_1 = T, S, R, E$ $M_2 = E, C, U$
	2			Other		
12	6		1	$[M_1, N(M_1), M_2, N(M_2), A]$	+	$M_1 = N, P, Q$ $M_2 = P, Q, R, S$
	4	1	2	$[M^1 = M_2, M_1, N(M_1),$ $M_2 = M_1, N(M_1), M_1, A]$		$M_1 = Q$
	1			Other		
13	5	6	1	$[M_1, N(M_1), M_1, M_2, N(M_2)]$	+	$M_1 = W, A;$
	1			Other		$M_2 = A, D$
14	10		1	$[M_1, N(M_1), M_1, M_2,$ $N(M_2), M_2]$	+	$M_1 = J, L, T, S$ $M_2 = Q, S, M, L$
	2			Other		
15	4	1	1	$[M_1, BN(M_1), M_2, BN(M_2),$ $M_3, BN(M_3)]$		$M_1 = P; M_2 = O$ $M_3 = N$
	1	3	2	$[M_1, BN(M_1), M_2 = M_1, M_1,$ $BN(M_1), M_1, M_1 = M_2]$		
	3			Other		

*Indicates agreement with the rule proposed by Simon and Kotovsky, 1963 (chapter 5.1 in this book).

†Example: $M_1 = A, D$; $M_2 = E, T$ reads: some subjects set memory cell M_1 at letter A on the alphabet, some set it at D; some subjects set memory cell M_2 at E and some set it at T when beginning their extrapolation. Information in this column is occasionally less certain than the other information in the table.

positions in the period of the sequence are represented by operations in the pattern description. Using this notation facilitates the comparison of the present data with the behavior of the program.

In coding the concepts, however, we did not force them into the Simon and Kotovsky scheme (chapter 5.1), but introduced new elements and mechanisms as dictated by the data, thus permitting an empirical test of how well the original theory fit the new evidence.

Overall Fit of Data to Model. The data on the concepts generated by the Ss are summarized in table 4. In the column headed "Program Concept," concepts that are identical to those proposed in chapter 5.1, table 2, are designated by +. For twelve of the fifteen problems, the pattern description most frequently generated by Ss (including one tie) is identical to that proposed in chapter 5.1.

Some 177 concepts are described at a moderate (24) or high (153) level of certainty (out of a possible total of 210). Of these, 103, or 58 percent, were in complete detailed agreement with those proposed in chapter 5.1, while 74 were different from those proposed there. Of the latter, 16 were minor variants of those proposed. The remaining 33 concepts which failed to reach a high enough certainty level for inclusion in table 4 do not noticeably differ, to the extent that partial information is available, from those included in the table.

The general qualitative agreement between the pattern descriptions attained by the Ss of this experiment and the pattern descriptions proposed by the model of chapter 5.1 supports hypothesis B3, that Ss possess a pattern generator that solves patterns by generating and fixating a pattern description associating the relations I, N, BN, with the several positions within the period of the sequence. This agreement, together with the fact that Ss were able to use those concepts to extrapolate the sequences correctly in 80 of 97 cases, confirms hypothesis B4 that Ss possess a sequence generator that can interpret such pattern descriptions.

Finally, the fact that most of the concepts (177 out of 210) were describable at moderate or high certainty levels in the pattern language, supports hypothesis B5 that the language (in a somewhat expanded form) proposed in chapter 5.1 gives an empirically valid explication of S's internal representations of patterns and the behavior attendant on their acquisition and use. Only one of the concepts ($S2$, P12) was not easily describable in terms of the expanded language).

Concept 1 on P3, and Concept 2 on P6 confirm, for at least some Ss, hypothesis B2 that Ss can induce a new alphabet from a given sequence and apply the N relation to extrapolate it.

The Circular Next Relation. Both model and most subjects treated alphabets in a circular fashion. That is to say, on the alphabet a,b, the N operator applied to a yields b, and applied to b yields a. The regular English alphabet is also usually treated circularly, the N of z being a. Some Ss encountered difficulties with circular alphabets.

The Backward Alphabet. The first change in the model that is necessary to fit the data is to eliminate the backward alphabet as a separate entity to which the NEXT operator applies. The behavior of even those Ss who could work backward through the alphabet is more accurately described by encoding the process by a backward next (BN), or predecessor, operator that is applied to the ordinary alphabet. The possible need for this alternative method of characterizing backward movement in the alphabet was mentioned in chapter 5.1. The additional BN operator appears mainly in P7, P10, and P15. With this change in the model, thirteen more Ss on P10 and two more on P15 would be brought into agreement with it, reducing the number of discrepant cases from 74 to 59 and increasing the number of positive agreements from 103 to 118 (67 percent).

The BN operator is not used by all Ss, and even where used, is usually not used with the same facility as the N operator.

In fact, some *S*s only perform "quasi-BN" operations. They pick a point in the alphabet somewhat ahead of the letter they want to perform a BN upon; then moving down the alphabet, using N, they remember the immediately preceding letter as well as the current letter; so that when they reach the target letter, they also retain in memory the one before it, i.e., the BN of the target letter.

Hierarchic Patterns. A second change in the original model is necessary to describe more accurately the organization of the pattern descriptions used by many *S*s on P7, P11, and P14. A means must be provided for describing the hierarchic organization of these *S*s' pattern descriptions. In the pair of similar problems, P11 and P14, the second concept in each case involves a memory chunk we have labeled M_k, which points to a position on a two-item list. One item on this list names the subpattern (M1, N(M2), M2). Thus, the pattern description for these problems (rscdstde . . . . . and jkqrklrs . . . . .) involves a higher level switching between the two subpatterns—$(M_k N(M_k))$—and the production of different alphabetic sequences by each subpattern—(M1, N(M1), M1) and (M2, N(M2), M2). The introduction of such hierarchic elements in the descriptions of concepts constituted the only difference between eight pattern descriptions in this study and those predicted by chapter 5.1.

Counting Procedures. In addition to the two changes in the language for describing pattern descriptions discussed above, a third change was introduced to describe the pattern descriptions some *S*s generated on P7 as well as on P2, P3, and P15. On these problems they used counting procedures of various sorts. Thus in problem 2 the most frequent rule was (3M1, N (M1)), which seemed more appropriate for those seven *S*s than the related (M1, M1, M1, N(M1)) used by four *S*s and predicted in chapter 5.1. Other counting procedures involve keeping tallies in memory (designated M_t and M_s).

Extensions of the Model: Summary. The use of a tally combined with hierarchic pattern descriptions in P7 accounted for the differences between the concepts of four *S*s and those predicted in chapter 5.1. These together with the seven concepts using the counting procedure in P2, the eight concepts using hierarchic pattern descriptions, and the fifteen concepts using BN instead of N on the backward alphabet account for 34 of the 74 concepts identified in the current study that differ in any respect from those predicted in chapter 5.1. Thus the introduction of these three changes substantially improves the predictive capacity of the model without a great proliferation of new mechanisms.

Short-term Memory. A few of the concepts used by *S*s require more than two chunks, or place-keepers, to be held in short-term memory. We will have more to say below about the burden this places on short-term memory.

A different point concerning memory allocation that is only implicit in chapter 5.1 is that a recurring letter (the I relation determining M in abmcdmefm, for example) is assumed to be held in long-term memory, hence not to add a chunk to the short-term memory load. Short-term memory is used only for those portions of the pattern description that involve N and BN operators associated with continually changing positions on alphabetical lists. In the computer model also, application of the I relation involves a simple set of computer operations compared to the relatively involved operations for applying N or BN. A related distinction was made by Gregg (1967), who differentiated between the direct and indirect production of items from memory (operations M and $D(M_1)$) in the meta-language he used for his sequential patterns.

Whether the M_k chunks postulated for hierarchic patterns impose a short-term memory load is not easy to determine. The *S*s tend to use auxiliary procedures that have the effect of reducing the load of this information on short-term memory. Thus rhythmical shifts in voice pitch, or separate and independent extrapolation of the two sequences (even though the *S* has previously achieved a unified pattern description) reduce the simultaneous demands on short-term memory. Further experiments will be needed to confirm this conjecture, although in the present experiment *S*s using hierarchic procedures made fewer errors on problems involving two (P7) or three (P11 and P14) chunks in short-term memory than did the other *S*s. We will look later at the exact process they used for extrapolating.

Initialization

Once *S* has attained a pattern description from the sequence, he then uses that pattern description to extrapolate the sequence. Occasionally this temporal order is not followed strictly. Instead, *S* obtains part of a pattern description—say, for one position of the period—and extrapolates it; then obtains another part and extrapolates it; then obtains another part and extrapolates it.

Generally, in order to use a pattern description to produce an extrapolation, *S* first has to initialize—that is, set "pointers" in short-term memory to specific letters in alphabets associated with the pattern. Table 5 describes the 147 (of a possible 210) initializations about which information was obtained at a moderate (17) or high (130) level of certainty. The table indicates whether *S* initialized his memory cells at the beginning (B) of the presented sequence (thus reproducing the sequence as well as extrapolating it), at the end (E) of the sequence (thus producing only the extrapolation), or at some point in the middle (M) region of the sequence. Again, the initializations not included on the table (not discernible at a 3, 4, or 5 certainty level) do not, at rough inspection, appear different in this respect from those that do appear.

*S*s tend to use B or M initializations on harder problems and E initializations on easier problems. A majority of *S*s used E

Table 5. Initialization.

Problem		B	M	E	Other
P1	cdcdcd			4	
P2	aaabbbcccdd	1	1	5	
P3	atbataatbat	3		4	
P4	abmcdmefmghm	1	1	7	1
P5	defgefghfghi	2	1	7	
P6	qxapxbqxa	3	4	2	
P7	aduacuaeuabuaf	4	1	4	3
P8	mabmbcmcdm	3	2	5	
P9	urtustuttu	7		3	1
P10	abyabxabwab	3		7	
P11	rscdstdetuef	3		7	2
P12	npaoqapraqsa	5	1	4	1
P13	wxaxybybzczadab	5	3	4	2
P14	jkqrklrslmst	7		3	1
P15	pononmnmlmlk	6		3	
		53	14	69	11

Note: B = beginning; M = middle; E = end.

or in one case E and M initializations on seven of the eight easiest problems, but B or M initializations on all but one of the seven hardest problems. The exceptions were easy P14 and hard P3. There is no significant difference discernible between good and poor *S*s in their choice of types of initializations.

Extrapolation

Table 6 contains information about the last operation performed by the *S*s: the actual extrapolation from the initialized pattern description. Information is presented in the table for 174 extrapolations (out of a possible 210), 137 at a high certainty level, and 37 at a moderate certainty level. Table 6 distinguishes extrapolations by positions, from those by period, and from mixtures of the two.

In extrapolating by *position*, the letters occupying a specific position in the period of the answer are initialized and extrapolated separately from the letters occupying other positions. When a problem is classified as extrapolated by position, every position for that problem was initialized and extrapolated separately. In contrast,

Table 6. Extrapolation.

Problem		STM Chunks	Extrapolation Method			Percent within period
			By Position	Mixed	Within period	
P1	cdcdcd	one			7	100
P2	aaabbbcccdd	one			14	100
P3	atbataatbat	one	2	1	7	70
P4	abmcdmefmghm	one		3	10	77
P5	defgefghfghi	several		1	11	92
P6	qxapxbqxa	one	2	1	9	75
P7	aduacuaeuabuaf	several	7	3	3	23
P8	mabmbcmcdm	one		3	9	75
P9	urtustuttu	one	1	2	9	75
P10	abyabxabwab	one	1		10	91
P11	rscdstdetuef	several		10	1	9
P12	npaoqapraqsa	several	7	1	4	33
P13	wxaxybyzczadab	several	1	4	7	58
P14	jkqrklrslmst	several	1	9	3	23
P15	pononmnmlmlk	several	6		6	50
All problems	Total		28	38	110	62
	One chunk		6	10	75	84
	Several chunks		22	28	35	41

other Ss extrapolated the sequence *by period*, that is, by iterating through the complete pattern description to generate sequentially a letter for each position. Of the 176 entries on table 6, 110 are extrapolations by period, 28 extrapolations by position, and the remaining 38 are mixed.

Ss may (and often do) extrapolate a sequence correctly without ever assembling a complete pattern description, when extrapolating either totally or partly by position. Even when they obtain a complete pattern description, they do not in these cases of extrapolation by position use the pattern description as a unified memory structure to produce the extrapolation, but rather use it piecemeal. $S2$'s verbalizations on P11 illustrate the point: "Letters are in groups of two by two.... We start off with a CD then something like a TU and this alternates. Each little series advancing by one letter each time," or $S14$ on P14, "... two series of two, each increasing." In some more extreme cases, S describes part of the sequence, extrapolates it before generating any sort of total pattern description, and then proceeds to

do the same for another part of the sequence.

In the sixty-six cases where Ss extrapolate by position, wholly or partly, they need not store a complete pattern description along with all the short-term memory pointers and their associated lists. In doing piecemeal extrapolation, the load on memory is therefore much reduced. In addition, the tasks of assembling and arranging the parts of a total pattern description in memory are substantially reduced. While the use of piecemeal extrapolation was suggested by various pencil marks on the problem sheets administered to the earlier groups of twelve and sixty-seven Ss, the data from the present study constitute the first strong evidence for this practice.

In all cases where more than two short-term memory cells were used in a pattern description, the extrapolations were either partially or totally by position. Thus what seemed to be a violation of the hypothesized limitations on short-term memory (hypothesis A3) was not, since piecemeal extrapolations do not require all the pointers to be retained simultaneously in memory.

The method of extrapolation also affects problem difficulty, as will be seen in the next section.

A similar question arises of the memory burden imposed by M_t or M_k tallies. There were (see table 4) seven uses of M_k tallies, three uses of M_t tallies, and four uses of an M_k and M_t tally within the same pattern description. Initialization information of moderate or high certainty was obtained for eleven of these fourteen cases. In all but one of the eleven cases, the sequence was extrapolated, in whole or part, by position. In the one remaining case ($S6$ and $P3$) S erred in his extrapolation. Thus in no case did S use an M_k or M_t tally in his pattern description to produce a successful extrapolation, except by piecemeal extrapolation. Hence the apparent memory load on S in these cases, inferred from the pattern description, is substantially higher than the actual load. Of course, the causal arrow may have run in the opposite direction: the high memory load implied by the description forcing the piecemeal extrapolation.

In the majority of cases (110 out of 176) Ss extrapolate the total pattern description (extrapolation by period) in support of hypothesis B4; that Ss in performing the final part of their task, do possess a "sequence generator" that utilizes the list processes previously discussed.

Errors and Sources of Problem Difficulty

Table 7 presents data on those mistakes made by the Ss that could be diagnosed at moderate and high certainty levels. Of the 54 mistakes made by the Ss, 35 were analyzed at a high level of certainty, and 8 with moderate certainty. Eleven additional mistakes contained too little data for analysis.

Extrapolation Errors and Concept Errors. The most frequent errors were in extrapolating correct concepts. There were 27 extrapolation errors, 11 errors in concepts, and 5 identifiable errors in both the concept and the process of extrapolation.

Of the 27 extrapolation errors, 15 occurred when Ss began their extrapolation at an incorrect part of the sequence. The next most frequent type of extrapolation error involved Ss who obtained a correct pattern description, but who were unable to use it to produce a correct extrapolation. Problem 9 caused 7 of the 27 extrapolation errors, because the repeated U in position

Table 7. Analysis of Diagnosable Errors (by Problem).

Problem		Chunks	Concept	Extrapolation	Both
				Error in	
P1	cdcdcd	one			
P2	aaabbbcccdd	one		3	
P3	atbataatbat	one	1		
P4	abmcdmefmghm	one		1	
P5	defgefghfghi	several	1	1	
P6	qxapxbqxa	one	2	2	
P7	aduacuaeuabuaf	several	1	3	1
P8	mabmbcmcdm	one	1	2	1
P9	urtustuttu	one		7	
P10	abyabxabwab	one	1		
P11	rscdstdetuef	several	2		1
P12	npaoqapraqsa	several		1	
P13	wxaxybyzczadab	several	2	3	
P14	jkqrklrslmst	several		1	1
P15	pononmnmlmlk	several		3	1
			11	27	5

1 conflicted with the U of the RSTU series in position 2. Six *S*s initially obtained correct concepts but altered them when they tried actually to use them in extrapolating. These errors all occurred on problems 8, 11, 13, and 14, which are analogous to double-alternation problems. In these cases, the *S*s tended to simplify the patterns, converting them to straight alphabetic sequences.

The remaining major sources of errors involve incorrect concepts, including approximations. These approximations all involve selecting certain parts or features of the presented sequence, ignoring other features or parts, and producing an extrapolation that fits the selected parts. In most cases, the problem is reduced to a simpler one by ignoring information that would contravene a proposed pattern.

The remaining cases in which *S*s did not obtain correct concepts involved failure to find the correct periodicity.

An examination of hypotheses A3 and D1, which postulated sources of problem difficulty, shows good agreement with the data. The only major source of difficulty not adequately predicted by the hypotheses is the frequent occurrence of the "double alternation" mistakes.

The relative paucity of instances where an *S* was unable to apply BN or use the alphabet correctly accounts for the poor agreement between the performance of newer variants of the computer program, which were designed to simulate these specific deficiencies, and the behavior of individual *S*s. Thus when specific abilities (to recognize and record N or BN relations either by position or by period) are removed from the program, or their order of application is changed, the resulting "crippled" versions of the program miss different problems (appendix 1) from those most often missed by the *S*s. The primary sources of problem difficulty for human *S*s are the presence of spurious relations, the inability to keep place on initialization, the failure to record a coherent pattern description that accurately keeps track of positions within the period, and the difficulty of simultaneous placekeeping on two series;

rather than ignorance of particular alphabets or relations.

Placekeeping as a source of error. A more detailed examination of hypothesis A3, which predicts that *S*s will have difficulty utilizing more than one placekeeper (memory cell) during extrapolation, reveals that while this difficulty caused some mistakes, it was more frequently seen (1) in its contribution to the *S*s' inability to assemble and/or use coherent pattern descriptions, and (2) in the *S*s avoidance of the memory burden by extrapolating by position. Thus, from table 6, on problems P1, P2, P3, P4, P6, P8, P9, and P10, where the *S*s almost always used no more than one placekeeper in short-term memory, they extrapolated partly or wholly by position 16 percent of the time, while on the remaining problems (P5, P7, P11, P12, P13, P14, and P15), where they usually used more than one chunk in their pattern descriptions, they extrapolated partly or wholly by position 59 percent of the time. This tendency for *S*s to extrapolate in piecemeal fashion when the pattern description involves more than one chunk in short-term memory strongly supports hypothesis A3.

A comparison of the difficulty rankings of the fifteen problems for the present group of *S*s with the average of their rankings for the two previous groups of *S*s casts further light on the relation of placekeepers to difficulty. For the comparison, we use the rankings, in table 1, by numbers of *S*s who solved the several problems correctly. The more difficult problems have the higher rankings.

In the two previous studies, the seven problems calling for multiple placekeepers in their descriptions ranked among the top eight problems in difficulty. (Average rank for these seven problems was 11.7; for the other eight problems, 4.75). In the present study, the same seven problems ranked only slightly higher than the remaining eight in difficulty. (Average ranks, from table 1, 8.4 and 7.6, respectively.)

The main reason for the difference appears to be that, in the present study, the *S*s often avoided the difficulty of retaining two or more placekeepers by extrapolating by position, instead of by period. Of the three *S*s who used two placekeepers in their description of the concept for problem 6, two made errors; only two of the nine who used a single placekeeper for this problem made errors. Presumably, the anticipation of these difficulties made *S*s avoid procedures which required them to keep several chunks in short-term memory when they could avoid it.

Summary. Our findings support hypotheses A3 and D1. An additional source of error not previously hypothesized is the tendency for subjects to convert double alternations to straight alphabet sequences. The tendency of the "poor" *S*s occasionally to use three or more placekeepers in contrast to other subjects solving the same problems is another source of error for these subjects.

CONCLUSION

The current study attempts to record details of human behavior in the problem solving process so as to test the hypotheses generated by the theory and computer model presented in chapter 5.1.

The data on *S*s' behavior were obtained in two main ways: from verbalizations and from records of a presentation device that required subjects to observe one letter at a time. This sequential presentation can be expected to influence the concept-forming behavior exhibited by the *S*s, especially noticing behavior, on problems involving N/ or BN/ relations. Thus, the single letter presentation task is a little different from that used in the earlier study. The general and specific areas of agreement between *S*s' performance in the current task and the previous two groups' performances, however, together with the data on *S*s' eye movements during problem solving in which the total sequence was visible (Williams, 1969), yield strong evidence for the similarity of most of the behavior exhibited in the two types of situations. No important differences were found between the *S*s' behavior in the eye movement study and that obtained with the more controlled single letter presentation modes. We conclude that the experimental task in this study is similar enough to the task used previously to constitute a reasonable test of the theory derived from *S*s' performances on the earlier task. Some modest changes in the model of chapter 5.1 are suggested by the findings of this study, specifically, an enlargement of the pattern description language both to handle counting or tally operations and to reflect the hierarchical nature of certain concepts.

If the model is to simulate more accurately the errors made by the *S*s, plausible means must be found for decreasing its ability to keep its place in the initialization and iteration of the pattern description and its ability to relate positions in the periodicity of the sequence. Another substantial difference between the error behavior of the model and that of the *S*s is that the computer always initializes its pattern description at the beginning of the sequence, while the *S*s do this only two-fifths of the time. On problems where no mistakes are made, this difference in behavior yields no difference in the output. But on problems involving a mistake, the difference in starting point of the extrapolations often produces gross differences between the computer's erroneous extrapolation and the *S*s.

On the other hand, many of the *S*s making errors of initialization did so because of a built-in rigidity somewhat similar to that of the computer. They tended to start their extrapolations at the beginning of a period rather than at the end of the presented sequence.

The last change needed in the model to reproduce more adequately the *S*s' errors is a double alternation mechanism that would cause the insertion of extra Ns in those concepts that contain such double alternation sequences.

The testing of the individual hypotheses deduced from the model against the behavior of the *S*s yielded excellent agreement between the hypothesized behavior and the actual behavior in all respects save those noted above. In addition, the experiment demonstrates the fruitfulness of the pattern description language for decribing behavior in tasks of this type.

The analysis of human behavior presented in the present study demonstrates that the specific hypotheses incorporated in the computer program, the Concept Former, and generated by the behavior of that program provide a useful framework for organizing observations of behavior, are testable, and are (with the exceptions and additions previously noted) confirmed.

In addition, the broad applicability to quite different tasks (Gregg, 1967; Simon and Sumner, 1968) of the mechanism and relations that constitute our model of sequential pattern recognizing behavior argues for the possibility of using the model to go beyond the prediction of specific behaviors to the discovery of general mechanisms that operate over broad ranges of human behavior.

Appendix 1. Problems Missed by Different Variants of the Computer Model.

Variants of the Program	No. of Major Abilities (Subroutines) included in this Version of the Model[†]	Problems Missed														
		1	*2*	*3*	*4*	*5*	*6*	*7*	*8*	*9*	*10*	*11*	*12*	*13*	*14*	*15*
A*	4		x		x	x		x	x	x	x	x	x	x	x	x
B*	4			x		x		x				x	x	x	x	x
C*	4			x		x		x					x	x	x	x
D*	4			x				x								
E	4	x	x		x			x								x
F	4	x	x		x			x								x
G	4			x				x								
H	4							x								
I	4	x			x			x								x
J	4							x								
K	4															
L	3			x	x			x								
M	3	x	x		x			x								x
N	3			x				x								
O	3			x				x								
P	2		x	x				x								
Q	2		x	x				x								
R	1	x		x	x		x	x	x	x	x		x			
S	1		x		x	x		x	x	x	x	x	x	x	x	x
T	1		x	x	x	x		x	x	x	x	x	x	x	x	x
U	1	x	x	x	x	x	x	x	x	x	x	x	x	x	x	x

*Variants reported in Simon and Kotovsky, 1963 (chapter 5.1 in this book).

[†]The order of their use in attacking a problem was independently varied as was the degree of refinement of individual subroutines in a few cases.

References

Gregg, L. W. Internal representations of sequential concepts. In B. Kleinmuntz (Ed.), *Concepts and the structure of memory*. New York, Wiley, 1967, 107–42.

Klahr, D., & Wallace, J. G. An information processing analysis of some Piagetian experimental tasks. *Cognitive Psychology*, 1970, 1, 358–87.

Kotovsky, K. An empirical test of the Simon & Kotovsky "concept former" model of human letter series sequence extrapolation behavior. Unpublished M. S. thesis, Carnegie-Mellon University, 1970.

Newell, A., & Simon, H. A. *Human problem solving*. Englewood Cliffs, N.J.: Prentice-Hall, 1972.

Pivar, M., & Finkelstein, M. Automation using LISP, of inductive inference on sequences, 125–216. In E. C. Berkeley & D. Bobrow (Eds.), *The programming language LISP*. Cambridge, Mass.: Information International, 1964.

Restle, F. Theory of serial pattern learning. *Psychological Review*, 1970 (November), 77, 481–95.

Simon, H. A., & Kotovsky, K. Human acquisition of concepts for sequential patterns. *Psychological Review*, 1963, 70, 534–46. Reprinted as chapter 5.1 in this book.

Simon, H. A., & Newell, A. Information processing in computer and man. *American Scientist*, 1964, 52, 281–300.

Simon, H. A., & Sumner, R. K. Pattern in music. In B. Kleinmuntz (Ed.), *Formal representation of human judgment*. New York: Wiley, 1968, 219–50.

Thurstone, L. L., & Thurstone, T. G. *Factorial studies of intelligence*. Chicago: University of Chicago Press, 1941.

Van de Geer, H. P., & Jaspers, J. F. M. Cognitive function. In P. R. Farnswort, O. McNemar & Q. McNemar (Eds.), *Annual Review of Psychology*, 1966, 17, 145.

Williams, D. S. Computer program organization induced from problem examples. Doctoral dissertation, Carnegie-Mellon University, 1969. Revised version published in H. A. Simon & L. Siklóssy (eds.), *Representation and meaning*. Englewood Cliffs, N.J.: Prentice-Hall, 1972, 143–205.

5·3

Complexity and the Representation of Patterned Sequences of Symbols (1972)

In the pages of *Psychological Review* alone, at least four apparently distinct theories have been proposed during the past decade to explain how human subjects process patterned sequences of symbols (Leeuwenberg, 1969; Restle, 1970; Simon and Kotovsky, 1963; Vitz and Todd, 1969). Additional theoretical proposals have appeared in other journals and books (e.g., Feldman, 1959, 1961; Feldman, Tonge, and Kanter, 1963; Glanzer and Clark, 1962; Gregg, 1967; Klahr and Wallace, 1970; Laughery and Gregg, 1962; Pivar and Finkelstein, 1964; Simon and Sumner, 1968; Williams, 1969). These theories differ radically from earlier explanations (in the traditions of S-R theory or stochastic learning theory) by postulating specific encodings of the sequences and by predicting from the hypothesized encodings a number of characteristics of subjects' behavior (e.g., loci of their errors, the relative difficulty of different problems, judged complexity of patterns, and so on).

In this chapter it will be shown that these various theoretical proposals, so different in their surface appearance, derive from a common central core and that it is this commonality that accounts for their success in explaining behavior. Our analysis requires us to pay careful attention to the notations in which the patterns of sequences

are described (by subjects and by theorists); hence, the analysis may cast some light on the general psychological significance and implications of notational devices.

Representational (or "information processing") explanations of serial pattern processing generally postulate some kind of language or notation[1] for expressing or describing the patterns and one or more processes for inducing pattern descriptions from sequences, for storing descriptions, for reproducing sequences, and for extrapolating them. Not all the theories incorporate all these elements.

The theories have been applied to various kinds of sequential material, including binary sequences (Feldman, 1959, 1961; Glanzer and Clark, 1962; Restle, 1967),

---

This work was supported in whole or in part by Public Health Service Research Grant MH-07722 from the National Institute of Mental Health. I am grateful to William G. Chase, Lee Gregg, David Klahr, Kenneth Kotovsky, Allen Newell, and Paul C. Vitz for comments on an earlier draft.

1. I will not distinguish systematically between the terms "language" and "notation," but will generally use the former to refer to the broader features of a representation and the latter to refer to the more particular features of a representation.

sequences of letters and/or digits (Restle, 1970; Simon and Kotovsky, 1963; Vitz and Todd, 1969), linear geometric figures (Leeuwenberg, 1969), intelligence test items (Williams, 1969), and musical scores (Restle, 1970; Simon and Sumner, 1968).

The tasks that have been used to test the various representational theories differ not only in the kinds of patterned sequences they use but also in what they ask the subject to do. In some cases, he must remember and reproduce a finite (or cyclically recurring) sequence (e.g., Gregg, 1967; Laughery and Gregg, 1962; Restle, 1967, 1970; Vitz and Todd, 1969); in others, he must extrapolate a partial sequence—that is, predict its continuation (e.g., Feldman, 1959; Simon and Kotovsky, 1963; Williams, 1969); in still others, he must rank different sequences by complexity (e.g., Leeuwenberg, 1969; Vitz and Todd, 1969).

Several of the basic elements that are incorporated in the representational languages can be found in work that predates these theories. Runs of identical symbols, for example, and simple and double alternations were discussed by earlier theorists (see e.g., Estes and Burke, 1955; Goodnow and Pettigrew, 1955). I limit this comparison, however, to contemporary information processing analyses of the phenomena.

INFORMATION PROCESSING AND INFORMATION THEORY

Information theory provides one direct method for measuring the complexity of sequences, by equating complexity with amount of information. Among the approaches under discussion here, the theory of Vitz and Todd (1969) is based on this information theoretic measure of complexity.

The amount of information in a patterned sequence, in information theoretic terms, is equal to the number of symbols required to describe the sequence when the maximally efficient code is used. If the coding alphabet consists of the binary digits, 0 and 1, then the information content of a sequence is equal to the number of

such digits, or bits, in its code when it is coded efficiently. What code will be most efficient for representing a set of sequences depends both on the collection of sequences that belong to the set and on the relative frequency with which they occur. An encoding can be made more efficient for a given set of sequences by assigning short codes to sequences that occur frequently.

Suppose, for example, that five sequences have been encoded by the twelve-symbol binary strings: 111100001111, 111111100000, 110000110000, 111111111111, and 010101010101, respectively. Suppose that the first and fourth of these sequences occur somewhat more frequently than the second and third, and that the fifth is exceedingly rare. Then we can encode them more efficiently by making the transformations: $1111 \rightarrow 111$, $0000 \rightarrow 110$, $111 \rightarrow 101$, $000 \rightarrow 100$, $11 \rightarrow 011$, $00 \rightarrow 010$, $1 \rightarrow 001$, and $0 \rightarrow 000$. With this scheme the first four sequences are encoded: 111110111, 111101110000, 011110011110, and 111111111, respectively. The second and third sequences have codes of length twelve, as before, but the first and fourth now have codes of only length nine. If complexity is measured by code length, then in the original encoding, all the sequences were of the same complexity; while in the new encoding, the first and fourth are simpler than the second and third. But while these particular four sequences all have codes of the same or shorter length in the new encoding as compared with the original one, this is dramatically untrue of the fifth sequence. The pattern 010101010101, also twelve symbols in length, would be recorded as 000001000001000001000001000001000001—a string of thirty-six symbols. The price paid for shortening the codes of some sequences is to lengthen the codes of others. The total number of encodings that can be represented by binary strings of length n is exactly 2^n, independent of the code used. The recoding will nevertheless increase average code efficiency if the fifth sequence is sufficiently rare.

Thus, information theory does not provide us with an unambiguous index of sequence complexity, but only measures complexity relative to some particular code. The complexity rankings of the sequences in a set can be changed at will by altering the encoding scheme on which the index of complexity is based. If an index of complexity is to have significance for psychology, then the encoding scheme itself must have some kind of psychological basis.

Encoding Alphabet

Also, it is not obvious why, in measuring code lengths, the binary alphabet, consisting only of the symbols 0 and 1, should be employed, rather than richer alphabets —the ten-decimal digits, for example, or the digits supplemented by the letters of the Roman alphabet. If we measure complexity by code length in *symbols* instead of code length in *bits*, then the complexity of sequences can be reduced by using a larger coding alphabet, each symbol of which can convey several bits of information. The alphabet of digits allows more than three bits to be encoded per symbol ($10 > 2^3$), while the Roman alphabet can encode between four and five bits per symbol ($2^4 < 26 < 2^5$).

Psychological theory provides good reasons why code length should be measured in terms of symbols rather than bits. If we replace the term "symbol" by "chunk," then we see that this observation is at the root of Miller's (1956) chunking hypothesis. The chunking hypothesis asserts that human short-term memory is limited in the number of symbols (or chunks) it can hold, not in the number of bits of information it can hold. Similarly, the EPAM (elementary perceiver and memorizer) theory of verbal learning asserts (Simon and Feigenbaum, 1963) that fixation of information in human long-term memory requires a constant time per symbol (or chunk), and not a constant time per bit.

Of course, when measuring complexity by code length, we cannot admit arbitrarily large coding alphabets, for these would allow us to reduce complexity to any desired level. In the limit, we could assign one letter of the alphabet to each sequence in the population to be encoded, with the result that each sequence would have a complexity of exactly one symbol. The solution to this dilemma, derivable from the EPAM theory, is to admit anything as encodable in a single symbol that has become familiar through prior learning. Anything recognizable by a subject as a "chunk," as the result of previous training or experience, is assumed to be codable into a symbol. The available coding alphabet then consists of the set of such symbols.

That the complexity of sequences must be measured relative to the psychological characteristics of the subject can be demonstrated in a variety of ways. Perhaps the most trivial is to observe that literate persons in a culture that uses the Roman alphabet will judge the sequence A B C D E to be simpler than the sequence A C E D B. Illiterate persons, and monolingual Chinese and Russians may judge the two sequences to be equally complex. Clearly, then, the presence or absence of a particular alphabet stored in long-term memory can have a major influence on judgments of complexity.

Code Length and Pattern Complexity

The theory to be proposed here takes code length as the basic measure of sequence complexity. It is postulated that most subjects in our culture will use approximately the same coding alphabets and encoding procedures. The code length of a sequence, then, means the number of symbols in the encoding when the alphabets and coding procedures common to the culture are used. We may call this encoding the *common pattern* of the sequence, and we will measure the complexity of the sequence by the length, in symbols, of this pattern.

From this point of view, any particular pattern language implies a psychological (or sociological) assertion about the alphabets and coding procedures that a subject will use when instructed to process certain sequences. While subjects' pattern language is not directly observable, it has observable consequences. If two or more pattern languages predict different complexity orderings of the sequences in some set, then empirical observations of the relative difficulty that the subject experiences with members of the set allow, at least in principle, a choice to be made of the language that corresponds most closely to the actual encoding scheme he is using. This is the underlying logic of virtually all experiments using patterned sequences as stimuli.

Now, in fact, there is almost always a high correlation among different measures of pattern complexity when several such measures are applied to the same set of patterns. Since the presence of correlation is not logically necessary, it must result from the fact that the coding schemes actually invented by investigators share some basic common features, which also lie at the base of the coding schemes used by subjects.

The next section discusses the common elements that are incorporated in the coding schemes of Simon and Kotovsky (1963), Glanzer and Clark (1962), Simon and Sumner (1968), Leeuwenberg (1969), Vitz and Todd (1969), and Restle (1970), as well as the specific differences among these schemes. These six papers represent fairly well the range of alternative coding schemes that have appeared in the literature.

Pattern Languages

In serial tasks, both terminating and nonterminating sequences have been used. To simplify the treatment, regard all sequences as nonterminating. Thus, a sequence of finite length (e.g., 12321) will be assumed to repeat indefinitely (1232112321 12···). As is customary in programming notation, the asterisk, *, will be used as superscript to denote indefinite repetition: (12321)*.

Conventional and Descriptive Pattern Names

A sequence of symbols can be designated by a conventional name or by a descriptive name. (We call the latter the *pattern* of the sequence.) Thus "Fibonacci Numbers" is the conventional name of the sequence: 1 2 3 5 8 13 21 34 ····. This sequence can be named descriptively as "the sequence

each of whose members is the sum of the two preceding members." A descriptive name for a sequence, its pattern, provides the information required by an appropriate encoder to extrapolate the sequence indefinitely. A conventional name does not provide this information; hence if only the conventional name is communicated to a decoder, the latter must already have stored the description (or its informational equivalent) if it is to be able to extrapolate the sequence.

If a pattern consisting of a finite string of symbols is to describe an infinite sequence, then the pattern must define one or more relations between each element of the sequence and preceding elements, or between each element and its order number in the sequence. An example of a pattern of the first kind is provided by the familiar formula for the Fibonacci Numbers: $F(i) = F(i-1) + F(i-2)$. An example of a pattern of the second kind is provided by a formula for the sequence of squares, 1, 4, 9, 16 ···: $S(i) = i^2$.

A pattern, then, is a finite string of symbols that states the rule governing the indefinite continuation of a nonterminating sequence. The symbols of the sequence are numbered in order, beginning with 0. The pattern must express relations between the *i*th symbol as the dependent variable and one or more preceding symbols and/or constant symbols as independent variables. Thus, the language must be capable of expressing the relations themselves, the names of the symbols that enter as dependent variables, and the names of the symbols that enter as independent variables.

Consider, by way of example, the simple sequence:

$$ABCD \cdots \qquad (1)$$

In the pattern to describe a sequence, the letters of the alphabet employed in the sequence can represent themselves. The letter *n* will represent the relation of *next* on an alphabet. The *i*th symbol in the sequence will be represented by Si; and the relations of sum and difference of pairs of integers, by + and −, respectively. Using these notational devices, a pattern for sequence 1 is

$$So = A; Si = n(S(i - 1)); i(1:*) \quad (2)$$

where the last relation indicates that i is to range from 1 to infinity. Counting all punctuation marks as symbols, this pattern has length 24, which number we may therefore take as a measure of the complexity of sequence 1 in this encoding.

Let us consider, in turn, each of the components of such an encoding scheme: the relations it admits, the way in which it names symbols, and the way in which it notates iteration.

Relations

What relations are available for defining the pattern of a sequence depends on the properties of the set of symbols, S, from which the sequence is constructed. For any set of symbols, S, we can define the identity relation (s, for "same") on the product set $S \times S$. Using this relation, we can describe simple patterns. Thus the pattern:

$$AQAQAQ \cdots \quad (3)$$

can be defined by:

$$So = A; S1 = Q;$$
$$Si = s(S(i - 2)); i(2:*) \quad (4)$$

[This pattern can also be defined simply by: $S(2i) = A; S(2i + 1) = Q; i(0:*)$.]

If the symbol set, S, is ordered, that is, constitutes an alphabet, then we can also define on $S \times S$ the successor relation (n, for "next"), and its inverse (p, for "immediate predecessor"). Moreover, these two relations, together with s, are the only relations that are common to all ordered sets.[2] With two exceptions, discussed below, they are also the only relations that enter into the serial pattern tasks that have been used in psychological experiments and tests.

The relations s and n are central to the

pattern language developed by Simon and Kotovsky (1963) and extended by Simon and Sumner (1968) and by Williams (1969). Both play an equally central role in Leeuwenberg's (1969) pattern language[3] and in Restle's (1970). Restle calls the s relation r (for "repeat") and the n relation t (for "transpose").

Glanzer and Clark (1962) and Vitz and Todd (1969) limit themselves to binary and ternary sets of symbols (the sets 0,1; a,b; and a,b,c), hence make no use of the n relation, but only of the s relation. Therefore, their pattern languages are both simpler and more limited in range of application than the languages used by the other authors.

We come now to two additional kinds of relations that are used by Simon and Sumner (1968; and subsequently by Restle, 1970) to describe certain patterns—relations that are relevant only to the alphabet of integers. With the integers, we may use, first of all, the relations of *sum* ($+$) and *difference* ($-$). These can be defined in terms of the successor and predecessor relations, as in the Peano axiomatization of arithmetic [e.g., $(i + 2) = n(i + 1) = n^2(i)$; $(i - 1) = p(i)$], but it is often more convenient, notationally, to retain the arithmetic relations as well as the successor and predecessor relations.

Finally, with the alphabet of integers, we may also define the *complement* relation (denoted ck, where k is an integer). To see what this means, consider the sequence:

$$123321 \quad (5)$$

Here $S5 = So$, $S4 = S1$, $S3 = S2$, or, in general, $Si = S(5 - i); i(0:5)$. Defining

---

2. More precisely, all other relations that are common to all ordered sets can be defined in terms of these, for these are the only relations required for the definition of an ordering.

3. The resemblance of Leeuwenberg's language to the others is not easy, at first, to detect underneath his notation. An integral sign plays the role of n in his language, and parentheses the role of s. Thus, the pattern $\int(1)$ describes the sequence $1234\cdots$ in his notation. That is to say, (1) denotes $(1)^*$, and the integral sign designates successive summations: 1, $1 + 1$, $2 + 1$, etc. In the notation of Simon and Kotovsky (1963), this same sequence would be encoded as $[\mu \leftarrow \text{integers}] (n(\mu))^*$; in Restle's (1970) notation, it would be encoded as $\mathcal{N}^*(1)$.

$ck(i)$ as the k's complement of i, we can write instead: $Si = S(c_5(i))$.

Restle (1970) introduces a relation which he calls m (for "mirror") in order to permit complementation. He does not, however, use the relation consistently, and hence his various examples do not all fit the same definition of it.[4]

In the example above, the complementation relation is applied to the postscripts designating the locations of symbols. If the sequence uses the alphabet of integers, the relation can also be applied to the symbols themselves. That is to say, sequence 5 can also be described by $Si = c_4(S(i - 3))$; $i(3:5)$; $Sj = (j + 1)$; $j(0:2)$.

In summary, all the pattern languages under consideration describe sequences with the help of the relations s, n, p, $+$, $-$, and ck, or some subset of these. The latter three relations are defined only on integers and are in any case definable in terms of n and p. The first three relations are defined on pairs of symbols drawn from any alphabet (ordered set); hence, they are common structural elements for virtually all kinds of linear patterns.

Designation of Symbols

While all the pattern languages use essentially the same small set of relations, they differ widely in the notation they employ to name or designate the symbols that enter into the relations. There appear to be three different ways to designate symbols: (1) naming them explicitly by their positions in the sequence (e.g., S_4 is the symbol that follows S_3 and precedes S_5), (2) displaying relations in the pattern in the order in which the corresponding symbols appear in the original sequence, so that the pattern becomes a "template" for the sequence,[5] and (3) noting successive runs of identical symbols by numbers corresponding to the run lengths.[6] In the examples thus far, we have used the first method,

naming each symbol explicitly by postscripting "S" with its order number in the sequence (numbering from zero). This is a very flexible notation, but it is not compact. Consider the sequence:

$$\text{ABMCDM} \cdots \qquad (6)$$

In this notation the sequence would be described by the relations:

$$\begin{aligned} &S_0 = \text{A}; \; S_{3i} = nS(3i - 2); \\ &S(3i - 2) = n(S_3(i - 1)); \qquad (7) \\ &S(3i - 1) = M; \; i(1:*) \end{aligned}$$

The postscripts do not reflect very clearly the periodic or hierarchic structure of sequence 6, in which each triad of symbols repeats the relations of the previous triad. The periodicity becomes more visible if each symbol is designated by a double postscript, the first component denoting the period, and the second, the location (0, 1, or 2) within the period. With this scheme, the second symbol in the sixth period would be designated $(S(5,1))$. The pattern can now be rewritten as:

$$\begin{aligned} &S_0 = A; \; S(i + 1, 0) = nS(i,1); \\ &S(i,1) = nS(i,0); \qquad (8) \\ &S(i,2) = M; \; i(0:*) \end{aligned}$$

This notation, employed by Simon and Sumner (1968), still does not fully reveal the structure of sequence 6, which consists of a simple alphabetic sequence (the first two symbols of each period) interwoven with a repetition of the letter M. The notation can be further simplified, using the second method of designating symbols, by writing down the relations in a definite order, and by introducing names for *working memories*.

---

4. The example in his figure 2, as well as the first two examples in his table 1, is inconsistent with his definition of the relation m.

5. More formally, this scheme retains some of the information about the order of symbols in the sequence by an order-preserving many-one mapping of symbols of the sequence onto subsequences of the pattern. The number of symbols mapped onto successive subsequences of the pattern defines the *period* of the sequence.

6. As we will see, this scheme is a specialization and abstraction of the preceding one that eliminates redundant symbols from the pattern, retaining only the superscripts that denote numbers of iterations.

A working memory, call it μ, contains the name of an alphabet and a pointer to a particular location of the alphabet. Moving the pointer locates the *next* location on the alphabet. Using this idea, we can notate the pattern of sequence 6 by:

$$[\mu\!\leftarrow\!\alpha]\,(n(\mu)\,n(\mu)\,\text{M})* \qquad (9)$$

which can be read: "Set the pointer in μ to the name of the Roman alphabet, α. Move the pointer one place down the alphabet [i.e., to $n(\mu) = \text{A}$], then one more place [i.e., to $n(\mu) = \text{B}$]; then produce the letter M; repeat these three processes indefinitely." (The square brackets in pattern 9 denote an operation that does not produce a symbol.)

This new notation abandons entirely the use of postscripts to designate symbol locations. Instead, the rules for the three positions in the basic triad are written down, one following the other, in order.

As a result of these two changes in notation—introducing working memories and dispensing with the explicit names for symbols at designated locations—the description is greatly abbreviated. In place of the 52 symbols in pattern 7, or the 51 in pattern 8, pattern 9 contains only 17 symbols. The notation of pattern 9 is essentially that introduced in Simon and Kotovsky (1963).

Restle (1970) later introduced a different device to permit the suppression of explicit names for symbols. He employed operations upon *sequences* of symbols, the effect of such an operation being to change all the symbols in the sequence in exactly the same way. To see the relation between his notation and that of Simon and Kotovsky, we denote by S_i a sequence of symbols, $S_1, S_2, \cdots$. Then we can define, for any operator, o,

$$o\{S_i\} = \{o(Si)\} \qquad (10)$$

so that, for example,

$$n\{\text{A,B,C}\} = \{n(\text{A}), n(\text{B}), n(\text{C})\}$$
$$= \{\text{B,C,D}\}.$$

Restle also allows concatenation of operators:

$$(o1, o2)\{S_i\} = o1\{S_i\}o2\{S_i\} \qquad (11)$$

that is, the effect of applying the concatenated operator, $(o1,o2)$, to a sequence $\{S_i\}$ is to produce the sequence $o1\{S_i\}$ followed by the sequence $o2\{S_i\}$.

Restle introduces one other useful notational device. Let a lowercase letter, o, designate any operator; then the corresponding capital letter, O, designates the concatenation of s with o. That is,

$$O = s,o \qquad (12)$$

so that $O\{S_i\} = s\{S_i\}o\{S_i\} = \{S_i\}\{o(S_i)\}$. While Restle's notational innovations are applicable only to very special classes of patterned sequences, they permit sequences belonging to these classes to be described perspicuously and compactly. Consider, for example,

$$\text{DEFGEFGHFGHI}\cdots \qquad (13)$$

In Restle's notation, this can be described by:

$$\mathcal{N}*(\mathcal{N}^3(\text{D})) \qquad (14)$$

where

$$\mathcal{N}^i\{S_i\} = \{S_i\}\mathcal{N}^{i-1}\{n(S_i)\};$$
$$\mathcal{N}\{S_i\} = \{S_i\}\{n(S_i)\}$$

whence:

$$\mathcal{N}*(\mathcal{N}^3(\text{D})) \rightarrow \mathcal{N}*(\text{D}\mathcal{N}^2(\text{E}))$$
$$\rightarrow \mathcal{N}*(\text{DE}\mathcal{N}(\text{F}))$$
$$\rightarrow \mathcal{N}*(\text{DEF }n(\text{F})) \rightarrow \mathcal{N}*(\text{DEFG})$$
$$\rightarrow [\text{DEFG }\mathcal{N}*(\text{EFGH})]$$
$$\rightarrow [\text{DEFGEFGH }\mathcal{N}*(\text{FGHI})] \rightarrow \text{etc.}$$

In the Simon and Kotovsky (1963) notation, the description of sequence 13 might take the form:

$$[\mu_2 \leftarrow \text{D}]\,([\mu_1 \leftarrow \mu_2]\mu_1[n(\mu_1)]^3[n(\mu_2)])* \qquad (15)$$

Pattern 14 requires only nine symbols, while pattern 15 requires twenty-seven to describe sequence 13.

On the other hand, many sequences cannot be described at all in Restle's special notation—sequence 6 being a simple example. The reason is easy to see. In sequence 6, unlike sequence 13, the symbols of the ith period cannot be obtained by applying the same operator to the corresponding symbols of the previous period.

The notation used by Leeuwenberg

(1969) resembles most closely that of Simon and Kotovsky (1963). In fact, when the fifteen patterns of the Thurstone Letter Series Completion Test are encoded in both notations, the pattern length in the Simon and Kotovsky notation has a 0.8 correlation with the pattern length in Leeuwenberg's notation. Leeuwenberg used a rather elaborate system of punctuation to obviate the need for naming working memories explicitly. Essentially, his idea in encoding a pattern like sequence 6 is to describe separately each of the intertwined subpatterns, then to indicate which of the symbols in each period belongs to each of the subpatterns. Sequence 6, for example, is constructed from two subpatterns, one providing the first two symbols in each period; the other, the third symbol. [Details of Leeuwenberg's encoding, which involves the notation of "runs" of the subpatterns (see below) can be found in his paper.]

In the schemes of Glanzer and Clark (1962) and Vitz and Todd (1969), matters become simpler because of the restriction to binary (or ternary) alphabets and to the relation s. In the binary case, a periodic pattern can be described in terms of the successive run lengths of 1s and 0s, respectively. Thus, the sequence

$$001000111111 \cdots \qquad (16)$$

can be encoded as $(02135)^*$. (By convention the sequence starts with a run of 1s, in this case, of length zero.) The longer the runs, on average, the more efficient is this encoding. The least parsimonious description—that for a simple alternation—is simply a sequence of 1s.

With a ternary alphabet, each run can be described by juxtaposition of the symbol and run length. Thus,

$$AAABBBCCC \cdots \qquad (17)$$

can be described as $(A3B3C3)^*$.

In terms of our previous notations, we could describe sequence 16 by:

$$((s(0))^2 (s(1))^1 (s(0))^3 (s(1))^5)^* \qquad (18)$$

Thus the run-length notation can be derived from the more general one by omitting all the redundant, predictable symbols

in the explicit notation and retaining only the superscripts.

Still more complicated codes may facilitate the description of special classes of binary patterns. If patterns consist, for example, of runs *and* simple alternations on a binary alphabet, then it may be efficient to recode into a ternary alphabet—$1 \to \alpha$, $0 \to \beta$, $01 \to \gamma$—and then use the ternary code suggested above for sequence 17 (cf. Feldman, 1961).

Where one symbol occurs much more frequently than the other in a binary sequence, a more efficient coding may be achieved by simply mentioning those positions in the sequence the are occupied by the rarer symbol, for example $S_1 = S_{12} = S_{19} = 1$. By convention, any symbol not explicitly mentioned is the common one (in the example, 0). This method of abbreviation is a special case of a more general Principle of Exceptions. Normal values are defined for certain symbols, and the symbol is not explicitly mentioned when it takes on its normal value. Thus, in the Simon and Kotovsky (1963) notation, we can take s as the normal value of the operator on a working memory, and simply write μ in place of $s(\mu)$ wherever the latter occurs.

Basically, all the representations we are considering describe sequences by defining the relations that determine symbols in terms of preceding symbols. The length of code for any given sequence (hence the complexity of the pattern) depends basically on the number of relations that must be defined. However, some coding economies can be realized for special classes of sequences by using the devices just mentioned; for example, by omitting mention of common elements, or by exhibiting explicitly only nonnormal values of symbols.

These devices are used by human subjects to achieve succinct descriptions of sequences. Glanzer and Clark (1962), whose method involved asking subjects to report patterns verbally, found that the subjects generally described binary patterns either in terms of runs (i.e., in a language like that used above to describe sequence 16) or by naming the location of the "exceptional" symbols (e.g., 1s in positions 2 and

Table 1. Correlation of Code Length, Information Content, and Judged Complexity of Four Sets of Patterned Sequences.

Variable		*Set of Sequences*			
		1	*2*	*3*	*4*
1. H_{VT} × complexity	r_{HC}	0.98	0.95	0.94	0.91
2. H_{VT} × code length	r_{HL}	0.92	0.79	0.91	0.88
3. Code length and complexity	r_{LC}	0.91	0.79	0.89	0.90
4.	r'_{LC}	0.90	0.75	0.85	0.80

Note: H_{VT} = Vitz-Todd information measure; code length = number of runs of identical symbols; complexity = judged complexity (sets 1–3), or number of reproduction errors (set 4). Data for the four sequence sets from Vitz and Todd (1969), tables 6, 7, 8, and 9, respectively. r'_{LC} = predicted correlation between code length and complexity. $r'_{LC} = r_{HC} \times r_{HL}$.

6—a simplification, for binary sequences, of the Simon and Sumner, 1968, language).

Vitz and Todd (1969), as previously noted, constructed an information-theoretic measure of pattern complexity. The encoding system underlying their measure was based on the detection in sequences of runs of individual symbols and runs of subpatterns (see Vitz and Todd, 1969, pp. 435–36). As a result, there is a very high correlation between their information measure and a simple count of runs. Table 1 shows, for four sets of data presented by Vitz and Todd, the correlation coefficients (1) between Vitz and Todd's information measure (H) and sequence complexity (C) as judged by subjects; (2) between H and length of code (L), based on runs; and (3) between C and L.

We see from table 1 that H accounts for from 80 percent to 95 percent of the variance in judged C of the sequences. Except in one case, where the correlation is 0.79, the correlation of H with L is around 0.9. Hence variation in code length accounts for about 80 percent of the variance in amount of information contained in these sequences. If H were the "true" estimator of C, and L an approximate surrogate for H, otherwise unrelated to C, then the correlation between L and C would be $r'_{LC} = r_{HC} \times r_{HL}$. As table 1 shows, the actual correlation, r_{LC}, is always larger than r'_{LC}. Hence code length makes a (small) independent contribution to the prediction of

complexity, over and above the part explanable by the relation of L to H.

In summary, the pattern languages we are examining use a variety of notations to designate the symbols between which specified relations hold. There is a trade-off, in general, between the generality of a notation—the range of pattern types it can describe—and its efficiency in describing particular types of patterns. Of the notations reviewed here, that of Simon and Sumner (1968) is the most explicit and general, but also the most "verbose" in designating locations. The Simon and Kotovsky (1963) notation is considerably more concise, giving up only a little generality. The notation of Restle (1970) is quite specialized but parsimonious where applicable. The coding schemes considered by Glanzer and Clark (1962) and Vitz and Todd (1969) are even more specialized and concise. They are obtained by omitting all the information that is redundant for the special sequences to which they are applicable.

Iteration and Hierarchy

Most of the coding schemes use numerical superscripts or subscripts to indicate repetition of pattern elements—operators, symbols, or subpatterns. Thus n^2 is a convenient notation for "next of next," so that $n^2(A) = n(n(A)) = C$. Similarly, $[\mu \leftarrow A](n(\mu))^3$ provides a shorthand for $[\mu \leftarrow A](n(\mu)$-

$n(\mu)n(\mu)) = $ BCD. We have seen how a run-length code can be derived by abstraction from such a notation for iteration:

$$11100111100 \rightarrow (1)^3(0)^2(1)^4(0)^2 \rightarrow 3242$$

The structure of patterns is not limited to simple periodicity, but may involve a hierarchy of periods. Restle (1970) has paid particular attention to hierarchic patterns, which were earlier used to a limited extent by Kotovsky and Simon (1973) and extensively by Simon and Sumner (1968) in their description of music.

Consider Restle's (1970) example:

$$1212232312122323\,65655545465655454 \tag{19}$$

The hierarchic phrase structure of this sequence can be made visible by punctuation:

$$(12\ 12)\ (23\ 23),\ (12\ 12)\ (23\ 23);\ (65\ 65)\ (54\ 54),\ (65\ 65)\ (54\ 54) \tag{20}$$

With our adaptation of Restle's notation, we can describe the sequence succinctly, thus:

$$C_7(S(N(S(N(1)))))), \tag{21}$$

and from this pattern we can regenerate the sequence again by successive steps:

$$
\begin{aligned}
&C_7(S(N(S(N(1))))) \\
&\rightarrow C_7(S(N(S(12)))) \\
&\rightarrow C_7(S(N(12\ 12))) \\
&\rightarrow C_7(S(12\ 12\ 23\ 23)) \\
&\rightarrow C_7(12\ 12\ 23\ 23\ 12\ 12\ 23\ 23) \\
&\rightarrow (12\ 12\ 23\ 23\ 12\ 12\ 23\ 23 \\
&\qquad 65\ 65\ 54\ 54\ 65\ 65\ 54\ 54) \tag{22}
\end{aligned}
$$

There is a serious objection to taking pattern 21 as a hypothesis of how a subject might encode sequence 20. As sequence 22 shows, regenerating the sequence from the pattern calls for a short-term memory capacity of at least sixteen symbols of the sequence as input.

An alternative encoding, based on the Simon and Kotovsky (1963) notation, avoids this difficulty. To explain it, it is necessary to introduce the concept of *push-down list*. A push-down list is simply a sequence that can be altered only by adding a symbol to, or taking a symbol from, its front end. Let us call *push* the operation of duplicating the first symbol of a push-down list, and *pop* the operation of removing the first symbol. Then push(ABC) = AABC, while pop(ABC) = BC.[7] We can use a working memory, μ, holding a push-down list, and these operations to encode sequence 19 as:

$$[\mu \leftarrow 1]\,((\,\text{push}\,((\,\text{push}\,\mu\,n(\mu)\,\text{pop})^2 \\ [n(\mu)])^2\,\text{pop})^2\,[C_7(\mu)\,;\,n \leftarrow p])^2 \tag{23}$$

where $[n \leftarrow p]$ replaces operation n by operation p everywhere throughout the pattern.

Let us follow step by step (see table 2) the generation of the sequence from pattern 23, indicating also the correspondence between these steps and Restle's operators in pattern 21.

Now in this process, unlike Restle's, only the symbols in the push-down list need be held in short-term memory (a maximum of three symbols), not all the symbols of the sequence already produced (a maximum of sixteen symbols). From this standpoint, the representation employing the push-down list provides a more plausible model of the psychological process than the recursive representation. The same argument applied to patterns 14 and 15 for generating sequence 13 shows that the former pattern (Restle, 1970) calls for a maximum of four symbols in short-term memory, the latter (Simon and Kotovsky, 1963), a maximum of two. With the use of a push-down list, pattern 15 could be rewritten:

$$[\mu \leftarrow D]\,(\text{push}\,\mu(n(\mu))^3\,\text{pop}\,[n(\mu)])* \tag{24}$$

In Restle's (1970) recursive scheme, the short-term memory requirements depend on the length of the period at the highest

---

7. Push-down lists were invented along with computer list-processing languages in the mid-1950s. They have been used widely in implementing parsing programs (so-called "push-down automata") for computing languages and natural languages. Hence, the notion that a push-down list may be part of the organization of short-term memory already has some currency and support in psycholinguistics (see Yngve, 1960).

Table 2. Results of Operation.

Operations	Push-down List	Symbols Produced	Restle's Operators
$[\mu \leftarrow 1]$	1	1	
A push	1 1		
B push	1 1 1		
$\mu\, n(\mu)$	2 1 1	1 2	N
Pop	1 1		
C ( )²	(Repeat from B to C)	1 2	S
$[n(\mu)]$	2 1		
D ( )²	(Repeat from B to D)	23 23	N
Pop	1		
E ( )²	(Repeat from A to E)	12 12 23 23	S
$[C7(\mu)\,;\, n \leftarrow p]$	6		
F ( )²	(Repeat from A to F)	$(65\ 65\ 54\ 54)^2$	C7

level of the pattern hierarchy. This number can be expected to increase (approximately) geometrically with number of levels. In the scheme using a push-down list, the short-term memory requirements increase only linearly with number of levels in the hierarchy.

Restle has produced some data that demonstrate quite convincingly (e.g., Restle, 1970, figure 3) the psychological reality of the hierarchic phrase structure of patterns. However, his data are equally compatible with the encodings represented by patterns 21 and 23, for both postulate the same phrase structure in the pattern.

In summary, various of the encoding schemes make provisions for iteration of subpatterns and for hierarchic phrase structure of patterns. Empirical evidence can be (and has been) produced to demonstrate that subjects, in fact, encode some patterns hierarchically. The different encoding schemes place quite different demands on short-term memory, however, in generating sequences from their patterns.

ADDITIONAL PSYCHOLOGICAL IMPLICATIONS

The analysis up to this point has been concerned mainly with describing different languages that have been proposed for encoding patterned sequences. We have introduced behavioral evidence only occasionally to elucidate some particular point of comparison or contrast. The remainder of this chapter is concerned with additional implications of coding languages for psychological theory.

If a particular sequence can be encoded, and represented internally, in several different ways, then it is important to explain what determines which encoding a human subject will use. If different subjects use different encodings, it is important to explain the causes for the difference and its consequences in terms of task performance.

The tasks that subjects have performed in the laboratory with patterned sequences include: (1) ranking sequences according to complexity, (2) inducing patterns from sequences, (3) describing sequences verbally, (4) learning and remembering sequences, and (5) extrapolating sequences.

Task 1 only produces observable behavior when combined with 3, 4, or 5. Any one of the latter can be used, in turn, to produce measures of sequence "difficulty" —that is, difficulty can be measured by the time required to perform any one of these tasks with a given sequence, or by number of errors. (Not only the number of errors, but also the precise nature of the errors can be determined.)

A priori measures of sequence complexity

can also be constructed and these can be correlated with sequence difficulty as measured by subjects' behavior. As we have seen, sequence complexity may be measured by code length or by information content; the two kinds of measures are mutually translatable, the one into the other; and both kinds of measures are defined relative to a specific encoding scheme.

Correlation of A Priori Complexity Measures

When two or more a priori complexity measures are computed for the same set of sequences, the correlation among these will indicate the similarities of the encodings or, conversely, the sensitivity of the measures to details of encoding.

We have already seen that Leeuwenberg's (1969) measure correlates 0.8 with Simon and Kotovsky's (1963) when both are applied to a set of fifteen sequences from the Thurstone Letter Series Test and that this high correlation is a consequence of the basic similarities in the coding concepts underlying both schemes.

Similarly, a simple computation verifies that Vitz and Todd's (1969) information measure correlates at about the 0.9 level with code length when binary and ternary sequences are encoded in terms of simple run lengths.

Since we emphasized at the outset that code length is relative to the coding language, it is not obvious why these high correlations occur. They occur because the various coding schemes are not unrelated but are all based on the same set of relations (n, p, s, c) and on notation for iteration. When we compare patterns 14 and 15 for sequence 13, for example, we see that, however more compact pattern 14 is, each symbol in that pattern corresponds to a symbol, or set of symbols, in pattern 15. Thus, we have the correspondences:

$$N^* \leftrightarrow ([\mu_1 \leftarrow \mu_2] \ldots [n(\mu_2)])^*$$
$$N^3 \leftrightarrow \mu_1 (n(\mu_1))^3$$
$$D \leftrightarrow [\mu_2 \leftarrow D]$$

As long as we do not change the basic relations used, we can expect that *relative*

complexity of sequences will be rather insensitive to details of the coding, providing that the sequences under consideration are not too heterogeneous. Hence, our ability to predict measures of behavior may not depend on our knowing in detail the exact encoding scheme that subjects use. If this is so, it will be difficult to choose among alternative encoding hypotheses without sophisticated analysis of the behavioral data.

Correlation of A Priori with Judged Complexity

A major use of complexity measures (see e.g., Vitz and Todd, 1969) has been to predict complexity as judged by subjects from an a priori measure of complexity. For the reasons just stated, the achievement of high correlations cannot be taken as a validation of the specific a priori measure used. Rather, the high correlations should be interpreted to imply: (1) that subjects confronted with sequences do in fact encode them with the aid of the relations we have discussed, and (2) that the length of the encoded pattern is the basis for the subjects' judging the complexity of the sequence.

This general hypothesis was put forth independently by Glanzer and Clark (1962) and by Simon and Kotovsky (1963). Glanzer and Clark went further, however, and, in their "verbal loop hypothesis," asserted that the encoding was verbal (i.e., consisted of a sequence of English words and phrases). They said, specifically:

[The subject] carrying out a perceptual recall task puts the information through a verbal loop. (1) He translates the visual information into a series of words. (2) He holds the verbalization and makes his final response on the basis of that.... Complexity, under this hypothesis, becomes identified with the length of the S's [subject's] verbalization [p. 295].

There is nothing in the data, however, to demonstrate that the internal representation is verbal. The verbal descriptions that Glanzer and Clark elicited from their subjects could equally well have been a fairly direct recoding into verbal form of the internally represented symbolic (but nonverbal) structures. It seems preferable, therefore, to adopt the more neutral stance of Simon and Kotovsky (1963) regarding the nature of the internal representation:

Subjects attain a serial pattern concept by generating and fixating a pattern description of that concept.... [Subjects] have stored in memory a program capable of interpreting and executing descriptions of serial patterns [p. 538].

Complexity and Difficulty

A second use of complexity measures, whether a priori or judged complexity, is to predict the relative difficulty subjects will experience in performing specific tasks on different sequences.

It is not obvious that the ranking of sequences by difficulty will be the same for all tasks—the same for describing sequences verbally as for learning periodic sequences as for extrapolating nonperiodic sequences. To describe a sequence verbally, the subject must (1) discover the pattern and (2) hold the pattern in memory (short-term or long-term) while he produces it (Glanzer and Clark, 1962). To learn a periodic sequence he must either (1) fixate the sequence by rote or (2) discover the pattern, hold it in memory, and use it to generate the sequence (Gregg, 1967). To extrapolate a nonperiodic sequence he must (1) discover the pattern, (2) remember it, and (3) use it to generate the sequence (Simon and Kotovsky, 1963).

An EPAM-like learning theory would suggest that three or four different sources of task difficulty are present in different combinations in these tasks: (1) difficulty of *discovering* a pattern, (2) difficulty of *fixating* either a sequence or a pattern in *long-term memory*, and (3) difficulty of holding in *short-term working memory* the placekeepers or pointers required to produce the sequence from the pattern.

However, disentangling these components of difficulty empirically is not at all easy. In general, the more complex the pattern (as measured by code length), the more relations it is necessary to induce from the sequence in order to find the pattern, the more symbols it is necessary to fixate in order to store the pattern in long-term memory, and the more working memories are necessary in order to produce the sequence from the pattern. Because of this confounding of components of difficulty, all investigators have found code length to be a reasonably good predictor of difficulty, in whichever way difficulty is measured. Thus, Glanzer and Clark (1962) report a correlation of -0.826 between mean verbalization length (code length) and accuracy of recall; Vitz and Todd (1969), using the same data, find a correlation of -0.82 between information content (which is interpreted here as an alternative estimate of code length) and accuracy of recall. Leeuwenberg's (1969) data show correlations of 0.65 and 0.66 between two measures of difficulty (errors and time, respectively, for a group of twelve subjects) on the Thurstone Letter Series Task and code length, using his encoding scheme; there are similar correlations, of 0.74 and 0.61, between these same two measures of difficulty and code length with the Simon and Kotovsky (1963) coding scheme.

Direct Evidence of Encoding

Three kinds of "direct" evidence have been sought to determine the actual encodings used by subjects. Glanzer and Clark (1962) simply instructed the subject to describe each sequence, with the results already mentioned. Kotovsky (1970) and Kotovsky and Simon (1973) obtained verbal protocols and other evidences of subjects' sequential behaviors while discovering the patterns in a set of sequences. Williams (1969) obtained a combination of verbal protocols and eye-movement data. The patterns inferred from this direct evidence generally fit well the Kotovsky and Simon coding language. While numerous individual differences were found, these almost all fell within the general range of concepts allowed by the formal language—that is, it was usually possible to express the variant encodings in that language.

For example, in the specific case of

sequence 13, some eight of Kotovsky and Simon's fourteen subjects used a pattern description corresponding closely to pattern 15 or 23, and only one a description resembling pattern 14. On the other hand, with the slightly simpler pattern, PON ONM NML . . . , four subjects used an encoding resembling Restle's (1970). Restle's description only requires three working memories to handle the latter pattern, but four to handle pattern 14, and this difference in the demands upon working memory may account, in whole or part, for the preferences among encodings.

Gregg (1967) has also provided direct evidence on how subjects describe a pattern they are trying to discover and, more important yet, how their mode of description affects the ease or difficulty of learning the pattern.

CONCLUSION

A survey of the principal alternative formulations of a theory to explain human performance in tasks involving patterned sequences shows all these formulations to be mild variants on a basic theme. The formulations agree in proposing the following: (1) that subjects perform these tasks by inducing pattern descriptions from the sequences; and (2) that these pattern descriptions incorporate the relations of *same* and *next* (on familiar alphabets) between symbols, iteration of subpatterns, and hierarchic phrase structure.

As a result of this consensus on fundamentals, measures of the relative complexity of different patterns can be expected to be nearly the same, independently of which specific encoding languages are used in computing them. A little direct evidence is now available to help us understand in what circumstances subjects will use one or another of these encodings (or others).

It is quixotic to seek crucial experiments to determine *the* coding language, because (1) different subjects almost surely use different representations for the same sequences, and (2) the representations used may well be modified by task instructions, previous experience, and the character of

the set of sequences used in the task. Empirical evidence on these points has already been mentioned. The same conclusion is suggested by the fact that the correlations between subjects in ratings of complexity are far from perfect. (In their paper, Vitz and Todd, 1969, mention mean or median among-subject correlations of 0.67 and 0.84 for two sets of data.) Instead of seeking to discover "the" pattern code or "the" complexity measures, we need to determine the conditions (sociological and psychological) under which subjects will adopt one or another coding scheme in handling patterned sequences.

References

Estes, W. K., & Burke, C. J. Application of a statistical model to simple discrimination learning in human subjects. *Journal of Experimental Psychology*, 1955, **50**, 81–88.

Feldman, J. An analysis of predictive behavior in a two-choice situation. Unpublished doctoral dissertation, Carnegie-Mellon University, 1959.

Feldman, J. Simulation of behavior in the binary choice experiment. *Proceedings of the Western Joint Computer Conference*, 1961, **19**, 133–44. Reprinted in E. A. Feigenbaum & J. Feldman (Eds.). *Computers and thought.* New York: McGraw-Hill, 1963, 329–46.

Feldman, J., Tonge, F. M., Jr., & Kanter, H. Empirical explorations of a hypothesis-testing model of binary choice behavior. In A. C. Hoggatt & F. E. Balderston (Eds.), *Symposium on simulation models.* Cincinnati, Ohio: South-Western Publishing, 1963, 55–100.

Glanzer, M. S., & Clark, H. H. Accuracy of perceptual recall: An analysis of organization. *Journal of Verbal Learning and Verbal Behavior*, 1962, 1, 289–99.

Goodnow, J. J., & Pettigrew, R. F. Effect of prior patterns of experience upon strategies and learning sets. *Journal of Experimental Psychology*, 1955, **49**, 381–98.

Gregg, L. W. Internal representations of sequential concepts. In B. Kleinmuntz (Ed.), *Concepts and the structure of memory.* New York: Wiley, 1967, 107–42.

Klahr, D., & Wallace, J. G. The development of serial completion strategies; an information processing analysis. *British Journal of Psychology*, 1970, **61**, 243–57.

Kotovsky, K. An empirical test of the Simon

and Kotovsky "concept former" model of human letter series sequence extrapolation behavior. Unpublished master's thesis, Carnegie-Mellon University, 1970.

Kotovsky, K., & Simon, H. A. Empirical tests of a theory of human acquisition of concepts for sequential patterns. *Cognitive Psychology*, 1973, **4**, 399–424. Reprinted as chapter 5.2 in this book.

Laughery, K. R., & Gregg, L. W. Simulation of human problem-solving behavior. *Psychometrika*, 1962, **27**, 265–82.

Leeuwenberg, E. L. L. Quantitative specification of information in sequential patterns. *Psychological Review*, 1969, **76**, 216–20.

Miller, G. A. The magical number seven, plus or minus two: Some limits on our capacity for processing information. *Psychological Review*, 1956, **63**, 81–97.

Pivar, M., & Finkelstein, M. Automation, using LISP, of inductive inference on sequences. In E. C. Berkeley & D. G. Bobrow (Eds.), *The programming language LISP*. Cambridge, Mass.: Information International, 1964, 125–216.

Restle, F. Grammatical analysis of the prediction of binary events. *Journal of Verbal Learning and Verbal Behavior*, 1967, **6**, 17–25.

Restle, F. Theory of serial pattern learning: Structural trees. *Psychological Review*, 1970,

77, 481–95.

Simon, H. A., & Feigenbaum, E. A. Elementary perceiver and memorizer: Review of experiments. In A. C. Hoggatt & F. E. Balderston (Eds.), *Symposium on simulation models*. Cincinnati, Ohio: South-Western Publishing, 1963, 101–10.

Simon, H. A., & Kotovsky, K. Human acquisition of concepts for sequential patterns. *Psychological Review*, 1963, **70**, 534–46. Reprinted as chapter 5.1 in this book.

Simon, H. A., & Sumner, R. K. Pattern in music. In B. Kleinmuntz (Ed.), *Formal representation of human judgment*. New York: Wiley, 1968, 219–50.

Vitz, P. C., & Todd, R. C. A coded element model of the perceptual processing of sequential stimuli. *Psychological Review*, 1969, **76**, 433–49.

Williams, D. S. Computer program organization induced from problem examples. Unpublished doctoral dissertation, Carnegie-Mellon University, 1969. Revised version published in H. A. Simon & L. Siklóssy (Eds.), *Representation and meaning*. Englewood Cliffs, N.J.: Prentice-Hall, 1972, 143–205.

Yngve, V. A model and a hypothesis for language structure. *Proceedings of the American philosophical Society*, 1960, **104**, 444–46.

5·4

Process Models and Stochastic Theories of Simple Concept Formation (1967)

with L. W. Gregg

Psychologists who wish to formalize a theory today have two major alternatives: they may construct either a mathematical theory, usually stochastic, or an information processing model in the form of a computer program. The work of Bower and Trabasso (1964) on concept attainment, carried out in the former mode, provides an opportunity to compare these two techniques in order to gain a deeper understanding of the contribution each can make to theory construction and testing. This chapter undertakes such a comparison, to test whether information processing models can cast additional light on experiments that have already undergone sophisticated analysis in terms of stochastic learning theory.

THE BOWER-TRABASSO THEORY

In the first instance, we will limit our discussion, as do Bower and Trabasso, to concept attainment experiments employing an N-dimensional stimulus with two possible values on each dimension and having a single relevant dimension (i.e., simple concepts). On each trial, an instance (positive or negative) is presented to the subject; he responds "Positive" or "Negative"; and he is reinforced by "Right" or "Wrong," as the case may be.

Bower and Trabasso's mathematical theory, devised to explain the results of their main experiments, may be described as follows (Atkinson, Bower and Crothers, 1965, pp. 33–34; Bower and Trabasso, 1964, p. 51):

1. On each trial the subject is in one of two states, K or $\overline{K}$. If he is in state K (he "knows" the correct concept), he will always make the correct response. If he is in state $\overline{K}$ (he "does not know" the correct concept), he will make an incorrect response with probability p.

2. After each correct response, the subject remains in his previous state. After an error, he shifts from state $\overline{K}$ to state K with probability π.

Bower and Trabasso derive mathemati-

Preparation of this chapter and the research on which it is based was supported by the Public Health Service, Department of Health, Education and Welfare, under Grant MH-07722.

307

Table 1. Experiments Analyzed in Bower and Trabasso (1964).

Exper. No.	Page Reference	Attributes			Reversal	Number of Subjects*	Average Total Errors	Probability of Errors in K (p)
		Number	Type	Relevant Attribute				
1	38–43	5	Consonant strings	—	None	25	12.16	0.523
2	61–65	3	Geometrical 4 values paired	Color	None	22	13.36	0.493
3	66–69	4	"Letter wheels"	Particular letters	Single	C 18	19.11	0.491
						R 18	19.11	
						N 18	18.28	
4	72–74	6	Geometrical	Color	Single	C 10	12.9	0.50
						R 10	14.9	
						N 10	14.0	
5	77–79	5	Geometrical	Color	Alternate errors	C 15	8.0	
						R 15	7.81	
6	80–82	5	Geometrical	Color	After errors	(8 of 11 failed) 3	47.7	0.499

*C, R, N stand for Control, Reversal, and Nonreversal, respectively. For details, see text and Bower and Trabasso (1964), at the pages indicated in the second column.

cally a number of consequences from this theory: in particular, expected values and variances of a large number of statistics. They then proceed to show that in a substantial number of experiments, of which we will discuss six in some detail, these expected values and variances are quite close to the sample statistics.

Estimates of the parameters p and π play a central role both in the analysis of the mathematical theory and in its fit to the empirical data. We will focus our attention, as do Bower and Trabasso, primarily on them. In this, we agree with Atkinson *et al.* (1965), who say of this model (p. 69):

The fundamental statistics of importance to the concept model are (1) stationarity and independency [of the estimates of p] prior to the last error and (2) the distribution of total errors or trial number of last error [determining π]. If these statistics conform to the predictions of the model, then we have found in practice that the remaining statistics accord well with predictions.

Once the subject has entered state K, he can no longer, according to the theory, make an error or return to state $\overline{K}$. Therefore we can be sure that the subject is in state $\overline{K}$ on every trial up to and including

that on which he made his last error (and in state K on every subsequent trial). Hence, pooling data for all subjects in state $\overline{K}$ for each trial, we can obtain independent estimates of p for each trial. The theory asserts that these are all estimates of the same population parameter, hence that the observed p should not vary significantly from trial to trial. In the experiments reported by Bower and Trabasso (except possibly Experiment 2 in Table 1, below). the observations confirm this prediction.

Since, whenever he makes an error, the subject has a probability, π, of moving from state $\overline{K}$ to state K, and since no errors will be made once state K is reached, the expected total number of errors will simply be $1/\pi$. The theory also asserts that π is constant from trial to trial, an assertion that implies that, on the average, the fraction of subjects still in state $\overline{K}$ who move to state K will not change over trials. Bower and Trabasso report little data on this point, commenting (p. 40) that:

No available data are sufficiently free of sampling error to permit quantitative decisions between the [constant-π] assumption and the [increasing-π] assumption [when there are a large number of stimulus dimensions]. However, some of the results reported later in this paper contradict the notion that [π] changes appreciably over trials.

Bower and Trabasso use the reciprocal of the total number of errors to estimate π (or *average* π, if it changes), on the basis of the simple relation stated above.

We see that the whole of the rather formidable array of mathematical derivations in the Bower-Trabasso analysis can be summed up, for practical purposes, in the informal calculations we have just carried out. The only strong predictions of the theory (and, as we will see, the only predictions with substantial psychological content) that are critically tested by the empirical data are the predictions of stationarity and independence of p from trial to trial.[1]

Process Descriptions

The mathematical theory of Bower and Trabasso is equivalent to the two numbered statements of the previous section, taken together with the ordinary laws of algebra and probability theory. The first statement determines the probability distribution of responses on each trial as a function of the subject's state; the second statement defines the conditions under which the state of the subject will change.

In a very aggregative sense, this theory can be regarded as a process model for the subject's behavior. The first statement describes, in terms of the probabilities of outcomes, a response process; the second, a learning process, also probabilistic. However, the theory states nothing about the subject's information processes that generate the probabilities. In this section we will describe an alternative model of concept attainment that makes somewhat more detailed assumptions about these processes. Before we do, some methodological remarks about the credibility of theories are in order.

One point of view is that theories gain their credibility solely from the accuracy of their predictions, account being taken of their parsimony in making these predictions. Each experiment is treated as an island unto itself, ignoring any knowledge about the world the experimenter might have had prior to making his predictions. From this point of view it is not relevant to ask how Bower and Trabasso came to write down their particular hypothetical description of the system. The only valid questions are whether the system's predictions are correct and whether they are achieved parsimoniously. (We will have more to say about parsimony later.)

There is another point of view on credibility, however: that the credibility of a theory depends on its plausibility as well as the accuracy of its predictions. This point of view, which has strong support in contemporary statistical decision theory, has been formalized along the following lines, based on Bayes' Theorem. Suppose that two alternative theories are under consideration and that we wish to judge their relative credibility after certain empirical events (E) have occurred. Let $p(E \mid H_1)$ and $(p(E \mid H_2)$, respectively, be the probabilities that the *actually observed* events would have occurred if H_1 and H_2, respectively, were the correct theory. We wish to compare $p(H_1 \mid E)$ with $p(H_2 \mid E)$—i.e., the relative probabilities that H_1 or H_2, respectively, are true, given E. Let $p(H_1)$ and $p(H_2)$, respectively, be the probability of H_1 and H_2, respectively, prior to the observations E. We may think of these probabilities as the "plausibilities" of the two theories on the basis of all facts known to us prior to the new observations. Then by Bayes' Theorem:

$$\frac{p(H_1 \mid E)}{p(H_2 \mid E)} = \frac{p(E \mid H_1)\, p(H_1)}{p(E \mid H_2)\, p(H_2)}. \quad (1)$$

Thus, the credibility of each theory after the observation is quite as dependent on the plausibility, $p(H)$, of that theory, as upon the likelihood, $p(E \mid H)$, of its producing the observation.

In practice, theorists almost always behave in accordance with Bayes' Theorem:

---

1. This is not a criticism of the experiments, which were aimed primarily at testing the all-or-none hypothesis. For this hypothesis, the stationarity of p and π are the critical issues.

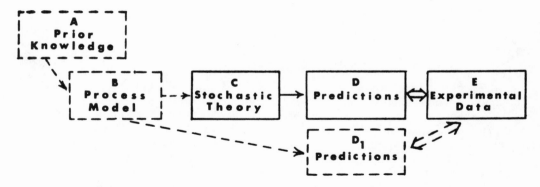

Figure 1. Theoretical structure (explicit and implicit) employed by Bower and Trabasso. Solid lines and boxes enclosed by solid lines depict the formal derivations and formal propositions, respectively. Broken lines and boxes enclosed by broken lines depict the informal derivations and propositions.

as though they thought the plausibility of their formalisms to be relevant to their credibility. An important argument for high prior plausibility of a theory is to show that it follows (formally or informally) from assumptions that are plausible, i.e., assumptions that accord with prior knowledge. Bower and Trabasso do precisely this— they show informally that the stochastic theory we have outlined can be derived from plausible assumptions about the subject's information processing strategy. There are a number of such discussions in their paper, the principal ones occurring on pages 39, 51, 81, 83–85, and 88–91. Since it will be relevant to our subsequent discussion, we quote the first of these at length:

The subject in a concept-identification experiment is viewed as testing out various hypotheses (strategies) about the solution of the problem. Each problem defines for the subject a population of hypotheses. The subject samples one of these hypotheses at random and makes the response dictated by the hypothesis. If his response is correct, he continues to use that hypothesis for the next trial; if his response is incorrect, then he resamples (with replacement) from the pool of hypotheses. . . .

Let us call the quoted statement a process model, P_0. The model P_0 lends plausibility to the stochastic theory, for it is obvious

that, if we identify "subject is in state K" of the latter with "subject holds the correct hypothesis" of the former, then the stochastic theory can be derived from P_0. But the assumptions of P_0 agree with our previous experience of human behavior—that is what, no doubt, suggested them in the first place. The situation is depicted in figure 1.

It is of some interest to note that the stochastic theory is only slightly more economical of words than the process model. In fact, we stated the former in sixty-five words (excluding parentheses), Bower and Trabasso stated the latter in seventy-seven. On the other hand, the process model makes more and stronger predictions than the stochastic theory (lower dotted path in figure 1). We mention two of these as examples:

1. If there are $2N$ possible hypotheses, and if the correct hypothesis is determined in each experiment at random, with equal probability for each hypothesis, then it follows from P_0 that $\pi = \frac{1}{2}N$.

2. If the subject, on each trial, verbalizes his hypothesis as well as his response, then he will change the verbalized hypothesis only if he made an error on the previous trial.

While the stochastic theory can be derived from P_0, the converse, as we have just seen, is not true. Indeed, it is easy to construct variants of P_0 from which the same stochastic theory is derivable. A simple variant would be to asume (local nonreplacement) that after each error, the subject selects a hypothesis at random from the possible hypotheses *excepting* the hypothesis he held on the previous trial. Call this variant P_1. A slightly more complex variant, which we will call P_2, would be to assume (local consistency) that the subject selects a hypothesis from the subset of hypotheses that are consistent with the last instance presented to him. A still more complex variant, P_3, would assume (global consistency) that the subject selects the new hypothesis randomly from the subset of hypotheses consistent with *all* the instances that have been presented to him. Moreover, in any of these sampling schemes, the different hypotheses might have unequal, instead of equal, probabilities of selection.

All four variant processing models, and others as well, imply the stochastic theory of Bower and Trabasso, or something almost indistinguishable from it. It follows that tests of that theory can contribute nothing to choosing among the variants—if the theory is consistent with the data, the actual behavior of the subject might correspond with any (or none) of the variant models.

This does not mean that the models are empirically indistinguishable or untestable. On the contrary, we have already seen that, if the experimenter chooses the correct concept and the instances at random, P_0 (replacement sampling) implies that $\pi = \frac{1}{2}N$. By parallel reasoning, it is easy to see that P_1 (local nonreplacement sampling) implies $\pi = 1/(2N - 1)$; while P_2 (local consistency) implies $\pi = 1/N$; and P_3 (global consistency) implies an increasing π, varying from $1/N$ after the first error to 1 after about $\log_2 N$ errors. Since, in all cases, the expected number of total errors is proportional to $1/\pi$, it should be easy to choose among these models except possibly between P_0 and P_1—between replacement and local nonreplacement sampling.

FORMALIZATION OF THE PROCESS MODEL

We have seen that Bower and Trabasso gave *a priori* plausibility to their stochastic theory by deriving it informally from an informal process model. By making use of a simple programming language we can formalize the process model. We require some variables, a few constants, and some processes. Following the conventions of ALGOL (McCracken, 1963) names of variables, called identifiers, represent computer cells upon whose contents the usual arithmetic operations can be performed. Additionally, the language incorporates the list processing features of IPL-V (Newell et al., 1964) so that the contents of a cell may also refer to names of lists of symbols.

Variables

> *Instance:* Its value is a *list* containing a value (e.g., "large," "square") for each of N attributes.
> *Attribute Structure:* Its value is a *list* of pairs of values (e.g., "red-blue") for each of N attributes.
> *Correct Response:* Its value is one of the two *constants:* "Positive," "Negative."
> *Correct Hypothesis:* Its value is one of the $2N$ attribute values.
> *Current Hypothesis:* Its value is one of the $2N$ attribute values.
> *Response:* Its value is one of the two constants: "Positive," "Negative."
> *Reinforcement:* Its value is one of the two constants: "Right," "Wrong."
> *New Hypothesis:* Its value is one of the $2N$ attribute values.
> *List of Possible Hypotheses:* Its value is the list of $2N$ attribute values.
> *Tally:* Its value is a positive *integer*.

Constants

"Positive," "Negative," "Right," "Wrong"; the integers; K, the criterion of solution; and the symbols for the $2N$ attribute values.

Processes

The symbol "←" is read "is set equal to,"

and the symbol "∈," "is a member of." Processes numbered E1–E4 describe the experimenter's behaviors, and S1–S5 the subject's behaviors; while E0 is the "executive process," controlling their alternation. Where "random" is not otherwise qualified, it means "with equal probabilities."

E1 :   Do E3; then do E4.
        [E3 and E4 are defined below]

S1 :   If Current Hypothesis ∈ Instance,
            then Response ← "Positive,"
            else Response ← "Negative."

E2 :   If Response = Correct Response,
            then Reinforcement ← "Right,"
            else Reinforcement ← "Wrong."

S2 :   If Reinforcement = "Wrong,"
            then Current Hypothesis ← S5.

E3 :   Generate an instance by sampling
            randomly from each pair on At-
            tribute Structure.
            Instance ← List of Attribute
                                Values

E4 :   If Correct Hypotheses ∈ Instance,
            then Correct Response
                        ← "Positive,"
            else Correct Response
                        ← "Negative."

S5 :   Generate New Hypothesis by sam-
            pling randomly from List of Possi-
            ble Hypotheses:
            Current Hypothesis
                        ← New Hypothesis.

E0 :   Do E1, then S1, then E2;
            If Reinforcement = "Right,"
            then Tally ← Tally + 1,
            else Tally ← 0;
            If Tally = K,
            then halt;
            else do S2, then repeat E0.

On examination, this model will be recognized as a formalization of P_0. P_1 differs from it only in replacing S5 by S51.

S51 :   Generate New Hypothesis by sam-
            pling randomly from List of Possi-
            ble Hypotheses;
            If New Hypothesis
                = Current Hypothesis
            then sample again,
            else Current Hypothesis
                        ← New Hypothesis.

A slightly more complex version, S52, corresponds to P_2.

S52 :   Generate New Hypothesis by sam-
            pling randomly from List of Possi-
            ble Hypotheses;
            If Response = "Positive,"
            If New Hypothesis ∈ Instance,
                then sample again,
                else Current Hypothesis
                        ← New Hypothesis.
            Else if New Hypothesis ∈ Instance,
                then Current Hypothesis
                        ← New Hypothesis,
                else sample again.

Similarly, S53, corresponding to P_3, might have the following structure:

S53 :   If Response = "Positive,"
            Generate values from Instance
                and remove each from List of
                Possible Hypotheses (if still on
                list);
            Else generate complements of values
                on Instance and remove each
                from List of Possible Hypotheses
                (if still on list);
            Generate New Hypothesis by sam-
                pling randomly from List of Possi-
                ble Hypotheses;
            Current Hypothesis
                        ← New Hypothesis.

These are, of course, not the only possible process hypotheses for the subject's behavior. But they will serve to illustrate: (1) that the process models can be formalized as fully as we please (i.e., we can formalize B of figure 1); (2) that these process models are empirically distinguishable (i.e., we can deduce direct connections between B and E of figure 1); (3) that they make stronger predictions of behavior than do the stochastic theories (including predictions about the subject's current hypothesis), and (4) that stochastic theories can be derived from them as formally as we please (i.e., we can formalize the relation of B to C in figure 1).

A CLOSER COMPARISON OF MODEL WITH THEORY

The relation between the stochastic theory and the process models can be stated even more precisely than it was in the previous section. For, we can formulate the stochastic theory in the same programming language as the process models; and, alternatively, we can extract a stochastic model from each of the process models that preserves all its detail.

First, we give the process-language version of the stochastic theory:

M1: If State = "Learned,"
      then Reinforcement ← "Right,"
      else generate item randomly, with
        probabilities $(1 - p)$ and p,
        from
      Reinforcement List, and
      Reinforcement
          ← Generator Output.
M2: If Reinforcement = "Wrong,"
      then generate item randomly,
      with probabilities π and $(1 - \pi)$,
      from
      State List, and
      State ← Generator Output.
M0: Do M1,
    If Reinforcement = "Right,"
      then Tally ← Tally + 1,
      else Tally ← 0;
    If Tally = K,
      then halt;
      else do M2, then repeat M0.

Comparing this description with the earlier process models, we see that the new process M1 telescopes and simplifies the processes E1, S1, E2, E3, and E4 of the process model; while M2 telescopes S2 and S5.

Conversely, a Markov process corresponding to the stochastic theory can be defined by considering the state of the subject after he has made a response, i.e., after execution of M1 and just before execution of M2. He is in one of three possible states: Learned-Right (LR), Unlearned-Right (UR), and Unlearned-Wrong (UW).[2] The matrix of transition probabilities is:

$$
\begin{array}{c c c c}
 & \text{LR} & \text{UR} & \text{UW} \\
\text{LR} & \begin{bmatrix} 1 \\ 0 \\ \pi \end{bmatrix} & \begin{matrix} 0 \\ (1-p) \\ (1-\pi)(1-p) \end{matrix} & \begin{matrix} 0 \\ p \\ (1-\pi)p \end{matrix}\end{bmatrix}
\end{array}
$$

Now in similar fashion, we can define a set of states for the subject in the process model P_0 after he has made a response, i.e., after execution of E2 and just before execution of S2. Number the hypotheses 1 for the correct one, 2 for its alternative value on the same attribute, and $3, \ldots,$ $2N$ for the remainder. Then the possible states are 1R, 2W, 3R, 3W, $\ldots$, $2N$R, $2N$W—a total of $4N-2$ states (since with hypothesis 1 the subject will necessarily make the correct response, and with hypothesis 2, the wrong one). The matrix of transition probabilities is

	1R	...	iR	...	jR	...	2W	...	iW	...	jW	...
1R	1	...	0	...	0	...	0	...	0	...	0	...
iR	0	...	$\frac{1}{2}$	...	0	...	0	...	$\frac{1}{2}$	...	0	...
jR	0	...	0	...	$\frac{1}{2}$	...	0	...	0	...	$\frac{1}{2}$	...
2W	$\frac{1}{2N}$	...	$\frac{1}{4N}$	...	$\frac{1}{4N}$	...	$\frac{1}{2N}$	...	$\frac{1}{4N}$	...	$\frac{1}{4N}$	...
iW	$\frac{1}{2N}$	...	$\frac{1}{4N}$	...	$\frac{1}{4N}$	...	$\frac{1}{2N}$	...	$\frac{1}{4N}$	...	$\frac{1}{4N}$	...
jW	$\frac{1}{2N}$	...	$\frac{1}{4N}$	...	$\frac{1}{4N}$	...	$\frac{1}{2N}$	...	$\frac{1}{4N}$	...	$\frac{1}{4N}$	...

(See footnote 2 overleaf)

where $k = (2N + 1)$.

If the only behavior observed in this system is whether the response is "Right" or "Wrong," then all the states beyond $1R$ and $2W$ can be collapsed into a pair of states—call them AR and AW, respectively, and an aggregate matrix derived strictly from the previous one:

$$
\begin{array}{c}
 \\
1R \\
AR \\
2W \\
\\
AW \\
\\
\end{array}
\begin{array}{cccc}
1R & AR & 2W & AW \\
\end{array}
\left[
\begin{array}{cccc}
1 & 0 & 0 & 0 \\
0 & \frac{1}{2} & 0 & \frac{1}{2} \\
\dfrac{1}{2N} & \dfrac{(N-1)}{2N} & \dfrac{1}{2N} & \dfrac{(N-1)}{2N} \\
\dfrac{1}{2N} & \dfrac{(N-1)}{2N} & \dfrac{1}{2N} & \dfrac{(N-1)}{2N}
\end{array}
\right]
$$

By a final step of aggregation, we can then aggregate the state AW, obtaining an approximation to the Bower-Trabasso matrix, with $\pi = \frac{1}{2}N$ and $p = \frac{1}{2}$:

$$
\begin{array}{c}
\\
1R \\
AR \\
W \\
\end{array}
\begin{array}{ccc}
1R & AR & W \\
\end{array}
\left[
\begin{array}{ccc}
1 & 0 & 0 \\
0 & \frac{1}{2} & \frac{1}{2} \\
\dfrac{1}{2N} & \dfrac{(N-1)}{2N} & \frac{1}{2}
\end{array}
\right]
$$

Comparing this matrix with the one for the Bower-Trabasso theory, we see two differences, one large and one small. The big difference is that the Bower-Trabasso matrix has two free parameters, the new aggregate matrix has none—it predicts exact numerical values for π and p. The small difference is that the Bower-Trabasso matrix predicts no difference, prior to learning, between the probability of a right guess following a right guess and a right guess following a wrong guess, respectively. The matrix derived from P_0 predicts that the former probability will equal $\frac{1}{2}$, the latter $(N-1)/(2N-1)$.[3] This difference, of course, could be detected only in very large samples.

Derivation of Theory for Modified Experiment

The process language description of the aggregated stochastic theory shows that the postulated aggregated processes intermingle the behaviors of E and S: M1 was

derived from E1, S1, E2, E3, and E4 of the process model; while M2 was derived from S2 and S5. Hence there is no clear separation between those processes that define the experimental design, on the one hand, and those that define the subject's behavior on the other. If the experiment is altered in any respect, there is no direct way, in this representation, of deriving the corresponding changes in the process description or in the transition matrix.

Matters are quite different with the detailed model. For any change in the design of the experiment *which does not cause the subject to change his response strategy*, the process model can be used to predict outcomes simply by modifying the input constants and the experimenter processes to fit the new description of the experiment. This procedure does not introduce any new degrees of freedom into the assumptions about the subject's behavior, since the modifications are strictly determined by the conditions of the experiment.

For example, Bower and Trabasso describe an experiment in which, for one group of subjects after each Reinforcement of "Wrong," the value of Correct Hypothesis was reversed. To represent this experimental condition, we simply modify E2 to E2_1 as follows:

E2_1:   If (Response) = (Correct Response)
          then Reinforcement ← "Right,"
          else Reinforcement ← "Wrong,"
          and Correct Response ↔ Opposite Response;

[where "↔" means "is interchanged with."]

In an even more trivial way, by changing

---

2. Bower and Trabasso call their theory a two-state process, but this refers only to the state of the subject before responding, not to the state of the entire system. See Bower and Trabasso (1964, pp. 51–52).

3. If the subject has not learned, the *relative* probabilities of a correct and wrong response (from the third line of the table) will be $(N-1)/2N$ and $\frac{1}{2}$, respectively. Multiplying these by $2N/(2N-1)$, to normalize them so that they add to unity, we get the conditional probabilities $(N-1)/(2N-1)$ and $\frac{1}{2}[2N/(2N-1)]$, respectively.

the value of Attribute Structure, the number of stimulus dimensions or, for that matter, the number of values on each dimension, can be altered. Thus the experimental conditions can readily be replicated for all the experiments described by Bower and Trabasso. Then, stochastic theories can be written for these new process models and, where feasible, more aggregative stochastic theories derived from them.

Testing Models Empirically

In table 1 are listed six experiments described by Bower and Trabasso, yielding the data they use to support their theory. In each case they compute about a dozen statistics from the experimental data and compare these with the corresponding statistics predicted by the theory after the free parameters have been estimated from the data. In a number of cases, they apply statistical tests to determine whether the differences between observed and predicted values can be attributed to chance.

The first two experiments and the controls in experiments 3–5 correspond to the experimental conditions we have described previously. We will speak of these as the "standard experiment." For each experiment, Bower and Trabasso examine the stationarity of p, estimate π from the observed data, then proceed to predict the remaining statistics.

Testability of the Models

There are, as we have seen, only two strong assumptions in the stochastic theory—if these are satisfied, the rest of the data will pretty much follow. The first is, that so long as the subject does not hold the correct hypothesis, he will have a constant probability, p, of making an error. The data support this prediction well. Note that all variants of the process model make the much stronger prediction that p will be close to 0.5 (not exactly 0.5, as we have already shown). The data also bear out this much stronger prediction, which does not follow from the Bower-Trabasso theory.

The second assumption, and the more

interesting one, is that π, the probability of hitting on the correct hypothesis is a constant. Again, the Bower-Trabasso theory does not predict the value of π, which the authors estimate directly from the data. Under the assumption, however, that the experimenter randomizes the choice of *correct hypothesis*, or that the subject selects hypotheses at random with equal probability, or both, we have already seen that the numerical value of π can be derived from any of the process models (although it will not be constant in P_3) and, in general, will be different for each of the models; P_0, P_1, P_2, and P_3. Thus, it is possible to use the empirical data to choose among the process models.

This point is important, because it has genuine psychological import. The alternative assumptions, S_5, S_{5_1}, S_{5_2}, and S_{5_3}, respectively, about the subject's behavior place quite different loads on his memory, and in particular on his short-term memory.

Under assumption S_5, the subject need keep only his current hypothesis in short-term memory. Under assumption S_{5_1}, he must retain the current hypothesis long enough to compare it with new hypotheses as he generates them; thus, for part of the time, he must hold two items in short-term memory.

Under assumption S_{5_2}, the subject must also retain in memory the current instance, unless that instance is displayed by the experimenter during the entire duration of the trial. The amount of short-term memory required will vary with the number of attributes in the stimulus.

Finally, under assumption S_{5_3}, the subject must, in addition to items mentioned previously, hold in memory the list of hypotheses not yet eliminated by previous instances. The length of this list will again depend on the number of stimulus dimensions. (It should be noted that these differences in assumption about memory requirements are explicit in the formal process models.)

Consideration of the psychological import of these assumptions, and especially their implications for short-term memory, calls attention to several aspects of experimental design whose significance is not apparent from the structure of the more abstract stochastic theory. We mention three of these:

First, it is important for the experimenter to vary the correct hypothesis across subjects, in order to wash out culturally or physiologically determined subject preferences for particular attributes. Without such randomization, π cannot be predicted (unless the additional assumption is made that the subjects' preferences are randomly and uniformly distributed). In the actual experiments, the correct hypothesis was not randomized and hence, interpretation of the observed values of π is ambiguous for the Bower-Trabasso experiments, and these values have lessened utility for choosing among the alternative process models.

Second, the length of time that the instances are exposed for the subject, the consequent amount of opportunity for memorization, and the presence or absence of visual props holding information about current or previous instances of hypotheses all become critical in determining what the burden of short-term memory will be on the subject for the models incorporating S_5, S_{5_1}, S_{5_2}, S_{5_3}, respectively, and consequently, which of these processes the subject can or will employ.

Finally, other variables that affect the short-term memory requirements, and the differential salience of different stimulus dimensions, may also alter the strategies employed by subjects, hence the values of π. As we will show in our discussion of experiments 2 and 3, these variables may be important sources of noncomparability among experiments and among the parameters of stochastic models describing their outcomes.

It can be seen that the predicted value of π will tend to be larger the greater the amount of information the subject retains in short-term memory or has available to him in displayed information. There is no way in which these parameters can be represented formally in the stochastic theory, hence no way in which predictions of changed π resulting from changes in

experimental design can be derived formally from that theory. These kinds of variables, on the other hand, are readily accommodated in process models—and can be accommodated formally by placing limits on the number of variables the subject can use.

Inconsistencies in Informal Derivations. Now let us consider experiments 3–6, whose conditions deviate from the standard experiment. In order to predict what effects the changes in experimental design will have on the subject's behavior, Bower and Trabasso have to resort to informal argument, that is to say, to reasoning in terms of an implicit process model (B in figure 1) that is nowhere stated formally.

The difficulties to which such informal treatment can lead are illustrated by the analysis of experiment 6, a pilot experiment. In order to explain why most subjects were unable to reach criterion on this experiment, Bower and Trabasso (1964, pp. 80–82), in effect, assumed the process model with S_{5_2}. (Models S_5 and S_{5_1} both predict that the reversal will cause no difficulty for subjects in this experiment.) But if, for consistency, we also apply S_{5_2} in experiment 4, we predict total errors of 6 or 7, while the observed value was 13 to 14.

Formalizing the process model would have made it obvious that no single one of the alternative processes we have defined will explain the data in both experiments 6 and 4. Either a modified process model has to be introduced to remove the contradition, or some essential difference must be found between the experiments to explain the subjects' use of different strategies. Let us sketch out some of the directions in which such an extension might lead.

None of these questions is raised by the stochastic theory, which is compatible with any and all of the process models. They arise only when an attempt is made to interpret the gross behavior of the subjects in terms of specific underlying psychological processes.

Abandoning the assumption of random, equiprobable selection of hypotheses would

Table 2. Predictions of Total Errors Four Models and Six Experiments.*

Experiment No. (From Table 1)

Model	1	2	3 C	3 R & N	4 C	4 R & N	5 C	5 R & N	6
P_0	10✓	6	8	8	12✓	12✓	10✓	10✓	10
P_1	9✓	5	7	7	11✓	11✓	9✓	9✓	10
P_2	5	3	4	5	6	7	5?	5?	∞✓
P_3	2.1	1.4	2	2	2.3	2.3	2.1	2.1	∞✓
Actual Errors	12.2	13.4	19.1	18.7	12.9	14.5	8	7.8	48—∞

*The entries in the table are the average number of errors per subject predicted by each model for each experiment. The numbers followed by a check mark (√) are reasonably compatible with the actual data shown in the last line; the numbers followed by a question mark are conceivably consistent with the data; the remaining entries are incompatible with the data.

salvage S_{52} in experiment 4, but only if color (the relevant dimension) has extremely low salience as compared with the other dimensions of the stimulus. For stimuli as simple and clear as those used in this experiment, this is not likely. For the moment, we put this possibility aside and retain the assumption of at least approximate equiprobability of sampling.

The entire situation is summarized in table 2. In this table are recorded the actual average numbers of errors per subject for each experiment and the predicted number for each experiment for each process model. Checks (√) designate those predictions that are close to the observed values, while question marks (?) designate two predictions that are perhaps "tolerable" if not close. The remaining predictions are certainly disconfirmed by the observations.

Consider first the subjects run under "standard conditions": 1, 2, 3C, 4C, and 5C. In three of these five cases (1, 4C, and 5C) the two models, P_0 and P_1, that assume that the subject uses little or no information about the specific content of the current or prior instances, predict well; in the other two cases (2 and 3C) they predict far too few errors. The models, P_2 and P_3, which assume more generous provision of short-term memory fail to predict correctly in all five cases. From the observations we conclude: (1) that subjects may behave as described in models P_0 or P_1, but

certainly not as described in P_2 or P_3, and (2) that there must be some circumstances in experiments 2 and 3C that are not reflected in any of the models.

Before we try to dispel all the mystery of the outcomes under standard conditions, let us turn to the remaining conditions, in which the experimenter, on one or more occasions in the course of the experiment, changed the correct hypothesis before the subject had learned it. Since we have combined the reversal and nonreversal variants of these conditions, we will designate them as 3E, 4E, 5E, and 6. In the first three cases, the data for experimental subjects were substantially indentical with data for the subjects in the corresponding control conditions; in the pilot experiment, 6, no control was run. Bower and Trabasso interpret the results, in experiments 3–5, as confirming their theory. We now see that the results in experiments 4 and 5 are consistent with models P_0 and P_1 (and 5 possibly with P_2), but that 3E is no more compatible than is 3C with *any* of the models, unless we modify them by assuming that the salience of the relevant attribute was much lower than the random sampling processes assume.

Detailed Analysis of Experiment 6. Next let us turn to experiment 6. Bower and Trabasso explain at some length why the outcome of this experiment is just what should be expected. In their words (p. 80):

Although this procedure represents only a minor modification of that used in the prior reversal study [experiment 5], analysis shows that the modifications are critical and that learning would be expected to be extremely slow.

The "analysis" to which they refer, and which they carry out on pp. 80–82, is not a formal derivation from the stochastic theory, but an informal derivation from a specific process model that differs from our P_2 only in supposing that the subject occasionally forgets part of the information he is holding in short-term memory. Specification of such a process model is, of course, the only basis on which the deviant results of experiment 6 could be "expected," since in the stochastic theory there is no way of expressing this interaction of experimental conditions with the subject's behavior—hence no way of predicting the large increase in number of errors with the change in conditions and the inability of most subjects to reach criterion.

On the other hand, table 2 shows that, by combining strategy S_{5_2} for the subject with an appropriate formal description of the experimenter's strategy (replacing E2 by $E2_1$, to be precise), the inability of the subject to solve the problem can be deduced formally. Bower and Trabasso's explanation of experiment 6 must be attributed wholly to the process model, whether used formally or informally, not to the stochastic theory.

Next, consider the relation of experiment 6 to the other experiments. Experiment 6 (and *possibly* experiment 5) is the only one that can be explained by models P_2 or P_3. The remaining experiments either require models P_0 or P_1, or are incompatible with all the models. Hence, unless some basis can be found for distinguishing experiment 6 from the other experiments, the Bower-Trabasso analysis must be regarded as *ad hoc*. We will not speculate as to what this basis might be. From the descriptions of the pilot experiment, we detect no change in procedure that might reduce the load on short-term memory imposed by strategy

S_{5_2}, and hence the feasibility of the subject conforming to P_2. In the presence of such a change we would be inclined to propose the following:

Strategy selection rule. The subject will select the most efficient strategy that does not overburden his short-term memory (i.e., strategies, if feasible, will be preferred in the order S_{5_3}, S_{5_2}, S_{5_1}, S_5).

Assume, for example, that a stimulus of three or more dichotomous attributes is too large to be held in short-term memory along with the other variable information the subject requires (e.g., his current hypothesis, his response, the reinforcement). Then the subject would employ S_{5_3} only if all previous stimuli remain visible while he is choosing a new current hypothesis, and S_{5_2} only if the most recent stimulus remains visible during this period. With a slight extension of the process models, we could incorporate the strategy selection rule and short-term memory limits formally, and thereby seek to predict the outcomes of experiments 1, 4C, 4R, 5C, 5R, and 6 within the framework of a single unambiguous model.[4]

The Anomalies in Experiments 2 and 3. This brings us back to the anomalous results of experiments 2 and 3, where the subjects made far more errors than were predicted by any of the models. Notice that they made two or three times as many errors as would have been made by model P_0, which is essentially a random device provided with a little bit of short-term memory.

When we examine Bower and Trabasso's descriptions of these experiments, we discover that the stimuli in these two experiments have complexities in their structures not shared by the stimuli in any of the other experiments. In experiment 2, each attribute is 4-valued, and is transformed

---

4. A control condition for experiment 6 would have provided valuable additional information to test this hypothesis. The prediction would be that total errors would average five per subject.

into a dichotomy by associating one response with a *pair* of values of the relevant attribute, the other response with the other pair of values. None of the process models would handle this situation without modifications.

In fact Bower and Trabasso also observe that their assumptions (i.e., the informal process model from which they derived the stochastic theory) do not fit the conditions in this experiment. In an appendix (Bower and Trabasso, pp. 87–92), they develop an entirely new process model, and a new stochastic theory derived from it, to give a better account of the data from this experiment. All the interpretations in the body of their paper of experiment 2 assume that π is the same for the 2-response and 4-response conditions, an assumption that does not follow from any of the process models, that does not fit the data well, and that is given up in their appendix.

In experiment 3, the stimulus letters are arranged in a "wheel," and the wheel orientations were randomly varied, since the experimenter intended only the letters as attribute values and not their locations. Subjects may well have interpreted the situation differently and could have behaved as though there were several more dimensions present than the experimenter thought he had put there. For example, subjects may have concluded that the position in which a letter occurred (e.g., "*T* at bottom") was part of the concept.

Hence, while we have not formally extended the process models to account quantitatively for the errors in experiments 2 and 3, it is easy to see why they should have been several times more numerous than predicted by models that took at face value the experimenter's abstract description of the stimulus. Clearly, the process models would need to be extended to include a perceptual "front end" to predict how the subject will encode for internal processing the actual stimulus configurations.[5]

Additional Tests of Process Models. Our discussion has shown that process models offer many advantages over more abstract stochastic theories for analyzing phenomena of the kind considered by Bower and Trabasso. They have a very important additional advantage, which we have not yet discussed, since its exploitation calls for the collection of data that were not gathered in the Bower-Trabasso experiments. They make predictions not made by the stochastic theory (i.e., they provide direct formal connections between B and E of figure 1).

Using the process models only to make numerical predictions of π requires the sometimes questionable assumption of approximately equal salience of attributes. More important, it does not take advantage of the real predictive strength of the process models as compared with the stochastic theory. The process models predict not only the probability that the subject will make an error on each trial, but they also predict: (1) what specific response he will make, (2) what hypothesis he holds, and (3) what information he retains about previous instances and responses.

There seems to be no reason why the subject should not at least record his current hypothesis as well as his response. If it is objected that asking him for these additional behaviors will change the results, this is an objection that can readily be evaluated by a controlled experiment. Its *a priori* probability does not seem high to us.[6]

---

5. There is substantial evidence (including experiment 3 here) that when the stimuli are complex, with "subtle" dimensions, differential salience of cues becomes very noticeable, and is moreover, subject to manipulation by pretraining (Trabasso, 1963). Under these conditions the assumption in the subjects' strategies that all hypotheses are equiprobable is certainly incorrect. On the other hand, using simple and clearly structured stimuli substantially the same as those in experiments 4–6, the number of errors reported by Bourne and Haygood (1959) are nearly those predicted by S5 (actual errors tend to exceed predicted, but usually not more than by 10 percent, rarely 20 percent). (*See footnote 6 overleaf*)

If these or equivalent data are recorded, the task of determining which (if any) model fits the behavior, for individual subjects as well as groups, becomes very much easier. To take just two examples, if a subject more than rarely stated a hypothesis (or gave a response) that was inconsistent with the previous instance, model P_2 and model P_3 clearly would not fit his behavior. And if he retained the same hypothesis after making an error, model P_0 would fit his behavior, but not P_1 or the others.

We can draw two main conclusions from our discussion of the empirical data. First, most of the interesting psychological content in these experiments relates to subject strategies: that is, to matters on which the process models make definite assumptions (hence yield behavioral predictions), but on which the stochastic theory is silent. This is shown by Bower and Trabasso's informal use of process models as well as our more formal analysis. The stochastic theory is simply irrelevant to most of these issues, hence largely lacking in psychological content.

Second, to test process models effectively calls not only for manipulating conditions experimentally, as in the six experiments examined here, but also for obtaining more detailed behavioral data bearing directly on the hypotheses entertained by individual subjects on each trial. Gross performance data leave open—unnecessarily—too many questions about what the subjects actually are doing.

---

6. Levine (1966) has devised a method using blank (nonreinforcement) trials for determining from the responses what hypothesis the subject is using. Thus, even without using "introspective data," as subject reports of hypotheses are sometimes called, the strategy assumptions of the process models can be tested quite directly. They can also be tested, more weakly, without blank trials by analyzing the relation of responses to instances—strategy S_{52}, for example, would definitely rule out certain "inconsistent" responses. Levine, using simple four-dimensional stimuli and self-paced trials, was able to demonstrate clearly that subjects in his experiment were using strategies somewhat "between" S_{52} and S_{53}.

COMMENTS ON TESTING THEORIES STATISTICALLY

In the remaining two sections of this chapter, we will undertake to discuss the formal criteria for choosing among alternative theories and then apply our conclusions to the choice between process models and abstract stochastic theories. The present section is mainly devoted to explaining why contemporary statistical theory gives us little help in the matter. The following section approaches the comparison of theories in terms of "degrees of falsifiability"—a concept most fully developed by Popper (1959). We will see that the notion of falsifiability does, indeed, cast considerable light on the problem.

We will first dispose of a rather specific statistical topic, then turn to a more general one. The former has to do with our reasons for considering only the stationarity and independence of p and the magnitude of π in comparing the predictions of the stochastic theory with the data. We have already quoted Atkinson et al. as taking the same point of view. Bower and Trabasso, although they compare for each of the experiments the predicted and observed values of a whole range of "fine-grained" statistics, seem to share this viewpoint also.

> Most of the fine-grain statistics we have calculated are primarily sensitive to the existence of a stationary Bernouilli trials process prior to the last error.... Since this property characterizes a large portion of the sequence of responses obtained from a subject, we were actually trying to differentiate the models according to their assumptions about the remaining portion of the data. This is surely a losing strategy.... (Bower and Trabasso, 1964, p. 61)

The Prediction of Standard Deviations

Let us make the point more explicit. Consider, for example, the errors made by a subject, all of which will occur while he is in state $\bar{K}$. Under a very wide range of assumptions, the distribution of these errors will be exactly or approximately geometric, with a standard deviation nearly equal to the mean.[7] That is what Bower and Trabasso predict for their experiments, and the observed standard deviations lie very close to the predicted ones.

Now this result might well seem puzzling, even if we were prepared to accept the basic ideas of the stochastic theory, for the following reason: As used for prediction, the theory assumes the same value of π for all the subjects—it makes no allowance for individual differences. Since there is every reason to suppose that individual differences in fact exist, why are not the actual standard deviations substantially larger than the predicted values? If V_T is the total variance in number of errors, V_B the "Bernoulli variance" from the assumption of constant probability, of shifting from state $\overline{K}$ to state K, and V_D the variance due to differences among subjects, then we should have approximately (since variances of mutually independent variables are additive, and these variables are nearly independent):

$$V_T = V_B + V_D \qquad (2)$$

But notice that, since standard deviations are square roots of variances, as long as V_D is not almost as large as V_B, the total standard deviation will remain very close to the Bernoulli standard deviation. Suppose, for example, that $\sigma_D = k\sigma_B$, so that $V_T = (1 + k^2)V_B$. Then:

$$\sigma_T = (1 + k^2)^{\frac{1}{2}}\sigma_B \qquad (3)$$

For $k = \frac{1}{2}$, this means that σ_T will only be about 11 percent larger than σ_B, for $(1 + k^2)^{\frac{1}{2}} = 1.11$. If $k = \frac{1}{4}$, $\sigma_T = 1.02\sigma_B$. Thus, if the intersubject standard deviation of π is even as much as one-half or one-quarter of its mean value, the augmentation of the variance will hardly be observable unless the samples are enormous.

We can be even more precise in showing how insensitive the statistics are to individual differences. In experiment 5, summarized in table 1, there were 16 subjects who started their criterion run on or before trial 5, in addition to the 10 subjects each in the C, R, and N conditions. For the data of these 46 subjects point predictions were made. Bower and Trabasso (p. 75) have this to say:

For these predictions, $p = 0.50$ and $\pi = 0.087$. The predictions are very accurate. Especially impressive are the predictions of the variance of total errors and the variance of the trial of the last error.

Now the only way that individual differences can enter into the formalized mathematical theory is through variation in p or π. Since π, as we have seen, can take on a range of values depending on the psychological assumptions about processing, we give the expression for the variance of total errors assuming a rectangular distribution of π.[8]

Given the geometric distribution for total errors with parameter,

$$g(T, \pi) = \pi(1 - \pi)^{T-1}, \qquad 0 < \pi < 1 \qquad (4)$$

Let

$$\varphi(\pi) = \frac{1}{\pi_2 - \pi_1} = \frac{1}{\Delta}, \qquad \pi_1 < \pi < \pi_2 \qquad (5)$$

be the rectangular distribution for π over the range π_1–π_2. Then the joint distribution is

$$F(T) = \frac{1}{\pi_2 - \pi_1} \int_{\pi_1}^{\pi_2} \pi(1 - \pi)^{T-1} d\pi \qquad (6)$$

$$= \frac{1}{(\pi_2 - \pi_1) T(T + 1)} \left[-(1 + T\pi)(1 - \pi)^{T} \right]_{\pi_1}^{\pi_2} \qquad (7)$$

---

7. It is not at all uncommon to find in learning experiments that a very large part of the variance in the data can be explained by the assumption of pure guessing behavior prior to the trial on which the correct response is fixated. This result is often guaranteed by the experimenter (independently of whether the subject actually is behaving "randomly") when he randomizes stimulus sequences to avoid position preferences and the like. "Explaining" such data, then, is more a matter of verifying the laws of probability than testing psychological theories. See Simon (1957; 1962).

8. We wish to thank Professor Tarow Indow, Keio University, who developed these equations and has kindly consented to our using them.

The expected value for total errors becomes

$$E(T) = \sum_{T-1}^{\infty} TF(T)$$

$$= \frac{1}{\pi_2 - \pi_1}$$

$$\left[\sum_{T-1}^{\infty} \frac{-(1 + T\pi)}{(T + 1)} (1 - \pi)^T \right]_{\pi_1}^{\pi_2} \tag{8}$$

$$= \frac{1}{\pi_2 - \pi_1} \ln \frac{\pi_2}{\pi_1} \tag{9}$$

and the variance is

$$\sigma^2(T) = \frac{2}{\pi_1 \pi_2} - E(T) - [E(T)]^2 \tag{10}$$

In the limit, these expressions are the same as equation (14) of Bower and Trabasso (p. 52).

$$\lim_{C_2 \to C_1} E(T) = \frac{1}{\Delta} \ln \left(1 + \frac{\Delta}{\pi_1} \right)$$

$$= \frac{1}{\Delta} \left(\frac{\Delta}{\pi_1} - \frac{\Delta^2}{\pi_1} + \cdots \right)$$

$$= \frac{1}{\pi_1} \tag{11}$$

where $\pi_2 = \pi_1 + \Delta$,

$$\lim_{\pi_2 \to \pi_1} \sigma^2(T) = \frac{1 - \pi_1}{\pi_1^2} \tag{12}$$

Returning now to the specific example when $\pi = 0.0873$. Then, the limiting value of

$$E(T) = \frac{1}{0.0873} = 11.45 \tag{13}$$

and the limiting value of

$$\sigma(T) = [\sigma^2(T)]^{\frac{1}{2}}$$

$$= \frac{1}{\pi} (1 - \pi)^{\frac{1}{2}}$$

$$= E(T)(1 - \pi)^{\frac{1}{2}}$$

$$= 11.45(0.9127)^{\frac{1}{2}}$$

$$= 10.96 \tag{14}$$

These are the point estimates, when π is estimated from the observed value of 11.45 mean errors obtained from the data of the forty-six subjects.

Now, doubling and halving the mean value of 0.087, we assume a distribution of π extending over a four-to-one range, with $\pi_1 = 0.0453$ and $\pi_2 = 0.174$. Substituting these values into equations (9) and (10) yields

$$E(T) = \frac{1}{(0.174) - (0.0435)} \ln \frac{0.174}{0.0435}$$

$$= 10.60 \tag{15}$$

$$\sigma^2(T) = \frac{2}{(0.174)(0.0435)} - 10.6$$

$$- (10.6)^2$$

$$= 146 \tag{16}$$

and the estimate of the standard deviation of total errors becomes

$$\sigma(T) = (146)^{\frac{1}{2}} = 12.08 \tag{17}$$

Compared with the value of 10.96, this is an increase of only 10 percent in σ, due to the assumed individual differences, for a fourfold range in variation of the learning parameter. For these large individual differences the increase in variance is barely detectable.

Prediction of the Other "Fine-grain" Statistics

By similar arguments we can show that almost all the "fine-grain" statistics reflect mainly the random component introduced into the experiment by the experimenter, through the initial guessing behavior of the subject. Hence, the statistics are insensitive to individual differences, or, for that matter, to any other psychological aspects of the subject's behavior that might be expected to affect the statistics.

To demonstrate this, we compare in table 3 actual and predicted statistics for one of Bower and Trabasso's experiments with the statistics of an unbiased coin flipped a number of times equal to the average number of learning trials of the experimental subjects. It can be seen that the coin-flipping statistics fit the observations about as well as do the statistics from the stochastic theory. The only difference, of course, between the pure guessing model and the stochastic learning model is that

Table 3. Comparison of Stochastic Theory with Pure Guessing Model.

	Pure Guessing	Observed*	Predicted (Stochastic)*
Total Errors	20.97	20.85	20.85
Errors before First Success	1.00	1.01	0.99
σ	1.41	1.39	1.37
Errors before Second Success	2.00	2.17	2.05
σ	2.00	2.29	2.07
Trial of Last Error	40.94	40.94	40.94
Successes between Adjacent Errors	1.00	1.04	1.04
σ	1.41	1.42	1.45
Probability of Error Following Error	0.50	0.46	0.48
Alternation of Success and Failure	21.47	22.04	21.06
Runs of Errors R	10.48	11.23	10.72
Runs of k Errors, r_1	5.24	6.33	5.54
r_2	2.62	2.52	2.68
r_3	1.31	1.20	1.30
r_4	0.66	0.52	0.62
Error pairs C_1	10.00	9.56	10.11
C_2	9.75	9.67	9.86
C_3	9.50	9.12	9.63
C_4	9.25	9.20	9.40
C_5	9.00	8.75	9.17

*The "Observed" and "Predicted" data are from Bower and Trabasso's first reversal experiment (p. 73, table 2), the "Pure Guessing" predictions are explained in the text.

the former terminates the series of trials at a predetermined point, while termination in the latter is itself a random phenomenon with an exponential distribution over trials. Hence this demonstration does not show that the stochastic theory is wrong, merely that it has minimal psychological content.

Statistical Tests of Extreme Hypotheses

We turn next to the more general question of how to evaluate the deviations between predictions and observations—how to decide whether they are small enough to ignore or large enough to invalidate the theory. Bower and Trabasso follow common practice in this matter: they treat the stochastic theory as a null hypothesis and use such statistics as chi-square or the Kolmogorov-Smirnov statistic to find the probability that observations as deviant as the actual ones could have arisen by chance.

It is generally agreed today among mathematical statisticians that this procedure is wholly inadmissible. We will not repeat the argument at length, since it has been put forth several times in the statistical and psychological literature. A well-known statement was published by Grant (1962). When a mathematical theory is taken as the null-hypothesis, the testing procedure has two unpleasant characteristics: (1) the poorer the data (small samples or "noisy" data), and the weaker the power of the test, the more likely is the hypothesis to be accepted; and (2) the better the data, and the more powerful the test, the more likely the rejection even of a hypothesis that is an excellent first approximation (say, within a few percent) to the "true" theory, e.g., the $1/2N$ hypothesis. Use of distribution-free statistics, like the Kolmogorov-Smirnov, is particularly objectionable under these circumstances, since such statistics almost invariably have low power. All that can be said for them is that they are unlikely to reject a theory that is even roughly correct. Using only such weak tests, a student in the sophomore physics laboratory might be unable to "disprove" Galileo's law of falling bodies, which he could more likely do with chi-square and reasonably precise apparatus. As others have suggested, the best way to deal with this dilemma is to dispense with significance tests entirely.

This, properly, is what Bower and Trabasso do, making only a formal bow in the direction of tests of significance, and placing their main reliance on finding "critical" experiments that separate alternative hypotheses radically. But this brings us back to the discussion of the previous section, for the variant predictions in the critical experiments come, as we have seen, not from the stochastic theory but from the informal, and only partially stated, process models that stand behind the theory.

ON THE CHOICE OF THEORIES

There is general agreement on at least one criterion for rejecting a theory: if it fails badly in its empirical predictions it should be repaired or discarded. What constitutes a "bad" fit is, as we have just seen, a debatable question.

A long interval of days, months, or years often intervenes between the moment when a theory is first conceived and the moment when it can definitively be rejected or accepted (the latter, of course, only until a better theory comes along). To guide our behavior during this interval, we need not only criteria for accepting and rejecting theories, but also criteria to tell whether to "entertain" theories. As a matter of fact, much of the debate about the relative merits of different theories is debate not about which theory to *accept* (since the evidence is inconclusive), but debate about which theory or theories to *entertain*.

Falsifiability

Universality and Precision. There is a connection between the criteria for accepting and rejecting theories and the criteria for entertaining them. Popper (chap. 6), after a careful analysis of these criteria, concludes that the best reason for entertaining a theory is that it is testable (more accurately "falsifiable")—i.e., that it makes strong predictions that are readily capable of

being refuted by evidence if the theory is, in fact, false. Putting the matter more vividly, you can't get into much trouble proposing a theory, however fantastic on its face, if there are numerous opportunities to demonstrate its ridiculousness empirically.

Let us, following Popper, restate the criterion in a number of other forms, to show that it really agrees with common sense and common belief on the matter. Ignoring whatever we may know about the facts of the matter, consider the two following theories:

T1. All heavenly bodies move in circles.
T2. All planets move in ellipses.

Theory T1 is decidedly stronger than theory T2, on two grounds: (1) in applying to all heavenly bodies, and not just planets, it is the more *universal*; (2) in specifying circles, which are special cases of ellipses, it is more *precise*. The falsifiers of T2 are a subclass of the falsifiers of T1; any observation that would falsify T2 (e.g., observation of a planet not moving in an ellipse) would also falsify T1, but not conversely. Since in a theory it is desirable to obtain the maximum of prediction from the minimum of assumptions, the more universal and precise a theory, hence the more falsifiable, the better.

The greater precision of T1, as compared with T2, may be viewed in a slightly different way. Suppose all the bodies we are observing move in a plane in Euclidean space. Then, since three points determine a circle, there is a possibility of disconfirming T1 with as few as four observations of the position of a heavenly body. Since five points determine a ellipse, T2 could never be disconfirmed with fewer than six observations of a planet. Thus, a theory is stronger the fewer the free parameters at our disposal in fitting it to data. Precision, in the context of curve fitting, varies inversely with numbers of degrees of freedom. Again, the intuitive criteria we apply in judging the "plausibility" of theories lead us to prefer the stronger theory.

Simplicity. Another consideration leads to exactly the same conclusion (Popper, 1959, chap. 7). "Simple" theories are generally thought preferable to "complex" theories. A number of reasons have been put forth for preferring simplicity, but the most convincing is that a simple theory is not as easily bent, twisted, or molded into fitting data as is a complex theory. This is merely a variant form of the argument for fewer rather than more degrees of freedom—i.e., for the more precise rather than the less precise theory.

Of course, no matter how two theories may compare in precision or universality, we will always prefer one that fits the empirical evidence to one that is falsified by the evidence. Hence, in the case of two theories related as T1 and T2, we will entertain the weaker, T2, only if the stronger, T1, is falsified.

Application of the Criteria. It is often objected to process models in general, and computer simulation models in particular, that they are too "flexible," hence weak and not falsifiable. They have, it is argued, too many degrees of freedom so that, by simple adjustment of parameters, they can be made to fit the data no matter how the data come out.

This impression seems to arise from the fact that simplicity is sometimes equated with parsimony, and that process models, when compared with mathematical theories, have the appearance of being decidedly garrulous and not parsimonious at all. For example, Bower and Trabasso's stochastic theory appears to be based on only two equations containing two parameters; while a computer program that is a literal translation of model P_0 contains about 200 instructions in IPL-V, a list processing programming language, in addition to a substantial amount of input data to specify the stimulus structure.

Appearances in this case are decidedly deceptive. A large part of the program and data in the process model are required to make explicit things that are only implicit—but of necessity assumed—in the stochastic theory. Our earlier comparison of the formalized descriptions of the models with the program implementing the theory shows that the differences in parsimony are more apparent than real as soon as both formulations are held to the same standards of explicitness.

Far more crucial than the number of words it takes to state a theory are the criteria for measuring its falsifiability. We have shown in detail that in terms of these criteria, the process models are stronger (more precise) theories than the stochastic theory, since the latter can be deduced (at least approximately) from P_0 and several of its variants. Hence, any observation that would falsify the stochastic theory would falsify the process models. Hence, until the process models are falsified by data, they are the preferable ones to entertain.

Flexibility. There still remains a slight aura of paradox about this conclusion, for we have demonstrated at least one kind of flexibility in the process models: we have shown how, by modifying S5, we could fit a number of different experimental outcomes. Yet all these variants are (approximately) consistent with the stochastic theory. Hence, the process models (1) appear to offer more points of adjustment, and (2) appear to be easy to change to avoid falsification (though not to a greater extent than is admitted by the vagueness of the stochastic theory).

The paradox disappears if we are careful to distinguish between parameters available within a *single* theory, on the one hand, and alternative theories within a *class* of theories, on the other. The process models do not contain any free parameters. (The stimulus structure is not a free parameter, since this is dictated by the nature of the actual stimulus, defined in the experimental design.) If one of them is falsified by experimental data, the only recourse is to replace it by a different process model—another theory.

On the other hand, the stochastic theory contains two free parameters, which can be used to fit the observed values of p and π. This is precisely why the single stochastic theory is consistent with the whole set of process models, and hence is weaker than they are. Furthermore, if it is impossible to fit the data with the two free parameters, recourse may be had to the same expedient that is admitted by the process models: to change the theory. If a one-element theory does not fit, perhaps a two-element theory will, or a theory modified in some other way. This is, quite properly, the procedure that Bower and Trabasso adopt in their appendix in order to provide a better explanation for the data of experiment 2. They construct a new informal process model and then derive from it a new stochastic theory that fits the data better than does the theory in the body of their paper.[9]

Formally, it is very difficult and perhaps impossible to distinguish between parameter-fitting and replacing a theory with a different, but similar one. Thus it would not be formally wrong to regard a process like S5 as a "parameter" to be fitted and the whole class of process models as a single one-parameter theory. But if we play this game, we must play it symmetrically: we can equally well view the stochastic theory as a particular member of a wider class of *n*-parameter theories, in which all but two of the parameters have zero as their particular value.

More important, we do not have to play the game at all. If we prefer strong theories to weak, then the precision of each individual process model is a definite asset. It gives us many opportunities to falsify the

model. (And many additional opportunites not available for the stochastic theory, if we observe the subject's choices of hypotheses and his specific responses.) Second, because the model specifies the experimental instructions as well as the subject's strategy, it gives (without introducing free parameters) a full range of predictions over many experimental conditions. Third, if it turns out, as it has with the data we have examined, that no one of the models fits all the data, we may be able to strengthen the theory again by incorporating several of the models in it, but adding also a process that determines the conditions under which the strategies of each model will be evoked. We have sketched out how this might be done in the case at hand. If all the submodels in the composite are consistent with the stochastic theory then, at worst, the composite model will be as strong as the stochastic theory, and almost always considerably stronger, for in any *particular experiment* it will make specific predictions without using any free parameters.

We add one comment of a more pragmatic kind. Persons who claim that it is "easy" to modify a process model, because of its garrulousness, to fit experimental data simply have never tried. The usual result of modifying a computer program, for any reason, is that the program behaves nonsensically. A program that is put together at random will give every evidence of being a random device—until it stops entirely or loops. Hence, modifying a program to fit particular discrepant observations without destroying the fit elsewhere is a good deal harder than estimating parameters, and probably at least as hard as modifying a mathematical theory by introducing new degrees of freedom via new parameters. Even if we give the theorist wide privileges of "fitting" them, process models in the form of computer programs are highly falsifiable—and most of the time demonstrably false.

Conclusion

In this chapter we have used a concept attainment experiment previously studied

---

9. Trabasso and Bower (1966) adopt the same strategy again to explain the data of some of their cue reversal experiments. Apparently they explore a number of (informal) process models before accepting one as the basis for their revised stochastic theory, for they comment (p. 169): "This rule is the only one we have been able to devise which is consistent with the results of our prior experiments on presolution reversals." The new model involves specific, and rather elaborate assumptions about the information the subject holds in short-term memory while executing the strategy we have called S5. As in their other experiments, Bower and Trabasso use none of the detailed information about each subject's individual choices that would provide much stronger tests of the model than the statistical aggregates actually used.

in considerable detail by Bower and Trabasso in order to compare stochastic theories, on the one hand, with process models formalized as computer simulation programs, on the other.

We have constructed a class of process models from which the stochastic theory proposed by Bower and Trabasso can be derived. We have demonstrated how the stochastic theory can be translated into a very aggregative process model; and we have demonstrated how one of the process models can be expressed as a stochastic theory, and that stochastic theory, in turn, aggregated, until the Bower-Trabasso theory is obtained in close approximation.

We have shown that Bower and Trabasso in fact make use of informal process models, closely related to the ones we have formalized, in carrying out their analysis; and that the analysis could not have been carried out without them, or some equivalent. They use these informal models (1) to provide grounds of plausibility for the stochastic theories, (2) to make predictions of detail not encompassed in the stochastic theories, and (3) to make predictions for new experimental conditions to which the stochastic theories do not apply. Formalizing the process models makes it easy to detect where Bower and Trabasso were led into unconscious inconsistencies while applying process assumptions (in particular, assumptions about subjects' strategies) to specific experiments.

We have reviewed the statistical evidence for the validity of the stochastic theories and have shown that the accurate predictions of fine-grain statistics that have been achieved with them must be interpreted as validations of the laws of probability rather than of the psychological assumptions of the theories and that the classical tests of statistical significance cannot properly be applied to testing theories of this kind.

Finally, we have discussed the criteria that might be used in choosing between relatively detailed process models, on the one hand, and highly aggregated stochastic theories, on the other, as vehicles for explaining concept attainment. We have shown that, in the case at hand, the process models are to be preferred as being stronger and more readily falsified than the stochastic theories. The process models are more universal, in permitting predictions over a wider range of experimental situations without introducing new, *ad hoc*, assumptions. They are more precise, in making more definite predictions and predictions about many aspects of the subjects' behavior that have been abstracted away in the stochastic theories. They are simpler and more parsimonious, in allowing fewer degrees of freedom to fit them to the data.

The distinction between process models and stochastic theories is, of course, a matter of degree—we have shown that the stochastic theory can be treated as a very gross process model, but one with only modest psychological content. The process models that have been described here are themselves relatively uncomplicated, not so much because they abstract from the subject's behavior (although they certainly do not contain any detailed assumptions about his microprocesses), as because the class of situations they were designed to handle is extremely simple. Perhaps one of their most promising characteristics is that they can gradually be expanded to handle wider ranges of situations, and handle them in detail, without damaging their efficacy in simple situations. In this way they provide a means, not previously available, for gradually integrating our theoretical models over wider and wider ranges of behaviors until that happy day arrives when we will have a theory of the whole cognitive man.

References

Atkinson, R. C., Bower, G. H., and Crothers, E. J. *An introduction to mathematical learning theory.* New York: Wiley, 1965.

Bourne, L. E., and Haygood, R. C. The role of stimulus redundancy in concept identification. *Journal of Experimental Psychology*, 1959, **58**, 232–38.

Bower, G. H., and Trabasso, T. R. Concept identification. In R. C. Atkinson (Ed.), *Studies in mathematical psychology.* Stanford: Stanford University Press, 1964. Pp. 32–94.

Grant, D. A. Testing the null hypothesis and the strategy and tactics of investigating theoretical models. *Psychological Review*, 1962, **69**, 54–61.

Levine, M. Hypothesis behavior by humans during discrimination learning. *Journal of Experimental Psychology*, 1966, **71**, 331–38.

McCracken, D. *A guide to Algol programming.* New York: Wiley, 1963.

Newell, A., Tonge, F. M., Feigenbaum, E. A., Green, B. F., and Mealy, G. H. (Eds.) *Information processing language-V manual.* (2nd ed.) Englewood Cliffs, N.J.: Prentice-Hall, 1964 (referred to hereafter as IPL-V).

Popper, K. R. *The logic of scientific discovery.* London: Hutchinson, 1959.

Simon, H. A. Amounts of fixation and discovery in maze learning behavior. *Psychometrika*, 1957, **22**, 261–68. Reprinted as chapter 2.1 in this book.

Simon, H. A. A note on mathematical models for learning. *Psychometrika*, 1962, **27**, 417–18. Reprinted as chapter 3.4 in this book.

Trabasso, T. R. Stimulus emphasis and all-or-none learning in concept identification. *Journal of Experimental Psychology*, 1963, **65**, 398–406.

Trabasso. T. R., and Bower, G. H. Presolution dimensional shifts in concept identification. *Journal of Mathematical Psychology*, 1966, **3**, 163–73.

5·5

Problem Solving and Rule Induction (1974)

with Glenn Lea

Discussions in the psychological literature of cognitive processes generally treat separately a category of behavior called "problem solving," on the one hand, and a category called "concept attainment," "pattern induction," or "rule discovery," on the other. We will use the phrase "rule induction" to refer to any of the diverse tasks in the second category. We find this division already in the 1938 edition of Woodworth's *Experimental Psychology*, where the penultimate chapter is devoted to problem solving behavior, and the final chapter primarily to rule induction. In explanation of this organization, Woodworth comments:

> Two chapters will not be too many for the large topic of thinking, and we may make the division according to the historical sources of two streams of experimentation, which do indeed merge in the more recent work. One stream arose in the study of animal behavior and went on to human problem solving; the other started with human thinking of the more verbal sort [Woodworth, 1938, p. 746].

This work was supported by Public Health Service Grant MH-07722, from the National Institute of Mental Health. We are grateful to James Greeno and Allen Newell for helpful comments on an earlier draft of this chapter.

Far from merging, the two streams are still treated as quite distinct in more recent works. For example, in his 1968 *Annual Review* survey of artificial intelligence studies and their relevance to psychology, Earl Hunt devotes separate sections to "deductive problem solving" and "inductive problem solving," his categories corresponding closely to those introduced above. Similar categories appear in the principal contemporary textbooks.

This dichotomization cannot be regarded as satisfactory, for it fragments theories of thinking into subtheories with no apparent relation between them. In proposing information processes to account for problem solving, the theorist then assumes no responsibility for the relevance of these processes to concept attainment or other rule induction tasks, and vice versa. It is of course possible that these two kinds of thinking activity are entirely separate and independent, but possibility is not plausibility. It would be much better if we could show just how they are related; or, if they are not related, if we could provide a common framework within which the two classes of activities could be viewed.

Hunt's (1968) dichotomy of "deductive" and "inductive" will not do, for it is easy to show that from a logical standpoint the processes involved in problem solving are inductive, not deductive. Hunt may have been misled by the fact that the earliest artificial intelligence systems for problem solving (e.g., the Logic Theorist) dealt with the task environment of theorem proving. To be sure, the proof of a theorem in a formal mathematical or logical system is a deductive object; that is to say, the theorem stands in a deductive relation to its premises. But the problem solving task is to *discover* this deduction, this proof; and the discovery process, which is the problem solving process, is wholly inductive in nature. It is a search through a large space of logic expressions for the goal expression—the theorem. Hence, both a theory of problem solving and a theory of rule induction must explain inductive processes—a further reason for believing that these theories should have something in common.

Recent developments in the theory of problem solving (Newell, 1968; Newell and Simon, 1972; Simon, 1972b) give us a clue as to how to go about building a common body of theory that will embrace both problem solving and rule induction, including concept attainment. It is the aim of this chapter to outline such a theory. We will not adduce new empirical evidence, nor even refer to particular experiments in the literature. Instead, we will take as our starting points the recent formulation of the theory of problem solving mentioned above (Newell and Simon, 1972) and a recently formulated and rather general process model of concept attainment (Gregg and Simon, 1967) and show how both of these relate to the more general framework that is our goal. Since these theories have substantial empirical underpinnings, the discussion will be tied firmly to empirical data, albeit indirectly.

Preliminary Remarks

Before proceeding, we need to say more clearly what we mean by "common body of theory." A theoretical explanation of

the behavior of a subject confronted with a problem solving task or a concept attainment task might take the form of a program, an organization of information processes, more or less appropriate to carrying out the task. This is, in fact, the form of the problem solving theory of Newell and Simon and the concept attainment theory of Gregg and Simon mentioned in the last paragraph. To the extent that two programs explaining behavior in these two kinds of task environments employ the same basic processes, or to the extent that the processes are organized isomorphically, we may say they express a common theory.

But we must be more specific about what is common to them. The fact that two physical theories can both be stated in terms of differential equations connects them only superficially. Even less should we be surprised or impressed to find that two theories of human information processing performance can be written in the same programming language. Computer languages—IPL-V, LISP, SNOBOL—are almost completely general, capable of describing any organization of information processes. Anything that can be done by a Turing Machine can be described in any of these languages. When we speak of a common theory for problem solving and rule induction we intend to assert more than that man is a Turing Machine.

Nor is it sufficient—or very informative—to show that it is possible to write a single program that will simulate and describe human behavior in both a problem solving and a concept attaining environment. That kind of generality could be achieved by a "big switch"—a pair of subprograms joined only by a simple test to identify the task environment and to select from the pair the appropriate subprogram to deal with it.

The generality we seek, then, is not the nearly vacuous generality of either the Turing Machine or the Big Switch. Our aim is to show a much closer relation between problem solving processes and rule inducing processes than is implied by either of these. Exactly what this means will become clear as we proceed.

Because "problem solving" and "rule induction" are themselves heterogeneous domains with ill-marked boundaries, we will make matters more concrete by referring to some specific illustrative tasks. For problem solving, we will pay special attention to two tasks analyzed at length in Newell and Simon (1972): cryptarithmetic and discovering proofs for theorems in logic. For rule induction we will use as examples the standard concept attainment paradigms (Bruner, Goodnow, and Austin, 1956; Gregg and Simon, 1967; Hunt, 1962), extrapolation of serial patterns (Feldman, Tonge, and Kanter, 1963; Simon and Kotovsky, 1963; Simon, 1972a), and induction of the rules of a grammar (Klein and Kuppin, 1970; Solomonoff, 1959; Siklóssy, 1972).

Our undertaking is a little more ambitious than has been indicated thus far. For, not only have distinct bodies of theory grown up to deal with problem solving and rule induction, respectively, but there has been relatively little unity in theorizing across the whole of the latter domain. In particular, previous theoretical treatments of concept attainment do not include extrapolation of patterned sequences, and theories of sequence extrapolation do not encompass the standard experimental paradigms for studying concept attainment. Here we will aim at a unified treatment of the whole range of things we have here been calling "rule induction" and a comparison of these, in turn, with the activities called "problem solving."

We will begin by outlining the basic features of the information processing theory of problem solving and then use these features to construct the broader theory.

```
          1
   5ONAL5              D=5
   GERAL5              T=0
   ROBERO              R > 5, odd
```

Figure 1. A knowledge state in a cryptarithmetic task. (The figure shows what the problem solver knows after the initial processing of the sixth, fifth, and first columns of the display.)

PROBLEM SOLVING

In solving a well-structured problem (and this is the only kind we will deal with), the problem solver operates within a *problem space*. A problem space is a set of points, or nodes, each of which represents a *knowledge state*. A knowledge state is the set of things the problem solver knows or postulates when he is at a particular stage in his search for a solution. For example, at a certain point in his attempt to solve the cryptarithmetic problem, DONALD + GERALD = ROBERT, the problem solver may know that the number 5 must be assigned to the letter D, the number 0 to T, the number 9 to E; and he may know also that R is odd and greater than 5. The conjunction of these bits of knowledge defines the particular node he is currently at in his problem space, and the space is made up of a collection of such nodes, each representing some set of pieces of knowledge of this kind.

Problem solving activity can be described as a search through the space (or maze, or network) of knowledge states, until a state is reached that provides the solution to the problem. In general, each node reached contains a little more knowledge than those reached previously, and the links connecting the nodes are search and inference processes that add new knowledge to the previous store.

Thus, in the cryptarithmetic problem, the solution state is one in which each letter has been assigned a digit and in which it has been verified that these assignments provide a correct translation of the encoded addition problem. The problem solver moves from one state to another by inferences (or conjectures) and by visual searches of the problem display. For example, knowing that E = 9 and that R is odd and greater than 5, he may infer that R = 7. Or knowing that E = 9, he may discover, by scanning, the E in ROBERT, and replace this by a 9, obtaining: A + A = 9 (apart from carries) for the third column from the right.

Similarly, in discovering the proof for a theorem, a problem solver organized like

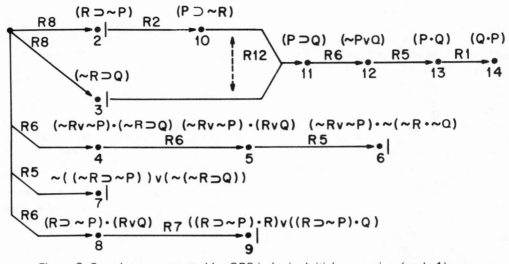

Figure 2. Search tree generated by GPS in logic. Initial expression (node 1) was (R ⊃ ~P) · (~R ⊃ Q). Above each node (knowledge state) is shown the new expression that has been derived here. Below each node is shown the order in which it was generated. On each link is shown the operator used to generate the next node. (See Newell and Simon, 1972, pp. 420–25.)

the General Problem Solver (GPS) starts with some initial expressions (premises) and the goal expression (the theorem to be proved), and applies rules of inference to generate new expressions that are derivable from the premises, until an expression is generated that is identical with the desired theorem. In this case, the knowledge states of which the problem space is composed are sets of expressions that have been derived along particular inference paths.

The search through such a problem is generally highly selective, being guided by the information that becomes available at each successive knowledge state. Given that the problem solver has already visited a certain number of points in the problem space, he can determine the direction in which he will continue to search by two kinds of decisions: (1) selection, from among those already visited, of a particular knowledge state from which to continue his search and (2) selection of a particular operator (inference rule, or "move") to apply at that node in order to reach a new knowledge stage.

Means-ends analysis, which appears to

be used extensively by human subjects in many problem environments, is a particular kind of scheme for making the choice of operator. It is the key selection mechanism incorporated in GPS. For means-ends analysis, the information in a particular knowledge state that has already been reached is compared with the specification of the solution to discover one or more differences between them. Corresponding to one of these differences, an operator is selected that is known, from previous experience, often to eliminate differences of that kind. The operator is applied to reach a new knowledge state.

We may formalize and generalize this description of problem solving as follows:

1. There is a *problem space* whose elements are *knowledge states*.

2. There are one or more *generative processes* (operators) that take a knowledge state as input and produce a new knowledge state as output.

3. There are one or more *test processes* for comparing a knowledge state with the specification of the problem state and for comparing pairs of knowledge states and producing differences between them.

4. There are processes for *selecting* which of these generators and tests to employ, on the basis of the information contained in the knowledge states.

The crucial points in this characterization are the third and fourth postulates: that information contained in the knowledge state can be used to guide the generation of new knowledge states, so that the search through the problem space can be selective rather than random. The problem solving process is an information gathering process as much as it is a search process. The accumulation of information in the course of search permits the search to be selective and gives problem solving in very large problem spaces a chance of success. The processes for using this information to steer the search are generally processes of inductive inference. Being inductive, they do not provide certainty, but have only heuristic value in guiding the search and making it efficient.

Characterizing problem solving as information gathering gives us the framework we need to deal with the whole range of tasks in which we are interested. We will describe the process for all these tasks as a search through a problem space guided by information accumulated during the search. And we will undertake to show that the fundamental search processes (generation, test, and selection processes), as well as the inference processes, are of the same kind in rule induction tasks as in problem solving tasks and are organized in a very similar way. Finally, we will see that the basic *difference* between the two domains is that rule induction involves an alternation of activity between two distinct, but interrelated, problem spaces, while only a single space is involved in problem solving.

Information Gathering in Theorem Proving

Consider the following GPS-like system for discovering proofs for theorems in symbolic logic. Many subjects in the laboratory have been observed to follow essentially this process. The knowledge states are sets of logic expressions that have been derived from the initial premises. Two kinds of information are used to guide the search: (1) the degree of similarity or difference between the expressions contained in a given knowledge state and the goal expression and (2) the specific character of the differences between particular expressions in the knowledge state and the goal expression. The first kind of information measures the progress that has been made in reaching a knowledge state—if it contains an expression that is highly similar to the goal expression, then it can be taken as a likely starting point for further search. The second kind of information suggests how a closer approximation to the goal expression can be obtained—the specific differences that are detected suggest specific operators to remove them (see figure 3).

Information Gathering in Cryptarithmetic

We will use the cryptarithmetic task as a "bridge" from the topic of problem solving to the topic of rule induction because it is possible to give an interpretation to the task which places it in either of the two categories. Although the information gathering process in solving cryptarithmetic problems could be described in a manner very similar to our description of information gathering in theorem proving, we will look at matters in a slightly different way. Let us consider the knowledge states in cryptarithmetic to be made up of two distinguishable components: the *problem display* in which digits have replaced those letters to which assignments have already been made and the *list of assignments* themselves. The problem solving goal can then be described in two ways: (1) to replace all letters in the display by digits in such a way that the resulting problem in arithmetic is correct or (2) to complete the list of assignments of digits to letters so that each letter has a distinct digit assigned to it. Of course, both conditions must be satisfied to solve the problem, but if appropriate consistency checks are made when the display is modified, and when a new assignment is added to the list, then

Goal: Transform object A into object B

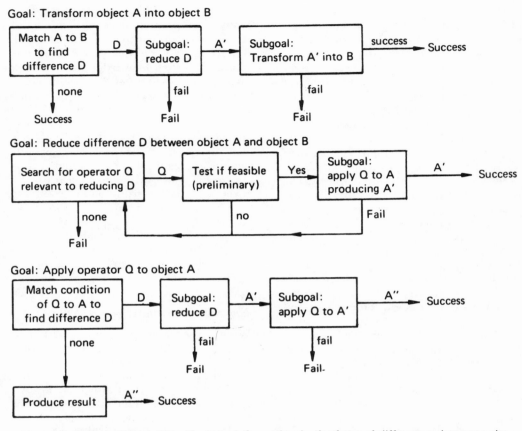

Figure 3. GPS methods—flow diagram. Information in the form of differences between the current knowledge state and the goal is used to select operators that may reduce the differences. (Reprinted with permission from Newell and Simon, 1972, figure 8.7, p. 417.)

reaching either goal will guarantee achievement of the other.

How is information extracted from knowledge states in the course of solving the problem? Whenever sufficient information has been accumulated in any column in the display, one or more new assignments of digits can be inferred from it by applying simple arithmetic processes. For example, in DONALD + GERALD = ROBERT, if D = 5 has been assigned, so that the display becomes: 5ONAL5 + GERAL5 = ROBERT, it can be inferred that the last T is o, so that T = o can be added to the list of assignments. The inference is made by a "Process Column" operator that takes the column of the display (together with information about

carries) as input and produces the assignment as output.

Conversely, whenever a new assignment is added to the list, the display can be changed by substituting the assigned digit for the corresponding letter whenever the latter occurs in the display. For example, suppose we have the display 5ONAL5 + G9RAL5 = ROB9Ro and the list of assignments: (D = 5, T = o, E = 9). Suppose we now add to the list the new assignment, R = 7. We can now alter the display to read: 5ONAL5 + G97AL5 = 7OB97o. Here, the input is an assignment from the list of assignments, the output is a modified display. The modification is made by a "Substitution" operator that searches the columns of the display for instances of the

```
  D O N A L D              D=5
 +G E R A L D
  R O B E R T
```

**Problem Display   List of Assignments
(Instance Space)   (Rule Space)**

Figure 4. Dual problem space interpretation
of cryptarithmetic task.

letter in question and substitutes the digit
for it wherever it is found.

Other inferential processes for producing
new information may operate internally to
the list of assignments or to the display
respectively. As an example of the former,
suppose that the list of assignments includes
the information: $E = 9$ and $R = 7$ v 9.
Then, if there is a process for examining
the consistency of assignments, that process
can draw the inference that $R = 7$, and
replace $R = 7$ v 9 on the list by this more
precise assignment. Similarly, processing
column 1 of the problem with the information that $D = 5$ leads both to the inference
that $T = 0$ and that a 1 is carried into the
second column. The latter piece of information can be entered directly on the
display.

The situation can now be redescribed in
the following way. We consider *two* problem spaces: a space of sets of assignment
rules (rules for substituting digits for letters
in the display) and a space of sets of
instances (columns of the display). The goal
is to complete the set of rules, so that there
will be a distinct assignment rule for each
letter. The proposed rules are tested against
the instances. Each column of the display,
which we are now interpreting as an
instance, provides a partial test of the
consistency of the rules. The situation so
described differs from the usual concept
attainment paradigm only in the fact that
the instances are not completely independent, but interact through the carries from
one column to the next (figure 5). In
every other respect, the task is now a
standard concept attainment task. Simply
by changing our way of viewing the problem space (or spaces), we have transferred

the cryptarithmetic task from the category
of problem solving to the category of concept attainment, pattern induction, or rule
discovery.

From this example, we hypothesize that
*the trademark that distinguishes these two classes
of tasks is the presence or absence of more than
one distinguishable problem space in which the
problem solving activity takes place*. If there is
only one space, we describe problem solving
as a search through that space, made more
or less selective and efficient by drawing
upon the information that is available at
each of the nodes that is reached. If there
are two spaces, we describe problem solving
as a search through one of them (usually,
as we will see, through the space of rules),
made more or less selective and efficient
by using information available in each
space to guide search in the other. By
focusing our attention on the processes for
obtaining and utilizing information, we
can provide the common framework that
we have been seeking for all these tasks.

RULE INDUCTION

If the theory of rule induction is to bear a
close relation to the theory of problem
solving processes, then it must be constructed of the same basic modules: one or
more generating processes, one or more
test processes, and one or more processes
to select the generators and tests to be
applied and to determine the order of their
application. Newell (1968, 1973a) has proposed a taxonomy of general problem
solving methods that lists the principal
ways in which these modules can be combined into operative systems. By "general

$$
\begin{aligned}
2D &= T + 10C2 \\
C2 + 2L &= R + 10C3 \\
C3 + 2A &= E + 10C4 \\
C4 + N + R &= B + 10C5 \\
C5 + O + E &= O + 10C6 \\
C6 + D + G &= R
\end{aligned}
$$

Figure 5. Space of instances in
cryptarithmetic, showing interdependence
of instances by virtue of carries, C2–C6.

methods" Newell means methods that make relatively unspecific demands upon the task environment, and hence, are widely applicable.

Some General Methods

We will be concerned with just three of the methods Newell defines: the generate-and-test method, the heuristic search method, and the induction (or hypothesis-and-match) method. We will see that the first two of these are characteristic of problem solving systems, the third of rule induction systems, but that they differ mainly with respect to the information flows among the modules. All these methods may draw upon one or both of two submethods: the matching method and the means-ends method.

At a minimum, any goal directed system must include a generator for producing new knowledge states and a test for determining whether a state produced by the generator is in fact a solution state. The simplest solution method is just this minimal *generate-and-test*. The power and efficiency of the method derives from information that is implicit in its structure. If, for example, the generator can produce only a very small set of states, and if this set is guaranteed to contain a solution, the method will be powerful, for the solution will be found promptly. If the test can reject inadequate solutions rapidly—say, by means of a matching process—then the cost of testing will be relatively small.

In the generate-and-test method, the order in which nodes are generated is independent of the knowledge that is gradually accumulating—the information is used only by the test process. Consider next a more sophisticated system, where the generator is no longer insensitive to knowledge that has been produced. Now information flows back from the test to the generator. This feedback requires the test to provide more information than just the success or failure of the match between the knowledge states generated and the specification of the desired knowledge state (the goal). Using the test information, the

generator produces a new knowledge state by modifying a state produced previously in the search. This dependency of generation upon the test outcome characterizes the *heuristic search* method.

We have already remarked on two kinds of information that can be used by the generator in heuristic search: first, information to select which of the previously generated states will be modified to produce the next state; second, information to select which of several available operators will be applied to the knowledge state to modify it. If the latter choice depends on the test's detecting specific differences between a state and the goal state, then we speak of the *means-ends* submethod.

Thus far everything that has been said applies equally well to problem solving and to rule induction. In the former case, the search ends with the discovery of the problem solution; in the latter, with the discovery of a rule that is consistent with a set of instances. In both cases, the key process is a search—an inductive process. The search for a rule can be (and usually will be) a heuristic search and can employ the means-ends submethod, as we will see.

What distinguishes rule induction tasks from problem solving tasks is the nature of the test process. In a rule induction task, the attainment of a solution is determined by applying the proposed rule to objects (*instances*), and by then testing whether the application gives a correct result. The test is not applied directly to the rule, but to another set of expressions, the instances. The evaluation of the rule thus takes an indirect path, and the feedback of information from test to generator retraces this path. A rule is rejected or modified if false instances are associated with it, or if there exist true instances that are not associated with it.

In a rule induction task we can define a space of sets of instances in addition to the space of sets of rules. The test process for the rule induction system operates within the space of instances. It can incorporate an instance generator (unless the instances are generated by the experimenter), as well as instance tests (which may or may not make use of knowledge of results provided by the experimenter). Suppose that the overall test process contains both generator and test subprocesses operating in the space of the instances. These subprocesses and their organization may, in turn, exhibit various levels of sophistication in their use of information—e.g., in the feedback of information from the test subprocess to the generator subprocess. A primitive test process would employ only the generate-and-test method; a more powerful one, heuristic search, possibly including the means-ends submethod.

In Newell's taxonomy, a system uses the induction method if there are separate generators for rules and instances and a match process to test whether an instance agrees with (is associated with) a rule. Since all heuristic search methods are inductive, as we have seen, it will be better to refer to this method as the *rule induction* method. It is clear that the rule induction method, so defined, is really a whole collection of methods. Nor is the locus of variation limited to the test process, as sketched in the last paragraph. There can also be various arrangements for the flow of information *between* the instance space

and the space of rules—i.e., between the test process and the generator process of the entire rule induction process (see figure 6).

In the most primitive system, there is no feedback of information from test to rule generator (Channel *e*, figure 6); the test simply eliminates rules that have been generated, but it does not provide information to help the generator select the next rule. In this case, the method is a rule induction version of the generate-and-test method, adapted to the dual problem space. On the other hand, if the rule generator does not create each rule anew, but produces it by modifying previous rule sets on the basis of information received from the test of instances (Channels *a* and *e*, figure 6), then we have a rule induction version of the heuristic search method.

Further, the existence of two spaces and two generators, one for rules and one for instances, opens up possibilities for methods that are not available when there is only a single problem space. For example, the instance generator need not be autonomous, but may instead derive information from the rules that have been generated and the previous tests that have been per-

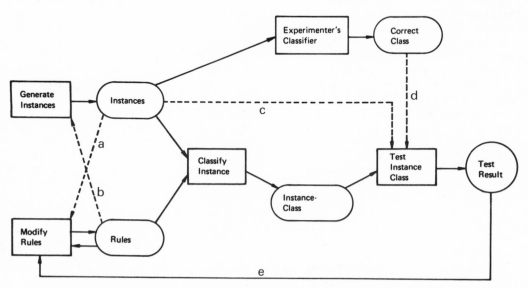

Figure 6. Information flows in rule induction processes. Broken lines show information channels used in some, but not all, variants of the rule induction task.

formed—a flow of information from rule space to instance generator (Channel *b*, figure 6) as well as from instance space to rule generator (Channel *a*). Thus, each new rule may be generated on the basis of the instances constructed up to that point (heuristic search for rules), while each new instance may be generated on the basis of the rules constructed up to that point (heuristic search for instances). This, in fact, is just what is happening in the cryptarithmetic solution method described earlier when we view the columns of the problem display as instances and the list of assignments as a list of rules.

A General Rule Induction Program

We are now ready to define a formal system that expresses the common theory we are seeking. Figure 7 gives the definition of a General Rule Induction (GRI) Executive Program. In order to make it as readable as possible, the definition is expressed in the informal programming language defined in Newell and Simon (1972, pp. 38–51).

The GRI system is extremely simple, consisting of a subprocess to generate rules and a second subprocess to generate and test instances. The output of the test (*test-result*) is available as an input to the rule generator, to help guide the next step of generation. Whether this information will be used, and in what way, depends on the internal structure of the rule generator, which is not specified. Thus GRI employs the generate-and-test method. Whether it employs heuristic search or even more elaborate methods depends on the specifi-

cation of the subprocesses and the information flows between them. Notice that just as the test results are available as input information to the rule generator, so the set of rules is available as input information to the instance generator.

Figure 7 makes patent that the only feature distinguishing a rule induction system from a problem solving system is that the tests of the rule induction system operate in a different space from the generator. Generator and test use the same space in a problem solving system. The fundamental generator-test alternation is identical for both kinds of systems, but the similarity between them extends much further. In both problem solving and rule induction systems, the selectivity of generators depends upon the feedback of information from the test processes. Because the rule induction system may contain two generators, rather than just one, there is a larger number of possible channels of information flow, hence, a richer taxonomy of possible specialized systems.

In figure 6, we have shown the flows of information in GRI. Some of these (shown by broken lines) are "optional," in the sense that variants can be devised that include or exclude them. We will illustrate this point in the next sections, when we discuss how GRI would handle some of the standard paradigms for concept attainment, series extrapolation, and grammar induction.

GRI is capable of performing the whole range of tasks just mentioned. We must be careful as to what we mean by this claim. The space of concepts appropriate to the usual concept attainment tasks is different

```
General Rule Inducer:
1. generate rules ( → rules);
   generate instances ( → instance);
      classify instance by rules ( → instance-class);
      test instance-class ( → test-result).
      if test-result = "correct" tally = tally + 1,
         else set tally = 0;
      if tally = criterion exit,
         else go to 1.
```

Figure 7. Executive program for the General Rule Inducer.

from the space of grammar rules or the space of sequential patterns. For a program to undertake to solve problems in any one of these domains, it will require—in addition to its general mechanisms and organization, common to all the domains— particularized equipment for dealing with the specific domain before it.

The situation here is the same as the situation confronting the General Problem Solver. GPS is a general organization for performing means-ends analysis, and for guiding search through a space of knowledge states. Before GPS can go to work on any specific problem, it must be provided with a specification of the problem domain: the objects, the definition of the knowledge states, the operators, the differences, and the associations of operators with differences. The General Rule Inducer needs the same kinds of problem specification in order to tackle specific tasks. GRI itself is an executive program providing an organization within which the specialized subprocesses can operate. We now present some examples of such specialized subprocesses that are applicable to the specific task domains of concept formation, series extrapolation, and grammar induction, showing how each operates within the general scheme.

Concept Attainment

In the commonest laboratory form of the concept attainment task, the subject sees a sequence of stimuli that differ along one or more dimensions (e.g., "large blue square"). Certain of these stimuli are instances of a concept (e.g., "square"), others are not. The subject guesses whether each is an instance, and is told whether he is right or wrong. His task is to induce the concept so that he can classify each successive stimulus correctly. In heuristic search terms, the subject searches through a space of possible concepts for the right one. The information that guides this search, however, is not information about concepts, but information about whether certain stimuli are instances of concepts or not.

The behavior of subjects in concept at-

tainment tasks of the kinds studied by Bower and Trabasso (1964) and others has been formalized by Gregg and Simon (1967) in a family of programs whose individual members differ only with respect to the amount of information the subject is assumed to retain as a basis for guiding the concept generator (Channels *a* and *e* of figure 6). The programs described by Gregg and Simon conform to the organization of the GRI executive.

In those variants of the program where no information is fed back (Channel *a* inoperative), whenever a guess has been wrong, the generator selects a concept at random from the set of available concepts. A slightly more efficient generator (which, strictly speaking, requires feedback via Channel *e* only to signal whether or not the last instance was classified correctly) samples randomly from the set of available concepts, but without replacing those already eliminated. A somewhat more efficient generator, using also feedback via Channel *a*, produces a concept consistent with the correct classification of the most recent instance. A still more efficient generator produces a concept consistent with the classifications of all previous instances. Empirical data in the literature indicate, according to Gregg and Simon, which of these methods will be employed by a human subject depends on the limits of his short-term memory and the availability of time to fixate information or of external memory to record it.

The paradigm described by Gregg and Simon's program does not incorporate a flow of information from the space of concepts to the generator of instances (Channel *b* in figure 6), since the instances in those experiments are produced by the experimenter independently of the subject's problem solving processes. The two spaces are linked only through the problem solver's guesses (*Classify Instance*, figure 6 and 7) as to the correct classification of the instances as they are produced. In fact, these guesses are irrelevant, since the information is actually provided by the experimenter's reinforcement of each guess as correct or incorrect. The same problem

Modify rules (→ rules):
   set tally = 0;
1. delete rules from hypothesis-list;
      select item randomly from
         hypothesis-list (→ rules);
      classify instance (→ instance-class);
      test instance-class (→ test-result);
      if test-result = "right" exit,
         else go to 1.

Generate instances (→ instance);
   if parity = "odd" set parity = "even",
      else set parity = "odd";
   produce instance randomly
      from instance-description (→ instance);
   classify instance (→ instance-class);
   if parity = "even"
      then if instance-class = "positive" exit,
         else set complement(rules) = rules in instance & exit;
      else if instance-class = "negative" exit,
         else set rules = complement(rules) in instance & exit.

Classify instance (→ instance-class):
   if rule ∈ instance set instance-class = "positive" & exit,
   else set instance-class = "negative" & exit.

Test instance-class (→ test-result);
   if correct-rule ∈ instance
      set correct-class = "positive",
         else set correct-class = "negative";
   if instance-class = correct-class
      set test-result = "right"
      set tally = tally +1 & exit,
         else set test-result = "wrong" & exit.

Figure 8. Program for concept attainment task. (Subroutines for executive program of figure 7.)

solving methods would work if the experimenter simply classified each instance as corresponding or not corresponding to the concept, without demanding a response from the problem solver. The flow of information is entirely from the instances to the concept generator and not in the opposite direction.

However, in other forms of the concept attainment experiment (Bruner et al., 1956) the problem solver himself generates the instances. He may, of course, generate them randomly; but he may also select instances so constructed as to choose between two classes of hypotheses. This information flow, from the space of rules to the generator of instances (channel *b*), enables solution methods that are more efficient than any with a one-way flow of information. Notice that the criterion for selection of instances is indirect and sophisticated: instances are valuable for solving the problem (finding the correct concept) to the degree that information on their classification imposes new restrictions on the domain of the rule generator.

The programs of Gregg and Simon do not cover the concept attainment paradigm in which the subject selects the instances. However, it is easy to generalize their programs to cover this case within the executive program of figure 7. A set of processes that accomplishes this is shown in figure 8. Each of the four processes— modify rules, generate instances, classify instance, and test instance-class—is extremely simple. The rule generator and instance generator embody particular assumptions about the subject's strategy for using information to enhance selectivity. The rule generator remembers which hypotheses have already been rejected and also requires the new hypothesis to be consistent with the previous instance. The particular instance generator that is provided here generates instances that are positive for the current rule on half the trials and negative on the other half. As a guarantee of the completeness of the analysis, a SNOBOL version of the program of figures 7 and 8 has been written and tested. By modifying the several processes in simple ways, always employing the executive of figure 7, a wide range of experimental paradigms and of subject strategies within each of those paradigms can be simulated.

Extrapolation of Patterned Sequences

A theory of how human subjects discover the patterns implicit in sequences of letters or numbers and use these patterns to extrapolate the sequences was developed in the form of a computer program by Simon and Kotovsky (1963—chapter 5.1 in this book). The relation of this theory to other theories of performance in this task and to the empirical data has been reviewed by Simon (1972a). The pattern discovery program is also an instance of the schema of figure 7.

In the sequence extrapolation task, the subject is presented with series of symbols followed by one or more blanks (e.g., "ABMCDM–"). His task is to insert the "right" symbols in the blanks—that is, the symbols that continue the pattern he detects in the given sequence. The goal object, then, is a sequence of symbols in

which all the blanks have been replaced "appropriately." But to fill in the blanks "appropriately," we must employ the notions of "same" and "next" between pairs of symbols, and perhaps other relations, in order to characterize the pattern as a basis for extrapolating it.[1] If the problem problem solving is to be characterized as a search, the search goes on in the space of patterns, and not in the space of extrapolated sequences.

To extrapolate the sequence, ABMCDM . . . , given as an example above, the problem solver must induce the pattern underlying that sequence: in each period of three letters, the first letter is *next* (N) in the English alphabet to the second letter (2) in the previous period (p); the second letter in each period is next (N) to the first letter (1) in the same period (s); the third letter in each period is the constant letter "M", i.e., is the *same* (S) as the third letter (3) in the previous period (p). The pattern might be described as "$N2p$ $N1s$ $S3p$." The sequence is initialized by supplying the beginning "A" and the constant "M."

Clearly, the elements of the sequence itself in the extrapolation task are the counterparts of the instances in the concept attainment task; while the pattern is the counterpart of the concept. What are the flows of information? As in the simple concept attainment paradigm, the sequence is provided by the experimenter rather than the problem solver. However, in his search for pattern, the problem solver can choose which elements of the sequence he will test for relations at any given moment. If, in the previous example, he is provided with three periods instead of

---

1. Ernst and Newell (1969) have proposed an ingenious scheme for handling the sequence extrapolation task as a GPS problem solving task, that is, in terms of a single problem space that accommodates both the sequences and the patterns. We will not discuss this scheme here, since an analysis in terms of a dual problem space seems more natural and simpler. However, their proposal shows again the close affinity between problem solving and rule induction, as these terms are commonly used.

two—ABMCDMEFM . . . —then, having discovered the second "M" three symbols beyond the first, he can test whether an "M" occurs again three symbols later. To this extent, there can be a flow of information (Channel *b*, figure 6) from a hypothesized pattern component (the repetition of "M") to a choice of which instance (which part of the sequence) to examine next.

The flow of information in the opposite direction, from sequence to pattern (Channel *a*), is even more critical for the efficiency of the solution method. The problem solver need not generate "all possible hypotheses," but can instead detect simple relations ("same" and "next") between pairs of symbols in the sequence and then hypothesize patterns constructed from those relations (an example of the *matching* method). Although obviously inductive, the process need not involve any considerable amount of search.

Induction of Grammars

As our final example of a rule induction task, we consider the induction of a grammar for a language, from examples of sentences and nonsentences. This task has received some attention in the artificial intelligence literature (e.g., Biermann and Feldman, 1971; Klein and Kuppin, 1970; Siklóssy, 1972; Solomonoff, 1959). In the grammar induction task, the subject generates a succession of symbol strings that may be sentences in a language possessing a formal grammar. He is then told whether or not each string is a sentence. His task is to induce the rules of the grammar so that he can predict infallibly whether any given string will be classified as a sentence. The commercially marketed game QUERIES 'N THEORIES provides a version of this task that is readily adapted to the laboratory.

In this problem domain, the examples of sentences and nonsentences constitute the space of instances, while the grammar rules correspond to the space of concepts. In the most common form of the task, the

problem solver selects the sentences against which to test his system of rules, hence there is a flow of information from the the space of rules to the space of instances (channel *b*, figure 6) as well as a reverse flow from instances to rules (channel *a*).

Let us illustrate these information flows more concretely. Consider a grammar with two components: a set of base sentences and a set of replacement rules that allow the construction of a new sentence by replacing certain symbols or sequences of symbols, in any sentence where they occur, by a new symbol or sequence. A simple example of such grammar is given by:

Base sentence: Y
Replacement rule: Y ← BY

This grammar has a single base sentence, Y, and a single replacement rule, Y ← BY. Applying the replacement rule to the base sentence, then to the resulting sentence, and so on, we obtain, as additional sentences of the language, BY, BBY, BBBY, and so on.

Suppose that it was already known, by previous tests, that Y and BY were sentences. Then, by supplying information from the instances to the rule generator, the possible replacement rule Y ← BY could be constructed directly. Reversing the flow of information, the rule itself can now be used to generate instances of predicted sentences, and the correctness of these can be checked by the "native informant" (the experimenter).

To match the various concept attainment paradigms, the task could be modified, for example, to supply the set of instances of valid sentences in advance. Or the experimenter could supply instances of sentences and nonsentences and require the problem solver to classify them. The two classes of tasks are in every way identical with respect to the ways in which information can be made available to the problem solver.

Figure 9 shows processes for performing the grammar induction task that again operates with the GRI executive of figure 7. These processes are a little more com-

Modify rules (→ rules):
  if test-result = "wrong"
    delete new-rule from rules;
  if basic-sentence-tally = "done" go to 1,
    else generate basic-sentence (→ rule)
      set new-rule = rule & exit;
1. if replacement-rule-tally = "done" exit,
    else generate replacement-rule (→ rule) &
      set new-rule = rule & exit.

Generate instances (→ instance):
  if new-rule ∈ basic-sentences
    set instance = new-rule & exit,
    else generate item from positive-instance (→ item);
      apply new-rule to item (→ instance)
      if instance ∉ positive-instance exit,
        else continue generation;
      if positive-instances exhausted
        set signal = "finished" & exit.

Classify instance (→ instance-class):
  generate basic-sentences (→ basic-sentence):
    if instance = basic-sentence set instance-class = "positive"
      & exit from routine,
      else continue generation;
  generate derived-sentences with length = length (instance)
    (→ derived-sentence):
    if instance = basic-sentence set instance-class = "positive"
      & exit from routine,
      else continue generation;
  set instance-class = "negative" & exit.

Test instance-class (→ test-result):
  if instance ∈ legitimate-instances add instance
    to positive-instances & set correct-class = "positive",
    else set correct-class = "negative";
  if instance-class = correct-class
    set test-result = "right",
    else set test-result = "wrong";
  add instance to tested-instances & exit.

Figure 9. Program for grammar induction task. (Subroutines for executive program of figure 7.)

plicated than those of figure 8, mainly because they must generate and test two different kinds of rules: basic sentences and replacement rules. The specific generators for the two kinds of rules are not defined in the figure. This program, like the one for concept attainment, has also been written and debugged in SNOBOL (with specific versions of the generators for basic sentences and replacement rules). We have begun to gather some data on human behavior in the grammar induction task which, on first examination, fit the program of figures 7 and 9 relatively well, but we will have to postpone detailed analysis of these data to another paper.

The Tower of Hanoi: A Digression

We digress for a moment to comment on the Tower of Hanoi problem, discussed by Egan and Greeno (1974), for this task illustrates again how tricky is the distinction between problem solving tasks and rule induction tasks. The problem as usually stated—to find a sequence of moves that will transfer all the disks from one peg to another, subject to the usual constraints on moves—is clearly a problem solving task. If demonstration of this is needed, it has been provided by Ernst and Newell (1969), who programmed GPS to solve the problem by the means-ends method.

But the problem can be stated differently: to find a *rule* for transferring the disks from one peg to another. It may also be required that the rule work properly for an arbitrary number of disks. Just as clearly, this is a rule induction task. To solve it, one or more rule spaces must be formulated and searches conducted through these spaces. Knowledge to guide this search may be obtained by manipulating the disks—that

is, by searching through the space of arrangements of disks on pegs. Thus *this* Tower of Hanoi problem, as distinguished from the one described in the previous paragraph, involves a dual problem space.

Rules for the Tower of Hanoi can be stated in various forms. One (incomplete) rule is based on the sequence: 1 2 1 3 1 2 1 4 1 . . . , where the digits refer to the disks to be moved. With slight modification, the sequential pattern programs discussed earlier could discover this pattern. The recursive solution to the problem requires a different kind of rule generator—one that understands the concept of recursive definition.

Summary: Application of GRI to Specific Task Environments

Table 1 shows how we have interpreted the processes of GRI in the context of the specific tasks we have discussed: concept attainment, sequence extrapolation, and grammar induction. A fourth column in

Table 1. Application of GRI to Four Tasks.

Task Environments

	GRI	Concept Formation	Sequence extrapolation	Grammar Induction	Crypt-arithmetic	Problem Solving
Rule Space	Rules	Current hypothesis	Partial pattern	Partial grammar	List of assignments	Node in problem space
	Modify rules	Generate hypothesis	Modify pattern	Modify grammar	Modify list	Apply operator at node
Instance Space	Instances	Instances	Sequence elements	Predicted sentences	Column of display	—
	Generate instance	(Generate instance)	[Generate sequence]	Generate sentence	Update display	—
Test	Classify instance	Respond	Predict symbol	Query experimenter	Process column	Describe new node
	Test instance-class	[Reinforce response]	Match symbols	[Accept sentence]	Detect contradiction	Evaluate new node

Note: Processes in square brackets are executed by experimenter; processes in parentheses are sometimes executed by experimenter.

the table shows how the cryptarithmetic task can be handled within the same schema when viewed as a rule induction task; while the fifth column shows which components of the schema have counterparts in a problem solving task where only a single problem space is involved.

We have shown how the specific processes that describe subject behavior within the executive program of GRI vary as a function of the characteristics of the experimental paradigm and the level of complexity and sophistication of the strategy that the subject adopts for handling the task.

In concept attainment experiments, for example, the subject is usually instructed specifically as to what concepts are admissible, that is, he is given the space of rules. He is also provided with an explicit definition of the space of possible instances. In sequence extrapolation tasks much more is usually left to the subject. The space of rules and the rule generator are not usually discussed explicitly in the instructions, nor *a fortiori*, the test for the adequacy or correctness of the extrapolation. The experimenter provides the instances (the incomplete sequence) and an ill-defined goal (that the sequence is to be extrapolated). The subject evolves the rest: the space of rules and the test for correctness of an extrapolation, as well as the generator and test processes that define his strategy.

Variations in subject strategies relate particularly to the use of information from each of the problem spaces—the rule space and instance space—to guide the generator for searching the other. In paradigms where the experimenter provides one of the generators (e.g., the instance generator in the standard concept attainment paradigm) there is less room for variation in subject strategy than in paradigms where the subject must devise both generators (e.g., in the form of the concept attainment experiment used by Bruner et al., 1956).

CONCLUSION

In this chapter we have proposed a conceptualization of problem solving and rule induction that allows these two areas of human thinking to be brought within a common framework. We have seen that both problem domains can be interpreted in terms of problem spaces and information processes for searching such spaces. The generators of elements in a problem space may be more or less selective, depending on what use they make of information provided by the tests, and varying levels of selectivity can be observed in both rule induction systems and problem solving systems. What chiefly distinguishes rule induction tasks from problem solving tasks is that the former call for a pair of problem spaces—one for rules and one for instances—while the latter commonly require only a single problem space. Our analysis of the cryptarithmetic task shows it to lie midway between the two main classes, and hence to provide a useful bridge for translating each of them in terms of the other.

To test the conceptualization, and to guarantee that it is more than a set of analogies, we constructed a formalization, the General Rule Induction program, together with subprocesses for concept attainment and grammar induction that operate within that program.[2] By means of GRI, each of the tasks can be mapped formally on the others. The basic components of these programs are generator and test processes organized into generate-test, heuristic search, means-ends, and matching methods.

References

Biermann, A. W., & Feldman, J. A. A survey of results in grammatical inference. *Conference on Frontiers in Pattern Recognition.* Honolulu: January 1971.
Bruner, J. S., Goodnow, J. J., & Austin, G. A. *A study of thinking.* New York: Wiley, 1956.

2. Since this was written, Dennis E. Egan and James G. Greeno have written SNOBOL routines that operate within GRI for discovering sequential patterns (personal communication). Thus the GRI scheme has now been implemented for the three main rule induction tasks discussed in this chapter.

Egan, D. E., & Greeno, J. G. Theory of rule induction: Knowledge acquired in concept learning, serial pattern learning, and problem solving. In L. W. Gregg (Ed.), *Knowledge and cognition*. Potomac, Md.: Erlbaum, 1974, pp. 43–103.

Ernst, G. W. & Newell, A. *GPS: A case study in generality and problem solving*. New York: Academic Press, 1969.

Feldman, J., Tonge, F., & Kanter, H. Empirical explorations of a hypothesis testing model of binary choice behavior. In A. Hoggatt & F. Balderston (Eds.), *Symposium on simulation models*. Cincinnati: Southwestern Publishing Co., 1963, pp. 55–100.

Gregg, L. W., & Simon, H. A. Process models and stochastic theories of simple concept formation. *Journal of Mathematical Psychology*, 1967, 4, 246–76. Reprinted as chapter 5.4 in this book.

Hunt, E. B. *Concept learning: an informational processing problem*. New York: Wiley, 1962.

Hunt, E. B. Computer simulation: Artificial intelligence studies and their relevance to psychology. *Annual Review of Psychology*, 1968, 19, 135–68.

Klein, S., & Kuppin, M. A. An intermediate heuristic program for learning transformational grammers. (Tech. Rep. No. 97), Computer Science Department, University of Wisconsin, Madison. August, 1970.

Newell, A., On the analysis of human problem solving protocols. In J. C. Gardin and B. Jaulin (Eds.), *Calcul et formalisation dans les sciences de l'homme*. Paris: Centre National de la Recherche Scientifique, 1968, pp. 146–85.

Newell, A. Artificial intelligence and the concept of mind. In R. Schank & K. Colby (Eds.), *Computer models of thought and language*. San Francisco: Freeman, 1973(*a*), pp. 1–60.

Newell, A. Production systems: Models of control structures. In W. G. Chase (Ed.), *Visual information processing*. New York: Academic Press, 1973(*b*), pp. 463–562.

Newell, A., & Simon, H. A. *Human problem solving*. Englewood Cliffs, N.J.: Prentice-Hall, 1972.

Siklóssy, L. Natural language learning by computer. In H. A. Simon & L. Siklóssy (Eds.), *Representation and meaning*. Englewood Cliffs, N.J.: Prentice-Hall, 1972, pp. 288–328.

Simon, H. A. Complexity and the representation of patterned sequences of symbols. *Psychological Review*, 1972(*a*), 79, 368–82. Reprinted 29 chapter 5.3 in this book.

Simon, H. A. The theory of problem solving. *Information Processing, 71*. Amsterdam: North-Holland, 1972(*b*), pp. 261–77.

Simon, H. A., & Kotovsky, K. Human acquisition of concepts for sequential patterns. *Psychological Review*, 1963, 70, 534–46. Reprinted as chapter 5.1 in this book.

Solomonoff, R. A new method for discovering the grammars of phrase structure languages. *Information Processing 59*. (Proceedings of the International Conference on Information Processing) Paris: UNESCO, 1959.

Woodworth, R. S. *Experimental Psychology*. New York: Holt, 1938.

6

Perception

Only blurred boundaries separate the traditional domains of sensation, perception, and cognition. In an information processing account of these domains the boundaries become even more blurred. A stimulus received on the retina, say, undergoes a whole series of encodings before it is stored in STM or LTM as some kind of symbol structure. The first stages of encoding take place in the sense organ itself, succeeding stages in those areas of the brain to which that organ communicates, later stages in less directly connected areas. Moreover, the process is not linear, for various kinds of feedback, including those that cause accommodation of the sense organ, influence the way in which the stimulus will be encoded.

The chapters of this section deal largely with the later stages of perceptual encoding and the recognition and memory processes associated with them. Nothing will be said here about the initial stages of boundary or object detection in the eye or about phoneme detection in the ear. Rather, we will assume that the incoming stimulus has been encoded as a collection of features and relations among those features. Thus, we will be concerned with exactly the same aspects of the perceptual system as we were in our account of EPAM, in section 3 of this book, and our theory of perception will use EPAM as its central mechanism.

Chapter 6.1 shows how some common perceptual illusions can be explained by postulating that visual images are encoded in memory as associative networks of nodes and links. The next four chapters, 6.2 through 6.5, discuss chessplayers' perception of the board in the game of chess and the relation of perceptual processes to expert skill in that game. Chapter 6.6 shows how spelling errors in English can be understood and predicted in terms of the same EPAM-like mechanisms that explain the chess perception phenomena.

ILLUSIONS AND VISUAL IMAGERY

Visual imagery continues to pose difficult problems for cognitive psychology. Only the most devout Skinnerian could doubt that the phenomenon exists, but characterizing it in operational terms is not a simple matter. If we make of the visual image too literal a picture inside the head, then we are forced to invent a homunculus to view that picture—indeed, an infinite sequence of such homunculi, each peering at the picture in the head of his predecessor.

From an information processing point of view, an attractive possibility is to suppose that visual images are like everything else in LTM: that they are associative, node-link structures. In this view, their peculiarly "visual" character is due to the facts (1) that they represent pictorial attributes of the stimuli (e.g., colors and shapes) and (2) that the node-link structure is a topological map of the visual stimulus. Thus, a red square could be represented by a node-link structure whose components denoted the corners, edges, and surface of the square, adjacent components being joined by links, and the node for the surface being joined to the node "red" by a link labeled "color."

The empirical question is whether visual images represented in this way would have the properties that such images are observed, by laboratory test, to have. For example, would such a node-link structure exhibit the common visual illusions? Chapter 6.1 undertakes to answer that question by creating a node-link representation of the Necker cube and of the well known "impossible figures." The illusions are readily created (indeed, it is difficult to see how such a representation could avoid them). Proceeding in a similar vein, the chapter also indicates how apparent motion could be produced in a memory of this kind.

Several studies at Carnegie-Mellon University have carried this inquiry further since the date when chapter 6.1 was published. Baylor (1971) demonstrated how a node-link representation could be used to explain human performance in Guilford's Block Visualization Test, while Farley (1974) and Moran (1974) built systems for visualizing line drawings of geometric figures. Just and Carpenter (1976) have used eye-movement data to support an information processing interpretation of the Shepard figure rotation phenomena.

Other accounts of visual imagery that are generally consistent with the views of this section, and in particular with the idea of representing visual images as node-link structures, include chapter 6.5 and the chapters by Chase and Clark (1972) and myself (1972) in the proceedings of the Fifth Annual Carnegie Symposium on Cognition, titled, *Cognition in Learning and Memory*. For a dissenting view, see Shepard and Podgorny (1978).

SCENE ANALYSIS

The process of converting the patterns of colored light that strike the retina into a "scene" composed of objects possessing clear boundaries and having intelligible locations in space relative to each other is not well understood. Much remains unknown about how the eye accomplishes this, and artificial intelligence efforts to imitate the natural process have thus far had only limited success. Almost the same can be said about encoding speech sounds, although research has progressed farther in this domain than in the domain of vision.

Without denying either the interest or the difficulty of these problems of initial encoding, we will simply bypass them in this book and concern ourselves solely with stimuli that have already been encoded symbolically. The visual stimuli treated in chapter 6.1 are sets of connected line segments, or are dots. The chessboard of chapters 6.2 through 6.5 (which is identical with the one used in chapter 4.3) is a structure of nodes, representing squares, and links, representing the visual paths along which one can move from any square to adjoining ones. The chessmen are represented as symbols having a few simple features, and associated with nodes. The spelling words of chapter 6.6 are represented as strings of letters, each letter, in turn, being encoded as a collection of features.

Even when we suppose that the visual stimulus has been encoded as a line drawing, it is not a trivial matter to interpret such a drawing as a representation of solid geometric objects located in three-dimensional space. The Artificial Intelligence Laboratory at MIT has carried on a long sequence of investigations, begun by Roberts (1963) and continued by Guzman (1968), Waltz (1975), and others, to design an information processing system capable of carrying out such an interpretation. Our present state of knowledge about this problem is summarized in the second, third, and fourth chapters of Winston (1975). The discussion of the Necker cube and impossible figures in chapter 6.1 is based on a system such as that proposed by Roberts.

PERCEPTION IN CHESS

Chapters 6.2 through 6.5 describe a series of investigations of how chessplayers encode and use the visual information they acquire from chessboards. Chapter 6.2 reports work done in collaboration with Michael Barenfeld; chapters 6.3 through 6.5, work done in collaboration with William G. Chase and Kevin Gilmartin.

The initial motivation for this line of research was provided by the claims of Gestalt psychologists, and particularly O. K. Tichomirov (Tichomirov and Poznyanskaya, 1966), that computer chess programs in general, and the MATER program in particular, were unable to represent the chess master's holistic grasp of the essential relations present in a chess position. Chapter 6.2 is a direct answer to that claim. The answer, as is usual in information processing psychology, takes the form of a computer program, PERCEIVER, that demonstrably does the things it was claimed could not be done.

As is recounted in chapter 6.2, the PERCEIVER program quite naturally brought to mind de Groot's (1978) well known experiments on the ability of chessmasters to retain visual information about chess positions, and thus led to the work reported in the succeeding three chapters. That work had a theoretical part and an experimental part. The theoretical part, reported in chapter 6.3, called for combining the mechanisms of PERCEIVER with the mechanisms of EPAM (section 3) to produce a new system, MAPP (Memory-Aided Pattern Perceiver), that would explain the phenomena revealed by the experiments on position memory. The experimental part, reported in chapters 6.4 and 6.5, called for replicating and extending the chessboard memory experiments to obtain more direct evidence for chunking as an explanation for the superior performance of chess masters in these experiments.

The hand-me-down character of the MAPP program is worth emphasizing, for it is an excellent example of the parsimony that is attainable from information processing models when they are extended from one task domain to another. MAPP is composed almost entirely of components that were first devised to solve different problems in quite remote task domains. The representation of a chess board for MAPP is borrowed from MATER, a program designed to demonstrate the power of selective search for solving problems in large spaces. The processes in MAPP for scanning the board come directly from PERCEIVER, which was constructed to explain the eye movement data published by Tichomirov and Poznyanskaya. The chunking mechanisms for MAPP were available in EPAM, a program originally designed to simulate behavior in rote verbal learning experiments. Thus, the chess perception phenomena were explainable in terms of existing information processing theories, without a need to postulate new mechanisms.

SPELLING SKILLS

Chapter 6.6, written in collaboration with Dorothea P. Simon, uses information processing concepts to understand the problem of spelling correctly in English and to evaluate some proposals for spelling instruction. It illustrates again the parsimony of using a few basic mechanisms (once more, EPAM) to explain a wide range of phenomena.

SPEL, a computer model for the spelling process, predicts successfully the kinds of errors that are typically made in spelling, and it provides some diagnostic principles for distinguishing among different deficiencies in spelling skills that may cause errors. A central component of SPEL is an EPAM-like word recognition memory that holds incomplete information about orthography. (Complete information is not generally necessary for word recognition in reading.) Spelling errors, tabulated by position in the word, exhibit a clear serial position effect of the kind we would expect EPAM to produce. In fact, the location of errors can be predicted quite accurately as the product of two factors: (1) expected errors calculated from the standard serial position curve and (2) phonemic ambiguity (the number of plausible alternative orthographic encodings of the phoneme). That is to say, a phoneme is likely to be misspelled if it is *both* in the interior of the word, instead of near its beginning or end, *and* if it is capable of being spelled phonetically in a variety of different ways.

The analysis of chapter 6.6 shows that most spelling errors lie in the direction of substituting a phonetically permissible spelling for the spelling that has come to be accepted as correct. Hence training in phonetic analysis can produce at most a limited improvement in spelling. Instead, techniques are needed for directing the learner's visual attention to the interior portions of words.

References

Baylor, G. W. A treatise on the mind's eye: An empirical investigation of visual mental imagery. Unpublished doctoral dissertation, Carnegie-Mellon University, 1971.
Chase, W. G. & H. H. Clark. Mental operations in the comparison of sentences and pictures, *In* L. W. Gregg (ed.), *Cognition in Learning and Memory*, New York: Wiley, 1972, pp. 205–32.
Farley, A. M. VIPS: A visual imagery and perception system. Unpublished doctoral dissertation, Carnegie-Mellon University, 1974.
de Groot, A. *Thought and Choice in Chess* (2nd ed.) The Hague: Mouton & Co., 1978.
Guzman, A. Computer recognition of three-dimensional objects in a visual scene. Ph.D. thesis, MAC-TR-59, Project MAC, Massachusetts Institute of Technology, 1972.
Just, M. A. & P. A. Carpenter. Eye fixations and cognitive processes, *Cognitive Psychology*, 8:441–80 (1976).
Moran, T. P. The symbolic imagery hypothesis: An empirical investigation. Unpublished doctoral dissertation, Carnegie-Mellon University, 1974.
Roberts, L. G. Machine perception of three-dimensional solids. *In* J. T. Tippet et al. (eds.), *Optical and Electro-Optical Information Processing*, Cambridge, Mass.: M. I. T. Press, 1965, pp. 159–97.
Shepard, R. N. & P. Podgorny. Cognitive processes that resemble perceptual processes, *In* W. K. Estes (ed.), *Handbook of Learning and Cognitive Processes*, Vol. 5, Hillsdale, N.J.: Lawrence Earlbaum Associates, 1978, pp. 189–238.
Simon, H. A. What is visual imagery? An information processing interpretation. *In* L. W. Gregg (ed.), *Cognition in Learning and Memory*, New York: Wiley, 1972, pp. 183–204.
Tichomirov, O. K. & E. D. Poznyanskaya. An investigation of visual search as a means of analyzing heuristics, *Soviet Psychology*, 5:2–15 (1966–67).
Waltz, D. Understanding line drawings of scenes with shadows. *In* P. H. Winston (ed.), *The Psychology of Computer Vision*, New York: McGraw-Hill, 1975, pp. 19–92.
Winston, P. H. *The Psychology of Computer Vision*, New York: McGraw-Hill, 1975.

An Information Processing Explanation of Some Perceptual Phenomena (1967)

INTRODUCTION

Contemporary schemes for using computers to process "visual" two-dimensional and three-dimensional representations, along with the recent information processing theories of human cognition, provide significant new clues to a number of perceptual phenomena hitherto regarded as somewhat mysterious and inexplicable. This chapter undertakes to show how some of the common visual "illusions," and one auditory illusion, would arise in an information processing system similar to those proposed recently to explain other aspects of cognition.

Newell, Shaw, and Simon (1960) have advanced a theory of human problem solving expressed in information processing terms, Feigenbaum and Simon (1964) have proposed a theory of rote memory, and a number of investigators have proposed theories of concept attainment that are closely similar to one another (Hovland and Hunt, 1960; Laughery and Gregg, 1962; Feldman, 1963; Simon and Kotovsky, 1963; Johnson, 1964). While these theories have not been completely unified, they all share certain common assumptions. First, they assume that representations of stimuli and problem situations can be stored in memory in structures isomorphic with lists and branching list structures. These structures have the properties of associations, more precisely, of the "directed associations" of the Würzburg School and Otto Selz. Secondly, the information processing theories assume that active cognitive processes store and modify these structures, admitting communication between the central nervous system and the environment, and between short-term and long-term memory, and that the active processes are fundamentally *serial* processes which can handle only a small

This work was supported in part by grant MH-07722-01 from the National Institutes of Mental Health to the Carnegie Institute of Technology. I am indebted for many of the ideas incorporated in these schemes to notions derived from B. F. Green's Baseball program; from Robert K. Lindsay's "Inferential memory as the basis of machines which understand natural language" (1963); from my own work on the Heuristic Compiler; and from work of Thomas G. Evans of MIT, e.g. "A heuristic program to solve geometry-analogy problems" (1964). My interest in applying these ideas to perception was stimulated by conversations with Jacob Beck, and I have benefited from comments from him and from E. G. Boring, E. J. Gibson, and Julian Hochberg. Needless to say, my gratitude for their help does not imply their agreement with the theory presented here.

amount of material at a time (e.g. the "seven chunks" of George Miller, 1956).

Information processing theories have not progressed very far in accounting for sensation, but have been concerned largely with the activity of the central nervous system. Hence, using these theories to explain perceptual phenomena will be compatible with some recent approaches that emphasize the common parts of perception and cognition. Clearly, this is not the whole story of perception, but it may well be an important segment of it.

The reversibility of the Necker cube provides an introductory example for an information processing explanation of a visual phenomenon. The "impossible" drawings for which the artist M. C. Escher is known make a second type of example, the phenomena of depth perception make a third example, and apparent motion, visual and auditory, is discussed as a final example.

The basic approach is to show that almost any serial information processing system that is capable of storing complex symbolic structures will "perceive" stimuli, i.e. encode and store them, in such a way as to produce some of the phenomena that have been observed in human beings. In several cases, actual running computer programs serve as examples, even though these programs were not written with simulation of human perception as a specific objective.

The explanations proposed appear to be consistent with a number that have been put forth in the recent literature on visual form recognition: for example, those of Gibson (1950) and Hochberg (1962). What distinguishes the present account is explicitness with respect to the character of the information processes needed by the viewer and neutrality on the question of whether these processes are innate or acquired.

The Necker Cube

The Necker cube provides a familiar demonstration of central control over visual perception. The subject is shown the two-

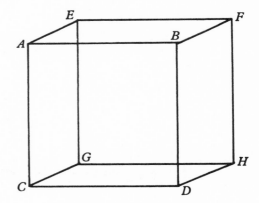

Figure 1. The Necker cube.

dimensional diagram of figure 1 and asked to "interpret" it as a three-dimensional cube. By asking him such questions as whether the square face on the lower left (*ABCD*), is in front of or behind the square face on the upper right (*EFGH*), it can be shown that two alternative interpretations are possible. Most subjects can learn to alternate "voluntarily" (and will alternate involuntarily) between these two interpretations at a maximum rate of perhaps one alternation per second.

From a subjective point of view, there is seldom any doubt in a subject's mind as to what is meant by *ABCD* being "in front of," or "behind" *EFGH*. When the subject is asked such a question, he can generally answer without hesitation. His report, however, is subject to all the objections that can be raised against introspection in general. Is it reliable? How can its reliability be tested? And, operationally, what does it mean to say that the one square is "in front of" or "behind" the other? (As any fool can see, they both actually lie in in the same plane!)

No answer is proposed to the question of reliability. That question has not often been raised about the Necker cube, possibly because the subjective reports are so readily produced and because the experimenter himself, looking at the cube, is hard-pressed to call them illusory. The operational meaning of the interpretation is another matter. To deny that the three-dimensional interpretation of the two-dimensional stimulus can be given operational meaning, would be to deny the whole possibility of an organism with two-dimensional sensory organs behaving "as if" it lived in a three-dimensional world.

A Mechanism for Interpreting Visual Stimuli

One way of providing operation meaning for the interpretation is to specify a mechanism for carrying it out. The mechanism might or might not resemble closely the actual human mechanism. It would show decisively how such a mechanism is possible and could provide explanations for some of the phenomena in which this mechanism is implicated. Such a mechanism is to be specified.

A memory is postulated that is organized in terms of names of "objects" and is capable of storing symbolized information about properties of objects and of relations between and among objects. In the case of the Necker cube, names of objects would include "the point C," "the angle AEF," "the plane $AEBF$," "the cube $ABCDEFGH$," and so on. Associated with the name "C," for example, might be information like: "C is a point," "line AC joins points A and C," "C lies on the lower left-hand corner of square $ABCD$," "GCD is a right angle." How information of this kind can be stored in a memory has just been illustrated: as English sentences on a piece of paper. It is easy to store the same information, in a wide variety of ways, in a digital computer.

One way in which the information could be stored in a computer is an analogical *image* of the diagram. In this phrase, the noun "image" denotes that information inside the memory will not necessarily *state* (explicitly) the information about the stimulus, as it was stated in the English sentences above. Instead, the information in the memory will *represent* the stimulus, providing some of the information explicitly, some implicitly. The meaning of this distinction will become clear as we proceed. The image is described as "analogical", to emphasize that the memory does not have to *be* three-dimensional (it does not contain a model of the cube), but has only to be capable of *representing* three dimensions symbolically:

A simple kind of analogical image for visual stimuli is provided by the coordinates of analytic geometry. A set of coordinates (x, y, z) can be associated with the name of each point in Figure 1:

A	0, 1, 0		E	0, 1, 1
B	1, 1, 0		F	1, 1, 1
C	0, 0, 0		G	0, 0, 1
D	1, 0, 0		H	1, 0, 1

This representation of the cube contains, in fact, all of the information needed for a particular three-dimensional interpretation of the stimulus—the interpretation which places $EFGH$, as a vertical plane, behind the vertical plane $ABCD$. A little bit of the information is explicit: the locations of the points. Most of the information is implicit. For example, the fact that points A, B, C and D lie in the same vertical plane is deducible from the fact that they all have the same z-coordinate, and similarly for points E, F, G and H. The fact that the former plane lies in front of the latter plane is deducible from the fact that the z-coordinate of the former, 0, is smaller than the z-coordinate, 1, of the latter. To deduce other facts—for example, that EGC is a right angle—requires slightly more complicated procedures.

A different set of coordinates could, of course, equally well have been assigned to the points, for example:

A	0, 1, 1		E	0, 1, 0
B	1, 1, 1		F	1, 1, 0
C	0, 0, 1		G	0, 0, 0
D	1, 0, 1		H	1, 0, 0

Applying the same deductive processes to the new coordinates, $ABCD$ and $EFGH$ are still vertical planes, but $ABCD$ now lies *behind EFGH*. In fact, the Necker cube has been reversed.

It is not suggested that the representations of visual stimuli in human memory are numerical or that information is extracted from them by doing analytic geometry. It is suggested that a representation analogical to the one just described, and with processes analogical to those of analytic geometry for interpreting the implicit information contained in the information, can account in general for human three-dimensional interpretation of two-dimensional stimuli, and in particular for the reversal of the Necker cube.

The explanation is not yet complete, however. A representation for three-dimensional objects has been provided that encodes such concepts as "in front of," "behind," "right angle." But how the perceptual processes might transform a stimulus into this encoding has not been explained, nor how the two alternative encodings corresponding to the two ways of viewing the Necker cube might arise. Consider a process of the following kind:

1. A scanner moves over the stimulus and detects simple configurations. By "simple configurations" are meant figures like those the Gestalt psychologists call "good": straight lines, especially if horizontal or vertical, right angles, squares, circles, closed symmetrical forms.

2. When a simple configuration has been detected, the scanner proceeds from it to the other elements of the stimulus, providing them with simple interpretations in relation to the initially discovered simple configuration. This process continues until an internal representation has been constructed for the entire stimulus, or a contradiction has been encountered.

3. If a contradiction is encountered, the interpretation is rejected and step (1) is repeated—usually with a different initial position of the scanner.

The example of the Necker cube enables the various elements of this scheme to be made more specific and more nearly operational. It is first assumed that a subject's physical orientation and environmental cues define for him the horizontal and vertical directions on the plane of the stimulus (so that he can notice that *CD* is horizontal and *EG* is vertical for instance). Suppose the scanner first encountered point *F*. It could then recognize the horizontal (*EF*) and vertical (*FH*)

lines from *F*, and hence the right angle, *EFH*. *EF* and *FH*, further, define a plane, which, since *FH* is vertical, and *EF* horizontal is interpreted as a vertical plane, parallel to the surface of the paper.

Following the closed line, *FEGHF*, in this plane, the square *EFGH* is detected. Returning to point *F*, the line *FB* must be accounted for. The angles it makes with *EF* and *FH* are not right angles. Line *FB* can be given a "simple" interpretation, however, by interpreting *B* as lying behind the plane of square *EFGH*. The "simple" interpretation of *BFDH*, then, is that it is a vertical square behind the plane of the paper and perpendicular to it. (*B* could equally well have been interpreted as *lying in front of* the plane of *EFGH*. Whichever interpretation is taken, provided that it is taken consistently, the Necker cube phenomena will appear. Empirically, it seems that subjects generally interpret such points as lying behind the previously defined plane.) A continuation of the same processes finally leads to the cube with *EFGH* as its front face and *ABCD* as its rear face.

If exactly the same processes had been applied, starting with point *C* instead of point *F*, the stimulus would again have been interpreted as a cube, but with *ABCD* as its front face and *EFGH* as its rear face. Thus the alternation of cubes can be produced by starting the scanner alternately at points *C* and *F* (or points *B* and *G*). It is well known that this is actually one procedure that subjects consciously use to produce rapid alternation of the two interpretations.

The scheme described, while adequate to account for the reversibility of the Necker cube would undoubtedly run into difficulty in simulating the way human beings interpret complex visual displays. It has been developed in detail to illustrate the kinds of information processes that are involved. A scheme capable of far more complex and realistic performances, but based on the same general principles, has been developed and implemented on an electronic computer by Roberts (1963) and by Kirsch (1964), to the last of which the reader is referred for a detailed description.

Even Roberts's (1963) scheme, as he was careful to point out, fell short of using all the perceptual cues that humans have been shown, by Gibson (1950) and others, to employ. For example, it does not use texture to estimate distance. Addition of these cues to the scheme is entirely feasible and would represent no change in the point of view. The question of specifically what cues the human viewer uses, and the extent to which these are innate or learned, can be separated from the question of whether the human viewer is fundamentally the kind of serial information processor that has been described.

"Impossible" Figures

The proposed explanation can be tested further by applying it to other phenomena of the same general kind as alternation of the Necker cube. As a preliminary, it is important to explain what is meant by "contradictory" interpretations (see step 3 of the interpretive scheme). Suppose that, for some reason, scanning of the Necker cube had begun independently at *both* points *C* and *F*. Then an interpretation might have been arrived at (see figure 2), in which both *ABCD* and *BDFH* might be interpreted as the front and right side of one cube. A subject can, in fact, rather easily train himself to "see" the figure in precisely this way. (This possibility is predicted by the theory proposed here and, as far as the writer is aware, has not previously

been noticed.) As long as the figure is interpreted as a set of four planes, perpendicular in pairs, the interpretation causes no difficulty. The moment, however, that the scanner seeks to interpret, say, the edge *AC* in relation to these planes, a contradiction arises. For *AC*, as an edge of square *ACEG*, lies *behind* the surface plane, while *AC*, as an edge of *ABCD*, lies *in* the surface plane. If the scanner focuses on *AC*, it cannot maintain the interpretation of the two intersecting cubes. The interpretation is readily maintained by alternating attention between, say, *EG* and *BD*, each of which has a single, unambiguous location in the interpretation.

The phenomena of consistency and contradiction may be described thus. The scanning process operates locally, gradually building up an interpretation of the stimulus and extending this interpretation to adjoining parts. If the same part is reached by two different routes, the two interpretations it thus acquires may be identical or different. In the latter case, a perceptual contradiction has occurred, and the original interpretation that led to it will be maintained with difficulty; more precisely, it will only be maintained by restricting the scanning to the noncontradictory portions of the stimulus.

This explanation of the perception of "contradiction" applies also to the "impossible" figures that have been constructed by the painter M. C. Escher, and by Penrose and Penrose (1958) and others. (See figures 3 and 4.) If the scanner starts at *A* in figure 3, for example, it might arrive at an interpretation of *ABC* and *DKL* as lying in one plane (say, a vertical plane), *BGF* and *BML* as lying in a second (horizontal) plane perpendicular to the first, and *CEF* and *IKN* as lying in a third plane, perpendicular to the other two. But an attempt to assign coordinates to the points on this basis would lead immediately to contradictory assignments, for the points *O* and *I* would both have to lie at the intersection of all three planes, which is patently impossible.

The "plausibility" of these figures, in the sense of the immediate reaction that

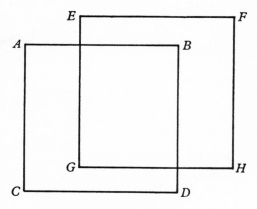

Figure 2. Partial Necker cube.

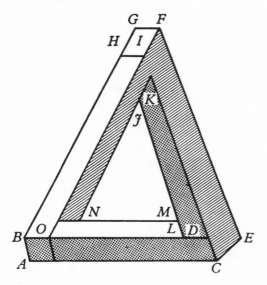

Figure 3. "Impossible" figure.

Figure 4. "Impossible" figure.

they can be interpreted as three-dimensional, arises from the fact that they are locally interpretable. The contradiction arises from the fact that no local interpretation can be extended to the figure as a whole. The scanner finds itself in the position of a surveyor who, after going around the three sides of a triangle dis-

covers that the sum of the angles does not equal 180°. He is advised, thereby, that the figure he has been measuring cannot be interpreted as a triangle in the Euclidean plane.

The explanation for the interpretation of two-dimensional stimuli as representing three-dimensional objects, and for the concept of contradiction, can readily be applied to familiar "illusions," such as those produced by the Ames rooms. The main property required of the scanner to produce these illusions is a strong tendency to interpret angles as right angles, wherever possible. In a photograph of an Ames room showing two persons of apparently quite different sizes, the illusions can, with effort, be "reversed" by focusing attention on the pair of human figures and ignoring the walls of the room until the figures appear to be of the same actual size, but at different distances. If this is done, the angles in the room will appear to lose some of their rectilinearity. In fact, the mechanisms that have been described seem generally adequate, with little amplification, to handle all the perceptual phenomena discussed by Ittelson and Kilpatrick (1952).

Two-dimensional and Three-dimensional Interpretations

The stimulus of figure 5 is more often than not interpreted by subjects as a two-dimensional regular hexagon. It can also, of course, be interpreted as a three-dimensional cube with front face *ABGF* or a cube with front face *CDEG*. The theory should explain why most subjects arrive first at the former, two-dimensional interpretation rather than one of the three-dimensional interpretations.

The scanner, starting at *A* would discover the vertical line *AB*, but no horizontal line. Further, it would discover the line *AGD* extending across the figure. It would discover that each of the three lines, *CF*, *AD*, and *BE* are axes of bilateral symmetry and that the six triangles about *G* are equilateral and equal. Hence, the figure, interpreted as two-dimensional, would be composed of symmetrically disposed simple subfigures. Any attempt to reinterpret the

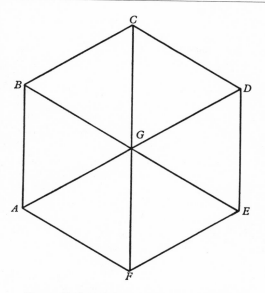

Figure 5. Special case of Necker cube.

stimulus in three dimensions would destroy a number of these properties. The six triangles no longer exist in the three-dimensional figure; the halves of the six diameters become distinct line segments, parallel but not colinear.

The foregoing explanation is not unlike those commonly given by Gestalt theorists. What distinguishes it from them is that operational meaning has been given to notions like "good figure" and that a definite process has been described for discovering properties in the stimulus corresponding to "goodness" which have been used to construct the interpretation and internal representation. It is consistent with measures that have been proposed for the three-dimensionality of drawings (cf. Hochberg and Brooks, 1960). The process is by no means "holistic" in any simple sense. It proceeds sequentially to examine local properties of the stimulus. Its apparent "holism" arises from its ability to compare interpretations of the same part of a stimulus arrived at by alternative paths.

STIMULUS CHANGE THROUGH TIME

A mechanism has been described that explains certain perceptual phenomena,

specifically the way in which stimuli are interpreted as representing objects in three-dimensional space. The explanation rests on the assumption that a scanner examines the stimulus serially, part by part, and attempts "simple" interpretations of these parts. In the present section a second-level explanation of the interpretive process itself is proposed, i.e., an explanation of why the process might be expected to have the properties it does, in fact, possess.

The organism's perceptual processes may be conceived as one part of an information storage and retrieval system. Suppose that a subject is given the laboratory task of observing a stimulus, reporting what he has observed; observing a second, reporting about it; and so on. Or, to change the situation slightly, but significantly, suppose he is given the task of observing a series of stimuli and, after observing all of them, reporting what he has seen. With both tasks, the subject must have some means of storing what he has seen until he reports. In the second task, since the reporting is delayed, efficiency in the storage and retrieval processes becomes critically important. How can efficiency be increased?

The means available for increasing efficiency in information processing depend on the nature of the successive stimuli. Redundancy from one stimulus to the next is the principal means of reducing storage requirements. One form of redundancy occurs when parts of successive stimuli can be set in correspondence with each other, that is, when they can be interpreted as belonging to the "same object." Consider the following series of stimuli:

A relatively succinct interpretation is that a dot moves from the left-hand to the right-hand side of an interval. An information processing system could accomplish this interpretation as follows: In the first stimulus, names are created for "the dot" and "the interval." The stimulus might be described by: "the dot is at the left end of the interval." Alternatively, the interval might be divided into locations, numbered from 1 to 6, from left to right, and the stimulus could be described by: "the dot is at location 1." The entire sequence of stimuli is then simply: "the dot moves from location 1 to location 6 at a constant rate." A slightly more formal translation would be "$\text{Loc}(d, t) = t$." As before, it is not being proposed that the description that is stored is actually verbalized in any of these ways, simply that what is stored might be roughly isomorphic with one of these verbalizations.

The central device used here to capitalize on the redundancy is that of treating the stimuli as though they consisted of objects and changes in, or actions upon or by objects, or of relations among objects (cf. Michotte, 1946). Linguists are almost in agreement that virtually all languages have noun-like words and verb-like words— names and processes or actions. The noun-verb distinction has essentially been used in describing the stimulus in the present case.

One can imagine a world in which this distinction would not be very useful, a world of clouds constantly forming and dissolving, for instance. Our world is quite different. It is a world in which it is usually quite easy to designate "objects" that, properly described, retain their properties over considerable stretches of time and change in simple, orderly ways, moving continuously, for example, and in smooth paths. In such a world, an information processing system can exploit the redundancy that is present by storing information as descriptions of the objects it has identified and named. This storage scheme will both reduce the storage required and, what is often more important, reduce the amount of processing needed to update the information and to keep it current. Consider the following variant on the previous stimulus:

In this case the stimulus can be interpreted as two dots, one moving from right to left, the other from left to right; alternatively, it can be interpreted as two dots moving toward the middle of the interval, colliding, and rebounding. With either interpreta-

tion, the identities of the two dots are preserved throughout.

The usefulness of this scheme, in our world, requires effective procedures for identifying objects, and effective procedures for describing them "properly," i.e., in ways that will leave their properties most nearly invariant over time. The problem of proper description is considered first.

Suppose that the stimulus is a cube of wire. If it is held in a fixed position, it is equivalent, in stationary monocular vision, to a two-dimensional drawing of a Necker cube. Let is be rotated, however, and, as is well known, it becomes vividly three-dimensional. It is obvious that, under rotation, three-dimensional representation of the cube is far more parsimonious than two-dimensional, for the three-dimensional figure can be described as an invariant cube, subject to a simple rotation.

In kinematics it is shown that a rigid body has only six degrees of freedom. No matter how irregular the shape of the body, nor how complex its motion, that motion, and the totality of information about the body, can be described by giving the time paths of six coordinates. Hence, in a world like ours, description of a stimulus as a collection of three-dimensional rigid bodies will generally be much more parsimonious than description of the same objects in two dimensions.

With the three-dimensional representation, objects in visual space will generally have a well-defined shape, which changes slowly if at all, and a well-defined size, which also tends to be invariant through time. Of course, illusions and difficulties in interpretation can be created by introducing contradictory clues, as has been noted previously; but such clues will seldom be present in nature.

The scheme proposed requires that the information processing system should have means for identifying objects. Motion is again exploited, by peripheral as well as by central processes, for motion generally provides more reliable cues than are provided by color, tone or hue contrasts. In modern painting the Impressionists, in particular, exploited the unreliability of the cues of tone and hue to "dissolve" the world of real objects into a television screen that was supposed to represent the "real" impact on the retina. (The Impressionist approach, and pointillism in particular, nevertheless, incorporated some erroneous views about perception. In particular, the Impressionists were unaware, apparently, of the peripheral encoding of cues derived from movement to determine object boundaries; cf. Gombrich, 1960.)

In a world of rigid, moving objects, where cues from movement are more important than cues of tone and hue in fixing object boundaries, how would an information processing system be expected to record color information? One important generalization is that "color," would be expected to be associated with each object, to remain relatively constant over the object, and to remain relatively invariant under movement and changing conditions of light and shade. This color might, of course, contain cues as to the position of the object in space, the "blueing" of distant objects for instance, but one would expect it to be rather independent of those aspects of lighting that can change rapidly. Hence, the well-known phenomena of color constancy, whatever the exact peripheral or central mechanisms that produce them, are generally consistent with the principle of efficiency in information storage and retrieval (cf. Helson, 1943).

Shepard (1964) has recently demonstrated an amusing and striking auditory illusion that can be interpreted in a parallel manner to the foregoing interpretation of apparent movement. His demonstration adds further credence to the hypothesis that such illusions arise centrally rather than peripherally, and that they are strongly moulded by requirements of parsimony. The familiar "barber's pole" illusion fits the earlier discussion of the apparent motion of dots along a line. Shepard (1964) has constructed an auditory "barber's pole" by presenting a mixture of tones and by gradually increasing the pitch of each component of the mixture while fading out the higher components and introducing new components of lower pitch. The hearer perceives the sound as continually rising in pitch although, after it has "risen" a full octave, the mixture of tones is again identical with the initial mixture. The perceptive reader will note that the phenomenon has been described as it might be by a listener who was taken in by the illusion, for to speak of "each component" of the mixture as gradually rising in pitch, is to give particular components at one moment the same name as the corresponding components at the next moment. But this naming procedure is not intrinsic to the physical sounds; it is imposed by the listener—it is precisely what creates the illusion.

Conclusion

This chapter has shown how a wide range of the known phenomena of visual perception can be accounted for by a mechanism that encodes information from the stimulus into an internal representation having certain efficient characteristics from an information processing and retrieval standpoint. A detailed account has been given of the Necker cube and related phenomena, and the theory has been extended in more general terms to other perceptual phenomena, including constancy of size, shape, and colour.

In many respects the proposed theory is far from novel. It is anticipated by many discussions of perceptual phenomena by Gestalt theorists and others. What is perhaps new is the demonstration that a small number of particular, operationally definable mechanisms can be specified that will produce many of the known effects. Realization of these mechanisms on a computer and simulation of the perceptual behaviour, as has been begun by Kirsch (1964) and others, would provide evidence as to whether these mechanisms perform, qualitatively and quantitatively, in a way that is consistent with the known phenomena.

References

Evans, T. G. (1964). A heuristic program to solve geometry—analogy problems. *Proc. 1964 Spring Joint Computer Conf., AFIPS Conf. Proc.* **25**, 327–38.

Feigenbaum, E. A. & Simon, H. A. (1964). An information-processing theory of some effects of similarity, familiarization, and meaningfulness in verbal learning. *J. verb. Learn. verb. Behav.* **3**, 385–96. Reprinted as chapter 3.2 in this book.

Feldman, J. (1963). Simulation of behavior in the binary choice experiment. In *Computers and Thought*, ed. E. A. Feigenbaum and J. Feldman. New York: McGraw-Hill. Pp. 329–46.

Gibson, J. J. (1950). *The Perception of the Visual World*. Boston: Houghton-Mifflin.

Gombrich, E. H. (1960). *Art and Illusion*. New York: Pantheon Books.

Helson, H. (1943). Some factors and implications of color constancy. *J. opt. Soc. Am.* **33**, 555–67.

Hochberg, J. (1962). The psychophysics of pictorial perception. *Audio-vis. Commun. Rev.* **10**, 22–52.

Hochberg, J. & Brooks, V. (1960). The psychophysics of form: reversible-perspective drawings of spatial objects. *Am. J. Psychol.* **73**, 337–54.

Hovland, C. I. & Hunt, E. B. (1960). The computer simulation of concept attainment. *Behavl. Sci.* **5**, 265–67.

Ittelson, W. H. & Kilpatrick, F. P. (1952). Experiments in perception. *Scient. Am.* **185**, 50–55.

Johnson, E. S. (1964). An information-processing model of one kind of problem solving. *Psychol. Monogr.* no. 581.

Kirsch, R. A. (1964). Computer interpretation of English language text and picture patterns. *IEEE Trans. on Electronic Computers*, EC-13, 363–76.

Laughery, K. W. & Gregg, L. W. (1962). Simulation of human problem solving behavior. *Psychometrika* **27**, 265.

Lindsay, R. K. (1963). Inferential memory as the basis of machines which understand natural language. In *Computers and Thought*, pp. 217–36, ed. E. A. Feigenbaum and J. Feldman. New York: McGraw-Hill.

Michotte, A. (1946). *La Perception de la Causalité*. Paris. [English translation by T. R. Miles & E. Miles (1963). *Perception of Causality*. New York: Basic Books.]

Miller, G. A. (1956). The magical number seven plus or minus two: Some limits on our capacity for processing information. *Psychol. Rev.* **63**, 81–97.

Newell, A., Shaw, J. C. & Simon, H. A. (1960). Report on a general problem-solving programme. *Proc. Int. Conf. Information Processing, Paris, June 1959*. London: Butterworths, pp. 256–54. Reprinted in R. D. Luce, R. R. Bush and E. Galanter, *Readings in Mathematical Psychology*, vol. 2. New York: Wiley, 1965, pp. 41–57.

Penrose, L. S. & Penrose, R. (1958). Impossible objects: a special type of visual illusion. *Br. J. Psychol.* **49**, 31–33.

Roberts, L. G. (1963). *Machine Perception of Three-Dimensional Solids*. In J. T. Tippet et al. (eds.). *Optical and Electro-Optical Information Processing*. Cambridge, Mass.: M.I.T. Press, pp. 159–97.

Shepard, R. N. (1964). Circularity on judgments of relative pitch. *J. acoust. Soc. Am.* **36**, 2346–53.

Simon, H. A. & Kotovsky, K. (1963). Human acquisition of concepts for sequential patterns. *Psychol. Rev.* **70**, 534–46. Reprinted as chapter 5.1 in this book.

6.2

Information Processing Analysis of Perceptual Processes in Problem Solving (1969)

with Michael Barenfeld

Information processing theories of human problem solving, particularly those employing computer simulation as their means of formalization and analysis, have emphasized the problem solver's selective search through the "tree" of solution possibilities. Both the authors of these theories and their critics agree that heuristic search, while a prominent feature of problem solving behavior, is by no means the whole of it—and perhaps not even the most crucial part. In particular, theories that describe problem solving only as search fail to capture and explain processes that are especially visible during the first 5 or 10 seconds after a problem situation is encountered.

There is evidence—some of which will be mentioned—that a great deal of structure may be imposed on the problem situation by subjects in problem solving experiments during those first seconds of exposure. Some critics of information processing theories have argued that this initial structuring activity, which they usually describe as "perceptual" rather than "cognitive," constitutes the really "significant" part of the problem solving process, the

subsequent heuristic search being relatively "routine." These critics have sometimes concluded that the initial perceptual processing would require information processing systems fundamentally different from those that have been postulated to explain heuristic search behavior (Tichomirov and Poznyanskaya, 1966).

Evidence for the existence and character of the initial perceptual activities comes largely from situations where problems are presented to subjects in visual form. The evidence takes at least two forms: (1) records of subjects' eye movements during the first few seconds after problems are presented to them, and (2) tests of subjects' abilities to retain information from complex visual displays after a few seconds' exposure.

It is the purpose of this chapter to propose an explanation in information processing terms of the initial perceptual phases of problem solving, to show that some existing computer simulation pro-

This work was supported by Public Health Service Research Grant MH-07722 from the National Institute of Mental Health.

363

grams for heuristic search and learning already contain the basic processes required for such perceptual activities, and to show how simple organizations of these basic processes enable the programs to parallel the behavior of human subjects.

Since the most extensive research on perception in problem solving deals with the perception of chess positions, the present analysis is made in terms of this task. The authors' aim is to describe a computer program that can explain, in information processing terms, the known empirical phenomena (1) relating to eye movements during initial view of a chess position and (2) relating to subjects' retention of information about a chess position after a few seconds' exposure to it. The emphasis will be on describing the theory. This chapter is not an attempt to review the considerable literature on eye movements and perception in chess; nor, except by way of illustration, will detailed comparisons of specific simulations with specific data be made. Instead, the authors state the central theoretical issues and propose a solution to them.[1]

PERCEPTION IN CHESS

Existing computer chess-playing programs, like most other problem solving programs,

1. Jongman (1968) has also sketched out, but not programmed, a process model to explain the perceptual phenomena. Jongman's dissertation was not available to the authors when the program described here was constructed, but some of the data gathered by de Groot, Jongman, and Noordzij in the Amsterdam project, including the data reported in de Groot (1966), and the project's eye movement films were accessible. Jongman's model, the details of which can be found in his thesis, especially page 142, focuses primarily on the determination of the initial features to be noticed rather than the subsequent eye movements, thus is complementary to the program described here, filling out some of the aspects that have been handled sketchily. The authors are grateful to their Amsterdam colleagues for collaboration and exchange of ideas on this subject that extends over a decade.

are based largely on the technique of selective heuristic search through the tree of legal continuations from the given game position. However, during the first moments—for example, 15 seconds more or less—during which he is exposed to a new position, a skilled human player does not appear to engage in a search of move sequences. Instead, he appears to be occupied with perceiving the essential properties of the position, which will suggest possible moves to him and help him to anticipate their consequences. He appears to be gathering information about the problem, rather than seeking an actual solution. In summing up his extensive empirical studies of the thought processes of chess players, de Groot (1965, p. 396), observes:

> From the analysis of protocols and from the additional experiments on chess perception we have learned that this is a first Phase of problem formation.
>
> The process in the first Phase is characterized by a perceptive and receptive, rather than actively organizing, attitude on the part of the subject....

Subsequent research by de Groot (1966) and his students (e.g., Jongman, 1968), provides additional support for this conclusion.

Superficially, it would appear that existing computer chess programs do not provide an explanation of these human behaviors—hence, they have questionable status as theories of human problem solving in chess. To be sure, if one makes a detailed examination of what is going on in the computer programs that play chess by selective search, one finds that they too contain processes that would be labeled "perceptual." If they did not, the programs could not search selectively. Consider, for example, MATER, a program that searches for checkmating combinations (Baylor, 1965; Baylor and Simon, 1966). Among the subroutines it contains—which are employed in the service of higher level routines for generating and testing moves—is one that finds the direction between two given squares (notices, e.g., whether they lie on the same file); a second determines whether there is a piece on the rank, file, or diagonal between two given squares; another, whether a specified piece is under attack; another, whether a given square is under attack; another, whether a given square is defended; and so on (Baylor and Simon, 1966, p. 446).

Eye Movements

While de Groot provided convincing evidence that his human subjects, during the first 5 or 10 seconds of looking at a position, were more concerned with extracting information about the position than with exploring sequences of moves, his experimental techniques (relying primarily on thinking-aloud protocols) did not permit him to establish the precise sequences of processing activities during this period. In order to obtain additional information about "noticing" behaviors during initial exposure of subjects to positions, Tichomirov and Poznyanskaya (1966), and subsequently, other researchers (de Groot, 1966; Winikoff, 1967), have recorded eye movements with sufficient accuracy to determine the location of each fixation within one or two squares of the chessboard.

Both the problems of calibrating the instruments and the nature of the human visual apparatus make it impossible to establish with assurance the precise square to which a subject is attending at any given moment. A single fixation may—and probably does—enable him to discover what pieces are standing on several neighboring squares. Peripheral vision permits some information to be gathered about the status of even more distant squares. Indeed, such peripheral information is necessary to direct the eyes to new fixation points if the eye movements are to be other than random. Records of eye movements can only show the succession of fixations; they cannot show precisely what information is being processed at each moment.

The eye-movement records gathered by Tichomirov and Poznyanskaya, as well as some gathered by Winikoff (1967, chaps. 6 and 7), and others by de Groot's students

in Amsterdam (personal communications), show rather consistently that the fixations of subjects move from one square of the board to another at a maximum rate of about four fixations per second. It appears that at each point of fixation the subject is acquiring information about the location of pieces at or near the point of fixation, together with information about pieces in peripheral vision (within, e.g., 7° of arc) that bear a significant chess relation ("attack," "defend," "block," "shield") to the piece at the fixation point.

PERCEIVER Program

To elucidate this hypothesis about the eye movements, and its implications, the authors have organized the "perceptual" processes already contained in MATER into a new chess-perception program, PERCEIVER, that can simulate the initial sequences of the eye movements of human subjects. This chapter describes PERCEIVER, then illustrates its behavior by comparing, for the same chess position, its initial simulated eye movements with an example of human data published by Tichomirov and Poznyanskaya (1966).[2] It should be emphasized that PERCEIVER is organized from processes that are present in the MATER program. (The processes are described in detail in Baylor, 1965; Baylor and Simon, 1966.)

Carrying out the simulation requires a stronger assumption than simply that the human subjects are "perceiving" the relations among the pieces on the board. It is

---

2. Comparisons are limited to the Tichomirov-Poznyanskaya data because (1) they are the only chess eye-movement data actually published to date, (2) they explicitly interpret their data as refuting computer-simulation models of problem solving, and (3) the other (unpublished) eye-movement data known to us were obtained either from weak players or players under instructions to "remember the position" rather than "select a move." The unpublished data gathered by Winikoff and by the Amsterdam group do not contradict any of the conclusions the present authors draw from the Russian data.

necessary, in addition, to posit processes that will generate these perceptions in some particular sequence. The two basic assumptions incorporated in the program are:

1. The information being gathered during the perceptual phase is information about relations between pieces—usually pairs of pieces—or between pieces and squares. When the eyes are fixated on a particular piece, it is possible to detect neighboring pieces (*a*) that defend the piece in question, (*b*) that attack it, (*c*) that are defended by it, and (*d*) that are attacked by it. (Other meaningful relations could be added to this list, but the experiment was limited to these four.)

2. When attention is fixed on piece A, and one of the four relations mentioned above is noticed, connecting A with another piece, B, attention may return to A without change in fixation. If it does not, B will be fixated next.

These two assumptions are, of course, not sufficient to determine all details of the program. By changing the order in which the various items are noticed, different sequences of eye movements can be produced in the same position. It is necessary also to specify an initial point of fixation (in the simulation to be described, this is

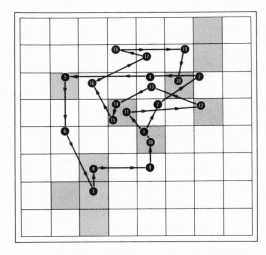

Figure 2. Record of eye movement for the first 5 seconds (expert player, from Tichomirov and Poznyanskaya, 1966). The ten squares occupied by the most active pieces (see figure 1) are shaded.

always a piece near the center of the board, but see Jongman, 1968, pp. 131–37). Finally, the program may be made to behave in various ways when it repeats the same cycle of fixations—it can be made more or less repetitive and stereotyped in its behavior. For the comparisons to be made here, the behavior of the program is not especially sensitive to such variations in the detail of its structure.

Illustrative Comparison with Eye-movement Data

Figure 1 shows the chess position used by Tichomirov and Poznyanskaya (1966, p. 5) in one of their experiments. Figure 2 shows the sequence of twenty fixations observed in a player of expert (just below master) caliber during his first 5 seconds of looking at this position. Figure 3 shows the sequence of fifteen simulated fixations produced by the PERCEIVER program before it began recycling and halted this phase of its exploration. On figures 2 and 3, the ten squares are shaded on which stand the pieces whose positions would be regarded by any good chess player as critical to understanding the structure of the position.

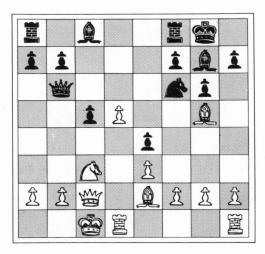

Figure 1. Middle game position used by Tichomirov and Poznyanskaya (1966). (Black to play.)

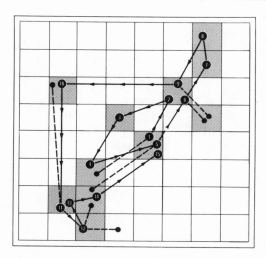

Figure 3. Record of simulated eye movements during period of initial orientation—PERCEIVER program. Solid line = eye movements; broken lines = relations noticed peripherally. The ten squares occupied by the most active pieces (see figure 1) are shaded.

Table 1. Sequence of Fixations and Noticing Acts; PERCEIVER Program.

1. Black pawn (K4)	attacked by defended by	White Knight Black Knight
2. Black Knight	attacks	White pawn (Q5)
3. White pawn (Q5)	defended by	White Knight
4. White Knight	attacks	Black pawn (K4)
5. Black pawn (K4)	attacked by defended by	White Queen Black Knight
6. Black Knight	attacked by defended by	White Bishop Black Bishop
7. Black Bishop	defended by	Black King
8. Black King	defended by	Black Knight
9. Black Knight	attacked by defended by	White Bishop Black Queen
10. Black Queen	attacks	White pawn (N2)
11. White pawn (N2)	defended by	White King
12. White King	defended by defended by defends	White Rook White Queen White pawn (N2)
13. White pawn (N2)	attacked by defended by	Black Queen White Queen
14. White Queen	attacks	Black pawn (K4)
15. Black pawn (K4)		

These are the pieces under attack (the two center pawns, Black's Knight, White's pawn on QN2), together with their attackers and defenders, and the two Kings.

It is obvious that both the human expert (figure 2) and the PERCEIVER program (figure 3) were mainly occupied with relations connected directly or indirectly with the Black pawn on White's K4, the Knight on B6, and the White pawn on QN2. By the construction of the program, all PER-CEIVER's fixations fell on squares occupied by pieces. Either for reasons of calibration, or from other causes, six of the human player's fixations fell on unoccupied squares. Nevertheless, the figures exhibit considerable concordance between the objects of attention in the two cases; and the eye-movement fixations, actual and simulated, reveal almost complete preoccupation with the ten critical pieces.

The trace printed by the PERCEIVER program shows the course of exploration over the board (table 1). On the left are shown the fifteen successive points of fixation of the program. For each fixation, on the right are listed the relations with other pieces that were noticed (centrally or peripherally) during the fixation.

The sequence can be divided into three main phases. The first five fixations relate directly to the Black pawn on White's K4, the Knight and Queen that attack it, the Knight that defends it, and the White pawn on Q5 that the same Knights attack and defend. The next four fixations concern the Black Knight, the Bishops that attack and defend it, respectively, and its other relations with Black's castled King's position. The defense of the Knight by the Black Queen shifts attention to the Queen, then to the White Knight's pawn she attacks. The next four fixations have to do with that pawn and its defense. The final two fixations return, via the White Queen, to Black's King's pawn.

Note that the Black Queen links the two main arenas—the one around the Black pawn on K4 and Knight on B6 and the one around the White pawn on QN2. The two situations are also linked by the White Queen, which appears in the first, third, and last episodes of the sequence. The Tichomirov-Poznyanskaya sequence reveals the same two foci of attention (though with less emphasis on the situation around QN2) and the same dual relations of the Queens connecting them.

PERCEIVER'S focus of attention on these particular relations does not rest on subtle or complex evaluations of what is "important" on the board. If attention follows a train of associations in such a web of relations, it will simply be brought back repeatedly to the points in the web where the density of relations is highest.

In the position shown in figure 3, the sequence of fixations identifies the Black pawn on K4 as underdefended—attacked by Knight and Queen, but defended only by a Knight. At the end of the initial perceptual phase, PERCEIVER undertakes a new exploration to find moves that would protect the pawn. The same perceptual processes are used as before, but in a slightly more complex way. Working from the pawn that is under attack, and following the ranks, files, and diagonals that converge on it, PERCEIVER discovers squares from

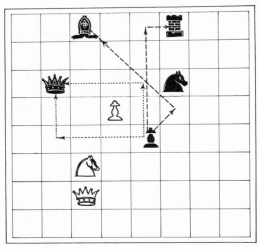

Figure 4. Record of simulated eye movements subsequent to orientation period—PERCEIVER program.

which a piece of an appropriate kind can defend the pawn, then searches for a piece that can be brought to the square. Thus, following the King's file to K8, PERCEIVER finds a square from which a Rook or Queen could defend the pawn, then discovers the Rook on B8 which can move to that square. In this way (figure 4), PERCEIVER discovers the Rook move, the move of the Bishop from QB8 to KB5, and two Queen moves that will protect the pawn. The eye movements of the human expert show the Rook move being discovered in the same way—fixations begin at the pawn, move up the file to K8, then over to the Rook (Tichomirov and Poznyanskaya, 1966, p. 6, figure 2).

REPRODUCTIONS OF POSITIONS FROM MEMORY

The example shows that a very simple program, using perceptual processes of the kinds already employed in computer chess programs, moves its attention about the board in a way that resembles the eye movements of a human subject. Since our central concerns are theoretical, a more extensive comparison of the program's behavior with eye-movement data will not undertaken. The authors simply assert that there is nothing particularly "atypical" about the position used for illustration and that the program will behave in a similar manner when faced with other board positions from chess games.

The broader question is whether the information that can be extracted from the position by these perceptual processes is adequate to account for the known ability of chess masters to reproduce chess positions after brief exposure (5 or 10 seconds) to sight of the board. Notice that there are two parts to the human performance: (1) extracting from the chessboard the totality of information about the chess position, and (2) retaining all this information long enough to reproduce the position from memory. The PERCEIVER program is concerned principally with the extraction of information from the board. To deal with the retention, another component of the information processing theory of cognition must be referred to—the EPAM (Elementary Perceiver and Memorizer) theory of rote learning (Gregg and Simon, 1967). EPAM simulates the recognition and fixation processes in learning at a finer level of detail than do the programs that simulate problem solving, hence it is more relevant than they are to questions of short-term memory.

Experimental Results

In a series of striking experiments, it has been shown that the ability of a subject to reproduce a chess position after a few seconds' exposure to it depends sensitively on (1) the subject's chess proficiency and (2) the "meaningfulness" of the position (de Groot, 1965, pp. 321–34; de Groot, 1966, pp. 35–48; Jongman, 1968, pp. 35–43). "Meaningfulness" can be manipulated by contrasting the reproduction of positions from actual games (but games not known to the subjects) with the reproduction of boards having the same pieces as the game positions, but placed at random.

In summary, de Groot and Jongman report that (1) after 5 seconds' sight of the board, a grandmaster or a master can reproduce a chess position almost without error; (2) the weaker the player below this level, the more errors he makes in the reproduction—very weak players can place only half a dozen pieces correctly; and (3) with random boards, the performances of grandmasters and masters sink to the level of weak players, while the weak players perform as well (or as poorly) with random boards as with boards from game positions.

An explanation of chess perception must be consistent with these data if it is to be regarded as satisfactory. At the same time, the explanation must also be compatible with what is known about short-term and long-term memory. It is rather well established that (1) "seven plus-or-minus two" *chunks* can be held in short-term memory; (2) probably not more than one chunk can be transferred from short-term to long-term memory in as short a time as 5 seconds.

A chunk here means any configuration that is familiar to the subject and can be recognized by him. (For a discussion of these facts, together with references, see Gregg and Simon, 1967.)

If these two facts are accepted, then the information that allows a subject to reproduce a chess position after only 5 seconds' exposure must be mainly in short-term memory; and if the position is reproduced perfectly, or nearly perfectly, it must somehow be encoded as not more than, say, nine chunks of information.

Proposed Explanation

The PERCEIVER program, taken by itself, does not satisfy these requirements. To describe a chessboard, containing 28 pieces, with the relations of "attack," "defend," and so on, would require an initial location plus at least 27 relations—even if the direction between the pieces were encoded as part of the relation. For this information to be retained in short-term memory, it must be recodable into familiar chunks, each containing, on average, three of four relations.

The mechanisms employed in the EPAM (Gregg and Simon, 1967), theory of discrimination constitute a theory of how such an encoding can be accomplished. Stimuli presented to EPAM are sorted through a discrimination net on the basis of perceivable characteristics. Stimuli, or portions of stimuli that are found to match in their characteristics with stimuli stored previously in the memory are "recognized" and are replaced in short-term memory by a single chunk that designates them. Thus, if a configuration of relations in a stimulus is recognized as familiar, the whole configuration, consisting of as many parts as there are perceived relations, can be represented in memory by a single chunk. Hence, the short-term memory, limited to holding a specified maximum number of chunks, can retain many more relations if they occur in familiar configurations than if they must be held independently in memory.

The EPAM theory of discrimination has

been shown (Gregg and Simon, 1967) to make correct predictions on the effects of familiarity in rote verbal learning, hence provides an "in-principle" explanation of the chessboard reproduction phenomena. According to this explanation, clusters of related pieces in a position are recognized by chess masters as familiar constellations; hence each cluster is stored as a single chunk; less skilled players have to describe the board in a larger number of simpler chunks—hence cannot hold all the information required to reproduce the board in short-term memory. Moreover, when the same number of pieces is arranged on the board at random, few of the resulting configurations are familiar even to grand masters. Hence, they then need more chunks to describe the position than can be held simultaneously in short-term memory, and hence perform as poorly as weaker players.

Several considerations support the plausibility of this explanation of the experimental data.[3] First, the quantities involved are of the right order of magnitude. Mastership in chess requires at least several years of serious occupation with the game. In that time, a player might be expected to acquire a "vocabulary" of familiar subpatterns comparable to the visual word recognition vocabularies of persons learning to read English, or the Kanji (or Kanji-pair) recognition vocabulary of persons learning to read Chinese or Japanese. But these vocabularies are of the order of 10^4–10^5 "words" in size. Hence, sequences of seven such subpatterns could be used to encode 10^{28}–10^{35} (i.e., $(10^4)^7$ or $(10^5)^7$) different total board positions.[4] The number of chess positions that could arise from sequences of "reasonable" moves has been estimated to lie in the range 10^{10} to 10^{15} (see Jongman, 1968, p. 33), hence well within the estimated vocabulary limits. A vocabulary of the postulated size is sufficient to supply distinct seven-chunk names to distinct chess positions.

Second, everyday chess experience, supported by de Groot's laboratory data (e.g., de Groot, 1965, pp. 324–34), suggests that the familiar chunks are configurations of several to a half-dozen pieces. But seven

configurations averaging three or four pieces each can describe a board on which there are 20–30 pieces. Further, the number of different three-to-four-piece configurations that have to be posited is again consistent with the estimate of 10^4–10^5 given above. The Tichomirov-Poznyanskaya position can be used to illustrate these points—not to "prove" them, for the present authors will make free use of chess knowledge gleaned from experience and the literature. The following are configurations that would likely be familiar to a chess master (cf. figure 1):

1. The two center pawns, the two Knights and Queen attacking and defending them, and the blocking White pawn on K3 (6 men).

2. Black's Knight, the Bishop attacking it, and Queen and Bishop defending it, and the two center pawns on which it bears (6 men).

3. White's Queen's Knight's pawn, the Queen attacking it, the King and Queen defending it, and the Knight it defends (5 men).

4. White's castled position on the Queen's side: 2 pawns, King, and Rook (4 men).

5. White's Bishop on King 2 (1 man).

6. White's King's side: Rook and 3 pawns (4 men).

7. Black's castled position: King, Rook, Bishop, Knight, and 3 pawns (7 men).

8. Black's Queen's side: Rook, Bishop, and 3 pawns (including the typically ad-

---

3. The analysis of Jongman, not available when the following paragraphs were written, again provides strong direct empirical support for these hypotheses about encoding, and especially the stereotyped nature of the patterns for the castled Kings (see Jongman, 1968, pp. 83–112).

4. A more conservative estimate would take account of the fact, to be mentioned presently, that the configurations in the corners of the board are highly stereotyped, hence perhaps only about 10^2 in number. The number of different positions made up of four such subpatterns and three other, less stereotyped, subpatterns describing the center of the board would then be about $(10^2)^4 \cdot (10^5)^3 = 10^{23}$, which still provides sufficient variety.

vanced Bishop's pawn) (5 men).

The authors do not assert that every chess master will break up the position into exactly the same configurations, but those listed above have been seen by any master many times. The first three chunks correspond essentially, to the three episodes in the PERCEIVER sequence. Each focuses on a critical man and its relations. Of the remainder, four describe the relatively stereotyped configurations in the four corners of the board, which would have to be picked up by PERCEIVER peripherally. The most complex is the seventh, describing the situation of Black's castled King. Yet this identical pattern for Black arises in 5–10 percent of all chess games between masters—the percentage varying from one era to another. (Seven configurations account for about half the castled positions in master games.)

Notice that there is redundancy in the description—many pieces enter into more than one configuration. De Groot (1965, pp. 321–22) observes that this redundancy contributes to error correction, and that in the absence of redundant relations, isolated pieces (such as the White King's Bishop) are the most easily omitted in reproduction (see also Jongman, 1968, pp. 92–93).

Obviously, there are different ways in which the relations on the board could be organized into familiar chunks. The purpose here is simply to show that the information known to be extracted by masters and grand masters in their first perception of chess positions is consistent, in quantity and quality, with a hypothesized mechanism that (1) notices relations, in the manner of PERCEIVER, then (2) recognizes and chunks configurations of such relations, in the manner of earlier programs for simulating human memory processes, such as EPAM (see Gregg and Simon, 1967). No significant new mechanisms have to be postulated to account for these data on chess perception.

CONCLUSION

In this chapter the authors have offered a theoretical account of the information proc-

essing that occurs in human problem solving during the initial attack on the problem, prior to the beginning of heuristic search. It was shown how perceptual processes employed in earlier problem solvers can be organized to make initial analysis of problem structure, using previous experience stored in memory to reorganize and recode a complex stimulus into a smaller number of familiar chunks.

The theoretical explanation was made more concrete by developing it for a specific task environment: chess playing. A PERCEIVER program was constructed to extract information from a chessboard, and the way the program behaves in comparison with a record of human eye movements was illustrated. The authors have shown how this program, combined with EPAM-like recoding mechanisms, can account for the ability of chess masters to reproduce chessboards after brief exposure. The processes used by PERCEIVER are very similar, also, to the processes postulated recently by Simon (1967—chapter 6.1 in this book) to account for such well-known perceptual phenomena as the reversibility of the Necker cube and the perception of "impossible" figures.

The significance of these results does not lie in the detail of the processes, which will surely need revision as knowledge grows, but in the demonstration for both of these realms that essentially the same elementary processes that have been employed to simulate problem solving and learning, operating in essentially the same kind of serial information processing system, produce the main known features of the human perceptual performances. In these task domains, no radically different principles would appear to govern perceptual processing from those governing other central processing.

References

Baylor, G. W. Report on a mating combinations program. *SDC Paper* No. SP-2150, 1965, System Development Corporation, Santa Monica, California.

Baylor, G. W., & Simon, H. A. A chess mating combinations program. In, *AFIPS Conference*

Proceedings, 1966 Spring Joint Computer Conference, 1966, 28, 431–47. Reprinted as chapter 4.3 in this book.

De Groot, A. D. Perception and memory versus thought: Some old ideas and recent findings. In B. Kleinmuntz (Ed.), *Problem solving*. New York: Wiley, 1966, pp. 19–50.

De Groot, A. D. *Thought and choice in chess*. The Hague: Mouton, 1965.

Gregg, L. W., & Simon, H. A. An information-processing explanation of one-trial and incremental learning. *Journal of Verbal Learning and Verbal Behavior*, 1967, 6, 780–87. Reprinted as chapter 3.3 in this book.

Jongman, R. W. *Het oog van de meester*. Am-

sterdam: van Gorcum, 1968.

Simon, H. A. An information-processing explanation of some perceptual phenomena. *British Journal of Psychology*, 1967, 58, 1–12. Reprinted as chapter 6.1 in this book.

Tichomirov, O. K., & Poznyanskaya, E. D. An investigation of visual search as a means of analyzing heuristics. *Soviet Psychology*, Winter 1966–67, 5, 2–15. (Trans. from *Voprosy Psikhologii*, 1966, 2(4), 39–53).

Winikoff, A. W. Eye movements as an aid to protocol analysis of problem solving behavior. Unpublished doctoral dissertation. Carnegie-Mellon University, 1967.

6.3

A Simulation of Memory for Chess Positions (1973)

with Kevin J. Gilmartin

Chapter 6.2 proposed an information processing theory, in the form of a computer program, to explain data on the eye movements of a chess player viewing a game position previously unknown to him. The program, PERCEIVER, which was built upon previously developed elementary processes for detecting basic chess relations of attack and defense (Baylor and Simon, 1966), simulated the subjects' eye movements over a 5-second interval, fixating on the same parts of the board as did the subject, and executing similar saccades. Chapter 6.2 sketched out a program combining PERCEIVER, which extracts visual information and controls attention, with EPAM (Feigenbaum, 1961), which learns by storing information in long-term memory, to account for the experimentally confirmed ability of chess masters to reproduce chess positions after brief exposure to sight of the board (de Groot, 1966; Chase and Simon, 1973).

In this chapter, we will describe a development and implementation of the Simon and Barenfeld (chapter 6.2) proposal in a program that represents a simplified concatenation of PERCEIVER and EPAM,

and we will compare the performance of the program with the performance of human subjects in reconstructing a chessboard which they have seen briefly.

The MAPP Program

We have named the new program MAPP (Memory-aided Pattern Perceiver). MAPP contains a *learning* component and a *performance* component. The learning component, which uses the learning mechanisms of EPAM, simulates the storage in long-term memory of varying amounts of information about simple, recurring patterns of pieces on a chessboard. Thus it can attempt to simulate the long-term pattern memory of a weak chess player (few patterns stored) or of a chess master (many patterns stored).

The performance program is itself made up of three parts. One part detects the

This work was supported by Public Health Service Grant MH-07722 from the National Institute of Mental Health. We are grateful, also, to our colleague, William G. Chase, for many discussions on the topic of this chapter.

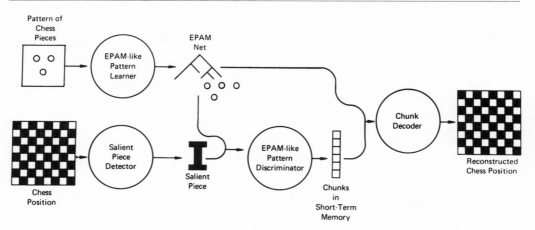

Figure 1. Principal processes of MAPP. The learning component is shown in the upper half of the figure; the three parts of the performance component in the lower half.

salient pieces in a chess position, hence performs roughly the same function as was performed by the part of the PERCEIVER program that directed attention to different areas of the board.[1] The second part of the performance program recognizes patterns —that is, groups of pieces around the salient pieces—and stores the labels, or internal names, of the patterns in short-term memory. Short-term memory is supposed to be limited in capacity, so that only a small number, say seven, of such names can be stored. The recognition process uses the EPAM net built by the learning component; hence, what chunks will be held in short-term memory depends on what patterns have previously been stored in long-term memory.

The third part of the performance program again decodes the information in short-term memory and reproduces as much of the original board position as this information covers. The overall structure of MAPP is depicted in figure 1.

A typical output of a MAPP performance run is shown in figure 2. The previously stored EPAM net is not shown. At the top

of figure 2 is the chess position to be remembered. The pieces are designated on their appropriate squares by pairs of letters; thus, "BQ" is Black Queen," etc. Next appears the output of the salient piece detector: two lists of pieces, one for primary attention, and one for subsequent attention if space remains in short-term memory. Here, "WC18" means "the White Castle on the *1st rank* and *8th file*" (i.e., at White's KR1). "WP41-WP56" means "the White pawn chain from White's QR4 (square 41) to his KB5 (square 56)."

Next appears the output of the pattern discriminator. It first (1) sought to recognize a pattern around the Black Knight at Black's QN3 (square 62) but failed to find such a pattern in long-term memory. It failed also to find patterns for the White King at 12, Castle at 18, and Queen at 47. It then (2) sought to recognize a pattern around the Black King at Black's KN8 (87), finding the set: "BK87BC86BP76BP78-BP67," i.e., the Black King, the Castle at KB8, and the pawn's at KB7, KN6, and KR7.[2]

---

1. There is an important difference between the attention strategies in PERCEIVER and MAPP, respectively. PERCEIVER simulates a subject scanning the board preparatory to making a move; MAPP simulates a subject scanning the board prepartory to reconstructing it from memory. Eye movements are typically somewhat different in the two cases.

2. Patterns and their "mirror images"—i.e., the corresponding patterns for Black and White —are stored together in the EPAM net, and only the Black patterns are represented explicitly. Hence "BP51BP62BP53" describes the triad of Black pawns at Black QR4, QN3, and QB4, and the triad of White pawns on the corresponding White squares.

```
OO  BC  OO  OO  OO  BC  BK  OO
OO  BP  OO  OO  OO  BP  OO  BP          Chess
BP  BN  OO  BP  OO  BP  BP  OO          Position
OO  OO  BP  WP  OO  WP  OO  OO
WP  OO  WP  OO  WP  OO  WQ  OO
OO  WP  BQ  OO  OO  OO  OO  WP
OO  OO  OO  OO  OO  OO  WP  OO
OO  WK  OO  WC  OO  WB  OO  WC
```

ATTENTION IS DIRECTED TO THE FOLLOWING   Salient
PIECES FOR POSSIBLE PATTERNS: Pieces
WK12, WC18, WQ47, BN62, BK87,
    WP41-WP56, BP76-BP78   Primary List
IF FEW PATTERNS HAVE BEEN RECOGNIZED,
ATTENTION WILL BE DIRECTED TO:
BC82, WP27-WP38, BP61-BP72, BP53-BP64,   Secondary List
EXIT AT 81   Pattern
62   (A)
EXIT AT 62
12   Discrimination
EXIT AT 12
18   Process
EXIT AT 18
47
EXIT AT 47
87   (B)
RECOG: N1187 = BK87BC86BP76BP78BP67   Pattern N1187
EXIT AT 67
56
RECOG: N265 = BP46BP55   Pattern N265
EXIT AT 45
53
RECOG: N155 = BP53BP64   Pattern N155
EXIT AT 64
82
EXIT AT 82
72
RECOG: N275 = BP72BP61   Pattern N275
EXIT AT 61
27
RECOG: N5 = BO77BP68   Pattern N5
EXIT AT 38
EXHAUSTED POSSIBILITIES W O FILLING STM
STM: BN1187 WN265 BN155 BN275 WN5   Patterns in
                                                   Short-term Memory

XX XX XX XX XX BC BK XX
XX BP XX XX XX BP XX BP
BP XX XX BP XX XX BP XX   Reconstructed
XX XX BP XX XX WP XX XX   Chessboard
XX XX XX XX WP XX XX XX
XX XX XX XX XX XX XX WP
XX XX XX XX XX XX WP XX
XX XX XX XX XX XX XX XX
```

Figure 2. Example of a MAPP run. Position M1. Net N15.
```

Continuing in this way, the pattern discriminator recognized five patterns in all. The five patterns were stored by name (N1187, N265, N155, N275, N5) in short-term memory. Finally, they were again decoded, and a diagram (bottom of figure 2) of the position constructed. In this case, the five chunks recognized and stored incorporated 14 of the 26 pieces in the original position.

THE COMPONENTS OF MAPP

We next describe more explicitly the structure of the main components of MAPP: the discrimination net, the pattern learner, the salient piece detector, the pattern discriminator, and the chunk decoder.

The EPAM Net

The EPAM net is stored in memory as a description list structure that forms a tree as depicted in figure 3. Each *node* of the structure specifies (1) a chessboard location (the rank and file of a square) where a test is to be performed and (2) a pair of *branches* (*positive* and *negative*) pointing to the next pair of nodes. The output of a test performed at a node is positive if a specified *color* and *type of piece* is found at that location and is negative if a different piece is on that square or the square is

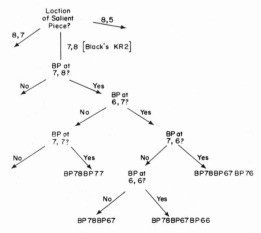

Figure 3. Segment of EPAM net showing structure of nodes.

unoccupied. Each *terminal node* of the EPAM net corresponds to a known pattern of chess pieces, and the name for that pattern is the name of that terminal node (e.g., N155).

The Pattern Learner

The input to the Pattern Learner is a list of pieces (one of which is marked as a salient piece), with a specification of the location of each on the chessboard. The pattern is always described in the EPAM net as a Black pattern, but once it is learned, the corresponding White pattern can be recognized also. A particular configuration of pieces is sometimes learned twice, each time with a different piece salient (e.g., either end of a pawn chain may serve as a salient piece for a pattern).

The Pattern Learner increases the size of the EPAM net by adding branches to what had previously been a terminal node. This is accomplished by specifying a test (for a piece at a location) to be performed at that node and adding a pair of branches (positive and negative) pointing to two new terminal nodes. When confronted with a new pattern to learn, the Pattern Learner starts at the top of the EPAM net and progresses from node to node conducting tests on that pattern. When a terminal node is reached, additional tests (and additional nodes) are added to the net so as to incorporate those pieces in the pattern that have not previously been tested for. If the pattern that is presented to MAPP has been learned previously, no additional tests are necessary and the EPAM net is not changed.

The Salient Piece Detector

When presented with a chessboard position, MAPP assigns a saliency score to each piece (excluding pawns). The saliency score of a piece is a function of its *type*, the number of *adjacent pieces* of the *same color*, and the number of nearby pieces that it defends. (Chase and Simon, 1973, found that pieces within a single chunk are bound by relations of defense, proximity, and common color and type.) If a piece has a relatively high saliency score, and is not adjacent to a piece with a higher score, it is marked as a salient piece. Both end pawns of a pawn chain are also marked as salient pieces.

The nodes of the top of the EPAM net are tested for the type and location of the piece that was salient in each learned pattern, i.e., each known pattern is categorized by its salient piece. When a configuration of pieces is encountered on a chessboard, it will be recognized as a familiar pattern only if the salient piece by which it is indexed in the EPAM net is also salient in the context of the whole chessboard. Thus a configuration of pieces that was previously learned by the Pattern Learner, with a certain piece as the salient one, will not be recognized in the context of a position in which a different piece is more salient in that part of the board.

The Pattern Discriminator

The Pattern Discriminator directs attention to a salient piece on the chessboard. Then a search is made in the vicinity for a known pattern that includes that salient piece. The search is directed by the EPAM net which serves as long-term memory. Each test in the EPAM net specifies a square on the chessboard, and the results of the test determine which test is performed next and where. Thus the pieces that are on the chessboard and the patterns that have been learned determine jointly which squares in the vicinity are scanned. If a pattern is recognized, its label (the name of the terminal node in the EPAM net) is placed in *short-term memory*. Short-term memory is a list with no internal structure, which can hold only a limited number of labels or chunks. Regardless of whether the Pattern Discriminator succeeds or fails in recognizing a pattern, attention is next directed to a new salient piece which is nearby. This process is continued until either (1) attention has been directed to all the salient pieces or (2) short-term memory is full.

It will be observed that the mechanism

which carries out the recognition process in EPAM is essentially the same as the recognition mechanism recently proposed by Noton and Stark (1971) to account for phenomena of visual attention. The basic idea in both theories is that recognition of an element in a visual stimulus retrieves from long-term memory information that directs attention to the next element to be considered. Thus, a mechanism first proposed by Feigenbaum in 1961 to account for phenomena in standard verbal rote learning experiments, without any direct concern for attentional phenomena, now also proves relevant to theories of visual perception and the control of attention (Simon and Barenfeld, 1969; Noton and Stark, 1971).

The Chunk Decoder

After scanning a chessboard position, MAPP reproduces as much of that position as it can remember, i.e., as much as can be retrieved with the information that is retained in short-term memory. The meanings of labels in short-term memory are held in the EPAM net in long-term memory. In order to reproduce the chess position, the Chunk Decoder must use each label from short-term memory as an entry point into the EPAM net, from which it can extract a list of the pieces comprising that pattern. These pieces then are placed on an empty chessboard.

Performance of MAPP

MAPP's ability to reconstruct chess positions by recognizing familiar patterns and holding their names in short-term memory was studied by, first, growing several EPAM nets in long-term memory, then presenting MAPP with chess positions at the same time the program was given access to one of the stored nets.

Acquiring the Nets

A large number of subpatterns of pieces that appear frequently in chess positions (drawn from games in the published literature) were presented to MAPP, one by one. Each pattern, as presented, was added by the Pattern Learner to the EPAM net in the manner described above.

An initial net was grown containing 1,526 nodes, of which 447 were terminal nodes, each naming two patterns, a Black one and its White counterpart. One copy of this net was stored, and additional patterns were then presented to a second copy until the latter grew to contain 1,909 nodes, and about 572 pattern pairs. These two nets, which we will call N12 and N15, respectively, were used for the experiments. N15, as we have just seen, contained about 28 percent more patterns than N12.

The patterns used to grow the nets contained from two to seven chessmen each. The bulk of the patterns were (1) pawn chains and (2) sets of pieces about a castled King's position; but a variety of other patterns that recur frequently were also included. The patterns were assembled from published chess games, but without a systematic attempt to sample the literature statistically. Hence, some patterns that occur in play rather rarely may be included, and some that occur commonly may be omitted. However, it is believed that a substantial fraction of common patterns from the opening and middle game are included. Since, in any event, no two chess players will encounter exactly the same patterns in play, it was thought that this method of assembling a large collection of patterns was adequate for an initial investigation.

Recognizing Patterns

To facilitate a comparison with human performance, which will be reported in the next section of this chapter, the experiment made use of fourteen middle game positions on which human players had previously been tested (Chase and Simon, 1973). These consisted of one set of five positions at the twentieth move, from published games: and nine positions from Reinfeld's *Win At Chess*. The latter are positions in which the player on move can secure a decisive tactical advantage.

In addition, four positions were examined at the tenth move of the openings of grandmaster games. We do not have human data for these four positions.

Table 1 summarizes the results of the simulation runs with the five middle game positions; table 2, the results with the nine positions from Reinfeld; and table 3, the results with the four opening game positions.

Table 1 shows that MAPP succeeded in reproducing from 39 percent to 43 percent of the pieces in these five positions, depending on which net was used. Replacing the smaller by the larger EPAM net brought about an increase of about 10 percent in the number of pieces placed correctly (from 9.8 to 10.8 pieces per position).

An examination of the data for individual positions in table 1 reveals a range of more than two to one in number of pieces placed per position, and shows that the changes in the EPAM net affected the performance in two of the five positions.

In the last column in table 1, which refers to the most powerful program variant, we see that MAPP recognized an average of 4.4 patterns per position, and that the patterns averaged 2.45 pieces each in size.

Comparable data for the nine tactical positions are provided in table 2. The same two EPAM nets were used as before. The percentage of pieces correctly placed has now increased to 53 and 55, from the 39 and 43, respectively, of the positions of table 1. Since the average number of patterns recognized per position remained almost the same (4.5 as compared with 4.4 in table 1), the improvement was mainly caused by an increase in average size of pattern, from 2.45 pieces per pattern to 2.78.

The positions of table 3, using the larger net, N15, show a still higher level of performance of the program, 73 percent of all pieces being placed correctly. There has been an increase both in average number of patterns recognized (to 5.75) and in average size of pattern (3.9 pieces per pattern). These increases reflect the more "stereotyped" character of positions

Table 1. Performance of MAPP in Reconstructing Five Middle Game Positions.

Positions	Total No. of Pieces	Pieces Reproduced		Patterns Found
		N12	N15	N15
M1	26	13	13	5
M2	25	8	11	5
M3	26	10	12	3
M4	24	12	12	6
M5	24	6	6	3
Total	125	49	54	22
Average	25	9.8	10.8	4.4
Percent		39	43	(2.45 pieces/pattern)

Table 2. Performance of MAPP in Reconstructing Nine Tactical Middle Game Positions.

Positions	Total No. of Pieces	Pieces Reproduced		Patterns Found
		N12	N15	N15
63	26	15	15	5
65	27	12	12	4
67	17	8	8	4
69	17	10	11	3
71	23	12	12	5
73	26	12	13	5
75	23	18	18	6
77	23	12	13	5
79	27	12	12	4
Total	209	111	114	41
Average	23.2	12.3	12.6	4.5
Percent		53	55	(2.78 pieces/pattern)

Table 3. Performance of MAPP in Reconstructing Four Opening Game Positions (at 10th move) Net N15.

Positions	Total No. of Pieces	Pieces Reproduced	Patterns Found
Steinitz-Bardeleben	28	23	6
Flohr-Lustig	32	25	6
Alekhine-Rubenstein	30	21	5
Steinitz-Blackburne	32	20	6
Total	122	89	23
Average	30.5	22.25	5.75
Percent		73	(3.9 pieces/patterns)

after only ten moves have been played. The positions of tables 1 and 2 represent later stages of the game, where a greater variety of possible dispositions of pieces can occur.

THEORETICAL ANALYSIS

Let us see what can be inferred about the variety of patterns that occur in chess positions from actual games. In games between masters, a player on the average has a choice among two to four acceptable moves. Some data gathered by de Groot (1966, pp. 39–40) even suggest that the average number of good alternatives is less than two. The numbers of different games that are possible at two, three, and four branches per alternative are shown in table 4.

Table 4. Estimates of Numbers of Distinct Master-Level Chess Games.

	Stage of Game	
Branches per Choice	*10 Moves (20-ply)*	*20 Moves (40-ply)*
2	1.04×10^6	1.1×10^{12}
3	3.8×10^9	1.2×10^{19}
4	1.1×10^{12}	1.2×10^{24}

The reasonableness of these estimates can be cross-checked in several ways. First, I. J. Good (1953) on examining games published by the *British Chess Magazine* in 1951, estimated, from this sample, that there were, in all, $1,132 \sim 10^3$ openings three moves (6-ply) deep. But three branches per choice would give $3^6 = 729$, while four branches would give $4^6 = 4,096$. Hence, the number of reasonable alternatives per move at the outset of the game appears to be a little more than three. Second, in the opening or early middle game, each piece finds itself almost always on one or another of a very small number of "normal" squares (e.g., the Queen's Knight on its original square, on QB3, on QN2, or absent from the board). If we estimate that at the twentieth move, there are four plausible squares for each piece (a generous estimate that does not allow for interdependencies of location), we arrive at $4^{32} \sim 1.8 \times 10^{19}$ possible positions. A similar estimate was made by de Groot (1966, p. 37, item 7) using a procedure for optimal binary encoding of positions.

Size of Required Pattern Repertory: Equiprobable Patterns

It is known that a chess master can reproduce a game position almost perfectly (holding it in short-term memory) after having seen it for only 5–10 seconds (Chase and Simon, 1973). How many patterns would have to be stored in order to recognize completely this variety of positions? For definiteness, we will assume there are 10^{10} possible positions, with 30 pieces each, at the end of 10 moves, and 10^{18} positions, with 24 pieces each, at the end of 20 moves. We will further assume that all patterns contain the same number of pieces, so that a 30-piece position can be represented by six 5-piece patterns or 7 patterns averaging 4+ pieces each, while a 24-piece position can be represented by 8 patterns of 3 pieces each, or 6 of 4 pieces each.

Table 5 shows the number of stored patterns required for these and other combinations of parameters. The entries are calculated as follows: Let k be the number of distinct patterns available for each component in the representation of the position; c, the number of components; and n, the number of distinct positions to be represented. Then the total number of patterns, π, that must be stored is $\pi = ck = c \times n^{1/c}$. The number of components, c, is P/p, where P is the total number of pieces in the position and p is the number of pieces per pattern. From table 5 we see that to represent 10^{10} positions would require about 280 patterns if each position were factored into six components (i.e., six chunks in short-term memory), but only 190 patterns if each were factored into seven components. To represent 10^{18} positions would require about 6,000 patterns if each were factored into six components, but only 1,400 patterns if each were factored into eight components. The table provides similar estimates for other combinations of n and c, thus giving an indication of the sensitivity of π, the number of patterns required, to variations in those parameters.

From these estimates, we conclude that a system that had stored some hundreds of patterns, four or five pieces in size, should be able to reproduce most positions reached in master games after ten moves; and if it has stored some thousands of patterns, three or four pieces in size each, it should be able to reproduce most positions reached in master games after twenty moves. This

Table 5. Numbers of Patterns (π) Required To Represent n Distinct Positions
Factored in c Components* ($\pi = c \times n^{1/c}$).

Number of Distinct Positions (n)	Number of Components (c)				
	4	5	6	7	8
10^8	4×10^2	2×10^2	1.3×10^2	0.98×10^2	8×10
10^9	7×10^2	3.2×10^2	1.9×10^2	1.4×10^2	1.1×10^2
10^{10}	1.3×10^3	5×10^2	2.8×10^2	1.9×10^2	1.4×10^2
10^{12}	4×10^3	1.2×10^3	6×10^2	3.6×10^2	2.5×10^2
10^{15}	2.2×10^4	5×10^3	1.9×10^3	0.98×10^3	6×10^2
10^{18}	1.3×10^5	2×10^4	6×10^3	2.6×10^3	1.44×10^3
10^{20}	4×10^5	5×10^4	1.3×10^4	0.5×10^3	2.5×10^3
10^{22}	1.3×10^6	1.2×10^5	2.8×10^4	0.98×10^4	4.5×10^3

*The number of pieces per position is $c \times p$, where p is the average number of pieces per pattern.

assumes that the system can hold six to eight chunks, corresponding to familiar patterns, in short-term memory.

The estimates are consistent with the observed fact that MAPP was able to restore about 55 percent of the pieces in games after twenty moves, but 73 percent in games after only ten moves. The fact that performance in the latter case was not perfect suggests that the number of positions reasonably attainable after ten moves may be somewhat larger than the estimate of 10^{10}. Notice, however, that to reproduce a thirty-piece position with six patterns requires an average pattern size of five, while the average size of patterns found by MAPP was just under four pieces. Hence the difficulty may lie in the fact that MAPP has an insufficient number of *large* patterns stored in its EPAM net. The data now available do not indicate a clear choice between these possible reasons for the imperfect performance.

Size of Pattern Repertory: Unequal Pattern Frequencies

To refine further the analysis of the size of net required for various levels of performance it is necessary to take into account the fact that not all patterns will occur in game positions with equal frequency. In the 18 positions taken together, MAPP recognized a total of 86 patterns, but only 64 *distinct* patterns. Some 47 patterns were

recognized once each, 12 twice each, and five three times each.

Since the patterns that were recognized averaged a little over three pieces in size, we can regard each position as analyzable into eight 3-piece components or a total of 144 components for the 18 positions. Hence the most frequent patterns, those that were recognized three times each, occurred with about 2 percent frequency (3/144) among the totality of patterns (recognized and unrecognized) in these positions.

We do not know the population frequency distribution of the different patterns, and our sample is too small to allow us to estimate it with any great confidence, but we can make some plausible conjectures about it. It is almost certainly a highly skewed distribution, perhaps something like the distribution of words, by frequency, in natural langague text, or the distributions of scientists by numbers of papers authored, or of chess openings by frequency of occurrence (Good, 1953).

One of these extremely skewed distributions is the harmonic distribution, which usually provides at least an approximate fit to data of the sorts just mentioned. If items from a harmonic distribution are ranked in order from the most frequent, then the frequency of the ith ranking item f_i, is given by

$$f_i = \frac{f_1}{i} \qquad (1)$$

Where f_1 is the frequency of the top-ranking item. Since $(d \log x)/dx = 1/x$, it follows that the total frequency of the first i items grows approximately with $\log i$:

$$\sum_{j=1}^{i} f_j \cong a \log_e i \qquad (2)$$

If we assume that the relative frequencies of patterns, when the patterns are ranked in order of frequency, can be approximated by the harmonic distribution, then we can estimate the total number of patterns required to permit near-perfect reproduction of chessboards. For boards after 20 moves, we saw that a repertory of about 1,144 patterns gave 55 percent accuracy of reproduction. We have, therefore:

$$0.55 = a \log_e 1,144 \qquad (3)$$

where a is a constant. If π_{20} is the number of patterns required for perfect reproduction,

$$\frac{\log \pi_{20}}{\log 1,144} = \frac{1}{0.55}, \text{ or} \qquad (4)$$

$$\log \pi_{20} = \frac{\log 1,144}{0.55} \qquad (5)$$

On carrying out the computation we obtain $\pi_{20} = 363,000$.

Boards after ten moves were reproduced with 73 percent accuracy. The corresponding calculation for this case give $\pi_{10} = 15,500$.

Thus, we see that to raise the standard of performance in the reproduction experiment to the level of perfect reproduction would require a repertory of patterns in the tens of thousands (for boards after ten moves) or hundreds of thousands (for boards after twenty moves). Masters are not, however, able to achieve perfection in this task (see table 6). In the nine positions where the program achieved an accuracy of 55 percent, a chess master achieved 81 percent; and in the five positions where the program achieved an accuracy of 43 percent, the same master achieved 63 percent (Chase and Simon, 1973). From these results, (2) and (3) give an estimate of $\pi_{20M} = 31,700$ for the master's repertory of patterns in the former case, and $\pi_{20M} = 25,100$ in the latter.

The hypothesis that the position repro-

Table 6. Percentage of Pieces Placed Correctly by Master, MAPP(N15), and Class A Player in Two Sets of Positions.*

	Master	MAPP	Class A Player
Five positions (table 1)	62	43	34
Nine positions (table 2)	81	54	49
Ratio	1.305	1.255	1.438

*The last line of the table shows the ratio of the percentages for the second to the first set of positions. Human data from Chase and Simon, 1973.

duction scores varies with the logarithm of the number of patterns stored gains some further support from the comparison between MAPP's performance with nets of 894 (N12) and 1,144 (N15) patterns, respectively. Log 1,144/log 894 = 1.07. In the fourteen positions of tables 1 and 2, 168 pieces were correctly placed when the larger net was used, but only 160 when the smaller was used. Since 168/160 = 1.05, there is reasonably good agreement between the two ratios.

All the estimates based on the harmonic distribution are a good deal higher than the ones arrived at in the previous section on the assumption of equal probability of patterns. If the pattern frequencies are skewed, then improving performance from any given level requires storing large numbers of additional (rare) patterns. Since the harmonic distribution assumes a very high degree of skewness in the pattern frequencies, the estimates given in this section of the pattern repertories required for high levels of performance are almost certainly on the high side. With a less skewed distribution, they would be substantially lower. For example, assuming that the cumulative frequencies grow with the square of the logarithm reduces the previous estimate of $\pi_{20} = 363,000$ patterns for reproduction of boards after twenty moves to about $\pi_{20} = 13,500$ patterns.

There are other respects in which the analysis here is very approximate, calling for caution in interpretation. A major consideration is that there is no guarantee that all the most frequent chess patterns are included in the nets that have been grown. However, this and most of the other assumptions that have been introduced are on the conservative side—that is, would tend to overestimate the size of the net required for specified levels of performance.

In summary, it appears safe to conclude that the performance of master and grandmaster chess players can be accounted for by postulating that they have a repertory of less than 100,000 patterns; and possibly their performance can be explained if they have a repertory of only about 10,000 patterns. The conclusions derived from the simulation are fully consistent with those reached previously in chapter 6.2 on the basis of sketchier evidence.

FURTHER COMPARISON WITH HUMAN PERFORMANCE

In the previous section allusions were made to the performance of a chess master in some of the positions whose reproduction was attempted by MAPP. We now add some additional comparisons of MAPP's performance with human performance.

Table 6 shows the performance, measured by percentage of pieces placed correctly, of the chess master, a Class A player and MAPP on the positions reported in Tables 1 and 2. (The human data, involving reproducing the position from memory after 10-second exposure to it, are from Chase and Simon, 1973.) MAPP was somewhat more effective in reproducing the positions than was the Class A player, but decidedly inferior to the master. Both human players and MAPP performed better on the nine positions of table 2 than on the five positions of table 1. The Class A player showed the greatest relative gain, the master the next greatest, and MAPP the least; but the relative gains of master and MAPP were roughly of the same magnitude.

Table 7 provides some data on the correlations of correct piece placements and errors between MAPP and the chess

Table 7. Number of Pieces Placed Correctly by Master and MAPP(N15) in Two Sets of Positions.*

	MAPP +	−	Total		MAPP +	−	Total
Master				Master			
+	40	38	78	+	101	68	169
−	14	33	47	−	13	27	40
Total	54	71	125	Total	114	95	209
	A				B		
	Five positions (from table 1)				Nine positions (from table 2)		

* + = Correctly placed pieces; − = pieces omitted or placed incorrectly. The table shows the numbers of pieces placed correctly by the master, by MAPP, by both, and by neither (human data from Chase and Simon, 1973).

master. In the first positions from table 1, MAPP scored 51 percent on the pieces placed correctly by the master, but only 30 percent on the pieces missed by the master. In the nine positions from table 2, MAPP scored 60 percent on the pieces placed correctly by the master, but only 32.5 percent on the pieces that he missed. Thus MAPP performed almost twice as well on the one set of pieces as on the other. From this we can conclude that there is a considerable degree of similarity between the patterns MAPP recognizes and those recognized by the chess master. It should perhaps be mentioned that the patterns for MAPP were extracted from the chess literature by Gilmartin, who had not previously examined the master's chunking data collected by Chase and Simon, although he was aware of the general kinds of chunks that the latter authors had identified.

Of the twenty-two patterns that MAPP recognized in the positions of table 1, seven (all of them pawn chains) were identical with chunks (as identified by Chase and Simon) in the chess master's reproduction of the positions, six were subpatterns of the master's chunks, and five overlapped chunks retained by the master (i.e., incorporated a large part of one of his chunks together with one additional piece

Table 8. Relations between Successive Pieces in Reconstructing Positions
Comparison of Master with MAPP on Positions of Table 1.

Relations	Within-chunk Sequences			Between-chunk Sequences		
	MAPP Number	Percentage	Chess Master Percentage	MAPP Number	Percentage	Chess Master Percentage
—			0.03	2	0.13	0.26
A			0.01			0.02
P			0.00*			0.01
C			0.09	3	0.20	0.22
S			0.03	6	0.40	0.07
AP			0.02			0.02
AS			0.01			0.01
DC			0.05			0.06
PC	2	0.06	0.03			0.03
PS			0.01			0.00*
CS	2	0.06	0.05	2	0.13	0.05
APS			0.00*	1	0.07	0.00
DPC	7	0.21	0.20	1	0.07	0.19
DCS	1	0.03	0.08			0.02
PCS	6	0.18	0.22			0.01
DPCS	16	0.47	0.18			0.03

* Less than 0.005.

—in one case, two additional pieces). In three of these last five cases, the overlap amounted to three or four pieces. Thus, in 16 of the 22 cases, the patterns that MAPP recognized were familiar patterns for the master, or very close to components of such familiar patterns. The remaining six patterns were not in any way peculiar—described rather common configurations which the master, in these instances, either missed or reproduced incorrectly.

The close similarity between MAPP's chunks and those of the chess master shows up in yet another way. Chase and Simon (1973) analyzed the relations [proximity (P), attack (A), defend (D), same color (C), same type (S)] holding between pairs of pieces placed on the board successively when reconstructing a position from memory. They showed that the frequencies of occurrence of particular combinations of relations are quite different when the two successive pieces belong to the same chunk than when they belong to different chunks. The within-chunk and between-chunk relations from MAPP's reconstructions show highly similar distributions to those of the chess master.

Table 8 compares the frequencies of within-chunk and between-chunk relations between master and MAPP in the five positions of table 1. It can be seen from the first three columns of table 8 that the five most frequent combinations of relations encountered in the chess master's within-chunk data (PCS, DPCS, DPC, C, DCS) account for 30 of the 34 within-chunk observations for MAPP. Likewise, the five most frequent combinations in the master's between-chunk data (no relation, C, DPC, S, and DC) account for 12 of the 15 between-chunk observations for MAPP. Moreover, as the table shows, there is relatively little overlap (12 of 49 observations belong to common categories) between the between-chunk and within-chunk distributions. That the relation DPCS is relatively overrepresented in the MAPP within-chunk sequences; and the relations S and CS in the between-chunk sequences probably reflects the overrepresentation of pawn chains in the set of patterns stored in the EPAM net. Except for this discrepancy, the match between theory and data is as good as the small sample size will support.

In sum, there are substantial correlations between chess master and MAPP as to which pieces from briefly exposed positions are remembered, as to the organization of these pieces in chunks, and as to the sequence with which pieces are replaced on the board.

CONCLUSION

In this chapter we have described an information processing model (MAPP) that simulates and thereby seeks to explain the processes that human subjects use to remember and reproduce chess positions to which they have been exposed for 5 or 10 seconds. The processes incorporated in the model were not constructed *ad hoc*, but were adapted from mechanisms previously devised to simulate and explain eye movements in initial exposure to a chessboard (PERCEIVER) and rote verbal learning phenomena (EPAM).

By comparing the performance of the model with the performance of a chess master and a Class A player in identical tasks, we have demonstrated the qualitative resemblances between the human and simulated behavior, and the adequacy of the mechanisms incorporated in MAPP to account for the main features of the human performances. We have also derived estimates of the size of the repertory of familiar patterns that chess players hold in long-term memory.

The MAPP theory is able to explain the chess data parsimoniously by bringing together into a common system basic mechanisms, for chunking in short-term and long-term memory and for managing attention, whose significance had already been demonstrated in accounting for behavior in experimental paradigms and tasks quite remote from the present one.

References

Baylor, G. W., Jr., & Simon, H. A. A chess mating combinations program. *AFIPS Conference Proceedings, 1966 Spring Joint Computer Conference*, 1966, **28**, 431–47. Reprinted as chapter 4.3 in this book.

Chase, W. G., & Simon, H. A. Perception in chess. *Cognitive Psychology*, 1973, **4**, 55–81. Reprinted as chapter 6.4 in this book.

Feigenbaum, E. A. The simulation of verbal learning behavior. *Proceedings of the 1961 Western Joint Computer Conference*, 1961, 121–32. Reprinted in E. A. Feigenbaum and J. Feldman (Eds.). New York: McGraw-Hill, 1963, pp. 297–309.

Good, I. J. The population frequencies of species and the estimation of population parameters. *Biometrika*, 1953, **40**, 237–63.

De Groot, A. D. Perception and memory versus thought: Some old ideas and recent findings. *In* B. Kleinmuntz (Ed.), *Problem Solving*. New York: Wiley, 1966, pp. 19–50.

Noton, D., & Stark, L. Scanpaths in eye movements during pattern perception. *Science*, 1971, **171**, 308–11.

Simon, H. A., & Barenfeld, M. Information-processing analysis of perceptual processes in problem solving. *Psychological Review*, 1969, **76**, 473–83. Reprinted as chapter 6.2 in this book.

6.4

Perception in Chess (1973)

with William G. Chase

What does an experienced chess player "see" when he looks at a chess position? By analyzing an expert player's eye movements, it has been shown that, among other things, he is looking at how pieces attack and defend each other (See chapter 6.2). But we know from other considerations that he is seeing much more. Our work is concerned with just what the expert chess player perceives.

The most extensive work to date on perception in chess is that done by de Groot and his colleagues (de Groot, 1965, 1966, Jongman, 1968). In his search for differences between masters and weaker players, de Groot was unable to find any gross differences in the statistics of their thought processes: the number of moves considered, search heuristics, depth of search, and so on. Masters search through about the same number of possibilities as weaker players—perhaps even fewer, almost certainly not more—but they are very good

This work was supported by Public Health Service Research Grant MH-07722 from the National Institute of Mental Health. We are indebted to Hans Berliner for his masterful performance as a subject.

at coming up with the "right" moves for further consideration, whereas weaker players spend considerable time analyzing the consequences of bad moves.

De Groot did, however, find an intriguing difference between masters and weaker players in his short-term memory experiments. Masters showed a remarkable ability to reconstruct a chess position almost perfectly after viewing it for only 5 seconds. There was a sharp drop-off in this ability for players below the master level. This result could not be attributed to the masters' generally superior memory ability, for when chess positions were constructed by placing the same numbers of pieces randomly on the board, the masters could then do no better in reconstructing them than weaker players. Hence, the masters appear to be constrained by the same severe short-term memory limits as everyone else (Miller, 1956), and their superior performance with "meaningful" positions must lie in their ability to perceive structure in such positions and encode them in chunks. Specifically, if a chess master can remember the location of twenty or more pieces on the board, but has space for only about five chunks in short-term memory, then each chunk must be composed of four or five pieces, organized in a single relational structure.

One key to understanding chess mastery, then, seems to lie in the immediate perceptual processing, for it is here that the game is structured, and it is here in the static analysis that the good moves are generated for subsequent processing. Behind this perceptual analysis, as with all skills (cf., Fitts and Posner, 1967), lies an extensive cognitive apparatus amassed through years of constant practice. What was once accomplished by slow, conscious deductive reasoning is now arrived at by fast, unconscious perceptual processing. It is no mistake of language for the chess master to say that he "sees" the right move; and it is for good reason that students of complex problem solving are interested in perceptual processes (cf., Newell and Simon, 1972). Our main concern here is to discover and characterize the structures, or chunks, that are seen on the board and stored in short-term memory.

SCOPE OF THE STUDY

The previous studies of chess perception make highly plausible the hypothesis that the chess master encodes information about a position in chunks but provides no direct methods for delimiting the chunk boundaries or detecting the relations that hold among the components of a chunk. Evidence is needed on these points in order to discover how many pieces typically constitute a chunk, what the relative sizes are of the chunks of masters and weaker players, and how many chunks players retain after a brief view of a position.

The player's perceptual processing of the board is so rapid (and probably unavailable to conscious introspection) that it is impossible to obtain an accurate verbal description of the process from him. Although eye movements give us a record of how the board is scanned (de Groot, 1966; Simon and Barenfeld, 1966; Tichomirov and Poznyanskaya, 1966; Winikoff, 1967), they don't tell us precisely which pieces are observed (especially in peripheral vision) and in what order; they only tell us the general area being aimed at by the fovea. And, of course, data on eye movements can't tell us what information is being abstracted from the display.

There are, however, other techniques, which have been used with verbal materials, that would appear promising for the problem at hand. Tulving (1962) has looked at clusters in free recall protocols; and Bower and Springston (1970) have looked at the timing relations and pauses in the output. McLean and Gregg (1967) have used pauses to define chunks in rote learning. Ein-Dor (1971) has studied chunking of visual stimuli in the form of Chinese ideograms, using a method essentially identical with our perception experiment.

The central objective of this chapter, then, is to isolate and define the chunks into which information is hypothesized to be encoded in chess perception tasks. We use two techniques. In the *perception task*, we ask chessplayers to reconstruct a chess position while it remains in plain view, and we use subjects' successive glances at the board as an index of chunking. The basic assumption is that, under the conditions of the experiment, the subject will encode only one chunk per glance while reconstructing the position.

In the *memory task*, which is very similar to de Groot's task, we ask chessplayers to reconstruct a position from memory after brief exposure to it, and we use the timing or clustering in recall to segment the output into chunks.

The memory task permits us to replicate the basic findings of de Groot and Jongman. These results are so important that it is essential to have an independent replication; moreover, the empirical results for the case of the random boards have never been reported in detail in the literature.

By using two different tasks, we obtain some protection against artifacts that might compromise the interpretation of our findings. One important question we will investigate is whether the chunks defined by the data from the perception task are essentially of the same size and character as the chunks defined by the data from the memory task.

In the following sections of this chapter, we will report and analyze the main body of data obtained by presenting the two tasks to a chess master and to weaker players. Then we will investigate in somewhat greater detail the data for the chess master in middle game positions. In a final section, we will summarize our findings and our interpretation of them.

METHOD

Three chess players, a master (M), a class A player (A), and a beginner (B), were used as subjects. Twenty games were selected from chess books and magazines to generate the stimuli. These were games between advanced players (masters, experts, and perhaps a few Class A players). Ten were middle game positions, at about White's 21st move, with 24–26 pieces remaining on the board. Ten were endgame positions, at about the 41st move, with 12–15 pieces remaining on the board. Not all the positions were "quiet," i.e., some of them caught games at a point where an exchange of pieces was in progress.

In addition to the positions from actual games, eight random positions were generated, four from middle games and four from end games, by taking actual positions and replacing the pieces randomly on the board.

Perception Task

In this task, two chessboards were placed side by side, separated by about 6 inches: One of the 28 chess positions was set up on the subject's left, and the other board, free of pieces, was placed directly in front of him. A full set of pieces was placed to the right of the blank board. A partition between the two boards prevented the subject from seeing the position on the left. When the partition was removed, the subject's task was to reconstruct the position on the board in front of him as quickly

and accurately as possible, glancing at the position on the left as often as he wished. His behavior was recorded on videotape.

Memory Task

The procedure in the memory task was similar to that used by de Groot (1965), except that the subject was given multiple trials in each position. The boards were set up exactly as in the perceptual task. When the partition was removed, the subject was allowed to view the position on the left for 5 seconds, and the partition was then placed in position again. The subject then recalled, by placing pieces on the board in front of him, what he could remember of the position on the left, being allowed as much time as he wished (subjects rarely took more than 1 minute). If the position was not reconstructed perfectly, the board in front of the subject was cleared and a second trial was conducted in the same way: 5 seconds of viewing, followed by free recall of the position. Additional trials followed until the subject recalled the position perfectly, except for the random positions, which were too difficult to continue to criterion.

In the perception task, each subject processed five middle game positions, five end game positions, two randomized middle game positions, and two randomized end game positions. He also processed the same number of each kind of position in the memory task.

RESULTS

The videotape records for both tasks were analyzed by recording each piece as it was placed on the board, and by recording the time, within 0.1 second, between the placing of that piece and the next one.

The time intervals were used to segment the protocols, in order to test the hypothesis that long pauses would correspond to boundaries between successive chunks, while short time intervals between pieces would indicate that the pieces belonged to the same chunk in memory.

The nature of the chess relations between

successive pieces, separated by long and brief pauses, respectively, were analyzed for information that would reveal how pieces are chunked perceptually. The occurrence of each of five chess relations between successively placed pieces was recorded: (1) *attack*: either one of the two pieces attacks the other; (2) *defense*: either one of the two pieces defends the other; (3) *proximity*: each piece stands on one of the eight squares adjacent to the other; (4) *common color*: both pieces are of the same color; and (5) *common type*: both pieces are of the same type (e.g., both are pawns, rooks, etc.).

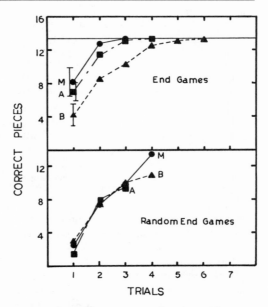

Figure 2. Learning curves for the end game and random end game positions. The brackets are standard errors based on five positions.

Accuracy of Reconstruction

The accuracy with which the subjects reconstructed positions on the first trial in the memory task was analyzed for comparison with the previous findings of de Groot and Jongman. Accuracy was measured by the number of pieces placed on the correct squares of the board on the first trial after a 5-second view of the board. The number of pieces correct on subsequent trials was also computed, but chief interest for our purposes centers on the first-trial results.

Figure 1 shows the results for the middle game positions, actual and random. Figure 2 shows the results for the end game positions, actual and random. The figures show the average number of pieces placed correctly by each subject on successive trials for all positions of the type in question. The standard errors, based on five scores, are shown for the first trial of middle and end game positions.

In the actual middle game positions, M was able to place an average of about sixteen pieces correctly on the first trial,

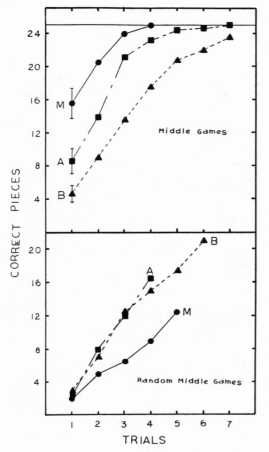

Figure 1. Learning curves of the master (M), class A player (A), and beginner (B) for the middle game and random middle game position. The brackets are standard errors on five positions.

while A and B placed about eight and four, respectively. M was able to reproduce the board perfectly in three or four trials, while A typically required about one or two more trials than M, but B took considerably more trials (as many as fourteen in one case). M showed no such superiority in *additional* pieces placed in successive trials. In trials just beyond the first, M typically added about four more pieces to his previous reconstruction, while the gains for A and B averaged five or six pieces per trial. Of course, A and B, because of their poorer first-trial performance, had much more room for improvement than did M; this difference disappears when the learning curve reaches the level of M's first-trial performance.

In the end game positions, M placed an average of about eight pieces correctly on trial 1, while A and B placed about seven and four, respectively. In these positions, M required two or three trials to reconstruct the positions perfectly; A, about three or four; and B, between four and seven trials. Thus, in both middle and end game positions from actual games, ability to retain information from a 5-second view of the board was closely related to playing strength.

In the random, unstructured positions there was no relation at all between memory of the position and playing strength. Moreover, the first-trial performances of all three subjects on the random positions was even *poorer* than B's performance on the actual game positions.

There is some quantitative difference between M's performance on the actual middle game positions and the performance reported by de Groot for grandmasters and masters in middle game positions. Typically, de Groot's grandmaster and master subjects were able to replace about 23 or 24 pieces out of 25 correctly after 5 seconds (or less!) view of the board. M, as we have seen, averaged only 16 pieces. The most plausible explanation for the difference lies in the nature of the positions used in the tests. De Groot used positions from relatively recent grandmaster games (not known to the subjects) and excluded positions that were not "quiet," i.e., positions where exchanges of pieces were in midstream. Some of the positions we used were from games between players of less than master caliber, and in several of them exchanges were under way.

On the hypothesis that memory of positions depends on recognizing familiar configurations or chunks of pieces, a grandmaster or master would find it easier to remember positions like those he encounters in his play and study. Our subject, M, when interviewed after the experiment, reported that he was troubled by positions that looked "unreasonable." He also reported difficulty with positions that were not quiet, complaining that he couldn't get the "sense" of the position when it was in the middle of an exchange.

Accordingly, our subjects were tested on nine new positions taken from a book of chess puzzles from actual master games (Reinfeld, 1945). Although the positions were tactical in nature, they were not in the middle of an exchange. For each subject, nine positions were chosen at random, and a single 5-second trial was conducted. For these new positions, B, A, and M averaged 33, 49, and 81 percent correct, respectively, as compared to 18, 34, and 62 percent, respectively, on the first trial of the previous positions. These figures are in very close agreement with those published by de Groot (1966), and, taking the differences in stimuli into account,[1] our data unequivocally replicate de Groot's important results.

One unexpected result deserves note at this point. M recognized four of the nine new positions, and always within the first

---

1. There were other differences between de Groot's procedure and ours. For example, de Groot always informed his subjects about who was on move (white or black), and the subject always viewed the board from that perspective, whereas our subjects didn't know who was on move and they always viewed the board from the perspective of the white player. These differences would seem to be minor, however, compared to the differences in quiet positions.

second of exposure, yet M's performance was virtually identical for recognized versus unrecognized positions: 83 versus 79 percent, respectively. Also, for one of the previous middle game positions, M suddenly recognized the game after he had placed the pieces on trial 1. This discovery did not, however, improve his recall of the position in any way.

Time Intervals

In the perception task, the first thing to look at is the distribution of times between successive pieces placed on the board. These times were analyzed separately for: (1) *within-glance intervals*, intervals between pieces placed without looking back at the original position; and (2) *between-glance intervals*, intervals between two pieces separated by a glance back at the original position. These frequency distributions are shown in figure 3 for each subject.

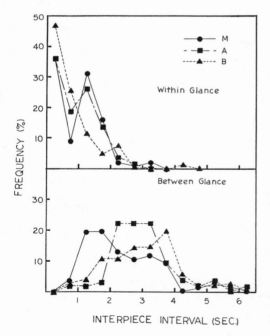

Figure 3. The frequency distributions, for each subject, of the interpiece intervals for the within glance and between glance times of the perception task.

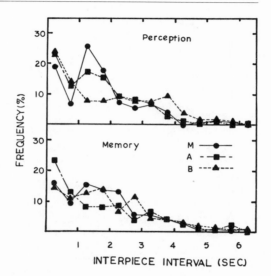

Figure 4. A comparison of the frequency distributions of the interpiece intervals for the perception and memory experiments.

The results are straightforward and roughly the same, with one exception, for all three subjects. Within-glance intervals seldom exceeded 2 seconds and the modal intervals were 0.5 seconds or less. For the between-glance intervals, there was a tendency for the better players to take less time: the mean latencies were 2.8, 3.2, and 3.5 seconds for M, A, and B, respectively. The differences between these means are statically significant ($p < 0.05$) when tested against a pooled error term.

In the memory task, of course, there is no observable behavior that corresponds to the within-glance, between-glance distinction. If we wish to compare the time intervals for the two tasks, we must use the combined frequency distribution for the perception task. Figure 4 compares the combined distributions for each subject in the perception task with the trial 1 distributions of the memory task.

The distributions of time intervals for the two tasks are not dissimilar. In the perception task, there is a preponderance of intervals under 2 seconds, but a "tail" of longer intervals. In the memory task, there are numerous intervals up to about 2.5 seconds, and again a tail of longer intervals. The very short intervals in the distributions, 0.5 seconds or less, are almost all cases where the subject picked up more than one piece of a kind (pawns or Rooks) at once, and placed them on the board in rapid succession. In general, it took at least 1 second to retrieve a piece from the side of the board.[2]

The similarity of the distributions encourages us to consider the following hypothesis about the nature of the perceptual chunks:

1. The pieces placed on the board by the subject in the perception task after a single glance correspond to a single chunk. About 2 seconds is required to recognize a chunk and store a label for it in short-term memory. Since short-term memory appears to have a relatively fixed capacity, measured in chunks, it is most reasonable to assume that what is held in short-term memory is not the content of the chunks, but an identifier (label) that allows the content, in long-term memory, to be located and assessed. When the label of a chunk is held in short-term memory, successive elements of the chunk can be recovered from long-term memory in some hundreds of milliseconds.

2. A sequence of pieces placed on the board by the subject in the memory task with intervals of less than 2 seconds between successive pieces corresponds to a single chunk. The times required for the underlying processes are essentially the same in the memory task as in the perception task.

The hypothesis gains some plausibility from measurements in previous experiments of the times required to transfer information into short-term memory. In particular, Dansereau (1969), studying times of performance of mental arithmetic and related tasks, estimated that about 2 seconds was needed to begin processing a chunk whose label was held in short-term memory, and only about 300 msec to transfer to short-term memory each successive element of the chunk. Intervals even shorter than 300 msec intervals are familiar from other experiments on the speed with which subjects can count down familiar lists (Landauer, 1962; Pierce and Karlin, 1957).

If our hypothesis is correct (that time intervals of 2 seconds or more correspond to boundaries between chunks) then an examination of the chess relations between successive pieces within single chunks should show these relations to be quite different from the relations between successive pieces across chunk boundaries. Furthermore, if we are right in equating the significance of long and short time intervals in the two distinct tasks (perception and memory) then the within-chunk and between-chunk chess relations in the perception task should be highly similar to the corresponding relations in the memory task (none of our results would be essentially changed if we had adopted a 2.5 instead of a 2-second boundary). We turn next to these tests of the hypothesis.

Chess Relations: Perception Task

Table 1 shows, for each subject, the within-glance probabilities and mean interpiece latencies for each of the sixteen possible combinations of attack (A), defense (D), same color (C), same piece (S), and proximity (P) relations. For example, the first row shows latencies and probabilities for successive pieces which have no relation; they are of opposite color, are not proximate to each other, and are not of the same type. The second row is for pieces that have only an attack relation. The last row (DPCS) is for pieces that have a defense relation, are within one square of each other, are of the same color, and are of the same type. This last row is comprised almost totally of pawn chains. Notice also that the color relation is carried redun-

---

2. A possible artifact in this experiment is the time required actually to pick up the pieces. We have replicated the experiment as an oral task (pointing to squares and naming the pieces on them) and a paper-and-pencil task (writing the names of the pieces on the proper squares of a diagram on the board) without altering the results. We will report on these later experiments in chapter 6.5.

Table 1. Chess Relations: Within-glance Latencies (RT) and Probabilities (p) for Each Subject (M,A,B), and Total Frequencies (N), Average Latencies ($\overline{RT}$), Standard Error of Average Latencies ($SE_{\overline{RT}}$), Observed Probabilities (P_o), a Priori Probabilities (P_e), and Deviation Scores (Z) for Combinations of the Five Chess Relations: Attack (A), Defense (D), Spatial Proximity (P), Same Color (C), and Same Piece (S).

Relations	M		A		B		All Players					
	RT	p	RT	p	RT	p	N	$\overline{RT}$	$SE_{\overline{RT}}$	P_o	P_e	Z
—	4.63	0.044	1.48	0.035	—	0	8	3.05	1.321	0.028	0.320	−30.1
A	1.60	0.011	1.90	0.009	1.40	0.013	3	1.63	0.119	0.010	0.0201	−1.6
P	1.30	0.011	1.80	0.009	—	0	2	1.55	0.177	0.007	0.0057	0.3
C	1.53	0.099	1.40	0.060	1.75	0.125	26	1.58	0.173	0.091	0.255	−9.7
S	0.80	0.022	1.35	0.017	0.80	0.013	5	1.02	0.163	0.017	0.148	−16.9
AP	1.23	0.044	1.85	0.052	1.78	0.063	15	1.65	0.206	0.052	0.0077	3.4
AS	—	0	—	0	—	0	0	—	—	0	0.0025	—
DC	1.53	0.099	1.44	0.103	1.38	0.100	29	1.45	0.104	0.101	0.0423	3.3
PC	1.17	0.033	1.51	0.060	0.72	0.063	15	1.18	0.126	0.052	0.0159	2.8
PS	2.10	0.022	0.77	0.026	0.30	0.013	6	1.13	0.322	0.021	0.0075	1.6
CS	1.44	0.077	1.08	0.043	0.58	0.050	16	1.11	0.190	0.056	0.0939	−2.8
APS	—	0	—	0	—	0	0	—	—	0	0.0022	—
DPC	1.30	0.132	1.19	0.190	1.04	0.113	43	1.19	0.081	0.150	0.0469	4.9
DCS	1.50	0.044	0.50	0.017	—	0	6	1.17	0.385	0.021	0.0057	1.8
PCS	0.41	0.154	0.46	0.155	0.41	0.188	47	0.43	0.043	0.164	0.0105	7.0
DPCS	0.53	0.209	0.41	0.353	0.48	0.263	66	0.47	0.033	0.230	0.0162	8.6
	1.22		0.99		0.89			1.04				

dantly with the defense relation (pieces defending one another are of the same color). Table 2 shows the corresponding data for between-glance probabilities and latencies.

The first thing to notice is that these data are quite similar for all subjects. The latencies show the same systematic trends, and, for the probabilities, the product moment correlation between subjects are quite high: M versus A = 0.93, M versus B = 0.95, and A versus B = 0.92. The same is true for the between-glance data, shown in table 2, and the correlations for the probabilities are about the same size: M versus A = 0.89, M versus B = 0.89, and A versus B = 0.90. Thus, the same kinds and degrees of relatedness between successive pieces holds for subjects of very different skills.

The marginal row statistics, shown in the last six columns of tables 1 and 2 are, therefore, representative of all subjects. The first summary column shows the total frequency for each type of event. The second and third columns show the mean

and standard error of the interpiece latencies. The fourth column shows the probabilities, based on the frequencies of the first column. The fifth column shows the *a priori* probabilities, which would prevail if successive pieces were chosen at random.[3] The last column shows a deviation score (the observed probability minus the *a priori* probability, divided by the standard error) assuming the normal approximation to the binomial. The *a priori* values can be considered exact since they are based on about 12,000 observations.

A comparison of tables 1 and 2 reveals quite different patterns for the within-glance and between-glance probabilities. An examination of the z scores shows that

3. The *a priori* probabilities were calculated by first recording, for each position, all relations that exist between every possible pair of pieces; the *a priori* probability for a relation, then, is simply the total number of occurrences of a relation divided by the total number of possible pairs. The *a priori* probabilities were based on thirty positions, and the random *a priori* probabilities were based on eight random positions.

Table 2. Chess Relations: Between-glance Latencies (RT) and Probabilities (p) for Each Subject (M,A,B), and Total Frequencies (N), Average Latencies ($\overline{RT}$), Standard Error of Average Latencies ($SE_{\overline{RT}}$), Observed Probabilities (P_o), a Priori Probabilities (P_e), and Deviation Scores (Z) for Combinations of the Five Chess Relations: Attack (A), Defense (D), Spatial Proximity (P), Same Color (C), and Same Piece (S).

	M		A		B		All Players					
Relations	RT	p	RT	p	RT	p	N	$\overline{RT}$	$SE_{\overline{RT}}$	P_o	P_e	Z
—	3.76	0.213	3.25	0.255	5.20	0.156	43	4.00	0.434	0.203	0.320	−4.2
A	2.50	0.013	3.80	0.055	3.63	0.052	8	3.55	0.926	0.038	0.0201	1.4
P	2.35	0.025	4.60	0.036	3.52	0.065	9	3.50	0.527	0.042	0.0057	2.7
C	2.94	0.338	3.15	0.236	3.38	0.260	60	3.14	0.182	0.283	0.255	0.9
S	2.63	0.050	2.75	0.036	3.43	0.052	10	2.97	0.311	0.047	0.148	−6.9
AP	1.25	0.025	3.05	0.036	3.70	0.052	8	2.92	0.638	0.038	0.0077	2.3
AS	—	0	—	0	—	0	0	—	0	0	0.0025	—
DC	1.63	0.050	2.91	0.127	3.33	0.156	23	2.91	0.277	0.108	0.0423	3.1
PC	1.27	0.038	1.20	0.018	3.00	0.026	6	1.83	0.346	0.028	0.0159	1.1
PS	4.63	0.038	3.10	0.018	—	0	4	4.25	1.121	0.019	0.0075	1.2
CS	4.06	0.063	8.10	0.055	2.75	0.026	10	5.01	1.435	0.047	0.0939	3.2
APS	—	0	—	0	—	0	0	—	0	0	0.0022	—
DPC	1.55	0.138	2.58	0.073	2.51	0.117	24	2.08	0.157	0.113	0.0469	3.0
DCS	—	0	0.90	0.036	—	0	2	0.90	0	0.009	0.0057	0.6
PCS	3.50	0.013	—	0	5.20	0.026	3	4.63	0.484	0.014	0.0105	0.5
DPCS	—	0	1.90	0.018	0.70	0.013	2	1.30	0.424	0.009	0.0162	−1.0
	2.86		3.30		3.58			3.24				

the between-glance probabilities are much closer to the chance levels than are the within-glance probabilities. In contrast, the within-glance probabilities are higher than chance for pairs of pieces with several relations, and lower than chance for pairs with few relations. In particular, the relations AP, DC, DPC, PCS, and DPCS have high probabilities, C, S, and null (—) relations have lower-than-chance probabilities.

These probabilities are informative about the underlying structures that the subjects are perceiving. As mentioned before, the relation DPCS is almost totally composed of pawn chains, and the relation PCS consists almost totally of rows of pawns on the same rank. Note also that these two relations have much shorter latencies than the others. The relation DPC consists of pieces placed on adjacent squares which have a defense relation, and the relation DC consists simply of a defense relation which, of course, also implies the same-color relation. The low frequencies for the A relation suggests that attacks are

noticed only if the pieces are in close spatial proximity (but see later the additional comments on this point in the discussion of the Perceptual Chunks of a Chess Master). The C, S, and null relations are low because subjects are placing pieces which usually have multiple relations. Thus, from the within-glance relations, it appears that subjects are noticing the pawn structure, clusters of pieces of the same color, and attack and defense relations over small spatial distances.

There is some indication from the between-glance probabilities that subjects are looking back at the chess position in order to complete some partially forgotten information or to obtain new information about a partially completed structure. For example, the DPC, CS, and DC relations are slightly higher and the S and null relations are down somewhat from the chance level. Subjects also report that sometimes they look back at the chess position for specific partial information. But the striking thing about these data is that between-glance frequencies are much

Table 3. Chess Relations for the Random Positions: Frequency (N), Average Latencies ($\overline{RT}$), Standard Error of Average Latencies ($SE_{\overline{RT}}$), Observed Probabilities (P_o), a Priori Probabilities (P_e), and Deviation Scores (Z) for the Five Chess Relations: Attack (A), Defense (D), Spatial Proximity (P), Same Color (C), and Same Piece (S).

	Within-glance						Between-glance					
Relations	N	$\overline{RT}$	$SE_{\overline{RT}}$	P_o	P_e	Z	N	$\overline{RT}$	$SE_{\overline{RT}}$	P_o	P_e	Z
—	2	1.95	0.672	0.018	0.298	−22.4	24	4.58	0.736	0.214	0.298	−2.2
A	1	1.20	0.001	0.009	0.0265	−2.0	1	1.50	—	0.009	0.0265	−2.0
P	2	1.30	0.141	0.018	0.0046	1.1	3	2.93	0.314	0.027	0.0046	1.4
C	7	1.09	0.172	0.063	0.287	−9.8	26	2.99	0.277	0.232	0.287	−1.4
S	2	0.80	0.212	0.018	0.150	−10.5	11	2.99	0.620	0.098	0.150	−1.8
AP	16	1.25	0.124	0.143	0.0351	3.3	9	4.59	1.166	0.080	0.0351	1.8
AS	2	1.90	0.001	0.018	0.0013	1.3	2	3.10	0.001	0.018	0.0013	1.3
DC	6	1.12	0.136	0.054	0.0238	1.4	6	2.30	0.253	0.054	0.0238	1.4
PC	10	1.17	0.178	0.089	0.0126	2.8	7	2.27	0.351	0.063	0.0126	2.2
PS	10	0.97	0.141	0.089	0.0139	2.8	3	2.17	0.446	0.027	0.0139	1.7
CS	6	0.65	0.087	0.054	0.101	−2.2	6	2.30	0.230	0.054	0.101	−2.2
APS	0	—	—	0	0.0053	—	0	—	—	0	0.0053	—
DPC	19	0.77	0.160	0.170	0.0265	4.1	12	2.77	0.206	0.107	0.0265	2.8
DCS	6	1.07	0.195	0.054	0.0013	2.5	6	1.07	0.195	0.054	0.0013	2.5
PCS	20	0.51	0.082	0.179	0.0060	4.8	2	3.65	0.601	0.018	0.0060	0.9
DPCS	3	0.43	0.152	0.027	0.0066	1.3	3	0.43	0.152	0.027	0.0066	1.3
		0.94						3.29				

closer to the chance level than within-glance frequencies.

Table 3 shows the summary data for the between and within-glance data for the randomized positions. Although there weren't many observations on individual subjects, the pattern of probabilities was still the same across subjects. The interesting thing about these data is that they look very similar to the data from real positions. Notice that frequencies of the PCS, DPC, and AP relations are higher than chance, and of the S, C, and null relations are lower than chance for the within-glance relations, whereas frequencies of the between-glance relations are very close to chance. Apparently, subjects are noticing the same kinds of structures in the random positions as in the game positions even though such structures are rare in the random positions.

The procedure of the perception experiment offers no absolute guarantee that the subject did not pick up more than one chunk at a glance. However, subjects reported that it was most comfortable to glance frequently at the board and not to retain much information in short-term memory. Moreover, especially with M, there was no evidence of perseveration in glances. The duration of most of his glances, including time for the head movement and time to place the next piece, was close to the 2-second boundary, and almost none was more than 4 seconds long. But the main test of the one-glance-one-chunk hypothesis lies in comparison of the data between perception and memory experiments.

Chess Relations: Memory Task

Table 4 shows the memory data for individual subjects.[4] Again the patterns of latencies and probabilities look the same for all subjects, and the correlations are about the same as in the perception data: M versus A = 0.91, M versus B = 0.95, and A versus B = 0.95.

---

4. Only the chess relations from actual game positions were analyzed for the memory task. Trial 1 recall of the random positions was so poor that there simply weren't enough data to make any comparisons.

Table 4. Chess Relations for the Memory Experiment: Average Latencies ($\overline{RT}$), Observed Probabilities (P_o), Frequency (N), Standard Error of Average Latencies ($SE_{\overline{RT}}$), a Priori Probabilities (P_e), and Deviation Scores (Z) for Combinations of the Five Chess Relations: Attack (A), Defense (D), Spatial Proximity (P), Same Color (C), and Same Piece (S).

	M		A		B		All Players					
Relations	$\overline{RT}$	P_o	$\overline{RT}$	P_o	$\overline{RT}$	P_o	N	$\overline{RT}$	$SE_{\overline{RT}}$	P_o	P_e	Z
—	6.67	0.147	5.18	0.117	4.53	0.124	114	5.81	0.552	0.132	0.320	−16.4
A	2.86	0.012	4.94	0.019	3.60	0.010	12	3.85	1.026	0.014	0.0201	−1.6
P	2.53	0.010	3.20	0.004	8.00	0.005	6	3.55	0.886	0.007	0.0057	0.4
C	3.57	0.150	6.28	0.140	3.04	0.163	129	4.19	0.426	0.149	0.255	−8.7
S	3.24	0.065	7.35	0.039	1.22	0.025	41	4.00	0.726	0.047	0.148	−13.9
AP	2.80	0.007	2.80	0.012	5.00	0.025	16	3.18	0.552	0.018	0.0077	2.4
AS	2.40	0.010	1.60	0.012	1.80	0.005	8	2.02	0.289	0.009	0.0025	2.1
DC	3.99	0.070	2.96	0.035	3.18	0.064	50	3.60	0.627	0.058	0.0423	2.0
PC	3.37	0.027	6.10	0.019	2.90	0.045	25	3.75	0.840	0.029	0.0159	2.3
PS	0.40	0.002	0.80	0.008	4.60	0.010	5	2.24	1.135	0.006	0.0075	−0.7
CS	2.86	0.055	4.83	0.027	1.90	0.054	40	2.94	0.585	0.046	0.0939	−6.7
APS	0.50	0.005	—	0	—	0	2	0.50	0	0.002	0.0022	0.1
DPC	2.22	0.175	2.69	0.214	3.01	0.213	168	2.58	0.207	0.194	0.0469	11.0
DCS	1.19	0.035	0.65	0.078	2.28	0.050	44	1.19	0.128	0.051	0.0057	6.0
PCS	0.63	0.107	0.92	0.167	0.67	0.114	109	0.75	0.116	0.126	0.0105	10.2
DPCS	0.97	0.122	1.08	0.109	0.73	0.094	96	0.95	0.111	0.111	0.0167	8.9
	2.98		3.19		2.68			2.97				

The first question of interest concerning the memory data is the relationship between interpiece latencies and the perceptual chunks: What evidence is there that pauses are associated with retrieval of new structures? The evidence seems fairly good on this point. It can be seen in Table 4 that longer latencies are associated with fewer interpiece chess relations, and figure 5 illustrates the relation between average interpiece latencies and the number of chess relations between the pieces. Another indication of this relationship is that latencies are correlated − 0.73 with the z scores of $(P_o − P_e)/SE_{P_0}$.

We should also note in passing that errors usually occur toward the end of the protocol; subjects usually report first what they know, and fast, and these errors generally have long latencies and few relations. Also, the results remain the same if we score only correctly placed pieces.

A closer look at table 4 reveals that the lowest latencies (except for APS, but we will not consider it because it occurred only twice, and both of those for M) occur for pawn formations (PCS and DPCS) and for pairs of Rooks or pairs of Knights that mutually defend each other (DCS). The other relation that occurred much more than chance was that of adjacent pieces

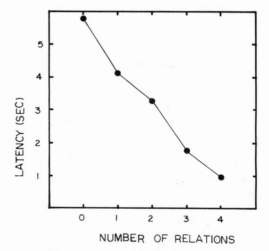

Figure 5. The relation between interpiece latencies and the number of relations between pairs of successively placed pieces in the memory task.

Table 5. Chess Relations for the Memory Data for Long and Short Interpiece Latencies for Combinations of the Five Chess Relations: Attack (A), Defense (D), Spatial Proximity (P), Same Color (C), and Same Piece (P).

	Less Than 2 Seconds						Greater Than 2 Seconds					
Relations	N	$\overline{RT}$	$SE_{\overline{RT}}$	P_o	P_e	z	N	$\overline{RT}$	$SE_{\overline{RT}}$	P_o	P_e	z
—	15	1.75	0.062	0.031	0.320	−36.4	99	6.42	0.612	0.258	0.320	−2.8
A	5	1.50	0.188	0.010	0.0201	−2.1	7	5.53	1.452	0.018	0.0201	−0.3
P	2	1.75	0.177	0.004	0.0057	−0.5	4	4.45	1.073	0.010	0.0057	0.9
C	43	1.48	0.052	0.089	0.255	−12.7	86	5.54	0.586	0.224	0.255	−1.5
S	14	1.23	0.121	0.029	0.148	−15.5	27	5.43	0.994	0.070	0.148	−6.0
AP	7	1.39	0.168	0.015	0.0077	1.3	9	4.58	0.670	0.023	0.0077	2.0
AS	5	1.44	0.100	0.010	0.0025	1.7	3	3.00	0.245	0.008	0.0025	1.2
DC	26	1.22	0.082	0.054	0.0423	1.1	24	6.17	1.079	0.063	0.0423	1.6
PC	13	1.48	0.114	0.027	0.0159	1.5	12	6.20	1.444	0.031	0.0159	1.7
PS	4	1.00	0.300	0.008	0.0075	0.2	1	7.20	—	0.003	0.0075	−1.9
CS	22	1.18	0.120	0.046	0.0939	−5.1	18	5.10	1.096	0.047	0.0939	−4.4
APS	2	0.50	0	0.004	0.0022	0.7	0	—	—	0	0.0022	—
DPC	95	1.28	0.045	0.198	0.0469	8.3	73	4.28	0.392	0.190	0.0469	7.2
DCS	38	0.91	0.071	0.079	0.0057	6.0	6	2.97	0.259	0.016	0.0057	1.6
PCS	104	0.57	0.044	0.216	0.0105	11.0	5	4.58	1.564	0.013	0.0105	0.4
DPCS	86	0.68	0.046	0.179	0.0162	9.3	10	3.34	0.583	0.026	0.0162	1.2
		1.02						5.40				

that have a defense relation (DPC), although these latencies were relatively long. It seems clear, however, that if there is a long pause in the recall, the pieces are not likely to be closely related.

We next turn to the hypothesis that time intervals of roughly 2 seconds or more correspond to boundaries between chunks. If this hypothesis is correct, the chess relations with latencies greater than 2 seconds ought to look like chance occurrences, whereas the relations occurring within 2 seconds ought to show even more structure. Table 5 shows the memory data of table 4 partitioned into relations for latencies less than (or equal to) 2 seconds and chess relations for latencies greater than 2 seconds. It is clear from table 5 that the hypothesis is essentially correct.

For the long pauses, the only relation that is considerably above chance is that of adjacent pieces with a defense relation (DPC). Apparently, a chunk isn't retrieved from memory completely at random. Subjects use the partially constructed board to retrieve new information, and the new information often consists of the DPC relation. Also it is clear from subjects' verbal reports and from watching subjects that the overall recall pattern is systematic, e.g., counterclockwise or clockwise recall, and that local proximities are very important.

A second hypothesis we wish to consider is that the short and long time intervals of the memory task have the same meaning as the within- and between-glance distinctions, respectively, of the perception task. The similarity of these patterns becomes evident when we lay the probabilities side by side, as in table 6, and contrast them with the a priori probabilities. There are some slight differences between the perceptual and memory probabilities, but these differences are everywhere small compared to their differences with the a priori probabilities. Table 7 illustrates this similarity more sharply by showing the matrix of correlations derived from table 6. There are two clusters of correlations in this table. First, the within-glance probabilities (perception task) from actual game positions are highly correlated with the probabilities for the short pauses in the memory task, and the within-glance probabilities from random games are moder-

Table 6. A Comparison of the Perceptual, Memory, and *a Priori* Chess Relation Probabilities for Combinations of the Five Chess Relations: Attack (A), Defense (D), Spatial Proximity (P), Same Color (C), and Same Piece (S).

Chess Relations	Perception Within-glance (Random)	Perception Within-glance (Games)	Memory Less Than 2 Seconds	Perception Between-glance (Random)	Perception Between-glance (Games)	Memory Greater Than 2 Seconds	A Priori (Games)	A Priori (Random)
—	0.018	0.028	0.031	0.214	0.203	0.258	0.320	0.298
A	0.009	0.010	0.010	0.009	0.038	0.018	0.0201	0.0265
P	0.018	0.007	0.004	0.027	0.042	0.010	0.0057	0.0046
C	0.063	0.091	0.089	0.232	0.283	0.224	0.255	0.287
S	0.018	0.017	0.029	0.098	0.047	0.070	0.148	0.150
AP	0.143	0.052	0.015	0.080	0.038	0.023	0.0077	0.0351
AS	0.018	0	0.010	0.018	0	0.008	0.0025	0.0013
DC	0.054	0.101	0.054	0.054	0.108	0.063	0.0423	0.0238
PC	0.089	0.052	0.027	0.063	0.028	0.031	0.0159	0.0126
PS	0.089	0.021	0.008	0.027	0.019	0.003	0.0075	0.0139
CS	0.054	0.056	0.046	0.054	0.047	0.047	0.0939	0.101
APS	0	0	0.004	0	0	0	0.0022	0.0053
DPC	0.170	0.150	0.198	0.107	0.113	0.190	0.0469	0.0265
DCS	0.054	0.021	0.079	0.054	0.009	0.016	0.0057	0.0013
PCS	0.179	0.164	0.216	0.018	0.014	0.013	0.0105	0.0060
DPCS	0.027	0.230	0.179	0.027	0.009	0.026	0.0162	0.0066

ately correlated with these two. Second, the between-glance probabilities in random positions, between-glance probabilities in game positions, probabilities for long pauses of the memory task, and *a priori* probabilities are all highly intercorrelated.

On the basis of these data, it is reasonable to conclude that the time intervals in the two variants of the experiment, perceptual and memory, have basically the same information processing significance. The processes that occur during an interval of more than 2 seconds between the placing of two pieces appear to be significantly different from the processes that occur during an

interval of less than 2 seconds. Moreover, the nature of the differences in frequencies of relations in the two cases makes it reasonable, at least tentatively, to apply the term "chunk" to the set of pieces placed on the board in either experiment within the boundaries of a pair of long time intervals.

One final comparison between the perception and memory task concerns the chunk size. Recall that in the perception task there was a systematic difference in the duration of the glances as a function of chess skill, with less time being taken by the more skilled players. But the average

Table 7. Intercorrelation Matrix for the Perceptual, Memory, and *a Priori* Chess Relation Probabilities.

	1	2	3	4	5	6	7
1. Within-glance (random) } Perception		.49	.59	.06	.02	.09	−.19
2. Within-glance (games) } Perception			.89	.06	.12	.18	−.04
3. Less than 2 seconds } Memory				.08	.10	.23	−.03
4. Between-glance (random) } Perception					.92	.93	.91
5. Between-glance (games) } Perception						.91	.81
6. Greater than 2 seconds } Memory							.87
7. *A priori*							

number of pieces per glance did not vary systematically as a function of chess skill. For the middle game positions, the average number of pieces per glance was 2.0, 2.8, and 2.0, respectively, for M, A, and B. For the memory experiment, however, the corresponding number of pieces per chunk was 2.5, 2.1, and 1.9, respectively. Thus, it appears that the chunks are about the same size in both tasks, but that chess skill is reflected in the speed with which chunks are perceived in the perception task and the size of the chunks in the memory task.

We undertake next to examine further evidence that will help us decide whether the chunks defined by long pauses have the properties we would expect from our previous experimental knowledge of perceptual chunking.

CHUNK SIZE AND MEMORY SPAN

Having segmented the recall protocol into chunks, we are now in a position to test the hypothesis that recall is limited by the number of chunks that can be held in short-term memory. We interpret this hypothesis to mean that M's superior recall should be associated with larger chunks, but that the number of chunks should be a small constant within the memory span (7 ± 2) for all subjects.

One problem with this analysis must be dealt with first: The recall protocols generally consist of two phases: an initial recall phase, followed by a reconstruction phase. The general practice of the subjects was to place first those groups of pieces they thought they remembered well, then to search memory for additional pieces. During the first phase, placing pieces in recall without "problem solving," chunks tended to be relatively large and errors relatively few. During the second phase, pieces tended to be placed one by one (pawns sometimes by pairs or triads), time being taken for deliberation between pieces. Errors were relatively frequent, and in many instances the player appeared to be determining where pieces ought to be (i.e., where they would function well, or where they are often posted in actual games) rather than recalling where he had actually seen them. This behavior was more true of M than the other subjects. De Groot (1966) points out, in fact, that subjects can average better than 44 percent simply by putting down the "average" or prototype position derived from master games.

To avoid inflating our estimate of the number of chunks, we need a way of distinguishing the recall phase from the reconstruction phase. To identify the reconstruction phase, we adopted the criterion of an extremely long pause (10 seconds or more) followed by mostly errors, or a series of long pauses (5 seconds or more) with errors. Based on this criterion, table 8 shows, for each of the subjects in the memory experiment, the average sizes of eight successive chunks on the first trial for the actual middle game and end game positions. The last column of the table shows the average number of chunks recalled for the first trial in each of these positions.

We observe, first, that chunk size is related to chess skill for the first few chunks,

Table 8. Average Sizes of Successive Chunks for Each Player, Middle Game and End Game Positions. Memory Experiments, First Trial.

| | | *Successive Chunks* | | | | | | | | *Average Chunks/Trial* |
		1	*2*	*3*	*4*	*5*	*6*	*7*	*8*	
Middle Games	M	3.8	3.0	2.5	2.3	1.9	1.5	2.2	2.0	7.7
	A	2.6	2.5	1.8	1.6	1.7	1.7	2.1	2.5	5.7
	B	2.4	2.1	2.0	1.6	1.4	1.5	1.0	2.0	5.3
End Games	M	2.6	1.6	1.4	1.8	1.8	1.2	2.3	1.0	7.6
	A	2.4	1.4	2.0	2.0	1.0	1.0	1.0	1.0	6.4
	B	2.2	2.4	2.2	1.0	1.0	1.0	1.0	0	4.2

but that this difference disappears in later chunks of the protocol. This relation is less true of the end game positions, and chunks are also smaller for the end games. The middle game-end game difference simply reflects the fact that end games are less structured than middle games.

The gradual drop in chunk size during recall could be due to several things. First, it may be that subjects simply recall their larger chunks first. Second, it is well known that recall has an interfering effect on short-term memory, and it may be that interference causes large chunks to break up into smaller chunks as some of the relations are forgotten. Third, the later chunks may be contaminated by some of the piece-by-piece reconstructions that are missed by our criterion; perhaps the first guesses are the best and are more likely to be correct.

We observe, second, that the average number of chunks for each subject is well within the memory span, as hypothesized; but, contrary to our expectation, the number of chunks is related to chess skill.

Taken at face value, these data suggest that M achieves his superior performance by recalling both more chunks and larger chunks. This seems a rather surprising result; we know from the performance on randomized positions that M does not have a superior memory capacity.

Where, then, do these extra chunks come from? There are at least two possibilities. First, it may be that M does not store a small number of unrelated chunks in short-term memory. Rather, he may be able to organize the chunks on the board in some as yet undetermined way so that more chunks can be stored. In this way, M will get more information from the partially reconstructed board than weaker players about what the rest of the position should be. In other words, the data should make us skeptical of an overly simple theoretical position that postulates that short-term memory consists of a linear list of seven or so unrelated chunk slots.

A second possibility, discussed earlier, is that M is reconstructing part of the position from his general knowledge of such

positions, and our criterion for these reconstructions doesn't pick up all these responses because they are more likely to be correct for M than for the other players.

In summary, the data on chunk size and memory span confirm the hypotheses that chunk size is larger for more skilled chess players, and that the number of chunks is within the memory span. However, the hypothesis that the number of chunks is invariant over different levels of chess skill is not supported.

PERCEPTUAL CHUNKS OF A CHESS MASTER

De Groot and Jongman have made some observations on the nature of the perceptual chunks into which grandmasters and masters encode information. In their experiments, however, these authors had no objective means for detecting chunk boundaries. Our data give us an operational method of characterizing chunks, which we will apply to the middle game memory experiments of subject M.

Table 9 shows for M the sizes of successive chunks for the five middle game and nine puzzle positions for trial 1 of the memory experiments. The great bulk of the 77 chunks (two or more pieces within 2 seconds) in these 14 positions belong to a very small number of types. Of the 77 chunks, only 17 couldn't be classified into the following three categories: Pawn chains, castled-King positions, or clusters of pieces of the same color. Over half the chunks (47) contained a Pawn chain, sometimes with nearby supporting pieces and sometimes with blockading pieces or contains more than one of these categories. For example, a castled-King position (a strong and often-used defensive structure) includes a King, a Rook, and three Pawns, sometimes with nearby pieces. Twenty-seven chunks consisted of clusters of pieces of the same color (exclusive of castled-King positions), and 18 of these were of very familiar types: nine chunks consisted of pieces on the back rank (rank 1 or 8), often in their original undeveloped position; and nine chunks consisted of connected Rooks (mutually supporting), or the Queen con-

Table 9. Size of the Master's Successive Chunks for the Five Middle Game and Nine Puzzle Positions. Memory Experiment, First Trial.

Successive Chunks

	1	2	3	4	5	6	7	8	9	10	11	12	13
M1	6	7	1	2	2	2	1	3	1	1			
M2	3	2	1	2	2	1	3	1	1	2	2	1	2
M3	4	2	5	2	4	1	1	1	2				
M4	4	2	1	1	1	1	5	1	2				
M5	2	2	2	4									
P1	3	7	4	2	1	2	1	2	2				
P2	4	5	1	2	1	3							
P3	2	2	2	4	3	3	2						
P4	6	3	5	2	1								
P5	5	2	3	3	2	1	1	1	1	1	1		
P6	3	4	4	1	1	1	4	4					
P7	8	4	5	3	3								
P8	2	1	2	4	4	1	2	2	2				
P9	3	2	1	2	2	2	2	3	2	3	3	1	
	3.9	3.2	2.6	2.6	2.1	1.6	2.2	2.0	1.6	1.8	2.0	1.0	2.0

SE = 0.46.

nected with one or two Rooks—a very powerful attacking structure. These categories are not mutually exclusive, since some chunks contain more than one of these categories. For example, a castled-King position also contains a Pawn chain, and sometimes Pawn chains and clusters of pieces occur within the same chunk. The point is, however, that over 75 percent of M's chunks belong to only three types of chessboard configurations, all highly familiar and stereotyped.

One further analysis was carried out on M's protocols. From an examination of the chess relations, it appears that subjects were not attending to the attack relation as much as the defense relation. Recall that the attack relation appeared more often than chance only if the attacking piece was also on an adjacent square. But a casual look at M's protocols indicated that some attacking pieces were clustered in his protocols.

Therefore, to test this hypothesis more objectively, the 14 middle game and puzzle positions were analyzed by the authors to find the strongest attacks; 18 such attacks were found, consisting mostly of pieces attacking the opponent's King position.

Of these 18 attacks, 11 were chunked in M's protocols, in the sense that at least two of the attacking pieces appeared within the same chunk; rarely did the attacked pieces also appear in the same chunk with the attackers. Of the 11 attacks, six consisted of Rook and Queen-Rook combinations—one chunk also contained a Pawn in combination with the Queen and Rook, and the other five chunks consisted of a Knight in combination with a Queen or Rook.

Thus, it appears that there are two kinds of attacks that get chunked. The first kind is a fortuitous attack characterized by an attack relation between two adjacent pieces. The second kind of attack is more abstract and involves combinations of pieces of the same color converging, usually, on the opponent's King position. The relation between the attacking pieces wouldn't appear as an attack relation; these pieces would either have no relation or a defense relation. These attack chunks would also be stereotyped, often involving classic maneuvers against a stereotyped defensive position.

M would be able to recognize all these chunks provided that he has stored in long-term memory a modest vocabulary of variant patterns for each of a half dozen types of configurations. The estimates given in chapter 6.2 as to the size of vocabulary required appear now to be, if anything, somewhat too large.

Thus, we can account for M's performance in recalling positions he has seen for 5 seconds if we postulate that he has a short-term memory of average capacity, but a long-term memory capable of recognizing:

1. A variety of chunks consisting of Pawns (and possibly Rooks and minor pieces) in common castled-King configurations.

2. A variety of chunks consisting of common first-rank configurations.

3. A variety of chunks consisting of common Pawn chain, Rook pair, and Rook and Queen configurations.

4. A variety of common configurations of attacking pieces, especially along a file, diagonal, or around an opponent's castled-King position.[5]

CONCLUSION

By confronting chess players of varying strength, from master to novice, with a perception task and a memory task, we have shown that the amount of information extracted from a briefly exposed position varies with playing strength, thus confirming earlier experiments of de Groot, Jongman, and others.

By measuring the time intervals between placements of successive pieces when the subjects attempted to reconstruct the positions, we were able to identify the boundaries of perceptual chunks. The data suggest that the superior performance of stronger players (which does not appear in random positions) derives from the ability of those players to encode the position into larger perceptual chunks, each consisting of a familiar subconfiguration of pieces. Pieces within a single chunk are

bound by relations of mutual defense, proximity, attack over small distances, and common color and type.

There is also some evidence that chunks may be held together by more abstract relations. There are more chunks in recall for the stronger players, yet the frequencies of between-chunk relations (of the kinds we recorded) are all close to chance. This may derive from a hierarchical organization of the chunks, related to chess skill, that is more abstract than the simple chess relations we have measured. Further, in M's protocol there is good evidence that pieces converging on the opponent's King position (or sometimes on other vulnerable positions) are chunked—a more abstract but fairly well-defined attack relation.

Finally, the number of chunks retained in short-term memory after brief exposure to chess positions is about of the magnitude we would predict from immediate recall of common words (Miller, 1956) and copying of visual patterns (Ein-Dor, 1971).

References

Bower, G. H., & Springston, F. Pauses as recoding points in letter series. *Journal of Experimental Psychology*, 1970, **83**, 421–30.
Dansereau, D. An information processing model of mental multiplication. Unpublished doctoral dissertation. Carnegie–Mellon University, 1969.
Ein-Dor, P. Elements of a theory of visual information processing, Unpublished doctoral dissertation. Carnegie–Mellon University, 1971.
Fitts, P. M., & Posner, M. I. *Human Performance*. Belmont, CA: Brooks/Cole, 1967.
De Groot, A. D. *Thought and choice in chess*. The Hague: Mouton, 1965.
De Groot, A. D. Perception and memory versus thought: Some old ideas and recent findings. In B. Kleinmuntz (Ed.) *Problem solving*. New York: Wiley, 1966, pp. 19–50.
Jongman, R. W. *Het oog van de Meester*. Amsterdam: van Gorcum, 1968.
Landauer, T. K. Rate of implicit speech. *Perceptual and Motor Skills*, 1962, **15**, 646.
McLean, R. S., & Gregg, L. W. Effects of induced chunking on temporal aspects of serial recitation. *Journal of Experimental Psychology*,

5. The master's vocabulary of recognizable configurations inferred by Jongman (1968) is very similar to the list above.

1967, **74**, 455–59.

Miller, G. A. The magical number seven, plus or minus two: Some limits on our capacity for processing information. *Psychological Review*, 1956, **63**, 81–97.

Newell, A., & Simon, H. A. *Human problem solving.* Englewood Cliffs, N.J.: Prentice–Hall, 1972.

Pierce, J. R., & Karlin, J. E. Reading rates and the information rate of a human channel. *Bell Telephone System Technical Publications*, 1957, **36**, 497–516.

Reinfeld, F. *Win at chess.* New York: Dover, 1945.

Simon, H. A., & Barenfeld, M. Information-processing analysis of perceptual processes in problem solving. *Psychological Review*, 1969, **76**, 473–83. Reprinted as chapter 6.2 in this book.

Tichomirov, O. K., & Poznyanskaza, E. D. An investigation of visual search as a means of analyzing hueristics. *Soviet Psychology*, Winter 1966–67, **5**, 2–15.

Tulving, E. Subjective organization in free recall of "unrelated" words. *Psychological Review*, 1962, **69**, 344–54.

Winikoff, A. W. Eye movements as an aid to protocol analysis of problem solving behavior. Unpublished doctoral dissertation. Carnegie–Mellon University, 1967.

6.5

The Mind's Eye in Chess (1973)

with William G. Chase

In this chapter, we would like to describe additional progress we have made toward understanding chess skill.[1] In the two previous chapters we have provided a theoretical formulation to characterize how expert chess players perceive the chessboard, and we have reported a series of experiments on perception in chess. In this chapter, we will first report some additional analyses we have made of the data discussed in chapter 6.4. Then we will describe some new tasks that also correlate well with chess skill; and finally, we will give a more complete account of our current thinking about the cognitive processes of skilled chess players.

ADDITIONAL ANALYSES OF PREVIOUS EXPERIMENTS

In this section we comment and enlarge upon the data that were discussed in chapter 6.4.

The Experimental Subjects

In the previous chapter, we did not indicate as specifically as we might have the relations of the chess-playing skills of our various subjects. We studied three chess players of varying strength in these experiments: a master, a Class A player, and a beginner. The master was at the time of the experiment, one of the top twenty-five players in the country, and he has also won the World Correspondence Chess Championship. The Class A player ranks at about the eighty-fifth percentile of players

This research was supported by a grant from the National Institutes of Mental Health (MH-07722), from the Department of Health, Education and Welfare. We wish to thank Larry Macupa for his help in running subjects, analyzing data, and drawing graphs. We are especially indebted to Hans Berliner for serving as our Master subject and for his many conversations about, and insights into, the mental life of a chess Master. We thank Michelene Chi for her patience as the beginner subject, and for her helpful comments concerning the perspective of a novice chess player. We owe a special debt of gratitude to Neil Charness, who performed a major portion of the work in setting up and conducting the experiments, analyzing data, and who greatly contributed conceptually to all phases of the research program.

1. This chapter has been substantially abridged to eliminate overlap with Chapter 6.4.

rated by the United States Chess Federation. The beginner has never competed in any tournaments and has played very little chess. The three players are otherwise roughly equated for intelligence: the Class A player has a PhD and the master and beginner are both candidates for the PhD. The probability that the Class A player could beat the master, or the beginner could beat the Class A player, is extremely small—perhaps one in a thousand. By a rough estimate, the amount of time each player has spent playing chess, studying chess, and otherwise staring at chess positions is perhaps 10,000 to 50,000 hours for the master; 1,000 to 5,000 hours for the Class A player; and less than 100 hours for the beginner.

Differences in Procedure

In chapter 6.4, we noted that the procedure we used was not exactly the same as that used by de Groot (1978). We have now explored one further difference between our procedure and de Groot's. We asked for immediate recall from our players, whereas de Groot encouraged his players to "concentrate for some time (with eyes closed) . . . " to "integrate" his data. The usual result of such delays, if anything, is to weaken the memory for material that has been most recently attended to (the recency portion of the serial position curve), presumably because this material is less well organized and therefore susceptible to retroactive interference. To investigate this possibility, the Class A player was shown twenty diagrams from Reinfeld's (1945) book for 5 seconds each; half the positions were recalled immediately and half were recalled after a 30-second delay. There was no significant difference in recall between these two procedures: 60 percent correct for immediate recall and 58 percent correct for delayed recall. We can therefore discount this minor difference in procedures.

Errors

One clue to the underlying representation

Table 1. Percentage of Various Types of Placement Errors for Real and Random Positions.

Errors	Real Positions	Random Positions
Translation	76.7	74.7
Wrong piece	6.6	8.2
Wrong Color	1.6	3.5
Other	15.1	13.5

is found in the kinds of errors that occur. Most errors are errors of omission, but there are some interesting aspects to the errors of commission. Given that a piece is incorrectly recalled, what kind of information is still present? We classified the misplaced pieces into four categories: (1) Translation errors: the right piece is misplaced by a square or two. (2) Wrong piece: a piece is placed on a square that requires a different piece of the same color. (3) Wrong color: the correct piece is placed on the correct square, but it is the wrong color. (4) Other: errors that can't be classified into the above three categories.

Table 1 shows the relative percentages of each of the four types of errors for the nineteen real positions and four random positions. Since there weren't any differences among the three players, the errors were summed over the three levels of chess skill. These percentages are based on 305 errors in the real positions and 170 errors in the random positions.

At least 85 percent of the placement errors still preserve some information about the location, identity, and color of the pieces. Almost all the information-preserving errors were translation errors, and there were very few wrong-piece and wrong-color errors. These translation errors often occurred as units (e.g., Pawn chains), so that several pieces were displaced one or more squares, but the correct configuration of pieces still remained intact. Another type of translation error occurred when pieces were displaced along paths that they control, such as Bishops along diagonals or Rooks along ranks or files. This kind of error still preserves an important function: the control of squares within the scope of a piece. These errors suggest that the absolute location of pieces is not as important as their relative location— relative to other pieces in a configuration and relative to squares under their control.

Stability of Chunks over Trials

An interesting aspect of the between-glance latencies, shown in the bottom of figure 3, chapter 6.4, is that the master generally took only a second or two to gather new information by looking back in the perception experiment whereas the beginner's modal "look-back" time was about 4 seconds. The Class A player's times were generally intermediate between the master and the beginner. The speed with which players can perceive information on the chessboard depends, then, upon their chess skill.

One fairly strong prediction of our chunking hypothesis is that a chunk, defined by our 2-second criterion, should have a tendency to remain a chunk on subsequent trials. The tendency to recall pieces in the same order from trial to trial did increase over trials, but it is difficult to define chunks on subsequent trials because, as the position gets learned, the interpiece latencies become shorter and more uniform. Also, chunk boundaries probably disappear as new relations are learned.

Since we have developed an objective criterion for chunk boundaries only for the first trial, we analyzed the first two trials of the middle and end games to see if the pieces within a chunk on the first trial, defined by the 2-second criterion, tended to be recalled together on the second trial. Since there were so few chunks involving two or more pieces for the beginner, we present data only for the master and the Class A player.

As expected, there was a considerable tendency for chunks to remain intact on the second trial. A chunk was defined as intact on the second trial if at least two-thirds of its pieces were recalled together. Some 65 percent of the master's chunks and 96 percent of the Class A players's

chunks remained intact on the second trial. It is interesting, however, that pieces were recalled in the same order for only about half the intact chunks. A common example of this phenomenon is when a player recalls a Pawn chain in reverse order from the previous trial. We conclude from these data, therefore, that chunks, as we have defined them, show the necessary stability over trials, but that there is no stereotyped order of recall of pieces within a chunk.

Chunks on Random Boards

Table 7 of Chapter 6.4 shows that there was a moderate correlation between pairs of pieces placed within a single glance from random boards in the perception experiment and the highly structured pairs (the short pauses in the memory experiment and the within-glance pairs from real games of the perception experiment). It would seem that even in the randomized boards, players are noticing the same kinds of structures as those they perceive in the coherent positions, even though these structures occur rarely in randomized boards.

Apparently, our technique really does segment the output in terms of the perceptual structures. What kind of structures are they? They are things like Pawn chains and clusters of pieces of the same color that lie close together and usually also defend each other; the players see local clusters of pieces on the board. It is interesting to note that in addition to the chess relations such as defense and same piece (which is important for Pawn chains and for Rook and Knight pairs), visual properties, such as color and spatial proximity, seem also to be important. Even the same-piece relation may represent visual properties because of the physical identity of the pieces.

We were a little surprised at the importance of these visual properties and, related to this, we were surprised that the players made so little use of the attack relation. Granted that in real game positions attacking relations are relatively rare, they are of great importance when they do occur, and we would expect them to be

Table 2. A Sample of the Master's Recall of Pieces, Interpiece Latencies, and Chess Relations.

Piece and Square	Time (sec)	Relations
K$_w$ at KR3		
K$_b$ at KN1	1.3	S
	2.7	—
R$_w$ at K5		
	2.7	DPC
P$_w$ at KB4		
P$_w$ at KN3	0.3	DPCS
	3.4	S
P$_b$ at KB4		
P$_b$ at KN3	0.2	DPCS
P$_b$ at KR4	1.3	DPCS
P$_w$ at KR4	0.4	PS
*P$_w$ at QR3	2.1	CS
P$_b$ at QR2	1.5	S
P$_b$ at QN3	0.2	DPCS
	2.2	C
R$_b$ at Q4		
R$_b$ at Q1	1.2	DCS
Q$_b$ at Q2	1.6	DPC
	2.1	—
R$_w$ at K2		
Q$_w$ at Q1	1.6	DPC

*Incorrect

noticed. However, the data clearly indicate that the attack relation was not often noticed. Finally, we were a little surprised that there were no differences in the kinds of relations noticed by different players. For example, we expected the master to notice more attacks, but that was not the case. The only difference was that the structures were bigger for the better player.

Recall Protocol of Master

Table 2 gives an example of the recall protocol of the master for one of the positions in the memory experiment, and figure 1 illustrates the chunk-by-chunk recall of the position. The master made only a single mistake, placing White's Pawn at Queen's Rook 3. The notation in the first column of table 2 refers to the placed piece (K = King, Q = Queen, R = Rook, P = Pawn), its color (w = White, b = Black), and the square where it was placed (e.g., KN1 = King's Knight 1). The second and third columns give the interpiece latencies and chess relations, respectively. This position contains instances of Pawn chains, Rook- and Queen-

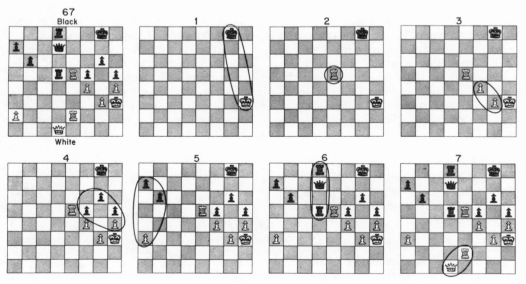

Figure 1. The chunk-by-chunk recall of Position 67 from Reinfeld (1945). Each new chunk is circled.

Rook connections, and some degenerate remnants of castled King positions. The recall protocol here is fairly typical of the kind of data we got from the master, and many of the stereotyped structures appear as chunks in the recall. So it does appear that these perceptual structures are very stereotyped and are seen every day when the master looks at the chessboard.

Differences in Chunk Size

If we want to retain the concept of a limited capacity short-term memory, then we must account for the fact that the master not only recalls larger chunks but recalls more chunks as well. If everyone has the same memory capacity, then where do these extra chunks come from? There are at least three possible explanations.

The first possibility is that the difference is due to a guessing artifact. The recall protocols generally consist of two phases: an initial recall phase where the players dump all they know from short-term memory and then a reconstruction phase where players tend to guess or "problem-solve" where the rest of the pieces ought to be. During the first phase, recall is fast and the chunks tend to be large and error-free, but during the second phase recall is piece-by-piece with long pauses and many errors. This second phase was more prominent in the master's protocols than in the others. We tried to remove this reconstruction phase from the data by eliminating the portion of the protocol following a long pause (10 seconds or more) followed mostly by errors, or the portion having a series of long pauses (5 seconds or more) with errors. However, we may have been unsuccessful in eliminating the reconstruction phase entirely, particularly if the master is very good at guessing. De Groot (1966), for example, has shown that players can average better than 44 percent pieces correct simply by putting down the most typical, or prototype, position derived from master games. And the master can undoubtedly reconstruct far better than 44 percent accuracy when partial information is already available.[2]

A second possibility is that the master's long-term memory is structured so that information associated with particular chunks serves as a cue to retrieve other chunks from memory. Thus, whenever the first member of such a pair of chunks is retrieved, the retrieval of the second member is thereby cued. In this way, a single chunk in short-term memory could permit the recall of several chunks from long-term memory.

For example, a Pawn at KR2 defending a Pawn at KN3 (a chunk) might later evolve the overlapping pattern: a Pawn at KN3 defending a Pawn at KB4. Or, in figure 1, the long-term memory representation of the Rook-Queen-Rook configuration (the sixth chunk) might have contained the information that there was a target piece on Q1, leading to the retrieval of the next Queen-Rook chunk (the seventh chunk).

We have no direct evidence to support this explanation, but the master did appear to find, in pieces already placed on the board, cues to additional chunks. Until we have additional data, the possibility remains speculative.

A third possibility, on which we will comment further below, is that a "chunk" is not a unit of quite uniform size. A highly overlearned structure of information may occupy only a little short-term memory (only its "name" need be held), while to hold a less well-learned structure of equal complexity may require several pieces of descriptive or relational information to be retained. For example, the Rook-Queen-Rook configuration in figure 1 (the sixth chunk) might be represented in long-term memory as a single chunk and only its name held in short-term memory. Or it

---

2. The Pennies-Guessing task is an interesting demonstration of how easy it is to reconstruct a position from partial information. This task involves selecting a quiet position from a master game and replacing all the pieces with pennies. The players's task is then to replace all the pennies with the correct pieces. The master is virtually perfect at this task, and the Class A player also scores well over 90 percent correct.

might be a composite of two chunks from long-term memory (e.g., Rook-Queen and Queen-Rook) and the chunk might be structured in short-term memory as a proposition involving the names of the two chunks plus the relation that holds them together. In the limit, the poorer player might have to represent this configuration in terms of even more elementary propositions about the two defense relations, the location of pieces relative to each other, and the location of the total configuration on the board. Thus, the efficiency of the code for a chunk in short-term memory would depend upon how much structure is available in long-term memory to build upon. Then, in short-term memory of given size, more overlearned chunks could be held than chunks that required partial descriptions.

The additional assumption we need to make is that the speed of recall of pieces within a chunk is fast, regardless of whether the chunk is stored in long-term memory as a single unit or assembled hierarchically in short-term memory out of several chunks from long-term memory.[3] A chunk, according to this view, is a collection of pieces related in some way, regardless of whether or not the relations are overlearned in long-term memory.

All these possibilities are quite plausible, they represent interesting processes in and of themselves, and there may be some truth to all three. However, the evidence is fairly strong in support of some kind of limited-capacity short-term memory where these structures or the internal names of familiar structures are stored.

---

3. There are probably subtle differences in the speed of recall for these different chunks. For example, Pawn chains, double rooks, etc., are usually recalled very fast (less than 0.5 second per piece), so that chunks containing these substructures would probably be recalled with a slight pause (but still less than 2 seconds) between substructures. Although there are some indications of this hierarchical organization in our data (e.g., in Castled King positions), we haven't studied this problem in any systematic way as yet.

EFFECT OF CHANGING THE STIMULUS NOTATION

The first round of experiments supports the hypothesis that much of the skilled processing in chess occurs at the perceptual front end. We have conducted some experiments to test this perceptual hypothesis against one possible artifact, and we were further interested in seeing how robust the perceptual processing is when the stimuli are subjected to a degrading transformation.

One possible alternative to our perceptual hypothesis is that the structures we are isolating actually arise from the organization of the output at recall rather than from the perceptual process, and the pauses really represent an artifact because players need to pause in order to pick up a new set of pieces before continuing their recall. This hypothesis has trouble explaining why pieces recalled together in time are also functionally related, but it is possible that this organization is somehow imposed at recall rather than at the time of perception.

We reasoned that if our perceptual hypothesis were true, then we ought to be able to disrupt these perceptual processes by perturbing the stimuli in some way. However, if the response organization hypothesis is true, then the way to disrupt

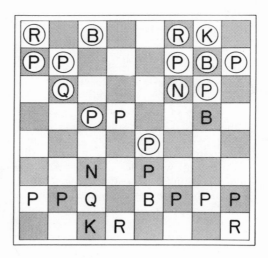

Figure 2. Example of a letter diagram.

Table 3. Percent Correct Recall for Boards vs Diagrams as Stimuli and as Responses.

| Trials | Response | | *Stimulus* | | |
			Written Diagram	*Board*	*Average*
1–16	Written Diagram		37	58	48
	Board		33	67	49
		Average	35	62	49
17–32	Written Diagram		50	46	48
	Board		48	55	51
		Average	49	50	50

performance is by changing the response mode.

We presented the Class A player with thirty-two new positions taken from Reinfeld (1945), but half the positions were presented as schematic diagrams in which a piece is represented by the first letter of its name, and black pieces are circled. Figure 2 shows an example of such a letter diagram position. The other sixteen positions were shown normally, as pieces on an actual board. Also, half the positions were recalled normally by placing pieces on a board, and the other half were recalled by writing letter diagrams like figure 2. Thus, we have a 2 × 2 design with boards versus letter diagrams as stimuli, and boards versus letter diagrams as responses.

The results, shown in table 3, are straightforward. Looking at the data on the first sixteen trials, it didn't make any difference, in response, whether pieces were placed on a board or a schematic diagram was drawn. On the stimulus side, however, it made a big difference whether real boards or letter diagrams were presented. The Class A player was getting almost twice as many pieces correct when real boards were presented as when diagram stimuli were shown. This result was highly significant statistically ($p < 10^{-6}$), and neither the response mode nor the stimulus-response interaction was significant.

The advantage of boards over letter diagrams was due to more chunks being recalled for boards than for diagrams (7.5

versus 4.0, respectively); the number of pieces per chunk was relatively constant for the different stimulus conditions (2.3 versus 3.0, respectively).

It appears, therefore, that the schematic diagrams slow down the perceptual process, so that fewer perceptual structures are seen in the 5-second exposure.

However, this effect washes out very quickly with practice, so that after about an hour or so the Class A player was seeing these schematic diagrams about as well as real board positions. Neither the main effects nor the interaction was significant for the second block of sixteen trials.

This experiment shows, first, that regardless of whether the player writes a letter diagram of the position or whether he picks up pieces at the side of the board and places them on the board, his performance is the same. This result eliminates the possibility that the pauses are artifacts due to picking up the pieces. Second, the fact that stimuli in the form of letter diagrams are initially disruptive suggests that performance in this task really depends upon perceptual rather than recall processes. The Class A player rapidly overcomes the difficulties of viewing the letter diagrams. Apparently some easy perceptual learning takes place so that the nonessential surface characteristics of the diagrams are ignored and the underlying invariant relations are perceived.

In a second experiment, we were interested in seeing how chess players of various strengths are affected by diagrams. In this

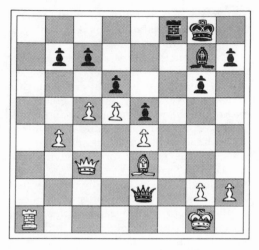

Figure 3. Example of a pictorial diagram (No. 169) taken from Reinfeld (1945).

experiment, we gave two Class A players and a beginner the same 5-second task, but this time we compared real board positions with printed (pictorial) diagrams from chess books. Figure 3 shows an example of these pictorial diagrams, selected from Reinfeld (1945), and in both cases real pieces were placed on a board at recall. Performance on pictorial diagrams is interesting because chess players spend a lot of time looking at diagrams like these when they read chess books and magazines.

Table 4 shows the basic results. Both Class A players did equally well for real boards and pictorial diagrams, but the beginner recalled real boards better than diagrams ($p < 0.001$). These limited data provide no evidence of a practice effect. These results presumably reflect the fact that the Class A players have had considerable experience with pictorial dia-

Table 4. Percent Correct Recall of Boards and Diagrams for two Class A Players and a Beginner.

| Player | *Stimuli* | |
	Boards	*Diagrams*
1. Class A	61	60
2. Class A	56	58
3. Beginner	35	24

grams (but not with letter diagrams), whereas the beginner has had little or none.

MEANINGFUL BUT UNFAMILIAR PATTERNS

In chapter 6.3, we proposed a theory in the form of a simulation model to account for the empirical data. Taken in perspective, what does the theory suggest about skilled chess performance? First, there is a very large repertoire of patterns in long-term memory—patterns that are held together by a small set of chess relations something like those we found in our earlier research. Second, there is a mechanism that scans the board, that recognizes pieces and the functional relations between pieces, and that finds the important pieces to build these little patterns around. And third, there are severe limits on the capacity of short-term memory, where the internal names of the patterns are stored.

There is one important mechanism, however, that is missing in the Simon-Gilmartin theory (chapter 6.3), as it is presently formulated. The simulation (unlike the earlier Simon-Barenfeld program —chapter 6.2) makes no provision for the perception of meaningful but unfamiliar patterns; only familiar patterns stored in long-term memory are recognized. As we mentioned earlier, there is a real possibility that if a player notices a relation between one or more pieces, this structural information may be stored in short-term memory. Such a structure is not a chunk, in the sense in which that term is now generally used, because in order to remember it, some details of the structure, and not just its internal name, must be retained in short-term memory.

The issue we are raising is that there must be some mechanism for perceiving meaningful structures—meaningful in the sense that the pieces comprising the structure are functionally related in some way— even though the structure is unfamiliar. This mechanism would be needed in order for such structures to become familiar in the first place. And the basic functions are undoubtedly the geometric and chess functions we have been studying.

One way of thinking about this mechanism is in terms of a set of production rules that create new structures, given certain inputs. For example, *if A attacks B and A attacks C, then A forks B and C.* The production in this case would consist of a condition side (*A attacks B, and A attacks C*) which needs to be fulfilled before any action is taken. The action in this case is to construct a new structure containing the pieces A, B, and C. This structure is meaningful because it is organized around the concept of a fork, but this particular fork need not be familiar. The structure would contain information about the relative locations of the three pieces, as well as the more abstract relation, *A forks B and C.* This relation might enter into a still more complicated production that takes a fork as a condition. And there must, of course, be more elementary productions that take pieces and the squares they control as input and construct relations like *A attacks B.*[4] A collection of rules of this form is called a production system (Newell and Simon, 1972).

Regardless of the organization of these rules, the perception of meaningful structures must be more rule-bound (generative) than is necessary for the familiar structures. In the latter case, the recognition relies heavily on a simple mechanism with a few rules—the interpreter for the EPAM net—to sort through a large set of familiar patterns. Since familiar patterns are also meaningful, a familiar pattern might be recognized in two ways, although the recognition mechanism for familiar patterns is probably much faster.[5] The

system for perceiving meaningful patterns is surely more elaborate for skilled players than for beginners.[6]

These processes are not necessarily organized as a production system or an EPAM net. That is a matter for further research. We merely wish to make the distinction between meaningful and familiar perceptual structures, and to point out that the simulation in chapter 6.3 has only a mechanism for perceiving the familiar patterns.

While this theory is simply a rough first approximation, it does offer a concrete application of cognitive principles to the task of playing skilled chess, and these principles are not derived or applied *ad hoc*: the basic elements of the theory—the EPAM organization of long-term memory, the elementary perceptual processes of PERCEIVER, and the limited capacity of short-term memory—are derived from an already existing body of theory about cognitive psychology that stands on a considerable data base of its own.

FURTHER EXPERIMENTS ON CHESS SKILL

We have presented an empirical and theoretical treatment of the immediate perceptual processing of a chess position which specifies cognitive processes to account for the remarkable ability of chess masters to remember so much from a brief exposure of a position. Other kinds of chesslike tasks show an equally dramatic effect of chess skill. In this section of the chapter, we present our experiments on these other tasks along with our speculations about the underlying processes.

---

4. We point out, again, that the structure contains the relative locations of the pieces as well as the underlying functional relationship.

5. It is quite possible that this dual process is responsible for the results of the experiment on letter diagrams, as follows. Letter diagrams are initially unfamiliar, so the player has to notice pieces and relations individually as they are decoded, and he then uses this information to construct unfamiliar chunks. With a little learning, however, the player is able to modify his recognition mechanism to substitute letters for pieces, and the familiar patterns in long-term memory then become accessible.

---

6. If it is true that some of the patterns are recalled because they are meaningful, and that the master is better at perceiving meaningful but unfamiliar patterns, then chapter 6.3 overestimated the size of the master's repertoire of familiar patterns. Also, in the present version of the program, patterns are associated with particular squares. However, it is probably the case that most patterns need not be tied to exact squares (cf. the data on placement errors in recall). If this restriction is relaxed, chapter 6.3's estimate could be substantially lowered.

Long-term Memory for Positions

In this experiment, we asked chess players to memorize a game until it was well learned, and then to reconstruct the position at a certain point in the game. The cue for recall was simply a move of the game, such as "White's twenty-third move: Bishop takes Knight." The player's task was then to reconstruct the position at that point.

We wanted to know if recall of these positions showed as large an effect of chess skill as the immediate recall of positions. We were further interested in the kind of chunks that would be revealed in this task. We conjectured that, in order to recall these positions, the players would have to rely in part on their memory for the dynamic move sequences, and we were therefore expecting a different kind of chunk in the recall of these positions than we found in the immediate recall experiments. We were expecting, for example, less reliance on spatial properties, such as proximity, and more reliance on the chess functions, such as attack.

For this experiment, our three chess players—the master, the Class A player, and the beginner—learned the moves of a 25-move game (50 plies) until they could reproduce the same perfectly twice in a row. The game was learned by the study-test method where each move (ply) was read out at the rate of 5 seconds per move, and the player then executed the move for himself on a chessboard. During the test phase, the player tried to recall each move for himself by playing it on a chessboard, and he was told the correct move if he made a wrong move or if 10 seconds had elapsed since the previous move. When the player had reproduced the whole sequence of moves perfectly, each move (ply) being made in less than 10 seconds, a second test trial was administered immediately. Upon successful completion of the second test trial, the player was then asked to reproduce the position after a specified move (e.g., after White's tenth move: Knight to Bishop Three). On five subsequent days following this learning session, the players returned for a single test trial on the same

Table 5. Recall of Positions from Long-term Memory.

Player	Percent Correct	Pieces per Chunk	Chunks per Position
Master	99	4.0	7.7
Class A	95	2.5	10.5
Beginner	90	1.2	22.8

game and then another reproduction of a different position from the game. We thus have six reproductions of positions taken from the same game, but widely spaced at different points throughout the game. All this behavior was videotaped and analyzed by the same methods as were used in the earlier experiments.

Table 5 shows the simple statistics on recall of positions after a game had been learned. First of all, the master just doesn't make many errors (99 percent correct) but the beginner does extremely well also (90 percent correct). The beginner, in fact, reproduces more of these positions than the master did after the 5-second exposure (81 percent). With respect to chunk size, defined by the same 2-second pause as previously, it turns out that the master recalls about 4 pieces per chunk, and the Class A player about 2 or 3 pieces per chunk. Thus, these chunks are about the same size as the first chunk recalled after the 5-second exposures of the middle game positions. However, chunk size is relatively constant here; it does not fall off with successively recalled chunks as it did for the 5-second exposures. Also, the number of chunks per position varies inversely with the chunk size since all players were able to recall most of the positions from long-term memory. (Clearly, number of chunks recalled in this experiment should be independent of short-term memory limits.)

Looking at the beginner's data, we see something very interesting. His chunk size is smaller than before; in fact, his average chunk size is hardly more than one piece. Some 82 percent of his chunks contained only a single piece, whereas this percentage was much smaller for the master and Class A player (26 and 37 percent, respectively). Apparently, the beginner doesn't have

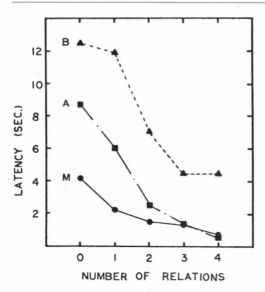

Figure 4. Average interpiece latencies for the Master (M), Class A player (A), and beginner (B) as a function of the number of relations between the two pieces.

access to many patterns in long-term memory. He virtually has to reconstruct the position piece by piece from the moves of the game.

The next thing we looked at was the relationship between the interpiece latencies and the chess relations. Figure 4 shows that there is a strong (negative) correlation between the number of relations between two pieces and their interpiece latency. But unlike the case of the 5-second recall data, there is an interaction with chess skill. When two pieces, placed sequentially in the output, are highly related, then both the master and the Class A player place them in rapid succession. However, with the pieces having few relations (0, 1, and possibly 2), the master's interpiece intervals are about half as long as the Class A player's intervals. The average intervals for the beginner are longer than the skilled players, even for the highly related pieces. This reflects the fact that the beginner had only a few intervals less than 2 seconds (18 percent), and these were for the highly related pieces (2, 3, and 4 relations).

Thus, the recall of positions from a game

is accelerated by recalling them in chunks of related pieces. Although there is also a difference in the amount of material recalled as a function of chess skill, this difference isn't nearly as impressive as in the 5-second recall task; but there is a striking difference in the speed of recall.

We interpret these data in the following way. Once a chunk has been retrieved from long-term memory, recall of the pieces is equally fast for all levels of chess skill (probably a second or less per piece). However, the differences in chess skill manifest themselves in the speed with which successive new chunks are retrieved from long-term memory: 3 or 4 seconds for the master, 6 or 8 seconds for the Class A player, and about 12 seconds for the beginner. This is tremendous range of times when it is considered that most simple mental operations take place in only a few tenths of a second!

Finally, when we ask what kinds of chunks are being recalled, we find that they look just like the chunks in the 5-second recall task. For short pauses (less than 2 seconds) there is a lot of structure, and the structure is the same: a preponderance of Pawn chains and local clusters of pieces of the same color that mutually defend each other. The expected more frequent appearance of the attack relation failed to occur. These data for the short pauses apply mostly to the master and the Class A player, since the beginner had few latencies under 2 seconds.

For the longer interpiece latencies

Table 6. Intercorrelation Matrix for Short-term Memory, Long-term Memory, and Random Chess Relation Probabilities.

Task	1	2	3	4	5
1. STM Less Than 2 Sec		0.86	0.23	0.26	−0.03
2. LTM Less Than 2 Sec			0.26	0.37	0.03
3. STM Greater Than 2 Sec				0.92	0.87
4. LTM Greater Than 2 Sec					0.81
5. Random					

(greater than 2 seconds), the relations again looked almost as if the two pieces were chosen randomly. Table 6 compares the frequencies of the sixteen possible inter-piece relations by examining the correlations between the various conditions involving long and short interpiece latencies for short-term and long-term recall tasks. There are two clusters of high correlations in this table: (1) between interpiece relations for short pauses in both long-term and short-term recall, and (2) between interpiece relations for long pauses in both long-term and short-term recall and the *a priori* random relations. In short, these data show that for skilled chess players (but perhaps not for the beginner), the same kinds of perceptual structures are recalled in short-term recall of briefly viewed positions and in recall of positions from the long-term memory of a game.

Another interesting finding that we haven't documented very well yet is worth mentioning at this point. From the verbal protocols it appears that the first piece in a chunk is recalled dynamically—in terms of the moves of the game—and then its neighbors are filled in by reference to the local features with strong spatial components that are characteristic of the perceptual structures we have been studying. The most common reasons given by players for remembering these initial pieces are in terms of a move made earlier in the game, together with the purpose of the move.

The fact that skilled chess players recall these positions from long-term memory by means of perceptual structures suggests that they are organizing the moves of the game in terms of these structures and their alternations as the game goes along. Of course, there is more to remembering a game than this: the moves themselves must be remembered, and these are un-doubtedly organized according to the semantics of the game (we will say more about this later). But part of the remem-bered organization of a game involves the perceptual structures.

The beginner, however, doesn't seem to make use of these structures, which suggests that he doesn't have a very large repertoire of chunks in long-term memory. When it comes to recalling a position from the game, the beginner is reduced to generating the positions of the pieces from his rote memory of the moves. This doesn't say that the beginner makes no use of perceptual structures. It means that he has to build such structures from pieces and relations that he notices on the board, since he doesn't have them familiarized for easy recognition in long-term memory. In the 5-second recall task, the beginner needs visual access to the board in order to build these structures, and, we have hypothe-sized, he has a smaller memory span than the skilled players for these structures be-cause they are not simple chunks. He has to store considerable information about the relations of pieces in short-term mem-ory. In the long-term recall of positions, however, the beginner doesn't have visual access to the position, so he can't build any structures, and he has long since lost from short-term memory any structures that he had originally assembled from the position.

Long-term Memory for Games

In this experiment, we asked how chess players organize a game in memory. When a player recalls the moves of a game, we suspect that here, too, he organizes his sequences of moves in bursts which are held together closely by chess relations, and which are segmented by longer pauses. We further hypothesized that forgetting ought to be very selective. That is, with forgetting, the game ought to come apart at the seams, so to speak, with long pauses and errors at those points in the game where new chunks begin.

The data we consider here are the learning and recall of moves for the twenty-five-move game mentioned in the previous section. We recorded the recall of moves, as well as positions, on videotape, including the trials to criterion on day 1 and the recall trials on the five subsequent days.

The results show conclusively that rates of learning and forgetting the moves of a

Table 7. Long-term Memory for Games.

Player	Trials to Criterion	Errors to Criterion	Learning Time (Minutes)
Master	2	4	10
Class A	5	13	29
Beginner	12	94	81

game strongly depend upon chess skill. In terms of trials to criterion, errors to criterion, and total learning time, the master learned very rapidly (as rapidly as the moves were given to him), whereas the beginner spent considerable time and effort memorizing the game, and the Class A player was intermediate between these two. Table 7 shows the actual data. So here is another task, like memory for positions, that shows a very strong effect of chess skill.

Further, if we categorize each move in terms of its chess function, the latencies are very different for moves with different functions. We categorized moves into six simple categories: (1) Opening: these are moves in the beginning of the game that develop the pieces. These moves usually follow fairly stereotyped patterns that are well known to skilled chessplayers. (2) Exchange: the exchange of one piece for another. (3) Defense: a move which defends an attacked piece or square. (4) Attack: a move that threatens to win material or gain a favorable position. (5) Counterattack: a move that counters an attacking move with a threat of its own. (6) Quiet: a move that is none of the above. In a game between skilled players, these latter moves generally represent the man-

euvering for a favorable position according to some strategic plan (e.g., to gain control of the dark squares on the King's side). Against weaker opponents, the "quiet" and attacking moves are the ones that masters make which usually lead to wins.

The latency data, shown in Table 8, indicate that latencies are generally longer for quiet moves and attacking moves than for the others. This seems to be true both for the test trials during learning and the recall trials over the five days following learning, although there are occasional deviations from this generalization. For example, the Class A player had repeated trouble recalling one move in the opening, and this single instance was enough to increase significantly his average opening-move latencies relative to the average latencies for exchange, defense, and counterattack moves.

Too much significance should not be attached to these data since they are based on a single game. The standard errors, for example, vary widely because the number of observations vary for different conditions. (For example, in the learning trials there were only two trials for the master and twelve trials for the beginner.) Also, there weren't many errors, particularly in the recall phase: 0.4, 1.7, and 2.1 percent for the master, Class A player, and beginner, respectively. The memory for this game was highly tenacious over a period of a week. Thus, with this one game, we were unable to see if forgetting would occur at the chunk boundaries.

However, one result seems fairly robust in these data: the relatively long pauses

Table 8. Move Latencies (Sec) and Their Standard Errors (in Parentheses)
for Long-term Recall of Moves.

Move	Learning			Recall		
	Master	Class A	Beginner	Master	Class A	Beginner
Opening	1.0 (0.08)	1.7 (0.18)	2.1 (0.13)	1.3 (0.11)	1.9 (0.31)	1.5 (0.08)
Exchange	1.8 (0.51)	1.6 (0.19)	2.5 (0.19)	1.1 (0.05)	1.2 (0.08)	1.5 (0.10)
Defense	2.0 (0.56)	2.2 (0.37)	3.4 (0.34)	1.2 (0.07)	1.6 (0.15)	1.4 (0.12)
Attack	3.0 (0.92)	2.5 (0.25)	3.9 (0.26)	1.6 (0.10)	2.1 (0.21)	2.4 (0.20)
Counterattack	1.6 (0.11)	2.5 (0.60)	3.3 (0.50)	1.0 (0.11)	1.1 (0.10)	1.6 (0.23)
Quiet	4.4 (0.81)	3.0 (0.33)	3.7 (0.23)	1.6 (0.10)	2.5 (0.21)	2.5 (0.25)

associated with the quiet and attacking moves. We take this to mean that chunks (sometimes involving only a single move) are organized around the ideas (semantics) behind the quiet and attacking moves. Recall of these moves is slow because the underlying idea must be retrieved from long-term memory. Associated with this idea may be a series of more or less stereo-typed moves—exchanges and defensive or counterattacking moves—which are chunked together by virtue of their relation (hierarchical) to the underlying idea. These chunks are generally only a few plies deep (say 2–4), whereas the openings usually run at least 10 plies. Although there are underlying semantics associated with the opening moves, these moves are over-learned by experienced players and usually are played by rote.

This leads us to consider how memory for games is organized. Skilled chess players have hundreds and perhaps thousands of sequences of moves stored away in long-term memory. The top players have thousands of opening variations—some running over forty plies deep—committed to memory. There are also hundreds, perhaps thousands, of traps and winning combinations of moves that every master knows. The question is whether most chunks comprising a game beyond the opening—simple exchanges, defensive moves, etc.—are also represented somewhere in this vast repertoire of move sequences, or whether these moves can be executed with a minimum of information because of the redundancy associated with the underlying idea behind the chunk. This is a question we can't resolve at the moment. It is clear, however, that the skilled player's recall of a game involves recognition memory for perceptual structures as well as sequences of moves, both of which must somehow be accessed in long-term memory.

Immediate Recall of Moves

In this experiment, we were interested in seeing if immediate recall of moves from a game yielded analogous results to those for immediate recall of a briefly exposed position. Specifically, we expected that immediate recall of a coherent sequence of moves from a real game would depend upon the level of chess skill, whereas memory for a random sequence of moves would be uniformly poor for all levels of chess skill. And we further expected that longer pauses and errors ought to occur on the same type of moves as in the previous section.

The master, Class A player, and beginner were each given twenty 10-move sequences (20 plies) for immediate recall.[7] Half the move sequences were taken from master games and half were random sequences. The initial positions were all taken from a book of Dr. Lasker's games (Lasker, 1935), with the restrictions that the sequence begin around move 20, that it begin with a move by White, that there be at least 10 more moves in the game, and that there be at least 18 pieces on the board. The real sequences of 10 moves were taken from the game from that point, and the random sequences were generated from that point by randomly selecting a piece of the correct color and then randomly selecting a move from the set of legal moves for that piece.

To familiarize the players with each initial position, they were required to set up the position on a board in front of them by viewing a diagram of the position. The players were then allowed 30 seconds to study the position before the sequence of moves was presented.

Following this initial familiarization, the next 10 moves (20 plies) were read to the player at the rate of 5 seconds per ply, and the player executed each move (ply) on the board as he heard it. Five seconds after the last move was executed, the board was removed, the videotape was turned on, and a new board containing the initial position was placed in front of the player. There was about a 10-second delay between removal of the final position and presentation of the initial position. The player then

---

7. We lost half the beginner's data due to a defective tape recorder, but the data we did obtain are enough for comparisons with the master and Class A player's data.

Table 9. Percent Errors for Short-term Recall of Moves.

Move	Real Moves			Random Moves		
	Master	Class A	Beginner	Master	Class A	Beginner
Exchange	0	0	29	10	23	73
Defense	4	0	25	25	13	50
Attack	3	11	39	25	28	67
Quiet	0	8	57	25	36	85
Average	1	6	43	22	31	85

immediately began to recall the sequence of moves by executing the moves on the board. The correct move was given to the player only if he made a wrong move, or if 10 seconds had elapsed since the previous move.

The first important result, shown in table 9, is that the master was virtually perfect at recalling the real game moves. The Class A player was also good at recalling the real move sequences, but the beginner made over 40 percent errors. This result confirms our expectation that immediate recall of moves is a function of chess skill. Contrary to our expectation, however, was the finding that even for the random sequences of moves, accuracy of recall depended upon the level of chess skill. Apparently, the skilled players were able to find some meaning in the randomly generated moves.

Second, there was some indication that errors were more likely to occur on the attacking and quiet moves than on the exchange and defensive moves. This is true only for the real moves, and only for those players who made errors—the master made only two errors on the real moves.

(We have eliminated the counterattacking moves from this analysis since they were so rare.)

The latency data, shown in table 10, reveal that for all levels of chess skill, the attacking and quiet moves from real games were recalled relatively more slowly, on the average, than the exchange and defensive moves. Not surprisingly, there were few systematic latency differences among the different moves when they were randomly generated. Also, the latency differences were not systematically related to chess skill; the only consistent difference was that between the beginner and the two skilled players. Finally, for all levels of chess skill, average latencies were longer for the random moves than for the real moves.

The results of this experiment parallel those of the 5-second recall task in that recall of a coherent sequence of moves from a game is far superior to that of a random sequence of moves, and further, performance depends upon the level of chess skill, with the master showing virtually perfect recall. However, unlike the 5-second recall task, performance on the

Table 10. Move Latencies (Sec) and Their Standard Errors (in Parentheses) for Short-term Recall of Moves.

Move	Real Moves			Random Moves		
	Master	Class A	Beginner	Master	Class A	Beginner
Exchange	2.2 (0.22)	2.2 (0.34)	4.2 (0.86)	4.3 (0.47)	3.6 (0.58)	6.9 (1.21)
Defense	2.1 (0.29)	2.0 (0.32)	4.4 (0.71)	2.8 (0.52)	4.5 (0.83)	4.8 (1.50)
Attack	2.5 (0.28)	3.4 (0.47)	6.4 (0.80)	4.0 (0.45)	4.2 (0.58)	7.1 (1.06)
Quiet	3.5 (0.23)	3.8 (0.27)	6.5 (0.58)	5.1 (0.33)	4.4 (0.35)	8.3 (0.56)
Average	2.8	3.1	5.7	4.6	4.3	7.3

random sequences also depends on chess skill.

We should point out that there is less reliance on short-term memory for immediate recall of moves than for recall of positions because total presentation time of moves is almost 2 minutes before recall. In this amount of time, a great deal of organization and more permanent storage almost certainly occurs.

Finally, these results, taken in conjunction with those in the previous section on long-term memory for moves, suggest that pauses and errors in recalling the moves of a game give a clue as to how this memory is structured. Memory for moves is probably segmented into little episodes, each organized around some goal. These episodes begin with a high information move which may represent a direct threat (attack), or some more subtle plan. These latter moves are categorized as "quiet" since the purpose or plan that motivates them is not always readily apparent. Sometimes, episodes are only a single ply deep—such is the nature of chess that the game can change completely with a single move —and sometimes these episodes continue with more predictable moves involving exchanges, defenses, counterattacks, and probably more attacks. It is probably true that the moves are organized hierarchically, with higher level plans involving episodes within episodes; our research represents only a modest beginning in understanding how these memories are structured.

The Knight's Tour

There is another task, described in a recent chess magazine (Radojcic, 1971), which purports to measure chess talent, i.e., the *potential* to play skilled chess. Figure 5 shows the task, which is to move the Knight from its initial position at Queen's Rook One to each successive square until it finally ends up on the Queen's Rook Eight square. The Knight can make only legal moves, and it must progress by touching successive squares in a rank. That is, it must go next to the QN1 square, which it

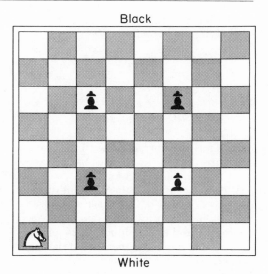

Black

White

Figure 5. Starting position for the Knight's tour.

can do via the route QB2-QR3-QN1. Then the next target square is QB1, and so on, until it reaches the KR1 square at the end of the First Rank. Then the Knight must traverse the Second Rank, starting with the KR2 square, which it can reach via KB2 and KN4. The Knight proceeds thus, rank by rank, until it ends up on the QR8 square. An additional requirement makes the task interesting: the Knight cannot go to a square where it can be taken by one of the black Pawns, nor can it capture a black Pawn. The strategically placed Pawns thus break up any stereotyped pattern of moves by the Knight, and they force the player to search for the right sequence of moves. The idea is to see how fast the player can do this.

This task was calibrated several years ago on a large sample of chess-playing school children in Czechoslovakia. Four children were far faster than all the others in their age group, and the boy who performed best on this test is currently one of the strongest players in the world and was a candidate for the World's Championship this year. The other three children who solved the problem rapidly all turned out to be grandmasters or international masters. Radojcic also reports that the times

Table 11. Pause Time (Sec) before
a Move Sequence.

		Sequence Length		
Player	*2*	*3*	*5*	*Average*
Master	1.5	2.6	10.5	2.9
Class A	2.1	5.6	28.6	7.4

on this task are correlated with the playing strengths of various masters. Masters usually complete the task in 2 to 5 minutes.

We have confirmed the fact that this task measures chess skill. Our master performed the task in 3 minutes, the Class A player in 7 minutes, and the beginner, in 25 minutes. Perhaps the task also measures talent, the potential for chess skill, but we don't have the right data to answer that question. Our main concern here is with understanding the cognition of already existing chess skill, and we will leave open the question of chess talent.

One additional interesting phenomenon was the manner in which players executed the Knight moves. The skilled players (master and Class A) invariably paused after reaching each successive target square. During the pause, they would search for the next series of Knight moves that would get the Knight to the next target square, and then execute these moves very rapidly (usually less than 0.5 second per move). It was at the pauses, when the players searched for the series of moves to the next target square, where chess skill had its effect. The master averaged about 3 seconds per pause whereas the Class A player averaged over 7 seconds per pause. These times are similar to the chunk retrieval times in the long-term memory task, but perhaps this is a coincidence. Further, the length of the pause was strongly correlated with the number of moves necessary to reach the next target square, and this time interacted with chess skill (table 11). For the short sequences, both players were about equally fast, but for the two longer sequences, the master showed increasing superiority over the Class A player. Also, the Class A player executed three sequences that were longer

than necessary.

For the beginner, there was no such neat division of the latencies, although his latencies did appear to consist of pauses followed by a series of more or less rapid moves. It seems fairly clear from the beginner's verbal report that he too was pausing to search for the correct path, but he often got lost. He sometimes executed partial solutions, and sometimes, after failing to discover a path, he would simply try to find a solution by trial and error.

We think the ability that underlies this task is very similar to that underlying the 5-second recall task: the ability to perceive a familiar pattern—in this case, the pattern of squares representing the Knight's path to the next target square. Here, too, the master's perceptual processes appear to be all-important.

COGNITIVE PROCESSES IN CHESS

All our studies point to the perceptual processing—the ability to perceive familiar patterns quickly—as the basic ability underlying chess skill. We have surveyed several tasks that measure chess skill, and we believe that in each case we were measuring similar perceptual abilities. We think that is true for the Knight's Tour, and true even for the memory of the moves of a game; we will outline our ideas on these tasks later in more detail. We first summarize our current thinking about the cognitive processes underlying chess skill.

The Contents of Thought

The slow, partly conscious, inferential processes that are available from verbal protocols just don't tell us very much about chess skill. Chess protocols are filled with statements like, "If I take him, then he takes that piece, then I go there . . ." and so on. De Groot showed that the structure of a player's thought processes while he is doing this are the same for all levels of chess skill. It is the *contents* of thought, not the structure of thought, that really makes the difference in quality of outcome. And we suggest that the contents of thought are mainly these perceptual structures that skilled chessplayers retrieve, for the most part, from long-term memory.[8]

Finding Good Moves

We believe we are in a position now to answer—albeit speculatively—the following question: Why, as has often been observed, does the master so frequently hit upon good moves before he has even analyzed the consequences of various alternatives? Because, we conjecture, when he stares at the chessboard, the familiar perceptual structures that are evoked from long-term memory by the patterns on the board act as move generators. In the master's long-term memory—at the end of his EPAM net, or wherever that information is stored—there is associated with the internal name structural information about the pattern that he can use to build an internal representation (a simulacrum in the mind's eye) and information about plausible good moves for some of the patterns. It is this organization of stored information that permits the master to come up with good moves almost instantaneously, seemingly by instinct and intuition.

We can conceive this part of long-term memory to be organized as a production system (see Newell and Simon, 1972, pp. 728–35). Each familiar pattern serves as the *condition* part of a production. When this condition is satisfied by recognition of the pattern, the resulting *action* is to evoke a move associated with this pattern and to bring the move into short-term memory for consideration.

Forward Search in Chess

When the master is staring at a chessboard trying to choose his next move, he is engaged in a forward search through some kind of problem space. The problem space

has generally been characterized as a branching tree where the initial node is the current board position, the branches represent moves, and the next nodes off these branches represent the new board positions reached by those moves (Newell and Simon, 1972, p. 665). But the master's problem space is certainly more complicated than this, because he doesn't have the board position organized in short-term memory as a single unitary structure. As we have shown, the board is organized into smaller units representing more local clusters of pieces. Since some of these patterns have plausible moves associated with them in long-term memory, the master will start his search by taking one of these moves and analyzing its consequences.

Since some of the recognizable patterns will be relevant, and some irrelevant, to his analysis, we hypothesize that he constructs a more concrete internal representation of the relevant patterns in the mind's eye and then modifies these patterns to reflect the consequences of making the evoked move. The information processing operations needed to perform this perturbation, whatever they are, are akin to the mental rotation processes studied by Shepard (cf. Cooper and Shepard, 1973) and the mental processes for solving cube-painting and cube-cutting puzzles studied by Baylor (1971). When the move is made in the mind's eye—that is, when the internal representation of the position is updated—the result is then passed back through the pattern perception system and new patterns are perceived. These patterns in turn will suggest new moves, and the search continues.

External memory (Sperling, 1960), eye movements, and peripheral vision are also important for the search. When the player executes a move in the mind's eye, he generally looks at the location on the actual, external board where the piece would be, imagines the piece at that location, and somehow forms a composite image of the generated piece together with pieces on the board. Peripheral vision is important because the fovea can resolve

---

8. Probably the moves derived from these structures, sequences of moves retrieved from long-term memory, and perhaps some strategic plans (e.g., center control) are also important.

only a very few squares (perhaps four), so that verification of the location of the pieces within the image requires detection of cues in the periphery. Thus, forward search involves coordinating information available externally on the visible chessboard with updating information held in the mind's eye. (For eye-movement studies of the coordination of external with internally stored information in a different problem-solving task, see Winikoff, 1967.)

If the master wants to reconstruct his path of moves through the problem space, all he needs to store in short-term memory are the internal names of the relevant quiet patterns along the path, since the rest of the information can be retrieved, as we have seen, from long-term memory. This provides a tremendous saving of space in short-term memory for other operations and time for the subsequent progressive deepening that is so often seen in the protocols.

We thus conceive of search through the problem space as involving an iteration of the pattern system's processes and repeated updating of information in the mind's eye. Only the barest outline of this complex process is explicit in the verbal protocols. Given the known time constants for the mind's eye and for long-term memory retrieval (cf. Cavanagh, 1972; Cooper and Shepard, 1973; Sternberg, 1969), each iteration takes perhaps half a second.

The Properties of the Mind's Eye

What goes on in the mind's eye, then, would seem to be of central importance for the search process, and we should spell out in more detail the properties of this system, as they are revealed by human performance in tasks calling for visualization.

We conceive of the mind's eye as a system that stores perceptual structures and permits them to be subjected to certain mental operations. The perceptual system then has access to these new structures in order to perceive the consequences of these changes. Although the repertory of operations that can be performed in the mind's eye is yet to be determined, they are often

analogous to external operations that cause visual-structural changes of objects in the real world. "Painting," "cutting," and rotating objects spatially are operations that have been shown experimentally to be performable.

Perhaps the most important (and "eye-like") property of the mind's eye is that spatial relations can be readily derived from the image. This property is illustrated as follows. Suppose an image is a structure describable in the two propositions: *A is to the left of B* and *B is above C*. Then people know directly from their image that *A* is above and to the left of *C*. By directly, we mean that people can use the perceptual system to abstract quickly from the mind's eye a new spatial proposition, something like *A is northwest of C*. Although people could also "problem-solve" such a proposition inferentially, this information is more quickly derived by taking advantage of the spatial operators of the mind's eye.

This property of the mind's eye probably also underlies much simple problem solving behavior. For example, DeSoto, London, and Handel (1965) were the first to point out that people seem to solve problems of the form *If A is better than B, and C is worse than B, then who is best?* by placing *A*, *B*, and *C* in a mental image and replacing *better* by the spatial relation *above*. Then to find *best* or *worst*, people find the top or bottom item, respectively, in the image. People seem to solve these problems faster by this "spatial paralogic" than by the use of deductive reasoning.[9]

There appear to be severe constraints on how much detail can be held at any moment in the mind's eye. It is not clear whether the source of this limitation is in the mind's eye itself or in short-term memory, which presumably contains the perceptual structure (the input), the instructions needed to generate and transform the image (the control structures),

---

9. We should point out that the relative difficulty of solving these syllogisms has been shown by Clark (1969) to be due primarily to the linguistic processes needed to comprehend the sentences in the first place.

and the new structures which are abstracted from the transformed image (the output). Because of this limited capacity, the mind's eye may image only part of a perceptual structure at a time.

Although an exact characterization of the mind's eye has yet to be worked out, we emphasize four properties of this system: (1) it is the meeting point where current visual information is coordinated and combined with remembered visual information stored in long-term and short-term memory; (2) it can be operated on by processes isomorphic to those that cause visual-structural changes of objects in the external world; (3) it can be operated on by the perceptual processes that abstract new information; and (4) it contains relational structures, hence the unstructured images and the feature-extractors of the visual system lie between it and the retina.

Characteristics of Perceptual Structures

Although the precise manner in which perceptual structures are represented internally is not known, some of their abstract properties have been determined by experiment. The psycholinguist tends to conceive of them as somehow analogous to "kernel sentences." "Propositions" would be a better term, provided we interpret it abstractly and provided we do not attribute specifically verbal or linguistic characteristics to the structures.

In artificial intelligence studies (e.g., Baylor, 1971; Baylor and Simon, 1966; Coles, 1972; Quillian, 1966; T. Williams, 1972), perceptual structures are represented as assemblages of description lists, the elementary components of which are propositions asserting that certain relations hold among elements (e.g., *A is to the right of B*). We will here refer to perceptual structures as relational structures whose components are propositions. It should be understood that they are generally weblike or networklike, rather than treelike in overall topology.

If this interpretation be accepted, then the "deep structures" postulated by psycholinguists, the "schemas" postulated by

psychologists of perception, and the "internal representations" postulated by information processing psychologists are not to be regarded as separate entities, but simply as different ways of naming a single system of representations and processes for acting on those representations. Images in the mind's eye can be generated from such structures derived from visual inputs, from verbal inputs (as in the experiments of Baylor), or from structures stored in long-term memory, by the processes we have just described.

For the representation of abstract information, most investigators have concluded that a propositional or relational format is necessary (see Baylor, 1971; Clark and Chase, 1972; Kintsch, 1972; Newell and Simon, 1972, pp. 23–28, for examples). We hypothesize that perceptual structures are organizations of propositions about the three-dimensional world we live in (e.g., *X is blue, X is above Y, X attacks Y*, etc.) where the relations (*blue, above, . . .*) and their arguments (*X, Y, . . .*) should be thought of as abstract symbols representing the meaning of objects, actions, spatial relations, and the like.

Relations and arguments in turn can sometimes be represented in terms of more elementary relational structures (Kintsch, 1972). *Above*, for example, might in turn be represented (+ *Polar*, + *Vertical*), semantic features for markedness and verticality (Clark and Chase, 1972). Objects can also have multiple representations. The symbol +, for example, might be represented as the single symbol representing "plus" or as a proposition with vertical and horizontal lines as arguments and their proper juxtaposition in space as the relation. Chess pieces (e.g., Queen) and chess relations (e.g., attack) can be represented in terms of more primitive features. Thus, there is no *a priori* reason why a sensory feature, such as a contour of a certain orientation, can't also appear as an argument in a perceptual structure. This hierarchical organization has certain practical advantages, since one would want to hold only the relevant propositions in short-term memory; other information in the hierarchy can be retrieved from long-term memory or generated from redundancy rules upon demand.

The most important question about these perceptual structures is how each is organized. Although this is an an empirical question, we think of these structures, for chess at least, as description list structures or directed graphs comprised of object-relation-object triples. In chess, the directed graph of a chunk would usually involve pieces or squares at the nodes and chess relations as pointers to new pieces or squares. The size of such a structure, the number of redundant relations, and the detail of information at the nodes depend upon how much learning (or forgetting) has taken place.

These perceptual structures contain the "meaning" of a position in both senses of the word: to the extent that the representations contain structure, they have meaning in the Gestalt sense; and to the extent that there are internal labels that stand for familiar configurations in long-term memory, they have meaning in the sense of designation (cf. Garner, 1962; Newell and Simon, 1972, p. 24). These representations are abstract in the sense that they are built out of functional chess relations (e.g., defense), but they also have strong geometric components.

The Mind's Eye in Recalling a Game

We have already discussed the presumptive role of the mind's eye in the search process when a skilled player is trying to find a good move. We hypothesize that these perceptual structures and the mind's eye play a similar role in recall of moves from a game. In this view, a player's memory for a game involves both perceptual structures and their changes during the course of a game. Players store the game as a series of quiet positions along with information, mostly in chunks in long-term memory, that allows the player to get from one quiet position to the next. There is no need to remember the intermediate positions if they can be regenerated from more general information, from the redundancy

of the position, or from plausible moves stored with these positions.

Thus, the perceptual structures relevant to the next move can be used to generate an image in the mind's eye, some transformation can be applied to the structure, and the next few moves can be abstracted from the mind's eye. A series of forced exchanges, for example, would be particularly suited to this process. The tendency of players to recall positions from a game in terms of chunks is evidence that these structures have been stored in memory as the game was memorized; and the inability of players to recall nonquiet positions is evidence that these positions are usually remembered only as transformations of quiet positions.

The Mind's Eye in the Knight's Tour

Performance in the Knight's Tour also depends upon basic processes involving perceptual structures and the mind's eye. The scope of the Knight—the eight squares of opposite color situated in a circle about the square containing the Knight—is stored as a perceptual structure in long-term memory. Perhaps the advantage of skilled players lies in the speed with which this structure can be retrieved from long-term memory, an image built in the mind's eye, and a new structure generated for the path of the Knight to its next location. As the search branches out, the skilled player holds an advantage in his ability to retrieve a sequence of moves as a chunk—in this case as a sequence of stereotyped moves to get the Knight to an adjoining square. The pattern of squares is generated in the mind's eye to see if the path works—that is, reaches the desired square without illegal intermediate moves.

Another principle illustrated by the Knight's Tour is the ability to superimpose a representation from memory onto the external representation. When the player is searching for the next series of Knight moves, he might imagine the Knight on successive squares and then construct the sequence of squares representing the potential next moves (phenomenally, these squares stand out as a pattern). From this pattern, he chooses the next move to be executed in the mind's eye, and the search continues.

This process is not unique to the Knight's Tour, but must also underlie the general ability to search ahead for a good move. In order to perceive chess relations, players must be able to visualize the path of a piece in order to see what lies in the path. This process is probably the same as that described by Hayes (1973), when people generate, as a mnemonic device, images of partial solutions imposed on visually presented arithmetic problems. This capacity to construct an image combining perceptual structures from internal memory with sensory features from external memory is probably one of the very basic cognitive processes.

Organization of the Perceptual Processor

The processes and representational structures we have outlined here are frankly speculative and sketchy. We have speculated in some detail about the nature of the representations that hold perceptual information, but we have been deliberately vague about the system of memories that holds this information and about the relation of the mind's eye to other memory structures. Our excuse for this vagueness is that the available empirical evidence does not choose among several alternative possibilities nor make one of them much more plausible than others.

The mind's eye is the meeting point where visual information from the external world is combined and coordinated with visual representations stored in short-term and long-term memory. Let us call the whole complex collection of visual processes and storage points for visual information that lie between the retina and this meeting point the "visual vestibule." The vestibular representation is by no means an unprocessed pictorial replica of the external world: contours are enhanced, the fovea is disproportionately represented, and there is a loss of resolution in the periphery. Within this vestibular passage

there take place, for example, the processes of feature extraction—colors, contours, and shapes that serve to identify pieces and squares on the chessboard—and probably also the short-term storage of visual information revealed by Sperling's (1960, 1963) experiments. Although we have not placed much emphasis on this vestibular memory in our research, evidence for such a memory in chess is provided, for example, by the difficulty an average player experiences in trying to play blindfold chess. The point we make here is that the mind's eye is located at the interface between this visual vestibule and the organized memories.

With this description of the visual system, imaging can be described as involving the interaction of three components, or memories: (1) An abstract representation in short-term or long-term memory where structural information about clusters of pieces is stored. (2) The "vestibule" memory, described above, where a fairly concrete representation of the board is maintained. (3) An image in the mind's eye that combines, in a common format, information from both short-term memory and vestibule. Unlike the vestibular memory, the image has structure based on meaning and familiarity, and unlike the representations in long-term and short-term memory, the image contains features in specific spatial locations.

The proposed theory has the attractive property that it explains why we should expect eye movements to accompany mental imaging. If the eyes normally extract information about the same part of the visual scene which short-term memory is structuring, and if these two sources of information are to be combined in the mind's eye, then it is essential that the imaging processes control eye movements to bring about this coordination.

Before we take our hypothesized memory systems too seriously, we will need to examine them in relation to many known perceptual phenomena. In particular, it is not obvious that the system, which postulates that the mind's eye contains relational structures similar to those in short-term and long-term memory, can accommodate the mental rotation experiments of Shepard (and perhaps the interference experiments of Brooks, 1968, and Segal and Fusella, 1970) which have sometimes been interpreted as implying an analog system (cf. Cooper and Shepard, 1973), rather than relational symbol structures, as the heart of visual memory. But further evaluation of these and other possibilities will have to be left to later studies.

CONCLUSION

Our specific aim in the experiments described in this chapter has been to explain why it has been impossible to find nonchess tasks (such as general memory span) that measure chess skill, and to give some account of where that skill lies. Our answer is that chess skill depends in large part upon a vast, organized long-term memory of specific information about chessboard patterns. Only chess-related tasks that tap this organization (such as the 5-second recall task) are sensitive to chess skill. Although there clearly must be a set of specific aptitudes (e.g., aptitudes for handling spatial relations) that together comprise a talent for chess, individual differences in such aptitudes are largely overshadowed by immense individual differences in chess experience. Hence, the overriding factor in chess skill is practice. The organization of the master's elaborate repertoire of information takes thousands of hours to build up, and the same is true of any skilled task (e.g., football, music). That is why *practice* is the major independent variable in the acquisition of skill.

References

Alekhine, A. *My best games of chess 1908–1923.* New York: McKay, 1927.

Baylor, G. W., Jr. A treatise on the mind's eye: an empirical investigation of visual mental imagery. Unpublished doctoral dissertation, Carnegie-Mellon University, 1971.

Baylor, G. W., Jr. & Simon, H. A. A chess mating combinations program. *AFIPS Conference Proceedings, 1966 Spring Joint Computer Conference,* 1966, 28, 431–47. Reprinted as chapter 4.3 in this book.

Brooks, L. R. Spatial and verbal components of the act of recall. *Canadian Journal of Psychology,* 1968, 22, 349–68.

Cavanaugh, J. P. Relation between the immediate memory span and the memory search rate. *Psychological Review,* 1972, 79, 525–30.

Chase, W. G., & Simon, H. A. Perception in chess. *Cognitive Psychology,* 1973, 4, 55–81. Reprinted as chapter 6.4 in this book.

Clark, H. H. Linguistic processes in deductive reasoning. *Psychological Review,* 1969, 76, 387–404.

Clark, H. H., & Chase, W. G. On the process of comparing sentences against pictures. *Cognitive Psychology,* 1972, 3, 472–517.

Coles, L. S. Syntax directed interpretation of natural language. In H. A. Simon & L. Siklóssy (Eds.), *Representation and meaning.* Englewood Cliffs, N.J.: Prentice-Hall, 1972, pp. 211–87.

Cooper, L. A., and Shepard, R. N., Chronometric studies of the rotation of mental images. In W. G. Chase (Ed.), *Visual information processing.* New York: Academic Press, 1973, pp. 75–176.

De Groot, A. D. *Thought and choice in chess.* The Hague: Mouton, 1965.

De Groot, A. D. Perception and memory versus thought: Some old ideas and recent findings. In B. K. Kleinmuntz (Ed.), *Problem solving.* New York: Wiley, 1966, pp. 19–50.

DeSoto, C., London, M., & Handel, S. Social reasoning and spatial paralogic. *Journal of Personality and Social Psychology,* 1965, 2, 513–21.

Feigenbaum, E. A. The simulation of verbal learning behavior. *Proceedings of the 1961 Western Joint Computer Conference,* 1961, 121–32.

Garner, W. R. *Uncertainty and structure as psychological concepts.* New York: Wiley, 1962.

Hayes, J. R., On the function of visual imagery in elementary mathematics. In W. G. Chase (Ed.), *Visual information processing.* New York: Academic Press, 1973, pp. 117–214.

Kintsch, W. Notes on the structure of semantic memory. In E. Tulving & W. Donaldson (Eds.), *Organization of memory.* New York: Academic Press, 1972, pp. 249–308.

Lasker, E. *Lasker's greatest chess games.* New York: Dover, 1935.

Miller, G. A. The magical number seven, plus or minus two: some limits on our capacity for processing information. *Psychological Re-*

view, 1956, 63, 81–97.

Newell, A., & Simon, H. A. *Human problem solving*. Englewood Cliffs, N.J.: Prentice-Hall, 1972.

Quillian, M. R. *Semantic memory*. In M. Minsky (Ed.), *Semantic information Processing*. Cambridge, Mass.: M. I. T. Press, 1968, 227–70.

Radojcic, M. What is your chess IQ? *Chess Life and Review*, December 1971, 709–10.

Reinfeld, F. *Win at chess*. New York: Dover, 1945.

Segal, S. J., & Fusella, V. Influence of imagined pictures and sounds on detection of auditory and visual signals. *Journal of Experimental Psychology*, 1970, 81, 458–64.

Simon, H. A., & Barenfeld, M. Information processing analysis of perceptual processes in problem solving. *Psychological Review*, 1969, 76, 473–83. Reprinted as chapter 6.2 in this book.

Simon, H. A., & Gilmartin, K. A simulation of memory for chess positions. *Cognitive Psychology*, 1973, 5, 29–46. Reprinted as chapter 6.3 in this book.

Sperling, G. The information available in brief visual presentations. *Psychological Monographs*, 1960, 74, [11, Whole No. 498].

Sperling, G. A model for visual memory tasks. *Human Factors*, 1963, 5, 19–31.

Sternberg, S. Memory-scanning: mental processes revealed by reaction-time experiments. *American Scientist*, 1969, 57, 421–57.

Williams, T. G. Some studies in game playing with a digital computer. In H. A. Simon & L. Siklóssy (Eds.), *Representation and meaning*. Englewood Cliffs, N.J.: Prentice-Hall, 1972, pp. 71–142.

Winikoff, A. W. Eye movements as an aid to protocol analysis of problem solving behavior. Unpublished doctoral dissertation, Carnegie-Mellon University, 1967.

6.6

Alternative Uses of Phonemic Information in Spelling (1973)

with Dorothea P. Simon

The well-known and frequently lamented idiosyncracies of English spelling raise serious doubts as to the role that information about the spellings of individual phonemes can play in learning to spell correctly. The purpose of this chapter is to distinguish several different ways in which phonemic information might be employed in spelling, to examine some empirical data on the consequences of using these different information sources, to formulate hypotheses about the underlying processes involved, and to suggest possible implications for the teaching (and learning) of spelling.

SPELLING PROCESSES—PHONEMIC AND OTHER

As a framework for examining empirical data about spelling, the next paragraphs will examine a number of different kinds of information which, if stored in memory, could be used to assist the spelling process.

Homonyms

The existence of numerous homonyms (e.g., MANE, MAIN) in English places an upper bound on the adequacy of phonemic information for indicating correct spelling. Since the members of a homonym set are, by definition, phonemically identical, the correct spelling cannot be inferred from the sound, but must be obtained from contextual information indicating meanings. Thus, in a context of lions, MANE can often be inferred; while a context of streets (or oceans) clues us to MAIN. We may sketch the spelling process in such cases by the diagram:

pronunciation + context → meaning → spelling

This research was supported by a grant from the National Science Foundation (NSF-GJ540-X-1) and by the Learning Research and Development Center, supported in part as a research and development center by funds from the United States Office of Education, Department of Health, Education, and Welfare; and by Public Health Service Research Grant MH-07722 from the National Institute of Mental Health (Department of Psychology, Carnegie-Mellon University). The opinions expressed in this publication do not necessarily reflect the position or policy of the sponsoring agencies, and no official endorsement should be inferred.

The arrow, in this and following diagrams, denotes an inference that may be derived from a stored direct association or by a complicated reasoning process. In the example above, the second arrow may denote a simple association stored in long-term memory, while the first arrow may denote a somewhat more complex process. We will postulate the detail of these processes only to the extent that it can reasonably be inferred from empirical evidence.

Phonemic Associations

Most people who have learned to read have acquired some kind of associations between particular phonemes and spellings that represent them. Notice that these associations can run in either of two directions:

$$\text{phoneme} \rightarrow \text{spelling}$$
$$\text{spelling} \rightarrow \text{phoneme}$$

Learning the association in one direction does not necessarily cause it to be learned in the opposite direction. If such associations are used as aids in reading, it is *presumably* the second association that is wanted and that is learned in the sounding-out method. It is *presumably* the first association, however, that is wanted if phonemic information is to aid spelling. The significance of the "presumably" will become clear as we proceed.

In neither direction, in English, is the association unambiguous. Thus, if the speller learns that a particular phoneme calls for a particular spelling, and uses that belief to spell, he will spell "phonetically" but often incorrectly.

If a speller knows that a particular phoneme may have several spellings, there are two further possibilities. On the one hand, he may simply have stored with the phoneme a list of possible spellings, ordered, say, by the frequency with which each spelling represents that phoneme. On the other hand, he may have stored in association with the phoneme a differentiated set of spellings—that is to say, an explicit or implicit set of rules that select one or another of the alternative spellings as a function of the phonemic context. We may distinguish these two possibilities by the diagrams:

$$\text{phoneme} \rightarrow sp_1, sp_2, sp_3, \text{etc.}$$
$$\text{phoneme} + (\text{phonemic context})_i \rightarrow sp_i$$

With the first of these two forms of information storage, phonemic information can be used either to spell phonetically (e.g., by choosing in each case the first spelling on the list of alternatives) or to generate *possible* spellings, from which the final choice is to be made by some subsequent selection process. We will be much concerned in this chapter with the use of phoneme-letter associations as *generators* of possible spellings.

The second form of information storage diagramed above has been studied extensively as a possible basis for teaching and learning English spelling. The work of Hanna and his associates sets some upper bounds on what can be expected from this process. We next summarize this evidence briefly.

Phonemic Rules

Hanna, Hanna, Hodges, and Rudorf (1966) have proposed that children be taught phonemic rules that would enable them, in most instances, to choose the correct spellings for words they have heard. They have set down a list of some 200 rules, and Rudorf (1965) has used a computer program to determine for what percentage of common words these rules would produce correct spellings.

The results are not very encouraging. A speller who used the 200 rules consistently would spell about 80 percent of all phonemes correctly, but since words contain several phonemes, this level of phonemic accuracy would allow him to spell correctly only about one-half (49.87 percent) of the 17,009 most common English words. As we will see, most children are able to spell at a much higher level of accuracy by the time they leave high school. Hence it is not clear that the 200 rules, even if they were learned thoroughly enough to be applied consistently, would help much. However, we will examine the evidence on this point more carefully in a later section of this chapter.

Recognition and Recall

To understand spelling processes, we need to remind ourselves of the fundamental distinction between recognition and recall. In order to *recall* a stimulus, we need complete information about that stimulus, else we could not reproduce it. In order to *recognize* the stimulus, we need only sufficient information about it to enable us to distinguish it from other stimuli that are possible in that context. In the extreme case, the context alone is enough. (What word other than "years" will satisfy for American readers the context: "Four score and seven . . . ago, our fathers brought forth. . . . "?)

As we are all aware from personal experience, the correctness or incorrectness of a spelling may be recognized in situations where we cannot recall the correct spelling. We may then hit upon the correct spelling by a trial-and-error procedure—generate alternative possible spellings, then test if they are recognized when written out.

Notice that this trial-and-error process has its precise counterpart in a procedure for sounding out words while reading:

generate alternative possible phonemes to correspond to the letters of the printed word, then test if the phoneme string, when pronounced, is recognized as a familiar word. The spelling scheme suggested above assumes that information for recognizing a written word can be evoked by presenting the written word or an approximation to it, while the sounding-out scheme assumes that information for recognizing a spoken word can be evoked by the spoken word or an approximation to it. The two processes are diagramed in figure 1.

Notice also that the information used in these processes is stored at two distinct levels of aggregation—for the generators, at the level of individual phonemes and letters (and correspondences between them) and for the recognizers, at the level of whole aural and printed words (and correspondences between them). Thus the information used to *generate* the trial spellings and trial pronounciations is stored in the form of phoneme-letter and letter-phoneme associations, respectively, while the recognition information, used to *test* the proposed spellings or pronounciations, is stored as structures of information for whole

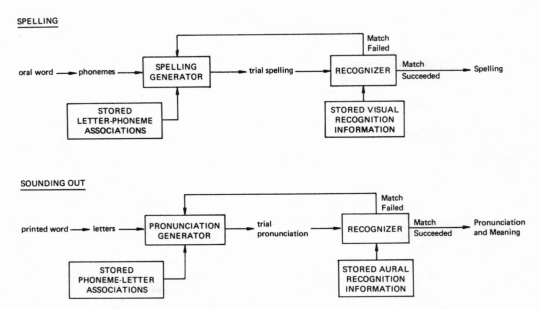

Figure 1. Spelling (above) and reading (below) by means of a generator-test process.

words. Thus, to use the sounding-out method, the printed word must be decoded letter by letter, recoded phoneme by phoneme, but *recognized* at the level of the whole word. To use the trial spelling method, the aural word must be decoded phoneme by phoneme, recoded letter by letter, but *recognized* at the level of the whole word.

Spelling Processes

It can be seen that there are a number of alternative routes along which the spelling of a particular word can be recalled. Each route requires different forms of information storage in long-term memory and different processes for using the information.

1. The simplest spelling route is *direct recall* of the spelling of the word, associated in long-term memory with its pronunciation and meaning (the latter essential because of homonyms). Probably most people spell most words that are highly familiar to them by this process.

2. Two quite different routes that have been mentioned above make primary use of phonemic information rather than direct association at the word level. The first of these is *direct phonemic spelling*, based on stored phoneme-letter associations, supplemented to a greater or lesser extent by rules that specify the conditions under which particular spellings are to be used with particular phonemes.

3. The second phonemic route is the *generate-and-test process* that was described in the last section—a generator of possible spellings, based on stored phoneme-letter associations combined with a recognizer of trial spellings, based on the stored information that is used in visual word recognition. As was pointed out above, this route is exactly analogous—with the roles of phonemes and letters interchanged—to the sounding-out process in reading.

4. Each of these routes may be modified by introduction of *morphemic information*. (See C. Chomsky, 1970, for a particular version of this idea). Here auditory recognition of morphemic components of words

gives access to spelling information (of any of the forms described above) about these components, which may be used to derive the spelling of the words containing the components. This process may also make use of conditional rules (e.g., "When adding ED or ING, double a final consonant preceded by a short vowel.").

Each of these possible spelling processes has obvious advantages and disadvantages that make it impossible, a priori, to predict which is the most advantageous and most easily learned. Direct recall requires the rote learning of thousands of spellings. Unless these are overlearned and actually used from time to time they may be forgotten relatively rapidly.

Direct phonemic spelling, without conditional rules, can produce spelling of only very low accuracy. Even when phonetic associations are supplemented by several hundred conditional rules—whose learning to a sufficient level of accessibility is itself a large task—the level of accuracy will not be acceptable.

The generate-and-test process, by itself, will not produce accurate spelling because the visual recognition information it uses to correct the phonetic generator is incomplete information. A reader need know much less than the full spelling of a word in order to recognize that word visually—and particularly in context. On the other hand, the generate-and-test process has the greatest attractiveness in that it enables the speller to draw upon a vast store of information he already holds in long-term memory—partial information about the spellings of all words that are in his reading vocabulary.

Little is known quantitatively about how these advantages and disadvantages of the different methods balance out. In the next section, however, we will consider computer programs that attempt to simulate two of the spelling processes described above—the rule-modified direct phonemic spelling process and the generate-and-test process. We will present some evidence that suggests strongly that most spellers make use of the generate-and-test process as an important tool in spelling.

Table 1. *Phoneme Code.*

Coded Form Phoneme	Graphemic Options	Example
A0	A-E AI AY A EIGH	*A*LE
A2	A AI A-E	C*A*RE
A3	A A-E	*A*DD
A5	A A-E EA	*A*RM
E0	E EE EA E-E I-E IE	*E*VE
E2	E EA EE E-E IE	H*E*RE
E3	E EA A E-E	*E*ND
E5	E U O A I	MAK*E*R
E7	A O I E OU U	*A*BOUT-(SCHWA)
I0	I-E I Y IGH IE Y-E	*I*CE
I3	I Y I-E A-E	*I*LL
O0	O O-E OA OW OU	*O*LD
O2	O AU AW O-E OUGH	*O*RB, S*O*FT
O3	O A O-E	*O*DD
O6	OO O U-E OU EW UE	F*OO*D
O7	OO U OU O U-E	F*OO*T
U0	U-E U EW EU UE	*U*NITE
U3	U O OU O-E U-E	*U*P
O8	OI OY	*OI*L
O9	OU OW OUGH	*OU*T
B0	B BB	*B*UT
D0	D DD LD	*D*AY
F0	F PH FF LF GH	*F*ILL
G0	G GG X GUE	*G*O
H0	H WH	*H*AT
J0	GE J DG DGE D DJ GI	*J*OKE
K0	C K CK CH X CC	*K*EEP
L0	L LL	*L*ATE
M0	M MM MB LM	*M*AN
N0	N NN KN GN	*N*OD
P0	P PP	*P*EN
R0	R RR WR	*R*AT
S0	S C SS CE CI SC X	*S*IT
T0	T TT ED BT	*T*O
V0	V LV F VE	*V*AN
W0	W U	*W*IN
Y0	I Y	*Y*ET
Z0	S Z ES X ZZ SS	*Z*ONE
C1	CH T TCH TI	*CH*AIR
W1	WH	*WH*AT
K1	CS CC X	BO*X*
L1	LE EL	TAB*LE*
M1	M	CHAS*M*
N1	EN ON IN	LIST*EN*
N2	NG N	SI*NG*
S1	TI SH CI SSI SI C CH T S	*SH*E
T1	TH	*TH*IN
T2	TH	*TH*EN
Z1	S Z ES X ZZ SS SI G Z TI	A*Z*URE
H1	H	*H*ONEST
K2	QU	*QU*ILT

THE RULE TABLE PROCEDURE FOR SPELLING

By storing in a computer memory the appropriate information and processes, we can simulate any one of the spelling processes that has been described above—or any combination of them. For most purposes, it will be satisfactory to simplify matters by presenting the spoken word as an encoded sequence of phonemes: thus KNOWLEDGE may be represented as /No/ /O3/ /Lo/ /E3/ /Jo/. Different speakers may produce different phoneme sequences for the same word, and different hearers may decode the same sound stream into different phoneme sequences, but we will ignore such variations as a first approximation. (See the later discussion of sources of spelling irregularity.) A simplified phonemic scheme for English which has proved satisfactory for the generate-and-test program is shown in table 1. This is a slight modification of the scheme that is used by Hanna et al. (1966) and Rudorf (1965) in their work.

The important difference between direct phonemic spelling which makes use of conditional rules and the generate-and-test process for spelling phonetically can be seen by comparing the computer programs that implement these two processes, respectively.

The Rule Table Algorithm

The program used by Rudorf (1965) to simulate phonetic spelling with conditional rules is based on a rule table associated with each phoneme. The rule table for a given phoneme lists a number of different spellings for the phoneme and states the conditions under which each of the spellings is to be used. The conditions may include the position of the phoneme in the word (e.g., initial, medial, syllable-final, word-final), the degree of accent, and the surrounding phonemes (e g., "preceded by /O7/," "followed by /T1/"). The relatively simple rule table (five rules) for /U2/ (the "u" in "urn") can be paraphrased:

(1) If initial, spell EA; (2) if preceded by /Wo/, spell O; (3) if preceded by /CHo/ /Bo/ or /Ko/, spell U; (4) if preceded by /T1/ /Go/ /HW/ or /KW/, spell I; (5) in all other cases, spell E.

Performance of the Algorithm

As was mentioned earlier, the complete algorithm contains about 200 rules and spells about one out of every two common words correctly. We present here several kinds of empirical evidence that enable us to judge the utility of the algorithm for improving spelling.

Masters (1927) gathered data on 268 words that occur within the first 5,000 of *A Basic Writing Vocabulary* and that had been found by Asbaugh to be misspelled by 40 percent or more of the eighth-grade pupils he tested. Of these words, 249 were attempted by the Rudorf (1965) program. It spelled correctly only 65, or about 26 percent. Yet Masters showed that generally 80 percent or more of twelfth-grade pupils spelled any one of these words correctly— not only the one in four words spelled correctly by the algorithm, but also the three in four that it missed. Since these pupils were drawing on stored information far more accurate than that provided by the algorithm, it is unlikely that knowledge of the algorithm would improve their spelling.

Let us next compare in detail the performance of the Rudorf (1965) algorithm with the actual performance of fifty pupils beginning a fourth-grade spelling course. The pupils themselves ranged from second through fifth grade and had been pursuing a program of individualized instruction in spelling. Table 2 compares the spellings by pupils and algorithm, respectively, on the 30 words in the first two spelling lessons of the fourth-grade book, 4 review words, and 14 supplementary words that were presumably relevant to other courses. The student scores and spellings are taken from a pretest given to the students *before* they had studied the words (except the review words).

On the 30 new words, the 50 children made a total of 126 errors, an average of

Table 2. *Comparison of Spellings by Elementary School Pupils and by Hanna-Rudorf Algorithm.*

Word	Students (N = 50) Errors	Common Error	Algorithm Error	Spelling	Grade for 80% Correct*
bag	0				5
wet	1				5
hid	4	hide			8
log	1				5
yet	3				5
bit	8	bite	×	bate	7
bus	0		×	buss	5
desk	3				5
pond	7	pound			6
tent	0				5
flat	1				5
held	4	hald			7
slid	4	slide			8+
spot	2				5
slip	0				6
tie	1		×	ty	6
ear	2				4
deep	6	deap			5
feel	11	feal	×	feal	7
laid	25	layed, lade	×	lade	8+
team	4	teem	×	teem	5
free	1				—
goat	2				5
coal	9	cool	×	cole	6
sweet	6	sweat	×	sweat	6
mean	4	meen			5
east	0				5
feast	4	feest, fest			7
dream	6				5
asleep	3	asleap			6
Review Words					
drank	0				—
drunk	4	dronk			6
wait	13	wate	×	wate	7
afraid	8	afriad	×	afrade	8+
Supplementary Words					
add	0		×	ad	4
addend	16	adden	×	adend	—
addition	41	addion, addtion	×	adition	8
plus	3	pluse	×	pluss	7
sum	5	some†			6
column	47	colum, colem	×	colum	8+
total	32	totel, totle			7
island	12	iland	×	iland	7
delta	11				—
gulf	18	golf†			8
bay	0				5
coast	18	cost	×	cost	7
dike	11	diek, dick			—
canal	27	canel, cannal	×	conal	8

*Lowest grade at which at least 80 percent of the children spelled the word correctly. From the *New Iowa Spelling Scale* (Greene, 1954).

† In these two cases the erroneous spellings are homonyms.

2.5 per child, or 8.4 percent of all the spellings. On the same words, the algorithm made eight errors in 30 words—26.6 percent. On the four review words, the children made 25 errors—12.5 percent; while the algorithm made two errors—50 percent. On the 14 supplementary words, the children made 241 errors—34.4 percent; the algorithm made eight errors—53.3 percent. In all three classes of words, the algorithm made far more errors than the average child. Thus, these fourth-grade students spell the words better than the algorithm even before they have studied them explicitly.

The same words that were misspelled by the algorithm tended to be difficult for the children. On the list of new words, eight words were misspelled by more than 10 percent of the children. Five of these eight words were also misspelled by the algorithm, together with three words that were spelled correctly by more than 90 percent of the children. In the case of three of the "difficult" words and one of the "easy" words misspelled by the algorithm, the erroneous spelling was identical with the most common, or one of the most common, spellings of the children who missed that word ("feal" for "feel"; "lade" for "laid"; "teem" for "team"; and "sweat" for "sweet"). The same thing may be said of four of the frequently misspelled review and supplementary words. In two cases ("sum" and "gulf") some of the children chose the wrong homonym, while the algorithm was luckier.

In the final column of table 2, we show, from Greene's (1954) data, the grade level by which 80 percent or more of all students can be expected to spell each word correctly. The single fourth-grade word on the list was misspelled by the algorithm, as were two of the 16 fifth-grade words and 3 of the 8 sixth-grade words. These are words the students might be expected to acquire soon, with or without the algorithm. Could the algorithm help, however, with the harder words? Hardly. It misspelled 6 of 9 seventh-grade words, 2 of 4 eighth-grade words, and 3 of 4 words on which mastery was not achieved by 80

percent of the students by the eighth grade.

Performance on Difficult Words

In his list of 268 difficult common words, Masters (1927) discovered 117 which, when misspelled, were misspelled in a relatively consistent way. That is, a single form accounted for more than half the misspellings of each of these 117 words. We can compare 51 of these words, their spellings and typical misspellings, with the spellings produced by the algorithm. (The remaining 66, mostly inflected forms, are not in the list that the algorithm spelled.)

The algorithm spelled only 15—less than one-third—of the 51 words correctly. In eight cases, its misspelling was identical with the typical human misspelling, and in nine other cases, algorithm and humans shared at least one error in common. In the remaining 19 cases, the errors made by the algorithm were different from the typical human errors. The words, together with the typical misspellings and the algorithm's spellings, are shown in table 3.

Even this small sample of words gives a good picture of the nature of typical human spelling errors. In nearly all cases, the typical misspelling implicates a single phoneme. Eighteen misspellings—more than one-third—involve a schwa (at least in some pronunciations of the word); eight involve other vowels; nine involve the choice between single and doubled consonants; three are consonantal errors of other kinds; nine involve homonyms or incorrect inferences from morphemes; and four involve miscellaneous difficulties. Hence, mistaken *phonetic* spellings predominate, and most of the remaining errors can be described as due to incorrect use of morphemic or semantic information. This is the same picture that emerges from Masters' (1927) analysis of his whole list of 268 words (see pages 71–74 of his monograph), and from the words from fourth-grade spelling lists shown in table 2. The evidence from all these sources is completely consistent.

Table 3. *Misspellings of "Hard Words" by Hanna-Rudorf Algorithm and by Typical Students.*

Word	Rudorf Algorithm (Blank if Correct)	Equal (=) or Similar (∼)	Typical Misspelling*
consistent			consistant
convenient	conveanient		convient
correspondence	corespondence		correspondance
curiosity			curiousity
decidedly	desidedly		dicidely
deem	deam	=	deam
delegate			deligate
despair	despare		dispair
disappoint	disapoint	∼	dissapoint
disappointment	disapointment	∼	dissapointment
divine	davine		devine
dormitory			dormatory
duly			duely
edition			addition
efficiency	efitionsy		effeciency
existence			existance
exquisite	exquisate		exquisit
fascinate	fasanate	∼	facinate
fundamental			fundemental
genius	geanious		genious
grateful			greatful
imitation			immitation
inconvenience	inconveanience		inconvience
indefinite	indefanate	∼	indefinate
infinite	infanate	∼	infinate
innocent	inosunt	∼	inocent
kindergarten			kindergarden
laboratory	laboritory		labratory
mortgage	morgage	=	morgage
mysterious	misterious	=	misterious
mystery	mistery	=	mistery
perceive	perseive		percieve
possess	pasess	∼	posess
procedure	prosegure		proceedure
psychology	sicology		Psychology
questionnaire	questicounaire		questionaire
rating	rateing	=	rateing
receiver	reseiever		reciever
reckon	recen	∼	recon
recommend	recomend		reccommend
recommendation	recomendation	=	recomendation
remembrance			rememberance
ridiculous			rediculous
romantic			romatic
seize	seas		sieze
specimen	spesamen		speciman
spiritual			spirtual
thorough	thiro		through
temporary	temporery		temperary
tonnage	tunage	∼	tonage
virtue	vertue	=	vertue
visible	visable	=	visable

*Masters (1927), 30–32.

Alternative Phonetic-Morphemic Schemes

The question may be asked whether the *right* phonetic rules were used in the Hanna-Rudorf scheme. In particular, N. Chomsky and M. Halle (1968) have proposed that English possesses a deep phonetic structure that is more closely related to orthography than is the surface structure. (For a brief discussion of their theory and its implications for spelling, see C. Chomsky, 1970.) Thus, for example, the lexical item, PRE-SIDE (/Po/ /Ro/ /Eo/ /Zo/ /Io/ /Do/) disambiguates the spelling of PRESI-DENT, where a surface phonetic variation has changed the long vowel, /Io/, to the schwa, /E7/.

It has been suggested (Chomsky, 1970, pp. 304–05) that the greater correspondence of orthography to phonetic deep structure can be used in teaching spelling. Thus, if the speller learned to generate several words having the same lexical base, these might help him resolve ambiguities. In the example above, the schwa in PRESI-DENT would not be misspelled if the derivation from PRESIDE were noticed.

There are two difficulties with this proposal. First, it can lead to wrong spellings, e.g., ABSTAINENCE for ABSTINENCE. Second, it applies to relatively few words. We have not determined systematically how many words misspelled by the Hanna-Rudorf algorithm could be handled by attention to phonetic deep structure, but examination of tables 2 and 3 suggests that there are relatively few. In table 2, the double D in ADDEND and ADDI-TION could be inferred by anyone who could spell ADD (which the Hanna-Rudorf algorithm could not). TOTAL, which the algorithm spelled correctly, could also be inferred, perhaps, from TO-TALITY. In table 3, LABORATORY (from LABOR), provides a positive instance, as does SPIRITUAL (SPIRIT), and perhaps the single C in RECOM-MEND (RE + COMMEND). On the other hand, the missing E in REMEM-BRANCE shows how the procedure can lead the speller astray (as does the missing E in PROCEDURE!).

We conclude that the Chomsky proposal might have some use in building a spelling program, but probably can play only a quite minor role.

Conclusions

What conclusions can be drawn from these data? As far as the Rudorf algorithm is concerned, the evidence is decisive that ability to use it would not help fourth-grade children to spell many of the words they do not already know how to spell (or can guess how to spell). On the totality of "new words" that the algorithm could spell—22 words—the children averaged only 1.2 errors per child. Hence, at best, the algorithm could only have improved spelling by 5 percent, even if its systematic use did not introduce errors in words that children had previously spelled correctly. Similarly, at more advanced levels, consistent use of the algorithm would degrade the spelling of all but the poorest human spellers.

We discuss these matters in detail because the results of the studies of phonetic regularity have been variously interpreted by the proponents and critics of phonetic approaches to spelling. We see that the facts do not justify reliance on the algorithm, per se. We will have to consider further, however, what they imply in general for uses of phonemic information.

It is important for our discussion that, with relatively few exceptions, the spelling errors made by humans (see tables 2 and 3) do not reveal any reluctance on their part to use phonemic cues. On the contrary, most of their errors, like the algorithm's, were made on words that are spelled in a phonetically ambiguous or irregular way.

GENERATE-AND-TEST PHONETIC PROCESSES

If phonemic information is not to be learned and applied in the form of an algorithm, how then can it be used at all? We have already discussed one alternative possibility—to use such information to generate *possible* spellings, these to be tested or screened with the aid of visual recognition. Before considering this process, we need to distinguish between two kinds of phonetic irregularities in spelling.

Sources of Spelling Irregularity

A spelling may be phonetically irregular when (1) it is ambiguous, or (2) it is nonphonetic. A spelling is ambiguous if one or more of its phonemes can be represented by several different letter combinations. The typical offender here is the schwa, which on different occasions can be represented by A, E, I, O, or U, to say nothing of more exotic combinations of these. A spelling is nonphonetic if one or more of its letters bear little or no relation to the phonemes. The S in "island" is a characteristic example.

Whether a spelling is nonphonetic is relative to the list of readings that is admitted for each of the phonemes. For example, by admitting "SL" as a (rare) reading for /Lo/, we can even regularize "island." Likewise, the K in "know" can be viewed as a nonphonetic element, or the readings for /No/ can be expanded to include KN. Observe that when a spelling is "phoneticized" by expanding the list of admissible readings for a phoneme, new ambiguity is introduced, for now the speller must choose between the alternative readings of the phoneme.

Ambiguity is also relative, and falls in several categories. First, a spelling may be ambiguous because pronunciation varies with dialect or with the degree of care exercised by the speaker. Second, even if a word is always pronounced in the same way, some of its phonemes have multiple admissible readings. This is also a relative matter (and not only because we may regularize irregularities as shown above), for by introducing *conditions* we may distinguish among the situations in which one or another reading is to be used, and hence, reduce the ambiguity, e.g., "I before E except after C." This is the route taken by the Rudorf algorithm, and the source of its 200 rules.

Non-deterministic Algorithms

The Rudorf spelling algorithm eliminates ambiguity entirely, proposing a specific spelling for every word presented to it, but it accomplishes this at the cost of spelling many words incorrectly. This suggests the possibility of reducing the conditionality of the algorithm, but retaining the alternate readings—that is, of making the algorithm *nondeterministic*. (Nondeterministic algorithms have theoretical and practical importance in several areas of computer science.)

A nondeterministic spelling algorithm will not propose a unique spelling for a word, but it will propose one or more spellings for each of the phonemes in the word. There are several ways to make a definite choice among the alternatives that are proposed. One way—the simplest—is always to choose the first alternative. Another way is to follow the generation of alternatives with a selection process to choose among them. We will examine this method in a moment.

Observe that conditionality in the spelling of a phoneme is compatible with a nondeterministic spelling algorithm. We can retain as many of the conditional rules as we like, leaving the indeterminacy only where additional conditions would appear to introduce more errors than they eliminate. For example, we might retain the distinction between initial and other positions in the spelling of /No/, and allow KN on the list of admissible readings only for the initial position. Thus, we can both have and eat our cake. We can have as much of the sophistication as we wish of a conditional algorithm, combined with as much of the flexibility as we wish of a nondeterministic algorithm.

The nondeterministic algorithm is also helpful in dealing with ambiguities due to variant pronunciation. We can handle these either by reducing the list of phonemes, combining similar phonemes into a single one (e.g., representing by a single phoneme the /E/ of "maker" and the /U/ of "urn," or the /L/ of "late" and the /L/ of "able"), or by enlarging the list of admissible readings for each phoneme, or by some combination of these two methods.

Word Recognition Information

We will now make these ideas more concrete by describing a specific spelling algorithm which uses a nondeterministic phonetic component to generate possible spellings of phonemes and a body of word-recognition information to test the correctness of proposed spellings. It will be argued that this nondeterministic algorithm is similar to the procedures used by human spellers for words whose direct spellings they do not know and that it can serve as a model for designing programs of spelling instruction. We will describe a particular, very simple version of the algorithm, which we have named SPEL, and which is written in the SNOBOL (sic!) programming language.

By word-recognition information we mean information stored in memory that enables a reader to recognize a word when it is presented to him visually. Even out of context, a word may be REC.G.Z.BLE when only a fraction of its letters are presented. When it is presented in context it may be R.........L. with even less information.

We can think of a reader's word-recognition information as stored in his memory in association with a kind of sorting net. When a word is presented visually, it is sorted down the net, which serves as an index to the memory, until the partial image of the word is found. A sorting net of this kind is at the core of the EPAM (Feigenbaum, 1961; Simon & Feigenbaum, 1964) theory of verbal learning, which has had considerable success in explaining a variety of phenomena from verbal learning experiments. An important feature of this kind of memory organization when applied to word recognition is that the information in the image can be retrieved *only* on presentation of an appropriate visual stimulus —that is, of the appropriate word, perhaps not quite correctly spelled.

Hence, the word-recognition information that a reader gradually accumulates with experience is available only in an indirect way to help him spell. If he can produce a spelling close enough to the correct one so that he can recognize the word in question, he can then retrieve such information about its form as is stored in memory. (It is *not* argued that this is the only information that spellers use. They may also have stored in memory direct associations from the spoken word and its meaning to the letter sequence; and they may also have stored some rule information to use as a mnemonic in some cases.)

By drawing on his word-recognition information, in combination with his phonetic knowledge, a child can use his growing reading vocabulary to bootstrap his spelling competence. It may be hypothesized that most correct spelling is learned by a combination of phonetics with reading. An important piece of supporting evidence is the fact that relatively few spelling errors on words within the reading vocabulary involve the first two or three letters— letters that are almost always a part of the word-recognition information that has been stored (Kooi, Schutz, and Baker, 1965).

Description of the SPEL Algorithm

The algorithm is given two inputs: (1) a list of the phoneme sequence for a word, and (2) a list providing the hypothesized word-recognition knowledge available for that word. For example, the phoneme list for "knowledge" might be "No O3 Lo E3 Jo" and the recognition list, "K N -". The latter list is to be interpreted as "a K followed by an N followed by (any) other letters." The word-recognition information is to be considered as part of the contents of long-term memory. The algorithm also has stored in its long-term memory a list of readings for each phoneme. For example, with the phoneme /No/ may be stored the list "N NN KN." At present, these lists are unconditional, but conditions could be introduced into them in a more sophisticated form of the program.

When instructed to spell a word, after presentation of the phoneme list and recognition list, SPEL take up each phoneme in sequence and seeks a spelling for it that is consistent with the recognition list. If it exhausts the list of readings for a particular phoneme without finding one that matches, it backs up and changes readings assigned earlier. If it encounters a "-", it seeks to match the letter, if any, that follows with one of the unused phonemes, and interpolates, ahead of the matching one, the first readings of each of the unused phonemes.

Consider the example of "knowledge," with the recognition information given above: K N -. The readings of N and NN for /No/ (see table 1) are rejected for failure to match the initial K, and KN is accepted. The algorithm finds the "-", but no specific letters beyond, hence adopts the first readings of each of the remaining phonemes: O for /O3/, L for /Lo/, E for /E3/, GE for /Jo/. Hence, it spells "knowledge" as KNOLEGE.

Any of the inputs to the algorithm—the phoneme list, the recognition list, or the lists of phoneme readings—can be altered to see what effect this would have on the spelling of the word. Thus, if the order of the /Jo/ list were changed to put the reading J first, the spelling of "knowledge" would change to KNOLEJ. If the second vowel in "knowledge" were interpreted as the schwa (encoded as /E7/), with the initial list of readings, the spelling would become KNOLAGE. If the recognition list were expanded to "K N - D G E," the spelling would be KNOLEDGE. In this case, the D beyond the dash would be matched by one reading of /Jo/, (DGE), and the OLE filled in. If the recognition list were blank, "-", the word would be spelled entirely phonetically—i.e., by using the first reading on each phoneme reading list—with a resultant spelling like NOLEJ, say.

A number of fussy programming details in the algorithm relate to keeping track of current locations in the phoneme list and recognition list, and keeping track of what readings have already been tried. These "programming details" may not be without psychological significance. Any child who undertook to use a procedure like this to test out possible spellings would also have to keep track of his matching process and of the alternatives he had already generated. The presence of the programming details will help remind us, therefore, that learning to use such a procedure to help spelling may be a nontrivial task.

Comparison of SPEL with Children's Spelling

Suppose that a speller were using this generate-and-test process. What kinds of spelling errors would we expect him to make? Since we know that the initial and final groups of letters in a word are the most important, and generally most used, for recognition, we would expect him to make relatively few errors on those letters and many more on letters in the middle (Feigenbaum and Simon, 1962; Jass and Gillooly, 1971a, 1971b; Kooi et al., 1965; cf., Jass and Gillooly, 1972). We might postulate something like the typical serial position curve to predict the relative frequencies of errors as a function of position within the word.

On the other hand, if phonemic associations alone are being used to generate possible spellings, many more errors will be made with ambiguous phonemes, those with many alternative spellings (e.g., the schwa or /S/), than with the phonemes that have few alternative spellings (e.g., /B/ or /D/). Suppose we had a predictive measure of the contributions of these two factors—position in word and phonemic ambiguity—to the probability of a misspelling of a phoneme. To take the simplest model, let p_{in} be the average probability that a phoneme in the ith position of an n-letter word will be misspelled; and let a_k be proportional to the average probability that the most common spelling of phoneme k will be an incorrect spelling in any particular instance. Then if the ith phoneme in a particular n-letter word is phoneme k, and assuming independence of the two probabilities, we would predict that it will be misspelled with probability $e_{in,k} = p_{in} \cdot a_k$.

Consider, for example, the word 'knowledge." Assume that the recognition list for that word is something like "KNO... GE" for most subjects. Then few errors will be made on the first three and last two letters (p_{in} will be close to zero for these); but many will be made on those remaining letters for which the ambiguity, a_k, is high (for these letters p_{in} will be close to unity). Three of the missing letters correspond to ambiguous phonemes (W from the /O3/, E from the schwa, and D from the /Jo/), hence have large a_k; while the remaining letter, L, corresponds to a relatively unambiguous phoneme, /Lo/, hence has small a_k. Therefore, we would predict that most of the errors in spelling "knowledge" would involve the W, E, and D; and that we would find frequently such spellings as KNOWLEGE, KNOLEGE, KNOLAGE, and so on.

These expectations are not disappointed when we look at the data from 47 fourth-graders who had attempted to spell "knowledge." About one-third, 15, produced the correct spelling. Of the remainder, 26 correctly transcribed /No/ as KN, and five transcribed it as N. Only one produced a nonphonetic transcription, KL. Apart from the correct spelling, the most common ones were KNOWLEGE, with the D omitted, and KNOWLAGE, with the D omitted and an A for the schwa. Of the 32 erroneous spellings, only 10 can be regarded as genuinely nonphonetic. These involved such errors as interchange of W and L (3 cases), W and O, G and D. Figure 2 shows the serial positions of the errors made by these 32 pupils. They lie exactly where we expected them—few errors in K, N, or O; many in W, but few in L; many in E and D; few in G and E. (See figure 2.)

These kinds of results are readily reproduced by the simulation program. Table 4 summarizes the results of a number of runs. The first column shows the phonetic list for "knowledge," the second, the word recognition list, and the third, the spelling produced. With completely phonetic spelling (blank recognition list), we get the spelling NOLAGE or NOLAJ, depending

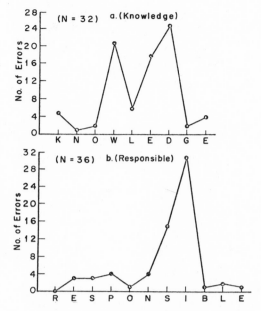

Figure 2. Distribution of spelling errors—grade 4 children. Errors were scored as follows: Children's spellings were transcribed onto a matrix of which columns were the correct letters, rows were individual misspellings; letters that were present and in correct order were entered in the appropriate column; one error was scored for each omission, substitution of single letter, or substitution of multiletter phonemic option.

on whether the admissible spellings of /Jo/ are listed in the order (GE, J, ...) or (J, GE, ...). Substituting /E3/ for the schwa as the fourth phoneme, we get NOLEGE or NOLEJ, respectively. If, now, the recognition information "KN-" is supplied, we get KNOLAGE, KNOLAJ, KNOLEGE, and KNOLEJ, respectively. If the recognition information is expanded to "KN-GE," only the forms ending in GE are produced. To obtain the correct spelling would require recognition information at least as complete as "KN-W-DGE." The 26 pupils who wrote the KNOW correctly may have used morphemic information—that "knowledge" is derived from "know." Eight children had the KNOW but not the D, while only one who wrote DGE missed KNOW.

Table 4. *Performance of SPEL Algorithm on "knowledge."*

Phonetic List	Recognition List	Spelling
/No O3 Lo E7 Jo/	"-"	NOLAJ
"	"-"	NOLAGE*
/No O3 Lo E3 Jo/	"-"	NOLEJ
"	"-"	NOLEGE*
"	"KN-"	KNOLEGE*
"	"KNOW-GE"	KNOWLEGE
"	"KN-W-DGE"	KNOWLEDGE

* Readings for /Jo/ changed from (J, GE, ...) to (GE, J, ...)

We have carried out a similar analysis for the spelling by these 47 pupils of the word "responsible." In this case, only 11 spelled the word correctly, and the vast bulk of the errors was concentrated on the schwa (a total of 31 errors for the spelling of this phoneme). As table 5 shows, the most likely misspelling, as indicated by the simulation, is RESPONSABLE. This was the most popular misspelling, produced by 11 pupils. The other phoneme accounting for many errors, seven in all, is the ambiguous /So/ preceding the schwa. Pupils represented this by S, CE, TS, and C, all of which can be produced by the algorithm by simple permutation of the list of readings for this phoneme. Five additional misspellings were phonetic; the remaining 13 largely involved the omission of transcriptions for one or more phonemes (e.g., REPOSABLE). These latter errors cannot be explained by our theory or produced by the simulation program. The others can be produced by permutations of the lists of admissible readings, or by varying the amounts of recognition knowledge provided. Table 5 gives examples.

By now the reader will see readily how the simulation program can be modified by simple changes and permutations of lists to produce such popular misspellings by these same 47 children of other words as FURTILIZER (1), FERTELIZER (2), and FERTALIZER (2), but not quite FERTERLIZER (4); ACOMADATE (6) and ACCOMODATE (3); OCASION (5) and OCCATION (2); ELAVATOR (6); SPECTATER (9); GRAMMER (19) and GRAMER (13).

We conclude that much of the spelling behavior of fourth-graders can be explained on the hypothesis that they use a phonetic generator combined with a recognition test in order to spell words of which they are not entirely sure. When the recognition information is insufficient to rule out phonetically correct, even though erroneous, spellings, the pupils use precisely those spellings. Many of the individual differences among students can be attributed to differences in the completeness of their recognition knowledge, differences in their phonetic rendition of the words, and differences in the content and ordering of

Table 5. *Performance of SPEL Algorithm on "responsible."*

Phonetic List	Recognition List	Spelling
/Ro E3 So Po O3 No So E7 Bo L1/	"-"	RESPONSABLE
"	"-"	RESPANSABLE*
"	"-"	RESPONCEABLE†
/Ro E3 So Po O3 No So E7 Bo Lo/	"-"	RESPONSABL
/Ro E3 So Po O3 No So E7 Bo L1/	"RESPON-BLE"	RESPONSABLE
"	"R-IBLE"	RESPONSIBLE

* Readings for /O3/ changed from (O, A, ...) to (A, O, ...)
† Readings for /So/ changed from (S, ...) to (CE, ...)

their lists of admissible readings for each phoneme.

CONCLUSIONS AND IMPLICATIONS

While the theory of spelling proposed here has empirical support, one should be cautious in inferring from it the effective ways to teach spelling. The data and theory give no encouragement to the idea that pupils should learn sophisticated rules for phoneme transcription. Most of their errors cannot be corrected by phonemic information. Instead, what is largely lacking is sufficient visual information about spelling —either in the form of direct associations or in the form of recognition information —to filter out the errors caused by phonetic ambiguity.

Perhaps the most valuable phonetic experience for pupils would be experience in generating possible *alternative* transcriptions for testing by recognition. This experience can be given without requiring pupils to learn complex systems of rules, since what is wanted are *lists* for each phoneme, and not unique transcriptions. The pupil can be encouraged to behave like a nondeterministic algorithm!

At the same time, spelling will only be learned if sufficient visual recognition information is also available. A considerable part of this information is normally acquired as a by-product of reading. Hence, by restricting spelling practice to words within the children's reading vocabularies, this information becomes available automatically to the generate-and-test process.

Since words can be recognized, however, without full information about their spelling, consideration should be given to techniques for getting children to attend to parts of words not normally used in recognition—particularly the central parts. Discussion of specific ways of doing this is beyond the scope of this chapter, but several such techniques are described and used in some of the standard spelling books.

It may be effective to make students explicitly aware of the generate-and-test technique for spelling, and to encourage them to try out alternatives rather than to

arrive immediately at the "one correct spelling." It would be highly desirable to have some empirical research aimed at testing the utility of such procedures.

Finally, we have focused on "typical" spelling errors, and have said relatively little about individual differences. As every teacher knows, the spelling errors of a minority of students are mainly non-phonetic in nature. There is no reason to suppose that the techniques that are best adapted to the majority of phonetically oriented students are also well adapted to this minority. The simulation technique discussed in this chapter may help to identify the spelling processes used by individual children and the information they hold in memory, and to diagnose and prescribe treatment for individual spelling problems. Again, these possibilities will only be realized if the technique is subjected to further empirical research.

The debate over the past decade or two on the utility of using phonic approaches in teaching spelling has no doubt led to the introduction of some innovative techniques in spelling instruction. However, the question of whether "phonics" should be taught as a part of the teaching of spelling is much too broad and vague. In this chapter, we have explored two main alternative processes for using phonemic information in spelling. Undoubtedly there are others. It is quite as important— perhaps more important—to learn *how* to introduce phonemic information, and to learn *how* the speller can best use it, as it is to learn *whether* to use phonemic information. It is time we turned from the latter question to the former, and designed research to answer it.

References

Chomsky, C., Reading, writing, and phonology. *Harvard Educational Review*, 1970, 40, 287–309.

Chomsky, N., & Halle, M. *The sound pattern of English.* New York: Harper & Row, 1968.

Feigenbaum, E. A. The simulation of verbal learning behavior. *Proceedings of Western Joint Computer Conference*, 1961, 121–132.

Feigenbaum, E. A., & Simon, H. A. A theory

of the serial position effect. *British Journal of Psychology*, 1962, 53, 307–20. Reprinted as chapter 3.1 in this book.

Greene, H. A. *The new Iowa spelling scale.* Iowa City: State University of Iowa, 1954.

Hanna, P. R., Hanna, J. S., Hodges, R. E., & Rudorf, E. H., Jr. *Phoneme-grapheme correspondences as cues to spelling improvement.* Washington, D. C.: U. S. Government Printing Office, 1966.

Jass, A. F., & Gillooly, W. B. The effect of phoneme-grapheme correspondences on the distribution of spelling errors. Paper presented at the American Educational Research Association, New York, February 1971.(a)

Jass, A. F., & Gillooly, W. B. The effect of instructions on the number and distribution of spelling errors. Paper presented at the Eastern Psychological Association, New York, April 1971.(b)

Jass, A. F., & Gillooly, W. B. The von Restorff effect on the number and distribution of spelling errors. Paper presented at the American Educational Research Association, Chicago, April 1972.

Kooi, B. Y., Schutz, R. D., & Baker. R. L. Spelling errors and the serial position effect. *Journal of Educational Psychology*, 1965, 56, 334–36.

Masters, H. V. *A study of spelling errors.* Iowa City: University of Iowa Studies in Education, vol. 4, series 1, no. 138, September 1, 1927.

Rudorf, E. H., Jr. The development of an algorithm for American-English spelling. (Doctoral dissertation, Stanford University) Ann Arbor, Mich.: University Microfilms, 1965. No. 65–6344.

Simon, H. A., & Feigenbaum, E. A. An information-processing theory of some effects of similarity, familiarization, and meaningfulness in verbal learning. *Journal of Verbal Learning and Verbal Behavior*, 1964, 3, 385–96. Reprinted as chapter 3.2 in this book.

7

Understanding

The three chapters of this section describe a model, UNDERSTAND, developed with J. R. Hayes, of the processes used by people to understand problem instructions prior to their initiating efforts to solve the problems. It is concerned with the way in which problem representations are generated and with the linkage between natural language stimuli and representations in long-term memory.

"Understanding," like "learning" and "thinking," is an umbrella word that refers to no single unique process. We judge understanding, as we do learning and thinking, by means of tests, and success on such a test in one task domain does not imply success in other domains. In a recent paper (Simon, 1977), I have proposed the following definitions—based on earlier ones by Moore and Newell (1974)—which make explicit the dependence of understanding on the task:

> S understands knowledge K if S uses K whenever appropriate.
> S understands task T if S has the knowledge and procedures needed to perform T.

Understanding is currently a popular topic of research, much of it focused on understanding natural language. Most measures of understanding that are used in this research test the ability to recall, paraphrase, or interpret information presented originally as natural language text—e.g., Schank and Abelson (1977); Kintsch (1974); Quillian (1968); Anderson (1976). It is not always clear as to what constitutes satisfactory performance on such tests. What is a good synopsis of a story? What inferences should a person be able to draw from information given him?

UNDERSTANDING PROBLEM INSTRUCTIONS

Our own research on understanding at Carnegie has, during the past five years, emphasized understanding written instructions for abstract puzzles—i.e., puzzles that do not call for real-world knowledge. We had several reasons for selecting these kinds of tasks for our work. First, there is a rather clear-cut criterion of whether the problem instructions have been understood: They are understood if the problem has been encoded in a form that makes it accessible to GPS-like general problem solving processes (see chapter 7.1). Second, by using puzzle-like domains of the sorts that have commonly been used in earlier problem solving research, we could build on the findings of that research. Third, we could avoid having to account for the subjects' substantive knowledge of a problem domain.

In the last couple of years, we have begun to extend the research into domains with substantial informational content, particularly chemical engineering thermodynamics (Bhaskar and Simon, 1977) and physics (Simon and Simon, 1978); but limits of space prevent the new work from being reported in this volume.

All three chapters in this section report work done with my colleague J. R. Hayes. Chapter 7.1 contains a description of our simulation program, UNDERSTAND, but does not undertake a detailed comparison of the program's behavior with the behavior of human subjects. Chapter 7.2 does carry out such a comparison, based mainly on verbal protocol data. Chapter 7.3 examines additional data on the fit between theory and behavior, this time obtained from experiments in which the form of the problem instructions was varied systematically. All the empirical data strongly support UNDERSTAND as an explanation of the main processes going on, although not always of the exact temporal sequence of those processes.

Our greatest insight into the human behavior on such tasks was gained by giving subjects different forms, all isomorphic, of the same problem. By isomorphic forms we mean forms that can be mapped into the same problem space, so that any solution path for the first will correspond to a solution path for the second and vice versa. Our goal was to discover whether changes in problem instructions, preserving isomorphism, would have any effects upon the way in which subjects represented the problems. Chapters 7.2 and 7.3 report clear-cut evidence of such effects. Moreover, they show that the change in representation caused a large difference (by a factor of two) in the difficulties of distinct isomorphs of the same problem. Hence, our data demonstrate both (1) that the way in which a person encodes a problem may have a major effect on the ease or difficulty of solution, and (2) that relatively "innocent" changes in the way in which the problem is stated may have major effects on the way in which people encode it.

The UNDERSTAND program predicts correctly the changes in problem representation that were induced by the changes in the problem instructions; but we do not have a satisfactory explanation of why the change in representation caused such a large change in problem difficulty. Some tentative explanations are offered in Chapters 7.2 and 7.3, none of which satisfy us. We are now engaged in a program of experimentation aimed at pinpointing the precise nature and locus of the change in difficulty and at finding a more adequate account of the differences in information processing strategies that lie at the root of these phenomena. We are not yet in a position to report on these new studies.

Semantic Information in Understanding

An important characteristic of the puzzles we have used in this research is that very little has to be understood about the semantics of the problem situations in order to understand the problems. Of course, UNDERSTAND has to be able to deal with the common English function words, such as "for" and "if" and "or." It also has to have some ability, mainly syntactic, to distinguish words that denote objects (mostly nouns) from words that denote relations (mostly verbs and prepositions).

But in a puzzle that concerns "monsters" holding "globes," the program does not need to know what monsters and globes are, beyond knowing that they are types of objects capable of being related (monsters hold globes). If the puzzle states that globes are transfered from one monster to another, the program needs to understand enough about the word "transfer" to know that a transfer dissolves the relation between a globe and one monster and creates a new relation of that globe with a different monster. Even this semantic understanding is very abstract, for internally all these objects and relations are represented in node-link memories, and changes in relations are simply changes in the linkages of those memories. Hence, UNDERSTAND can get along with a very lean semantic capability, and that is a major source of its flexibility and generality. However vividly the world outside is described by the problem statement, the world inside—the world of the internal representation—looks much the same everywhere. It consists solely of lists and list structures.

When we turn from puzzles to problems having genuine semantic content— even such restricted content as the domain, say, of kinematics—then the semantics must find some representation in the understanding program. Almost universally this is provided by storing in LTM semantic schemas containing the necessary information. These schemas serve as templates against which the information in the problem instructions can be matched in order to interpret those instructions. More than fifteen years ago, I built a primitive automatic programming system employing such devices (reported in Simon, 1972), and a number of contemporary understanding systems use schemas, including SAM (Schank and Abelson, 1977) and MEMOD (Norman and Rumelhart, 1975). In our own work on problem solving in chemical engineering thermodynamics, schemas hold information about working substances (e.g., air, steam, ammonia), and devices (e.g., pumps, condensers, pipes), which can be accessed when these substances and devices are mentioned in the problem statement (Bhaskar and Simon, 1977).

One of the most interesting systems built recently for understanding a semantically rich domain is Novak's ISAAC system (1977), which handles physics word problems: problems of statics stated in natural language. When ISAAC encounters a term such as "lever" in the text of a problem, it accesses a schema for levers in LTM and fills out that schema with the specifications of the particular lever mentioned in the text (the length of its arms, its points of attachment, and so on). It assembles the various instantiated schemas for the components of a problem into a coordinated representation that is a topological image of the problem situation, linking the components just as they are linked in the "real world." It then uses this linked structure to set up the algebraic equations for the problem. There is considerable evidence that·skilled human subjects generate some such internal image of the physical situation—indeed, that the ability to do so lies at the heart of what is usually called "physical intuition." As yet, we have very little empirical evidence as to how much psychological reality Novak's specific representation possesses.

Conclusion

The chapters of this section describe one of the currently active directions of research in the Carnegie-Mellon group. Comments in the introductions to various sections of this book have alluded to some of the other directions that seem especially promising to us at the present time. Without attempting an exhaustive list, I would like just to mention some of them: studying problem solving and understanding processes in semantically rich domains (and especially, in real-world domains); characterizing the internal representation of visual images; describing problem solving systems for ill-structured tasks such as architectural design; explicating the interaction of cognitive and esthetic components in artistic and other creative activity; investigating the interaction of cognition, on the one hand, with emotion and motivation, on the other; using adaptive production systems to explain human learning and discovery processes. I hope that in some years we will be able to issue another progress report on research that addresses some of these important and challenging questions.

References

Anderson, J. R. *Language, Memory, and Thought.* Hillsdale, N.J.: Erlbaum (1976).
Bhaskar, R. & H. A. Simon. Problem solving in semantically rich domains: An example from engineering thermodynamics, *Cognitive Science*, 1: 193–215 (1977).
Kintsch, W. *The Representation of Meaning in Memory*, N.Y.: Wiley, 1974.
Moore, J. & A. Newell, How can MERLIN understand? *In* L. W. Gregg (ed.), *Knowledge and Cognition*, Potomac, Md.: Erlbaum, 1974, pp. 201–52.
Norman, D. & D. Rumelhart, *Explorations in Cognition*, San Francisco: W. H. Freeman, 1975.
Novak, G. S. Representations of knowledge in a program for solving physics problems, *Proceedings of the 5th International Joint Conference on Artificial Intelligence*, 1977, Vol. 1, pp. 286–91.
Quillian, M. R. Semantic memory, *In* M. Minsky (ed.), *Semantic Information Processing*, Cambridge, Mass.: M.I.T. Press, 1968, pp. 227–70.
Schank, R. & R. Abelson. *Scripts, Plans, Goals and Understanding*, Hillsdale, N.J.: Erlbaum, 1977.
Simon, D. P. & H. A. Simon, Individual differences in solving physics problems, *In* R. S. Siegler (ed.), *Children's Thinking: What Develops?*, Hillsdale, N.J.: Erlbaum, 1978, chap. 13.
Simon, H. A. The heuristic compiler, *In* H. A. Simon & L. Siklóssy (eds.), *Representation and Meaning*, Englewood Cliffs, N.J.: Prentice-Hall, 1972, pp. 9–43.
Simon, H. A. Artificial intelligence systems that understand, *Proceedings of the 5th International Joint Conference on Artificial Intelligence*, 1977, Vol. 2, pp. 1059–73.

7.1

Understanding Written Problem Instructions (1974)

with John R. Hayes

Psychological experiments are usually carried out as follows: when the subject is brought into the laboratory, he is carefully introduced to the task he is to perform. He receives a set of instructions, written or oral or both, and then a series of practice tasks and examples. The experimenter answers any questions he may raise about points he does not understand. Only after the subject has completed these steps and the experimenter is satisfied that the subject understands the task, does the actual "experiment" begin.

For many experimental purposes, the procedure just described is perfectly reasonable. But if the object of study is the process known as "understanding," then the procedure discards from the data precisely the phenomena that are to be explained—how the subject comes to understand what task it is that he is supposed to perform. In the present research our aim has been to observe and record the behavior of the uninstructed subject—his behavior from the first moment that he receives the experimental instructions until the time when it appears that he understands the task fully.

While it is surely an elementary point

that the relevant data for the study of understanding are the records of behavior while understanding is being achieved, for years we have, in our studies of problem solving, been throwing away these data and examining only the protocols of subjects who have received and absorbed "proper training" in the task they are to perform. Of course we have not been alone in doing this. Studies of the behavior of naive subjects during the period when they are assimilating experimental instructions are almost nonexistent in the literature of psychology.

If a person is to solve a problem, there are several things he must know. First, he must know the set of problem elements—that is, the materials of the problem. Second, he must know the initial state of the problem and its goal. Third, he must know an operator or a set of operators for

This research has been supported by Public Health Service Grant MH-07722 from the National Institute of Mental Health and by National Science Foundation Grant GS-38533. The authors wish to express special thanks to Don Waterman who introduced us to the PAS-II system and who spent many hours advising us.

451

transforming the initial state into the goal. Finally, he must know the restrictions under which the operators may be applied.

Taken together, these essential items of information define what Newell and Simon (1972) have called a basic problem space. A problem space is a subject's representation of the task environment that permits him to consider different problem situations, to characterize these situations in ways that may help him decide what to do, and to apply the operators for changing one situation into another. A basic problem space is a minimal space that includes just those things that are essential for defining the problem, the solution, and the operators. Subjects may elaborate the problem space to incorporate other kinds of information that may be helpful to a solution. Hence, two subjects who set out to solve a given problem may use different spaces to do so. For example, one of the subjects may solve the problem by relatively inefficient trial and error procedures for searching the basic problem space; while the second, who identifies a cue for selecting the best operator at each step, may solve the problem in this augmented problem space (the space augmented, that is, by the descriptors that provide the cues) quickly and with little or no search. The problem space that the subject constructs will determine the manner of his search for a solution.

When a person solves a problem of a type with which he is already familiar, he will be able to recall and use elements of the problem space that he constructed while working on previous problems. This gives him an advantage over the naive subject who must construct the entire problem space from the beginning by extracting the necessary information (sometimes laboriously) from the problem instructions. Comparison of naive and sophisticated subjects makes it clear that the process of problem space construction may require considerable time and effort.

Our interest in the process of problem space construction derives in part from the above observation—that it is an essential aspect of problem solving which can be an important source of problem solving dif-

ficulty. Our interest also derives from observations that the form of the problem instructions may determine which of several alternative problem spaces the subject constructs. For example, Duncker (1945) has observed that information in the problem description in an active sentence may lead to the exploration of an entirely different set of alternatives than does the same information in a passive sentence. A better understanding of the process of problem space construction should help us to understand the relation between the problem instructions and the problem space that the subject constructs.

In this chapter, we will be concerned with the procedures that humans use to construct a new problem space when they are faced with an unfamiliar problem. We will present and analyze, in general terms, a problem solving protocol, propose a model of the process of problem space construction that appears to be generally consistent with the protocol, and describe a computer simulation of some of the central processes of that model. Finally, we will draw some conclusions from our work about the nature of the understanding process, as this process appears in the understanding of written task instructions.

THE TASK

Our subjects solved a problem called "The Tea Ceremony" shown below.

A Tea Ceremony

In the inns of certain Himalayan villages is practiced a most civilized and refined tea ceremony. The ceremony involves a host and exactly two guests, neither more nor less. When his guests have arrived and have seated themselves at his table, the host performs five services for them. These services are listed below in the order of the nobility which the Himalayans attribute to them.

> Stoking the Fire
> Fanning the Flames
> Passing the Rice Cakes
> Pouring the Tea
> Reciting Poetry

During the ceremony, any of those present may ask another. "Honored Sir, may I perform this onerous task for you?" However, a person may request of another only the least noble of the tasks which the other is performing. Further, if a person is performing any tasks, then he may not request a task which is nobler than the least noble task he is already performing. Custom requires that by the time the tea ceremony is over, all the tasks will have been transferred from the host to the most senior of the guests. How may this be accomplished?

The Tea Ceremony was constructed as an isomorph of the "Tower of Hanoi" problem (Rouse-Ball, 1962), the familiar puzzle in which disks of various sizes must be transferred among three pegs subject to restrictions on the set of legal moves. When we say that the Tea Ceremony is an isomorph of the Tower of Hanoi, we mean that it is the same problem as the Tower of Hanoi but disguised in different words. More precisely, we mean that any solution of the Tower of Hanoi puzzle may be translated, step by step, into a solution of the Tea Ceremony and vice versa by using the following correspondences:

TEA CEREMONY	TOWER OF HANOI
Three participants	Three pegs
Five tasks	Five disks
Nobility of tasks	Size of disks

The problem space information that the subject had to identify from the problem description included: (1) problem elements, such as the set of three participants in the Tea Ceremony and the list of five tasks, (2) the initial state in which the host was performing all the tasks and the goal state in which the senior guest performed them all, (3) the operator for requesting and effecting the transfer of tasks, and (4) the complex restrictions contained in sentences 6 and 7 under which a task could be transferred.

The problem was presented to the subject typed on an 8-inch-by-11-inch sheet. It was organized in two paragraphs—sentences 1 through 4, and sentences 5 through 9—rather than in the format shown. Our subject did not recognize that the Tea Ceremony was isomorphic to the Tower of Hanoi puzzle.

PRELIMINARY ANALYSIS OF THE PROTOCOL

The initial segment of the subject's protocol is reproduced in figure 1. While our discussion will include references to the whole protocol, the later portions have not been reproduced in detail because of its length (a total of 494 lines).

The Processing Sequence

When the subject received the instruction sheet containing the text, he first read through the sentences in their order of presentation, with only a single instance of backtracking (see figure 1, lines 2–4). We know that he was able to extract a good deal of information from sentences 1, 2, 3, 4, and 8 on his first pass through the text since he later makes use of information in these sentences before he returns to reread them. Indeed, he never rereads sentences 1, 2, and 3. In particular, during the first pass, he derives information about the set of participants, about the list of tasks, about the initial assignment of tasks to participants, and about the goal.

After reading through the text for the first time, the subject turns his attention to understanding sentences 5, 6, and 7, the sentences that contain information about the operator for transforming the initial state into the goal and information about the restrictions under which that operator may be applied (figure 1, lines 5–35). That these three sentences were relatively more difficult to understand than the others is suggested by the fact that the subject read them from nine to eleven times each in the course of the problem solving episode. In contrast, he read sentences 1, 2, 3, 4, and 9 only once or twice each, and sentence 8, four times.

The subject's behavior in interpreting these relatively difficult passages is of considerable interest. As we interpret them, the relevant sections of the protocol reflect two major processes which alternate with each other. The first is the *Language* process which reads short segments of text and extracts information from them through syntactic and semantic analysis. The sec-

The Initial Segment of the Problem Solving Protocol

1.	*S.*	Reads sentences 1, 2, and 3.
2.		"Now wait a minute. How many people are here? Let's go back."
3.		Reads sentence 2.
4.		"OK, the host isn't a guest, that's my problem."
5.		Reads sentences 3, 4, 5, 6, 7, 8, and 9.
6.		"Well, I don't understand the problem. Let's go back to the
7.		beginning of the last paragraph."
8.		Reads sentences 5, 6, and 7.
9.		"I'm beginning to get an idea of trying to order these tasks.
10.		Where . . . OK . . . there are five—fire, flames, cakes, tea, poetry."
11.	*E.*	"A little louder."
12.	*S.*	"OK. A person may request of another only the least noble of the
13.		tasks which another is performing—so if my friend is performing
14.		a bunch of tasks, I can request—wait a minute—something's
15.		fishy here. Look at this sentence. 'Honored Sir, may I perform
16.		this onerous task for you?'. So I'm going to perform a task
17.		for him."
18.		Reads sentence 6.
19.		(pause) "Let me get this straight. Let's assume there's someone
20.		across the table from me and I'm one of the guests and my host is
21.		on the left and the other guest is straight across the table. Now—
22.		now, if I'm the person, I may request of, say, the other guest only
23.		the least noble of the tasks which he is performing. So he is per-
24.		forming a bunch of tasks and I may ask him . . . But if all I can ask
25.		him is 'Honored Sir, may I perform this onerous task for you?' . . .
26.	*S.*	Hmm. What does this mean?"
27.		Reads sentence 6.
28.		"I'm not . . . I'm requesting to do something for him—or I am
29.		requesting to do something that he is already doing—for him.
30.		Oh, I see. So he's doing something and I'm going to do it for
31.		him, I guess."
32.		Reads sentence 7.
33.		"OK. So we got both of us here doing something and I can't
34.		ask to do something which is better than I'm already doing."
35.		Reads sentences 8 and 9.
36.		"To the most senior of the guests—I guess that means the oldest."
37.		(pause) "Hmm. OK. So from the host to the most senior of the
38.		guests. Ah. The transfer of the task means the doing of
39.		the tasks, I guess, so the host starts out doing all the tasks
40.		and we want to end up with the oldest guest doing all of the
41.		tasks, I suppose. Ahh . . . Let's think about that.
42.		Let's say the host is doing all five tasks.
43.		He's stoking the fire, fanning the flames, cakes,
44.		tea, poetry and the other two
45.		doing nothing."

Figure 1. The initial segment of the problem solving protocol.

ond is the *Construction* process in which the newly extracted information is checked against and added to the subject's develop-ing model of the situation described in the problem text. Passages in the protocol which illustrate alternation between these two processes may be seen in figure 1 at lines 1–2, 12–14, 15–17, 18–22, 23–25, 28–32, 33–35, and 36–42. Each of these eight passages begins with a short direct quote from the problem text. The reading of these quotes signals the initiation of the *Language* process.

The last part of each of the eight passages reflects the subject's attempt to interpret the information extracted from the segment of text he has just read. The subject's interpretations are clearly more than simple paraphrases of the text since they contain information which, while consistent with the text, was neither required nor suggested by it. For example, in lines 13–14 the subject introduces himself and his friend as participants in the Tea Ceremony. In lines 18–22, he assigns spatial relations to the three participants which were nowhere suggested by the text. Notice that the subject continues to appear as a participant in all the passages but the last one. These interpretations by the subject reflect the operation of the *Construction* process.

The transition between the first and the second process is frequently marked by the use of the conjunction, *so*. In four of the eight passages, *so* follows the quote immediately (lines 13, 16, 24, and 34). In two others, *so* also appears, but only after the meaning of a lexical element has been clarified (lines 29–31 and line 37). If we assume, as seems reasonable, that these lexical clarifications are part of the *Language* rather than the *Construction* or some other process, then *so* marks the transition between the two processes in six of the eight cases.

Examination of the sequence in which the subject reads the sentences of the text yields further suggestions about the nature of the processes which he employs in understanding the text. In the segment of protocol shown in figure 1, there are 22 transitions from one text sentence to another. Of these, 16 are in the forward direction—from an earlier to a later sentence—and six are in the backward direction. In all cases, the forward transitions are from a sentence to its immediate successor in the text—that is, the forward

transitions never skipped a sentence. Twelve of the 16 forward transitions occurred without intervening comment by the subject. These appear to reflect the normal process of reading sentences of text in sequence.

Of the remaining four transitions, three were associated with passages which we classified above as reflecting the *Construction* process. In all three cases, the process succeeded in the sense that the subject completed an interpretation of the text segment without discovering a contradiction. The three passages may be found at lines 16–17, 31–32, and 34–35. In the one remaining transition, seen at lines 26–28, the subject's comment, "Hmm. What does this mean?" suggests a failure to interpret the extracted information but does not indicate that the subject has discovered a specific area of conflict which might guide his search for new information.

Of the six backward transitions, two occur after the subject has read the last text sentence. At this point, of course, any transition would have to be a backward transition. Of the remaining four backward transitions, three were associated with failures of the *Construction* process. (In lines 2, 13–15, and 24–25 in figure 1, there is evidence of the failed construction processes. The fourth transition (figure 1, lines 8–12) is not obviously associated with such a failure. The box score is shown below.

		Construction Process		
		succeeds	fails	uncertain
transition	forward	3	0	1
	backward	0	3	1

These results suggest that forward transitions are associated with success of the *Construction* process and that backward transitions are associated with its failure.

While we will not focus on the later stages of problem solution in this chapter, we should comment on them here to place the *Understanding* process in appropriate context. The segment of protocol which we have examined above covers the beginning of the experimental session and is concerned entirely with understanding the problem and not at all with taking steps to solve it. We could as easily have selected a segment at the end of the experimental session which would be concerned entirely with solution and not at all with understanding. Such protocols, like the segment quoted below, consist largely of sequences of legal moves:

—the senior guest will ask to recite poetry from the host. OK. The junior guest then asks to pour the tea from the host. . . .

Between these two extremes, in the middle part of the experimental session, the protocol reflects both attempts to understand the problem and attempts to solve it.

The processes of *Solving* and of *Understanding* appear to alternate with one another much in the manner of the *Language* and *Construction* processes described above. That is, failure of the *Solving* process appears to cause the subject to return to the *Understanding* process.

We want to call attention to the rapid alternation between these two processes when the subject is attempting to interpret a difficult section of the text. This alternation of processes provides a key to the subject's procedures for constructing the problem space. A preliminary model of the relations among these processes is described below and summarized in the

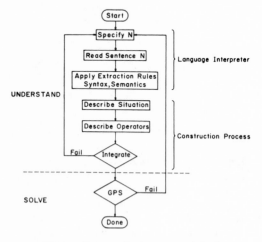

Figure 2. A preliminary model of understanding: flow diagram of the processes.

form of a flow diagram in figure 2. A simulation which we will describe later provides a detailed realization for the *Extraction* and *Construction* process, although not of the actual alternation process. Inside the boxes in figure 2 are the names of programs used in the simulation.

The Model

In the model (figure 2), we will view problem solution by the naive subject as employing two complex and interacting processes: an *Understanding* process that generates a problem space from the text of the problem, and a *Solving* process that uses the problem space to explore steps toward solving the problem. A problem solving episode is assumed to start with the *Understanding* process, to end with the *Solving* process, and to alternate frequently between these two processes in the intervening interval. The *Solving* process is assumed to control problem solving in the sense that it begins to run as soon as enough information has been generated about the problem space to permit it to do anything. When it runs out of things to do, it calls the *Understanding* process back to generate more specifications for the problem space. With this arrangement, the text of the instructions is interpreted only to the extent that is necessary in order for the *Solving* process to arrive at a problem solution. Any parts of the text that are irrelevant to that goal may remain uninterpreted or only partly interpreted.

The *Understanding* process consists of two subprocesses (figure 2): a *Language* interpreting process and a problem space *Construction* process. The process for interpreting *Language* reads the sentences of the problem text and extracts information from them, guided by a set of information extraction rules. These rules identify the moods of the text sentences, identify noun groups that refer to physical objects and activities, and assign such relations to them as "agent," "instrument," "property," "location," and so on, much in the manner of a case grammar (Fillmore, 1968). In the Tea Ceremony problem, the

Language process must recognize "the inns" and "a most civilized and refined tea ceremony" as noun groups, "in the inns" as a locative phrase, and so on.

The *Construction* process accepts information, sentence by sentence, from the *Language* interpreting process and builds a representation of the problem space, consisting of two parts: a *Situation* description and a set of *Operators*. The description of the *Situation*, based on information extracted from sentences in the indicative mood, represents the problem elements (e.g., inns, villages, host, and so on), relations among problem elements (e.g., The inns are located in the villages), and the initial and goal states of the problem.

The set of *Operators*, identified from information extracted from conditional statements and sentences in the subjunctive mood, constitutes a production system in which the conditions are represented as states (or aspects of states) of the *Situation*, and the actions are represented as processes for making changes in the *Situation*. As we will see, a major responsibility of the *Construction* process is to make certain that the representation of the *Situation* is compatible with the representation of the *Operators*, so that the *Operator* process will perform correctly in changing the *Situation*.

The problem *Solving* process works by running the *Operators* generated by the *Construction* process under the control of a problem solving strategy of some kind. If the *Solving* process fails to achieve a solution, either because it runs out of things to do, or because it encounters a contradiction, it calls back the *Understanding* process to elaborate or alter the problem space in order to resolve the conflict.

SIMULATING THE UNDERSTANDING PROCESS

In the previous section we examined the behavior of a human subject in the laboratory, confronted with instructions for a task with which he was not previously familiar. We have observed the subject as he gradually acquired an understanding of the task. On the basis of our examination of the subject's protocol, we then sketched out a model to describe his behavior.

Another approach to the understanding of understanding is to construct a computer simulation of the process. There already exist in the literature a number of examples of "understanding" programs, although these were constructed mainly as explorations in artificial intelligence and not as specific simulations of the human processes. Before we go on to describe the simulation program we have built to explain human behavior in the Tea Ceremony task, it will be instructive to take a brief look at these earlier efforts.

Previous Understanding Programs

The broad outlines of the understanding program described here derive from the HEURISTIC COMPILER (Simon, 1972), an early exploration of the possibilities of constructing a problem solving program capable of writing computer programs from English-language instructions. The problem solving component of the HEURISTIC COMPILER was modeled on the GENERAL PROBLEM SOLVER; that is, it accepted as input a formalized description of the program to be written and used means-ends analysis to produce code corresponding to the description. The "front end" of the HEURISTIC COMPILER, a rather primitive interpreter of natural language, accepted an English-language description of the programming problem and produced from it the formalized description that the problem solving component required as its input.

The HEURISTIC COMPILER's capabilities for interpreting natural language instructions were primarily semantic rather than syntactic in character. It was not capable of handling a wide range of English constructions, but only relatively simple descriptive prose; hence, it needed only relatively simple processes to discover the underlying phrase structure and convert the input sentences into internal list structures. Of more interest is the fact that it was capable of expanding these input sentences, supplying various omissions and ellipses, by matching them to information already stored in semantic memory. Thus if the input sentences referred to a "state description," the HEURISTIC COMPIL-ER would find in semantic memory a full and rather elaborate characterization of a state description and could use the information contained in that character-ization to supply missing information about state descriptions that was needed to formulate the programming problem for the problem solving component of the system. Since we will be using the same techniques in the present system (but with rather more elaborate syntactic capabi-lities), there is no need to describe here just how the HEURISTIC COMPILER accomplished this semantic analysis. The interested reader is referred to the published description (see Simon, 1972).

Bobrow (1968) constructed an early program for understanding natural lan-guage in algebra story problems in order to set up the equations for solving the problems. His program demonstrated that only relatively simple syntactic analysis was required when the task itself supplied a sufficiently rich semantic environment. Raphael (1964, 1968) constructed a ques-tion answering scheme, SIR, that accepted natural language questions and used var-ious kinds of stored semantic information to draw inferences and to answer the questions.

Another understanding program, the General Game Playing Program (GGPP), was constructed by T. G. Williams (1972) to show how the information contained in a source like Hoyle's Book of Games could be translated automatically into a program that would play (legally if not well) any one of the games described there. Thus, GGPP was confronted with exactly the same task we posed to our subjects in the present study—to extract from written instructions the description of a task and to program itself to perform that task. GGPP did not accept natural English text as input; the information had to be put into a proper language for it. But the inputs it accepted contained essentially

the same information about the game as was provided by Hoyle. The program had general capabilities for making moves or plays in board and card games, for sorting decks, and for matching patterns, and could store in semantic memory in-formation about decks of cards, and so on, that could subsequently be applied as an aid in interpreting the rules of par-ticular games. (For example, "a bridge hand consists of 52 cards, deuce through ace, in four suits.") GGPP could interpret the instructions for most kinds of card and board games.

An understanding program constructed by D. S. Williams (1972) programmed itself to perform tasks (to answer items on an intelligence test), but avoided the problem of natural language interpretation by inducing the task requirements, instead, from worked-out examples presented to it. Programs constructed by Coles (1972) and Siklóssy (1972) had capabilities for under-standing natural language input but em-ployed these capabilities to a rather different end than the one under considera-tion here. They are relevant, however, to the general problem of using semantic information as an aid to the interpretation of natural language. Coles used information derived from pictures to select the correct interpretations of sentences that were syntactically ambiguous. Siklóssy used matched pairs of pictures and sentences, in the manner of the Ogden and Richards "Language Through Pictures" series, to enable his program to induce the grammar of a natural language.

Moore and Newell (1974) describe a sys-tem, MERLIN, designed to perform vari-ous kinds of understanding tasks and to ex-plore the general nature of understanding processes. In a later section of this chapter, we will have some comparisons to make be-tween the notions of understanding that are embodied in MERLIN and those incorpo-rates in the program we are about to de-scribe. The schemes reviewed in the pre-ceding paragraphs, together with a number of other schemes for handling natural language are discussed and compared by Simon and Siklóssy (1972, chap. 2).

The state of the art of natural language processing, as of about 1972, is captured very well by Winograd's (1972) SHRDLU program. SHRDLU interprets statements and questions in English, using a case grammar that facilitates matching syntactic with semantic information. On the basis of the input questions or commands, SHRDLU then provides answers or carries out the commands, using for this purpose a reasoning program, PLANNER. Thus the language processing component and the problem solving component of SHRDLU stand in the same relation as the language processing component and the problem solving component of the HEURISTIC COMPILER, or of the system to be described here.

All the programs described in this section are to be viewed primarily as studies of artificial intelligence schemes.

The UNDERSTAND Program

We have written a computer program, UNDERSTAND, as a first approximation to the processes used by our human subjects to understand the instructions of the Tea Ceremony problem. As we stated earlier, the process of understanding a task begins with the presentation of the task instructions to the subject and ends when the subject has acquired a program that enables him to undertake to perform the task. If the task involves solving a problem, then the product of the understanding process is a problem solving program appropriate to the task in question.

In the UNDERSTAND program, we have not tried to simulate the alternation of phases between *Understanding* and *Solving* that we observed in the subject's protocol. and in this respect the program fails to capture the temporal sequence of the human processing. It seemed to us that, in this first approximation, the initial job was to see how information in the task instructions could be combined with semantic information assumed to be already available to the subject in such a way as to permit the subject to interpret the instructions as an appropriate input to his

problem solving processes. We leave the alternation of phases to a later time when this initial problem has been adequately solved, and we can undertake a second approximation.

The problem solving program that the subject acquires through the understanding process defines for him: (1) a basic problem space in which he can carry on a search for the problem solution. (2) one or more operators for moving through the problem space, and (3) one or more, tests for determining the presence or absence of particular features at any node in the problem space. The problem-solving program that is developed under these circumstances need not be manufactured out of whole cloth. The subject may come to the experimental situation already provided with more or less general problem solving capabilities. Under these circumstances, understanding means representing the new task to himself in such a way that some of these general problem solving capabilities can now be used for tackling it. We can imagine the *Solving* processes mentioned earlier as having two components: a more or less general program for solving problems and a set of specific inputs to that program which define a particular problem for it in such terms that it can go to work on the problem. If such a factorization is possible, then the task of the *Understanding* processes is to provide this second component, in proper format, to the problem solving program.

In the present instance, we will assume that the problem solving program which is the target of the understanding process resembles the General Problem Solver (GPS) (Ernst and Newell, 1969), in its general shape. The principal inputs that GPS requires, before it can go to work on a problem, are (1) a representation of the successive states of the problem solving situation (i.e., of the nodes in the problem space), (2) one or more processes or actions for changing one of these states into another (for making legal, and possibly illegal, moves), (3) a set of differences for describing states and comparing pairs of states, and (4) a table of connections between differences and actions, which prescribes the possible actions that may be taken when each kind of difference is encountered. Providing GPS with these four kinds of information about a task environment enables it to undertake problem solving activity in that enviroment.

Not all this information needs to be supplied to GPS from external sources. Equipped with appropriate learning programs, GPS might be expected to develop the third and fourth classes of information by itself, that is, to induce from the description of the problem space a list of differences and to induce from these and from the operator or operators for changing states a table of connections between differences and actions. Several investigators have discussed learning programs for GPS-like problem solvers that are capable of carrying out these learning tasks—of inducing differences and the table of connections. (A number of such learning programs are described and discussed in Eavarone and Ernst, 1970; Ernst and Newell, 1969; Newell, 1963; Newell, Shaw, and Simon, 1960.)

To strip our problem to its barest essentials, we will assume that GPS is equipped with such a learning program. Hence, what remains for the understanding process is to generate from the problem instructions the representation of problem states, one or more processes for changing states, and one or more tests for the presence or absence of particular features in a state. If the task, for example, were to learn to play checkers from a set of written instructions, the understanding program would have to be able, by reading the instructions, to generate a representation for the checker board and checker positions and to generate a process for making checker moves.

In the problem before us, the Tea Ceremony, the task for the understanding program is to find a way to represent the successive situations during the ceremony —specifically, to represent the distribution of tasks among the participants—and to construct a program for transferring a task from one participant to another. Moreover, the transfer program must operate properly

upon whatever representation has been constructed. The latter is a nontrivial requirement, for we will see that it is probably most expedient to generate the two main outputs of the understanding program—the representation of situations and the transfer process—more or less independently of each other. Hence, the transfer process must be sufficiently flexible to adapt itself to the particular representation that has been chosen, whatever that may be.

Whether the scheme described above and the program developed out of that scheme actually describe how human subjects go about understanding task instructions is, of course, an empirical question, to be settled by comparing the output of the understanding program with the subjects' protocols. In the present chapter we will not undertake a detailed comparison of the UNDERSTAND program with the protocol we presented and discussed in the previous section. Our main concern is to see whether we can in fact produce from the Tea Ceremony instructions an appropriate set of inputs for a GPS-like problem solver. As in other simulation environments, an important first step is to produce a set of processes that are sufficient for the task. Determination of how closely these processes approximate to the human processes can be postponed until this first step has been taken.

Processing Stages

The UNDERSTAND program carries out its work in two discrete stages which correspond to two of the components of the model described earlier (figure 2).

1. The task instructions are read and reread. They are analyzed syntactically and semantically to extract from them their "deep structure," as linguists use that term. As before, we will refer to the processes that do this as the *Language* processes.

2. The deep structures of the sentences describing the task are analyzed further by matching them against a set of requirements that specify the form of an accept-

able input to GPS. We can think of these requirements as a set of templates in long-term memory that provide a model for a well-formed problem, in the sense of GPS. We will call this second set of processes the *Construction* processes.

The input to the first stage is the text of the task instructions, and the output is the deep structure of the text (figure 5). The input to the second stage is the deep structure, the output is a task specification in a form suitable as input to GPS (figures 7, 8, and 9). Since the problem solving process can now go to work on this task specification, the latter represents the subject's understanding of the problem.

As before, we are oversimplifying when we describe the understanding process as proceeding in two sequential stages. We have seen in the human protocol strong evidences of alternation of processes from the *Understanding* to the *Solving* processes and back, and this surely implies, within the *Understanding* processes, some alternation between *Language* and *Construction*.

Language: Extracting Deep Structure from Text

That portion of the simulation which is concerned with extracting the deep structure from the text has been realized mostly in PAS-II (Waterman and Newell, 1973). PAS-II is a flexible interactive computer program designed as an aid to the process of protocol analysis. In particular, it was designed to take as input a problem solving protocol and a description of the problem space that the subject used to solve the problem and from these to trace the sequence of operators that the subject applied in solving the problem. For example, PAS-II will provide an analysis of a cryptarithmetic protocol if it is given a description of the subject's problem space, including both the knowledge elements that the subject identifies in the problem (e.g., letters, digits, parity, and so on), and a list of the operators that are available to the subject (e.g., operators that assign a value to a digit or that process a column).

In the present context, we have made use of PAS-II in a manner parallel to, but different from, its originally intended use. We have used it to accept as input the problem text and a set of text-reading rules, and to generate as output a set of syntactically and semantically interpreted elements from which the second part of the UNDERSTAND program can derive the problem space that is implied in the problem description.

Since PAS-II has convenient facilities for defining sets of processing rules (e.g., segmentation rules, grammar rules) that can be applied in an arbitrary order designated by the user, it is well adapted to this new task. PAS-II also provides compact notations for expressing grammatical and semantic relations, a number of editing, storage, and other utility functions, and interactive capabilities.

General Organization

We have divided the task of extracting the deep structure into three phases, accomplished in sequence: (1) a syntactic phase that parses sentences, (2) a semantic phase that identifies significant relations and assembles structures that have special meaning (e.g., lists and quotes), and (3) a cross-reference phase that handles inter-sentence relations such as anaphoric reference. The first two of these phases operate on the text one sentence at a time. In the third, or cross-reference, phase, the text is considered as a whole.

The Syntactic Phase. The syntactic analysis is accomplished by applying three types of rules to the input sentences. These are segmentation rules, grammar rules, and integration rules. The function of the segmentation rules is to break complex sentences into smaller, more easily handled, segments. For example, the segmentation rules separate the subject from the predicate of a sentence by breaking after a noun that is followed by a verb. This separation simplifies the identification of the object of the sentence by preventing confusion between the subject and the object. The segmentation rules also break after commas, colons, semicolons, and relatives such as "which" and "that."

For example, sentence 2 of "The Tea Ceremony" is broken into three parts by the segmentation rules:

"The ceremony"

"involves a host and exactly two guests,"

"neither more nor less."

The grammar rules assign grammatical classes to words and to groups of words. First, single words are classified as nouns, verbs, adjectives, determiners, and so on. Then more complex units are identified by the ordering and grammatical classes of the words that comprise them. For example, in parsing the segment of sentence 1, "a most civilized and refined tea ceremony," the words were classified respectively as determiner, adjective, adjective, conjunction, adjective, noun, noun. The string adjective-conjunction-adjective was classed as a conjoined adjective, and the two nouns were classed as a noun string. Then the whole structure, because it consisted of a noun string preceded by an optional adjective string preceded, in turn, by an optional determiner, was classed as a

noun-group with "ceremony" as its head. Finally, the structure was reclassified—as are all noun-groups and pronouns that are not possessive pronouns—as an object. The output of the grammar rules for this segment was the element (**OBJ CEREMONY**).

The output of the grammar rules for the segment, "is practiced, . . ." is the element (**VG IS PRACTICED**), indicating a verb-group with "practiced" as the main verb and "is" as the auxiliary. When there is no auxiliary, the marker, "aux" appears in the auxiliary position.

In addition to noun-groups and verb-groups, the grammar identifies prepositional phrases (" . . . to them . . . " = (PHR TO THEM)), time marks ("When . . ." = (TMARK)), modal auxiliaries (" . . . may . . . " = MODAL)), groups defined as a digit followed by a plural noun (" . . . two guests . . . " = (GR TWO GUESTS)), and about 20 others. Figure 3 shows the output of the grammar rules for each of the sentences of the problem text.

The integration rules are applied to the output of the grammar rules. These rules serve the function of assembling correctly

```
          : : SENTENCE 1
(PHR IN INNS) (PHR OF VILLAGES)
(VG IS PRACTICED) (OBJ CEREMONY)
          : : SENTENCE 2
(OBJ CEREMONY)
(GR TWO GUESTS) (VG < AUX > INVOLVES) (OBJ HOST) (AND)
(ADJNEG MORE) (ADJNEG LESS) (COMMA)
          : : SENTENCE 3
(OBJ GUESTS) (TMARK)
(PHR AT TABLE) (CONJVG (VG HAVE ARRIVED) (VG HAVE SEATED)) (OBJ
   THEMSELVES)
(OBJ HOST) (COMMA)
(GR FIVE SERVICES) (PHR FOR THEM) (VG < VAUX > PERFORMS)
          : : SENTENCE 4
(OBJ SERVICES)
(LIST) (EXTD NOBILITY)
(OBJ HIMALAYANS)
(PRH TO THEM) (VG < AUX > ATTRIBUTE) (COLON)
(ACT STOKING FIRE)
(ACT FANNING FLAMES) (COMMA)
(ACT PASSING CAKES) (COMMA)
(ACT POURING TEA) (COMMA)
(ACT RECITING POETRY) (COMMA)
```

```
              : : SENTENCE 5
(COTEMP CEREMONY)
(GROUP THOSE-PRESENT) (COMMA)
(VG < VAUX > ASK) (OBJ ANOTHER) (MODAL)
(OBJ SIR) (QUOTE) (COMMA)
(OBJ I) (MODAL) (COMMA)
(MEMB THIS ONEROUS TASK) (PHR FOR YOU) (VG < VAUX > PERFORM)
   (QUOTE) (QUEST)
              : : SENTENCE 6
(HOWEVER)
(OBJ PERSON) (COMMA)
(PHR OF ANOTHER) (VG < AUX > REQUEST) (MODAL)
(EXTM LEAST NOBLE TASKS) (ONLY)
(OBJ OTHER)
(VG IS PERFORMING)
              : : SENTENCE 7
(FURTHER)
(OBJ PERSON) (IF) (COMMA)
(GROUP TASKS) (VG IS PERFORMING)
(OBJ HE) (COMMA) (THEN)
(EXTD TASK) (VGNEG < AUX > REQUEST) (MODAL)
(MEMB NOBLEST < ADJ > TASK) (VG < AUX > IS) (OBJ HE) (COMP
   NOBLER < ADJ >)
(VG IS PERFORMING)
              : : SENTENCE 8
(OBJ CUSTOM)
(VG < AUX > REQUIRES) (REL)
(OBJ CEREMONY) (TMARK)
(VG < AUX > IS) (FINAL)
(GROUP TASKS) (COMMA)
(MEMB MOST SENIOR GUESTS) (PHR FROM HOST) (VG WILL
   TRANSFERRED) (PREP TO)
              : : SENTENCE 9
(OBJ THIS) (QWORD HOW) (MODAL)
(VG BE ACCOMPLISHED) (QUEST)
```

Figure 3. Output of the grammar rules
applied during syntactic processing of the
problem text.

parsed sentences from the grammatically classified elements. Included among the integration rules are rules that identify sets of objects (defined as a group or an object joined to another group or object by "and"), subsets of sets, and lists (defined as ordered sets). Other integration rules assemble predicates from verb groups, objects, phrases, and time markers, and then construct sentences by adding subjects to these predicates. The output of the integration rules for sentence 2 is

```
(SEN CEREMONY INVOLVES
(HOST (TWO GUESTS) ) D T)
(SET HOST (TWO GUESTS) )
   (SUBSET (TWO GUESTS) )
(NEGADJ MORE) (NEGADJ LESS)
```

In the first line of the output above, "D" is a place-holder for an indirect object and "T" is a place-holder for a time mark such as "Initial" or "Final". The negative adjectives will be ignored by the program hereafter, since they have failed to find

SEMANTIC 2 MODE

       :: SENTENCE 1
(REL LOC INNS VILLAGES) (REL LOC CEREMONY INNS)
(PRED (IS PRACTICED) CEREMONY D T))
       :: SENTENCE 2
(REL PART CEREMONY (MOST (TWO GUESTS)) D T)
(SET HOST (TWO GUESTS)) (SUBSET (TWO GUESTS))
(ADJNEG MORE) (ADJNEG LESS)
       :: SENTENCE 3
(TMARK Q) (REL LOC GUESTS TABLE) (SEN GUESTS (VG HAVE SEATED)
  GUESTS D Q) (SEN GUESTS (VG HAVE ARRIVED) NIL D Q)
(REL DO HOST (FIVE TASKS) (FOR GUESTS) Q)
(SET (FIVE TASKS))
       :: SENTENCE 4
(LIST TASKS (NOBILITY A) L)
(SEN HIMALAYANS (<AUX > ATTRIBUTE) (NOBILITY A) (TO THEM) T)
(STRING ((ACT STOKING FIRE) (ACT FANNING FLAMES) (ACT PASSING
  CAKES) (ACT POURING TEA) (ACT RECITING POETRY)))
       :: SENTENCE 5
(COTEMP CEREMONY) (MODAL)
(REL ASK (GROUP THOSE PRESENT) OB (OF ANOTHER) T)
(QUOTE) (INDIR SIR)
(QUEST) (REL DO I (MEMB THIS ONEROUS TASK) (FOR YOU) T
(QUOTE)
       :: SENTENCE 6
(HOWEVER) (MODAL)
(REL ASK PERSON (MEMB ONLY (LEAST NOBLE) (TASKS A)) (OF
  ANOTHER) T)
(REL DO OTHER (TASKS A) D T)
       :: SENTENCE 7
(FURTHER)
(IF) (MODAL) (REL DO PERSON (GROUP TASKS) D T)
(THEN) (REL (NO ASK) HE (TASK A) D T)
(SEN (TASK A) (IS (COMP NOBLER < ADJ >))
  (MEMB NOBLEST < ADJ > TASK) D T)
(REL DO HE OB D T)
       :: SENTENCE 8
(SEN CUSTOM (<AUX > REQUIRES) REL D FINAL)
(TMARK FINAL) (SEN CEREMONY (<AUX > IS) OB D FINAL)
(REL TRANS (GROUP TASKS) HOST (MEMB MOST SENIOR GUESTS)
  FINAL)
       :: SENTENCE 9
(QWORD HOW) (QUEST) (REL DO THIS OB D T)

Figure 4. Output of semantic processing.

a place in any structure of interest to the UNDERSTAND processes. Execution of the integration rules marks the end of the syntactic phase of the *Language* program.

Semantic Phase. Processing in the semantic phase is accomplished by two sets of rules which we will call the Semantic1 rules and the Semantic2 rules. The Semantic1 rules search for sentences that have verbs denoting important relations, such as ASK, DO, and PARTICIPATE and transform them into the corresponding relations. For example, the segment of sentence 7, "if a person is performing any tasks, . . . " which the syntactic phase has coded as:

(IF) (SEN PERSON PERFORMING
(GROUP TASKS) D T)

is transformed into:

(IF) (REL DO PERSON (GROUP
TASKS) D T)

Figure 4 shows the output of the Semantic1 rules for each of the sentences in the problem text.

The Semantic2 rules carry out the final stage of semantic processing. These rules use the special marks left in the text by the earlier processing stages, e.g, (QUOTE), (QUEST), (STRING X), to assemble complex structures (quotes, questions, and lists—ordered sets). For example, lines 12–15 figure 4 are transformed to:

(REL ASK (GROUP (THOSE
PRESENT)) LIT (OF ANOTHER) T)
(REL (ASK DO) I (MEMB THIS
ONEROUS TASK) (FOR YOU) T)

In the first line, the marker "LIT" indicates that the object of the relation "ASK" is a quote, the interpretation of which follows in the next line. The relation (ASK DO) stands for the complex relation of "asking to do" constructed from the "ASK" relation and the action of doing involved in the quote that the relation contained. Lines 7 and 8 figure 4 are transformed into:

(LIST TASKS NOBILITY ((ACT
STOKING FIRE) (ACT FANNING
FLAMES) (ACT PASSING CAKES)
(ACT POURING TEA) (ACT
RECITING POETRY)))

Cross-referencing. Currently, cross-referencing is handled by an auxiliary SNOBOL program called JTEA. This program performs two functions:

1. It traces anaphoric references and replaces pronouns with the referenced nouns.

2. It handles words such as "further" and "however" that link sentences together. It does this by (1) matching elements in the two sentences to be sure that the subscripts are assigned in a consistent way across sentences (e.g., that "PARTICIPANT.1" in sentence 5 refers to the same object as "PARTICIPANT.1" in sentence 6. The matching is accomplished by searching for an identical verb in the two sentences and establishing that the matched objects bear identical relations to it. (2) It then assembles the two sentences into a single sentence and deletes the linking word.

Figure 5 shows the final result of the processes for extracting the deep structure from the problem text. Now the *Construction* processes must be applied.

Construction: Representation and Transfer Processes

In figure 5 we show the interpreted text as it emerges from the parsing process, that is, in the form of the "deep structure" of the original problem instructions. In the present section, we describe the portions of the understanding program that take this interpreted text as input and produce a representation for the various states of the problem situation and a process for transferring tasks from one of the participants to another. The latter process will also incorporate tests for guaranteeing that the conditions stated in the problem for a "legal" transfer are satisfied; that is, that the task being transferred is the least noble of the tasks being performed by the person from whom it is taken, and is less noble than any of the tasks of the person who takes it.

Representing the Situation

In preparation for subsequent processing steps, the program examines the text to find the whole set of participants and the whole list of tasks, then it converts this set and this list into an appropriate internal representation, assigning to the set and list their

DEEP 2 MODE

(REL LOC INNS VILLAGES) (REL LOC CEREMONY INNS)
(PRED (IS PRACTICED) CEREMONY D T)
(REL PART CEREMONY (HOST TWO GUESTS) D T)
(SET HOST (TWO GUESTS)) (SUBSET (TWO GUESTS))
(ADJNEG MORE) (ADJNEG LESS)
(REL LOCA GUESTS TABLE) (SEN GUESTS (VG HAVE SEATED) GUESTS
   D Q) (SEN GUESTS (VG HAVE ARRIVED) NIL D Q)
(REL DO HOST (FIVE TASKS) (FOR GUESTS) Q)
(SET (FIVE TASKS))

(LIST TASKS (NOBILITY A) ((ACT STOKING FIRE) (ACT FANNING FLAMES)
   (ACT PASSING CAKES) (ACT POURING TEA)
   (ACT RECITING POETRY)))
(SEN HIMALAYANS (< AUX > ATTRIBUTE) (NOBILITY A) (TO THEM) T)
(COTEMP CEREMONEY) (MODAL)
(REL ASK (GROUP THOSE PRESENT) LIT (OF ANOTHER) T)
(REL (ASK DO) I (MEMB THIS ONEROUS TASK) (FOR YOU) T)
(HOWEVER) (MODAL)
(REL ASK PERSON (MEMB LEAST NOBLE (T ASKS A)) (OF ANOTHER) T)
   (REL (NO ASK) PERSON (MEMB NO (LEAST NOBLE) (TASKS A))
   (OF ANOTHER) T)
(REL DO OTHER (TASKS A) D T)
(FURTHER)
(IF) (MODAL) (REL DO PERSON (GROUP TASKS) D T)
(THEN) (REL (NO ASK) HE (TASK A) D T)
(SEN (TASK A) (IS (COMP NOBLER < ADJ >)) (MEMB NOBLEST
   < ADJ > TASK) D T)
(REL DO HE OB D T)
(SEN CUSTOM (< AUX > REQUIRES) REL D FINAL)
(SEN CEREMONY (< AUX > IS) OB D FINAL)
(REL TRANS (GROUP TASKS) HOST (MEMB MOST SENIOR GUESTS)
   FINAL)
(QWORD HOW) (QUEST) (REL DO THIS OB D I)

Figure 5. Deep structure of the problem
text.

types, to the list its ordering relation (OR-DER), and to the members of each their respective types. The resulting structures, obtained by processing sentences 2 and 3, respectively, are shown in figure 6.

The program searches the text for a sentence in the declarative mood that is labeled with a time tag, on the assumption that such a sentence will be descriptive of the situation at some stage in the problem. The first such sentence it discovers in the processed text is sentence 2, which describes the problem situation at the outset of the

Tea Ceremony. The program takes this as the information from which it will undertake to construct a representation of the situation. The sentence asserts a relation between the host and the tasks.

Now the program is ready to create a description of the initial situation. Sentence 2 asserts a relation, DO, between an object of the class, PARTICIPANT, and a list of objects of the class, TASK. The attribute, PARTICIPANT, is associated with the structure, SITUATION; and the list of participants is associated with this attribute

TASK = 'FIRE FLAMES CAKES TEA POETRY:, TYPE LIST, ORDER NOBILITY'
FIRE = ':, TYPE TASK'
FLAMES = ':, TYPE TASK'
CAKES = ':, TYPE TASK'
TEA = ':, TYPE TASK'
POETRY = ':, TYPE TASK'

PARTICIPANT = 'HOST GUEST.1 GUEST.2:, TYPE SET.'
HOST = ':, TYPE PARTICIPANT'
GUEST.1 = ':, TYPE PARTICIPANT'
GUEST.2 = ':, TYPE PARTICIPANT'

Figure 6. List structures obtained for sentences 2 and 3.

as its value. The participant on this list that is synonymous with "HOST" is assigned the attribute, TASK, and the list of tasks that, according to sentence 2, the host is performing is assigned as the value of this attribute. The resulting description of the situation is shown in figure 7.

The Transfer Process

The program next seeks information about the operators for the Tea Ceremony. Employing as its cue the use of the subjunctive mood, it discovers that sentences 5 through 7 of figure 5 have been tagged as a production—that is, as describing an action. In sentence 5 it discovers the rela-

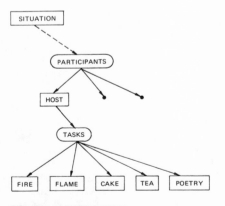

SITUATION = " : ,PARTICIPANT L1,"

L1 = " HOST GUEST.1 GUEST.2 : ,TYPE SET,"

HOST = " : ,TYPE PARTICIPANT,TASK L2,"

L2 = " FIRE FLAME CAKE TEA POETRY : ,TYPE LIST,ORDER NOBILITY,"

Figure 7. Description of the situation.

tion ASK:DO having three arguments: the task, the participant making the request, and the participant currently performing the task. That is, ASK:DO is of the form:

REL (TASK,PARTICIPANT.1,
PARTICIPANT.2).

The next step is to search semantic memory for the meaning of this relation—that is, for a known process having the same formal structure as ASK:DO and having associated with it a procedure for actually executing the process. In the present version of the system, the proper formal structure is identified by *Match*, a process that compares the given relation with a relational structure in semantic memory and determines whether the former is isomorphic with the latter. Here "isomorphic" means that the given relation has the same number of arguments as the relation in semantic memory and that these arguments are distributed in the same way among arguments of different types. To accomplish its task, *Match* makes use of a subroutine, *Class*, which identifies the types of the arguments in each relation and counts the number of arguments of each type.

In the instance before us, the given relation has three arguments, one of one type (TASK), and two of another type (PARTICIPANT). In semantic memory, we find the relation, *Transfer*, which also has three arguments, one of the type OBJECT, and two of the type ACTOR. The *Match* process therefore succeeds in

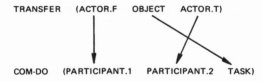

Figure 8. Matching the arguments of the transfer relation into the relation COM-DO.

mapping REL upon *Transfer*, with TASK corresponding with OBJECT, and PARTICIPANT.1 and PARTICIPANT.2 corresponding with ACTOR.F and ACTOR.T, respectively (see Figure 8).

Associated with the transfer process in semantic memory is a procedure for actually carrying out a transfer. We can now use that procedure, on the basis of the identification we have made of the components of ASK:DO with the components of *Transfer*, to execute the action called for by ASK:DO, that is to transfer a task from one participant to another. However, two things remain to be done: to add to ASK:DO the specific conditions for a legal move in the Tea Ceremony and to adapt the code for the transfer operation to the particular representation we have chosen for the problem space. We will take up these two points in reverse order.

Fitting Process to Representation. The coding procedure associated in semantic memory with *Transfer* is very general and flexible. If it is provided with information about the representation that has been selected, the procedure will perform a transfer operation appropriate to that representation. In the case before us, a task is a member of the value list of the attribute TASK of the participant who is performing it. To transfer that task from one participant to another, we must delete it from the list on which it appears and add it to the list of tasks that is the value of the attribute TASK of the participant who receives it.

The information that *Transfer* needs about the representation is provided by the process called *Describe. Describe* examines the representation of the situation and produces a description of the way in which the relation between a task and the participant who is performing it is represented (Figure 9). In the case before us, the description would read: TASK MEMBER VALUE TASK, which may be translated, "TASKS are stored as MEMBERS of the list of VALUES of the attribute TASK of the structure PARTICIPANT.X." The description produced by *Describe* also indicates where information about the participants is stored in relation to the structure, SITUATION. In the present case, the description would read: PARTICIPANT MEMBER VALUE PARTICIPANT, which may be translated, "PARTICIPANTS are stored as MEMBERS of the list of VALUES of the attribute PARTICIPANT of the structure SITUATION."

The *Transfer* process uses the latter description to *Find* the structure associated with PARTICIPANT.1, then uses the former description to find the task to be transferred on this structure and deletes it from the list. The *Transfer* process next uses the second description to *Find* the structure associated with PARTICIPANT.2, then uses the first description to add the task to the list of tasks associated with this structure.

The *Transfer* process will use the same method to carry out the transfer for other representations of the data—it will *Find* the first participant, delete the task to be transferred, *Find* the second participant, and add the task to those associated with him. The transfer will also be performed correctly if participants are associated with tasks instead of tasks with participants. In this case (which will be disclosed by the output of *Describe*) *Transfer* will *Find* the task to be moved, *Find* the participant associated with it, and change the latter to the participant who is to receive the task.

VSIT = ":, WHICH PARTICIPANTS, PARTICIPANTS MEMBER, TASKS MEMBER VALUE TASKS,"

Figure 9. The relation between a task and the participant who is performing it.

Conditions for a Legal Transfer

To define a complete process for a legal move (i.e., a legal transfer of a task) in the Tea Ceremony, the program must be able to test whether a particular task is the least noble of the tasks being performed by one of the participants (the donor); and whether this task is less noble than all the tasks being performed by another participant (the one requesting the task). The process LIST('TASK', 'PARTICIPANT.X') will produce a list, in order of nobility, of all the tasks that are being performed by PARTICIPANT.X. The *List* process, like *Transfer*, is independent of the particular representation that has been selected to describe the situation. It acquires this independence by making use of the description of the situation produced by *Describe* to find PARTICIPANT.X in the structure that describes the situation and then to find all the tasks assigned to PARTICIPANT.X. From the list, TASK, it obtains the tasks, ordered by the relation of NOBILITY.

List will operate equally well if the situation is described in terms of tasks and the participants responsible for them, as if it is described, inversely, in terms of participants and the tasks they are performing. In either case it produces an ordered list of those tasks that are being performed by the participant in question.

With the output of *List* in hand, it becomes an easy matter to determine whether a particular task is the least of an ordered list (i.e., its last member), and whether the task is less than all members of such a list. The former test is performed by the function LEAST, the latter by the function LESSA (for "less than all"). Thus to test whether the conditions are satisfied for transferring TASK.4 from PARTICIPANT.2 to PARTICIPANT.3, we first execute the test:

LEAST('TASK.4',LIST('TASK', 'PARTICIPANT.2'))

and then, if that test succeeds, the test:

LESSA('TASK.4',LIST('TASK', 'PARTICIPANT.3'))

Accommodating the Transfer and Find Processes

Making the *Transfer* process and the *Find* process that it employs independent of the representation exacts a heavy price in terms of processing time and complexity. Each time these processes are executed, the description of the representation must be reexamined, and a multitude of tests must be carried out to choose the correct path through the routines. The inefficiency is twofold: (1) only a small part of the total routine, *Transfer*, or *Find*, is relevant to any particular problem representation, and (2) tests on the description of the representation to determine which path to follow make up a considerable part of the processing. The processing could be carried out much more rapidly if these inefficiencies could be removed.

The phenomenon we are describing has a clear human counterpart. When a human subject learns a new procedure that is necessary for carrying out a task, he executes the procedure haltingly, stopping along the way to ask himself: "What do I do next?" or "Where am I?" As he executes the procedure repeatedly, he begins to transfer more and more of the steps to long-term memory, so that he can retrace the path "automatically," without these halts, hesitations, and tests. It is our hypothesis that his increasing speed and sureness of performance results specifically from replacing a "general purpose" program, replete with tests for selecting his path in a given situation, with a special program tailored to the current representation he is employing, and omitting the tests as inessential.

To simulate this hypothesized human assimilation process, we assume a gradual transfer to long-term memory of the steps in *Transfer* and *Find* that are actually executed, omitting those steps that are information gathering tests on the description of the representation. Thus, there are gradually created in long-term memory, streamlined versions of *Transfer* and *Find*—call them STRANFER and SFIND, respectively—that permit automatization of these operations.

RELATION OF PROTOCOL TO PROGRAM

Since the UNDERSTAND program is intended only as a first approximation of the process by which our subject understands the problem text, we did not expect (and have not observed) a detailed correspondence between the behavior of the subject and the behavior of the program. Indeed, we have not as yet attempted to derive a complete problem behavior graph from the protocol. However, we have observed some interesting correspondences between the protocol and some of the global features of program organization which suggest that at least the major processes are grouped together appropriately and that they are arranged in roughly the right order.

Earlier analysis of the protocol focused on the content of the subject's statements strongly suggested that the subject employs two distinct processes in understanding the problem—a *Language* process which extracts information from short segments of text and a *Construction* process which integrates the information derived from the text into a unified model. This conclusion was supported by two observations:

1. Transition from the *Language* process to the *Construction* process is frequently marked by use of the conjunction *so*.

2. The sequence in which the sentences were read was influenced by the subject's success or failure in finding an interpretation in his model for the information from the text. Thus, the *Language* process appeared to be controlled by the *Construction* process, and hence, to have a role distinct from it.

Further evidence concerning the differentiation of these two major processes may be obtained by examining the subject's difficulties in understanding sentences 5 and 6 of the problem text. In essence, what we will argue is that information analyzed in an earlier stage of processing by the *Language* process may be reanalyzed and given a new interpretation at a later stage of processing by the *Construction* process.

A major difficulty in interpreting sentences 5 and 6 stems from the ambiguity of the construction "perform . . . for" in the question "may I perform this onerous task for you?"[1] Suppose that A asks B, "May I pour tea for you?" This may mean that A has responsibility for pouring tea and that he wants to exercise that responsibility for B's benefit by pouring tea into B's cup. On the other hand, it may mean that B has responsibility for pouring tea and that A wants to relieve B of that responsibility. The first interpretation is the one most strongly suggested in the context of sentence 3. One expects a gracious host to perform activities for the benefit of his guests. Only the second interpretation, however, is consistent with sentences 6 through 8, since these sentences clearly require that responsibility for the tasks be transferred among the participants. Both interpretations are compatible with sentence 5.

We believe that the *Language* process assigned the first meaning to "perform . . . for" in sentences 3 and 5 and the second meaning in sentences 6 and 7. The disparity between these two meanings first became important when the subject attempted to integrate the information in sentences 5 and 6 into a single representation. The attempt at integration is first revealed in lines 13–15 of figure 1 when the subject says, "so if my friend is performing a bunch of tasks, I can request—wait a minute—something's fishy here." The subject is in the process of interpreting sentence 6 and has just assigned some tasks to "the other" represented in his model by his friend. Allowing ourselves to speculate freely about what the subject is thinking at this point, we generate the following scenario. The subject, trying to represent the request mentioned in sentence 6, imagines himself asking his friend if he

---

1. Webster's Collegiate dictionary (1961) lists eleven definitions of the preposition "for" of which only three are appropriately used with the verb "perform." In the first, "for" is synonymous with "instead of"; in the second, it is synonymous with "in behalf of"; and in the third, it expresses duration of time as in "for hours." Only the first two of these meanings are used in the protocol.

may perform one of the friend's tasks. The form of the request that he imagines, however, derives from sentence 5, and the meaning of "perform" in that request is different from the one required in sentence 6. At the moment when he says, ". . . I can request . . . . wait a minute . . . Something's fishy here," he recognizes that the request as he has formulated it is inappropriate for accomplishing the transfer required in sentence 6 and thus derives the first clue to the conflict in the meanings of "perform." After reexamining sentences 5 and 6, he responds to this inadequacy again in line 25 when he says, ". . . But if all I can ask him is . . . .".

The conflict between the two meanings is finally resolved in lines 29–32. In lines 29–30, the subject clearly recognizes that the critical difference in the meanings is whether the asker or the person asked has the initial responsibility for performing the task. In lines 31–32, he chooses the second meaning.

To summmarize, what we derive from this sequence is evidence consistent with our position that two distinct processes are involved in understanding the problem; a first process which assigns meanings to sentences taken one at a time and a second process which integrates the meanings of the sentences.

Another example which illustrates the integration of meanings may be found in lines 31–34 of figure 1. Sentence 6, which focuses on the tasks "the other" is doing, yields the interpretation in line 31, "So he is doing something. . . ." Sentence 7, which focuses on the tasks which the asker is doing, might be expected by itself to yield an interpretation such as, "So I am doing something. . . ." In fact, the interpretation of sentence 7 at line 34 is, "So we got both of us here doing something. . . ." This suggests the integration of information derived separately from sentences 6 and 7.

Evidence of the operaton of a *Describe-Situation* process may be found in lines 2–4, where the subject identifies the set of participants, in lines 9–10, where he identifies the list of tasks, and in lines 40–42, where he states the initial and final conditions of the problem. Evidence of the operation of a *Describe-Operator* process may be found in lines 39–40, when the subject says, "The transfer of the tasks means the doing of the tasks. . . ."

The evidence that we have presented here is extremely fragmentary and in no sense establishes the reality of the processes we have postulated. Only careful analysis of many problem solving episodes can provide the kind of evidence we require.

LESSONS FOR UNDERSTANDING

Moore and Newell (1974) provide a general discussion of what it means for a system to "understand." Their viewpoint is that a system understands knowledge to the extent that it uses the knowledge whenever it is appropriate. How well does the UNDERSTAND system that we have been describing in this chapter meet this criterion? And is the identical task with which we have confronted our human subjects properly regarded as a test of understanding?

Does This Task Require Understanding?

With respect to the second question, clearly learning about a task from written instructions is a test of understanding of those instructions. The instructions contain knowledge about the task imbedded in English prose, and the evidence that the subject has used the knowledge appropriately is that, after a time, he is able to try to perform the task. We say "try to perform" because the issue is not whether he can solve the Tea Ceremony problem, but whether he comes to know what the problem is.

The nature of the understanding so achieved is most evident from an examination of the UNDERSTAND program. "Using the knowledge when appropriate" means, in this context, using it to construct a problem representation that will serve as input to a problem-solving program. That the subject also constructed such a representation is evident from his verbalizations of his attempts to operate the model of the situation that he produced. We can say, therefore, that both computer program and human subject understood the task instructions, for they used the knowledge contained in them, successfully, for the purpose for which they were intended.

How Full is the Program's Understanding?

Understanding is not an all-or-none affair. One can speak of degree, range, and depth of understanding. Moore and Newell (1974) provide a useful checklist of dimensions of understanding. It will be instructive to apply this checklist to the UNDER-STAND program, to see what kinds of generality it possesses and along what dimensions it is limited. In assessing both generality and limitations, however, we need to bear in mind that the limitations will be of at least two different kinds. Certain kinds of understanding may be unachievable because of limitations built into the very structure of the program. A program might be so built, for example, as to be inherently incapable of forms of understanding that humans achieve through processes of visualization.

Other kinds of understanding may be lacking to a system not because of structural deficiencies but because it does not possess critical specific pieces of information that it needs to perform a task given it. For example, to perform the Tea Ceremony task, a system needs a certain knowledge of English vocabulary and English syntax. The brightest person in the world will not be able to understand the task instructions if he knows no English. But this kind of deficiency is less incorrigible than the kind first mentioned. If the system's structural capabilities are adequate, then it can be supplied with specific information of the second kind as it needs it for any given task.

One should not be too glib about "supplying" information to a system—whether computer or human. Computers are notoriously hard to program, and humans almost as notoriously hard to educate. Nevertheless, the distinction between structural limitations of understand-

ing systems and limitations stemming from remediable lacks of specific information is important for any evaluation of a system's performance and prospects.

Moore and Newell (1974) take up eight dimensions of understanding in their analysis: representation (completeness, "grain," multiplicity of representations), ability to convert knowledge to action, assimilation of the external environment, accommodation to the external environment, directionality, efficiency, tolerance of error, and depth of understanding. Let us see how UNDERSTAND fares with respect to each of these.

Representation

UNDERSTAND does not encode information into specialized formats, but holds it internally in the form of list structures, that is, lists and descriptions (alias semantic nets, association networks, colored graphs). It is well known that these are perfectly general structures: anything that can be symbolized can be symbolized with their help.

But to encode something is one matter, to encode it in such a way that it is usable is another. UNDERSTAND has no particular capabilities for selecting a problem representation that will facilitate solving the problem. It is, in fact, closely bound to the stimulus in the representation it constructs. Change in the wording of the text of instructions will cause UNDER-STAND to change its representation of the problem.

By the same token, UNDERSTAND is not capable of constructing more than one representation for a given problem—in the way, for example, that a person solving a mathematical problem may carry along both an algebraic and a geometric version of it. In general, we may say that, although UNDERSTAND can understand task instructions in order to construct a problem representation from them, it does not understand the design and modification of representations as a means for facilitating problem solution. It is not able to apply information toward that goal.

Efficiency

There is little we can say about the efficiency of the UNDERSTAND program, beyond what has already been said in the discussion of representation and accommodation. The chief efficiency issue for a program of this kind is probably not how efficiently it achieves an understanding of the text, but whether the understanding, once achieved, is in such form as to facilitate its subsequent problem solving efforts.

Error

The UNDERSTAND program has little or no capability for recovering from error. Its chief protection against erroneous interpretation of information is to leave it uninterpreted unless the interpretation is clear. This is an important technique that has not been much exploited in artificial intelligence programs (see Siklóssy, 1972), but which is probably much used by humans. When we do not understand a sentence, we can go back and read an earlier sentence that may help us interpret it, or we may continue reading until we gain other information that helps us understand it.

In contrast to the simulation program, the human subject gives evidence of having error-recovery capabilities. For example, he first appears to interpret "for him," in the expression "to do something for him," as meaning "on his behalf." Only after this interpretation leads him into difficulties does he explore the alternative: "in place of him."

Depth of Understanding

Does a human "understand" arithmetic if he can add two numbers and get the correct sum? Or does he understand only if he can state Peano's postulates for the integers and derive the sums table from them? Or do we have to test his understanding in some other way? We would probably be inclined to say that the second test implies deeper understanding than the first. It implies that the performer cannot merely

do something, but that he knows what makes it work.

We could ask a whole host of comparable questions about the UNDERSTAND program. It understands the text of instructions well enough to construct a problem representation, but it does not understand why it wants such a representation. It can "understand" the structure of a representation well enough to write a description of it, for use by the *Find* and *Transfer* processes, but not well enough to manipulate the representation into a more useful form. Understanding in complex environments of this kind is not a unitary thing; it can be tested in many ways, and passing one test offers no guarantee of passing others.

The Program and Human Understanding

If our main interest lay in artificial intelligence, then we would want the UNDERSTAND program to understand in the deepest, most efficient, most flexible way possible. However, we developed this program not as an exercise in artificial intelligence but as an attempt at a first-order approximation to human understanding in this task environment. A human being does not usually understand a difficult problem quickly, deeply, efficiently, and in the most flexible way possible. Part of our task is to identify the limitations—structural limitations and limitations of knowledge—of the human seeking to understand written instructions.

It is probable that humans, like the UNDERSTAND program, are severely stimulus-bound with respect to the particular representation they construct. For many problems—expecially puzzlelike problems—finding the good representation is the nub of the problem. What is the human capability for solving problems, like the problem of the mutilated checkerboard, that are of this kind? Inventing a new representation or shifting from one problem representation to a more appropriate one are acts of human creativity that occur rather rarely, even with intelligent persons. A program with strong capabilities of this kind, if we could invent one, would probably not provide a good simulation of human capabilities or limitations.

Similar comments could be made with respect to the other dimensions of understanding we have discussed. The real test of whether the UNDERSTAND program has the right characteristics to simulate humans is to compare its behavior in different task environments with records of the behavior of human subjects. The program may equally well fail by showing too much understanding as by showing too little. We would be hard pressed, until we have carried our analysis much farther than we have to date, to say whether the subject whose protocol we discussed here was more skillful or less skillful than the UNDERSTAND program in understanding the text of the Tea Ceremony instructions.

Converting Knowledge to Action

The UNDERSTAND program has a number of important capabilities for translating knowledge into action. These capabilities exist at two levels. In the first place, the central objective of the program is to translate static knowledge, in the form of English language prose, into an input suitable to a general problem solving program such as GPS. We can view the problem solving program itself as an interpreter and the input that defines a particular task domain and problem for it as a program to be interpreted. Thus, the translation process dynamicizes the knowledge contained in the static instructions— makes it interpretable.

The second way in which the UNDERSTAND program translates knowledge into action is by assimilating information in the task instructions that refers to task actions or moves (e.g., the transfer of a task from one participant to another in the Tea Ceremony). Stored in the program's long-term memory is information about how to execute certain quite general processes, like the TRANSFER process. Assimilating an action mentioned in the task instructions to such a general process stored in memory gives the UNDERSTAND program the

ability actually to execute that action in the context of the problem representation.

Assimilation

The generality of the UNDERSTAND program's assimilative powers depends on the generality of its capabilities for processing the English language and the repertoire of actions that is stored in its long-term memory. The actual program as it now stands is quite limited in these respects. We have limited its linguistic knowledge and its knowledge of actions pretty much to the specific needs of the Tea Ceremony task. But, in terms of our earlier distinction, the limits are mainly limits of education and not limits of educability.

The machinery of PAS-II makes it quite easy to supplement the syntactical and semantic rules with new or modified ones. To be sure, if we multiplied the amount of information about language now stored in PAS-II by 10 or 100, we would have to reorganize the memory storage somewhat, to avoid lengthy linear searches through it; but methods for searching efficiently through large memories, by providing them with appropriate accessing routes or "indexes" are now pretty well known, and this can hardly be regarded as a structural limitation on the system.

Similarly, while UNDERSTAND now possesses knowledge of only a few active processes (TRANSFER, LEAST, LESSA), there is no in-principle reason why this repertoire cannot be expanded. Moreover, examination of the *Transfer* process, and the matching procedure that underlies its application, suggests that the number of different processes that commonly arise in representing problem situations may not be large. The *Transfer* process as it now stands, for example, can be interpreted to handle all the kinds of processes that are defined as "moves" in common games.

Accommodation

The line between assimilation—taking in information from the external environment—and accommodation—adapting the internal system to the requirements of the external environment—is not easy to draw. If we think of constructing the problem space as assimilation, then the UNDERSTAND program does relatively little that can be interpreted as accommodation. It does not store the results of its understanding in long-term memory in such a way as to facilitate the solution of new problems that may be posed to it. The one process we have described that might be considered to be accommodation is the process for streamlining the *Transfer* process once it has been adapted to a particular problem representation.

Directionality

The UNDERSTAND program's strong sense of directionality derives from its single-purpose nature. It is designed to do just one kind of task: to translate problem instructions into a form that makes them suitable as inputs to a problem solver. It can do whatever the situation calls for, provided that this is what it does call for. This does not mean that the general principle underlying the UNDERSTAND program could not be used in programs with other goals. Indeed, the HEURISTIC COMPILER is an example of an earlier program that used the same idea to another end. The HEURISTIC COMPILER also derived its directionality from templates stored in longterm memory of the kind of object it was seeking to construct. In that case, the desired object was a computer program in a certain format.

Hence, we can say of directionality as we said of assimilation, that the underlying principle of the UNDERSTAND program is quite general, while its present implementation is quite limited and specific.

Conclusion

We have set ourselves the goal of describing the processes by which a person understands a set of written problem instructions. This chapter reports the first phase of our work toward that goal. We have made progress in two directions. First, through protocol analysis, we have identified, at least tentatively, a network of functions involved in the subject's attempts to understand the problem text. Second, in the UNDERSTAND program, we have provided a set of well-specified processes that perform some of the identified functions. In specifying these processes, we have made some choices that have theoretical implications for psychology, For example, the structure of the transfer process and the nature of the language analysis both make strong assertions about the understanding process—assertions that can be checked against data.

The work reported here represents only a first step toward the goal of discovering exactly how people extract meaning from task instructions. We may list some of the tasks that remain to be carried out:

1. An important feature of our subject's behavior. the alternation between the text-reading and the problem-solving functions. must be simulated. In its present form, the UNDERSTAND program may be viewed as simulating the subject's behavior through his first reading of the text up to the point at which he first attempts to run his model of the problem. The simulation must now be carried forward to include processes by which the subject's attempts to run the model, either through their success or their failure, provide new information to guide the text interpreting processes in returning again to the problem instructions.

2. We need to carry out protocol analyses formally and in detail, and we need to widen our data base. Data from other subjects and from a wider variety of problems (including variants of the instructions for the Tea Ceremony, as well as other isomorphs of the Tower of Hanoi problem) must be analyzed and compared in detail with simulation programs.

We are encouraged by our progress to date to believe that thinking-aloud protocols of naive subjects trying to interpret the instructions of a new task, combined with simulation programs embodying some of the processes we have incorporated in UNDERSTAND, provide us with powerful tools for examining the processes of human understanding.

References

Bobrow, D. G. Natural language input for a computer problem-solving system. In M. Minsky (Ed.), *Semantic information processing.* Cambridge, Mass: M.I.T. Press, 1968, pp. 146–226.

Coles, L. S. Syntax directed interpretation of natural language. In H. A. Simon, & L. Siklóssy (Eds.), *Representation and meaning.* Englewood Cliffs, N. J.: Prentice-Hall, 1972, pp. 211–87.

Duncker, K. On problem solving (trans. L. S. Lees, from 1935 original), *Psychological Monographs,* 1945, 58 (Whole No. 270).

Eaverone, D. S., & Ernst, G. W. A program that discovers good difference orderings and tables of connections for GPS. *Proceedings of 1970 IEEE Systems Science and Cybernetics Conference,* New York: IEE, 1970, pp. 226–34.

Ernst, G. W., & Newell, A. *GPS: A case study in generality and problem-solving.* New York: Academic Press, 1969.

Fillmore, C. J. The case for case. In E. Bach & R. T. Harms (Eds.), *Universals in linguistic theory.* New York: Holt, Rinehart & Winston, 1968, pp. 1–88.

Moore, J., & Newell, A. How can MERLIN understand? In L. W. Gregg (Ed.), *Knowledge and cognition.* Potomac, Md.: Erlbaum, 1974, pp. 201–52.

Newell, A. Learning, generality, and problem solving. *Proceedings of the AFIP Congress,* 1963, 62, 407–12.

Newell, A., Shaw, J. C., & Simon, H. A. A variety of intelligent learning in a general problem solver. In M. A. Yovitz & S. Cameron (Eds.), *Self-organizing systems.* New York: Pergamon Press, 1960, pp. 153–89.

Newell, A., & Simon, H. A. *Human problem solving.* Englewood Cliffs, N. J.: Prentice-Hall, 1972.

Raphael, B. A computer program which "understands". *Proceedings of the 1964 AFIPS Fall Joint Computer Conference,* 1964, pp. 577–89.

Raphael, B. SIR: Semantic information retrieval. In M. Minsky, (Ed.), *Semantic information processing.* Cambridge, Mass.: MIT Press, 1968, pp. 33–145.

Rouse-Ball, W. W. *Mathematical recreation and essays.* New York: Macmillan, 1962.

Siklóssy, L. Natural language learning by compter. In H. A. Simon & L. Siklóssy (Eds.), *Representation and meaning.* Englewood Cliffs, N. J.: Prentice-Hall, 1972, pp. 288–328.

Simon, H. A. The heuristic compiler. In H. A. Simon & L. Siklóssy, (Eds.), *Representation and meaning.* Englewood Cliffs, N. J.: Prentice-Hall, 1972, pp. 9–43.

Simon, H. A., & Siklóssy, L. (Eds.) *Representation and meaning.* Englewood Cliffs, N. J.: Prentice-Hall, 1972.

Waterman, D. A., & Newell, A. *PAS-II: An interactive task-free version of an automatic protocol analysis system.* Pittsburgh: Department of Computer Science, Carnegie-Mellon University, 1973.

Williams, D. S. Computer program organization induced from problem examples. In H. A. Simon & L. Siklóssy (Eds.), *Representation and meaning.* Englewood Cliffs, N. J.: Prentice-Hall, 1972, pp. 143–205.

Williams, T. G. Some studies in game playing with a digital computer. In H. A. Simon & L. Siklóssy (Eds.), *Representation and meaning.* Englewood Cliffs, N. J.: Prentice-Hall, 1972, pp. 71–142.

Winograd, T. Understanding natural language. *Cognitive Psychology,* 1972, 3, 1–191.

7.2

The Understanding Process: Problem
Isomorphs (1976)

with John R. Hayes

In the previous chapter and in Hayes and Simon (1975) the authors have developed a theory about human understanding of written instructions. The formal theory is embodied in a computer program, UN-DERSTAND, which simulates these understanding processes. UNDERSTAND takes written problem instructions in natural language as input and produces internal representations of the problems and the legal move operators as outputs. A program that is capable of simulating performance in the actual task requires that all component processes be specified completely. The construction of UNDER-STAND, therefore, called for a substantial number of choices among alternative processing assumptions. In some cases, little or no empirical evidence was available for preferring one processing alternative to another.

This research has been supported by Public Health Service Grant MH-07722 from the National Institute of Mental Health and by National Science Foundation Grant GS-38533. The authors are grateful to Don Waterman and David Kieras for many discussions on the subject of this paper.

Thus, several weakly motivated assumptions were, perforce, incorporated in the UNDERSTAND program. It is the main purpose of this chapter to analyze evidence that bears on the validity of some of the more important of these assumptions. The principal evidence to be examined consists of verbal thinking-aloud protocols obtained in an experiment in which different subjects were presented with different, but isomorphic, forms of a problem. (We will define "isomorphic" presently.) Some additional supporting evidence was obtained from an experiment, also using these isomorphs of the same problem, in which protocols were not recorded, but subjects were allowed to use paper and pencil in working the problem. In this latter experiment, the notations adopted spontaneously by the subjects are our primary data.

The subjects' task was to understand written problem instructions in natural language. There is, of course, no unique way to describe a given problem in natural language. Moreover, for any particular problem, it is usually easy to construct problem isomorphs—that is, problems whose solutions and moves can be placed in one-to-one relation with the solutions and moves of the given problem. By comparing and contrasting protocol data from subgroups of subjects presented with different classes of isomorphs, we can begin to see what particular aspects of the instruction text have major importance for task performance, and we can assess the validity of some of the basic assumptions incorporated in the UNDERSTAND program.

The problems used in this study were thirteen variants of a single problem, all formally isomorphs of the Tower of Hanoi puzzle. (See figure 1 for an example). That is to say, successive situations in these task environments could be mapped, in one-to-one fashion, on arrangements of disks on pegs in the Tower of Hanoi puzzle; and legal moves for each of the problems could be mapped into legal moves of the Tower of Hanoi. In fact, any of the problems could have been solved by mapping it into the corresponding Tower of Hanoi problem and then solving the latter. No subject did this, and only two or three even thought of trying or noticed the analogy. The problems, then, were identical in formal structure, but differed in their "cover stories."

PREDICTIONS OF THE UNDERSTAND
PROGRAM

The UNDERSTAND program postulates that understanding written instructions for a problem involves constructing an *internal representation* (in long-term memory) of the problem space and a set of *operators* for making "moves" from one situation to another in that problem space. Such an internal representation and such a set of operators constitute the principal inputs that a program such as the General Problem Solver (Newell and Simon, 1972, chap. 8) requires in order to set to work solving the problem. In the present form of the theory, there is no feedback from solution attempts to understanding—the problem is assumed to be fully understood before the solution processes begin their work. This is one of the assumptions of the theory we wish to test. As an alternative, it is easy to imagine a feedback loop, so that, after

initial interpretation of the problem instructions, unsuccessful attempts at solution reveal inadequate understanding of the instructions and lead to additional efforts of interpretation. Does understanding wholly precede solution attempts, as the present program assumes; or are these two processes intermingled, with the solution processes returning control, from time to time, to the understanding processes?

The UNDERSTAND program itself has two main components. The first is a set of language processes, which take the instruction text and, using both syntactic and semantic means, extract from it a deep structure. The second component is a set of construction processes, which take the deep structure produced by the language processes and construct from it the internal problem representation and the legal move operators. Again, language and construction processes are assumed to work sequentially, in that order, without feedback. We will have occasion to discuss here only some general features of these processes; a detailed description of the program is found in chapter 7.1.

The language processes incorporate a more or less conventional case-grammar parser. The system does have capabilities, however, for tracing anaphoric references across sentence boundaries. When a particular portion of the text cannot be parsed, it is simply dropped from consideration. Apart from anaphoric reference, little contextual meaning is carried across sentence boundaries; for the most part, the text is processed "locally," sentence by sentence.

The construction processes combine information extracted from the text by the language processes with several kinds of information already stored in semantic memory. First of all, the representation-constructing processes have built into them the assumption that problem situations can be represented as list structures expressing the relations among the objects and attributes mentioned in the problem instructions, and specifically, mentioned in the sentences that describe the initial problem situation. Hence, under this assumption, the representation is not created from the

S1. Three five-handed extraterrestrial monsters were holding three crystal globes.

S2. Because of the quantum-mechanical peculiarities of their neighborhood, both monsters and globes come in exactly three sizes with no others permitted: small, medium, and large.

S3. The medium-sized monster was holding the small globe; the small monster was holding the large globe; and the large monster was holding the medium-sized globe.

S4. Since this situation offended their keenly developed sense of symmetry, they proceeded to transfer globes from one monster to another so that each monster would have a globe proportionate to his own size.

S5. Monster etiquette complicated the solution of the problem since it requires:

S6. (1) that only one globe may be transferred at a time,

S7. (2) that if a monster is holding two globes, only the larger of the two may be transferred, and

S8. (3) that a globe may not be transferred to a monster who is holding a larger globe.

S9. By what sequence of transfers could the monsters have solved this problem?

Figure 1. Monster problem 1.

entire problem text but from particular specific sentences in that text.

Second, the operator-constructing processes assume that the problem's legal move operators can be described in terms of a few basic types of operations on list structures, like "Transfer A from X to Y," "Exchange X with Y," "Copy A from X to Y," "Erase A at X," "Insert A at X," and so on. These are the standard types of operations that appear as the primitives in any list-processing language, and they bear a strong resemblance, also, to the elementary types of "actions" postulated by Schank (1972) in his semantic parsing schemes. We will look for evidences in our data for the subjects' use of these sorts of basic operations or actions, abstracted from the particularities of the specific task described in the instructions.

The operator-constructing processes extract these legal move definitions from the corresponding sentences of the task instructions, but interpret them in the light of the representation that has previously been generated by the representation-constructing processes. Hence, the final form these operators take is much more context-dependent than the form of the represen-

tation; the former depends on several portions of the problem text, the latter only on one or a few sentences. In the case of the "Monster problem" text of figure 1, the problem representation would be constructed by the UNDERSTAND program from information extracted from the third sentence of the instructions; while the operators would be constructed from the fourth sentence and the three conditions following it—but formulated in such a way as to operate correctly on the representation already constructed.

Finally, in handling anaphoric reference, the UNDERSTAND system must adopt conventions for naming objects. For example, in the initial situation described in figure 1, the "small monster" may also be referred to as the "monster holding the large globe." In the program as it is now constructed, the selection of a representation automatically determines which of these names will be applied (in fact, the former). This is an important assumption that we will also wish to test from the data of our experiment. We will discuss the psychological meaning of the assumption in a later section.

In the main series of protocols to be

Problem				
Number	Type	Sentence 3	Sentence 4	Sentence 7
1	T	The small monster held the large globe.	. . . to teleport globes . . . monster would have a globe proportionate to his own size.	If a monster holds two globes . . . can transmit only the larger.
2	T	The small monster stood on the large globe.	. . . to teleport them-selves . . . monster would have a globe proportionate to his own size.	If two monsters are standing on the same globe, only the larger . . . can leave.
3	C	The small monster was holding the large globe.	. . . to shrink and expand the globes . . . monster would have a globe proportionate to his own size.	If two globes are of the same size, only the globe held by the larger monster . . . can be changed.
4	C	The small monster was holding the large globe.	. . . to shrink and expand themselves . . . monster would have a globe proportionate to his own size.	If two monsters are of the same size, only the monster holding the larger globe can change.
5	T	The monster with the small name was holding the large globe.	. . . to transfer names . . . monster would have a globe proportionate to the size of his name.	If a monster has two names, . . . can transmit only the longer.
6	T	The monster with the small tail was holding the large globe.	. . . to transfer tails . . . monster would have a globe proportionate to the size of his tail.	If a monster has two tails, . . . can transfer only the longer.
7	C	The small monster was originally large.	. . . to shrink and expand themselves . . . monster would have his original size back.	If two monsters are the same size, . . . only the monster who was originally larger can change.
8	T	The monster with the small name originally had the large name.	. . . to transfer names . . . monster would have his original name back.	If a monster has two names, . . . can transmit only the longer.
9	T	The small monster was originally large.	. . . to transfer sizes . . . monster would have his original size back.	If a monster has two sizes, . . . can transfer only the larger.

Figure 2. The Monster problems.

examined here, the problem isomorphs were created from a single basic "cover story"—all were Monster problems—by making carefully structured changes in the language of the sentences (see figure 2). Since these sentences are used in this problem by the UNDERSTAND program to construct the problem representation and define the operators, changes in their wording can be expected to alter the representation and operator definitions. Specifically, the UNDERSTAND program will represent certain of these isomorphs as Change problems (i.e., problems whose legal-move operator is of the form "Change X to Y"); while it will represent other isomorphs as Transfer problems (i.e., problems whose legal-move operator is of the form "Transfer A from X to Y").

As can be seen from figure 2, sentence 3 of each problem refers to two classes of objects (e.g., in problem 5, "monsters' names" and "globes"). Sentence 4 designates the objects of one class as fixed, of the other as variable (e.g., in problem 5, the globe held by each monster is fixed, his name is variable). By sentences 7 and 8, the legality of moves depends on the ordering of one of the attributes (e.g., in problem 5, the names are ordered by length). If the ordering refers to the variable objects, the problem is a Transfer problem; if it refers to the fixed objects, the problem is a Change problem. Thus, problem 5 is a Transfer problem.

A problem is constructed by selecting the two classes of objects and their relation (e.g., "holding"), assigning one class to be fixed and the other variable, and choosing the problem form (Transfer or Change). Once these choices have been made, the problem instructions are determined. The reader can test his understanding of figure 2 by making up a full problem instruction for problem 5, using the language in the figure to replace the language for problem 1 in figure 1, and making the corresponding changes in the remaining sentences.

Readers familiar with the Tower of Hanoi problem can construct a set of instructions for that problem by taking pegs as the fixed objects and disks as the variable

objects and regarding the disks as ordered by size. An exactly isomorphic problem (but in Change rather than Transfer format) can be obtained by making pegs variable and disks fixed (i.e., assigning pegs to disks), but ordering again by disk size.

The authors have demonstrated in another series of experiments, concerned with problem difficulty, that Transfer problems can be solved by subjects nearly twice as fast as isomorphic Change problems (see chapter 7.3). In those experiments, the differences in solution times were traced to differences in the difficulty of executing comparison processes when applying the rules for a legal move. The authors also found that transfer of training, when problem isomorphs were presented successively, varied markedly with the pair of isomorphs presented. The authors proposed that these differences in transfer of training were determined largely by the process of formulating the rules for legal moves.

The UNDERSTAND program predicts that subjects will adopt different representations and operator definitions for isomorphic Transfer and Change problems; and these differences could explain the observed differences in problem difficulty and transfer of training. It is important, therefore, to see if direct evidence can be found to test the program's predictions. (Since the UNDERSTAND program, first constructed and debugged in the context of the Tea Ceremony problem of figure 3, has not yet been fully extended to handle the input language for all the isomorphs of the Monster Problem, the predictions we make here from the theory involve a certain amount of hand simulation of the program's behavior.)

The assumptions embedded in the UNDERSTAND program that lead to these predictions, made before the experimental facts just described had been discovered, are by no means obvious. Recall that all the tasks under consideration are isomorphic, hence are capable of being represented in the same problem space and with the same operators for legal moves. Since some of these representations have

1. In the inns of certain Himalayan villages is practiced a most civilized and refined tea ceremony.

2. The ceremony involves a host and exactly two guests, neither more nor less.

3. When his guests have arrived and have seated themselves at his table, the host performs five services for them.

4. These services are listed below in the order of the nobility which the Himalayans attribute to them:

     stoking the fire,
     fanning the flames,
     passing the rice cakes,
     pouring the tea,
     reciting poetry.

5. During the ceremony, any of those present may ask another, "Honored Sir, may I perform this onerous task for you?".

6. However, a person may request of another only the least noble of the tasks which the other is performing.

7. Further, if a person is performing any tasks, then he may not request a task which is nobler than the least noble task he is already performing.

8. Custom requires that by the time the tea ceremony is over, all the tasks will have been transferred from the host to the most senior of the guests.

9. How may this be accomplished?

Figure 3. A Tea Ceremony.

now been shown to facilitate solving the problem, and others to delay solution, it might be supposed that an instruction understanding process would involve not only discovering *some* representation for a problem, but discovering a particular representation that was convenient or facilitative. Alternatively, there might be associated with each problem a canonical representation, independent of isomorphic transformations; and the UNDERSTAND program could construct the identical canonical representation, whichever isomorph was presented.

The UNDERSTAND program predicts that neither of these will be the case; instead, the problem solver will adopt the first representation to which the surface description of the problem leads him, and this will be a good or poor representation depending on the characteristics of that surface description. This prediction derives, in turn, from two characteristics of the program: (1) the absence of feedback from the solution processes to the UNDERSTAND program, and (2) the "local"

operation of that part of the UNDERSTAND program that constructs the representation from a limited portion of the text of the instructions. The prediction might be thought to conflict with findings (e.g., Bransford and Franks, 1971) that differences in surface structure are often lost when sentences are processed and stored in memory. However, there is no real contradiction here. The prediction does not assert that all surface information is retained, but simply that when isomorphic information structures are expressed in quite different natural language encodings, they may lead to correspondingly different deep structure interpretations.

Thus we will be chiefly interested, in this chapter, in evidence relating to four aspects of the UNDERSTAND program: (1) the assumption that understanding will be achieved prior to the start of solution attempts, (2) the assumption that subjects will represent legal moves in terms of basic, rather abstract, information processes that operate upon list structures, (3) the prediction that the verbal form of the instructions will affect the naming of objects in specified ways, and (4) the prediction that the representations used in Change and Transfer problems will differ in specified ways. With these explanations of the purposes of this study, and the nature of the assumptions embedded in the UNDERSTAND program and their consequences, we turn now to the data and their analysis.

MATERIALS AND METHODS

The Data

Each of twenty subjects was given a one-page description of a puzzlelike problem and asked to solve it, thinking aloud as he worked. The recorded verbal protocols for these twenty problems constitute the data that we will analyze.

The subjects were male and female graduate students and faculty members at Carnegie-Mellon University. They were not previously familiar with the particular problems on which they worked, although a few of them had encountered at least one problem that was formally isomorphic to the one on which the protocol was taken. In only one case could a subject be described as "experienced" with problems of this kind. In any case, there was no evidence that their limited experience affected their behavior in the task, and some positive evidence that it did not—at least along dimensions relevant to our present discussion.

The tasks were the thirteen problem isomorphs described above, providing two or three different protocols for a few problem variants and a single protocol for each of the remaining variants. Since the problems are all formal isomorphs, we can regard them, for purposes of analysis, as a sample of tasks drawn from a well-defined population. Lacking a taxonomy of isomorphs in this populations, there is no way to sample from it randomly. Instead, we have simply generated a collection of isomorphs that vary along a number of dimensions and have carried out our analysis (1) by examining properties that are shared by essentially all the isomorphs and

(2) by dividing the isomorphs into dichotomous subclasses according to variables we had reason to think were important and comparing the properties of these subclasses. In this way we are able to establish some of the differences between the subclasses as being statistically significant.

Figure 1 gives the problem text for the variant called "A Monster Problem 1." Figure 2 describes variants of the Monster problem that we will have occasion to examine in detail. Figure 3 gives the problem text for the variant called "A Tea Ceremony," while figure 4 is a complete list of problems and subjects.

Method of Analysis

The methods that we have used previously for analysis of problem solving protocols—in particular, the problem behavior graph—are not suitable for the present undertaking. Use of the problem behavior graph to depict and summarize a subject's behavior requires that the subject operate in a well-defined problem space. This requirement is generally only met when subjects are confronted with well-structured problems of a sort with which they are already familiar (Newell and Simon, 1972).

In the present instance, however, it is precisely the process whereby the subject first constructs a new problem space in the face of a novel problem that chiefly interests us. In this experiment, the subjects had no prior experience with the problem instructions. Understanding those instructions—constructing a problem space, describing the initial problem situation, and constructing operators for changing the situation (making moves)—constituted their first task. We wish to find in the protocols evidence that shows what kinds of problem descriptions the subjects built and how they went about building them.

The principal evidence we have found in the protocols for identifying the subjects' problem spaces are: (1) the frequency with which they reread each particular sentence in the problem statement prior to their

Problem	Variant	Subjects	
		Number	Identification
Tea Ceremony	—	3	S1, S8, SM
Academic Problem	—	1	J.C.1
Moving Experience	—	1	D.M.
Monster Problem	1	1	M.Y.
	2	1	C.J.
	3	1	I.B.
	4	3	J.C.2, D.D., M.Y.
	5	2	J.P., G.L.
	6	1	K.K.
	7	2	L.A., R.B.
	8	1	B.C.
	9	2	J.C.3, B.T.
Nonsense Problem	—	1	J.B.

Figure 4. Problems and subjects.

first move attempt; (2) their verbal exchanges with the experimenter, initiated either by subject or by the experimenter; (3) the way in which subjects described moves and named objects in their move attempts; and (4) the way in which subjects described the current situation before or after a move attempt. In addition, the protocols were examined for explicit comments of the subjects that might reveal something about their representations of the problems.

At the end of the solution attempt, whether successful or not, subjects were debriefed by the experimenter, and we have found some of the comments during debriefing to be illuminating. In general, however, we have relied upon the subjects' thinking-aloud behavior while they were actually working the problems as the source of our evidence, rather than upon their subsequent introspections or retrospections about what they had been doing.

RESULTS AND DISCUSSION

Reading the Instructions

Among the 20 protocols, there were 28 occasions when a subject reread the sentence describing the initial problem situation (sentence 3) prior to his first attempted move. (See table 1.) There were 42 occasions when a subject reread one or more of the sentences in the problem instructions that defined the conditions for legal moves (sentences 6 through 8). There were 10 occasions when a subject reread the sentence (sentence 4) defining the problem goal, There were six occasions when a subject reread one of the other sentences (sentences 1, 2, or 9).

A subject will presumably reread a sentence if (1) he believes the information in the sentence is relevant to his task and (2) he does not, at present, retain that information in short-term or long-term memory. For example, in the Monster problems, we observe that sentences 1 and 2 contain mostly irrelevant information; all that needs to be retained from these sentences is that three monsters are holding three globes, and that monsters and globes each come only in small, medium, and large sizes. The rest of the information is irrelevant, and even the relevant information is largely redundant, being repeated in later problem statements. Sentence 9, similarly, contains only an easily remembered statement of the task. These three sentences are reread only infrequently. In subsequent work to be reported elsewhere

Table 1. Number of Times Instructions Were Reread Prior to Solution Attempts.

Problem	Number of Protocols	*Number of Rereadings of Sentence*			
		S3	S4	S6–8	*Other*
Monster Problems	14	23	9	32	5
Other Problems	6	5	1	10	1
All Problems	20	28	10	42	6

(Hayes and Waterman, 1974), a simulation of the relevance-judging process, called ATTEND, made essentially the same judgments about sentences 1, 2, and 9.

Sentence 4, while relevant (at least in its second clause), describes the goal in terms of a single simple condition (e.g., that globe sizes should correspond with monster sizes), which is easily remembered. This sentence, also, is reread only infrequently.

Sentence 3, on the other hand, is relevant and, moreover, involves three pairings of objects which are listed (except in five of the variants of the Monster problem) in an arbitrary order not corresponding to the order of sizes of either set of objects. The conditions of sentences 6 through 8 (and especially 7 and 8) were similarly complex and correspondingly difficult to retain in memory. Subjects had to return to all these more complex sentences. We conclude that frequency of rereading depends mainly on the relevance of sentences and the difficulty of holding their contents in memory.

After the subjects have begun to make moves, they still need sometimes to refer back to the problem instructions. These references are predominately to the move conditions, sentences 6 through 8, but occasionally also to the initial situation, sentence 3. Virtually no other sentences are reread after the subjects have actually begun to make trial moves in efforts to solve the problems.

The only aspect of these particular findings that is nonobvious is that subjects appear to be able to make judgments about the relevance of particular sentences in the problem statement at a relatively early stage (see also Hayes and Waterman, 1974, for additional evidence of this ability).

The UNDERSTAND program behaves in a similar fashion, for it only continues to process those sentences (3 through 8) that are relevant to the construction of the representation and operators. The program (and perhaps also the human subjects) can do this because its programs and stored semantic information tell it what it is looking for, and it need not depend upon explicit indications in the problem instructions to separate wheat from chaff.

Exchanges between Subject and Experimenter

If, during the taking of a protocol, the subject asked a question, the experimenter replied briefly. If the subject made an illegal move that was noticed by the experimenter, and the subject was proceeding to carry out further moves without checking, the experimenter interrupted to ask him to recheck the legality of the last move. A total of 76 exchanges between experimenter and subject were noted in the twenty protocols. If we classify these exchanges by their content, rather than by who initiated them, we find that 40 were Task exchanges, resulting from questions or confusions the subject had about the exact nature of the task. The remaining 36 exchanges may be classified as Application exchanges because they occurred after misapplications of the rules that produced illegal moves. All the Task exchanges and some of the Application exchanges were initiated by the subjects. (See table 2)

In 12 protocols, representing 71 of the total of 76 exchanges, examples of both Task and Application exchanges occurred. In only seven cases among these 71 exchanges did a Task exchange occur after the first Application exchange. In four of the seven cases, when this happened the

Table 2. Exchanges between Subjects and Experimenters.

Type of Exchange	Number of Protocols	Number of Exchanges
All Kinds	20*	76
Task	14	40
Application	13	36
Both	12	71

*Includes five protocols having no exchanges.

subject started a new solution attempt from the beginning.

These data lend themselves to a rather straightforward interpretation. In general, subjects did not attempt a solution of the problem until they thought they understood the instructions. As postulated by the UNDERSTAND program, the understanding processes usually preceded the solving processes. In achieving their understanding, most subjects (15 of the 20) asked one or more clarifying questions of the experimenter.

Contrary to the assumption of the UNDERSTAND program, however, there was some evidence of feedback from the solution-seeking processes to the understanding processes and a consequent interweaving of the two. Many subjects, when they attempted to undertake a solution of the problem, made illegal moves, either because they had forgotten the conditions or the current situation, or (but less frequently) because they did not, in fact, have an accurate understanding of the problem instructions. In the latter case, recognition of the error often led to reinterpretation of the task instructions (and sometimes new Task questions), whereupon the subject began his solution attempts over again. As noted above, however, there were only seven instances of this interweaving of the two processes.

Of the 40 Task questions, three-quarters (31) refer to just seven topics (table 3). Three subjects asked if the problem had a unique solution. Three asked whether they might use pencil and paper. Although sentence 6 gives a clear negative answer, five asked whether two or more moves could be made simultaneously (e.g., whether globes could be "exchanged" between

monsters). Five asked whether a move from "large" to "small" had to pass, by two steps, through "medium." Five asked questions about the meaning of the ordering relation in sentences 7 and 8. Seven asked whether two or more globes could be held simultaneously (i.e., whether there was always a one-one relation between monsters and globes). The three subjects doing the Tea Ceremony problem all asked the meaning of "senior guest." The remaining nine questions covered a wide range of topics without any particular discernible pattern.

All these questions can be interpreted as responses to ambiguities in the task instructions (only occasionally do subjects fail to notice information that is explicit). Except for the question about the term "senior guest," the questions were not specialized to these particular problems; rather they were mostly questions about how the problem moves should be interpreted semantically, but at a relatively abstract level. Was simultaneity excluded?

Table 3. Number of Task Questions, by Topic.

Question	Number of Questions
Can hold several globes simultaneously?	7
Simultaneous moves (exchanges) legal?	5
Must moves pass through "medium" (continuity)?	5
Meaning of ordering relation?	5
Unique solution?	3
Paper and pencil?	3
Meaning of "senior guest"?	3
All other	9
Total	40

Was continuity implied? Was a relation one-one? Was a relation exclusive?

The abstract character of these questions is consistent with the assumption of the UNDERSTAND program that the subject is trying to map the concrete description of the problem situation onto an abstract list-structure representation and the description of legal moves onto the basic actions stored in semantic memory. The five questions asked most frequently fit this interpretation. (See table 3). One is a question as to whether the relation between the two types of objects (globes and monsters) is one-one or one-many. A second asks whether the basic legal move is to be classified as an exchange (simultaneous moves) or a transfer. A third asks whether the ordering on sizes implies that sizes must change continuously (i.e., pass through "medium" in going from "large" to "small"). A fourth seeks to clarify the restrictions placed on legal moves by the ordering relation. A fifth asks whether there is a single path to the goal in the problem space, or several paths.

The Problem Representations

The central objective of our inquiry is to determine how subjects represented the problem space that they generated in order to try to solve their problems. In particular, did changes in the problem statement, while retaining isomorphism, change the processing of the text in such a way as to change the representation that the subject created and used in his solution attempts. In answering this question, we will limit ourselves to the fourteen protocols for isomorphs of the Monster problems. Because the cover stories for these isomorphs are highly similar, it is easy to characterize the main differences among them (see figure 2 and table 4) and to sort them in dichotomous classes on the basis of salient characteristics whose effect upon the representations chosen can then be tested.

Consider a Monster problem in which the problem instructions describe monsters as holding globes. There are at least two obvious ways in which this problem can be represented by means of list structures: (1) a list of Monsters is kept in memory, and with each Monster, a list of the globes he is holding; or (2) a list of globes, and with each globe the name of the monster (as the value of an appropriate attribute) who is holding it. More briefly: globes can be associated with monsters, or monsters with globes.

Which of these two representations is chosen will determine, in turn, how moves are made. Consider the process of moving Globe A from Monster 1 to Monster 2. With the first representation, Globe A must be dissociated from Monster 1 and associated with Monster 2. With the second representation, the value of the monster associated with Globe A must be changed from 1 to 2. We will call the former representation a Transfer representation, and the latter a Change representation. With a Transfer representation something (e.g., a globe) moves from one location (a monster) to another. With a change representation, the object (monster) associated with a particular location (globe) is altered.

Names for Objects. Closely related to the form of the representation is the way in which the objects that appear in the problem can be named. In Monster Problem 1, for example, we can speak of "the large monster" or "the monster holding the small globe." The former name is *Permanent*, for in this problem, the size of a monster does not change as moves are made. The latter name is *Variable*: it changes as the globes are passed from one monster to another, for then different globes are associated successively with the same monster. Thus, for example, the monster who was initially holding the small globe may later become the "monster holding the large globe."

The name that is given to an object by sentence 3, in the description of the initial problem situation, will be called its *Initial* name. Regardless of whether the object is named permanently or transiently, the problem solver has the option of referring to it by its Initial name, and the protocols show that that option is often used. Thus

Table 4. Monster Problem Protocols: Predicted and Actual Representations and Names.

Protocol (1)	Primary Object (2)	Ordering of S3 (3)	Representation			Naming		
			Predicted from Program (4)	Actual		Initial		Subsequent (9)
				From Moves (5)	From Situations (6)	Predicted (7)	Actual (8)	
M1-MY	Monster	No	Transfer	Transfer	Transfer	Perm.	Var.[a,h]	Perm.
M2-CJ	Globe	Yes	Transfer	Transfer	Transfer	Perm.	Perm.	Perm.
M3-IB	Monster	No	Change	Change	Change	Perm.	Perm.	Perm.
M4-JC2	Monster	Yes	Change	Change	Change	Var.	Var.[b]	Perm.
M4-DD	Monster	Yes	Change	Change	Change	Var.	Perm.[h]	Perm.
M4-MY	Monster	No	Change	Change	Change	Var.	Var.[a]	Perm.
M5-JP	Monster	Yes	Transfer	Transfer	Transfer	Var.	Perm.	Perm.
M5-GL	Monster	Yes	Transfer	Transfer	Transfer	Var.	Var.	Perm.
M6-KK	Monster	No	Transfer	Transfer	Transfer	Var.	Var.	Perm.[c]
M7-LA	Monster	No	Change	Transfer	Transfer	Var.	Var.[d]	Perm.
M7-RB	Monster	No	Change	Change	Change	Var.	Var.[e]	Var.
M8-BC	Monster	No	Transfer	Transfer	Transfer	Perm.	Perm.[f]	Perm.
M9-JC3	Monster	No	Transfer	Transfer	Transfer	Var.	Var.[g]	Var.[h]
M9-BT	Monster	No	Transfer	Transfer	Transfer	Var.	Var.	Var.

Notes: M1 through M9 denote Monster Problems 1 through 9, respectively. Perm. = Permanent; Var. = Variable.

[a] Ordered, left to right, by size of globes.

[b] Referred to monsters as occupying "slots" in order of their current size and as moving from slot to slot.

[c] Numbered monsters in order of mention in S3.

[d] Represented size by vertical displacement.

[e] Explicitly and unsuccessfully tried to use visual imagery.

[f] Kept track by position on instruction sheet.

[g] Used finger to keep track of place on instruction sheet.

[h] Vacillated between variable and permanent naming.

we find many statements of the form: "The globe that was initially small." In sum, at any given time while he is working on a problem, a subject may refer to an object by its Permanent name, its Initial name, or its Variable name; or by some combination of these (e.g., "the large monster that is now holding the medium-size globe," or "the monster who was at the outset holding the large globe and is now holding the small globe.")

Sentence 3 in each of the Monster problems paired one set of things (e.g., monsters) of different sizes with another set of things (e.g., globes) of different sizes. In most of the problem statements, the sizes of both sets of things were listed in an irregular order—e.g., large; small; me-dium, but not small; medium, large. In five of the fourteen sets of instructions, however, the sizes of the things mentioned in the predicates were ordered from small through medium to large. (See table 4, column 3.) As we will see, subjects found it easier to keep track of the successive problem situations in the ordered than in the unordered condition and adopted some special naming tactics when they were confronted with the latter condition.

In the problem instructions, objects may be referred to by either Permanent or Variable names. For example, sentence 3 of Monster Problem 1 contains the clause, "the small monster held the large globe." In this variant of the problem, neither monsters nor globes change size, so the naming of both is permanent. In Monster problem 4, however, monsters change their sizes; hence the identical clause in sentence 3 refers to the monster by a Variable name. If the subject wishes to employ a Permanent name for a monster in this problem variant, he must use a phrase like "the monster holding the large globe," for monsters keep the same globe throughout the problem. Table 4, column 7, shows, for sentence 3 of each variant of the Monster problem, whether the subject of that sentence assigns a Permanent or a Variable name to its referent. In all cases where the sentence assigns a Variable name, the referent can be named permanently by referring to it in terms of the corresponding predicate—as in the example for Monster Problem 4, above. It will be observed that the subjects of the clauses of sentence 3 in problems 1, 2, 3, and 8 provide Permanent names for their referents, while the corresponding clauses in the other problem statements provide Variable names. Four subjects solved problems in which the Initial name was Permanent; ten solved problems in which it was Variable.

Transfer Problems and Change Problems. The variants of the Monster problems can also be dichotomized in another way. Sentence 4 of problem 1, which defines what is meant by a "move," states: "they proceeded to teleport globes from one to another." The UNDERSTAND program formalizes the move as a three-argument relation: TRANSFER (G, M1, M2), where the first argument denotes a globe, and the other two arguments monsters. In Monster problem 3, the corresponding clause of sentence 4 is: "they proceeded to shrink and expand the globes," which the UNDERSTAND program formalizes as: CHANGE (G, S1, S2), where the first argument denotes a globe and the other two arguments sizes.

In spite of the formal similarity between the moves of the two problems—both represented by three-argument relations— there is an important difference between them. The rules governing "moves" (sentences 4 through 8) in Monster problem 3 make no reference to the monsters who are holding the globes. Suppose, now, that the subject represents the situation in either of these problem variants as a list of monsters, and, associated with each member of the list, a list of the globes he is currently holding. Each monster would be further labeled by his size, as would each globe. Thus, the representation might look like this:

> Monster-list
>> Monster 1
>>> Size: Medium
>>> Globes
>>>> Globe A
>>>>> Size: Large
>> Monster 2
>>> Size: Large
>>> Globes
>>>> Globe B
>>>>> Size: Small
>> Monster 3
>>> Size: Small
>>> Globes
>>>> Globe C
>>>>> Size: Medium.

Now, to perform the operation TRANSFER (GA, M1, M2), we must locate M1 and M2 on the Monster-list, remove Globe A from the list of globes of Monster 1, and add Globe A to the list of globes of Monster 2. The operation is one of *transfering* a symbol from one list to another. On the other hand, to perform the operation CHANGE (GA, Large, Small), we must search the list of monsters until we find the one holding Globe A, then change the value of the size attribute of that globe from large to small. The operation is one of *changing* the value of an attribute of an object.

The UNDERSTAND program, reading the problem instructions of a Monster problem, would construct a representation from the information in sentence 3, and the particular representation chosen would depend upon the grammatical structure of that sentence. If the clauses of that sentence describe monsters holding globes, then the situation would be described as a list of monsters, and associated with each monster, a list of the globes it was holding. In problems 1 and 3, for example, the program would create precisely the representation that is depicted above. Because the form of the moves in these two problems is determined, as we have seen previously, by the structure of sentence 4 (and the similar structures of sentences 6 through 8), the UNDERSTAND program would interpret problem 1 as a Transfer problem and problem 3 as a Change problem.[1]

In table 4, column 4, the variants of the Monster problems are classified as Transfer problems or Change problems, respectively, in the manner we have just described. First, a representation is induced directly from sentence 3; then the legal move described in sentence 4 is described in terms of this representation. With this method of classification, problems 1, 2, 5, 6, 8, and 9 become Transfer problems, while problems 3, 4, and 7 become Change problems. If the UNDERSTAND program represents correctly the way in which human subjects go about interpreting the problem instructions, then we must predict that the same classification of the problems will be inferable from the data of the subjects' protocols. Eight subjects solved Transfer problems, six solved Change problems.

Legality Tests. The distinction between a Transfer problem and a Change problem has a further consequence. Not only are different processes required to make a move in the two kinds of problems, but the tests for legality of a move, defined by sentences 6 through 8 of the problem instructions, are different also. In the representation above, the legality of the move, $T(G, M_1, M_2)$ depends on the size of G compared with the sizes of other globes assigned to M_1 and M_2. To perform these tests, the globe lists of M_1 and M_2 must be accessed.

---

1. The assertions of this paragraph and the next are based upon a careful hand simulation of the UNDERSTAND program with these problem texts. We are now undertaking to verify these conclusions automatically by expanding the vocabulary and syntax of UNDERSTAND so that it will handle all the problem variants.

On the other hand, the legality of the move, $C(G, S_1, S_2)$, is ascertained by finding all the globes that are of size S_1 and determining if G is held by the largest of the corresponding monsters, then finding all the globes that are of size S_2 and making the same determination. Thus, it is a more complex and lengthier processing task to determine the legality of a move with the Change representation than with the Transfer representation, although it is perhaps no more complex actually to make the move once its legality has been determined. Figure 5 shows more precisely just why testing the legality of a Change is more complex than testing the legality of a Transfer.

In the Transfer operation, we test, for all other globes belonging to Monster 1, whether Globe A is greater than or equal to the other globe. If the test fails, the transfer is illegal (rule 2). If the test succeeds in all cases, we test, for all globes belonging to Monster 2, whether Globe A is greater than or equal to the other globe. If the test fails, the transfer is illegal (rule 3). If the test succeeds in all cases, the transfer is legal, Globe A is deleted from the globes of Monster 1 and added to the globes of Monster 2.

In the Change operation, we test, for all globes other than Globe A, whether these globes are equal in size to S_1. For each case where this test succeeds, we test whether the monster of Globe A is at least equal in size to the monster of the other globe. If the latter test fails, the change is illegal (rule 2). If the tests all succeed, we test, for all globes other than Globe A, whether these globes are equal in size to S_2. For each case where this test succeeds, we test whether the monster of Globe A is at least equal in size to the monster of the other globe. If the latter test fails, the change is illegal (rule 3). If the test succeeds in all cases, we set the size of Globe A equal to S_2.

In the Change operator, we have sets of nested tests, while in the Transfer operator, we do not. The UNDERSTAND program predicts that the form of sentence 3, in relation to the form of sentence 4, will determine whether a subject will represent

```
TRANSFER(Globe.A,Monster.1,Monster.2)
   For-all-other(Globe.A,Globe(Monster.1)):
      Test-GE(Size(Globe.A),Size(Globe(Monster.1))),
         If test fails, return "ILLEGAL", Halt.
   For-all(Globe(Monster.2)):
      Test-GE(Size(Globe.A),Size(Globe(Monster.2)))
         If test fails, return "ILLEGAL", Halt.
   Delete(Globe.A,Globe(Monster.1));
   Add(Globe.A,Globe(Monster.2)), Halt.

CHANGE(Globe.A,Size.1,Size.2)
   For-all-other(Globe.A,Globe):
      Test-Eq(Size(Globe),Size.1),
         If test succeeds, call Globe Globe.B),
            Test-GE(Size(Monster(Globe.A)), Size(Monster(Globe.B)))),
               If test fails, return "ILLEGAL", Halt.
      If test fails, go next.
   For-all-other(Globe.A,Globe):
      Test-Eq(Size(Globe),Size.2),
         If test succeeds, call Globe Globe.B,
            Test-GE(Size(Monster(Globe.A)),Size(Monster(Globe.B)))
               If test fails, return "ILLEGAL", Halt.
      If test fails, go next,
   Set-Eq(Size(Globe.A),Size.2),Halt.
```

Figure 5. Programs for *Transfer* and *Change* operators. "Test-Eq(X,Y)" means "Test if X is equal to Y." "Test-GE(X,Y)" means "Test if X is greater than or equal to Y." "For-all-other (X,Y)" means "for all the Ys other than X." "$X(Y)$" means "the X(s) of Y."

a problem as a Transfer problem or a Change problem, and hence, that the forms of these two sentences will be a major determinant of problem difficulty.[2]

There is nothing that *requires* a subject to represent any problem in the particular way we have indicated. In Monster problem 3, for example, the situation could be represented as a list of globe sizes and associated with each member of that list the globes of that size (the globes would be named, permanently, by the names of the monsters holding them). In this representation, the problem becomes a Transfer problem instead of a Change problem.

It would be possible for a subject to seek that representation which is simplest, ac-

cording to some criterion, or to translate all such problems into the same, canonical, representation. The postulate incorporated in the UNDERSTAND program, however, is that subjects will not employ such alternative strategies, even though they are available, but will adopt the representation that constitutes the most straightforward translation of sentences 3 and 4 of the instructions.

Empirical Evidence for Representations and Naming

In this section, we will compare the predictions with respect to problem representation and naming made by our hand simulation of the UNDERSTAND program with the behaviors of the human subjects as inferred from their protocols. We will first take up the evidence for representations, and then for naming.

The evidence was gathered by coding

---

2. In studies reported in chapter 7.3, the authors have found that Transfer problems require an average of 15.45 min for solution while Change problems require an average of 28.9 min.

each instance in the protocols where the subject described a *situation*, mentioned a *move*, or *named* one of the objects in the problem. The entire protocol was then classified, according to the representation the subject used and his naming practices, on the basis of the codings of the majority of the relevant instances. In almost all cases, the great preponderance of instances fell in the one category or the other; close divisions were rare. In three protocols where there was variability in the subjects' naming practices, we classified the protocols in the way that would be least favorable to the hypotheses we were testing. Hence, the statistics and significance levels given below are conservative.

Initially, the protocol elements were coded by a single judge, and later, independently, by a second judge. The two judges agreed on more than 90 percent of the individual protocol elements. With only four exceptions, they agreed fully on the classifications of the protocols. Three of the exceptions were the instances, mentioned above, where the subject was not consistent in *naming* objects by their Variable or Permanent names. The judges did not disagree on these protocols about the codings of individual elements, but found it difficult to classify the protocols as wholes. We have indicated above how we handled this problem. Finally, in one instance the second judge did not find enough evidence of the way in which *situations* were represented by the subject to classify the protocol from this evidence. However, on the basis of the subjects' descriptions of moves, both judges determined that this subject was using a Change representation of the problem.

Representations. We must ask first how we can determine empirically what representation a subject is using. If we limit ourselves to the initial portions of the protocols, the portions prior to the first attempted moves, we find relatively little concrete evidence about the nature of the representation the subject is constructing. This portion of the protocol typically consists largely of reading and rereading of the problem instructions, together with questions addressed to the experimenter about their meaning.

Once the subject begins to attempt moves, however, he provides much richer evidence about the representation he has constructed. This evidence comes from the way in which he names the moves, together with the way in which he describes the situations that are created by the moves. Consider the statement, "So the small globe goes over to the guy with the medium-size globe." This sentence describes globes as moving from one monster to another, hence implies a list of monsters, each with associated globes. Consider next the statement from a different protocol, "The medium-size monster changes his into a small globe." Here again, globes are the possessions of monsters; they change in size without changing ownership. Finally, consider, "I will move the monster which is on the medium-sized globe to the large globe." Here the relation is reversed: There is a list of globes and monsters are associated with globes, instead of vice versa.

The evidence from the way in which situations are described is equally clear. In a protocol from problem 1: "The small monster has the large, the medium has the small, and the large has the medium." A protocol from problem 4: "A small monster is holding a small globe, a large monster holding a medium-size globe, and a medium-sized monster holding a large globe." Or consider Monster problem 5, in which the monsters transfer names, and a monster can have more than one name (or none) at a time: "The guy with the long name now has a long name and a medium-size name."

Table 4, columns 5 and 6, summarizes the evidence about the subjects' representations from both their move statements and their situation descriptions. The table shows that both sources of evidence imply the same representations in all cases.[3] It shows further that, except for Monster

---

3. The departure from the null hypothesis of equally likely agreement or disagreement is significant at the 0.00006 level.

problem 2 (monsters standing on globes), monsters are always selected as the primary objects—i.e., the main list in the representation—then are further described by the globes they hold, their sizes, their names, and so on.[4]

There is another and more fundamental way of looking at the representations. We have seen that, by virtue of sentence 4 of the problem instructions, the UNDERSTAND program describes problems 1, 2, 5, 6, 8, and 9 as Transfer problems, and problems 3, 4, and 7 as Change problems. In all cases except one (subject L. A. on problem 7), that is also the way in which the subjects represented them internally.[5] The exceptional case, problem 7, stated in the instructions as a Change problem, was transformed by subject L. A. into a Transfer problem. There were no transformations in the other direction. The sample of one is too small to draw firm conclusions, but it is suggestive that the one example of problem transformation that we found was in the direction from the more difficult to the easier form of the problem.

It was observed earlier, and can be seen from the data in table 3, that most of the Task questions subjects asked were of a rather abstract nature, referring to formal properties of the relations among objects in the problem rather than to their concrete semantic interpretation. This, of course, was an appropriate reaction to these problems, whose solutions do not depend on the laws of quantum mechanics, the sizes of globes, or the social customs of monsters. The appropriate strategy was to strip away such semantic meanings and to abstract the problems down to their bare essentials. As several subjects pointed out explicitly, terms such as "quantum-mechanical" and the fact that monsters were described as five-handed were simply irrelevant.

Some additional studies to be reported in detail elsewhere (Hayes and Waterman, 1974) indicate that subjects can discrim-

inate between the "real" problem and the "cover story" quite early in the course of their exposure to the problem text. Subjects, viewing the text sentences one at a time, judged the relevance of each for solution of the problem. For the Tea Ceremony, subjects' judgments of relevance were correct in 77 percent of the cases on a first reading and 86 percent on second reading. Corresponding percentages for the Monster problem were 77 and 90 percent.

If the problems we had presented the subjects had been genuine problems in physics, or some other real-world subject, the abstracting behavior might not have been appropriate. In that case, it would have been necessary to retain the physical content of the problems and to draw upon knowledge of physics stored in long-term memory. What cued the subjects to respond in an abstract manner? We do not know for sure. It may have been the fact that these problems resembled other puzzlelike problems they had known and which required an abstracting strategy. It may have been the fact that the problems were presented in a psychological laboratory and not in a physics class. It may have been that the problem instructions appeared, on their face, to describe puzzles rather than genuine real-world problems.

Whatever the reason, 12 of the 14 subjects who were given Monster problems adopted a strategy of abstraction from the beginning. Two subjects, however, did not. One regarded the phrase "quantum mechanical" as probably significant and introduced notions of energy conservation in his attempts to solve the problem. A second subject avoided the complications of sentences 6 and 8 by allowing his monsters to enter into a mutual pact to define new sizes to which they could change. Then no two monsters would become the same size. We have no very convincing evidence that would tell us why these particular subjects behaved differently from the others. Both of the exceptional subjects are trained in the humanities and probably do not encounter many formal, abstract problems in their professional

---

4. Again, this agreement is significant at the 0.00006 level.

5. Agreement with the theory in 13 cases out of 14 is significant at the 0.00009 level.

activities. However, a number of the other subjects who immediately adopted abstract interpretations of the problems were also trained in the humanities. We simply mention these individual differences to indicate that there is nothing inevitable about the application of an abstracting strategy and that a fuller study of individual differences in this dimension of problem solving style might be instructive.

Further evidence on representations. In two experiments with Monster problems designed to test relative difficulty of Transfer and Change problems, and the amounts of transfer of training from one to the other, subjects did not provide thinking-aloud protocols but were allowed to use paper and pencil to record their successive moves (see chapter 7.3). In other respects, these experiments were conducted in the same way as those reported in detail in this chapter.

In these experiments, more than half the subjects spontaneously and without instruction or training adopted a notation ("state-matrix" notation) that permits an unequivocal determination of whether they were using a Transfer representation or a Change representation of the problem. Of 62 subjects who were presented with a Transfer version of the problem, 37 used the state-matrix notation for recording their moves; of 55 subjects who were presented with a change version of the problem, 30 used the state-matrix notation.

With the state-matrix notation, the problem solution is described by specifying the state of all the problem elements at each step of the solution. Most frequently, the subjects portrayed the sequence of states in a matrix like one of those shown in figure 6. Each column of the matrix represents an object of one type (globe or monster); entries in the matrix represent the object or objects of the other type associated with a column. Rows represent successive problem states after each move. Thus, in figure 6a, at the starting state (state 0), the large object of type 2 is associated with the medium object of type 1; while at state 1, the large and small objects of type 2 are associated with the large object of type 1 (representing a transfer of the large type 2 object from the medium to the large type 1 object).

A matrix like that in figure 6a gives clear evidence that the subject who employs it has a Transfer representation of the problem; while a matrix like that in figure 6b just as clearly denotes a Change representation. Note that in figure 6a relations between objects of type 1 and type 2 may be one-many, while in figure 6b they are many-one.

Now the striking finding of these experiments is that, without a single exception among the 67 subjects who used the state-matrix notation, every single one used the form of the notation consistent with the form of the problem presented him. Hence all 37 subjects who were given Transfer

	(Transfer Type)					(Change Type)		
	M	L	S			M	L	S
0	L	S	M		0	L	S	M
1	—	L,S	M		1	L	L	M
2	M	L,S	—		2	L	L	S
	(a)					*(b)*		

Figure 6. State-matrix notations used by subjects. (a) shows the notation used in solving *Transfer* problems, (b) the notation used in solving *Change* problems. The columns correspond to the fixed attribute, the rows to the successive problem situations after each move (0 is the starting situation). Within the cells are shown the current values of the variable attributes, which either (a) migrate from column to column (*Transfer* type) or (b) change value within a column (*Change* type).

Table 5. Summary of Naming Practices.

Type of Problem*	Initial Name		Intermediate or Final Name		Total
	Var.	Perm.	Var.	Perm.	Total
Transfer-Permanent	1	2	0	3	3
Transfer-Variable	4	1	2	3	5
Change-Permanent	0	1	0	1	1
Change-Variable	4	1	1	4	5
All Variable	8	2	3	7	10
All Permanent	1	3	0	4	4
All Transfer	5	3	2	6	8
All Change	4	2	1	5	6
All Problems	9	5	3	11	14

Note: Var. = Variable name; Perm. = Permanent name.

*For the distinction between Transfer and Change problems, see text. "Variable" problems are those in which the subject of sentence 3 has a Variable name; "Permanent" problems, those in which the subject of sentence 3 has a Permanent name.

forms of the Monster Problem gave evidence of adopting a Transfer representation of the problem; while all 30 who were given Change forms of the problem gave evidence of adopting a Change representation.

Naming. Table 4, some of whose contents are summarized in table 5, also tells us something about the way in which the subjects name objects. With three exceptions in fourteen protocols, in the early portions of the protocols, the name is determined by the form of sentence 3.[6] In those cases where the name so determined is a Variable name, the method of naming is usually (five cases in eight) changed by the subject in the course of his problem solving efforts so that the objects are subsequently referred to by Permanent names. There are no examples in the data of a progression in the opposite direction.

Thus, we see in table 5 that, in eight of the ten cases where the grammatical subject of sentence 3 was a Variable name, the initial name applied to it by the subject was also Variable. In five of these eight cases, however, the subject at some later point in the protocol was found referring to the same object by a Permanent name. In only one of the four cases where the grammatical subject of sentence 3 was a Permanent name was it referred to initially by a Variable name, and in all four cases it was referred to later by a Permanent name.[7] There were no differences in initial naming practice between Transfer problems and Change problems—the important variable was the form of sentence 3. In sum, the initial naming practices adopted by the subjects agree in eleven cases out of fourteen with the prediction of the UNDERSTAND program, but the program does not predict the adaptive shifts that many subjects made in the course of their problem solving activity from Variable naming to Permanent naming.

In the case of nine of the fourteen Monster problems, the pairs of objects in sentence 3 were listed in an arbitrary order not corresponding to the order of either set of objects. In seven of these nine cases,

6. The hypothesis that the naming is independent of sentence 3 is disconfirmed (11 cases out of 14) at the 0.028 level.

7. Again, if Permanent and Variable naming are equally likely, the chance of using a variable name three or fewer times in fourteen is only 0.028.

the subjects introduced some special method to keep track of the monster-globe relationships. In only one of the four cases where objects were ordered from small to large in sentence 3 did a subject make use of any such special placekeeping devices.[8] The special placekeeping methods were quite varied in nature. One subject assigned numbers to monsters in the order of their mention in sentence 3. Another subject referred to monsters as occupying "slots," in order of their current sizes, and as moving from slot to slot. A third represented size by vertical displacement on the page. A fourth (two protocols) reordered the globes by size, thus reformulating sentence 3. Two subjects kept track of pairings by their position on the instruction sheet, one using his finger for this purpose. Finally, one subject tried, explicitly and unsuccessfully, to use visual imagery to remember the pairings. These renaming methods gave the objects Permanent names, usually associated with spatial position of some kind. The UNDERSTAND program in its present form does not make provision for any reordering processes to conserve short-term memory.

CONCLUSIONS

We can draw several conclusions from these findings. First, both the way in which the subject names objects and the way in which he structures the internal problem representation are determined pretty directly by the language in which the problem instructions are written. Subjects initially adopt the naming conventions and representations that follow most directly from a parsing of the instructions. This is precisely what the UNDERSTAND program predicts, as against several alternative strategies mentioned earlier. If the problem is described as a Transfer problem, the subject will represent it as one; if it is described as a Change problem, he will

represent it in that way—even though, as we have seen, Change problems are more complex than the isomorphic Transfer problems.

On the other hand, there is some evidence that, as the problem solving efforts continue, inconvenient naming conventions are abandoned for more convenient conventions (Variable names abandoned for Permanent names). There is also one piece of evidence (the case of L. A.) that a subject may abandon a difficult representation for one that makes solving the problem easier.

Although we have not yet found a way of encoding this particular evidence, perusal of the protocols suggests that the main cue that subjects are responding to in considering a change of naming practice or representation is the load on short-term memory that is imposed by awkward naming or representation, either when it comes to applying the tests of legality of moves or when it comes to recalling the current problem situation, or both. The present version of the UNDERSTAND program is not capable of this kind of adaptive behavior and will have to be modified to incorporate it if it is to simulate this aspect of the human behavior.

The assumption incorporated in UNDERSTAND that understanding processes will precede solution attempts, without feedback, is partially, but not fully, borne out by the data. A more sophisticated simulation will have to take such feedback into account. Some evidence was found to support the assumption of UNDERSTAND that subjects interpret the instructions of these kinds of tasks by mapping them onto list structures and basic operators drawn from a repertory stored in long-term semantic memory.

References

Bransford, J. D., & Franks, J. J. The abstraction of linguistic ideas. *Cognitive Psychology*, 1971, 2, 331–50.

Hayes, J. R., & Simon, H. A. Understanding Written Problem Instructions. In L. W. Gregg (Ed.), *Knowledge and cognition*. Potomac,

---

8. As before, there were only three cases of fourteen that diverged from expectations, the probability of such an extreme outcome being only 0.028.

Md: Lawrence Erlbaum Associates, 1974, pp. 167–200. Reprinted as chapter 7.1 in this book.

Hayes, J. R., & Simon, H. A. Understanding tasks stated in natural language. In D. R. Reddy (Ed.), *Speech Recognition*. New York: Academic Press, 1975, pp. 428–54.

Hayes, J. R., & Simon, H. A. Understanding Complex Task Instructions. In D. Klahr (Ed.), *Cognition and instruction*. Potomac, Md: Lawrence Erlbaum Associates, 1976, pp. 269–86.

Hayes, J. R., & Simon, H. A. Psychological differences among problem isomorphs. In N. J. Castellan, D. B. Pisoni, and G. R. Potts (Eds.), *Cognitive theory*, vol. 2. Hillsdale, N.J.: Lawrence Erlbaum Associates, 1977, pp. 21–44. Reprinted as chapter 7.3 in this book.

Hayes, J. R., & Waterman, D. A. *Identifying the relevant aspects of a problem text* (Complex Information Processing Working Paper 273). Unpublished manuscript, Carnegie-Mellon University, 1974.

Newell, A., & Simon, H. A. *Human problem solving*. Englewood Cliffs, N.J.: Prentice-Hall, 1972.

Schank, R. C. Conceptual dependency: A theory of natural language understanding. *Cognitive Psychology*, 1972, 3, 552–631.

7·3

Psychological Differences among Problem Isomorphs (1977)

with John R. Hayes

The fact that two problems are exact iso-morphs—that legal moves can be mapped between them in one-to-one fashion—does not guarantee that they are of equal difficulty for human subjects. On the contrary, we will show in this chapter that changing the written problem instructions, without disturbing the isomorphism between problem forms, can affect by a factor of two the times required by subjects to solve a problem. This effect is produced because different problem instructions cause subjects to adopt different problem representations, even when the problems are formally isomorphic.

To understand a written problem text, a person must do two things. First, he must read the sentences of the text and extract information from them by grammatical and semantic analysis. Second, he must construct from the newly extracted information a representation of the problem that is adequate for its solution. This repre-

sentation must include the initial conditions of the problem, its goal, and the operators for reaching the goal from the initial state.

In earlier papers (Hayes and Simon, 1974; Simon and Hayes, 1976—see chapters 7.1 and 7.2), the authors presented protocol analyses of subjects' attempts to understand Tower of Hanoi-like puzzles and described the UNDERSTAND program—a simulation model of the process by which humans come to understand problem texts. The model, while imperfect, matched the gross structure of the subjects' behavior quite well.

The structure of the UNDERSTAND program implies that certain changes in the form of the problem text that do not change its meaning will lead to changes in the representation adopted for the problem. Thus, the sentence, 'The monster stood on the globe," would be represented as a monster having a globe as an attribute, while the sentence, "The globe supported the monster," would be represented as a globe having a monster as an attribute. Since it is known that changes in the *representation* of a problem can change the solution process significantly (Newell and

This research has been supported by Public Health Service Grant MH-07722 from the National Institute of Mental Health and by National Science Foundation Grant GS-38533.

Simon 1972), it is possible that changes in the *problem statement* can also have important effects on the solution process.

Problem Materials

The purpose of this study is to explore the influence of changes in the form of the problem text on the representation of problems, and consequently upon the process of solution of problems, by humans. To do this, we have employed sets of problem isomorphs. Two problems are isomorphic if they are essentially the same problem disguised in different words. More formally, two problems are isomorphs if any solution path of one may be translated step by step into a solution path of the other and vice versa. Problem isomorphs are of interest because they allow one to control such formal properties of a problem as the number of steps required for solution, or the number of blind alleys, while varying the way in which the problem is presented. Systematic differences among isomorphs can provide especially good clues, unconfounded with differences in formal properties, to determinants of problem difficulty, transfer of training, and manner of problem formulation.

The materials to be used here are eight "monster" problems, all of which are variants of the Tower of Hanoi puzzle. All the monster problems concern a set of objects that are transformed from one set of permissible states to another. The problems differ, however, in two systematic ways. First, in problems TA and TP, which will be called *transfer* problems, the transformation is a movement of something from one location to another. In problems CA and CP, which will be called *change* problems, the transformation is a change in property rather than a movement.

The second systematic difference among the problems involves agent-patient relations. In problems TA and CA, which will be called *agent* problems, the monsters are agents but not patients of the transformations. In problems TP and CP, which will be called *patient* problems, the monsters are both agents and patients of the trans-

formations. The key difference for the agent-patient variable, then, is whether the monsters transfer or change the globes or whether they transfer or change themselves.

The differences that have been incorporated into the problem set reflect our hypotheses about the kinds of changes in problem text that are likely to influence the internal representations of problems and the ways they are solved. Suppose that some underlying problem feature is represented in the text of one problem isomorph by element A and in the text of a second, by element B. Elements A and B will both be subjected to grammatical and semantic analysis early in the subject's attempt to understand the problems. If A and B are similar, for example, both are nouns designating animals, we would expect them to receive very similar analyses (and the UNDERSTAND program does so predict). However, if they are dissimilar, for example, if A is a verb and B a concrete noun, they would receive very different analyses. We hypothesize that if A and B receive similar grammatical and semantic analyses, then the two isomorphs will be represented and solved in similar ways and transfer of training between the isomorphs will be large. However, if A and B receive very different analyses, then the two isomorphs are likely to be represented and solved in disimilar ways and transfer of training will be small. In particular, we hypothesize that elements that are classified into different cases by a case grammar analysis such as Fillmore's (1968) will yield isomorphs (1) that are represented and solved differently and (2) that will consequently exhibit little mutual transfer of training.

Experiment 1

Experiment 1 employed eight monster problems. Monster problems TA, TP, CA, and CP are shown in Table 1. Problems TA′, TP′, CA′, and CP′ were identical, respectively, to problems TA, TP, CA, and CP except for sentence 3. In the unprimed problems, sentence 3 matches the medium-

Table 1. Four Monster Problems.

A. Monster problem TA

Three five-handed extraterrestrial monsters were holding three crystal globes. Because of the quantum-mechanical peculiarities of their neighborhood, both monsters and globes come in exactly three sizes with no others permitted: small, medium, and large. The medium-sized monster was holding the small globe; the small monster was holding the large globe; and the large monster was holding the medium-sized globe. Since this situation offended their keenly developed sense of symmetry, they proceeded to transfer globes from one monster to another so that each monster would have a globe proportionate to its own size.

Monster etiquette complicated the solution of the problem since it requires that:

1. Only one globe may be transferred at a time.
2. If a monster is holding two globes, only the larger of the two may be transferred.
3. A globe may not be transferred to a monster who is holding a larger globe.

By what sequence of transfers could the monsters have solved this problem?

B. Monster problem TP

Three five-handed extraterrestrial monsters were standing on three crystal globes. Because of the quantum-mechanical peculiarities of their neighborhood, both monsters and globes come in exactly three sizes with no others permitted: small, medium, and large. The medium-sized monster was standing on the small globe; the small monster was standing on the large globe; and the large monster was standing on the medium-sized globe. Since this situation offended their keenly developed sense of symmetry, they proceeded to transfer themselves from one globe to another so that each monster would have a globe proportionate to its own size.

Monster etiquette complicated the solution of the problem since it requires that:

1. Only one monster may be transferred at a time.
2. If two monsters are standing on the same globe, only the larger of the two may be transferred.
3. A monster may not be transferred to a globe on which a larger monster is standing.

By what sequence of transfers could the monsters have solved this problem?

C. Monster problem CA

Three five-handed extraterrestrial monsters were holding three crystal globes. Because of the quantum-mechanical peculiarities of their neighborhood, both monsters and globes come in exactly three sizes with no others permitted: small, medium, and large. The medium-sized monster was holding the small globe; the small monster was holding the large globe; and the large monster was holding the medium-sized globe. Since this situation offended their keenly developed sense of symmetry, they proceeded to shrink and expand globes so that each monster would have a globe proportionate to its own size.

Monster etiquette complicated the solution of the problem since it requires that:

1. Only one globe may be changed at a time.
2. If two globes have the same size, only the globe held by the larger monster may be changed.
3. A globe may not be changed to the same size as the globe of a larger monster.

By what sequence of changes could the monsters have solved this problem?

D. Monster problem CP

Three five-handed extraterrestrial monsters were holding three crystal globes. Because of the quantum-mechanical peculiarities of their neighborhood, both monsters and globes come in exactly three sizes with no others permitted: small, medium, and large. The medium-sized monster was holding the small globe; the small monster was holding the large globe; and the large monster was holding the medium-sized globe. Since this situation offended their keenly developed sense of symmetry, they proceeded to shrink and expand themselves so that each monster would have a globe proportionate to its own size.

Monster etiquette complicated the solution of the problem since it requires that:

1. Only one monster may be changed at a time.
2. If two monsters have the same size, only the monster holding the large globe may be changed.
3. A monster may not be changed to the same size as a monster holding a larger globe.

By what sequence of changes could the monsters have solved this problem?

sized monster with the small globe, the small monster with the large globe, and the large monster with the medium-sized globe. In the primed problems, sentence 3 matches the medium-sized monster with the large globe, the large monster with the small globe, and the small monster with the medium-sized globe.

We have included the primed as well as the unprimed problems in the experiment because there are slight differences in the solution paths for problems TA, TP′, CA′, and CP, on the one hand, and problems TA′, TP, CA, and CP′, on the other. Thus, the four problems in the first set are isomorphs of each other, as are the four problems in the second set. The two sets, however, are not isomorphic. Each of the sets is isomorphic to a Tower of Hanoi puzzle, but the two Tower of Hanoi puzzles do not have the same starting place. (See Nilsson, 1971, for a discussion of solution paths in the Tower of Hanoi puzzle.)

Procedure

In experiment 1, each subject was asked to solve two problems—one was a transfer problem (problem TA or TP) and the other a change problem (problem CA or CP). Four pairs of problems, involving one transfer and one change problem each, were employed. These pairs were problems TA and CA, problems TA′ and CA′, problems TP and CP, and problems TP′ and CP′. In half the cases, the transfer problem was solved before the change problem, and in the other half, the solution order was reversed.

Each problem was presented to the subject typed on a single sheet of paper. The subject was asked to solve the problem, to write his solution on the problem sheet in any notation he desired, and to bring it to the experimenter to be checked for correctness. If his solution was correct, the subject was given the next problem. If incorrect, he was told the location of his error, for example "step 3 is not correct:," and asked to try again. The solution times shown in table 2 are the sums of all the intervals during which the subject worked on the problem. They do not include the times required for the experimenter to check the solutions.

Results

Solution Time. Table 2 shows the mean solution time for each of the eight monster problems, both when the problem was

Table 2. Experiment 1: Mean Solution Times (min).

Problem for Which Solution Time is Given

Order in Pair	TA	TA′	TP	TP′	CA	CA′	CP	CP′
First								
Solution time	13.78	19.00	15.50	13.11	35.00	25.75	28.67	25.33
Number of Subjects	9	10	10	9	8	8	9	6
Pair in which problem occurred	TA-CA	TA′-CA′	TP-CP	TP′-CP′	CA-TA	CA′-TA′	CP-TP	CP′-TP′
Second								
Solution time	19.13	11.625	13.78	5.83	15.00	14.60	19.90	25.22
Number of Subjects	8	8	9	6	9	10	10	9
Pair in which problem occurred	CA-TA	CA′-TA′	CP-TP	CP′-TP′	TA-CA	TA′-CA′	TP-CP	TP′-CP′

solved first and when it was solved second. To provide a clear differentiation of the initial difficulty of the problems from transfer-of-training effects, a separate analysis was performed on the data for problems solved first.

An unequal-*n* three-factor analysis of variance (transfer-change × agent-patient × primed-unprimed) of the log transformed solution times for the problems solved first revealed that the main effect for transfer versus change was significant ($p < 0.00001$), but that no other main effects or interactions approached significance even at the 0.05 level. The transfer problems required an average of 15.45 min for solution, whereas the change problems required an average of 28.90 min or nearly twice as long. Thus, the nature of the transformation made a very large difference in solution time, while the agent-patient variation did not have a significant effect.

Errors. Thirteen subjects failed to solve the first problem presented to them within the 60-min time limit and two subjects failed to solve the second problem after having successfully solved the first. The analysis of solution times presented above and the analyses of notation presented below include no data from subjects who failed to solve either problem. The 13 failures to solve the first problem were distributed as follows: for TA problems there were no failures among 19 subjects; for TP problems, 2 failures among 21 subjects; for CA problems, 8 failures among 24 subjects; and for CP problems, 3 failures among 18 subjects. A chi-square test revealed a significant difference in error frequency between transfer and change problems ($\chi^2 = 1.7$, $df = 1$).

Transfer of Training. In interpreting the transfer results presented below, one should notice the different roles played by the agent-patient and transfer-change variations in each of the first two experiments. In experiment 1, transfer of training was always from a change to a transfer problem or from a transfer to a change problem with the agent-patient relation held constant.

In experiment 2, transfer of training was always from an agent problem to a patient problem or from a patient problem to an agent problem with the transfer-change relation held constant.

An analysis of variance was performed on the log transformed data for all sixteen conditions represented in table 2. Significant. main effects were found for order of presentation ($p < 0.00001$) reflecting strong transfer-of-training effects and for transfer versus change ($p < 0.00001$) confirming the result found in the analysis of problems solved first.

The analysis also revealed a significant interaction between transfer versus change and agent versus patient ($p < 0.01$) which was not found in the analysis of the solution times of problems solved first.

In the agent condition, transfer-of-training between transfer and change problems was quite asymmetric. Transfer from TA to CA problems was 51 percent on the average while transfer from CA to TA problems was only 6 percent. In the patient condition, the asymmetry was less marked and opposite in direction. Transfer from TP to CP problems was 18 percent while transfer from CP to TP problems was 26 percent.

Reed, Ernst, and Banerjii (1974), studying two river-crossing problems, also found asymmetry in transfer of training. In particular, they found that transfer-of-training from the harder problem to the easier problem (43 percent) was greater than transfer from the easier problem to the harder problem (1 percent). Notice, however, that for the agent condition in our experiment, transfer from the harder problem to the easier one, that is, from the change problem to the transfer problem, is less than from the easier problem to the harder problem. This may be seen in table 2 in the columns labeled TA, TA′, CA, and CA′. Solution time for the transfer problems is reduced only 6 percent on the average when they follow solution of a change problem. Solution time for the change problems, however, is reduced by 51 percent on the average when they follow solution of a transfer problem.

EXPERIMENT 2

A second experiment was performed to provide data on transfer of training from one transfer problem to another and from one change problem to another. The primed problems were not included in experiment 2 since no significant differences were detected between the primed and unprimed problems in experiment 1. Otherwise, the problems, procedures, and methods for selecting subjects were identical to those in experiment 1.

Results

Solution Time. Table 3 shows the mean solution time for the problems solved in experiment 2. Analysis of variance of log-transformed solution times for the first problem solved showed a very significant effect of transfer versus change ($F = 22.48$, $df = 1$, $p < 0.00002$) and a smaller effect for agent versus patient ($F = 4.82$, $df = 1$, $p < 0.04$). The interaction of these two variables was not significant. As in experiment 1, the change problems were about twice as difficult as the transfer problems; while agent problems were slightly easier than patient problems.

Errors. There were no failures to solve either TA or TP problems among 16 and 8 subjects, respectively. Two of 14 subjects failed to solve a CA problem presented first and 1 of 14 failed to solve a CP problem presented first. One of 13 subjects failed to solve a CP problem after successfully solving a CA problem.

Transfer of Training. Analysis of variance was performed on the log transformed data for all eight conditions represented in table 3. Significant main effects were found for order of presentation ($F = 41.26$, $df = 1$, $p < 0.00001$) indicating a strong transfer-of-training effect, an effect for transfer versus change ($F = 48.99$, $df = 1$, $p < 0.00001$), and an effect for agent versus patient ($F = 6.46$, $df = 1$, $p < 0.02$). The last two effects confirm the results of the analysis of solution times presented above. No interactions were significant.

Transfer of training was about equal in the change and transfer conditions. Among change problems, the second problem was solved in 48.2 percent less time on the average than the first; while among transfer problems, the second problem was solved 55.9 percent faster than the first. Within both change and transfer conditions, however, there was marked asymmetry in transfer of training between the agent and the patient problems. Transfer from the TA problem to the TP problem was 49.4 percent while transfer from TP to TA was 62.4 percent. Similarly, transfer from the CA problem to CP problem was 36.5 percent while transfer from CP to CA was 59.8 percent. In contrast to the results of experiment 1, transfer was greater from the more difficult problems (patient type) to the easier problems (agent type) than the reverse.

In general the transfer of training effects found in experiment 2 were larger than those found in experiment 1. The transfer results together with the solution time and

Table 3. Experiment 2: Solution Times (Min).

Order in Pair	Problem for Which Solution Time is Given			
	TA	TP	CA	CP
First				
Solution Time	10.88	16.63	28.08	31.50
Number of Subjects	16	8	12	12
Pair in Which Problem Occurred	TA-TP	TP-TA	CA-CP	CP-CA
Second				
Solution Time	5.5	6.25	17.83	12.67
Number of Subjects	8	16	12	12
Pair in Which Problem Occurred	TP-TA	TA-TP	CP-CA	CA-CP

error results indicate that the difference between transfer and change problems is much more important to the subject's solution processes than is the difference between agent and patient problems.

Influences of Problem Text on Representation in Experiments 1 and 2

The work sheets used by the subjects in experiments 1 and 2 were analyzed for evidences of differences among subjects in their manner of formulating the problem. Since no instructions were given to the subjects specifying the method for recording their answers, it was hoped that the notations they adopted spontaneously would yield evidence about their internal representations of the problems.

Types of Notation Observed. Subjects used three major types of notations to describe their solutions:

1. Operator-sequence notation: The solution is described as a sequence of applications of the operators, for example, "The large monster gives his globe to the small monster. Then the medium monster . . . ," etc.

2. State-matrix notation: The solution is described by specifying the state of all the problem elements at each step of the solution. Most frequently the subjects portrayed the sequence of states in a matrix like one of those shown in figure 1. The matrix of figure 1*a* is typical of those used

by subjects solving transfer problems. After each successive move, the symbol designating the object moved is literally transferred from one column of the diagram to another.

The matrix of figure 1*b* is typical of those used by subjects solving change problems. After each successive move, the value of a symbol in one of the columns is changed. From the figure it is seen that whether a matrix depicts a transfer representation or a change representation can be determined without ambiguity.

3. Labeled-diagram notation: The solution is described by presenting a diagram depicting the initial state of the problem together with a sequence of changes depicted either by numbered arrows or by a spatially ordered sequence of crossed-out and redrawn elements in the diagram. See figure 2 for an example of labeled-diagram notation.

Table 4 shows that the frequencies with which the three major notational types were used in the first solution in experiment 1 did not depend in any important way on the type of problem being solved. Further, the solution times for the problems did not appear to vary with the notation type used in the solution. Solution times for the first problem solved were classified by notation type and by problem type for those subjects who used either pure matrix notation or pure operator sequence notation. Labeled diagrams were not used frequently enough to allow analyses. An unequal-n analysis of variance of the log-transformed data re-

	(Transfer Type)				(Change Type)		
	M	L	S		M	L	S
0	L	S	M	0	L	S	M
1	—	L,S	M	1	L	L	M
2	M	L,S	—	2	L	L	S
		(a)				*(b)*	

Figure 1. State-matrix notations used by subjects in solving move and change problem: (*a*) *Transfer* type; (*b*) *Change* type. The columns correspond to the fixed attribute, the rows to the successive problem situation after each move (0 is the starting situation). Within the cells are shown the current values of the variable attributes, which either (*a*) migrate from column to column (*Transfer* type) or (*b*) change value within a column (*Change* type).

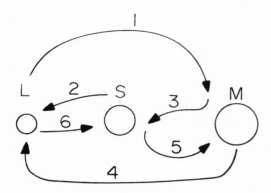

Figure 2. An example of labeled diagram notation from a solution for problem *TP'*. Letters indicate monsters. Circles indicate globes and numbers indicate the order in which transformations were applied.

vealed neither a main effect nor interactions due to notational type.

Generally, subjects used the same notation or mixture of notations for solving the second problem as for solving the first (91 cases out of 117). The changes that did occur are predominately shifts from operator sequence notation to matrix notation. For the first problem, 43 subjects used operator sequence notation and 57 used matrix notation. For the second problem, 30 subjects used operator sequence notation and 70 used matrix notation.

While the gross notational types described above did not vary in frequency across problem types, variants within notational types were associated with specific problem types. The matrix notation used

for move problems is characteristically different from that used for change problems. In all the problem solutions we have observed, the transfer form (figure 1*a*) was without exception used in solving the transfer problems and the change form (figure 1*b*) was always used in solving the change problems.

There is no formal reason that the transfer form of the matrix could not be used to represent a change problem. In solving problem 3 for example, one could let the columns of the matrix represent the globes of different sizes and the entries in the body of the matrix represent the sizes of the monsters holding the globes. While such a matrix, which has the form of figure 1*a*, is quite adequate for solving the change problems, it was never used by our subjects for those problems.

The operator-sequence notation also shows variants in form that are characteristic of the problem being solved. To identify a move in a monster problem using operator-sequence notation, it is sufficient to designate the object to be transformed and the new state it is to be transformed to. Thus, the subject may designate an operator application by specifying two elements. For example, in problem TA, a solution might consist of a sequence of statements such as "small globe to big monster." In many cases, however, the subjects specify three elements rather than just two. For example, in problem TA, statements in the solution frequently have the form "the medium monster gives the small globe to the large monster." Thus we can distinguish

Table 4. Use of Notations in Experiments 1 and 2.

Notation Type	Problem Type				
	TA	TP	CA	CP	Σ
State Matrix	18	12	12	15	57
Operator Sequence	13	9	11	10	43
Both State Matrix and Operator Sequence	2	3	2	1	8
Labeled Diagram	1	0	2	1	4
Labeled Diagram and State Matrix	1	1	0	0	2
Labeled Diagram and Operator Sequence	0	2	1	0	3
Σ	35	27	28	27	117

Table 5. Variations in Operator Sequence Notation in Experiments 1 and 2.

	Transfer				*Change*		
	Problems						
	TA		*TP*		*CA*		*CP*	
	Object Naming		*Object Naming*		*Object Naming*		*Object Naming*	
Number of Elements	*Direct*	*Indirect*	*Direct*	*Indirect*	*Direct*	*Indirect*	*Direct*	*Indirect*
2	5	0	14	0	0	11	4	7
3	9	1	0	0	2	1	1	0
	14	1	14	0	2	12	5	7

notations that mention two elements to identify a move from notations that mention three elements.

Another variation in the form of operator-sequence notation concerns the naming of objects. An object may be designated either by direct naming—that is by specifying an attribute of the object, for example, "the big globe"—or by indirect naming—that is, by specifying a relation of the object to another object or to an array of objects, for example, "the globe of the large monster," or "the globe on the left."

Table 5 shows the relation between the variant operator-sequence notations and the problem solved. Clearly, indirect naming is used more frequently in change problems (19 cases out of 26) than in transfer problems (1 case out of 29) ($\chi^2 = 25.79$, $p < 0.005$). Further, three elements are named far more frequently for specifying solutions for agent problems (13 cases out of 29) than for patient problems (1 case out of 26) ($\chi^2 = 10.07$, $p < 0.005$).

Process Explanations for the Findings

We have hypothesized that the notation a subject uses in solving a problem is related to his internal representation of that problem. We will now present a view of the relation between the internal representation and the notation that is consistent with the variant notations reported above. This view is consistent also with the structure and operation of the UNDERSTAND program.

We propose that the first three sentences of the monster problem text determine a representation of the initial situation which is essentially the same in all the monster problems. The initial situation has as its most prominent feature a set of monsters. Next in importance is a set of globes which bear a locative relation to the monsters. We suppose that the initial situation is represented as a list of monsters and that each monster has associated with it a list of globes. Early in the process of solution, many of the subjects draw a sketch of the monsters and globes like that shown in figure 3. Such sketches can be identified and distinguished from the notation that the subject used to solve the problem in about 60 percent of cases for the first problem solved. These sketches impose spatial relations of two sorts on the monsters and globes. The first is a spatial association representing the pairing of monsters and globes given in sentence 3 of the problem text. The second is an arbitrary arrangement of these pairs in a linear ordering which is arrayed either horizontally or vertically. The pairs are ordered either as they are in sentence 3 (text order), or in

Figure 3. An example of a monster-globe diagram for problem TP.

order of monster size (monster order), or in order of globe size (globe order).

When the subject begins to solve the problem, he chooses one of the three notations to record his answer. We have no information about what determines this choice except to note as we did above that subjects tend to use the same notation in both their problems. Whichever notation is chosen makes use of some information from the subject's representation of the initial situation.

Both the state-matrix and the labeled-diagram notations incorporate the two sets of objects in the initial situation together with their spatial relations. Thus, these two notations are always monster-globe notations and never monster-size or globe-size notations. Further, the spatial ordering of elements in the matrix or diagram is closely related to the spatial arrangement of elements in the sketch of the initial situation. Table 6 shows that in more than 80 percent of cases, the ordering of monster-globe pairs in the sketch matches that in the matrix or diagram. Table 7 shows that in more than 90 percent of cases, the horizontal-vertical orientation of the sketch is identical to the orientation found in the matrix or diagram. Thus, the matrix notation and the labeled-diagram notation are clearly dependent on the initial representation of the situation shown in the sketch.

The association between the forms of the matrix notation shown in figure 1 and the problem type depends not on the initial representation, which is the same in all cases, but rather on the relation of the operators in the problem to the initial

Table 6. Relation of Ordering in the Diagram of the Initial Situation and in the Matrix Used for Solution.

		Type of Orderiing in Matrix		
		Text	*Monster*	*Globe*
Type of Ordering in Diagram	*Text*	7	1	2
	Monster	0	12	2
	Globe	0	0	3

Table 7. Relation of Spatial Arrangement in the Diagram of the Initial Situation and in the Matrix Used for Solution.

		Spatial Arrangement in Matrix	
		Horizontal	*Vertical*
Spatial Arrangement in Diagram	*Horizontal*	21	1
	Vertical	1	4

representation. Thus the differences in notation related to problem type are due to differences in the way the operators are represented and not to the way the initial situation is represented.

The variations in operator-sequence notation bear a somewhat more complex relation to the initial representation than is the case for the other two notations. However, these variations may be accounted for reasonably well by the following two principles:

1. The monsters are the most important elements in the problem, being the agents of all actions, and therefore must be mentioned. (In 56 of the 59 instances of operator-sequence notation, the monsters are mentioned routinely).

2. Because the complete state is not recorded in this notation, objects should be provided with permanent names so as to identify them unambiguously. That is, an object should be named by a property or relation that does not change in the course of the problem solution. In the change problems, the size of the objects is changed in the course of solution. Thus the big monster at the beginning of the CP problem may become medium or small later in the problem. Hence, only indirect names for the objects are permanent in these problems. This principle, then, may be used to account for the high frequency of indirect naming in change problems.

In the agent problems the agent is distinct from the object being transformed and from the state to which the object is being transformed. In patient problems, however, the agent and the object are identical.

Our first principle, therefore, would lead us to expect that transformations would be designated by three elements in agent problems, that is, by agent, objects, and destination, but by two elements in patient problems. This expectation is fulfilled with few exceptions, except for CA problems. This case is largely explainable, however, by the relation between indirect naming and the designation of the agent. In the monster problems, indirect naming frequently involves specifying the relation between the object and the agent. In the CA problems, in fact, all indirect naming was of this sort. A typical transformation might be designated by the statement, "Large monster's globe to large size." Hence, although only two elements are mentioned, one of their names makes reference to the agent. While only two of the subjects used direct naming in the CA problems, both those subjects used three elements in specifying the transformation.

Models of Solution Time Differences

The models below are intended to account for the differences in solution time between transfer and change problems. We will present just two models here; a model for TA problems and a model for CA problems. Models could easily be derived for TP and CP problems but they would be identical to the TA and CA models respectively.

We assume that in solving TA problems, the subject makes use of the following three kinds of goals:

1. To move the globe of size A to the monster of size A.

2. To move a globe away from monster X, so that another globe also held by monster X may be moved.

3. To move a globe away from monster X, so that another globe, Y, can be moved to monster X.

Since the models for executing these three goals are very nearly identical, we will confine our attention to the model for goal 1.

To make the models concrete, we will assume that the subjects are using the matrix shown in figure 1a to represent

transfer problems and the matrix shown in figure 1b to represent change problems. For convenience, we will further assume that the subject first checks rule 2 and then rule 3 in testing the legality of a move. The order in which the rules are checked has no implications for our analyses.

Table 8 shows the model for TA problems and table 9 the model for CA problems. There are two differences between the models that might account for the difference in problem solving. The first is a difference in procedures used for checking whether there are (in TA problems) other globes at a given location or (in CA problems) other globes of a given size. These procedures are invoked in their respective problems at step A1 and again at step B1. To determine if there are other globes at a given location requires examining just one cell of the matrix (see figure 1a). On the other hand, to determine if there are other globes of a given size requires the subject to scan a row of the matrix (see figure 1b). For this reason, we would expect that steps A1 and B1 in model CA would take more time than the corresponding steps in model TA.

Table 8. Model for the Solution
of Problem TA.

Goal: Move globe X (of size A) to monster Y
(of size A)
A. Check rule 2
  1. Does the monster Z, now holding globe X, hold any other globes?
  2. If not, go to B.
  3. If so, is globe X larger than any of the other globes of monster Z?
  4. If so, go to B.
  5. If not, return and report "Blocked at origin, try to remove block."
B. Check rule 3
  1. Is monster Y now holding any globes?
  2. If not, go to C.
  3. If so, is globe X larger than any of the other globes of monster Y?
  4. If so, go to C.
  5. If not, return and report "Blocked at destination, try to remove block."
C. Transfer
  1. Delete globe X from monster Z.
  2. Add globe X to monster Y.

Table 9. Model for the Solution
of Problem CA.

Goal: Change globe *X* (size *A*) to size of own
 monster (size *B*).
A. Check rule 2
  1. Does any other monster hold other globes
   of size *A*?
  2. If not, go to *B*.
  3. If so, is monster holding globe *X* the
   largest of the monsters holding globes
   of size *A*?
  4. If so, go to *B*.
  5. If not, return and report "Blocked at
   origin, try to remove block."
B. Check rule 3
  1. Does any other monster hold other
   globes of size *B*?
  2. If not, go to *C*.
  3. If so, is monster holding globe *X* larger
   than any other monster holding a
   globe of size *B*?
  4. If so, go to *C*.
  5. If not, return and report "Blocked at
   destination, try to remove block."
C. Change
  1. Change size of globe *X* from *A* to *B*.

A second difference between the models
may be found in steps A3 and B3. In Model
TA, if there are other globes at the specified
locus, Globe *X* is compared in size to those
other globes. In model CA, if there are
other globes of the specified size, then
rather than comparing globe sizes, the sizes
of the monsters holding the globes are compared. This comparison requires one more
step of retrieval than does the corresponding comparison in model TA.

EXPERIMENT 3

Since either or both of these differences
could account for the differences in difficulty between move and change problems,
we performed experiment 3 in an attempt
to differentiate between these alternatives.

In designing problems TA2 and CA2,
shown in table 10, we attempted to produce
problems that differ in steps A1 and B1 in
the same way as problems TA and CA
differ, but that do not differ in steps A3
and B3. We have done this by introducing
an extra dimension, color. In problem

TA2, instead of comparing the sizes of
globes at a given location as in problem
TA, the subject must now compare the
colors of globes of specified sizes. In problem CA2, instead of comparing the sizes
of monsters holding globes of a given size
as in problem CA, the subject must now
compare the colors of the various globes of
a given size. Thus, in problem TA2, steps
A3 and B3 require comparing the size of
the globes, whereas in problem CA2 these
steps require comparing the sizes of the
monsters who are holding the globes.

If steps A1 and B1 are the main factors
determining problem difficulty then we
would expect problems TA2 and CA2 to
yield results like those for problems TA and
CA, respectively. However if steps A3 and
B3 are the main determinants of problem
difficulty, then we would expect both problem TA2 and problem CA2 to be about as
difficult as problem CA and considerably
more difficult than problem TA.

Procedure

In experiment 3, each subject solved only
one problem. In all other respects, the
procedures were identical to those in experiments 1 and 2. Fourteen subjects solved
problem TA2 and 13 subjects solved problem CA2. One subject in each condition
failed to solve the problem.

Results

The mean solution time for problem TA2
was 27.07 min and the mean solution time
for problem CA2 was 29.77 min. The
difference between the two was not significant by t-test. The solution times for these
problems are close to the solution times of
28.48 min for problem CA in experiment 1
and 28.08 min in experiment 2.

GENERAL DISCUSSION

The results of experiment 3 clearly support
the hypothesis that the difference in solution times between transfer and change
problems observed in experiments 1 and 2
may be attributed to differences in the

Table 10. Two Monster Problems.

A. Monster problem TA2

Three five-handed extraterrestrial monsters were holding three crystal globes. Because of the quantum-mechanical peculiarities of their neighborhood, both monsters and globes come in exactly three sizes with no others permitted: small, medium, and large. Furthermore, globes come in just three colors: white, gray, and black. The medium-sized monster was holding the small white globe; the small monster was holding the large black globe; and the large monster was holding the medium-sized gray globe. Since this situation offended their keenly developed sense of symmetry, they proceeded to transfer globes from one monster to another so that each monster would have a globe proportionate to its own size.

Monster etiquette complicated the solution of the problem since it requires that:

1. Only one globe may be transferred at a time;
2. If a monster is holding two globes, only the darker globe may be changed;
3. A globe may not be transferred to a monster who is holding a darker globe.

By what sequence of changes could the monsters have solved this problem?

B. Monster problem CA2

Three five-handed extraterrestrial monsters were holding three crystal globes. Because of the quantum-mechanical peculiarities of their neighborhood, both monsters and globes come in exactly three sizes with no others permitted; small, medium, and large. Furthermore, globes come in just three colors: white, gray, and black. The medium-sized monster was holding the small gray globe; the small monster was holding the large white globe; and the large monster was holding the medium-sized black globe. Since this situation offended their keenly developed sense of symmetry, they proceeded to shrink and expand globes so that each monster would have a globe proportionate to his own size.

Monster etiquette complicated the solution of the problem since it requires that:

1. Only one globe be changed at a time.
2. If two globes have the same size, only the darker globe may be changed.
3. A globe may not be changed to the same size as a darker globe.

By what sequence of changes could the monsters have solved this problem?

difficulty of executing the comparisons in steps A3 and B3. Further, they offer no support for the hypothesis that the differences are due to differences in difficulty in executing steps A1 and B1. In other words, the difference between transfer and change problems occurs not because it is harder in change problems to determine if any other globes need to be considered when making a move, but rather because when such globes are found, it is harder to make the appropriate comparisons among globes.

Experiments 1 and 2 have provided a considerable amount of information about transfer of training among the problems. We will discuss just two aspects of these data: (1) the observation that there was generally greater transfer of training in experiment 2 than in experiment 1, and (2) the asymmetry of the transfer effects observed in both experiments.

Reed, Ernst, and Banerjii (1974) offer two explanations for the asymmetry of transfer that they found in their study. The first explanation, which concerns a difference between the problem spaces of their two problems, is not applicable in the present study since we have used only isomorphic problems. The second explanation is that while the two problems were solved in the same number of steps, subjects spent more time on the more difficult problem. Thus, in the more difficult problem, the steps are better learned and provide more transfer than in the easier problem. This explanation is consistent with the results of experiment 2 in which transfer from patient to agent problems was greater than from agent to patient problems and the patient problems were slightly more difficult. However, it is not consistent with the results of experiment 1 in which the TA problems are much easier than the CA problems but transfer from TA to CA is much greater than transfer from CA to TA.

To analyze the transfer of training effects, we must identify the processes that are facilitated by previous training. Our analysis embodied in the UNDERSTAND program (see chapter 7.1) suggests three groups of processes to consider. These are:

1. Processes for formulating the initial situation.

2. Processes for identifying and representing the operators.

3. Processes for formulating the rules for a legal move.

Since the initial situation is essentially the same in all problems, we would expect that experience with any of the problems would facilitate formulation of the initial situation equally. Thus, it seems unlikely that either the differences in transfer between experiments 1 and experiment 2 or the asymmetries of transfer are traceable to the processes for formulating the initial situation.

Similarly, since the processes for identifying "move" and "change" operators are thoroughly overlearned in adults, it seems unlikely that these processes could either benefit enough from transfer or occupy enough time to account for the differences among problems which we have observed.

The final group of processes, the processes for formulating the rules for a legal move, is a much more likely locus for the transfer effects. First, the rules for a legal move are stated in a different way in the text of each of the problem types. Second, the formulation of these rules by the subjects takes considerable time and is known to constitute one of the most difficult parts of formulating the whole problem (see chapter 7.2). We assume that transfer occurs when the subject, in the course of formulating the rules for a legal move in the second problem recognizes and uses similarities to the formulation of the rules in the first problem. In doing this, the subject must recognize the similarity of two complex structures despite differences in them.

There are two differences between the statements of the rules either or both of which might be responsible for the differ-

ences in transfer. One is the difference in the operators—the transfer-change difference. The other is the difference in the way constraints are stated. Constraints are stated either in terms of properties—"The big globe"—or in terms of relations—"The globe of the big monster." Further research will be needed to evaluate the importance of these two differences.

CONCLUSION

We have shown that differences among the texts of isomorphic problems influence problem solving behavior strongly in three ways:

1. Problems involving transfer operators were solved much more quickly than problems involving change operators.

2. Both the agent-patient variation and the transfer-change variation influence the notation which the subjects use to solve the problems.

3. Transfer between two problems is greater when the difference between the problems is an agent-patient variation than when it is a transfer-change variation.

The differences in solution time between transfer and change problems can be attributed to differences in the difficulty of executing comparison processes when applying the rules for a legal move. The differences in the use of matrix notation in transfer and change problems can be attributed to differences in the relation between the subject's representation of the initial situation and his representation of the operators. Differences in transfer of training among the problems can be attributed to differences in the way the rules for a legal move are formulated.

References

Fillmore, C. J. The case for case. In E. Bach & R. T. Harms (Eds.), *Universals in linguistic theory*. New York: Holt, Rinehart & Winston, 1968, pp. 1–88.

Hayes, J. R., & Simon, H. A. Understanding written problem instructions. In L. Gregg (Ed.), *Knowledge and cognition*. Potomac, Md.: Lawrence Erlbaum Assoc., 1974, pp. 167–

200. Reprinted as chapter 7.1 in this book.

Newell, A., & Simon, H. A. *Human problem solving.*Englewood Cliffs, N.J.: Prentice-Hall, 1972.

Nilsson, N. J. *Problem-solving methods in artificial intelligence.* New York: McGraw-Hill, 1971.

Reed, S. K., Ernst, G. W. & Banerjii, R. The role of analogy in transfer between similar problem states. *Cognitive Psychology*, 1974, 6, 436–50.

Simon, H. A., & Hayes, J. R. The understanding process: Problem Isomorphs, *Cognitive Psychology*, 1976, 8, 165–90. Reprinted as chapter 7.2 in this book.

Index of Names

Index of Subjects